Lecture Notes in Computer Science 2683

Edited by G. Goos, J. Hartmanis, and J. van Leeuwen

T0142039

Springer
Berlin
Heidelberg
New York
Hong Kong
London
Milan
Paris
Tokyo

Anand Rangarajan Mário Figueiredo
Josiane Zerubia (Eds.)

Energy Minimization Methods
in Computer Vision
and Pattern Recognition

4th International Workshop, EMMCVPR 2003
Lisbon, Portugal, July 7-9, 2003
Proceedings

Springer

Series Editors

Gerhard Goos, Karlsruhe University, Germany
Juris Hartmanis, Cornell University, NY, USA
Jan van Leeuwen, Utrecht University, The Netherlands

Volume Editors

Anand Rangarajan
University of Florida
Dept. of Computer and Information Science and Engineering
Gainesville, FL, US 32611-6120, USA
E-mail: anand@cise.ufl.edu

Mário Figueiredo
Instituto Superior Técnico
Torre Norte, Piso 10, Av. Rovisco Pais, 1049-001 Lisboa, Portugal
E-mail: Mario.Figueiredo@lx.it.pt

Josian Zerubia
INRIA
Sophia-Antipolis, France
E-mail: Josiane.Zerubia@sophia.inria.fr

Cataloging-in-Publication Data applied for

A catalog record for this book is available from the Library of Congress

Bibliographic information published by Die Deutsche Bibliothek
Die Deutsche Bibliothek lists this publication in the Deutsche Nationalbibliografie;
detailed bibliographic data is available in the Internet at <http://dnb.ddb.de>.

CR Subject Classification (1998): I.5, I.4, I.2.10, I.3.5, F.2.2, F.1.1

ISSN 0302-9743
ISBN 3-540-40498-8 Springer-Verlag Berlin Heidelberg New York

Springer-Verlag Berlin Heidelberg New York
a member of BertelsmannSpringer Science+Business Media GmbH

http://www.springer.de

© Springer-Verlag Berlin Heidelberg 2003
Printed in Germany

Typesetting: Camera-ready by author, data conversion by DA-TeX Gerd Blumenstein
Printed on acid-free paper   SPIN 10927793   06/3142   5 4 3 2 1 0

Preface

This volume consists of the 33 papers presented at the International Workshop on Energy Minimization Methods in Computer Vision and Pattern Recognition (EMMCVPR 2003) which was held at Instituto Superior Técnico (IST), the Engineering School of the Technical University of Lisbon, Portugal during July 7–9, 2003. This workshop was the fourth in the series which started with EMMCVPR 1997 held in Venice, Italy in May 1997 and continued with EMMCVPR 1999 held in York, UK in July 1999 and EMMCVPR 2001 held in Sophia-Antipolis, France in September 2001.

Many problems in computer vision and pattern recognition (CVPR) are couched in the framework of optimization. The minimization of a global quantity, often referred to as the energy, forms the bulwark of most approaches in CVPR. Disparate approaches, such as discrete and probabilistic formulations on the one hand and continuous, deterministic strategies on the other, often have optimization or energy minimization as a common theme. Instances of energy minimization arise in Gibbs/Markov modeling, Bayesian decision theory, geometric and variational approaches and in areas in CVPR such as object recognition and retrieval, image segmentation, registration, reconstruction, classification and data mining.

The aim of the EMMCVPR workshops is to bring together researchers with interests in these disparate areas of CVPR but with an underlying commitment to some form of energy minimization. Although the subject is traditionally well represented in major international conferences on CVPR, this workshop provides a forum wherein researchers can report their recent work and engage in more informal discussions.

We received 66 submissions, from 23 countries, each of which was reviewed by three members of the program committee and the co-chairs. Based on the reviews, 24 papers were accepted for oral presentation and 9 for poster presentation. In this volume, no distinction is made between papers that were presented orally or as posters. The book is organized into six sections with section titles corresponding to the workshop sessions: *Unsupervised Learning and Matching*, *Probabilistic Modelling*, *Segmentation and Grouping*, *Shape Modelling*, *Restoration and Reconstruction*, and *Graphs and Graph-Based Methods*.

EMMCVPR 2003 also included keynote talks by three distinguished scientists: William Freeman (MIT), Alfred Hero (Univ. of Michigan), and Panos Pardalos (Univ. of Florida). The invited talks focused on recent results in the areas of Bayesian networks, entropy-based methods and global optimization, respectively. These researchers have played leading roles in the fields of optimization, computer vision, image processing and pattern recognition.

We would like to thank Marcello Pelillo and Edwin Hancock for their pioneering efforts in launching this series of successful workshops with EMMCVPR 1997 and for much subsequent advice, organizational tips and encouragement.

We also thank Anil Jain (co-chair of EMMCVPR 2001) for his support. We thank the program committee for careful and timely reviews which made our task easier.

We acknowledge and thank the following organizations that have provided support for EMMCVPR: the International Association for Pattern Recognition (IAPR) for sponsoring the workshop and providing publicity, Instituto Superior Técnico (IST) for hosting the workshop, Instituto de Telecomunicações (IT) for providing organizational support, and finally Springer-Verlag for including EMMCVPR under the LNCS rubric.

May 2003

Anand Rangarajan
Mário Figueiredo
Josiane Zerubia

Organization

Program Co-chairs

Mário Figueiredo   Instituto Superior Técnico, Lisbon, Portugal
Anand Rangarajan   University of Florida, Gainesville, FL, USA
Josiane Zerubia   INRIA Sophia Antipolis, France

Program Committee

Pedro Aguiar	Instituto Superior Técnico, Lisbon, Portugal
Yali Amit	University of Chicago, USA
Yuri Boykov	Siemens Corp. Research, USA
Joachim Buhmann	University of Bonn, Germany
Roland Chin	University of Science and Technology, Hong Kong
Laurent Cohen	Univ. Paris-Dauphine, France
Jose Dias	Instituto Superior Técnico, Lisbon, Portugal
Byron Dom	IBM Almaden Research Center, USA
Marie Pierre Dubuisson-Jolly	Siemens Corp. Research, USA
Davi Geiger	New York University, USA
Georgy Gimel'farb	University of Auckland, New Zealand
Christine Graffigne	Université René Descartes, France
Edwin Hancock	University of York, UK
Tin Ho	Bell Laboratories, USA
Vittorio Murino	University of Verona, Italy
Robert Nowak	Rice University, USA
Marcello Pelillo	University of Venice, Italy
Jose Principe	University of Florida, USA
Kaleem Siddiqi	McGill University, Canada
Richard Szeliski	Microsoft Research, USA
Alan Trouve	Univ. Paris 13, France
Baba Vemuri	University of Florida, USA
Laurent Younes	ENS Cachan, France
Alan Yuille	UCLA, USA
Ramin Zabih	Cornell University, USA
Song-Chun Zhu	UCLA, USA

Sponsoring Institutions

Instituto Superior Técnico (IST), Portugal
International Association for Pattern Recognition (IAPR)
Instituto de Telecomunicações (IT), Portugal

Table of Contents

III   Segmentation and Grouping

IV   Shape Modelling

V   Restoration and Reconstruction

VI   Graphs and Graph-Based Methods

Stochastic Search for Optimal Linear Representations of Images on Spaces with Orthogonality Constraints

Xiuwen Liu[1] and Anuj Srivastava[2]

[1] Department of Computer Science
Florida State University
Tallahassee, FL 32306
`liux@cs.fsu.edu`
Phone: (850) 644-0050, Fax: (850) 644-0058.
[2] Department of Statistics, Florida
State University, Tallahassee, 32306

Abstract. Simplicity of linear representations makes them a popular tool in several imaging analysis, and indeed many other applications involving high-dimensional data. In image analysis, the two widely used linear representations are: (i) linear projections of images to low-dimensional Euclidean subspaces, and (ii) linear spectral filtering of images. In view of the orthogonality and other constraints imposed on these representations (the subspaces or the filters), they take values on nonlinear manifolds (Grassmann, Stiefel, or rotation group). We present a family of algorithms that exploit the geometry of the underlying manifolds to find optimal linear representations for specified tasks. We illustrate the effectiveness of algorithms by finding optimal subspaces and sparse filters both in the context of image-based object recognition.

1 Introduction

High dimensionality of observed images implies that the task of recognizing objects (from images) will generally involve excessive memory storage and computation. It also prohibits effective use of statistical techniques in image analysis since statistical models on high-dimensional spaces are both difficult to derive and to analyze. In addition, representations based on full images seem too sensitive to perturbations that are not intrinsic to the objects, such as noise, illumination, obscuration etc. On the other hand, it is well recognized that images are generated via physical processes that in turn are governed by a small number of physical parameters. This motivates a search for representations that can reduce image dimensions or induce representations that are relatively invariant to the unwanted perturbations.

Within the framework of linear representations, two types of techniques have commonly been used. The first idea is to project images linearly to some predefined low-dimensional subspace, and use the projected values for analyzing

A. Rangarajan et al. (Eds.): EMMCVPR 2003, LNCS 2683, pp. 3– , 2003.
© Springer-Verlag Berlin Heidelberg 2003

images. For instance, let U be an $n \times d$ orthogonal matrix denoting an orthonormal basis of a d-dimensional subspace of $I\!R^n$ ($n >> d$), and let I be an image reshaped into an $n \times 1$ vector. Then, the vector $a(I) = U^T I \in I\!R^d$, also called the vector of coefficients, can be a d-dimensional representation of I. In this setup, several bases including principal component analysis (PCA) and Fisher discriminant analysis (FDA) have widely been used. Although they satisfy some optimality criteria, they may not necessarily be optimal for a specific application at hand. Their optimality criterion is often not related to the application performance, or if related, is based on unrealistic assumptions (such as normality of image pixels). The second idea is to project spectral transforms of images onto local linear bases, i.e. linear filters, through convolution and then analyze filter responses. Examples include wavelets, steering filters, Gabors etc. An important principle for deriving the filters in the past has been to maximize the sparseness of filter responses [,]. However, the resulting filters may not provide optimal performances in specific applications.

The main goal of this paper is to present a family of algorithms for finding *linear representations of images that are optimal for specific tasks and specific datasets.* Our search for optimal linear representation is based on a stochastic optimization process that maximizes the performance function. To be computationally effective, the optimization process has been modified to account for the geometry of the underlying space by formulating the problem on several manifolds that are manifested in linear representations.

This paper is organized as follows. In Section 2 we set up the problem of optimizing the recognition performance over the set of subspaces on a Grassmann manifold, and describe a stochastic gradient technique to solve it. Section 3 generalizes the algorithm to other manifolds. Experimental results on optimal subspaces and optimal filters are shown in Section 4. Section 5 concludes the paper with a summary discussion.

2   Specification of Optimal Subspaces

2.1   Problem Formulation

We start by formulating a restricted problem of finding optimal linear representations in cases where the performance function does not depend on the choice of basis in a subspace. Let $U \in I\!R^{n \times d}$ be an orthonormal basis of a d-dimensional subspace of $I\!R^n$, where n is the size of an image and d is the required dimension of the optimal subspace ($n >> d$). For an image I, considered as a column vector of size n, the vector of coefficients is given by $a(I, U) = U^T I \in I\!R^d$. Let $F(U)$ be a performance function associated with a system that uses U as a linear representation, and assume that $F(U) = F(UO)$ for any $d \times d$ orthogonal matrix O.

Let $\mathcal{G}_{n,d}$ be the set of all d-dimensional subspaces of $I\!R^n$; it is called a Grassmann manifold [ ]. It is a compact, connected manifold of dimension $d(n-d)$ and can be studied as a quotient space $SO(n)/(SO(n-d) \times SO(d))$, where $SO(k)$ is the special orthogonal group of $k \times k$ orthogonal matrices with determinant $+1$. An element of $\mathcal{G}_{n,d}$, i.e. a subspace, can be represented either by a basis (non-uniquely) or by a projection matrix (uniquely). Choosing the former, let U be an orthonormal basis in $\mathbb{R}^{n \times d}$ such that $span(U)$ is the given subspace. Then, for any $d \times d$ orthogonal matrix O, UO is also an orthonormal basis of the same subspace. Therefore, we have an equivalence class of bases that span the same subspace:

$$[U] = \{UO | O \in \mathbb{R}^{d \times d}, \ O^T O = I_d, \ \det(O) = 1\} \quad \in \mathcal{G}_{n,d} \ .$$

Let the given performance function be $F : \mathcal{G}_{n,d} \mapsto \mathbb{R}_+$ and we want to search for the optimal subspace: $[\hat{U}] = \mathrm{argmax}_{[U] \in \mathcal{G}_{n,d}} F([U])$.

Since the set $\mathcal{G}_{n,d}$ is compact and F is assumed to be a smooth function, the optimizer $[\hat{U}]$ is well defined. Note that the maximizer of F may not be unique and hence $[\hat{U}]$ may be set-valued rather than being point-valued in $\mathcal{G}_{n,d}$. We perform the search in a probabilistic framework by defining a probability density function

$$f([U]) = \frac{1}{Z(D)} \exp(F([U])/D) \ , \tag{1}$$

where $T \in \mathbb{R}$ plays the role of temperature and f is considered a probability density with respect to the Haar measure on the set $\mathcal{G}_{n,d}$.

2.2   Optimization via MCMC-Based Simulated Annealing

We have chosen a simulated annealing process to seek an optimal subspace $[\hat{U}]$. In fact, we adopt a Markov chain version of simulated annealing using acceptance/rejection at every step, while the proposal states come from a stochastic gradient process. Gradient processes, both deterministic and stochastic, have long been used for solving non-linear optimization problems[,]. Since the Grassmann manifold $\mathcal{G}_{n,d}$ is a curved space, as opposed to being a (flat) vector-space, the gradient process has to account for its intrinsic geometry, similar to work presented in [ ]. Deterministic gradients such as Newton-Raphson method, on such manifolds with orthogonality constraints have also been studied in [ ]. We will start by describing a deterministic gradient process (of F) on $\mathcal{G}_{n,d}$ and later generalize it to a Markov chain Monte Carlo (MCMC) type simulated annealing process.

Deterministic Gradient Flow The performance function F can be viewed as a scalar-field on $\mathcal{G}_{n,d}$. A necessary condition for $[\hat{U}]$ to be a maximum is that for any tangent vector at $[\hat{U}]$, the directional derivative of F, in the direction of that vector, should be zero. The directional derivatives on $\mathcal{G}_{n,d}$ are defined next. Let J be the $n \times d$ matrix made up of first d columns of the $n \times n$ identity matrix I_n; $[J]$ denotes the d-dimensional subspace aligned to the first d axes of $\mathbb{R}^n$.

1. **Derivative of F at $[J] \in \mathcal{G}_{n,d}$:** Let E_{ij} be an $n \times n$ skew-symmetric matrix such that: for $1 \le i \le d$ and $d < j \le n$,

$$E_{ij}(k,l) = \begin{cases} 1 & \text{if } k = i,\ l = j \\ -1 & \text{if } k = j,\ l = i \\ 0 & \text{otherwise} \end{cases} \tag{2}$$

Consider the products $E_{ij}J$; there are $d(n-d)$ such matrices that form an orthogonal basis of the vector space tangent to $\mathcal{G}_{n,d}$ at $[J]$. That is: $T_{[J]}(\mathcal{G}_{n,d}) = \text{span}\{E_{i,j}J\}$. Notice that any tangent vector at $[J]$ is of the form: for arbitrary scalars α_{ij},

$$\sum_{i=1}^{d} \sum_{j=d+1}^{n} \alpha_{ij} E_{ij} J = \begin{bmatrix} 0_d & B \\ -B^T & 0_{n-d} \end{bmatrix} J \quad \in \mathbb{R}^{n \times d}, \tag{3}$$

where 0_i is the $i \times i$ matrix of zeros and B is a $d \times (n-d)$ real-valued matrix. The gradient vector of F at $[J]$ is an $n \times d$ matrix given by $A([J])J$ where:

$$A([J]) = \left(\sum_{i=1}^{d} \sum_{j=d+1}^{n} \alpha_{ij}(J)E_{ij} \right) \quad \in \mathbb{R}^{n \times n}$$
$$\text{and where } \alpha_{ij}(J) = \lim_{\epsilon \downarrow 0} \left(\frac{F([e^{\epsilon E_{ij}} J]) - F([J])}{\epsilon} \right) \quad \in \mathbb{R}. \tag{4}$$

α_{ij}s are the directional derivatives of F in the directions given by E_{ij}, respectively. The matrix $A([J])$ is a skew-symmetric matrix of the form given in Eqn. (to the left of J) for some B, and points to the direction of maximum increase in F, among all tangential directions at $[J]$.

2. **Derivative of F at any $[U] \in \mathcal{G}_{n,d}$:** Tangent spaces and directional derivatives at any arbitrary point $[U] \in \mathcal{G}_{n,d}$ follow easily from the above discussion. For a given $[U]$, let Q be an $n \times n$ orthogonal matrix such that $QU = J$. In other words, $Q^T = [U\ \ V]$ where $V \in \mathbb{R}^{n \times (n-d)}$ is any matrix such that $V^T V = I_{n-d}$ and $U^T V = 0$. Then, the tangent space at $[U]$ is given by:

$$T_{[U]}(\mathcal{G}_{n,d}) = \{Q^T A : A \in T_{[J]}(\mathcal{G}_{n,d})\}.$$

and the gradient of F at $[U]$ is a $n \times d$ matrix given by $A([U])J$ where:

$$A([U]) = Q^T \left(\sum_{i=1}^{d} \sum_{j=d+1}^{n} \alpha_{ij}(U)E_{ij} \right) \quad \in \mathbb{R}^{n \times n}$$
$$\text{and where } \alpha_{ij}(U) = \lim_{\epsilon \downarrow 0} \left(\frac{F([Q^T e^{\epsilon E_{ij}} J]) - F([U])}{\epsilon} \right) \quad \in \mathbb{R}. \tag{5}$$

The deterministic gradient flow on $\mathcal{G}_{n,d}$ is a solution of the equation:

$$\frac{dX(t)}{dt} = A(X(t))\ J, \quad X(0) = [U_0] \in \mathcal{G}_{n,d}, \tag{6}$$

with $A(\cdot)$ as defined in Eqn. . Let $G \subset \mathcal{G}_{n,d}$ be an open neighborhood of $[\hat{U}]$ and $X(t) \in G$ for some finite $t > 0$. Define $\{[U] \in \mathcal{G}_{n,d} : F([U]) \ge \gamma, \gamma \in \mathbb{R}_+\}$ to be the level sets of F. If the level sets of F are strictly (geodesically) convex in G, then the gradient process converges to a local maximum, i.e. $\lim_{t\to\infty} X(t) = [\hat{U}]$. As described in [ ], $X(t)$ converges to the connected component of the set of equilibria points of the performance function F.

Numerical Approximation of Gradient Flow: Since F is generally not available in an analytical form, the directional derivatives α_{ij} are often approximated numerically using the finite differences:

$$\alpha_{ij} = \frac{F([Q^T e^{\epsilon E_{ij}} J]) - F([U])}{\epsilon}, \tag{7}$$

for a small value of $\epsilon > 0$. Here, the matrix $\tilde{U} \equiv Q^T e^{\epsilon E_{ij}} J$ is an $n \times d$ matrix that differs from U in only the ith-column which is now given by $\tilde{U}_i = \cos(\epsilon)U_i + \sin(\epsilon)V_j$, where U_i, V_j are the ith and j^{th} columns of U and V respectively.

For a step size $\Delta > 0$, we will denote the discrete samples $X(t\Delta)$ by X_t. Then, a discrete approximation of the solution of Eqn. is given by:

$$\begin{aligned} X_{t+1} &= Q_t^T \exp(\Delta A_t) J \\ \text{where } A_t &= \sum_{i=1}^{d} \sum_{j=d+1}^{n} \alpha_{ij}(X_t) E_{ij} \text{ and } Q_{t+1} = \exp(-\Delta A) Q_t . \end{aligned} \tag{8}$$

In general, the expression $\exp(\Delta A_t)$ will involve exponentiating an $n \times n$ matrix, a task that is computationally very expensive. However, given that the matrix A_t takes the skew-symmetric form before J in Eqn. , this exponentiation can be accomplished in order $O(nd^2)$ computations, using the singular value decomposition of the $(d \times d)$ sub-matrix B contained in A_t. Also, Q_t can be updated for the next time step using a similar efficient update.

The gradient process $X(t)$ has the drawback that it converges only to a local maximum, which may not be useful in general. For global optimization or to compute statistics under a given density on $\mathcal{G}_{n,d}$, a stochastic component is often added to the gradient process to form a stochastic gradient flow, also referred to as a diffusion process [ ].

Simulated Annealing Using Stochastic Gradients We are aiming for an MCMC version of the simulated annealing technique that uses stochastic gradients for sampling from the proposal density [ ]. We begin by constructing a stochastic gradient process on $\mathcal{G}_{n,d}$ and then add a Metropolis-Hastings type acceptance-rejection step to it to generate an appropriate Markov chain.

One can obtain random gradients by adding a stochastic component to Eqn. according to

$$dX(t) = A(X(t))J dt + \sqrt{2D} \left(\sum_{i=1}^{d} \sum_{j=d+1}^{n} E_{ij} J \ dW_{ij}(t) \right), \tag{9}$$

where $W_{ij}(t)$ are real-valued, independent standard Wiener processes. It can be shown that (refer to [ ]), under certain conditions on F, the solution of Eqn. , $X(t)$, is a Markov process with a unique stationary probability density given

by f in Eqn.   . For a numerical implementation, Eqn.   has to be discretized
with some step-size $\Delta > 0$. The discretized time process is given by:

$$dA_t = A(X_t)\Delta + \sqrt{2\Delta D} \sum_{i=1}^{d} \sum_{j=d+1}^{n} w_{ij} E_{ij},$$

$$X_{t+1} = Q_t^T \exp(\Delta dA_t) J,$$
$$Q_{t+1} = \exp(-\Delta dA_t) Q_t , \tag{10}$$

where w_{ij}'s are *i.i.d* standard normals. It is shown in [ ] that for $\Delta \to 0$, the
process $\{X_t\}$ converges to the solution of Eqn.   . The process $\{X_t\}$ provides a
discrete implementation of the stochastic gradient process.

In case of MCMC simulated annealing, we use this stochastic gradient process
to generate a candidate for the next point along the process but accept it only
with a certain probability. That is, the right side of the second equation in
Eqn.   becomes a candidate Y that may or may not be selected as the next
point X_{t+1}. **Algorithm 1 MCMC Simulated Annealing**: Let $X(0) = [U_0] \in$
$\mathcal{G}_{n,d}$ be any initial condition. Set $t = 0$.

1. Calculate the gradient matrix $A(X_t)$ according to Eqn.   .
2. Generate $d(n - d)$ independent realizations, w_{ij}s, from standard normal
   density. Using the value of X_t, calculate a candidate value Y according to
   Eqn.   .
3. Compute $F(Y)$, $F(X_t)$, and set $dF = F(Y) - F(X_t)$.
4. Set $X_{t+1} = Y$ with probability $\min\{\exp(dF/D_t), 1\}$, else set $X_{t+1} = X_t$.
5. Modify D_t to D_{t+1}, set $t = t + 1$, and go to Step 1.

The resulting process X_t forms a Markov chain and let X^* be a limiting point of
this Markov chain, i.e. $X^* = \lim_{t \to \infty} X_t$. This algorithm is a particularization of
Algorithm A.20 (p. 200) in the book by Robert and Casella [   ]. Please consult
that text for the convergence properties of X_t.

3   Linear Representations with Orthogonality Constraints

So far we have described an algorithm for finding optimal subspaces under a performance function F that is invariant to changing bases of a subspace. In contrast
to this situation, many applications have performance functions that depend
not only on the choice of subspaces but also on the particular basis chosen, i.e.
$F(U) \neq F(UO)$ for any $O \in SO(d)$. In some other cases the basis vectors may
not even be required to be orthogonal to each other. Imposition of these different constraints leads to different manifolds on which the search for optimal
representation is performed. Within the framework of linear representations the
following manifolds seem most relevant.

We are interested in generalizing our optimization process to these different
manifolds. Algorithm 1 applies to these cases with simple modifications. First,
the gradient evaluation Eqn.   is modified to account for the tangent space of

Table 1. Linear Representations Under Orthogonality Constraints

Parametrization	Manifold	Search space	Application/Examples
Subspace	Grassmann [ ]	$d(n - d)$	Optimal subspace/ Principal components
Orthonormal basis	Stiefel [ ]	$d(n - \frac{d+1}{2})$	Optimal orthonormal filters
Directions	Direction manifold (d Grassmann $\mathcal{G}_{n,1}$)	$d(n - 1)$	Optimal filters for recognition/ Independent components
Directions with scaling	Euclidean	dn	Linear basis with weights

that manifold. Secondly, the discrete updating rule given by Eqn.   is modified according to one-parameter flow of that manifold.

In some of the above mentioned cases a multi-flow technique [ ] may prove useful for optimization. The basic idea is to divide the search space into cartesian products of smaller spaces, and then perform optimization in each smaller space iteratively. For example, the Stiefel manifold $\mathcal{S}_{n,d} = SO(n)/SO(n - d)$ can be viewed as the product $\mathcal{G}_{n,d} \times SO(d)$. Therefore, the optimization can be performed in two step iterations: (i) Update the subspace according to a gradient term while keeping the basis parallel to the current basis (in $\mathcal{G}_{n,d}$), and (ii) update the basis according to a gradient term by keeping the subspace fixed (in $SO(d)$). The second step involves a gradient on a $d(d - 1)/2$-dimensional space and is computationally efficient since d is typically small. For the case of direction manifold, we can iterate optimization along each direction which is an element of $\mathcal{G}_{n,1}$ or the real-projective space $I\!RP^{n-1}$. This can be implemented directly using d replicates of Algorithm 1. For the last case of Euclidean manifold, it is a flat space and so the Eqn.   and   can be implemented directly using classical Euclidean techniques.

Similar to many numerical methods, the choice of free parameters, such as Δ, ϵ, d, and U_0, may have a significant effect on the results of Algorithm 1. While limited theoretical results are available to analyze the convergence of such algorithms in $I\!R^n$, the case of simulated annealing over the space $\mathcal{G}_{n,d}$ is considerably more difficult. Instead of pursuing asymptotic convergence results, we have conducted extensive numerical simulations to demonstrate the convergence of the proposed algorithm, under a variety of values for the free parameters.

4   Empirical Investigations of Algorithm 1

We have applied Algorithm 1 to the search for optimal linear bases in several different contexts. Note that these algorithms require evaluation, exact or approximate, of the performance function F for any linear representation $[U]$. So far we have not specified a performance function F but will do so now to illustrate the experimental results. We present two sets of results: (i) for finding optimal linear subspaces for recognition in the context of object recognition, and

(ii) for finding linear filters with optimal recognition performance/sparseness in the context of image coding.

Datasets: Before we proceed, we briefly describe the three image datasets that have been used in our experiments: the ORL face recognition dataset , the COIL dataset [ ], and a Brodatz texture dataset . The ORL dataset consists of faces of 40 different subjects with 10 images each. The full COIL database consists of 7200 images at different azimuthal angles of 100 3-D objects with 72 images each. In this paper, we have used a part of the COIL database by involving only the first 20 objects, with a total of 1,440 images. The texture dataset consists of 40 textures. It is a difficult dataset for classification in the sense that some of the textures are perceptually quite similar to other textures, and some are inhomogeneous with significant variations across spatial locations.

Specification of Performance Function F: To recognize a class we choose the nearest neighbor rule under the Euclidean metric on the coefficients $a(I,U)$ as the classifier. It is easier to implement and, given sufficient amount of training data, the asymptotic error under this rule is bounded to be within two times of the Bayesian error.

Let there be C classes to be recognized from the images; each class has k_{train} training images (denoted by $I_{c,1}, \ldots, I_{c,k_{train}}$) and k_{test} test images (denoted by $I'_{c,1}, \ldots, I'_{c,k_{test}}$) to evaluate the recognition performance measure, for $c = 1, 2, \ldots, C$. In order to utilize Algorithm 1, F should have continuous directional derivatives. Since the decision function of the nearest neighbor classifier is discontinuous, the resulting recognition performance function is discontinuous and needs modification. To obtain a smooth F, we define $\rho(I'_{c,i}, U)$ to be the ratio of the between-class-minimum distance and within-class minimum distance of a test image i from class c, given by

$$\rho(I'_{c,i}, U) = \frac{\min_{c' \neq c,j} d(I'_{c,i}, I_{c',j}; U)}{\min_j d(I'_{c,i}, I_{c,j}; U) + \epsilon}, \tag{11}$$

where $d(I_1, I_2; U) = \|a(I_1, U) - a(I_2, U)\|$ as given before, and $\epsilon > 0$ is a small number to avoid division by zero. Then, define F according to:

$$F(U, \beta) = \frac{1}{Ck_{test}} \sum_{c=1}^{C} \sum_{i=1}^{k_{test}} h(\rho(I'_{c,i}, U) - 1, \beta), \quad 0 \le F \le 1.0 \tag{12}$$

where $h(\cdot, \cdot)$ is a monotonically increasing and bounded function in its first argument. In our experiments, we have used $h(x, \beta) = 1/(1 + \exp(-2\beta x))$ where β controls the degree of smoothness of F.

4.1   Experimental Results: Representations Using Subspaces

In this subsection, we present a set of results on finding optimal linear subspaces and compare performance with commonly used ones such as PCA and FDA. The

---

[1] http://www.uk.research.att.com/facedatabase.html
[2] http://www-dbv.cs.uni-bonn.de/image/texture.tar.gz

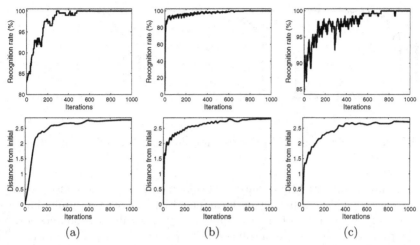

Fig. 1. Plots of $F(X_t)$ (top) and distance of X_t from X_0 (bottom) versus t for different initial conditions. (a) $X_0 = U_{PCA}$, (b) $X_0 = U_{ICA}$, (c) $X_0 = U_{FDA}$. For these curves, $n = 154$, $d = 5$, $k_{train} = 5$, and $k_{test} = 5$

comparisons as they are presented here can be deemed unfair since all the data (test and training) is used to estimated our optimal subspaces (X^*) while only the training data is used to learn PCA, ICA, or FDA. In future publications, we will correct this drawback by restricting to only the training set for finding X^*.

As a first set of results, we ran Algorithm 1 starting with different initial conditions. Fig. - show the results on the ORL database with different initial conditions and Fig.   shows similar examples on the COIL-20 database.

1. Fig.   shows the cases when X_0 is set to U_{PCA}, U_{ICA}, or U_{FDA}. Here U_{FDA} was calculated using a procedure given in [ ] and U_{ICA} using a FastICA algorithm proposed by Hyvärinen [   ]. In these experiments, $n = 154$, $d = 5$, $k_{train} = 5$, and $k_{test} = 5$. While these commonly used linear bases provide a variety of performances, the proposed algorithm converges to a perfect classification solution regardless of the initial condition. Using $\|U_1 U_1^T - U_2 U_2^T\|$ to compute distances between subspaces, we also plot the evolution of the distance between X_0 and X_t. The distance plots highlight the fact that the algorithm moves effectively on the Grassmann manifold going large distances along the chains. Note that the maximum distance between any two d-dimensional subspaces can only be $\sqrt{2d} = 3.16$ in this case. We found multiple subspaces that lead to perfect classification.
2. Fig.   shows three results when the initial condition X_0 is selected randomly from $\mathcal{G}_{n,d}$. As earlier, we have $n = 154$, $d = 5$, $k_{train} = 5$, and $k_{test} = 5$. For different initial conditions, the search process converges to a perfect classification solution and moves effectively along the Grassmann manifold.
3. We have studied the variation of optimal performance versus the subspace rank denoted by d. We set $k_{train} = 5$, $k_{test} = 5$, and a random value is used

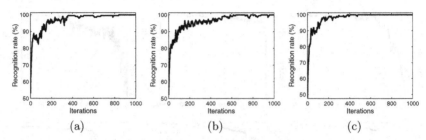

Fig. 2. Performance of X_t versus t for three random initial conditions

for X_0. It is expected that a larger d leads to a better performance, or makes it easier to achieve a perfect performance. Fig. shows the results for three different values of d. In Fig. (a), for $d = 3$, it takes about 2000 iterations for the process to converge to a solution with perfect performance. In Fig. (b), for $d = 10$, it takes about 300 iterations while in Fig. (c), for $d = 20$, it takes less than 200 iterations.

4. Next, we have studied the variation of $F(X^*)$ against the training size k_{train}. Fig. shows two results with different values of k_{train}. In this experiment, $n = 154$, $d = 5$ and random bases were used as initial conditions. Also, the division of images into training and test sets was random. In view of the nearest neighbor classifier being used to define F, it is easier to obtain a perfect solution with more training images. The experimental results support that observation. Fig. (a) shows the case with $k_{train} = 1$ ($k_{test} = 9$) where it takes about 3000 iterations for the process to converge to a perfect solution. In Fig. (c), where $k_{train} = 8$ ($k_{test} = 2$), the process converges to a perfect solution in about 300 iterations.

5. We have also tried the COIL dataset obtaining results similar to ones described earlier for the ORL dataset. Fig. shows three representative results. Fig. (a) shows a case with random basis as initial condition, $n = 64$, $d = 5$, $k_{train} = 4$, and $k_{test} = 68$. The process converges to an optimal solution with perfect classification. Fig. (b) shows a case with $X_0 = U_{ICA}$, $n = 64$,

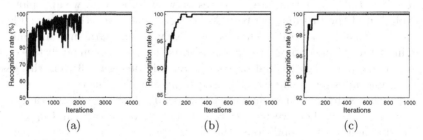

Fig. 3. Performance of X_t versus t for three different values of d. (a) $d = 3$. (b) $d = 10$. (c) $d = 20$

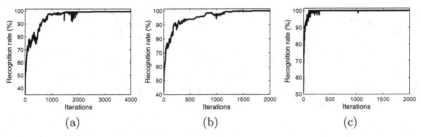

(a)   (b)   (c)

Fig. 4. $F(X_t)$ versus t for three different divisions of database into training and test sets (keeping $n = 154$, $d = 5$ fixed). (a) $k_{train} = 1$, $k_{test} = 9$. (b) $k_{train} = 2$, $k_{test} = 8$. (c) $k_{train} = 8$, $k_{test} = 2$

$d = 5$, $k_{train} = 8$, and $k_{test} = 64$. The process moves very effectively initially as $F(U_{ICA})$ is small. Again it converges to a perfect classification solution. Fig. (c) shows a case with random basis as initial condition and $n = 64$, $d = 10$, $k_{train} = 8$, and $k_{test} = 64$. With $d = 10$, the initial random basis X_0 gives a performance of 87.5% and the process converges to a perfect classification solution.

These plots underscore two important points about Algorithm 1: (i) the algorithm is consistently successful in seeking optimal linear basis from a variety of initial conditions, and (ii) the algorithm moves effectively on the manifold $\mathcal{G}_{n,d}$ with the final solution being far from the initial condition.

We have also compared empirically the performances of these optimal subspaces with the frequently used subspaces, namely U_{PCA}, U_{ICA}, and U_{FDA}. Again, keep in mind that the comparison is biased since the search of X^* uses the whole database and not just the training set. Fig. (a) shows the recognition performance F (for the ORL database) versus d for four different kinds of subspaces: (i) optimal subspace X^* computed using Algorithm 1, (ii) U_{PCA}, (iii) U_{ICA}, and (iv) U_{FDA}. In this experiment, $k_{train} = 5$ and $k_{test} = 5$ are kept fixed. In all the cases, optimal basis X^* results in a better performance than the

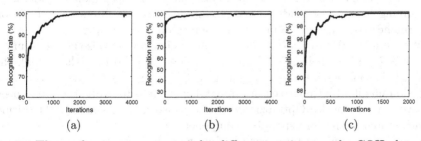

(a)   (b)   (c)

Fig. 5. The performance versus t under different settings on the COIL dataset. (a) $k_{train} = 4$, $k_{test} = 68$, $d = 5$, and X_0 is random. (b) $k_{train} = 8$, $k_{test} = 64$, $d = 5$, and $X_0 = U_{ICA}$. (c) $k_{train} = 8$, $k_{test} = 64$, $d = 10$, and X_0 is random

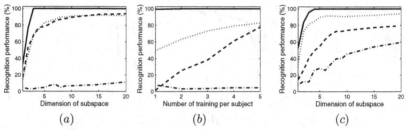

Fig. 6. The performance of different linear subspaces with respect to the dimensionality and the number of training images on the ORL and COIL-20 dataset. Here solid line is the optimal basis from the gradient search process, dashed line FDA, dotted line PCA, and dash-dotted line ICA. (a) The performance versus d with $k_{train} = 5$ on the ORL dataset. (b) The performance versus k_{train} with $d = 5$ on the ORL dataset. (c) The performance versus d with $k_{train} = 8$ on the COIL dataset

standard ones. We have compared the values of $F(X^*)$ with $F(U_{PCA})$, $F(U_{ICA})$, and U_{FDA}) for different values of k_{train} and k_{test}, on the ORL database. Figure (b) shows the performance of the proposed method as well as standard linear subspace methods with d set at 5. We also compared the different subspaces using the COIL-20 datasets and have obtained similar results. As an example, Fig. (c) shows the recognition performance of different bases with respect to d. These examples illustrate the importance of using optimal representations in algorithms.

4.2 Experimental Results: Representations Using Linear Filters

Now we consider the search for linear filters that are optimal under some pre-specified criteria. Studies of natural image statistics have shown that sparse filters of natural images share the important characteristics of receptive fields found in the early stages of the mammalian visual pathway [ ]. It was argued [ ] that these filters should be important for visual recognition as it is the central task of the visual system. While sparseness has been a common consideration in deriving filters, few studies have attempted to relate filters to recognition performance. We attempt to make this connection in this paper.

With a slight abuse of notation we denote the linear filters also by the columns of matrix U. Since there is no requirement here for U to be orthonormal, the matrix U is considered to be an element of $\mathcal{G}_{n,1}^d$, a space we termed earlier as a Direction manifold. (To derive a meaningful sparseness measure, the filters need to have a fixed length.) Optimization is performed using d copies of Algorithm 1, each search in the corresponding component $\mathcal{G}_{n,1}$.

To setup recognition by linear filtering, we utilize a spectral representation framework [,] where each filtered image is represented by its histogram and the recognition is performed by imposing a χ^2-metric on the histogram space.

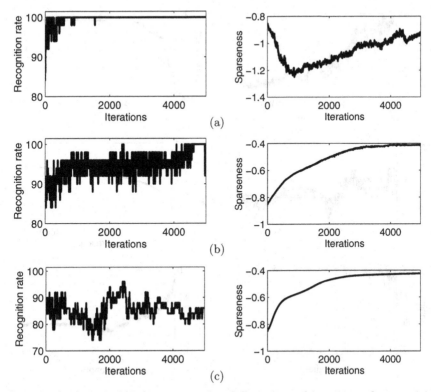

Fig. 7. $F(X_t)$ and $S(X_t)$ versus t for different combinations of recognition performance and sparseness. (a) $\lambda_1 = 1.0$ and $\lambda_2 = 0.0$. (b) $\lambda_1 = 0.2$ and $\lambda_2 = 0.8$. (c) $\lambda_1 = 0.0$ and $\lambda_2 = 1.0$

As shown by Liu and Cheng [ ], this representation is sufficient for representing textures as well as non-texture images such as faces. To define the performance function F, the formula in Eqn.   applies with ρ now obtained using this χ^2 metric in Eqn.   . We have further generalized by using a linear combination of recognition performance and sparseness of the resulting coding:

$$R(U) = \lambda_1 F(U) + \lambda_2 S(U), \tag{13}$$

where $S(U)$ is the sparseness of the resulting coding on the given dataset. $S(U)$ is defined as $S(U) = -\sum \log(1 + x^2)$ where x denotes the pixel values in the filtered images and the sum is taken over all pixels. Note that this definition of $S(U)$ is the negative of the one given in [ ].

   Three classes of filters have been studied and compared to the receptive fields of the visual system. The first class is the Gabor filter family, which localizes optimally jointly in the spatial and frequency domain. Filters with sparse response have been proposed to be important for recognition and have been compared with Gabor filters [ ]. In contrast to sparse filters, filters that lead to be com-

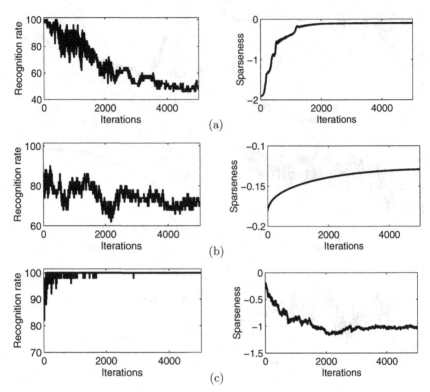

Fig. 8. $F(X_t)$ and $S(X_t)$ versus t with different initial conditions and coefficients on the ORL face datset. (a) $\lambda_1 = 0.0$ and $\lambda_2 = 1.0$ with PCA filters. (b) $\lambda_1 = 0.0$ and $\lambda_2 = 1.0$ with sparse filters. (c) $\lambda_1 = 1.0$ and $\lambda_2 = 0.0$ with sparse filters

pact coding are also used. The main purpose of the following experiments is to study empirically the relationship between recognition performance and sparseness of linear filters with an optimal performance measure given by Eqn.   . Also, in the literature there exist several algorithms for maximizing sparseness, and hence we can compare our results with these existing methods.

To study and compare these pre-specified filters using our algorithms, Fig. shows three examples with Gabor filters as the initial condition (at $t = 0$). Here filters are with size 7×7 ($n = 49$) with $d = 6$. These examples demonstrate clearly that Gabor filters provide neither optimal recognition nor maximum sparseness. Our optimization algorithm seems to be effective in all the cases we have studied in the sense that the performance measure is maximized and the search space is traversed effectively. In Fig.   (a), where only the recognition performance is maximized, the performance is improved quickly to give a perfect recognition on the dataset. Because the sparseness does not play a role in this case, the change in sparseness indicates the solutions are moving effectively along the manifold. Fig.   (c) is also an interesting case; by maximizing the sparseness, the performance remains relatively low compared to the other two cases, indicating that sparseness is not be directly related to performance at the least in the spectral representation framework. Fig. (b) shows a case by maximizing a weighted combination of performance and sparseness. Compared to the other two cases, this one results in a set of relatively sparse filters and perfect recognition performance.

To evaluate the effectiveness of the proposed algorithms, we have also compared our results with existing algorithms to maximize the sparseness. Fig. (a) shows the performance and sparseness with respect to t where the initial filters are compact filters, calculated as principal components of image windows of size 7×7. The plots show that those filters are compact in that the filter responses are not sparse with a sparseness measure of -1.912 but with good recognition performance. As in Fig. (c), maximizing sparseness gives worse recognition performance. The best sparseness measure resulting from our algorithm is -0.098. Fig. (b) and (c) show two cases with sparse filters as the initial condition. The algorithm we used here is the FastICA algorithm by Hyvarinen [ ]. The algorithm indeed gave sparse filters with sparseness measure of -0.181 and recognition performance 82%. Our algorithm can still improve the sparseness measure to -0.129 as shown in Fig. (b). By maximizing the performance, our algorithm also converges to a set of filters with perfect recognition performance, which is shown in Fig. (c).

We have also applied the algorithm on the texture dataset and obtained similar results. However, the resulting sparseness measure is much lower compared to the ORL face dataset case as image windows in textures change signicantly. Fig. shows three examples. As in the previous cases, our algorithm can find filters with better sparseness measure. Also by maximizing a weighted performance and sparseness measure, we can obtain sparse filters with close to perfect recognition performance on the given dataset as shown in Fig. . The performance is considerably better than previous classification results on the same dataset.

5   Discussion

In this paper, we have proposed a family of MCMC simulated annealing algorithms on different manifolds to find the optimal linear subspaces and linear filters according to a performance function F, which can be computed numerically. They provide an effective tool to study problems using linear representations, where two such examples are provided. Our extensive experiments demonstrate their effectiveness. These algorithms make it possible to study and explore the generalization and other properties of linear representations for recognition systematically, which could lead to significant performance improvement within the linear representation framework.

The proposed algorithms can also be viewed as learning algorithms in an integrated learning framework. While feature extraction has been an important step for pattern recognition applications, in most cases features are found based

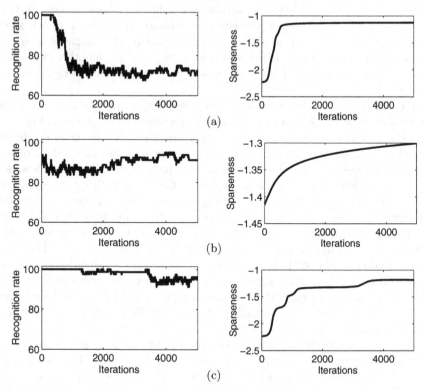

Fig. 9. $F(X_t)$ and $S(X_t)$ versus t with different initial conditions and coefficients on the Brodatz texture dataset. (a) $\lambda_1 = 0.0$ and $\lambda_2 = 1.0$ with initial PCA filters. (b) $\lambda_1 = 0.0$ and $\lambda_2 = 1.0$ with initial sparse filters. (c) $\lambda_1 = 0.2$ and $\lambda_2 = 0.8$ with initial PCA

on empirical comparisons among existing features and the one with the best performance is often used. Such an example is the face recognition based on linear subspaces such as PCA and LDA. This methodology is also reflected by dividing a pattern recognition system into a feature extraction stage and a classifier design stage, where learning is often adopted only in the second stage. The proposed algorithms, on the other hand, can be seen as algorithms that learn features and classifiers within the same framework, which is implemented as two iterative steps. In theory, one can also formulate the problem in the joint space of features and classifiers and perform the optimization in the joint space. The feasibility as well as the effectiveness of the joint search needs to be further studied.

Acknowledgments

We thank the producers of the ORL and COIL datasets for making them available to the public. This research has been supported in part by the grants NSF DMS-0101429, ARO DAAD19-99-1-0267, and NMA 201-01-2010. We would like to thank Prof. Kyle Gallivan of FSU for his help in computing the exponential of the skew-symmetric metrics encountered in this research.

References

[1] Y. Amit. A multiflow approximation to diffusions. *Stochastic Processes and their Applications*, 37(2):213–238, 1991. ,

[2] P. N. Belhumeur, J. P. Hepanha, and D. J. Kriegman. Eigenfaces vs. fisherfaces: Recognition using class specific linear projection. *IEEE Transactions on Pattern Analysis and Machine Intelligence*, 19(7):711–720, 1997.

[3] William M. Boothby. *An Introduction to Differential Manifolds and Riemannian Geometry*. Academic Press, Inc., 1986. ,

[4] A. Edelman, T. Arias, and S. T. Smith. The geometry of algorithms with orthogonality constraints. *SIAM Journal of Matrix Analysis and Applications*, 20(2):303–353, 1998.

[5] D. J. Field. What is the goal of sensory coding? *Neural Computation*, 6(4):559–601, 1994. ,

[6] S. Geman and C.-R. Hwang. Diffusions for global optimization. *SIAM J. Control and Optimization*, 24(24):1031–1043, 1987.

[7] U. Grenander and M. I. Miller. Representations of knowledge in complex systems. *Journal of the Royal Statistical Society*, 56(3), 1994. ,

[8] D. J. Heeger and J. R. Bergen. Pyramid-based texture analysis/synthesis. In *Proceedings of SIGGRAPHS*, pages 229–238, 1995.

[9] U. Helmke and J. B. Moore. *Optimization and Dynamical Systmes*. Springer, 1996.

[10] A. Hyvarinen. Fast and robust fixed-point algorithm for independent component analysis. *IEEE Transactions on Neural Networks*, 10:626–634, 1999. ,

[11] X. Liu and L. Cheng. Independent spectral representations of images for recognition. *Journal of Optical Society of America A*, 20(7), 2003.

[12] S. K. Murase and S. K. Nayar. Visual learning and recognition of 3-D objects from appearance. *International Journal of Computer Vision*, 14(1):5–24, 1995.

[13] B. A. Olshausen and D. J. Field. Emergence of simple-cell receptive field properties by learning a sparse code for natural images. *Nature*, 381:607–609, 1996. ,

[14] C. P. Robert and G. Casella. *Monte Carlo Statistical Methods*. Springer Text in Stat., 1999. ,

[15] A. Srivastava, U. Grenander, G. R. Jensen, and M. I. Miller. Jump-diffusion markov processes on orthogonal groups for object recognition. *Journal of Statistical Planning and Inference*, 103(1-2):15–37, 2002.

[16] A. Srivastava, M. I. Miller, and U. Grenander. *Ergodic Algorithms on Special Euclidean Groups for ATR*. Systems and Control in the Twenty-First Century: Progress in Systems and Control, Volume 22. Birkhauser, 1997.

[17] F. W. Warner. *Foundations of Differentiable Manifolds and Lie Groups.* Springer-Verlag, New York, 1994.

[18] S. C. Zhu, Y. N. Wu, and D. Mumford. "Minimax entropy principles and its application to texture modeling". *Neural Computation,* 9(8):1627–1660, November 1997.

Local PCA for Strip Line Detection and Thinning

Zhi-Yong Liu, Kai-Chun Chiu, and Lei Xu

Department of Computer Science and Engineering
The Chinese University of Hong Kong
Shatin, N.T. Hong Kong, P.R. China

Abstract. We solve the tasks of strip line detection and thinning in image processing and pattern recognition in help of an energy minimization technique called rival penalized competitive learning (RPCL) based local principal component analysis (PCA). Due to its model selection and noise resistance ability, the technique is shown to outperform conventional Hough transform and thinning algorithms via a number of simulations.

1   Introduction

Strip line detection and thinning are two basic problems in image processing and pattern recognition. In this paper, we introduce an energy function minimization based technique for solving both tasks.

Strip line detection concerns identifying a thick, linear pattern from an image. This can be achieved by detecting the main axis of the strip line concerned. In literature, Hough transform [,] is an important tool for line detection. Its further advances in term of randomized Hough transform [,] not only considerably reduces the time and space complexity of the conventional Hough transform, but also increases the resolution of parameterization and the robustness to outliers. However, neither Hough transform nor randomized Hough transform can be directly used to detect thick strip lines. The problem is usually resolved by either adopting edge detection for preprocessing or instead, extending Hough transform on strip band detection [ ]. The first approach actually converts the problem of strip line detection to edge line detection and thus make Hough transform applicable. However, what we desire is detecting the main axis of the strip line itself, instead of its edges. Though we may further extend Hough transform to direct the main axis as in [ ], the resulted performance is still far from satisfactory when used for detecting a set of parallel, thick strip lines, especially under the conventional normal or uniform noises.

Image thinning [ ] is used for eliminating redundant pixels in image. In general, thinning is effected via iteratively deleting the successive layers of pixels on the boundary of the pattern until the skeleton remains [ ]. However, such a pixel-by-pixel approach has no noise tolerance ability and thus performs poorly in a noisy environment. Moreover, its performance would deteriorate greatly for the blurred pattern that has some deformation on the skeleton.

A. Rangarajan et al. (Eds.): EMMCVPR 2003, LNCS 2683, pp. 21–   , 2003.

Recently, energy minimization methods become more and more popular in the fields of computer vision and pattern recognition (see, for instance, [,   ,]). Energy minimization methods usually consist of two steps. The first step is to formulate an objective function, or called energy function, which is then minimized in the second step. A typical example of such approach is the least mean square error reconstruction (LMSER) [ ] proposed to locally detect the main axis from each of the multiple clusters as via minimizing the following energy function [ ],

$$E_{MW} = \sum_{i=1}^{N_c} E_{mw}^{(i)}, E_{mw}^{(i)} = \sum_{X \in S_i} \|(X - m_i)(I - w_i w_i^t)\|^2 \tag{1}$$

where $m_i = \frac{1}{\#S_j} \sum_{X \in S_i} X$, and w_i is the first principal component vector of the ith cluster at minimum. Incidentally, under the assumption of gaussian distribution and restricting the number of interesting principal component to be one only for each cluster, local principal component analysis (PCA) actually performs the function of locating the main axes of all gaussian clusters. From this perspective, local PCA can be considered as a special case of the local LMSER.

In this paper, we introduce how the tasks of stirp line detection and thinning can be achieved by RPCL-based local PCA, in view of its robustness under gaussian noise as compared to Hough transform related approaches. For the problems of detecting lines or strips on images, however, pixels spreading from its main axis are more likely from a uniform distribution instead of a gaussian distribution. In this paper, we further investigate the problem of detecting the main axis of strip lines on images. First, in section 2 we mathematically show that the main axis found by PCA is also the main axis of pixels uniformly distributed on a strip, which thus justifies directly using local PCA for strip line detection. Second, in section 3 we choose the recently proposed RPCL-based local PCA model for implementation. The performance has been shown by experiments in Section 4 to outperform both that of Hough transform based and line thinning based approaches. Finally we conclude in Section 5.

2   A Mathematical Justification on Using Local PCA for Strip Pattern Detection and Thinning

The term local PCA [, , , ,   ] comes from the extension of PCA. Principal component analysis [ ] involves a mathematical procedure that linearly transforms a number of correlated variables into a (smaller) number of uncorrelated variables called principal components. It is frequently adopted for dimensionality reduction as the mean square error (MSE) upon reconstruction error is minimized. However, when the data is from multi-modes, performing PCA can be far from satisfactory and thus its local extension is preferable. Fig.   and Fig.   are two simple examples generated from three gaussian's, where it is better to perform PCA locally on each of multiple clusters to detect its main axis

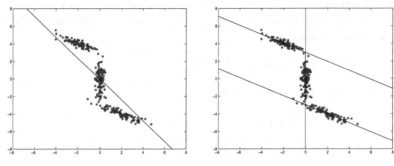

Fig. 1. By PCA description   **Fig. 2.** By local PCA description

as a detected line [,]. A similar concept for curve detection was also discussed in [ ] from the perspective of clustering analysis, with an efficient model selection ability in help of the RPCL learning. Such local PCA based approaches are more robust under gaussian noise in comparison with the Hough transform related approaches, when the first principal component can be described by the main axis of a cluster of samples from a gaussian distribution as shown in Fig. . However, for a problem of detecting strip line on image, pixels spreading from its main axis are more likely from a uniform distribution instead of a gaussian distribution.

Here we mathematically prove the following theorem, which states that the main axis, or the first principal component found by PCA on a strip line with the uniformly distributed pixels is also its main axis, which thus justifies directly using local PCA for strip line detection.

Theorem 1. *The first principal component obtained by PCA on a strip line with uniformly distributed pixels is its main axis.*

Proof. Without loss of generality, assume pixel distribution being bivariate uniform, symmetrical with being $U(-m, m)$ and $U(-n, n)$ on x and y direction respectively, as shown in Fig. .

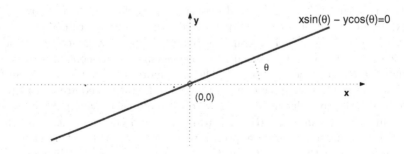

Fig. 3. Uniform distribution of line pixels

Let the first principal component pass through origin $[0,0]^T$ and in the direction $[\cos\theta, \sin\theta]^T$. Denote any pixel $s = [x,y]^T$. Transformation via the first principal component results in

$$\tilde{s} = [\cos\theta, \sin\theta][x,y]^T = x\cos\theta + y\sin\theta. \qquad (2)$$

This implies the reconstructed signal $\hat{s}$ is

$$\hat{s} = [\cos\theta, \sin\theta]^T \tilde{s}$$
$$= \begin{bmatrix} x\cos^2\theta + y\cos\theta\sin\theta \\ y\sin^2\theta + x\cos\theta\sin\theta \end{bmatrix}. \qquad (3)$$

MSE of the reconstructed data is

$$e = (\hat{s} - s)^T(\hat{s} - s)$$
$$= x^2\sin^2\theta + y^2\cos^2\theta - 2xy\cos\theta\sin\theta. \qquad (4)$$

Take expectation of ( ) over all the reconstructed pixels. The expected MSE is

$$E = E_s\{(\hat{s} - s)^T(\hat{s} - s)\}$$
$$= E_{x,y}\{x^2\sin^2\theta + y^2\cos^2\theta - 2xy\cos\theta\sin\theta\}$$
$$= \sin^2\theta\mathrm{Var}(x) + \cos^2\theta\mathrm{Var}(y)$$
$$= \frac{m^2}{3} - \frac{(m^2 - n^2)}{3}\cos^2\theta \qquad (5)$$

With $m > n$, expected MSE of the reconstructed data eqn( ) is minimized when $\cos^2\theta = 1$, which implies that the first principal component is the x-axis, or the main axis of the strip line.

3   An Algorithm for RPCL-Based Local PCA

Local PCA can be implemented in several ways. One direct way is to make clustering or estimate a gaussian mixture as the first step and then to perform PCA on each cluster or gaussian as the second step [ ]. A better way is to make the two steps coordinately such that the first step and the second step are performed alternatively [, ,]. Moreover, instead of using the full covariance matrix, each covariance matrix is represented either in a constrained covariance matrix in term of the principal component and the noise variance [,] or an equivalent way that directly considers each principal component and the noise variance in a reconstruction cost [ ]. They are more preferred especially in the case of small sample size, since free parameters to be estimated are considerably reduced. An adaptive algorithm on how to estimate each principal component is given in [ ] via combining RPCL learning [ ] and Oja rule. Also, in help of the RPCL learning a clustering approach was proposed for detecting curve [ ], which performs exactly local PCA in the 2-dimensional case, but becomes local minor principal analysis (MCA) in high-dimensional case. This can be compared with other local PCA approaches, which actually perform local subspace analysis when used on high-dimensional data. Recently, an improved RPCL learning based local PCA approach was proposed in [ ].

As preliminarily described in [ ], a salient advantage of RPCL learning based local PCA is being able to automatically determine the number of clusters (lines) during learning its parameters, which is also shared by the Hard cut local LMSER algorithm in [ ]. However, such an advantage is not shared by the maximum likelihood learning based models [, ,], for which the task of selecting the number of lines should be achieved via some model selection criteria, e.g., the Akaike's information criterion (AIC) [ ],

$$\min AIC(k) = -2\log(\mathcal{L}_{ML}) + 12k - 2, \tag{6}$$

where $\mathcal{L}_{ML}$ denotes the maximized likelihood function value. However, it involves enumerating the objective function for different k's and thus is computationally expensive.

Based on the above discussion, this paper chooses the RPCL learning based local PCA in [ ] for our strip line detection task.

The key idea behind RPCL is that for each sample point, not only the winner cluster center is pulled toward the point, but also the rival (2nd winner) one is pushed slightly away from it. Mathematically, it consists of the following two steps [,]:

Step 1: Find the winner cluster center i_c and the rival one i_r as

$$i_c = \arg\min_i \gamma_i d_i(x), i_r = \arg\min_{i \neq i_c} \gamma_i d_i(x), \tag{7}$$

where $\gamma_i = n_i / \sum_{j=1}^{k} n_i$ with n_i denoting the cumulative times of the cluster i being winner and $d_i(x)$ denotes distance between sample x and cluster i.

Step 2:

$$\theta_{i_c}^{new} = \theta_{i_c}^{old} - \eta_c \nabla_{\theta_{i_c}} d_{i_c}(x), \theta_{i_r}^{new} = \theta_{i_r}^{old} + \eta_r \nabla_{\theta_{i_r}} d_{i_r}(x) \tag{8}$$

where θ_i denotes the parameter under consideration, e.g., the cluster center, $\nabla_{\theta_i} d_i(x)$ denotes the derivative of $d_i(x)$ with respect to θ_i, and the learning rate $\eta_c \gg$ de-learning rate η_r.

Learning via RPCL will not only possess model selection ability via pushing the redundant cluster centers far away from the data, but also avoid the so-called dead unit problem for clustering due to the introduced de-learning mechanism [ ].

Consider the gaussian mixture model

$$p(x|\theta) = \sum_{i=1}^{k} \alpha_i G(x|\mu_i, \Sigma_i) \tag{9}$$

where $\alpha_i > 0$, $\sum_{i=1}^{k} \alpha_i = 1$, $G(x|\mu_i, \Sigma_i)$ denotes a gaussian density with mean vector μ_i and covariance matrix Σ_i. In this case, $d_i(x)$ in the above step 1 is specifically given by the following general *distance* metric (Xu, 2001):

$$d_i(x_t) = -\ln[G(x_t|\mu_i, \Sigma_i)\alpha_i] \tag{10}$$

For the task of strip line detection and thinning where only the first principal component is under consideration, we consider a special case of the elliptic RPCL algorithm (i.e., eqn(33) given in [ ]) by focusing on a covariance matrix as follows:

$$\Sigma_i = \varsigma_i I + \sigma_i \phi_i \phi_i^T \tag{11}$$

where $\phi_i^T \phi_i = 1, \varsigma_i > 0, \sigma_i > 0$, and the first principal component is ϕ_i. Then, similar to the energy function eqn( ) for the local LMSER, we can get the following energy function for the local PCA based strip line detection and thinning approach,

$$rclE_\Theta = \sum_{i=1}^{N_c} E_\theta^{(i)}, \tag{12}$$

$$E_\theta^{(i)} = \sum_{X \in S_i} d_i(X),$$

$$d_i(x_t) = -\ln[G(x_t|\mu_i, \Sigma_i)\alpha_i],$$

$$\Sigma_i = \varsigma_i I + \sigma_i \phi_i \phi_i^T$$

In this energy function, the parameters to be determined are $\Theta = \{\alpha_i, \mu_i, \phi_i, \sigma_i, \varsigma_i\}_{i=1}^{k}$. Thus, for the step 2 for RPCL learning, we find the gradients of $d_i(x_t)$ with respective to Θ as follows:

$$\nabla_{\alpha_i} = -1/\alpha_i, \nabla_{\mu_i} = -e_{i,t} \tag{13}$$

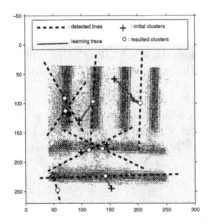

Fig. 4. ML-based local PCA with wrong number of clusters

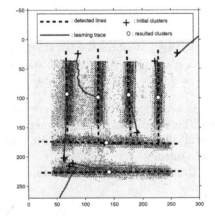

Fig. 5. Result by RPCL-based local PCA with model selection

$$\nabla_{\varsigma_i} = 0.5\mathrm{Tr}(\Sigma_i)^{-1}(\mathrm{I} - S_i(\Sigma_i)^{-1}) \tag{14}$$

$$\nabla_{\sigma_i} = 0.5\phi_i^T(\Sigma_i)^{-1}(\mathrm{I} - S_i(\Sigma_i)^{-1})\phi_i \tag{15}$$

$$\nabla_{\phi_i} = \sigma_i(\Sigma_i)^{-1}(\mathrm{I} - S_i(\Sigma_i)^{-1})\phi_i \tag{16}$$

where $S_i = e_{i,t}e_{i,t}^T$ with $e_{i,t} = x_t - \mu_i$. $\varsigma_i = e^{\varrho_i}$ and $\sigma_i = e^{\omega_i}$ can be introduced to constrain $\varsigma_i > 0$ and $\sigma_i > 0$ respectively, and the constraints $\sum_{i=1}^k \alpha_i = 1$ and $\phi_i^T\phi_i = 1$ can be satisfied via no more than one step of normalization.

4   Simulations

We present four experiments to illustrate the RPCL-based local PCA for strip line detection and thinning. The first experiment aims to illustrate the model selection ability of the RPCL-based local PCA, the second and third ones to demonstrate the strip line and thinning respectively, and the last one to illustrate how the RPCL-based local PCA can be used to aid container recognition.

4.1   On Model Selection

This experiment aims to illustrate the importance of model selection for the strip line detection and thinning. We base our comparison on two algorithms. They are respectively the maximum likelihood learning based local PCA algorithm [   ] with and without model selection by AIC and the RPCL-based local PCA with embedded model selection. The original image is extracted from an image of striped shirt (Fig. 9.25(a) in [   ]). For the maximum likelihood learning without model selection by AIC and RPCL-based local PCA algorithms, we randomly initialize 8 cluster centers; for the maximum likelihood learning with model selection by AIC, we enumerate the AIC function by increasing k from 1.

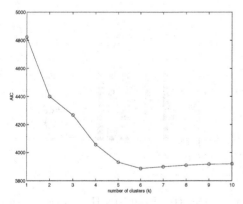

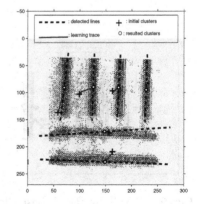

Fig. 6. AIC varies as the number of clusters k

Fig. 7. ML-based local PCA with correct number of clusters

Fig. 8. The original real image

Fig.   and Fig.   respectively illustrate the line detection results of the maximum likelihood learning based local PCA without model selection by AIC and RPCL-based local PCA. Without model selection, the maximum likelihood learning based local PCA cannot drive the redundant cluster centers away. Some cluster centers occupy more than one cluster while on the other hand, two or more cluster centers share one cluster or some centers occupy nothing at all. The later is closely related to the problem of dead unit. Consequently, not only the 6 lines in the original image is incorrectly detected as 7, but also the position of the 4 lines are misplaced. Although maximum likelihood learning based local PCA with model selection by AIC can detect the right number of clusters, as shown in Fig.   and   , its time complexity growths greatly, which ($\sim$ 179s) is about 7 times of the RPCL-based local PCA ($\sim$ 26s). On the other hand, pushing force on the rival resulted from the de-learning of the RPCL learning can be traced from the paths of the redundant cluster centers in Fig.   . As a result, the RPCL-based local PCA succeeds in line detection via a more efficient model selection ability.

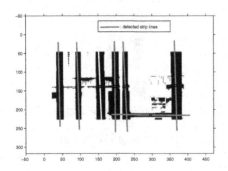

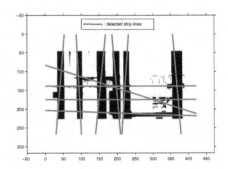

Fig. 9. Result by RPCL-based local PCA

Fig. 10. Result by Hough transform

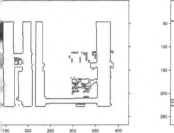

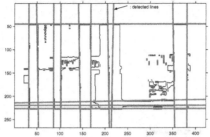

ulted image via edge de-   **Fig. 12.** Result by Hough transform

ip Lines Detection

n aims at comparing the effectiveness of RPCL-based local PCA
ansform for strip line detection. The effectiveness performance of
d Hough transform is similar on such a task. Fig. shows the
taken in our campus. The image threshold is set according to the
ogram approach [ ]. Here we use Hough transform in two ways
a, i.e., first directly on the image and then with preprocessing by
. We initialize 10 random cluster centers for the RPCL-based local
n at the beginning of the simulation.

Hough transform without edge detection are shown in Fig.
) "peaks" in Fig. correspond to the 10 lines in Fig. , which is
ith the original 7 strip lines. Results of the Hough transform after
are shown in Fig. ,   and respectively. The 14 "peaks" in
ond to the 14 lines in Fig. , from which it is also hard to obtain

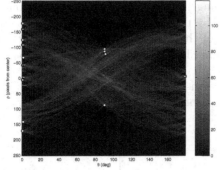

ks" of Hough transform   **Fig. 14.** "Peaks" of Hough transform
detection   after edge detection

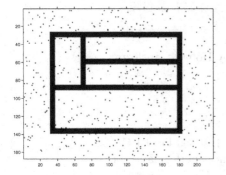

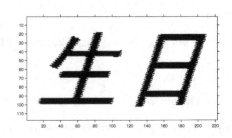

Fig. 15. Original table image with background noise

Fig. 16. Original blurred Chinese character image

the 7 original strip lines. The results can be compared with the successful one by RPCL-based local PCA shown in Fig. .

4.3   On Strip Lines Thinning

This experiment compares the performance of RPCL-based local PCA and conventional thinning algorithm [ ] on strip lines thinning when image is affected by uniform background noise, as the *table* image shown in Fig.   , or is blurred due to scanning, as the Chinese characters shown in Fig.   .

Results of thinning for the *table* by the conventional approach are shown in Fig.   and that by the RPCL-based local PCA in Fig.   and   . On the other hand, results of thinning for the Chinese characters by the conventional approach are shown in Fig.   and that by the RPCL-based local PCA in Fig. and   .

From Fig.   we can see that the RPCL-based local PCA not only can outline the main skeleton of the original *table* image, but also remove background

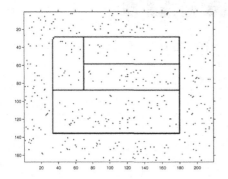

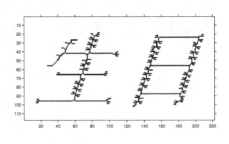

Fig. 17. Result by thinning algorithm

Fig. 18. Result by thinning algorithm

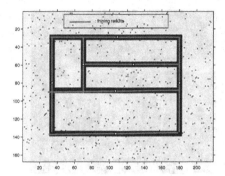

Fig. 19. Result by RPCL-based local PCA

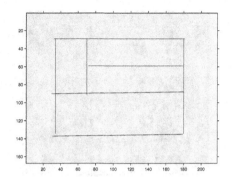

Fig. 20. Skeleton by RPCL-based local PCA

noise. On the contrary, as shown in Fig.   , the conventional pixel-by-pixel thinning approach fails to remove the background noise. Also, when the skeleton of Chinese characters is blurred as shown in Fig.   , the conventional thinning algorithm cannot obtain the main axis via *magnifying* its distorted outliers. This can be contrasted with the success by RPCL-based local PCA in capturing its main structure as shown in Fig.   .

4.4   On Container Recognition

Automatic container recognition system is very useful for customs or logistic management. Here we illustrate how the RPCL-based local PCA can be employed in such a system. Container recognition is usually based on the captured container number located at the back of the container. For example, the container in Fig.   can be recognized by the number "OCLU 152277 0". The whole process can be roughly broken down into two subtasks. The first one involves locating and extracting a rectangular area of the raw image that contains the number, and the second one concerns actually recognizing the number via some image processing and pattern recognition techniques.

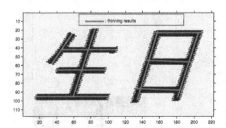

Fig. 21. Result by RPCL-based local PCA

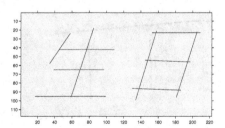

Fig. 22. Skeleton by RPCL-based local PCA

Fig. 23. Original container image   **Fig. 24.** Pre-processed image

Using the container in Fig.   as an example, we first preprocess the image by sharpening, erosion, and threshold, with the resulted image shown in Fig.   . For the first subtask, we may adopt the RPCL-based local PCA to roughly locate the container number via detecting several (four in this example) standard strip lines as shown in Fig.   . Based on the lowest detected strip line (the dashed one in Fig.   ), area with roughly a rectangular shape as shown in Fig.   can be extracted from the raw image. Then, the number can be subsequently recognized using some other popular image processing and pattern recognition techniques.

5   Conclusion and Future Work

In this paper, we introduce how the RPCL-based local PCA, an energy minimization approach, can be novelly applied to two traditional image processing tasks, i.e, strip lines detection and thinning, respectively. In particular, its model selection property is beneficial for automatically determining the line number and its

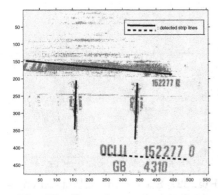

Fig. 25. Four detected strip lines   **Fig. 26.** Detected interesting area

noise resistance property is helpful for thinning. Because the focus of this paper is on the study of linear structure, future research effort may be directed to its nonlinear extension.

Acknowledgement

The work described in this paper was fully supported by a grant from the Research Grant Council of the Hong Kong SAR (Project No: CUHK 4336/02E).

References

[1] H. Akaike. A new look at statistical model identification. *IEEE Trans. Automatic Control*, 19(2):716–723, 1974.

[2] D.H. Ballard. Generalizing the hough transform to detect arbitrary shapes. *Pattern Recognition*, 13(2):111–122, 1981.

[3] E. R. Davies and A. P. N. Plummer. Thinning algorithms: A critique and a new methodology. *Pattern Recognition*, 14:53–63, 1981.   ,

[4] S. Geman and D. Geman. Stochastic relaxation, gibbs distributions, and the bayesian restoration of images. *IEEE Transaction on Pattern Analysis and Machine Intelligence*, 6:721–741, 1984.

[5] G.E. Hinton, M. Revow, and P. Dayan. Recognizing handwritten digits using mixtures of linear models. *Advances in Neural Information Processing System*, 7:1015–1022, 1995.   ,   ,

[6] T. Hofmann, J. Puzicha, and J. M. Buhmann. Unsupervised texture segmentation in a deterministic annealing framework. *IEEE Transaction on Pattern Analysis and Machine Intelligence*, 20(8):803–818, 1998.

[7] P.V.C. Hough. Method and means for recognizing complex patterns. *U.S. Patent 3069654*, 18, Dec. 1962.

[8] I. T. Jolliffe. *Principal Component Analysis*. Springer-Verlag, New York, 1986.

[9] N. Kambhatla and T.K. Leen. Dimension reduction by local principal component analysis. *Neural Computation*, 9:1493–1516, 1997.   ,   ,

[10] R. C. Lo and W. H. Tsai. Gray-scale hough transform for thick line detection in gray-scale images. *Pattern Recognition*, 28:647–661, 1995.

[11] S. Marchand-Maillet and Y. M. Sharaiha. *Binary Digital Image Processing: A Discrete Approach*. Academic Press, 2000.

[12] J. D. McCafferty. *Human and Machine Vision*. Ellis Horwood, 1990.

[13] U. Otsu. A threshold selection method from gray-level histograms. *IEEE Trans. Systems, Man and Cybernetics*, 9(1):62–67, 1979.

[14] T. Poggio, V. Torre, and C. Koch. Computational vision and regularization theory. *Nature*, 317:314–319, 1985.

[15] M.E. Tipping and C.M. Bishop. Mixtures of probabilistic principal component analysis. *Neural Computation*, 11:443–482, 1999.   ,   ,   ,

[16] L. Xu. Least mse reconstruction: A principle for self-organizing nets. *Neural Networks*, 6:627–648, 1993.

[17] L Xu. Multisets modeling learning: An unified theory for supervised and unsupervised learning. *Proc. of 1994 IEEE International Conference on Neural Networks*, I:315–320, 1994.   ,   ,

[18] L Xu. Vector quantization by local and hierarchical lmser. *Proc. of 1995 International Conference on Artificial Neural Networks (ICANN)*, II:575–579, 1995.   ,

,
[19] L Xu. Rival penalized competitive learning, finite mixture, and multisets clustering. *Proc. of IEEE-INNS International Joint Conference on Neural Networks*, II:2525–2530, 1998.   ,

[20] L Xu. An overview on unsupervised learning from data mining perspective. *Advances in Self-Organizing Maps, Nigel Allison, et al eds, Springer-Verlag*, pages 181–210, 2001.   ,   ,

[21] L. Xu, A. Krzyzak, and E. Oja. Rival penalized competitive learning for clustering analysis, rbf net, and curve detection. *IEEE Trans. on Neural Networks*, 4:636–649, 1993.   ,   ,

[22] L. Xu and E. Oja. Randomized hough transform (rht): Basic mechanisms, algorithms and complexities. *Computer Vision, Graphics, and Image Processing: Image Understanding*, 57(2):131–154, 1993.

[23] L. Xu, E. Oja, and P. Kultanen. A new curve detection method: Randomized hough transform (rht). *Pattern Recognition Letter*, 11:331–338, 1990.

Curve Matching
Using the Fast Marching Method

Max Frenkel and Ronen Basri

Weizmann Institute of Science, Rehovot, Israel
{maksimf,ronen}@wisdom.weizmann.ac.il

Abstract. Common techniques for curve alignment find a solution in the form of a shortest network path by means of dynamic programming. In this paper we present an approach that employs Sethian's Fast Marching Method to find the solution with sub-resolution accuracy and in consistence with the underlying continuous problem. We demonstrate how the method may be applied to compare closed curves, morph one curve into another, and compute curve averages. Our method is based on a local curve dissimilarity function $F(t, s)$ that compares the two input curves $C_1(t)$ and $C_2(s)$ at given points t and s. In our experiments, we compare dissimilarity functions based on local curvature information and on shape contexts. We have tested the algorithm on a database of 110 sample curves by performing "best matches" experiments.

1 Introduction

Determining similarity is a problem that lies at the heart of computer vision. Given two line drawings of say a digit 2, one that has a loop at the bottom and the other that has a sharp corner, such as the curves in Fig. (a), how can we judge that they both depict the digit 2 and not two different digits? In order to answer this question, we need to define some sort of a similarity measure to relate objects of the same class and distinguish between objects of different classes.

Suppose that the input curves are given to us as a sequence of curve coordinates in the order in which they were produced by a pen. One way of assessing similarity between such curves is by means of dynamic programming (a brief review of past work is given in Sect.). Input curves are treated as if they were strings, and curve points - as if they were letters. Just like a string can be edited to transform it into another string by inserting, deleting and relabelling characters, the first curve is stretched, shortened, and bent to match the second curve. For instance, in order to match SHALL with HELLO, we can delete an S, change an A to an E and insert an O. If we associate a cost with each of the three basic operations, then by summing the costs during each edit sequence we obtain a way of comparing different sequences and picking the optimal edit operation. The *edit distance* between the strings is defined as the minimal such sum of local costs. The string-to-string correction algorithm [ ] employs dynamic programming to compute this distance between strings S_1 and S_2 and to

A. Rangarajan et al. (Eds.): EMMCVPR 2003, LNCS 2683, pp. 35– , 2003.

recover a *trace* or a *matching* - a set of non-crossing lines between the letters of S_1 and the letters of S_2, where each line corresponds to a relabel operation in the optimal edit sequence. In the above example, the matching would be {(S,ε), (H,H), (A,E), (L,L), (L,L), (ε, O)}, where ε corresponds to the empty character.

In a similar fashion, discretized curves can be compared using dynamic programming by summing up the local costs of curve deformation operations, and the optimal *curve matching* may be recovered. In this paper we intend to study the dynamic programming approach, point out its inherent drawback related to curve discretization, and suggest a different way of obtaining the solution using Sethian's Fast Marching Method that avoids the shortcoming of the edit distance approach. Possible areas of application of curve matching include handwritten character recognition [ ], image indexing [ ], and tracking [ ]. We will test our algorithm by comparing various handwritten digits and letters.

1.1   Past Work

Edit distances were used extensively in the past to compare curves. Here we only mention a few relevant examples. [ ] introduced a measure that relied on intrinsic properties of curves (such as curvature), and compared curves using dynamic programming. [ ] proposed a set of properties that a desired similarity function should possess. Among other things, these properties preferred the deformations that preserve the part structure of objects over those that modify the parts. [,] emphasized the importance of a symmetric treatment of curves. [ ] also presented an efficient method (based on [ ]) to treat closed curves.

A wide variety of other approaches have been taken to solve the problem of curve alignment. For example, [ ] compared non-rigid object shapes by measuring the amount of deformation required to register the shapes exactly. Assuming that the amount of deformation between shapes is small, they used gradient descent to determine the deformation parameters. [ ] described shapes by a list of properties and their relations and used pattern matching techniques to judge similarity. [ ] deformed shapes by aligning the principal modes of their mass and stiffness matrices.

Recently Belongie et al. [ ] introduced the *shape context*, a rich local shape descriptor that aids in judging shape similarity and in finding correspondences between similar shape points.

Matching Unordered Point Sets with Shape Contexts. The method employed by Belongie et al. solves a more general problem of matching an unordered set of n points $\mathcal{P} = \{p_1, ..., p_n\}, p_i \in \mathbb{R}^2$ sampled somehow (e.g., by an edge detector) from the given input image. We would like to match each point p_i from the first set to some point q_j from the second set. Consider the set of $n-1$ vectors that originate at p_i and extend to p_l, for $l \neq i$. A shape context h_i is a histogram of coordinates of p_l relative to p_i, namely $r_{li} = p_l - p_i$. In the experiments of Belongie et al., h_i is a 5 by 12 array. Length of r_{li} is quantized into 5 bins, and its orientation is quantized into 12 bins. Thus the shape context encodes the distribution of relative positions in a robust and compact way.

From here, Belongie et al. proceed to define $C_{ij} = C(\boldsymbol{p}_i, \boldsymbol{q}_j)$ as the cost of matching $\boldsymbol{p}_i$ with $\boldsymbol{q}_j$ and use the χ^2 test statistic to compare the histograms $h_i(k)$ and $h_j(k)$ at $\boldsymbol{p}_i$ and $\boldsymbol{q}_j$ as follows:

$$C(\boldsymbol{p}_i, \boldsymbol{q}_j) = \frac{1}{2} \sum_{k=1}^{K} \frac{[h_i(k) - h_j(k)]^2}{h_i(k) + h_j(k)} \ , \tag{1}$$

where K is the total number of bins in the histograms. Once the local matching cost is defined, the total cost $H(\pi)$ is minimized.

$$H(\pi) = \sum_i C(\boldsymbol{p}_i, \boldsymbol{q}_{\pi(i)}) \ , \tag{2}$$

where π is a permutation of the second shape indexes, i.e., the matching is one-to-one. The permutation π that achieves the above minimum can be obtained using various weighted bipartite graph matching algorithms that take the matrix C_{ij} as input.

The curve matching problem that we are facing is more specific in that it requires that the points in the input set be ordered. The order of the points is an extra piece of information that may be utilized. The edit distance algorithm that we review next does just that.

The Dynamic Programming Approach to Curve Matching. Denote the curve segments to be matched by $\mathcal{C}_1(t) = (x_1(t), y_1(t))$, $t \in [0, m]$ and $\mathcal{C}_2(s) = (x_2(s), y_2(s))$, $s : [0, n]$, where t is arc-length, x_1 and y_1 are the coordinates of curve points, m is curve length, and each is similarly defined for $\mathcal{C}_2$. A correspondence between $\mathcal{C}_1$ and $\mathcal{C}_2$ is specified by a function $s(t)$, which is a monotonic, one to one mapping from arc-length onto arc-length so that the point $\mathcal{C}_1(t)$ is matched with the point $\mathcal{C}_2(s(t))$. Given a correspondence $s(t)$, a similarity measure between $\mathcal{C}_1$ and $\mathcal{C}_2$ can be defined by a distance function $C(\mathcal{C}_1, \mathcal{C}_2)$ that judges the cost of deforming one curve into the other, e.g., [ ]:

$$C(\mathcal{C}_1, \mathcal{C}_2) = \int_{\mathcal{C}_1} F(\kappa_1(t), \kappa_2(s(t)), \frac{ds}{dt}) dt \ , \tag{3}$$

where $\kappa_1(t)$ is the curvature of $\mathcal{C}_1$ at t and $\kappa_2(s)$ is the curvature of $\mathcal{C}_2$ at $s(t)$. The cost function conveys the goodness of a correspondence between the two curves. C integrates over the curves a measure F of local differences of corresponding subsegments. The distance (dissimilarity) $C^*(\mathcal{C}_1, \mathcal{C}_2)$ between $\mathcal{C}_1$ and $\mathcal{C}_2$ is the distance that minimizes C over all possible matchings $s(t)$. One example of a local cost function is

$$F(\kappa_1, \kappa_2, s') = |\kappa_2 s' - \kappa_1| + \lambda |s' - 1| \ , \tag{4}$$

where the first term penalizes bending and the second term penalizes stretching.

To discretize the problem, the two input contours are represented as ordered chains: $T = \{u(t) : t = 0, 1, ..., m\}$ and $S = \{v(s) : s = 0, 1, ..., n\}$, where $u(t)$

are the coordinates of the first contour, parameterized by t, and $v(s)$ are the coordinates of the other contour, parameterized by s. We then seek to find the optimal matching $(\alpha_1, ..., \alpha_N)$, that minimizes $C(T, S)$. Here

$$\alpha_k = (u(t_k), v(s_k)), \; t_k \in \{1, ..., m\}, s_k \in \{1, ..., n\}, k = 1, ..., N \; , \qquad (5)$$

and if it is assumed that the endpoints of the curves match, then $\alpha_1 = (u(1), v(1))$ and $\alpha_N = (u(m), v(n))$.

Returning to the string matching problem described in the introduction, the *edit distance* between strings is defined as the cost of the optimal sequence of edit operations: relabelling, deleting, and inserting characters [ ]. In the curve matching problem, curve points serve as "characters". Bending a curve (changing the curvature) or stretching it at a point corresponds to relabelling a letter. Removing a point of $\mathcal{C}_1$ is analogous to a deletion, and removing a point on $\mathcal{C}_2$ - to an insertion. So the cost measure ( ) is related to the optimal amount of *deforming* needed in order to make the two curves identical [ ].

This problem can also be viewed as an optimal path problem. We let each match $w = (u(t), v(s))$ be a node in a graph G and link it to those nodes that correspond to predecessor matches $(u(t_p), v(s_p))$ of w. Further, we assign a weight to an edge between a predecessor match and the current match that corresponds to the cost of deforming the segment $[u(t_p), u(t)]$ so that it coincides with the segment $[v(s_p), v(s)]$. Then, finding the matching with the lowest cost reduces to finding an optimal path in G from the start node to the end node. An example of such a network path is shown in Fig. (b). Diagonal path segments signify a local "relabel" operation, while horizontal/vertical segments signify removing points on one of the curves. Stretching a curve at a point is marked by red (dotted in black and white production) diagonal segments that jump across several cells [ ].

Sethian [ ] discusses network path algorithms and mentions that the network imposes an unnatural metric on the problem. Imagine a rectangular graph with unit weights on all edges. If we were computing a path from the bottom left corner to the top right corner according to the L_1 distance metric, then several paths would qualify as "shortest" (see Fig. (c)). However, the true solution is a straight line diagonal between the source and the destination points (Fig. (d)), and none of the obtained network paths would be of desired length even if the resolution of the graph was refined (i.e. if the curves were sub-sampled). The drawback is in the discretization itself in that it is *inconsistent* with the underlying continuous problem. The true solution must be described by the underlying differential equation, and if we had managed to find a continuous solution then we would in fact solve the problem with sub-resolution accuracy. The Fast Marching Method provides the means to achieve that goal.

An interesting attempt to modify the dynamic programming procedure to allow for sub-pixel matching of curves has been proposed in [ ]. This method attempts to store a parametric description of the optimal cost at every node, and this limits the method to quite specific cost functions. The Fast Marching Method provides a simpler and more generic way to achieve this goal.

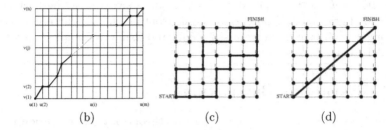

Fig. 1. (a) An example of a *2* drawn in different ways. (b) An example of a discrete alignment curve given as a shortest path in a graph. (c) Multiple "shortest" network paths and (b) the optimal diagonal path given by the Fast Marching Method

1.2   The Fast Marching Method

The Fast Marching Method is an $O(N \log N)$ technique for solving the Eikonal equation, $|\nabla T(x, y)| = F(x, y)$, for T given F on a rectangular grid, where N is the total number of grid points. An important property of the Fast Marching Method is that it converges to the continuous viscosity solution of the Eikonal equation as the rectangular numerical grid is refined [ ]. In computer vision, the Fast Marching Method has been applied to various applications including active contours [ ] and shape from shading [ ].

The algorithm is based on the following upwind approximation of the Eikonal equation:

$$((\max(D_{ij}^{-x}T, -D_{ij}^{+x}T, 0))^2 + (\max(D_{ij}^{-y}T, -D_{ij}^{+y}T, 0))^2)^{1/2} = f_{ij} , \qquad (6)$$

where $f_{ij} = F(i\Delta x, j\Delta y)$, and $D_{ij}^{-x}T = (T_{ij} - T_{i-1,j})/\Delta x$ is the standard backwards derivative approximation, $D_{ij}^{+x}T = (T_{i+1,j} - T_{ij})/\Delta x$ is the standard forward derivative approximation in the x direction, and similarly for the y direction. In the case of a uniform grid, we have $\Delta x = \Delta y = 1$. Then, the approximation ( ) may equivalently be written as

$$(\max(T_{ij} - T_1, 0))^2 + (\max(T_{ij} - T_2, 0))^2 = f_{ij}^2 , \qquad (7)$$

where $T_1 = \min(T_{i-1,j}, T_{i+1,j})$ and $T_2 = \min(T_{i,j-1}, T_{i,j+1})$, and the update step for $T_{i,j}$ consists of setting up the quadratic equation

$$T_{i,j} = T_1 + T_2 + \sqrt{2f_{ij}^2 - (T_1 - T_2)^2} . \qquad (8)$$

If the real solution does not exist, then we set $T_{i,j} = f_{ij} + \min(T_1, T_2)$, which corresponds to the case when one of the terms in the approximation is zero [ ].

The central idea behind the Fast Marching Method is to systematically construct the solution T using only upwind values. The upwind difference structure of Eqn. ( ) allows us to propagate the information *one-way*, from the smaller values of T to the larger values. The front is swept along by keeping a narrow band of grid points around the existing front in a heap structure and marching it forward bringing in unprocessed points and fixing the smallest computed values in the band [ ].

2   Theoretical Background

Next, we present some results from the theory of curve evolution that are necessary in order to formulate our equations of motion. The following material is based on [ ].

The optimal path between points A and B in $\mathbb{R}^2$ is defined by the weighted arc-length $d\tilde{\tau}^2 = F^2(t, s)d\tau^2$, where $d\tau = \sqrt{dt^2 + ds^2}$ is the Euclidean arc-length differential and $F(t, s)$ is the weight over the domain. We search for the path $\boldsymbol{c}(\tau) = (t(\tau), s(\tau))$, where τ is the arc-length parametrization of $\boldsymbol{c}$ with $|\boldsymbol{c}'(\tau)| = 1$. The necessary boundary conditions for $\boldsymbol{c}(\tau)$ are $\boldsymbol{c}(0) = A$ and $\boldsymbol{c}(L) = B$, where L is the total arc-length. The desired path should minimize $\min_{\boldsymbol{c}} \int F(\boldsymbol{c}(\tau))d\tau$, with $|\boldsymbol{c}'(\tau)| = 1$. For an arbitrary parametrization p of $\boldsymbol{c}$, the above geometric functional reads

$$\min_{\boldsymbol{c}} \int_0^1 F(\boldsymbol{c}(p))|\boldsymbol{c}'(p)|dp \ . \tag{9}$$

Lemma 1. *If a path $\boldsymbol{c}(p)$ satisfies the equation*

$$\nabla F|\boldsymbol{c}'(p)| = \frac{d}{dp}(F(\boldsymbol{c}(p))\boldsymbol{T}(p)) \ , \tag{10}$$

where $\boldsymbol{T}(p)$ is the unit tangent vector to $\boldsymbol{c}(p)$ defined as $\boldsymbol{T}(p) = \frac{\boldsymbol{c}'(p)}{|\boldsymbol{c}'(p)|}$, then $\boldsymbol{c}(p)$ achieves the minimum in ( ).

Thus, Eqn. ( ) is the Euler-Lagrange (EL) equation of the measure ( ). Next, let $T : \mathbb{R}^2 \to \mathbb{R}$ be a weighted distance function with $|\nabla T| = F(t, s)$, where $|\nabla T|$ is evaluated at (t, s), with given boundary conditions $T(0, 0) = 0$. Let us show that the gradient descent curves of T minimize the measure ( ).

Lemma 2. *The gradient descent curves $\boldsymbol{c}(p) = (t(p), s(p))$ defined by the ODE $\boldsymbol{c}'(p) = \nabla T$ satisfy the Euler-Lagrange equation of the measure*

$$\int F(\boldsymbol{c}(p))|\boldsymbol{c}'(p)|dp \ .$$

Proof. First, let us observe that $\boldsymbol{c}'(p) = (t'(p), s'(p)) = \nabla T = (\frac{\partial T}{\partial t}, \frac{\partial T}{\partial s}) = (T_t, T_s)$. Next, we have $F(\boldsymbol{c}(p))\boldsymbol{T}(p) = |\nabla T|\frac{\nabla T}{|\nabla T|} = \nabla T$. Hence, the right hand side of Eqn. ( ) has the form

$$\frac{d}{dp}(F(\boldsymbol{c}(p))\boldsymbol{T}(p)) = \frac{d}{dp}\nabla T = \frac{d}{dp}(T_t(t(p), s(p)), \ T_s(t(p), s(p)))$$
$$= (T_{tt}t'(p) + T_{ts}s'(p), \ T_{st}t'(p) + T_{ss}s'(p)) \ .$$

On the other hand,

$$\nabla F|c'(p)| = \nabla(|\nabla T|)|\nabla T| = \frac{(T_{tt}T_t + T_{st}T_s, \; T_{ts}T_t + T_{ss}T_s)|\nabla T|}{(T_t^2 + T_s^2)^{1/2}}$$
$$= (T_{tt}t'(p) + T_{ts}s'(p), \; T_{st}t'(p) + T_{ss}s'(p)) \; . \qquad \square$$

We have just seen that by solving the Eikonal equation $|\nabla T| = F(t, s)$ for $T(t, s)$ we can backtrack the optimal path by starting at the final location B and by stepping in the direction of the gradient of T. Note that if we set $F(t, s) = 1$, then the distance map $T(t, s)$ will be just a series of concentric circles corresponding to the Euclidean distance map, and the optimal path will be a straight line from B to A.

The weighted distance function $T(t, s)$ reconstructed from the point A may be thought of as the minimal cost required to travel from A to the point (t, s). In terms of the original functional, that is

$$T(t, s) = \min_c \int_A^{(t,s)} F(c(\tau))d\tau \; . \tag{11}$$

The level set curve $T(t, s) = C$ is the set of all points in $\mathbb{R}^2$ that can be reached with minimal cost C [ ].

3   The Distance between a Pair of Curves

Equipped with this theory, we can now proceed to define a distance measure between a given pair of curves $C_1(t) = (x_1(t), y_1(t))$, $t \in [0, m]$ and $C_2(s) = (x_2(s), y_2(s))$, $s \in [0, n]$, where s and t are arc-length parameters and m and n are the lengths of the curves. Assuming that the endpoints of the input curves match, and given some local dissimilarity measure F, we are interested in a path c through t, s-space from $(0, 0)$ to (m, n) such that

$$T(m, n) = \min_c \int_c F(c(\tau))d\tau \; . \tag{12}$$

For such a path we define a distance measure between C_1 and C_2 as

$$d(C_1, C_2) = T(m, n) - \lambda\sqrt{m^2 + n^2} + \left|1 - \frac{\min(m, n)}{\max(m, n)}\right| \; , \tag{13}$$

where λ is a *smoothing constant* such that $\lambda > 0$. Thus, we define the dissimilarity between C_1 and C_2 as the minimal sum of local dissimilarities between individual pairs of curve points, and here we note the similarity to the edit distance approach. The second term in this expression is needed for normalization and the third term penalizes global stretching of the curves. The significance of these terms will become apparent in the next section. Now, let us say a few words about our choice of F.

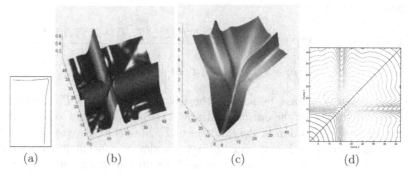

(a)   (b)   (c)   (d)

Fig. 2. Comparing a 7, the shape in (a), to itself using curvature information and $\lambda = 0.111$. The graph in (b) shows the resulting F, (c) shows the reconstructed $T(t, s)$, and (d) - the contour lines of T with the optimal path superimposed

3.1   First Attempt: Curvature-Based Dissimilarity Function

As mentioned in the previous sections, intrinsic properties of curves such as curvature are frequently used in curve alignment algorithms. Let us first study a local dissimilarity function based on curvature:

$$F(t, s) = |\kappa_1(t) - \kappa_2(s)| + \lambda \ . \tag{14}$$

Here, κ_1 and κ_2 are the curvatures of C_1 and C_2 respectively, and $\lambda > 0$. Hence, we have $F(t, s) > 0$ and the Fast Marching Method may be used to solve for $T(t, s)$, setting $T(0, 0) = 0$ since the first points of the curves are assumed to match. Notice that such a choice of F resembles somewhat the expression ( ) in that it penalizes bending. Stretching is also modelled by the resulting distance measure $d(\cdot, \cdot)$, since the more the optimal path c differs from the diagonal line, the higher the value of $T(m, n)$.

Proposition 3. *Let $C_1(t) = (x_1(t), y_1(t))$, $t \in [0, m]$ and $C_2(s) = (x_2(s), y_2(s))$, $s \in [0, n]$ be two curves of lengths m and n respectively, each parameterized by arc-length. Let $d(C_1, C_2)$ be defined as above. Then, the following hold:*

1. *$d(C_1, C_1) = 0$,*
2. *$C_1 \neq C_2 \Rightarrow d(C_1, C_2) > 0$,*
3. *$d(C_1, C_2) = d(C_2, C_1)$.*

Proof. To prove ., let $\check{c}(\tau) = (t(\tau), s(\tau)) = (\frac{\sqrt{2}}{2}\tau, \frac{\sqrt{2}}{2}\tau)$, $\tau \in [0, m\sqrt{2}]$. Then, $F(\check{c}(\tau)) = \lambda$, for $\tau \in [0, m\sqrt{2}]$. Let us show that $\check{c}(\tau)$ satisfies Eqn. ( ). Since $F(t, s) = \lambda$, on the left we have $\nabla F|\check{c}'(\tau)| = (0, 0)$. And since τ is the arc-length parameter of $\check{c}$, we have $|\check{c}'(\tau)| = 1$, and

$$\frac{d}{d\tau}(F(\check{c}(\tau))\boldsymbol{T}(\tau)) = \frac{d}{d\tau}(\lambda\frac{\check{c}'(\tau)}{|\check{c}'(\tau)|}) = \frac{d}{d\tau}(\frac{\sqrt{2}}{2}\lambda, \frac{\sqrt{2}}{2}\lambda) = (0, 0) \ .$$

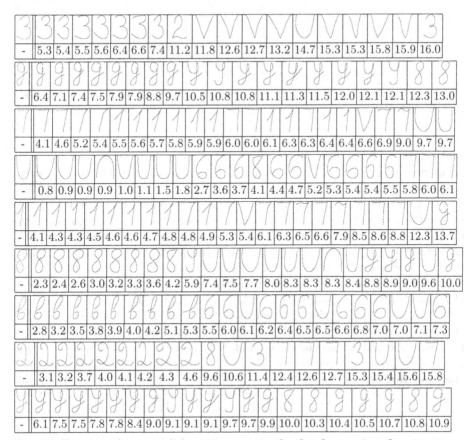

Fig. 3. Best matches out of the 110 curves in the database using the curvature-based dissimilarity function. The number underneath each curve represents its distance from the left-most curve. An average y curve was used as a y-class prototype

Since Eqn. ( ) is the EL equation of ( ), $\check{c}$ must achieve the minimum in $T(m,m)$. Finally, since the length of $\check{c}$ is $m\sqrt{2}$ we obtain $T(m,m) = \int_{\check{c}} F(\check{c}(\tau))d\tau = \lambda m\sqrt{2}$, which gives . To prove ., let $\bar{c}$ achieve the minimum in $T(m,n)$. First, suppose $m = n$. Since $\mathcal{C}_1 \neq \mathcal{C}_2$, $\exists\ \tau$ s.t. $\kappa_1(t(\tau)) \neq \kappa_2(s(\tau))$, which implies that $F(\bar{c}(\tau)) > \lambda$, and the length of $\bar{c}$, $\int_{\bar{c}} d\tau > m\sqrt{2}$, which in turn implies $T(m,m) = \int_{\bar{c}} F(\bar{c}(\tau))d\tau > \lambda m\sqrt{2}$. Property . then follows. If $m \neq n$, then we have $|1 - \min(m,n)/\max(m,n)| > 0$ and hence $d(\mathcal{C}_1,\mathcal{C}_2) > 0$. Property . is true by the symmetry of $F(t,s)$. $\qquad\square$

The above properties play an important role in applications such as handwritten character recognition. To illustrate with an example, let us compare a curve that has the shape of a digit 7 with itself (see Fig.).

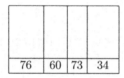

| 76 | 60 | 73 | 34 |

Fig. 4. Curvature test results. The curves shown did not place in their corresponding class tables

Using $\lambda = 0.111$ (see Sect.   for an intuition on how we chose λ and for more examples), we obtain a surface $T(t, s)$ that has two prominent ridges around otherwise smooth areas. The high-slope regions arise when one of the input curves has points of high curvature, and the other curve has regions of low curvature resulting in great local curvature differences - the high ridges in the graph of F. And since the Eikonal equation $|\nabla T| = F$ implies that the magnitude of the gradient is greater at the places where F is greater, we observe the high slopes on the graph of T in the areas around $t = 15$ and $s = 15$ and relatively low slopes in most other regions. Finally, the gradient descent path of T is a straight line from $(0, 0)$ to $(42, 42)$ as is expected.

For testing the algorithm, we have used a data-set of 110 sample curves. The curves were all drawn by a single subject with a mouse in an environment that tracked mouse motion and produced uniformly spaced curve points $C_i = (x_i, y_i)$ to simulate arc-length parametrization. The curvature κ_i at each curve point was computed as follows

$$\kappa_i = \frac{4(y_{i+1} - 2y_i + y_{i-1})\Delta x_i - 4(x_{i+1} - 2x_i + x_{i-1})\Delta y_i}{((\Delta x_i)^2 + (\Delta y_i)^2)^{3/2}},$$

where $\Delta x_i = \frac{1}{2}(x_{i+1} - x_{i-1})$, and $\Delta y_i = \frac{1}{2}(y_{i+1} - y_{i-1})$. Note that the above measure tends to infinity as $\Delta x_i \to 0, \Delta y_i \to 0$. Therefore, we bounded κ_i to make sure that it stayed well defined. The obtained curvature vectors were convolved with a one-dimensional Gaussian filter of width 7 in an attempt to lessen the presence of noise in the input data. The parameter λ was chosen automatically per each curve pair (see Sect.   ). The prototypes were chosen in a way so as to represent the associated class "best" in terms of the number of class members that place at the top. In some cases, curve averages were used (see Sect.   for a description of how averages were obtained). Since the average curves' points were not uniformly spaced, a variant of the Fast Marching Method had to be employed that operates on a non-uniformly spaced grid [ ]. Figure   shows the results of comparing some of the 110 curves in our data-set with the rest of the curves. The 13 best matches are shown together with their corresponding matching distances.

Notice that the results are intuitive. The β-shapes are the closest ones to the reference β-shape, the γ's are the closest ones to the reference γ, etc. Also, shapes that belong to different classes, but appear similar, such as a y and a g or a 6 and a U, have similar distance measures from the references. It is interesting to note

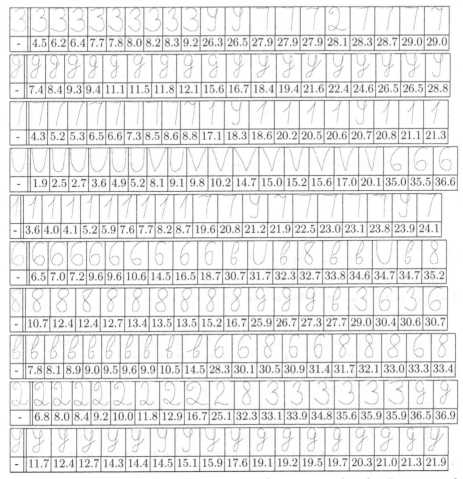

Fig. 5. Best matches using shape contexts. Average *y* and *8* shapes were used as class prototypes

that the upside-down *U*-shape ranks very high among the regular *U*-shapes. This phenomenon is due to the fact that curvature is an intrinsic curve property that is invariant with respect to rotation. The local nature of the curvature measure also causes six of the *1*-shapes to rank closer to a reference *7*-shape than some of the *7*'s whose corner is somewhat smoother than that of the reference *7*. This is due to the fact that curvature was bounded and that the *7* and the *1* sample shapes do not differ much *intrinsically* at other points.

Figure   shows the curves that did not place in their class tables. The corresponding ranks are also shown. Locality is also a major cause that misplaces the *3*'s with a loop in the middle (instead of a sharp corner that the others possessed), a *g* with a sharp corner instead of a loop, and a *2* with a sharp corner

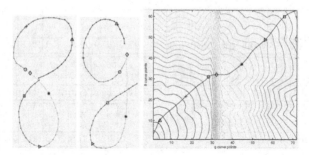

Fig. 6. Some sample curve point correspondences represented by coloring (curve density in black and white production) and by markers. The curve coloring is independent of the contour line coloring on the graph

instead of a loop. The misplaced *8* was drawn in such a way that the endpoints were not matched with the prototype *8*.

3.2   Second Attempt: Shape Contexts to the Rescue

The problems due to locality described above served as motivation to seek a dissimilarity measure that takes into account all the points in the curve instead of being confined to a local region. Shape contexts (see Sect.   ), being more descriptive in nature, proved also to be more effective in our experiments.

As we have mentioned, $C(\mathbf{p}_i, \mathbf{q}_j)$ in expression ( ) is a local cost of matching the points $\mathbf{p}_i$ and $\mathbf{q}_j$ that lie on the two input shapes. In the case when the two shapes are curves, C may be used in place of F, and the expression ( ) resembles ( ) in the sense that local dissimilarities are summed. The smoothing parameter λ was still employed and $d(\cdot, \cdot)$ remained otherwise unchanged so that Proposition   held.

During shape context computation, point distance was quantized into 5 bins, as in [ ], ranging from 0 to the maximum distance between a pair of points on a given curve, thereby achieving invariance to scale. The size of the bins increased exponentially as distance increased in order to give more weight to nearby points. Orientation was quantized into 12 bins.

Figure   shows the results of the top 13 experiment performed on the same database of 110 curves using the shape contexts. The first thing to notice is that the problems due to locality are solved. The *3* with a loop instead of a corner places third in the first table on top even though it is compared to a shape that has a corner. The *g* that was problematic before also places in the *g* class. Perhaps, most notably, the *2* that has a sharp corner instead of a loop on the second table from the bottom is given a rank of 25.1 which is closer to the *2*-class than the next closest shape, an *8* of rank 32.3. In general, curves from the same class place closer together and are easier to separate from the outliers than before. For example, the *7*'s with curly arms place well within the *7* class. The algorithm has some trouble with rotated shapes. As may be seen on the

Fig. 7. (a) Sample curve point matchings obtained using curvature differences. The matching points are color coded (or marked by density in black and white production). (b) Averaging two y's. The red shape is the *average* shape. We used a similar average as a y-class prototype in the "top matches" experiments (see Sects.   and   )

figure, one y is more slanted than the curves in the y class, and that causes it to place 17'th. That was not a problem before, since curvature is a rotation-invariant measure. Belongie et al., however, mention that shape contexts may be computed taking into account the direction of the curve tangents thereby achieving rotation-invariance.

3.3   Curve Point Correspondence

An extra feature that may be obtained once we have computed the distance between the input curves is a correspondence between the curve points. As mentioned in Sect.   , backtracking along the gradient from the final location (m, n) recovers the optimal path that achieves the minimum in (   ). Such gradient descent paths may be viewed as sub-pixel resolution curve point correspondences, since they are continuous paths in (s, t) space, and are analogous to the alignment curves α in (   ). Figures   and   (a) show several examples of correspondences obtained using the curvature-based measure. It is interesting to note that the high curvature parts of V and 3 match. Also the upper and lower loops of 8 and g that turn in the same directions (first to the left, then to the right) are matched regardless of g's corner. The corner is in a way "skipped" in favor of matching the loops as the descent path levels out to a horizontal slope.

Once a correspondence has been recovered, it can be useful in several ways. For instance, we can form weighted averages between the corresponding point coordinates, resulting in an *average* shape (see Fig.   (b)), that can, for instance, serve as a representative of a class of shapes. We have used averages in our experiments with a curve database (see Sects.   and   ). On the other hand, if we vary the weights in a sequence going from 0 to 1 using some small predefined step, interpolating the coordinates, we can generate frames of a *morphing sequence*. An example is shown in Fig.   .

3.4   The Choice of the Smoothing Parameter λ

Both choices of F - either based on curvature or on the shape contexts - contain the smoothing term λ. But how should we choose it? The parameter λ may be

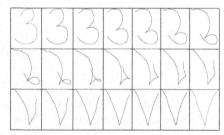

Fig. 8. *Morphing* a *3* into a *V*. The matching was obtained using a curvature-based measure, hence the sharp corners of *3* and *V* match

viewed as a driving force that makes sure that the Fast Marching Method keeps going even when the local dissimilarity term - either the difference of curvatures or the χ^2 test statistic - is zero. Thus λ should not be zero. As mentioned above, changing the parameter λ also has an effect of *smoothing out* the solution. As illustrated on Fig. , both the reconstructed surface T and the gradient descent curve are affected by the choice of λ. When λ is low, surface features are more pronounced. Plateaus tend to be flatter, making descent more difficult, and ridges sharpen up. On the other hand, setting λ too high to the point where it dominates the dissimilarity measure, tends to over-smooth the solution making the measure insensitive to the local differences, and leading to a distance map that is essentially a series of concentric circles. In our experiments, we chose λ automatically, driven by the intuition that it should be comparable in magnitude to the dissimilarity term so as neither of the terms would dominate the measure. The average value of F for a given pair of curves $\mathcal{C}_1$ and $\mathcal{C}_2$ of lengths m and n served that purpose relatively well in our tests:

$$\lambda(\mathcal{C}_1, \mathcal{C}_2) = \frac{1}{mn} \int_{\mathcal{C}_1} \int_{\mathcal{C}_2} F(t, s) ds dt . \tag{15}$$

3.5 Comparing Closed Curves

The original dynamic programming technique can handle closed curves in a manner similar to the edit distance approach of [ ] to comparing cyclic strings. The

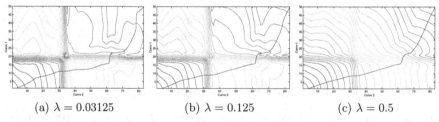

(a) $\lambda = 0.03125$ (b) $\lambda = 0.125$ (c) $\lambda = 0.5$

Fig. 9. The effects of increasing λ on T and on the resulting optimal path

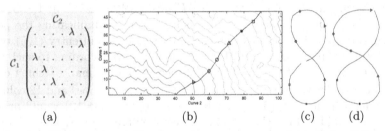

(a)   (b)   (c)   (d)

Fig. 10. (a) The matrix of F values given two curves C_1 and C_2 of six points, where C_2 is C_1 shifted by three points. (b) The matching curve obtained when comparing (c) with (d). Curve (c) points go along the y-axis, and curve (d) points go along the x-axis. Some matching points are shown. The gaps on the curves signify the starting points of curve parametrization

method finds the optimal solution in $O(nm \log m)$ steps. One way of applying the Fast Marching Method to closed curves would be to extend the dynamic programming technique, but that would require developing a version of the Fast Marching Method that restricts the computation to a section of the grid between two given curves and would result in at least a factor of $O(\log m)$ increase of the computation time.

Another approach that is more empirical in nature, but one that does not increase the complexity, is based on the following observation. Suppose we are comparing a closed curve C_1 discretized at six points with a version of itself (denoted C_2) re-parameterized such that its coordinates begin after a shift of three points. Then the matrix F where the rows are points of C_1 and the columns are points of C_2 (see Fig.   ) will have λ values along diagonals in places where

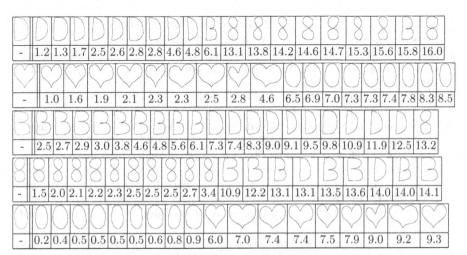

Fig. 11. Best matches of a data-set of closed curves using shape contexts

curve points match. Then, concatenating F with itself horizontally to obtain $\widetilde{F}$ that has 6 rows and 12 columns, which is equivalent to duplicating the points of C_2 along the x-axis produces a diagonal of λ values from entry $(1,5)$ to the entry $(6,10)$. Propagating a front from the point $(1,5)$ according to such an F and then backtracking from $(6,10)$ would recover the optimal matching curve. Concatenating $\widetilde{F}$ vertically twice to obtain $\overline{F}$ that has 18 rows and 12 columns, propagating a front from $(0,0)$, and backtracking from $(18,12)$ would produce a path that would include the optimal matching curve from $(1,5)$ to $(6,10)$. In order to compute the distance between two closed curves, given such a path, we can re-parameterize C_2 so that both curves start at the same point and run the regular algorithm. Fig.   shows an example of a matching curve (b) obtained when comparing two closed shapes (c) and (d). Fig.   shows the results of running the above procedure using shape contexts on a smaller data-set of 50 closed curves.

References

[1] N. Ayache and O. Faugeras, "HYPER: A new approach for recognition and positioning of two-dimensional objects," *IEEE Trans. on PAMI*, **8**(1) (1986) 44–54.

[2] S. Belongie, J. Malik, and J. Puzicha, "Shape Context: A New Descriptor for Shape Matching and Object Recognition," *NIPS* **13**: (2001) 831–837.   ,

[3] R. Basri, L. Costa, D. Geiger, and D. W. Jacobs, "Determining the Similarity of Deformable Shapes," *Vision Research*, **38**: (1998) 2365–2385.   ,   ,

[4] I. Cohen, N. Ayachi, and P. Sulger, "Tracking points on deformable objects using curvature information," In *ECCV*, (1992) 458–466.

[5] L. D. Cohen and R. Kimmel, "Global minimum for active contour models: a minimal path approach," *IJCV*, **24**(1) (1997) 57–78.

[6] E. Hildreth, *The Measurement of Visual Motion*, MIT Press, Cambridge (1983).

[7] R. Kimmel, J. A. Sethian, "Fast Marching Methods for Robotic Navigation with Constraints," Report, Univ. of California, Berkley, May (1996).

[8] R. Kimmel and J. A. Sethian, "Optimal algorithm for shape from shading and path planning," *Journal of Mathematical Imaging and Vision*, **14**(2) (2001) 237–244.

[9] M. Maes, "On a cyclic string-to-string correction problem," *Information Processing Letters*, **35** (1990) 73–78.   ,

[10] A. Pentland, and S. Sclaroff, "Closed-Form Solutions for Physically Based Shape Modeling and Recognition," *IEEE Trans. on PAMI*, **13**(7) (1991) 715–729.

[11] A. Pope, and D. Lowe, "Learning Object Recognition Models from Images," *ICCV* (1993) 296–301.

[12] T. Sebastian, P. Klein, B. Kimia, "On aligning curves," *IEEE Trans. on PAMI*, **25**(1) (2003) 116–124.   ,

[13] B. Serra and M. Berthod, "Optimal subpixel matching of contour chains and segments," *IJCV* (1995) 402–407.

[14] J. Sethian, *Level Set Methods: Evolving Interfaces in Geometry, Fluid Mechanics, Computer Vision and Materials Sciences*, Cambridge Univ. Press (1996).   ,   ,

[15] J. A. Sethian, "A fast marching level set method for monotonically advancing fronts," *Proc. Nat. Acad. Sci.*, **93**(4) (1996) 1591–1595.   ,

[16] H. D. Tagare, "Shape-based nonrigid correspondence with application to heart motion analysis," *IEEE Trans. Medical Imaging*, **18**(7) (1999) 570–578.

[17] C. Tappert, "Cursive script recognition by elastic matching," *IBM Journal of Research Development*, **26**(6) (1982) 765–771.

[18] R. Wagner, and M. Fischer, "The string-to-string correction problem," *Journal of the Association for Computing Machinery*, **21** (1974) 168–173.   ,

EM Algorithm for Clustering an Ensemble of Graphs with Comb Matching

Miguel Angel Lozano and Francisco Escolano

Robot Vision Group
Departamento de Ciencia de la Computación e Inteligencia Artificial
Universidad de Alicante, Spain
{malozano, sco}@dccia.ua.es
http://rvg.ua.es

Abstract. In this paper we address the unsupervised clustering of an ensemble of graphs. We adapt to the domain of graphs the Asymmetric Clustering Model (ACM). Firstly, we use an improvement of our Comb algorithm for graph matching, a population-based method which performs multi-point explorations of the discrete space of feasible solutions. Given this algorithm we define an incremental method to obtain a prototypical graph by fusing the elements of the ensemble weighted by their prior probabilities of belonging to the class. Graph-matching and incremental fusion are integrated in a EM clustering algorithm: In the E-step we re-estimate the class-membership variables by computing the distances of input graphs to current prototypes through graph-matching, and in the M-step we re-estimate the prototypes by considering the latter class-membership variables in order to perform graph fusions. We introduce adaptation: The algorithm starts with a high number of classes and in each epoch tries to fuse the two classes with closer prototypes. We present several results of Comb-matching, incremental fusion and clustering.

1   Introduction

We are interested in the problem of clustering a set of graphs (ensemble) into a few classes represented by their prototypes. Previous approaches have been mainly addressed to deal with attributed relational graphs (ARGs). This is the case of random graphs [ ][ ][ ] whose nodes and edges attributes are random variables and their joint probability distribution defines a probability measure over the space of all graphs inside a class (outcome graphs). However, as considering high-order dependencies between variables is computationally intractable, in practice it is usually assumed a first-order model relying on strong independence assumptions. As such assumptions may result in generating rare outcome graphs belonging to the class with high probability, the first-order model is usually extended. For instance, the function-described graph (FDG) model [ ] includes second-order dependencies, and in [ ] a chain graph capturing a sequence of observations is embodied into a hierarchical random graph (HRG).

A. Rangarajan et al. (Eds.): EMMCVPR 2003, LNCS 2683, pp. 52–   , 2003.
© Springer-Verlag Berlin Heidelberg 2003

Assuming that the latter models are used to represent graph prototypes, structural clustering algorithms rely on two key elements: a distance function to evaluate whether two graphs may be assumed to belong to the same class, and a method to build the temporary prototypes, that is, to merge graphs closer enough. The distance function is built on the cost function minimized or maximized by a graph-matching algorithm [ ][ ][ ], that is, in order to compute such distance between a pair of graphs we must solve a NP-complete problem. On the other hand, temporary prototypes are usually build through either incremental or hierarchical strategies [ ][ ] that use the common labelling between pairs of graphs provided by graph-matching to update the probabilities of the nodes and edges of the prototypes.

In this paper we adapt a EM clustering algorithm to the domain of graphs. Firstly, we present an improved a graph-matching algorithm that we have recently proposed [ ]. Basically, this algorithm optimizes the Gold and Rangarajan's cost function [ ] by embodying multi-point local search inside a global random algorithm that explores the discrete space of feasible solutions. Such an algorithm, known as Comb, was originally applied to solve MRF-labeling problems [ ]. Although in our earlier experiments we assume ARGs, in this case we will assume that input graphs have not node or edge attributes, that is, matching relies only on edge connectivity. In addition to test the Comb-matching algorithm in these conditions, we are interested in defining graph prototypes on the basis of structural information. Consequently, our prototypes will not be random graphs because they are not ARGs. Although attributes representing the frequency of each node or edge in a given class are considered while the prototype of the class is built, we only retain those nodes and edges with high probability, and thus our model is close to the median-graph model [ ].

Our un-supervised clustering approach relies on the Asymmetric Clustering Model (ACM) proposed by Hoffman and Puzicha [ ] [ ]. In [ ] we extended this model by making it adaptive, that is, able of identifying the optimal number of classes. In the E-step it is assumed that class prototypes are known and the distances between each graph in the ensemble and each prototype are computed on the basis of the Comb-matching algorithm. Such computations yield the re-estimation of the class-membership variables, and in turn those variables are used in the M-step to re-estimate the prototypes. The M-step relies on an incremental algorithm that builds the prototype of each class by considering the current probabilities of belonging to each class. Finally, adaptation is implemented by dividing the computation in epochs. Starting from a high number of classes, as in [ ], in each epoch we try to merge the two classes with closer prototypes.

The paper is organized as follows: In Section   we will present an improved version of the Comb-matching algorithm, and some matching results. In Section   we will describe a simple incremental method for building prototypes, illustrating how it works and showing some results. In Section   we will present our ACM clustering algorithm for graphs and some results both with the adaptive and non-adaptive version of the algorithm. Finally, in Section   we will summarize our conclusions and future work.

2   Graph Matching

2.1   Stochastic Search for Assignement

Given two graphs $G_X = (V_X, E_X)$, with nodes $a \in V_X$ and edges $(a, b) \in E_X$, and $G_Y = (V_Y, E_Y)$, with nodes $i \in V_Y$ and edges $(i, j) \in E_Y$, their adjacency matrices X and Y are defined by

$$X_{ab} = \begin{cases} 1 & \text{if } (a, b) \in E_X \\ 0 & \text{otherwise} \end{cases} \quad \text{and} \quad Y_{ij} = \begin{cases} 1 & \text{if } (i, j) \in E_Y \\ 0 & \text{otherwise.} \end{cases}$$

A feasible solution to the graph matching problem between G_X and G_Y is encoded by a matrix M of size $|V_X| \times |V_Y|$ with binary variables

$$M_{ai} = \begin{cases} 1 & \text{if } a \in V_X \text{ matches } i \in V_Y \\ 0 & \text{otherwise} \end{cases}$$

satisfying the constraints defined respectively over the rows and columns of M

$$\sum_{i=1}^{|V_X|} M_{ai} \leq 1, \forall a \quad \text{and} \quad \sum_{a=1}^{|V_Y|} M_{ai} \leq 1, \forall i . \tag{1}$$

Cost Function. Following the Gold and Rangarajan formulation we are interested in finding the feasible solution M that maximizes the following cost function,

$$F(G_X, G_Y; M) = \sum_{a=1}^{|V_X|} \sum_{i=1}^{|V_Y|} M_{ai} \sum_{b=1}^{|V_X|} \sum_{j=1}^{|V_Y|} M_{bj} X_{ab} Y_{ij} , \tag{2}$$

that is, when $a \in V_X$ matches $i \in V_Y$, it is desirable that nodes b adjacent to a (with $X_{ab} \neq 0$) and nodes j adjacent to i (with $Y_{ij} \neq 0$) also match, that is $M_{ai} = M_{bj} = 1$.

Constrained Maximization. In order to maximize the Gold and Rangarajan function we propose to apply a global population-based optimization strategy known as Comb (Common structure of the best local maxima) originally applied to labeling problems in MRF models, in order to explore the set feasible solutions.

The Comb algorithm maintains a population $P = \{M^{(1)}, \dots, M^{(L)}\}$ with the L (experimentally set to 10 individuals) best local maxima found so far. Such a population is initialized according to an uniform distribution over the space of feasible solutions. Each iteration begins by selecting, also randomly, a pair of local maxima $M^{(a)}$ and $M^{(b)}$. As this method relies on the assumption that local maxima share some matching variables with the global maxima, it derives a new candidate to local maximum $M^{(0)}$ by combining the latter pair. Such a combination consists of (i) retaining common variables, (ii) randomly generating new values for components with different variables and (iii) ensuring that the result is still a permutation matrix. In order to do that, if $M_{ai}^{(a)} = M_{ai}^{(b)}$ we will set $M_{ai}^{(0)} = M_{ai}^{(a)}$ with probability $1 - \tau$, where $\tau = 0.01$ allows to avoid premature convergence. Otherwise, we will set $M_{ai}^{(0)} = r$ with $r \in \{0, 1\}$ satisfying

$$(\textstyle\sum_{j=1}^{i-1} M_{aj} + r + \sum_{j=i+1}^{|V_X|} M_{aj}) \leq 1, \forall a$$
$$(\textstyle\sum_{b=1}^{a-1} M_{bi} + r + \sum_{b=a+1}^{|V_Y|} M_{bi}) \leq 1, \forall i ,$$

Each $M^{(0)}$ is considered the starting point of a hill-climbing process which consists of changing the value at a component at a time while ensuring that the resulting matrix satisfies the matching constraints and then testing whether it provides a better solution. In order to select such a component compute the matrix of partial derivatives

$$\triangle_{ai} = \frac{\partial F}{\partial M_{ai}} = \sum_{b=1}^{|V_X|} \sum_{j=1}^{|V_Y|} M_{bj} X_{ab} Y_{ij}, \tag{3}$$

and then identify

$$\triangle_{rc} = \max_{1 \leq a \leq |V_X|, 1 \leq i \leq |V_Y|} \triangle_{ai}. \tag{4}$$

that is, the component with maximum partial derivative. Then, we will set $M_{rc} = 1$ and repair the resulting matrix in order to satisfy all matching constraints, that is, if $\exists \tilde{c} \neq c$, $M_{r\tilde{c}} = 1$ then we will set $M_{r\tilde{c}} = 0$. Similarly, if $\exists \tilde{r} \neq r$, $M_{\tilde{r}c} = 1$ then we will set $M_{\tilde{r}c} = 0$. This is a rough discrete version of the Gold and Ranjarajan's deterministic annealing procedure which allows us to save the computational load of the Sinkhorn step devoted to enforce constraint satisfaction.

Once the new matrix is obtained we test whether the cost function is improved. If so, a new hill-climbing step starts. Otherwise, it is not possible to improve the current matrix and a new local maximum M^{local} is declared. Such a local maximum updates P as follows: If

$$F(G_X, G_Y; M^{local}) > M^{worst} \text{ where } M^{worst} = \arg \min_{M^{(k)} \in P} F(G_X, G_Y; M^{(k)}) ,$$
$$\tag{5}$$

then the worst local maximum so far M^{worst} is replaced by M^{local}. Otherwise the population does not change. Such an updating rule ensures that the quality of the individuals in P is improved, expecting that such an improvement eventually reaches the global maximum. Thus, if we detect all individuals in P are almost equal, we assume that the algorithm has found the global maximum (the best local maximum so far). The algorithm also stops when the latter termination condition is not satisfied after $I = 1000$ iterations.

2.2   Matching Results

In Figure   we show the result of matching two graphs with similar structure, whereas in Figure   we show the optimal matching for two different graphs. In

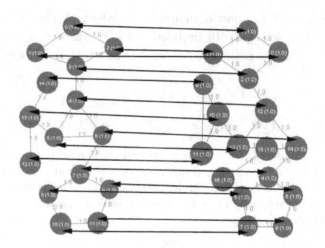

Fig. 1. Matching two similar graphs

the first case the normalized optimal cost is 0.80 and in the second it is 0.65. In Figure   we show a local maximum obtained after a steepest-ascent stage. Its normalized cost is 0.75 and the corresponding global maximum is the solution showed in Figure   . At least half of labels are common. Finally, in Figure   we show the evolution of the inverse normalized optimal cost (match error). First we match a randomly generated graph of 50 nodes with himself and next we randomly delete a given percentage of both the graph and its copy, repeat the match, and so on. We observe that the match error has a linear increment.

3   Graph Prototypes

3.1   Incremental Fusion

Suppose that we have N input graphs $G_i = (V_i, E_i)$ and we want to obtain a representative prototype $\bar{G} = (\bar{V}, \bar{E})$ of them. We define such a prototype as

$$\bar{G} = \bigoplus_{i=1}^{N}(\pi_i \odot G_i) \text{ where } \sum_{i=1}^{N} \pi_i = 1 \,. \tag{6}$$

Firstly, the $\odot$ operator implements the weighting of each graph G_i by π_i which we will interpret in terms of the probability of belonging to the class defined by the prototype. The definition of resulting graph $\tilde{G}_i = \pi_i \odot G_i$, with $\tilde{V}_i = V_i$ and $\tilde{E}_i = E_i$ is extended in order include a node-interpretation function $\tilde{\mu}_i : \tilde{V}_i \to [0,1]$, addressed to register the relative frequency of each node, and an edge-interpretation function $\tilde{\delta}_i : \tilde{E}_i \to [0,1]$ which must register the relative frequency of each edge. Then, weighting consists of assigning the following priors:

$$\tilde{\mu}_i(a) = \pi_i \; \forall a \in \tilde{V}_i \,, \text{and} \; \tilde{\delta}_i(a,b) = \pi_i \; \forall (a,b) \in \tilde{E}_i. \tag{7}$$

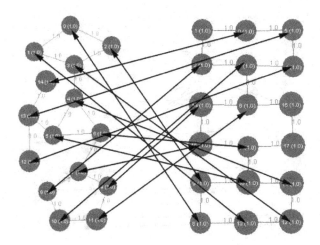

Fig. 2. Matching two different graphs

Secondly, given a set of weighted graphs, the $\oplus$ operator builds the proto-type $\bar{G}$ by fusing all of them. Ideally, the result should not depend on the order of presentation of the weighted graphs. However, such a solution would be too computational demanding because we need to find a high number of isomor-phisms, that is, to solve a high number of NP-complete problems. In this work we propose an incremental approach. Initially we select randomly a weighted graph $\tilde{G}_X = \pi_X \odot G_X$, as a temporary prototypical graph $\bar{G}$. Then we select, also randomly a different graph $\tilde{G}_Y = \pi_Y \odot G_Y$. The new temporary prototype results from fusing these graphs:

$$\bar{G} = \tilde{G}_X = \pi_X \odot G_X$$
$$\bar{G} = \tilde{G}_X \oplus \tilde{G}_Y = (\pi_X \odot G_X) \oplus (\pi_Y \odot G_Y)$$

$$\cdots$$

An individual fusion $\tilde{G}_X \oplus \tilde{G}_Y$ relies of finding the matching M maximizing

$$\tilde{F}(\tilde{G}_X, \tilde{G}_Y; M) = \sum_{a=1}^{|\tilde{V}_X|} \sum_{i=1}^{|\tilde{V}_Y|} M_{ai}(1 + \epsilon(\tilde{\mu}_X(a) + \tilde{\mu}_Y(i)) \sum_{b=1}^{|\tilde{V}_X|} \sum_{j=1}^{|\tilde{V}_Y|} M_{bj}\tilde{X}_{ab}\tilde{Y}_{ij}, \quad (8)$$

where $\tilde{X} = X$, $\tilde{Y} = Y$, are the respective adjacency matrices and $\epsilon > 0$ is a small positive constant closer to zero (in our implementation $\epsilon = 0.0001$). Such a cost function is an extension of Equation   addressed to deal with ambiguity: If there are many matchings with equal cost in terms of $F(\tilde{G}_X, \tilde{G}_Y; M)$, it prefers to choose the alternative in which the nodes with the higher weights so far are matched.

The fused graph, that is, the new prototype $\bar{G} = \tilde{G}_X \oplus \tilde{G}_Y$ registers the weights of its nodes and edges through its interpretation functions $\bar{\mu} : \bar{V} \to [0, 1]$

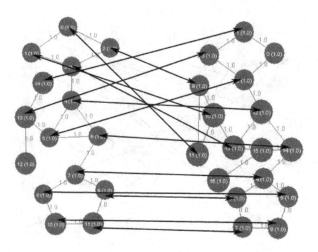

Fig. 3. A local maximum obtained by the Comb algorithm

and $\bar{\delta} : \bar{E} \to [0, 1]$. Such a registration relies on the optimal match

$$M^* = \arg\max_M \tilde{F}(\tilde{G}_X, \tilde{G}_Y; M) . \tag{9}$$

The weights of the nodes $m \in \bar{V}$ are updated as follows:

$$\bar{\mu}(m) = \begin{cases} \tilde{\mu}_X(a) + \tilde{\mu}_Y(i) & \text{if } (\exists a \in \tilde{V}_X, \exists i \in \tilde{V}_Y : M^*_{ai} = 1) \\ \tilde{\mu}_X(a) & \text{if } (a \in \tilde{V}_X) \\ \tilde{\mu}_Y(i) & \text{if } (i \in \tilde{V}_Y), \end{cases} \tag{10}$$

that is, we consider that $m = a = i$ in the first case, $m = a$ in the second and $m = i$ in the third.

Similarly, the weighs of the edges $(a, b) \in \bar{E}$ are updated by

$$\bar{\delta}(m, n) = \begin{cases} \tilde{\delta}_X(a, b) + \tilde{\delta}_Y(i, j) & \text{if } (\exists (a, b) \in \tilde{E}_X, \exists (i, j) \in \tilde{E}_Y : M^*_{ai} = M^*_{bj} = 1) \\ \tilde{\delta}_X(a, b) & \text{if } ((a, b) \in \tilde{E}_X) \\ \tilde{\delta}_Y(i, j) & \text{if } ((i, j) \in \tilde{E}_Y), \end{cases} \tag{11}$$

As before we consider that $(m, n) = (a, b) = (i, j)$ in the first case, $(m, n) = (a, b)$ in the second, and $(m, n) = (i, j)$ in the third. Consequently, weights are updated by considering that: (i) two matched nodes correspond to the same node in the prototype; (ii) edges connecting matched nodes are also the same edge; and (iii) nodes and edges existing only in one of the graphs must be also integrated in the prototype. In cases (i) and (ii) frequencies are added, whereas in case (iii) we retain the original frequencies.

Once all graphs in the set are fused, the resulting prototype $\bar{G}$ must be pruned in order to retain only those nodes $a \in \bar{V}$ with $\bar{\mu}(a) \geq 0.5$ and those edges $(a, b) \in \bar{E}$ also with $\bar{\delta}(a, b) \geq 0.5$. This results in simpler median graphs

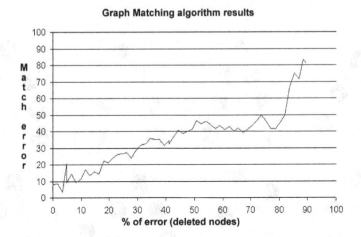

Fig. 4. Linear evolution of the match error

containing nodes and edges with significant frequencies, and these frequencies will be neglected in the future, that is, weights are also taken into account to obtain the prototype.

3.2 Fusion Results

In order to test our incremental fusion algorithm we have built three classes corresponding to the graphical models of characters A, B, and X. Each class has 8 samples. We show these samples in Figures , and . In Figure we present partial results of the incremental fusion of samples in class A. Nodes with high probabilities appear in black, whereas nodes with low probabilities appear in dark gray. Finally, in Figure we show the prototypes obtained for classes A, B, X, before and after pruning.

4 Graph Clustering

4.1 ACM for Graphs

Given N input graphs $G_i = (V_i, E_i)$ the Asymmetric Clustering Model (ACM) for graphs finds the K graph prototypes $\bar{G}_\alpha = (\bar{V}_\alpha, \bar{E}_\alpha)$ and the class-membership variables $I_{i\alpha} \in \{0, 1\}$ maximizing the following cost function

$$L(\bar{G}, I) = -\sum_{i=1}^{N} \sum_{\alpha=1}^{K} I_{i\alpha}(1 - F_{i\alpha}) , \qquad (12)$$

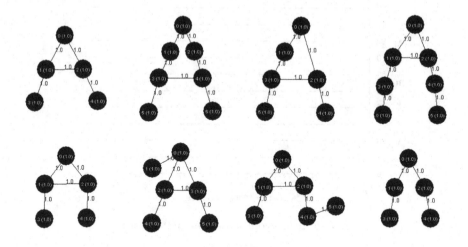

Fig. 5. Samples for class A

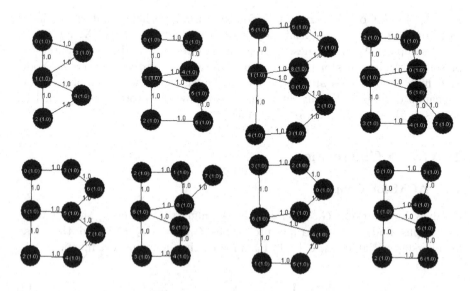

Fig. 6. Samples for class B

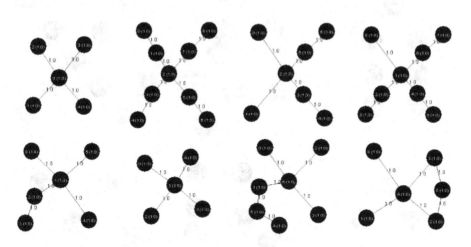

Fig. 7. Samples for class X

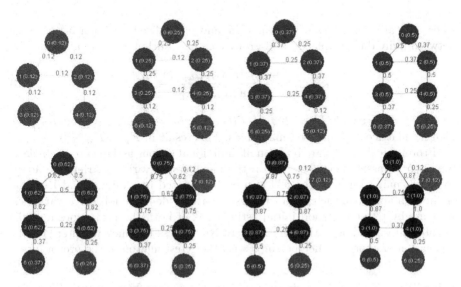

Fig. 8. Step-by-step results of fusing the samples of class A

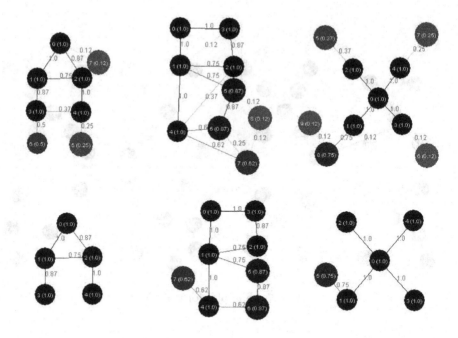

Fig. 9. Prototypes obtained for classes A, B, X before (up) and after pruning (below)

where $F_{i\alpha}$ are the values of a symmetric and normalized dissimilarity measure between individual graphs G_i and prototypes $\bar{G}_\alpha$. Such a measure is defined by

$$F_{i\alpha} = \frac{\max_M[F(G_i, \bar{G}_\alpha; M)]}{\max[F_{ii}, F_{\alpha\alpha}]} , \qquad (13)$$

where $F_{ii} = F(G_i, G_i; I_{|V_i|})$, $F_{\alpha\alpha} = F(\bar{G}_\alpha, \bar{G}_\alpha; I_{|\bar{V}_\alpha|})$, being $I_{|V_i|}$ and $I_{|\bar{V}_\alpha|}$ the identity matrices defining self-matchings. This result in $F_{i\alpha} = F_{\alpha i} \in [0, 1]$.

Prototypical graphs are built on all individual graphs assigned to each class, but such an assignment depends on the membership variables. Here we adapt to the domain of graphs the EM-approach proposed by Hoffman and Puzicha. As in such approach the class-memberships are hidden or unobserved variables, we start by providing good initial estimations of both the prototypes and the memberships, feeding with them an iterative process in which we alternate the estimation of expected memberships with the re-estimation of the prototypes.

Initialization. Initial prototypes are selected by a greedy procedure: First prototype is assumed to be a graph selected randomly, and the following ones are the most dissimilar graphs from any of the yet selected prototypes. Initial memberships $I_{i\alpha}^0$ are then given by:

$$I_{i\alpha}^0 = \begin{cases} 1 & \text{if } \alpha = arg\min_\beta[1 - F_{i\beta}] \\ 0 & \text{otherwise} \end{cases}$$

E-step. Consists of estimating the expected membership variables $I_{i\alpha} \in [0, 1]$ given the current estimation of each prototypical graph $\bar{G}_\alpha$:

$$I_{i\alpha}^{t+1} = \frac{\rho_\alpha^t \exp[(1 - F_{i\alpha})/T]}{\sum_{\beta=1}^{K} \rho_\beta^t \exp[(1 - F_{i\beta})/T]} \text{, being } \rho_\alpha^t = \frac{1}{N}\sum_{i=1}^{N} I_{i\alpha}^t \text{ ,} \tag{14}$$

that is, these variables encode the probability of assigning any graph G_i to class c_α at iteration t, and T is the temperature, a control parameter which is reduced at each iteration (we are using the deterministic annealing version of the E-step, because it is less prone to local maxima than the un-annealed one).

As in this step we need to compute the dissimilarities $F_{i\alpha}$, we need to solve $N \times K$ NP-complete problems.

M-step. Given the expected membership variables $I_{i\alpha}^{t+1}$, the prototypical graphs are re-estimated as follows:

$$\bar{G}_\alpha^{t+1} = \bigoplus_{i=1}^{N}(\pi_{i\alpha} \odot G_i) \text{ , where } \pi_{i\alpha} = \frac{I_{i\alpha}^{t+1}}{\sum_{k=1}^{N} I_{k\alpha}^{t+1}} \text{ ,} \tag{15}$$

where variables $\pi_{i\alpha}$ are the current probabilities of belonging to each class c_α. This step is completed after re-estimating the K prototypes, that is, after solving $(N - 1) \times K$ NP-complete problems. Moreover, the un-weighted median graph $\bar{G}_\alpha^{t+1}$ resulting from the fusion will be used in the E-step to re-estimate the dissimilarities $F_{i\alpha}$ through maximizing $F(G_i, \bar{G}_\alpha; M)$ with Comb-matching.

Adaptation. Assuming that the iterative process is divided in epochs, our adaptation mechanism consists of starting by a high number of classes K_{max} and then reducing such a number, if proceeds, at the end of each epoch. At that moment we select the two closest prototypes $\bar{G}_\alpha$ and $\bar{G}_\beta$ as candidates to be fused, and we compute h_α the heterogeneity of c_α

$$h_\alpha = \sum_{i=1}^{N}(1 - F_{i\alpha})\pi_{i\alpha} \text{ ,} \tag{16}$$

obtaining h_β in a similar way. Then, we compute the fused prototype $\bar{G}_\gamma$ by applying Equation   and considering that $I_{i\gamma} = I_{i\alpha} + I_{i\beta}$, that is

$$\bar{G}_\gamma = \bigoplus_{i=1}^{N}(\pi_{i\gamma} \odot G_i) \text{ .} \tag{17}$$

Finally, we fuse c_α and c_β whenever $h_\gamma < (h_\alpha + h_\beta)\mu$, where $\mu \in [0,1]$ is a merge factor addressed to facilitate class fusion (usually we set $\mu = 0.6$). After such a decision a new epoch begins. We wait until convergence before trying two fuse two other classes.

Testing whether two classes must be fused or not needs to solve $N - 1$ NP-complete problems, but if we decide to fuse the number of NP-complete problems to solve in each iteration of the next epoch will be reduced in $2N - 1$ (a reduction of N for each E-step and a reduction of $N - 1$ for each M-step).

4.2   Clustering Results

First of all we test the ACM algorithm for graph with classes A, B, X. First we consider A and B, that is those with more similar structure. In Figure   we show the evolution of their prototypes, in the top row and in the bottom row respectively. Only two A samples, and one of the B samples were misclassified. In Figure   we show the prototypes obtained for the three classes assuming a correct number of classes ($K_{max} = 3$). All A samples were classified correctly. Only one of the B samples was misclassified, and only three X samples were classified correctly. In Figure   we show the prototypes obtained with a non-adaptive version of the algorithm with $K_{max} = 5$ classes. Only the samples of classes A and B were used. Finally, in Figure   we show the improved results when the adaptive algorithm is applied.

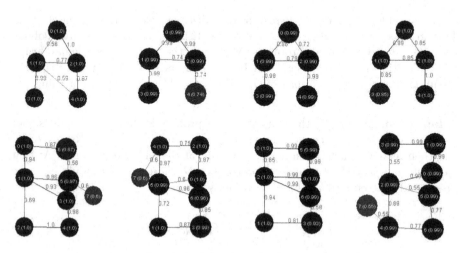

Fig. 10. Step-by-step clustering of classes A and B

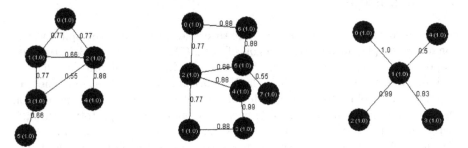

Fig. 11. Clustering results for A, B and X

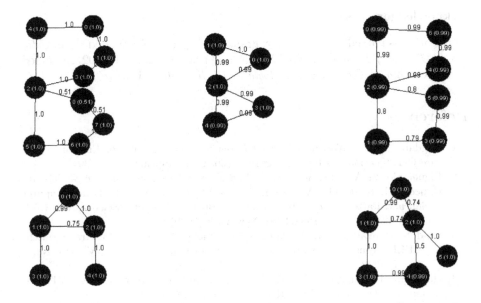

Fig. 12. Results of un-adaptive clustering of A, B and X with $K_{max} = 5$

Fig. 13. Results of adaptive clustering with $K_{max} = 5$

5   Conclusions

Our main contributions in this paper are threefold: First, we have applied to the domain of graphs an adaptive version of the ACM clustering model originally proposed for image segmentation. Second, our clustering algorithm relies on an improvement of our Comb-matching algorithm. Third, we have defined an alternative type of prototypical graph which relies only on structural information and it is close to the median-graph concept. We obtain such a prototype through incremental fusion. Future work includes the improvement of Comb-matching, and the application of this framework to cluster images, three-dimensional shapes and other learning domains in which structural information is key.

Acknowledgements

This work was partially supported by grant $TIC2002-02792$ funded by *Ministerio de Ciencia y Tecnología* and *FEDER*, and grant $CTBPRA/2002/25$ funded by the *Oficina de Ciencia y Tecnología de la Generalitat Valienciana*.

References

[1] Bagdanov, A. D., Worring, M.: First Order Gaussian Graphs for Efficient Structure Classification. Pattern Recognition (2002) (to appear).

[2] Figueiredo, M. A.T, Leitao, J. M.N, Jain, A. K.: On Fitting Mixture Models. In: Hancock, E. R., Pelillo, M. (eds.): Energy Minimization Methods in Computer Vision and Pattern Recognition. Lecture Notes in Computer Science, Vol. 1654. Springer-Verlag, Berlin Heidelberg New York (1999) 54-69.

[3] Gold, S., Rangarajan, A.: A Graduated Assignement Algorithm for Graph Matching. IEEE Trans. on Pattern Analysis and Machine Intelligence, Vol. 18, No. 4 (1996) 377-388.

[4] Hofmann, T., Puzicha, J.: Statistical Models for Co-occurrence Data. MIT AI-Memo 1625 Cambridge, MA (1998)

[5] Jiang, X., Münger, A., Bunke, H.: On Median Graphs: Properties, Algorithms, and Applications. IEEE Trans. on Pattern Analysis and Machine Intelligence, Vol. 23, No. 10 (2001) 1144-1151

[6] Kim, H. Y., Kim, J. H.: Hierarchical Random Graph Representation of Handwritten Characters and its Application to Hangul Recognition. Pattern Recognition 34 (2001) 187-201

[7] Li, S. Z.: Toward Global Solution to MAP Image Estimation: Using Common Structure of Local Solutions. In: Pelillo, M., Hancock, E. R.(eds.): Energy Minimization Methods in Computer Vision and Pattern Recognition. Lecture Notes in Computer Science, Vol. 1223. Springer-Verlag, Berlin Heidelberg New York (1997) 361-374.

[8] Lozano, M. A., Escolano, F.: Recognizing Indoor Images with Unsupervised Segmentation and Graph Matching. In: Garijo, F. J., Riquelme, J. C., Toro, M.(eds.): Advances in Artificial Intelligence - Iberamia 2002. Lecture Notes on Artificial Intelligence, Vol. 2527. Springer-Verlag, Berlin Heidelberg New York (2002) 933-942.

[9] Luo, B., Hancock, E. R.: Structural Graph Matching Using the EM Algorithm and Singular Value Decomposition. IEEE Trans. on Pattern Analysis and Machine Intelligence, Vol. 23, No. 10 (2001) 1120-1136.

[10] Puzicha, J.: Histogram Clustering for Unsupervised Segmentation and Image Retrieval. Pattern Recognition Letters, 20, (1999) 899-909.

[11] Shapiro, L. G., Brady, J. M.: Feature-based Correspondence-An Eigenvector Approach, Image and Vision Computing, Vol. 10 (1992) 283-288

[12] Sanfeliu, A., Serratosa, F., Alquézar, R.: Clustering of Attributed Graphs and Unsupervised Synthesis of Function-Described Graphs. In: Proc. of ICPR2000, 15th International Conference on Pattern Recoginition, Barcelona, Spain, Vol. 2 (2000) 1026-1029.

[13] Serratosa, F., Alquézar, R., Sanfeliu, A.: Function-described graphs for modelling objects represented by sets of attributed graphs, Pattern Recognition, Vol. 23, No. 3 (2003) 781-798

[14] Wong, A. K.C, Ghahraman, D. E.: Random Graphs: Structural-Contextual Dichotomy. IEEE Trans. on Pattern Analysis and Machine Intelligence, Vol. 2, No. 4 (1980) 341-348.

[15] Wong, A. K. C., You, M.: Entropy and Distance of Random Graphs with Application to Structural Pattern Recognition. IEEE Trans. on Pattern Analysis and Machine Intelligence, Vol. 7, No. 5 (1985) 599-609.

[16] Wong, A. K. C., Constant, J., You, M.:Random Graphs. In: Synthactic and Structural Pattern Recognition: Theory and Applications, World-Scientific, Singapore, (1990) 197-234

Information Force Clustering
Using Directed Trees[*]

Robert Jenssen[1,2], Deniz Erdogmus[1], Kenneth E. Hild II[1], Jose C. Principe[1],
and Torbjørn Eltoft[2]

[1] Computational NeuroEngineering Laboratory
Department of Electrical and Computer Engineering
University of Florida
Gainesville FL. 32611, USA
robertj@cnel.ufl.edu
Phone: (+1) 352-392-2682, Fax: (+1) 352-392-0044
[2] Electrical Engineering Group
Department of Physics
University of Tromsø
N - 9037 Tromsø, Norway

Abstract. We regard a data pattern as a physical particle experiencing a force acting on it imposed by an overall "potential energy" of the data set, obtained via a non-parametric estimate of Renyi's entropy. The "potential energy" is called the information potential, and the forces are called information forces, due to their information-theoretic origin. We create directed trees by selecting the predecessor of a node (pattern) according to the direction of the information force acting on the pattern. Each directed tree correspond to a cluster, hence enabling us to partition the data set. The clustering metric underlying our method is thus based on entropy, which is a quantity that conveys information about the shape of a probability density, and not only it's variance, as many traditional algorithms based on mere second order statistics rely on. We demonstrate the performance of our clustering technique when applied to both artificially created data and real data, and also discuss some limitations of the proposed method.

1 Introduction

In exploratory data analysis it is often desirable to partition a set of data patterns into different subsets, such that patterns within each subset are *alike* and patterns across subsets are *not alike*. This problem is known as clustering.

A wide variety of approaches to clustering have been made over the last four decades [ ]. In particular, one branch of clustering techniques utilize graph theory to partition the data. Graph theoretic clustering has the advantage that parametric assumptions about data distributions do not have to be made. In

---

[*] This work was partially supported by NSF grants ECS-9900394 and EIA-0135946

A. Rangarajan et al. (Eds.): EMMCVPR 2003, LNCS 2683, pp. 68– , 2003.

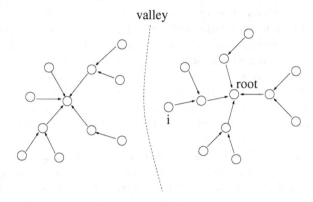

Fig. 1. Example of two directed trees, each corresponding to a cluster

addition, normally it precludes the need to know in advance the number of clusters to be formed.

In graph theoretic clustering, usually a proximity graph [ ] is constructed. In a proximity graph each node corresponds to a data pattern, which is considered a point in feature space. Between each pair of nodes an edge is formed, and the weight $d(i, j)$ on each edge is a measure of the similarity (proximity) of the nodes i and j. Clustering now becomes the problem of partitioning the proximity graph.

A common partitioning method consists of creating a hierarchy of threshold sub graphs by eliminating edges of decreasing weight in the proximity graph. Here under are included the well-known single-link [ ] and complete-link [ ] hierarchical clustering algorithms. Other methods form clusters by breaking inconsistent arcs in the minimum spanning tree [ ] of the proximity graph, or graphs constructed from limited neighborhood sets [ ]. Partitioning based on minimum cuts [ ], normalized cuts [ ] or variants thereof [ ], have also proven efficient in clustering, especially in an image segmentation context.

A somewhat different, and less explored graph theoretic approach for detecting clusters, is based on *directed trees* [,   ]. In a directed tree each node i initiates a branch pointing another node j, which is called the predecessor of i. Only one node does not have a predecessor, and this node is called the root. Starting from any node, the branches can be followed to the root. Note that each node except the root has one and only one predecessor, but each could be the predecessor of a number of nodes (its "children"), including zero [ ].

Figure   shows an example of two directed trees, each corresponding to a cluster. The two clusters are separated by a valley, where the density of data points is low. Nodes near the valley, like e.g. node i, must point away from the valley in order for the clusters to be formed.

In [ ] the predecessor j of node i is searched for along the steepest ascent of the probability density function, which is estimated based on points within a local region centered around i. Node j is found within the local region, as the node closest to the steepest ascent line from i. This method is sensitive to the size of the local region, especially in the important areas near the valley.

We propose a different view to this clustering problem, derived from recent developments in information theory [ ]. In our approach each data point can be considered a physical particle that experiences a force acting on it. This force is called an *Information Force* (IF), because it is the derivative (with respect to the particle) of an overall "potential energy", called the *Information Potential* (IP) [ ]. The IP is defined through a non-parametric estimate of Renyi's entropy, using Parzen kernel density estimation.

For a well chosen (Gaussian) kernel size, σ, in the Parzen density estimate, the information force acting on a particle points toward the cluster the particle belongs to. This happens irrespective of the shape of the probability density describing the data set. This property can be attributed to the underlying entropy metric. The issue now is to utilize the information forces to cluster the data. It should be noted that our clustering method has resemblance to other kernel based methods, such as e.g. spectral clustering [ ] and Mercer kernel based clustering [ ].

Our approach is to create directed trees, each corresponding to a cluster, according to the direction of the information forces. We show that σ can also be used when selecting the predecessor node j. We search for j in a neighborhood of i, where the size of the neighborhood is specified by σ, such that j is closest to the direction of the information force acting on i.

Obviously, the parameter σ is very important. It should be determined automatically from the data at hand, and preferably each data pattern should be associated with a unique kernel, adapted based on it's neighboring data. However, at this point in time, we use only one single kernel in the Parzen estimate. The kernel size is determined manually, such that the Parzen density estimate is relatively accurate.

In the next section we explain the information-theory enabling us to define the information forces, following the outline given in [ ]. In section   we discuss how the directed trees, which correspond to clusters, are created. We present some clustering experiments in section   , both on artificially created data and real data. Finally, in section   we make our concluding remarks.

2   Information Forces

In a 1957 classic paper Jaynes [ ] re interpreted statistical mechanics, providing a new viewpoint from which thermodynamic entropy and information-theory entropy [ ] appear as the same concept. This advance, however, is predicated on the specifications of the data distributions.

Avoiding unrealistic parametric assumptions about data distributions, recently Principe et al. [ ] combined a non-parametric density estimator with an easily computable information-theoretic definition of entropy, resulting in an entropy estimator with a very interesting physical interpretation as a potential energy field. The entropy definition used in [ ] was proposed by Renyi [ ], hence called Renyi's entropy.

Renyi's entropy for a stochastic variable $\mathbf{x}$ with probability density function (pdf) $f(\mathbf{x})$ is given by [ ]

$$H_R(\mathbf{x}) = \frac{1}{1 - \alpha} \log \int f^\alpha(\mathbf{x})d\mathbf{x}, \ \alpha > 0, \ \alpha \neq 1. \tag{1}$$

Specifically, for $\alpha = 2$ we obtain [ ]

$$H_R(\mathbf{x}) = -\log \int f^2(\mathbf{x})dx, \tag{2}$$

which is called Renyi's quadratic entropy [ ].

This expression can easily be estimated directly from data by the use of Parzen window density estimation, with a multidimensional Gaussian window function. We have available the set of discrete data points $\mathbf{x}_i$, $i = 1, \ldots, N$. Now, the pdf estimate based on these data points is given by [ ]

$$\hat{f}(\mathbf{x}) = \frac{1}{N} \sum_{i=1}^{N} G(\mathbf{x} - \mathbf{x}_i, \sigma^2 \mathbf{I}), \tag{3}$$

where we have used a symmetric Gaussian kernel, $G(\mathbf{x}, \boldsymbol{\Sigma})$, where the covariance matrix, $\boldsymbol{\Sigma}$, is given by $\boldsymbol{\Sigma} = \sigma^2 \mathbf{I}$.

By substituting ( ) into ( ), and utilizing the properties of the Gaussian kernel, we obtain an estimate of the entropy given by;

$$H_R(\mathbf{x}) = -\log V_R(\mathbf{x}), \tag{4}$$

where

$$V_R(\mathbf{x}) = \frac{1}{N^2} \sum_{i=1}^{N} \sum_{j=1}^{N} G(\mathbf{x}_i - \mathbf{x}_j, 2\sigma^2 \mathbf{I}). \tag{5}$$

Regarding the data points $\mathbf{x}_i$ and $\mathbf{x}_j$ as physical particles, we can regard $V_{ij} = G(\mathbf{x}_i - \mathbf{x}_j, 2\sigma^2 \mathbf{I})$ as an interaction law between particles, imposed by the Gaussian kernel. This interaction law is always positive and is inversely proportional to the distance between particles.

The sum of interactions on the i'th particle is $V_i = \sum_j V_{ij}$. The sum of all pairs of interactions, given by ( ), can now be regarded as an overall potential energy of the data set, where the local field strength between pairs of particles is governed by the width of the Gaussian kernel [ ]. This potential energy is called the information potential.

Just as in mechanics, the force acting on particle $\mathbf{x}_i$ is given by the derivative of the potential field with respect to the particle;

$$\mathbf{F}_i = \frac{\partial}{\partial \mathbf{x}_i} V_R(\mathbf{x})$$

$$= -\frac{1}{N^2 \sigma^2} \sum_{j=1}^{N} G(\mathbf{x}_i - \mathbf{x}_j, 2\sigma^2 \mathbf{I})(\mathbf{x}_i - \mathbf{x}_j)$$

$$= -\frac{1}{N^2 \sigma^2} \sum_{j=1}^{N} V_{ij} \mathbf{d}_{ij}, \tag{6}$$

where $\mathbf{d}_{ij} = \mathbf{x}_i - \mathbf{x}_j$. This is the net effect of the IP on particle $\mathbf{x}_i$, and will be called an information force.

Naturally, the behavior of the information forces and the quality of the pdf estimate inherent in the entropy estimator, are closely related. However, our concern at this stage is mainly whether a particle $\mathbf{x}_i$ experiences a force pushing it toward a cluster or not. Whether the pdf estimate is the most accurate possible, is of lesser concern.

In Fig.   (a) a data set consisting of three elongated clusters and one spherical cluster is shown, and the IF acting on each data point is indicated by an arrow. The arrows only convey information about the directions of the forces, not the magnitude. Before calculating the IFs the data set was normalized feature-by-feature to lie in a range $[-1, 1]$. A kernel size of $\sigma = 0.03$ was used in the pdf estimation. It can be seen that nearly all the IFs point inward to one of the clusters. A few outliers mostly interact with each other, because the kernel size is small. The corresponding pdf estimate is shown in Fig.   (c). This is a rather crude and noisy estimate, indicating that if our concern is solely density estimation, σ is probably too low.

Figure   (b) and (d) show the IFs and the corresponding pdf estimate for $\sigma = 0.09$. The IFs point inward to one of the clusters also in this case. The pdf estimate clearly shows the structure of the data, but the increasingly dominant smoothing effect resulting from a large kernel size is evident.

A close look at Fig.   (a) and (b) also shows that some of the IFs points to different clusters for the two different kernel sizes.

3   Creating Directed Trees

Our procedure for creating directed trees is very simple, once the IFs have been calculated. We examine every data point $\mathbf{x}_i$, $i = 1, \ldots, N$, one at a time, where $\mathbf{x}_i$ corresponds to node i in the final tree. For node i we determine whether it has a predecessor j, or whether it is a root, based on the following: Node j is the predecessor of node i if it satisfies

o Node j lies *closest to the direction of the force* $\mathbf{F}_i$ *acting on* i,

under the following constraints;

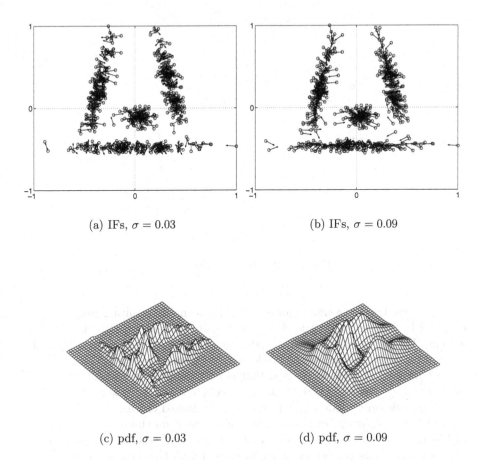

(a) IFs, $\sigma = 0.03$ (b) IFs, $\sigma = 0.09$

(c) pdf, $\sigma = 0.03$ (d) pdf, $\sigma = 0.09$

Fig. 2. (a) and (b): Example of a data set and the IFs acting on each particle for two different values of σ. (c) and (d): The corresponding Parzen pdf estimates

1. The distance $\mathbf{x}_i - \mathbf{x}_j \leq 3\sigma$.
2. $\mathbf{F}_i \cdot (\mathbf{x}_i - \mathbf{x}_j) \geq 0$.
3. Node j can not be one of i's children.

If there exists no node j satisfying the above constraints, then node i is defined to be a root, not pointing to another node.

The only free parameter, σ, is the same as the one already used when determining the IFs. The end result of this procedure is a set of directed trees, each corresponding to a cluster.

Constraint 1 is necessary in order to avoid linking together trees that are in fact part of different clusters. Consider Fig. . The tiny arrows show how nodes have been connected up to a point in time. The nodes with big arrows have not yet been examined, and the arrows show the direction of the IF acting on each

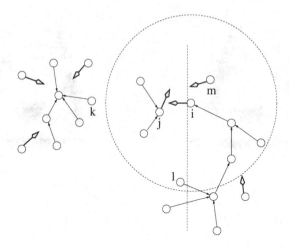

Fig. 3. Creating directed trees

one of them. Let us examine node i. Of all the nodes pointing inward to the cluster i belongs to, node j is closest to the direction of $\mathbf{F}_i$. However, node k, actually belonging to a different cluster, is even closer to the direction of $\mathbf{F}_i$. To avoid k being selected as the predecessor of i, we must restrict our search to a neighborhood of node i. We find that simply defining the neighborhood of i to be given by a hyper-sphere of radius 3σ centered at i, is reasonable. In Fig. the neighborhood of node i is indicated by the dashed circle.

Our choice of neighborhood is reasonable based on the inherent properties of Parzen pdf estimation. In order for the Parzen pdf estimate to be relatively accurate, the Gaussian kernels must be chosen such that the effective width of the kernels is sufficiently large, but not too large. If it is sufficiently large, a kernel centered at a data point also covers several other of its neighboring data points. But it doesn't cover distant data points, because that would result in to smooth an estimate. The effective width of a Gaussian kernel is given by 3σ, since 98% of its power is concentrated within 3σ of its center.

Constraint 2 is crucial, since it ensures that we really use the information provided by the direction of the IFs. Figure   illustrates this point. Node m, or any of the other nodes to the right of the dashed line, is not allowed to be selected as predecessor of node i. The reason for this is obvious, since the whole idea of our clustering technique is to use the IFs to create directed trees since the IFs point toward clusters, and not away from them.

Constraint 3 ensures that a node do not become one of its own children, contradicting the idea of a directed tree. For instance, in Fig.   , node l can not be a predecessor of node i, even though it is located within the neighborhood of i.

4   Clustering Experiments

We present some clustering experiments, both on an artificially created data set, and two real data sets. In all experiments the data have been normalized feature-by-feature to have a range $[-1, 1]$.

We create the directed trees, and for each tree assign the same label to its members. Outliers in the data set will tend to create trees with only one or a few members. Clusters with 5 members or less are kept in an outlier set, and are not assigned a label. Labeling these points can be done in a post-clustering operation, for example by simple nearest-neighbor classification.

4.1   Artificial Data Sets

First, we re-visit the data set considered in Fig. . Figure   (a) shows the same data set, where the data points belonging to the same cluster have been marked by the same symbol. It can be seen that three of the clusters are elongated, with a shape making this data set very difficult for variance based clustering methods.

Figure   (b) shows the clustering result our IF directed tree method produces when applied to this data set, for a kernel size $\sigma = 0.07$. The result is satisfying. Only three patterns have been assigned to the wrong cluster, and there is one outlier. Furthermore, the outlier would be assigned to the correct cluster after a nearest-neighbor classification.

Figure   shows the clustering results for a range of σ's. For $\sigma = 0.06$ there are three errors, and three outliers. When the kernel size increases the number of outliers decreases, while the number of errors increases as σ increases.

For $\sigma > 0.085$ our experiments show that clusters tend to be merged together across cluster boundaries. For $\sigma < 0.06$ the clusters tend to be split. E.g. for $\sigma = 0.055$ one of the clusters is split into two clusters. Even though clusters are split, the method can still be useful if a merging procedure is implemented.

However, we see that even though we previously have shown that the IFs point inward to clusters for at least $0.03 \leq \sigma \leq 0.09$, the overall clustering procedure is somewhat more sensitive to the size of σ.

For comparison we show in Fig.   the clustering result the K-means [ ] algorithm produces on the same data set. Since the K-means algorithm has a tendency to be trapped in local minima when minimizing the K-means cost, we have shown the best result out of 10 runs. Since K-means is based on a minimum variance criterion, it only works well for hyper-spherical, or at best hyper-elliptical data. This can be clearly observed, as K-means fails on our data set consisting of several elongated clusters.

The second artificially created data set consists of two highly irregular clusters. On this data set we are able to produce a perfect clustering for a kernel size in the range $0.1 \leq \sigma \leq 0.12$. Figure   (a) shows the result of our method for $\sigma = 0.1$.

In Fig.   (b) the result for K-means is shown. Again, K-means fails, since it can not handle clusters having a non-linear boundary between them.

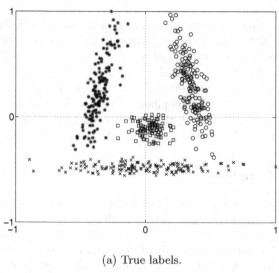

(a) True labels.

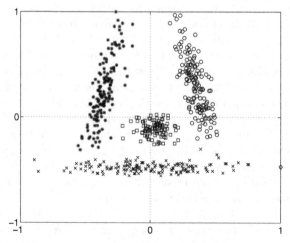

(b) Result of IF directed tree labeling. $\sigma = 0.07$.

Fig. 4. Two-dimensional artificially created data set used in clustering experiment

4.2   Real Data Sets

Next, we test our method on the WINE data set, extracted from the UCI repository database [ ]. This data set consists of 178 instances in a 13-dimensional feature space, where the features are found by chemical analysis of three differ-

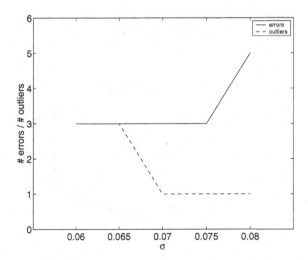

Fig. 5. # of errors and # of outliers for two-dimensional data set plotted as a function of σ

ent types of wines. We include this data set in our analysis, because it shows that our clustering method is capable of performing well in a high dimensional feature space.

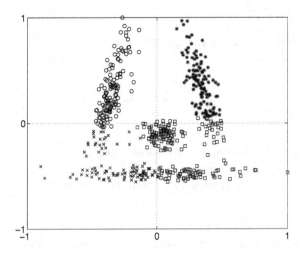

Fig. 6. Result of K-means clustering

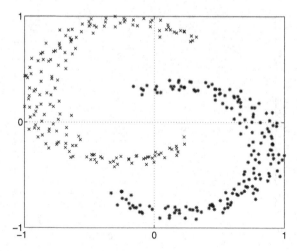

(a) Result of IF directed tree labeling for highly irregular clusters. $\sigma = 0.1$.

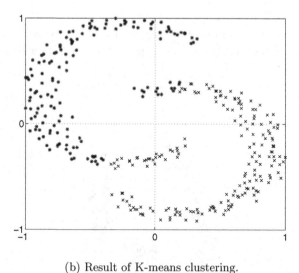

(b) Result of K-means clustering.

Fig. 7. Two-dimensional artificially created data set used in clustering experiment

For a range $0.29 \leq \sigma \leq 0.32$ we obtain satisfactory clustering results. The confusion matrix using $\sigma = 0.32$ is shown in Table . We denote each class by C_i, $i = 1, 2, 3$. The numbers in parenthesis indicate the number of instances actually belonging to each class. Table shows that there are 10 patterns as-

Table 1. Confusion matrix for wine data; $\sigma = 0.32$

		Result		
		C_1	C_2	C_3
	C_1 (59)	59	0	0
True	C_2 (71)	4	50	6
	C_3 (48)	0	0	46

Table 2. Confusion matrix for iris data; $\sigma = 0.095$

		Result		
		C_1	C_2	C_3
	C_1 (50)	49	0	0
True	C_2 (50)	0	42	3
	C_3 (50)	0	5	44

signed to the wrong class. The 10 patterns in fact belong to C_2, but some are assigned to C_1, and some to C_3. There are a total of 13 outliers. Again C_2 is the troublesome class, since 11 of the outliers belong to this class. We have not made any attempt to classify the outliers by other means, so we do not know whether they would be assigned to class C_2 or not in a post-clustering operation. The last two outliers belong to C_3.

Last, we have included an experiment clustering the well-known IRIS data set, also extracted from the UCI repository database. This data set contains three classes of 50 patterns each, where each class refers to a type of iris plant. It is characterized by four numeric attributes. The IRIS data set is known to be difficult to cluster, since two of the classes overlap to some degree, and the boundaries between classes are non-linear. In this case, our method is expected to have difficulty in producing a satisfying clustering result. When there is no clear boundary between clusters, the particles of the overlapped clusters will interact more with each other, and the information forces will seize to point toward the distinct clusters.

Consequently, in this case our clustering method is more sensitive to the kernel size than in the other experiments. The range of σ's for which we obtain reasonable results is narrow. However, choosing e.g. $\sigma = 0.095$, we obtain the confusion matrix shown in Table . In this case eight patterns are assigned to the wrong class. The incorrect labeled patterns clearly belong to the two clusters that overlap somewhat. In addition there are seven outliers.

5   Conclusion

We have presented a new graph-theoretic clustering method. The core idea is to utilize the information forces to create directed trees, each corresponding to a cluster.

The directed trees are created by searching for the predecessor of node i, in the direction of the information force acting on i. The information force can be regarded as a force acting on a physical particle, imposed by an overall potential energy. The potential energy is called the information potential, because of its information-theoretic origin.

The information forces contain global information about all data points. Hence, we avoid having to rely on local estimates of the gradient of the pdf, which is known to be sensitive to the size of the local region, especially in the important areas near the valleys of the data distribution.

A non-parametric estimator of Renyi's entropy is obtained via Parzen (Gaussian) kernel density estimation. The information potential is based on this estimator, and hence the information forces too. The main advantage of our approach is that the underlying clustering metric is based on entropy, which is a quantity that conveys information about the shape of a probability density, and not only it's variance, which many traditional clustering algorithms, e.g. K-means, rely on.

To determine the information forces a single $O(N^2)$ operation is required. Determining the neighbors of each pattern requires a further $O(N)$ search procedure in each case. The $O(N^2)$ operation is computationally demanding for large data sets. Still, our clustering method is less computationally expensive than a previous iterative clustering algorithm proposed by Gokcay and Principe [ ] based on the same theory underlying the Renyi entropy estimator.

At present, the major problem with our clustering algorithm is how to choose the kernel size σ. This is a problem encountered in all kernel based methods, both unsupervised and supervised. For our current clustering method to be useful in practice, an automatic procedure must be implemented, determining σ such that the Parzen pdf estimate is relatively accurate. Preferably, each data pattern $\mathbf{x}_i$ should be associated with a unique kernel, σ_i, adapted based on it's neighboring data. In regions of high density of data patterns the kernels should be relatively narrow, and in regions of low density the kernels should be relatively wide. The use of non-symmetric kernels, may also potentially help. The σ_i's could in this case e.g. be determined based on the covariance matrix estimated in a neighborhood of $\mathbf{x}_i$.

In our current method, it is also possible to avoid having to define the neighborhood of a pattern directly in terms of σ when creating the directed trees. Instead, the neighborhood of $\mathbf{x}_i$ could for example be defined in terms of the inverse of the magnitude of the IF acting on it. The magnitude of the IFs will be relatively large in areas of high density of data patterns, and relatively small in areas of low density. Decoupling the creation of the directed trees from σ could lead to improvements, since we have found that our algorithm may be more dependent on the value of σ when creating the directed trees, compared to it's effect on the actual information forces.

For clusters having a large degree of overlap, our current method will encounter increasing difficulty, because the information forces no longer points to distinct cluster centers. This was observed when trying to cluster the IRIS data set. The range of σ's giving satisfying results was narrow.

We have performed several clustering experiments both on an artificially created data set and two real data sets. We have shown that our method has the ability to discover clusters of irregular shape, also in a high dimensional feature space.

Finally, to put the clustering results of our graph theoretic information force clustering algorithm in some perspective, we compare the result we obtained on the most difficult data set for our algorithm to handle, namely the IRIS data set, with the results achieved by some other recent clustering methods on the same data set. The results are not straightforward to compare, because the data are often pre-processed in different ways. As an example Eltoft and deFigueiredo [ ] reported on the average six errors (or outliers), where clustering is based on the first and second principal components. Gokcay and Principe [ ] obtained 14 errors when normalizing the data the same way we did. Ben-Hur et al. [ ] report four errors when the clustering is based on the first three principal components, and 14 when the fourth principal component is added to the feature vectors. The information-theoretic approach of Tishby and Slonim [ ] leads to five mis classifications and the SPC algorithm of Blatt et al. [ ], when applied to the original data space, has 15 mis classifications. Horn and Gottlieb [ ] report five errors when the data is normalized in a certain manner. Without this normalization they obtained 15 errors. The best result to our knowledge is the kernel-based method of Girolami [ ], obtaining only three partition errors.

References

[1] A. K. Jain and R. C. Dubes, *Algorithms for Clustering Data,* Prentice-Hall, Englewood Cliffs, NJ, 1988.   ,

[2] P. H. A. Sneath and R. R. Sokal, *Numerical Taxonomy,* Freeman, London, 1973.

[3] B. King, "Step-wise clustering procedures," *J. Am. Stat. Assoc.,* pp. 86-101, 1967.

[4] C. T. Zahn, "Graph Theoretic Methods for Detecting and Describing Gestalt Clusters," *IEEE Trans. Comput.,* vol. 20, pp. 68-86, 1971.

[5] R. Urquart, "Graph Theoretical Clustering based on Limited Neighborhood Sets," *Pattern Recognition,* vol. 15, pp. 173-187, 1982.

[6] Z. Wu and R. Leahy, "An Optimal Graph Theoretic Approach to Data Clustering: Theory and Its Applications to Image Segmentation," *IEEE Transactions on Pattern Analysis and Machine Intelligence,* vol. 15, no. 11, pp. 1101-1113, 1993.

[7] J. Shi and J. Malik, "Normalized Cuts and Image Segmentation," *IEEE Transactions on Pattern Analysis and Machine Intelligence,* vol. 22, no. 8, pp. 888-905, 2000.

[8] C. H. Q. Ding, X. He, H. Zha, M. Gu, and H. D. Simon, "A Min-max Cut Algorithm for Graph Partitioning and Data Clustering," in *IEEE Int. Conf. on Data Mining*, 2001, pp. 107-114.

[9] W. L. G. Koontz, P. M. Narendra, and K. Fukunaga, "A graph-theoretic approach to nonparametric cluster analysis," *IEEE Transactions on Computers, vol. 25*, pp. 936-944, 1975.

[10] K. Fukunaga, *Introduction to Statistical Pattern Recognition*, Academic Press, New York, 1990.

[11] J. Principe, D. Xu, and J. Fisher, *Unsupervised Adaptive Filtering, vol. 1*, chapter 7 "Information Theoretic Learning", John Wiley & Sons, 2000.

[12] A. Y. Ng, M. Jordan, and Y. Weiss, "On Spectral Clustering: Analysis and an Algorithm," in *Advances in Neural Information Processing Systems*, 2002, number 14, pp. 849-856.

[13] M. Girolami, "Mercer Kernel-Based Clustering in Feature Space," *IEEE Transactions on Neural Networks, vol. 13*, no. 3, pp. 780-784, 2002.

[14] E. T. Jaynes, "Information Theory and Statistical Mechanics," *The Physical Review, vol. 106*, no. 4, pp. 620-630, 1957.

[15] C. E. Shannon, "A Mathematical Theory of Communication," *Bell Sys. Tech. J.*, vol. 27, pp. 379-423, 623-653, 1948.

[16] A. Renyi, "On Measures of Entropy and Information," in *Fourth Berkeley Symposium on Mathematical Statistics and Probability*, 1960, pp. 547-561.

[17] E. Parzen, "On the Estimation of a probability density function and the mode," *Ann. Math. Stat., vol. 32*, pp. 1065-1076, 1962.

[18] J. McQueen, "Some methods for classification and analysis of multivariate observations," in *Fifth Berkeley Symposium on Mathematical Statistics and Probability*, 1967, pp. 281-297.

[19] R. Murphy and D. Ada, "UCI Repository of Machine Learning databases," Tech. Rep., Dept. Comput. Sci. Univ. California, Irvine, 1994.

[20] E. Gokcay and J. Principe, "Information Theoretic Clustering," *IEEE Transactions on Pattern Analysis and Machine Intelligence, vol. 24*, no. 2, pp. 158-170, 2002.

[21] T. Eltoft and R. J. P. deFigueiredo, "A New Neural Network for Cluster-Detectionand-Labeling," *IEEE Transactions on Neural Networks, vol. 9*, no. 5, pp. 10211035, 1998.

[22] A. Ben-Hur, D. Horn, H. T. Siegelmann, and V. Vapnik, "Support Vector Clustering," *Journal of Machine Learning Research, vol. 2*, pp. 125-137, 2001.

[23] N. Tishby and N. Slonim, "Data Clustering by Markovian Relaxation and the Information Bottleneck Method," in *Advances in Neural Information Processing Systems*, Denver, USA, 2000, vol. 13, pp. 640-646.

[24] M. Blatt, S. Wiseman, and E. Domany, "Data Clustering using a Model Granular Magnet," *Neural Computation, vol. 9*, no. 8, pp. 1805-1842, 1997.

[25] D. Horn and A. Gottlieb, "The Method of Quantum Clustering," in *Advances in Neural Information Processing Systems*, Vancouver, Canada, 2001, vol. 14, pp. 769-776.

Watershed-Based Unsupervised Clustering

Manuele Bicego, Marco Cristani, Andrea Fusiello, and Vittorio Murino

Dipartimento di Informatica, Università di Verona
Ca' Vignal 2, Strada Le Grazie 15, 37134 Verona, Italia
{bicego,cristanm,fusiello,murino}@sci.univr.it

Abstract. In this paper, a novel general purpose clustering algorithm is presented, based on the watershed algorithm. The proposed approach defines a density function on a suitable lattice, whose cell dimension is carefully estimated from the data. The clustering is then performed using the well-known watershed algorithm, paying particular attention to the boundary situations. The main characteristic of this method is the capability to determine automatically the number of clusters from the data, resulting in a completely unsupervised approach. Experimental evaluation on synthetic data shows that the proposed approach is able to accurately estimate the number of the classes and to cluster data effectively.

1 Introduction

Unsupervised classification or clustering [,] is undoubtedly an interesting and challenging research area. It could be defined as the organization of a collection of patterns into groups, based on similarity. It is well known that data clustering is inherently a more difficult task if compared to supervised classification, in which classes are already identified, so that a system can be adequately trained. Clustering has been applied in several contexts, as, for example, data mining, DNA modeling, information retrieval, image segmentation, signal compression and coding, and machine learning. Hundreds of clustering algorithms have been proposed in the literature, mostly divided in two categories: iterative partitional and agglomerative hierarchical techniques. The former attempts to obtain a partition of data that minimizes the within-cluster scatter or the between-scatter matrix. The latter organizes the data in a nested sequence of groups organized in a dendrogram which is cut at the chosen depth level in order to obtain the desired number of clusters.

In this paper, a novel clustering scheme is proposed, based on the watershed segmentation algorithm [,] also called watershed transform. This is an effective and accurate method originally conceived in the Mathematical Morphology (MM) field [ ] and widely employed in recent years for intensity image segmentation, and video segmentation [,]. The watershed algorithm has also been used in the clustering context, in order to cluster histograms with the aim of color segmentation [ ]. The key idea is to consider the gray level picture as a topographic relief, in which to actuate an immersion process.

A. Rangarajan et al. (Eds.): EMMCVPR 2003, LNCS 2683, pp. 83– , 2003.

In this paper the use of watershed for general clustering purposes is investigated. From the clustering point of view, watershed presents some appealing characteristics: first, it is accurate, as the obtained image segmentation is typically highly informative. Second, and most important, it is an unsupervised method, as the number of clusters does not have to be determined *a priori*. Other techniques, like the K-means or the agglomerative hierarchical family of methods, require the number of clusters to be fixed *a priori*, or to be detected using index like the Davies-Bouldin criterion [ ] or some model selection analysis. Another appealing characteristic of the watershed algorithm is that it could be easily extended to deal with n-dimensional spaces [ ].

The watershed algorithm is defined over a discrete topological space, where a function defining the "height" of each point should be given. In the case of images, this function is the color intensity of each pixel, but in the clustering context there is no natural choice, and this function should be carefully defined.

In our approach, this function is derived by dividing the space in a set of cells, each of fixed dimension. The height of each cell represents the density of points in that cell, *i.e.* the number of points belonging to the cell. Clearly, the size of the cell is crucial: if too small it could lead to over-segmentation, a too large size could cause a coarse segmentation. In this paper, this problem is carefully addressed, by devising an automatic way for determining the cell size from data.

Preliminary experimental evaluation on synthetic data shows that the proposed approach is quite accurate in discovering the real structure of the data, detecting automatically the number of clusters and their composition.

The rest of the paper is organized as follows. In Section   the fundamentals of the watershed algorithms are summarized, and the whole strategy is detailed in Section . Section   presents experimental evaluation of the proposed method, and in Section   conclusions are drawn and future perspectives are investigated.

2   The Watershed Algorithm

In the field of image processing and more particularly in Mathematical Morphology (MM) [ ], gray-scale pictures could be considered as topographic reliefs, in which the numerical value of each pixel of a given image I represents the elevation at that point. In such a context, the image segmentation could be obtained by the watershed transform, a technique originally proposed by Digabel and Lantuejoul [   ]. The intuitive idea under this segmentation method is the following: imagine that the image-landscape I is immersed in a lake, with holes pierced in local minima. Basins (also called "catchment basins") will be filled up with water starting at these local minima, and, at points where water coming from different basins meet, dams are built. When the water level has reached the highest peak in the landscape, the process is stopped. As a result, the landscape is partitioned into regions or basins separated by dams, called *watershed lines* or simply *watersheds*. For the sake of clarity, we will use the expression "watershed transform" to denote a labeling of the topographic space, such that all points of a given catchment basin have the same unique label, and a special label, distinct from all the other labels of the catchment basins, is assigned to all point of the watershed.

Many sequential algorithms have been developed to compute watershed transform (see [ ] for a critical review). They can mainly be divided into two classes: the first one is based on the algorithm proposed by Vincent and Soille in [ ]; the second one is based on distance functions, and was firstly proposed by Meyer [ ]. For our clustering purpose, we prefer the first approach, that is very general: its adaptation to any kind of underlying grid (4-, 6-, 8-connectivity) is straightforward, and it can be easily extended to n-dimensional spaces.

The following subsections present the watershed algorithm, following a definition that is know in literature as *algorithmic definition*.

2.1   Definitions

Let I be the topographic space, 2D for simplicity, whose definition domain is denoted $D_i \subset \mathbb{Z}^2$. I is supposed to take discrete values in a given range $[0, N]$, $N \in \mathcal{N}$. Let $G \subset \mathbb{Z}^2 \times \mathbb{Z}^2$ denote an underlying digital grid, in 8-connectivity for example. We could define the following entities:

Definition 1. *A path P of length l between two points p and q in G is a $(l + 1)$-tuple of points $(p_0, p_1, \ldots, p_{l-1}, p_l)$ such that $p_0 = p$, $p_l = q$, and $\forall i \in [1, l], (p_{i-1}, p_i) \in G$. We will define $l(P)$ the length of a given path P, $N_G(p) = \{p' \in \mathbf{Z}^2, (p, p') \in G\}$ the neighbors of a point p, with respect to G.*

Definition 2. *A minimum M of I at altitude h is a connected plateau of points of height h from which it is impossible to reach a lower height point without having to climb:*

$$\forall p \in M, \forall q \notin M, \text{ such that } I(q) \leq I(p),$$
$$\forall P = (p_0, p_1, \ldots, p_l) \text{ such that } p_0 = p \text{ and } p_l = q,$$
$$\exists i \in [1, l] \text{ such that } I(p_i) > I(p_0). \tag{1}$$

Definition 3. *The geodesic distance $d_A(x, y)$ between two points x and y in A (set of points simply connected in G) is the minimum length of the paths which join x and y that are totally included in A:*

$$d_A(x, y) = inf\{l(P), P \text{ path between } x \text{ and } y \text{ which is totally included in } A\}. \tag{2}$$

Let $B \subset A$ made of several connected components $B_1, B_2, \ldots, B_k$.

Definition 4. *The geodesic influence zone $iz_A(B_i)$ of a connected component B_i of B in A is formed by those points in A whose geodesic distance to B_i is smaller than their geodesic distance to any other component of B:*

$$iz_A(B_i) = \{p \in A, \forall j \in [1, k]/\{i\}, d_A(p, B_i) < d_A(p, B_j)\}. \tag{3}$$

The points of A not belonging to any geodesic influence zone form the *skeleton by influence zones (SKIZ)* of B inside A:

$$\text{SKIZ}_A(B) = A/\text{IZ}_A(B) \text{ with } \text{IZ}_A(B) = \bigcup_{i \in [1;k]} iz_A(B_i). \tag{4}$$

2.2 The Watershed Transform

To reproduce the immersion procedure described above, we start from the set $T_{h_{min}}(I) = \{p \in D_I, I(p) \le h_{min}\}$ of the points first reached by the water. These points constitute the starting set of our recursion. Thus, we set

$$X_{h_{min}} = T_{h_{min}}(I). \tag{5}$$

$X_{h_{min}}$ is composed by the points of I which belong to the minima of lowest altitude. Let us now consider the threshold of I at level $h_{min}+1$, i.e., $T_{h_{min}+1}(I)$. Now, if Y is one of the connected components of $T_{h_{min}+1}(I)$, there are three possible relations of inclusion between Y and $Y \cup X_{h_{min}}$:

1. $Y \cup X_{h_{min}} = \emptyset$: Y is a new minimum of I. Indeed, according to the definitions above, Y is a plateau at level $h_{min} + 1$, since:

$$\forall p \in Y \begin{cases} p \notin X_{h_{min}} \Rightarrow I(p) \ge h_{min} + 1 \\ p \in Y \Rightarrow I(p) \le h_{min} + 1 \end{cases} \tag{6}$$

   Moreover, all the surrounding points do not belong to $T_{h_{min}+1}(I)$ and have a function value strictly greater than $h_{min} + 1$. The minimum discovered is "pierced", hence, its corresponding catchment basin will be progressively filled up with water.
2. $Y \cup X_{h_{min}} \ne \emptyset$ and is connected: in this case Y corresponds exactly to the pixels belonging to the catchment basin associated with the minimum $Y \cup X_{h_{min}}$ and having a gray level lower than or equal to $h_{min} + 1$:

$$Y = C_{h_{min}+1}(Y \cup X_{h_{min}}). \tag{7}$$

   where $C(M)$ is the catchment basin associated with a minimum M, and $C_h(M)$ is the subset of this catchment basin made of points having an altitude smaller or equal to h:

$$C_h(M) = \{p \in C(M), I(p) \le h\} = C(M) \cup T_h(I) \tag{8}$$

3. $Y \cup X_{h_{min}} \ne \emptyset$ and is not connected: we therefore notice that Y contains different minima of I. Denote $(Z_1, Z_2, \ldots, Z_k)$ these minima. In this situation, the best possible choice for $C_{h_{min}+1}(Z_i)$ is given by the geodesic influence zone of Z_i inside Y:

$$C_{h_{min}+1}(Z_i) = iz_Y(Z_i). \tag{9}$$

Since all possibilities have been discussed, we take as second set of our recursion:

$$X_{h_{min}+1} = \min_{h_{min}+1} \cup IZ_{T_{h_{min}+1}(I)}(X_{h_{min}}). \tag{10}$$

This relation holds for all levels h, and finally, we obtain the following definition:

Definition 5. *(Catchment basins and watershed by immersion): the set of the catchment basins of the function I is equal to the set $X_{h_{max}}$ obtained after the following recursion:*

$$a)X_{h_{min}} = T_{h_{min}}(I), b)\forall h \in [h_{min}, h_{max}-1], X_{h_{min}+1} = min_{h+1} \cup IZ_{T_{h+1}(I)}(X_h) \tag{11}$$

The watershed of I corresponds to the complement of this set in D_I, i.e. to the set of the points of D_I that do not belong to any catchment basin.

Our watershed algorithm is based on the above definitions, and is thoroughly described in [ ]. We consider the subsequent height levels of the topographic space examined, and compute the *geodesic influence zones* on the basis of the labeling of the previous level.

The watershed algorithm is realized in two steps: the first consists in an initial sorting in increasing order of the values of the pixels. In the second step, the flooding phase, the geodesic influence zones are computed by performing a breadth-first scanning of each height level. Suppose the flooding of the catchment basins has been done up to a given level h. Each catchment basin already discovered is supposed to have a unique label. Starting from the pixels that have at least one neighbor already labeled, we compute the geodesic influence zone in order to extend the labeled catchment basins. After this step, only the *minima* at level $h + 1$ have not been reached (they are not connected to any of the already labeled catchment basin). Therefore, a second scanning of the pixels at level $h + 1$ is necessary to detect and to label the new minima. This procedure stops when the highest pixel has been examined.

3   The Proposed Strategy

In this section, the proposed strategy is detailed. The first goal is to obtain a height function from data, in order to transform the feature space into the topographic space. To this end, the problem space is divided into cells of fixed squared size, and a function is defined over these cells. More formally, given a set of D-dimensional samples $\mathcal{Y} = \mathbf{y}_1, \mathbf{y}_2, ..., \mathbf{y}_N$, where each sample is $\mathbf{y}_i = y_{i,1}, y_{i,2}, ...y_{i,D}$, the discretization process defines a lattice $\mathcal{R}$ on this D-dimensional space. The origin O of this lattice is the minimum over all dimensions, *i.e.*

$$O = [\min_n y_{n,1}, \min_n y_{n,2}, ..., \min_n y_{n,D}] \tag{12}$$

A diagonal transformation is then performed, which stretches the scale of the axes of the data space in order to standardize the range of each feature, such that

$$\forall d \qquad \max_n y'_{n,d} - \min_n y'_{n,d} \equiv k \tag{13}$$

where $\{y'_{n,d}\}$ are the points in the transformed space. The constant k represents the maximum dimension width of the feature space, *i.e.*

$$k = \max_d \left(\max_n y'_{n,d} - \min_n y'_{n,d} \right) \tag{14}$$

In this way we could define the cells as D-dimensional hypercubes of fixed size $\ell_{\mathcal{R}}$. Let us denote the cell in the position $\mathbf{i} = (i_1, ..., i_D)$ as $R(\mathbf{i}) = R(i_1, ..., i_D)$. Obviously, the choice of the parameter $\ell_{\mathcal{R}}$ is critical. Before addressing the problem of calculating $\ell_{\mathcal{R}}$, let us define the function I used for watershed clustering.

Once fixed $\ell_{\mathcal{R}}$, we have a discrete-lattice of $\left(\frac{k}{\ell_{\mathcal{R}}}\right)^D$ cells, describing the feature space. The height function is then defined on this lattice: the value of the function in a cell is the number of points belonging to that cell. In other words, the function value in one cell measures the density of points in that part of the problem space. More formally, the function $I(R(\mathbf{i}))$ is defined as follows:

$$I(R(\mathbf{i})) = \sum_{\mathbf{y}_n \in \mathcal{Y}} \chi_{R(\mathbf{i})}(\mathbf{y}_n) \tag{15}$$

where χ is the characteristic function of the set $R(\mathbf{i})$, defined as

$$\chi_{R(\mathbf{i})}(\mathbf{y}_n) = \begin{cases} 1 & \text{if } \mathbf{y}_n \in R(\mathbf{i}) \\ 0 & \text{otherwise} \end{cases} \tag{16}$$

This function reflects the density properties of the clustering space: assuming that similar points (*i.e.* points that belong to the same cluster) are near in the feature space this function assumes high values in proximity of parts of the space where several similar points are present, while in the boundary (low density parts) assumes low values. By inverting all the values of this function, all the highest values are considered as local minima, from which the recursive process of the watershed transform can adequately start.

Let us now come back to the determination of the cell size $\ell_{\mathcal{R}}$. This represents obviously a crucial choice. If the cell is too small, this could results in a non informative representation, and the watershed algorithm will tend to produce an over-segmentation. On the other side, a too large value could lead to a coarse clustering; if the cell contains points too much far apart, the boundary could not be easily estimated, resulting in a quite rough separation between clusters. In our approach, the dimension of the cell is estimated by making a direct usage of the data. A good compromise between over-segmentation and rough clustering could be obtained by linking the choice of the $\ell_{\mathcal{R}}$ parameter to the median

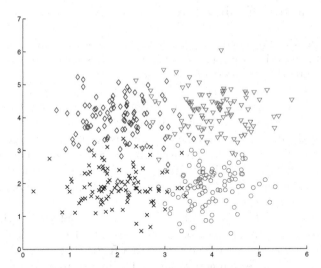

Fig. 1. Synthetic generated data, for a 4 clusters problem with a variance equal to 1

of the pairwise distances between all points. In particular, we compute all distances $d(\mathbf{y}_i, \mathbf{y}_j)$ ($\forall i, j \in 1..N$), then we extract the median value and fix the $\ell_{\mathcal{R}}$ parameter to

$$\ell_{\mathcal{R}} = \frac{\text{median}(d(\mathbf{y}_i, \mathbf{y}_j))}{m} \tag{17}$$

where m is a constant that has been experimentally fixed to 4, for all evaluated data sets . The use of the median, instead of the mean, allows to gain robustness against outliers. After defining the height function, the clustering is obtained applying to the lattice $\mathcal{R}$ the watershed algorithm described in Section . A problem that occurs is represented by the watersheds, *i.e.* the lines that divides the clusters. In our case, each watershed has width equal to one cell: the points in the cell are unlabeled, and have to be assigned to some clusters. To this end we use the following procedure. Starting from the consideration that each line divides only near clusters, we could decide to which of the near groups each point in the watershed belongs. In order to do that, we simply perform a new clustering on the watershed points, using the standard K-means algorithm. This clustering is really fast and quite accurate, since the watershed cells contain only few points, and the number of clusters is known (number of neighbors). After performing the sub-clustering, each mini-cluster is assigned to the nearest maxi-cluster, identified by determining the distance from the centroid of the nearest cells. By the use of this algorithm, the clustering boundaries are refined, and results are more accurate.

4 Experimental Evaluation

In this section, the proposed clustering method is tested, in order to assess its validity in synthetic cases. The following examples have been chosen to get some insight into the behavior of the watershed transform in the context of cluster analysis and to demonstrate the interest of this approach to pattern classification. The proposed approach is compared to the standard K-means algorithm [,]: this approach finds the optimal partition by evaluating, at each iteration, the distance between each item and each cluster descriptor, and by assigning it to the nearest class. At each step, the descriptor of each cluster is re-evaluated by averaging its cluster items. The system stops when no changes are produced in the clustering. In the K-means algorithm, the number of clusters should be decided *a priori*.

We present results obtained on different synthetic problems, varying the difficulty of the task and the number of the clusters. Fixed K the number of clusters, synthetic data are generated according to a K 2D Gaussians $\mathcal{N}(\mu_i, \sigma^2)$, $i = 1 \ldots, K$, sharing the same common variance. The means are randomly placed in the space, drawn from an uniform distribution in the interval $[-5, 5], [-5, 5]$. We vary the variance of the Gaussians in order to drive the difficulty of the problem: the higher the variance, the more overlapped the clusters, implying a more difficult task. For each Gaussian 200 elements have been drawn. An example of

Table 1. Clustering accuracies (means and standard deviations) for the synthetic experiment: (a) 2 clusters; (b) 3 clusters; (c) 4 clusters

(a)

variance σ^2	K-Means Accuracy		Watershed Accuracy	
	mean	std	mean	std
0.5	99.50%	2.08%	98.79%	1.95%
1.0	98.10%	3.88%	97.03%	5.20%
1.5	96.50%	4.54%	95.41%	4.53%
2.0	94.43%	4.57%	91.00%	2.56%

(b)

variance σ^2	K-Means Accuracy		Watershed Accuracy	
	mean	std	mean	std
0.5	91.90%	13.65%	96.22%	8.23%
1.0	93.86%	8.84%	87.01%	13.18%
1.5	91.53%	8.18%	80.16%	14.82%
2.0	90.05%	5.82%	71.85%	16.40%

(c)

variance σ^2	K-Means Accuracy		Watershed Accuracy	
	mean	std	mean	std
0.5	88.39%	13.71%	88.38%	11.02%
1.0	91.01%	9.21%	80.63%	9.06%
1.5	88.92%	5.84%	74.08%	10.32%
2.0	85.33%	4.54%	67.11%	11.19%

Table 2. Average number of clusters estimated by the proposed approach, for different variances and for different number of true clusters

	2 clusters	3 clusters	4 clusters
$\sigma^2 = 0.5$	2.02	3.08	3.72
$\sigma^2 = 1.0$	2.21	3.27	3.75
$\sigma^2 = 1.5$	2.31	3.60	4.26
$\sigma^2 = 2.0$	2.52	3.37	4.43

the generated data is presented in Fig. , where a 4 clusters problem is displayed (variance is 1). One can notice that there is a visible overlapping between these distributions, and the problem is quite difficult.

Experiments are repeated 100 times, in order to assess the statistical significance of the results and moreover to minimize the very poor performances of K-means due to wrong initialization. The accuracy of the clustering could be quantitatively assessed, by computing the number of wrongly composed clusters: a clustering error occurs if a pattern is assigned to a cluster in which the majority of the patterns are from another source. The obtained averaged accuracies, together with the standard deviations, are presented in Table , for different number of clusters. From this table it is evident that the accuracy of the proposed approach is slightly worse than that of the K-means. With our algorithm, nevertheless, the number of clusters is properly detected in almost all experiments, resulting in a completely unsupervised approach, differently than in the K-means case.

The watershed algorithms is more sensitive to higher variances, since the boundaries could not be easily estimated and the resulting clustering could be

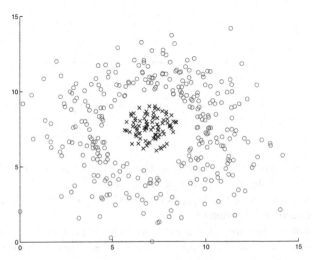

Fig. 2. Data generated from two concentric clusters

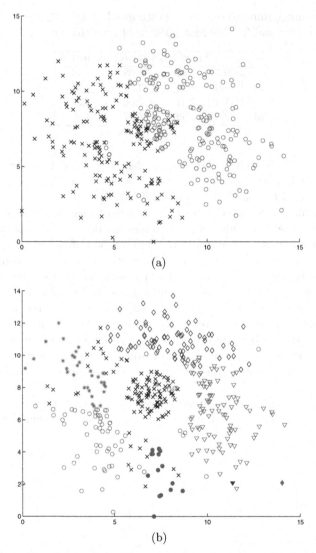

Fig. 3. Clustering obtained on the concentric clusters problem: (a) K-means; (b) Watershed algorithm

poor. Due to its unsupervised nature, the watershed algorithm performances worsen when increasing the number of true clusters.

Estimated numbers of clusters, determined in each problem, are shown in Table , for different Gaussians variance.

One can notice that the watershed algorithm is quite effective in estimating the number of clusters of the problem. Nevertheless, except than in the case of 5 clusters, it tends to over-estimate this number: this represents a well-known problem of the watershed algorithm, already encountered in the image segmentation literature. In [ ], this problem was faced by applying a Gaussian filter in the space: but this process, nevertheless, suppresses also some important minima, so it was not used here. In our approach, a smoothing process is performed during the lattice construction operation, since the size of the cell determines the smoothness of the resulting function.

We tested our approach on another synthetic example, with two concentric clusters, presented in Fig. . This clustering experiment is rather difficult. It is well known [ ] that the K-means algorithm is not able to deal with this problem: the obtained segmentation is proposed in Fig. (a), and is a completely wrong clustering. We applied our watershed algorithm to this problem: the obtained clustering is presented in Fig. (b). We can note that the central cluster is correctly identified, but the outside cluster is over segmented. Nevertheless, this represents an improvement with respect to the clustering obtained with the K-means approach, since at least some part of the semantic information is discovered, considering also the fact that this approach is completely unsupervised.

5 Conclusions

In this paper, a novel method for clustering points has been proposed, based on the watershed algorithm. The system automatically derives a discrete lattice from the feature space, and defines a height function. Watershed is then performed in that lattice. Boundary situations are then addressed with a intra-cell analysis, able to remove the watershed lines not needed in the clustering process. The main advantage of this method is its completely unsupervised nature, since it is able to automatically discover the number of clusters of the data. The main problem of this approach is the tendency to produce an over-segmentation, which is intrinsic in the nature of the watershed algorithm. In our opinion, this could be faced by working on the lattice definition, and this will be an issue of a future investigation.

References

[1] Jain, A., Dubes, R.: Algorithms for clustering data. Prentice Hall (1988)   ,   ,

[2] Jain, A., Murty, M. N., Flynn, P.: Data clustering: A review. ACM Computing Surveys **31** (1999) 264–323

[3] Beucher, S.: Watersheds of functions and picture segmentation. In: IEEE Proc. of Int. Conf. Acoustics, Speech and Signal Processing. (1982) 1928–1931

[4] Vincent, L., Soille, P.: Watersheds in digital spaces: an efficient algorithm based on immersion simulations. IEEE Trans. on Pattern Analysis and Machine Intelligence **13** (1991) 583–589   ,   ,   ,

[5] Serra, J.: Image Analysis and Mathematical Morphology. Academic Press, London (1982)   ,

[6] Patras, I., Hendriks, E., Lagendijk, R.: Video segmentation by map labelling of watershed segments. IEEE Trans. on Pattern Analysis and Machine Intelligence **23** (2001) 326–332

[7] Hung, Y. P., Tsai, Y. P., Lai, C. C.: A bayesian approach to video object segmentation via merging 3D watershed volumes. In: IEEE Proc. of Int. Conf. on Pattern Recognition. Volume 1. (2002) 496–499

[8] Geraud, T., Strub, P. Y., Darbon, J.: Color image segmentation based on automatic morphological clustering. In: IEEE Proc. of Int. Conf. on Image Processing. Volume 3. (2001) 70–73   ,

[9] Davies, D., Bouldin, D.: A cluster separation measure. IEEE Trans. on Pattern Analysis and Machine Intelligence **1** (1979) 224–227

[10] Digabel, H., Lantujoul, C.: Quantitative analysis of microstructures in materials sciences. Dr. Riederer-Verlag GmbH, Stuttgart (1978)

[11] Roerdink, J. B. T. M., Meijster, A.: The watershed transform: Definitions, algorithms and parallelization strategies. Fundamenta Informaticae **41** (2000) 187–228

[12] Meyer, F.: Topographic distance and watershed lines. Signal Processing **38** (1994) 113–125

[13] Ball, G., Hall, D.: A clustering technique for summarizing multivariate data. Behavioral Science **12** (1967) 153–155

Active Sampling Strategies for Multihypothesis Testing

Stéphane Herbin

ONERA

Département Traitement de l'Information et Modélisation
29, avenue de la Division Leclerc, BP 72, 92322 Châtillon Cedex, France
Stephane.Herbin@onera.fr

Abstract. This paper presents a rationale for the design of optimal sequential sampling procedures for multi-hypothesis discrimination where a system selectively queries the environment based on the current state of the discrimination process.

The environment is modelled as a controlled i.i.d. process conditionned by various hypotheses. Recognition is achieved when the test identifies the correct hypothesis describing the environment behavior.

As the testing proceeds, hypotheses may be rejected with infinite confidence when feature values with zero probability are observed. The sampling strategy is stationary but is updated each time a hypothesis is rejected. It is chosen according to a criterion measuring the recognition error speed of convergence to zero when the number of samples goes to infinity. This criterion is obtained by Large Deviation Theory techniques and characterizes globally the multi-hypothesis discrimination problem. An application on 2D rotation invariant shape recognition with non-closed noisy contours illustrates the approach.

Keywords: multihypothesis decision process, optimal sampling strategies, large deviations theory, shape recognition.

1 Introduction

1.1 The "Active" Approach

The principle of an "active" testing or recognition approach is to identify the behavior of a possibly dynamic and random environment and assign it to a predefined set of models or labels.

There are several reasons for using an active approach for recognition: a first one is philosophical, since we believe that the true origin of the intelligence of natural systems such as animals or humans lies in the interactive control of their environment, which must be described as a genuine time-dependent process. This question will not be addressed further in this paper.

A second reason, more engineering oriented, is the limitations of the ability of the algorithms embedded in artificial systems to deal with complex objects or environments. Most of the time, the usual approach consists in capitalizing all

A. Rangarajan et al. (Eds.): EMMCVPR 2003, LNCS 2683, pp. 97–   , 2003.

possible data about the environment and, in a posterior phase, try to make it informative by reducing or transforming it in a goal oriented way.

The informative step is often produced either through the participation of human expertise or knowledge, or automated. In this last option, the design is either constrained by the availability of a huge number of pre-identified data or limited to a small number of hypotheses. However, interesting problems must handle a significant number of hypotheses represented by a small number of exemplars.

We believe that one of the key problems to overcome these limitations is the dynamic management of informative data. Indeed, there is no such a thing as a universal set of object characteristics able to discriminate a priori all kinds of hypotheses. The idea of an active testing approach is to control *on line* in a goal oriented way the choice of the useful features based on a current state of achievement.

1.2   Objectives

We investigate in this paper the optimal design of decision processes based on sequentially querying the values of several features or measures. The testing procedure is said to be "active" since the querying depends on the past collected data.

At each time T, a query or action a_T is generated towards the environment which returns a feature value s_T. All those variables may be random and time dependent.

Given a sequence of action/measurements $\Phi_T = (a_1, s_1, a_2, s_2, \ldots a_T, s_T)$ specific to a hypothesis, the procedure of active testing is based on the exploitation of the following recursion:

$$P[\Phi_T] = P[s_T \mid a_T, \Phi_{T-1}]P[a_T \mid \Phi_{T-1}]P[\Phi_{T-1}] \tag{1}$$

meaning that the likelihood of observing a sequence Φ_T depends on the past likelihood and on the new measurement.

Once the feature values have been collected, a final decision $B(\Phi_T)$ will identify or reject a hypothesis among a predefined set $\Omega = \{\omega_k\}_{k=1}^N$, or decide to generate new actions to improve the decision safety. We will not deal in the following with this last choice, and take T to be a non random stopping time.

Designing an active decision process consists in solving three problems:

1. Model the action-conditioned probability of observing a feature value given the past: $P[s_T \mid a_T, \Phi_{T-1}]$
2. Define the sequence of actions or queries to be generated : $P[a_T \mid \Phi_{T-1}]$
3. Define a decision procedure based on the collected data : $B(\Phi_T) \in \Omega$

The goal of this paper is to propose several directions to solve those three questions under given assumptions.

1.3   Paper Organization

Section   discusses the choice of a controlled i.i.d. process for modelling the interactions between the recognition system and the environment. Section   describes
the structure of the selective testing procedure based on rejecting hypothesis
with null likelihood. The description of the on-line sampling strategy based on
Large Deviations exponential error rates is presented in . An application on
noisy shape recognition exploiting the distribution of pairs of contour points is
described in . Several mathematical results and sketched proofs about large
deviations techniques are summarized in the appendices   and   .

1.4   Related Work

Many recognition algorithms can be described in the "active testing" framework. The differences depend on the choices that have been made to model the
environment.

Classification trees [, ,], which are inherently sequential algorithms, may
be the of closest type. They model functional dependence to the past collected
feature values as a branch and assign a query to each internal nodes. In their
usual setting, however, actions generated and return feature values are deterministic. Similarly to the approach taken in this paper, the design of the querying
strategy follows a local optimal construction by minimizing a hypothesis scat-
tering function such as the entropy.

Large deviation theory applied to pattern recognition has been used on a few
papers; the main issues have usually been to design bounds able to control the
behavior of empirical learning processes [ ]. In computer vision, several authors
have applied basic large deviation theory results to the analysis of specific algorithms. [ ] studies several numerical quantities able to characterize the de-
tectability of simple objects such as curves in a noisy image. [ ] uses large deviation theory and statistical mechanics concepts to characterize texture discrimination.

This work is a continuation of previous studies on active recognition [ ] and
application of Large Deviation Theory techniques to 3D object aspect graph
comparison [ ] and texture similarity measures [ ].

2   Controlled i.i.d. Processes

This section examines the type of model used to describe the behavior of the
environment when queried by an action a_T: $P[s_T \mid a_T, \Phi_{T-1}]$.

It is assumed in this paper that the environment has no memory, is stationary and is purely reactive to the actions generated by the system. However,
feature values are random, i.e. repeated queries produce an answer according
to a probabilitic law. This is an important difference with most of the pattern
recognition approaches where answer to the queries are determinisitic — they
may only differ from one realization to the other.

An environment under hypothesis ω_k is modelled as a controlled independent identically distributed process and is completely described by a transition law $P[s \mid a, \omega_k]$. We also restrict the spaces of features $a \in \mathcal{A}$ and feature values $s \in \mathcal{S}$ to be finite.

The complexity of the environment will be rendered by the diversity of features examined. Randomness is used as a way to model the possibly composite structure of environments with uneven number of elements or dimensions. In general, the modelling step will try to resolve a trade-off between number of features, number of hypotheses and number of available labelled data.

When assuming a controlled i.i.d. process for each hypothesis, the likelihood ( ) conditionally to the hypothesis ω_k becomes:

$$P_k[\Phi_T] = P_k[s_T \mid a_T]P[a_T \mid \Phi_{T-1}]P[\Phi_{T-1}] \qquad (2)$$

where for the sake of notation clarity, a probability conditioned on the hypothesis ω_k is written : $P_k(.)$.

3   Adapted Selective Testing

This section examines the structure of the testing procedure. The central idea is the management of null likelihoods for several observations.

3.1   Likelihood-Comparable Observations

A basic setting for the final decision exhibiting the candidate hypothesis is a maximum likelihood test :

$$B(\Phi_T) = \arg\max_k P_k(\Phi_T) \qquad (3)$$

The active decision process is sequential and potentially controlled at each time. The formula ( ) shows however that the only useful contribution to the computation of ( ) is the product of terms $P_k[s_T \mid a_T]$ since the choice of the action a_T sampled according to $P[a_T \mid \Phi_{T-1}]$ is independent from any hypothesis.

We introduce the notion of "selective testing" based on the fact that a hypothesis can be discarded with infinite confidence when the corresponding conditional likelihood of an observed feature is null ($P_k[s_T \mid a_T] == 0$). The basic idea of selective testing is to make a "comparative" test based on likelihood comparison only for the hypotheses that cannot be discarded readily.

We introduce now the following notations: $x = [s, a]$ is the composite observation state (feature value, action), S is the space of these observations and $S_k = \{x \in S \,/\, P_k[x] > 0\}$ the support of each conditional probability where $P_k[x] = P_k[s \mid a]$.

The structure of selective testing depends on three elements: the hypotheses, the observations and the conditional likelihoods. We define a series of subsets of the observations $\mathcal{U} = \{U_p\}_{p=1\ldots|\mathcal{U}|}$ such that, in each subset U_p, the elements share the same likelihood-comparable hypotheses :

$$U_p = \{x \in S \,/\, \forall k \in \Omega_p, x \in S_k\} \tag{4}$$

where the coupled subsets of hypothesis indices Ω_p are defined as

$$\Omega_p = \{k \in \{1\ldots N\} \,/\, \forall x \in U_p, x \in S_k\} \tag{5}$$

Given the conditional probability supports, there are several couples of sets $(S, \mathcal{U})$ sharing the definition above. The mathematical object $(S, \mathcal{U})$ is usually called a *hypergraph* in combinatorics [ ]. We choose among the possible candidates the one with minimal size, which is also maximal when the sets are ordered by inclusion.

There are two consequences of this choice. The first one is that, for any subset of observations, there is a unique U_p containing all of them:

$$\forall U \subset S, \exists! \, p \in \{1, \ldots |\mathcal{U}|\} \text{ s.t. } U \subset U_p$$

This property implies that for any sequence Φ_T, there exists a unique element in $\mathcal{U}$ noted $U(\Phi_T)$ which contains all the observations $(x_1, x_2, \ldots x_T)$.

A second consequence is that the subsets U_p's define a restricted one to one mapping between subsets of observations 2^S and subsets of hypothesis indices 2^N: $U_p \to \Omega_p$. These two properties will be used by the selective test to handle the variation of active hypotheses.

3.2   Sampling Law Based on Active Hypotheses

As the previous section pointed out, given a set of hypotheses and corresponding conditional probabilities, there exists two different kinds of states: selective and likelihood-comparable.

At each time T, the collected feature generated by the environment may be selective for several hypotheses. The current set of active hypotheses, i.e. that have not been discarded by previous selective states, may either remain unchanged if $x_T \in U(\Phi_{T-1})$ or reduced by the new observation.

The idea underlying a selective testing procedure is to reduce as soon as possible the number of active hypotheses by issueing actions likely to generate selective states. Indeed, the difficulty of identifying the true hypothesis depends strongly on the number of candidates. This fact will become more visible in the next section devoted to the construction of an optimal sampling strategy.

Ideally, the choice of the action generated at each time should depend on the whole past observed features. Instead, the statitics $U(\Phi_T)$, i.e. the current set of active hypotheses, will be assumed to summarize what really counts in a selective testing procedure and determine the feature sampling law.

3.3   Testing Procedure

The testing procedure will issue actions towards the environment sampled from the same law until no new selective observation is encountered. Each newly observed feature value may generate a reorganization of the sampling law if it happens to be able to reject with infinite confidence one or several hypotheses.

The hypergraph $(S, \mathcal{U})$ depends on the set of active hypotheses. As the selective testing proceeds, elements from the set of edges $\mathcal{U}$ are desactivated each time hypotheses are removed from the list of candidates. Removing a hypothesis is equivalent to removing all its connected edges in the hypergraph on the hypotheses labels $(\{1 \ldots N\}, \{\Omega_p\})$. Since there is a one to one mapping between the subsets of hypotheses labels $\{\Omega_p\}$ and the subsets of observations $\{U_p\}$, removing a hypothesis is equivalent to removing the corresponding subsets in $\mathcal{U}$. Both the set of active hypotheses and subsets of likelihood-comparable observations have to be updated when a new feature value is observed.

Given a fixed maximal number of observations $T_{\max}$, the selective testing procedure can be described the following way:

1. Update the current stationary sampling law based on the current set of active hypotheses.
2. Issue an action a_T sampled from the current stationary sampling law.
3. Collect the feature value s_T and append $[a_T, s_T]$ to the current sequence Φ_{T-1}.
4. Update the set of active hypotheses and subsets of likelihood-comparable observations.
5. If there are more than one active hypotheses or if $T < T_{\max}$ go to 1.
6. Compute the likelihoods of the remaining hypotheses.
7. The winning hypothesis is the one with highest likelihood.

The choice of the sampled actions depends therefore on the past collected feature values through the *on line* management of a set of active hypotheses. The next section describes on what optimality grounds will be constructed the corresponding stationary sampling laws.

4   Optimal Stationary Sampling Law

The general principle for designing a sampling strategy is to find the basis for a trade-off between exploration of selective states and comparison of likelihoods. This will be achieved by computing the rate of convergence of selective testing given the active set of hypotheses and the conditional probabilities.

4.1   Asymptotics of Selective Testing with Fixed Sampling Law

The global Bayes probability of error generated by the test ( ) is defined as:

$$P_e = \sum \pi_k P_k [B(\Phi_T) \neq k]$$

where the π_k's are the priors.

Each term can be decomposed into: $P_k[B(\Phi_T) \neq k] = \sum_{k' \neq k} P_k[B(\Phi_T) = k']$ stating that the global probability of error is a linear combination of terms of the form $P_k[B(\Phi_T) = k']$.

One can decompose one step more the probability of error using the subsets of observations $\mathcal{U}$ defined in ( ). Indeed, given a sequence Φ_T, there exists a unique set $U(\Phi_T)$ containing all the observations, and we have:

$$P_k[B(\Phi_T) = k'] = \sum_{p=1}^{|\mathcal{U}|} P_k[B(\Phi_T) = k' \,|\, U(\Phi_T) = U_p]\, P_k[U(\Phi_T) = U_p] \quad (6)$$

In this paragraph, we are interested in studying the asymptotics of the error when the observations are generated by a fixed sampling law. If $\mu(a)$ is this law, the couple $x_T = [s_T, a_T]$ becomes i.i.d. with a probability transition equal to:

$$P_k[x] = \mu(a)P_k(s \,|\, a) \quad (7)$$

Given the assumptions defined above (i.i.d. control process and fixed stationary sampling law) one can prove:

Proposition 1. *The probability of deciding a wrong hypothesis when the observations generated by a fixed stationary sampling law belong to a selective set U_p decreases to zero exponentially fast as the number of observations goes to infinity. The rate of convergence is defined as:*

$$\lim_{T \to \infty} -\frac{1}{T} \log P_k[B(\Phi_T) = k' \,|\, U(\Phi_T) = U_p] = \rho_p(k, k') > 0 \quad (8)$$

This result is an application of Large Deviations Theory [,   ]. See appendix ( ) for a sketched proof. The key point here is that this rate is computable with an explicit formula and can be used in numerical calculations.

The second term $P_k[U(\Phi_T) = U_p]$ contributing to the error is also decaying to zero exponentially fast. Indeed, it is easy to check that:

$$\lim_{T \to \infty} -\frac{1}{T} \log P_k[U(\Phi_T) = U_p] = -\log \sum_{x \in U_p} P_k[x] = \tau_p(k) \quad (9)$$

We therefore have the global result :

$$\lim_{T \to \infty} -\tfrac{1}{T} \log P_k[B(\Phi_T) = k' \,|\, U(\Phi_T) = U_p]P_k[U(\Phi_T) = U_p]$$
$$= \rho_p(k, k') + \tau_p(k) > 0$$

stating that the probability of wrong guessing when the observations belong to the same selective set decreases to zero exponentially fast. This global rate is the sum of two terms: one qualifying the probability of staying in the same subset of observations, one quantifying the capacity of discriminating using a maximum likelihood test. The trade-off between exploration of selective states and comparison of likelihoods appears naturally in this formulation.

The probability of error P_e, as a linear combination of terms decreasing to zero exponentially fast, is therefore itself converging to zero with a rate equal to the slowest, i.e. smallest. We have the proposition:

Proposition 2. *The probability of error of the maximum likelihood selective test decreases to zero exponentially fast when the number of observations goes to infinity with a rate equal to:*

$$\lim_{T \to \infty} -\frac{1}{T} \log P_e = \min_{k \neq k'} \min_p \left(\rho_p(k, k') + \tau_p(k) \right) \tag{10}$$

The rate ( ) measures globally the complexity of discriminating between a set of hypotheses using a fixed sampling strategy and a selective testing procedure. It is therefore a straightforward candidate for a criterion — an energy — to optimize. The next section examines the possibility of using this criterion to find an optimal sampling strategy.

4.2 Sub-optimal Fixed Sampling Strategy

In the process of selective sampling, the only free parameter is the sampling law μ. The probability transitions $P_k(s \mid a)$ describe the environment and are only used in the calculation of the likelihoods.

Given the conditional probabilities, the global convergence rate ( ) depends on the fixed sampling law $\mu(a)$ through ( ). If we consider this rate to be a good criterion able to measure the discriminative capacity of a selective testing process, the best sampling strategy μ^* should be defined as:

$$\min_{p, k \neq k'} \left(\rho_p(k, k'; \mu^*) + \tau_p(k; \mu^*) \right) = \sup_{\mu} \min_{p, k \neq k'} \left(\rho_p(k, k'; \mu) + \tau_p(k; \mu) \right) \tag{11}$$

where we have made explicit the dependency of the rates ( ) and ( ) on the sampling law. The supremum in ( ) is actually a maximum since the rates ρ_p and τ_p are bounded and the sampling law is constrained to belong to the space of positive measures.

The optimization of ( ) is a difficult problem. There is one straightforward situation — 2 hypotheses and no selective observations — for which the optimal rate is obtained when sampling the best feature: $\mu^*(a) = \mathbf{1}_{a=a^*}$ (see appendix   ). In the general case, however, each elementary rate $\rho_p(k, k'; \mu)$ is itself the result of an optimization and makes the calculation of ( ) computer intensive.

The convergence of the test errors to zero is warranted for any sampling strategy. What is sought out is a good sampling law, not necessarily uniform and querying all the features. We propose to generate a sub-optimal sampling strategy by using a linear approximation of the function $\mu \to \rho_p(k, k'; \mu)$. It is obtained by computing the rates ( ) for each feature a and summing them according to:

$$\rho_p(k, k'; \mu) + \tau_p(k; \mu) = \sum_a \mu(a) \cdot \left(\rho_p(k, k'; \mathbf{1}_a) + \tau_p(k; \mathbf{1}_a) \right) \tag{12}$$

where $\mathbf{1}_a$ is the sampling law having a 1 at th a-th position and 0 elsewhere.

Fig. 1. The six types of shapes in random orientations. From left to right: Jaguar, F16, Mig 29, Mirage, Rafale, Sukhoi 27

The linear approximation ( ) makes the optimization ( ) a constrained linear min-max problem which can be solved efficiently for any current set of active hypotheses. In general, for discriminative features, the structure of the hypergraph $(S, \mathcal{U})$ is rather sparse and limits the number of min-max problems to solve.

Due to the constraint $\sum_a \mu^*(a) = 1$, a sampling law solution will often have several null coordinates, meaning that only a few features are really useful for the discrimination of a given set of hypotheses. However, as the number of candidate hypotheses decreases due to the observation of selective feature values, the set of useful features may vary with the number of likelihood-comparable sets $\mathcal{U}$ still active at each step. This means that the "optimal" set of features depends on the nature of the recognition problem and must be adapted on line. The optimization ( ) can be understood as a feature selection phase adapted to the recognition of controlled i.i.d. processes.

5 Noisy Shape Contour Recognition

5.1 Contour Detection

The application illustrating the active sampling approach is a 2D shape recognition problem based on noisy contour detection.

The shapes we are trying to discriminates are shown Fig. . They consist of 6 planes observed from above in any orientation. The typical applicative context is remote sensing from an aerial camera.

It is assumed that the distance from the camera to the object is known from another source of information. Scale invariance is therefore not an issue here. The only nuisance parameters are clutter, object rotation and sub-pixel position.

Contour is a graphical primitive assumed to be quite stable to illumination variations and is often detected in a preliminary phase prior to shape representation. In practice, extracted contours are seldom closed, limiting the pertinence of many common shape representations based on their boundary [ ].

Figure   shows some examples of contours produced by a standard algorithm (Canny) on several noisy images. The images tested were synthesized using a sensor model characterized by a gaussian transfer function, additive white

Fig. 2. Influence of noise and aliasing in contour detection. The shapes have the same orientation but various sub-pixel positions and noise outcomes

noise (SNR = 15dB) and uniform random spatial sub-sampling to account for aliasing. In the sensor model studied, shapes are between 25 to 60 pixels wide depending on the size of the plane observed and on the quality of the image feature extraction.

The contour detection process used is purposively elementary. Indeed, contour extraction generates "imperfections": areas with high local curvature are often thresholded out and sub-pixel sampling at the object boundary produces non-linear perturbations. No specific procedure to improve them by morphological closing or region growing, for instance, is attempted. Furthermore, in the application of interest, it seems illusory to base the hypothesis testing on a prior segmentation which would define the set of pixels associated with a shape: in general, the background is potentially complex and unevenly contrasted with the object. Segmentation produces often artefacts in this context difficult to neutralize. The contour imperfections generated by the detector used in this application are expected to be generic.

5.2   Contour Distribution Coded as a Controlled i.i.d. Process

Contour points are local elements spatially ordered. One simple way to describe their arrangement is to exploit the distribution of specific features attached to *pairs* of points.

Bipoint feature distributions have been used in several studies to describe shapes made of random spatial arrangements of pixels or edgels. In perceptual grouping, elements are associated according to similarity, colinearity or proximity and characterized by a global grouping likelihood [ ]. Random graphs between local contrast detectors, which are collections of bipoint features, can also be used for shape modelling [ ].

We use bipoint feature value distributions conditioned on specific bipoint orientations to model shapes as a controlled i.i.d. processes. Bipoint orientation conditioning will be function of grey-level gradients and bipoints directions. Let P be a contour point, ∇P the gradient computed at location P in global coordinates and Θ the function returning the direction of a vector in global

Fig. 3. Distribution of contour bipoints for various angles $\theta \in \{0, \pi, 3\pi/2\}$

coordinates. Gradients can be computed on the whole image using standard algorithms. A set of contour points will be represented by two kinds of distributions, bipoint lengths and gradient angles, conditioned by the angle between local gradient and bipoint direction $\theta = \Theta(\nabla P_1) - \Theta(P_2 - P_1)$ and bipoint length intervals $\|P_1 - P_2\| \in [l_{\min}, l_{\max}]$.

The pixel size of the shapes (20 to 60) and their erratic repartition forbids the usage of discrete approximation of continuous geometric features. In this graphical context, most of the methods derive recognition from template matching [ ]. These are usually not rotation invariant and require a preliminary model space compression. It is easy to check that the conditional distributions defined above are rotation invariant.

Given a set of contour points, we define a control, i.e. an action, as a direction θ and a length interval $[l_{\min}, l_{\max}]$ coupled with a type of feature — gradient angles or bipoint length. Active sampling is the operation of choosing a control and collecting the random bipoint feature value.

Figure   shows the set of bipoints selected by various angles θ. It is expected that this way of analyzing the contour point arrangement will allow shape parts to be specifically observed while ensuring more global shape comparison for certain other types of of bipoint conditioning.

5.3   Experiment

The shapes were modelled using three types of length intervals ($[3, 10]$, $[10, 20]$ and $[20, 70]$) and 12 bipoint orientations resulting in 48 different types of queries. The gradient angles were uniformly quantized with a 15° step resulting in 24 values. The bipoint lengths were quantized with a 4 pixel length step resulting in 21 values. The controlled i.i.d. model was estimated using 400 simulated images per model.

The overall estimated model contains 25 comparative sets of hypotheses following definition ( ). The corresponding sampling laws computed using the linear approximation (   ) selected between 1 and 20 queries among the 48 possible types. The maximum number of query types is associated with the comparative set containing all the hypotheses. This seems logical since the process should

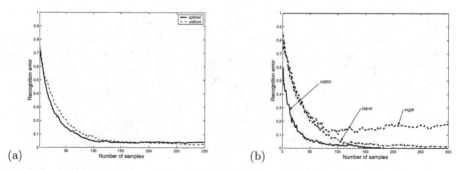

Fig. 4. Recognition error versus number of sample bipoints. (a) Using sub-optimal and uniform sampling strategies for all hypotheses. (b) For three targets

explore the maximum number of possible features to discriminate the maximal number of hypotheses.

In the experiment, the rejection of a hypothesis was declared official when the testing process encountered 3 selective observations for that hypothesis. This modification in the decision process aims at controlling the possibly noisy contour point detections which were found very influential in the first experiments.

Selective testing was empirically evaluated on 1200 synthesized images (random orientation, SNR = 15dB, sub-pixel uniform sampling). Figure (a) shows the error decay for two sampling laws: sub-optimal computed using ( ) and uniform. The sub-optimal strategy generates slightly faster error decrease, but using much fewer features. Both generate a recognition rate of 92% using 300 samples.

The errors differ according to the hypotheses. Tab. shows the confusion matrix obtained after having sampled 300 bipoint feature values. The errors originate mainly from one target: Mig 29. Figure (b) shows the evolution of the recognition error for three different targets. The "Mig29" curb behavior appears rather different from the others: the error decreases then increases with the number of samples, showing non-monotonic variations.

Table 1. Confusion matrix using 300 sample bipoints by image

	m2000	mig29	su27	jaguar	rafale	f16
m2000	**1.0**	0	0	0	0	0
mig29	0	**0.73**	0.23	0.04	0	0
su27	0	0	**1.00**	0	0	0
jaguar	0	0	0	**1.00**	0	0
rafale	0	0	0	0.04	**1.00**	0
f16	0	0	0.03	0.06	0	**0.91**

One possible explanation of this behavior is the difference between bipoint distribution of a single shape and the mixed distribution estimated from the learning examples. The selection of optimal features concentrates the sampling process on very few sources of information. Model estimation should be able to remove the use of features when they happen to be badly characterized by an i.i.d. law.

From these first experiments one should retain that model estimation must be carefully conducted. There are potentially two types of errors: the validity of the i.i.d. assumption, and the consequences of a small number of learning examples on the selective states. These are issues for future work.

6 Conclusion

The specific aspects of multi-hypotheses discrimination has not been given much attention in the litterature. Global decision is often reduced to a series of binary comparisons for which, indeed, possible methods abound. The goal of this paper was to propose a general framework genuinely dedicated to the discrimination of multiple hypotheses on complex data which settles on a rigorous mathematical ground. The approach was demonstrated on a 2D noisy shape recognition problem and shows promising preliminary results.

The coupling of optimal active sampling and selective testing can be understood as unifying two different questions: *feature selection* since the optimal sampling strategy selects the best queries according to a multi-hypothesis discrimination criterion, and *data fusion* since the final test gathers the feature values collected in a global maximum likelihood decision.

The basic setting developed in this article can be improved in several ways. A notion of memory, e.g. a Markov dependence or a short-term buffer, may be introduced in both the sampling law and the environment modelling in order to design more flexible strategies. The accuracy of model estimation is very influential and necessitates further studies to control its impact on the decision process.

References

[1] Breiman, L., Stone, C., Olshen, R., Friedman, J.: Classification and Regression Trees. Wadsworth (1984)
[2] Amit, Y., Geman, D.: Shape quantization and recognition with randomized trees. Neural Computation **9** (1997) 1545–1588 ,
[3] Geman, D., Jedynak, B.: An active testing model for tracking roads in satellite images. IEEE Trans. Pattern Analysis and Machine Intelligence **18** (1996) 1–14

[4] Azencott, R., Vayatis, N.: Refined exponential rates in Vapnik-Chervonenkis inequalities. C. R. Acad. Sci., Paris, Math., Ser. I **332** (2001) 563–568
[5] Yuille, A., Coughlan, J., Wu, Y., Zhu, S.: Order parameters for detecting target curves in images: When does high level knowledge help? International Journal of Computer Vision **41** (2001) 9–33

[6] Wu, Y., Zhu, S., Liu, X.: Equivalence of julesz ensembles and FRAME models. International Journal of Computer Vision **38** (2000) 245–261

[7] Herbin, S.: Recognizing 3D objects by generating random actions. In: IEEE Conference on Computer Vision and Pattern Recognition. (1996) 35–40

[8] Herbin, S.: Combining geometric and probabilistic structure for active recognition of 3D objects. In: European Conference on Computer Vision. Volume 1407 of Lecture Notes in Computer Science., Berlin, Springer Verlag (1998) 748–764

[9] Herbin, S.: Similarity measures between feature maps - application to texture comparison. In: Proceedings of the Texture 2002 workshop. (2002) 67–72

[10] Berge, C.: Graphes et hypergraphes. Dunod (1970)

[11] Kazakos, D.: Asymptotic error probability expressions for multihypothesis testing using multisensor data. IEEE Trans. Systems, Man and Cybernetics **21** (1991) 1101–1114   ,

[12] Dembo, A., Zeitouni, O.: Large Deviations Techniques and Applications. Jones and Bartlett Publishers, Boston (1993)   ,

[13] Loncaric, S.: A survey of shape analysis techniques. Pattern Recognition **31** (1998) 983–1001

[14] Amir, A., Lindenbaum, M.: A generic grouping algorithm and its quantitative analysis. IEEE Trans. Pattern Analysis and Machine Intelligence **20** (1998) 168–185

[15] Olson, C., Huttenlocher, D.: Automatic target recognition by matching oriented edge pixels. IEEE Trans. Image Processing **6** (1997) 103–113

[16] Shimkin, N.: Extremal large deviations in controlled i.i.d. processes with applications to hypothesis testing. Adv. Appl. Probab. **25** (1993) 875–894

A   Calculation of the Error Rate of Convergence

A.1   Maximum Likelihood Test

The rates of convergence can be computed exactly thanks to tools developed in the Large Deviation Theory of empirical processes. This section is devoted to presenting the basic useful results. Refer to [,   ] for a more complete presentation.

Define a rate function as:

$$I(\boldsymbol{y}) = \sup_{\boldsymbol{\theta} > 0} \left[\langle \boldsymbol{\theta}, \boldsymbol{y} \rangle - \log M(\boldsymbol{\theta}) \right] \tag{13}$$

The Laplace transform $M_k(\boldsymbol{\theta})$ is defined as:

$$M(\boldsymbol{\theta}) = \mathrm{E}\left[\exp\langle \boldsymbol{\theta}, \boldsymbol{l}(x) \rangle \right] \tag{14}$$

where $\boldsymbol{l}(x)$ is a vector valued function in $\mathbb{R}^k$ of the observations x, and the expectation is computed on their distribution.

The fundamental result (Cramér Theorem) characterizes the occurence of rare deviations from the empirical mean:

$$L_T = \frac{1}{T} \sum_{t=1}^{T} l(x_t)$$

Theorem 1. *For any set $A \subset \mathbb{R}^d$, we have*

$$\liminf_{T->\infty} -\frac{1}{T} \log P\{L_T \in A\} \geq \inf_{\boldsymbol{y} \in \bar{A}} I(\boldsymbol{y})$$

$$\limsup_{T->\infty} -\frac{1}{T} \log P\{L_T \in A\} \leq \inf_{\boldsymbol{y} \in A^\circ} I(\boldsymbol{y})$$

If the two bounds coincide, which is the case in the application we are studying, we have:

$$\lim_{T->\infty} -\frac{1}{T} \log P\{L_T \in A\} = \inf_{\boldsymbol{y} \in A} I(\boldsymbol{y})$$

In the multihypothesis likelihood test, we are studying the random behavior of the log-likelihood vector in $\mathbb{R}^N$ defined by:

$$\boldsymbol{l}(x) = \log\left(P_1[x], \ldots P_N[x]\right)$$

when the samples are drawn from hypothesis k.

As a direct consequence of the above theorem, we have:

Proposition 3. *The error rate of the probability of deciding a wrong hypothesis k' is:*

$$\rho(k, k') = \inf_{\boldsymbol{y} \in C(k')} I_k(\boldsymbol{y}) \tag{15}$$

where the convex constraint is defined as:

$$C(k') = \{\boldsymbol{y} \, / \, \forall j \neq k', y_{k'} > y_j\}$$

The practical computation of ( ) is managed using elementary convex analysis. Indeed, one can prove:

Theorem 2. *The rate of convergence ( ) can be computed as:*

$$\rho(k, k') = -\inf_{\boldsymbol{\lambda} > 0} \log M_k(-\tilde{\boldsymbol{\lambda}}_{k'}) \tag{16}$$

where $\boldsymbol{\lambda}$ is the vector of $N-1$ Lagrange multipliers, and $\boldsymbol{\lambda}_{k'}$ is the vector of Lagrange multipliers augmented by a normalizing factor at the k'-th position:

$$\tilde{\boldsymbol{\lambda}}_{k'} = (\lambda_1 \ldots \lambda_{k'-1}, -\sum_j \lambda_j, \lambda_{k'+1} \ldots \lambda_{N-1}).$$

The Laplace transform based on the Lagrange multipliers is now defined as:

$$M_k(-\tilde{\boldsymbol{\lambda}}_{k'}) = \sum_x P_k[x] \prod_{l \neq k'} \left(\frac{P_{k'}[x]}{P_l[x]}\right)^{\lambda_l} \tag{17}$$

The numerical value of the rate is obtained using optimization ( ).

A.2   Mixing Active Sampling and Selective Testing

The results from the previous section assumed that the log-likelihood vector was defined for any observation. The principle of selective testing is to exploit the probability that some of its coordinates become infinite. The active sampling principle consists in randomly examining a family of random laws.

We assume now that the state x is composite $x = [s, a]$ where s is assumed to be a finite value, and a a given action governed by a sampling strategy μ:

$$P_k[x] = P_k[s, a] = \mu(a)P_k(s \mid a)$$

Define a likelihood-comparable set U_p of states, and $U_p(a)$ the feature values which are comparable for a given sampling a action:

$$U_p(a) = \{s / [s, a] \in U_p\}$$

and the normalized conditional probability as:

$$\tilde{P}_k(s \mid a) = \frac{P_k(s \mid a)}{\sum_{a'} \mu(a') \sum_{s \in U_p(a')} P_k(s \mid a')} \tag{18}$$

In the calculation of the error rate $P_k[B(\Phi_T) = k' \mid U(\Phi_T) = U_p]$, the only change appears in the definition of the Laplace transform ( ):

$$\tilde{M}_k(-\boldsymbol{\lambda}_{k'}) = \sum_a \mu(a) \sum_{s \in U_p(a)} \tilde{P}_k(s \mid a) \prod_{l \neq k'} \left(\frac{P_{k'}[x]}{P_l[x]}\right)^{\lambda_l} \tag{19}$$

where the expectation is now taken over the likelihood-comparable observations. The optimization ( ) remains unchanged and we have:

$$\rho_p(k, k') = -\inf_{\boldsymbol{\lambda} > 0} \log \tilde{M}_k(-\tilde{\boldsymbol{\lambda}}_{k'})$$

The dependence of the rate $\rho(k, k')$ on the sampling law μ is strongly influenced by the presence of selective observations. If all the observations are likelihood-comparable, the rate function ( ) has interesting properties [ ]:

- the Laplace transform ( ) is concave in μ;
- the rate function ( ) is jointly convex in y and μ;
- the error rate $\rho(k, k')$ is convex in μ.

These properties make the two-hypothesis case search for optimal decay rate easy: the best achievable rate is obtained at the vertices of the sampling law. In the multi-hypothesis case, however, the search for the best achievable rate appears to be a non convex problem.

When there is a chance to observe selective observations, the convexity properties of the rate function are no longer true due to the normalizing ( ). This makes the search for an optimal sampling law even more difficult, and justifies the use of a linear approximation in the computations.

Likelihood Based Hierarchical Clustering and Network Topology Identification[*]

Rui Castro and Robert Nowak

Rice University, Electrical and Computer Engineering Department
6100 Main St., MS366, Houston, TX 77005, U.S.A.
{rcastro,nowak@rice.edu}

Abstract. This paper develops a new method for hierarchical clustering based on a generative dendritic cluster model. The objects are viewed as being generated through a tree structured refinement process. In certain problems, this generative model naturally captures the physical mechanisms responsible for relationships among objects, for example, in genetic studies and network topology identification. The networking problem is examined in some detail, to illustrate the new clustering method. In general, the generative model is not representative of actual physical mechanisms, but it nonetheless provides a means for dealing with errors in the similarity matrix, simultaneously promoting two desirable features in clustering: intra-class similarity and inter-class dissimilarity.

1 Introduction

A clustering algorithm is a process designed to organize a set of objects into various classes, such that elements within the same class have similar characteristics. Let R denote a set of objects, called input objects. Associated with this set is an $|R| \times |R|$ matrix $\mathbf{X}$ of estimated pairwise similarity measures between the objects. While for some clustering problems, the goal is to partition the set of input objects into disjoint classes (k-clustering), for some other problems one desires to obtain a hierarchical structure, where each class of objects is also partitioned into sub-classes and so on. In this last case one can represent the clustering of objects as a tree, also called *dendrogram*, in which the nodes represent subsets of the input set R. The leaf nodes correspond to the individual elements of R, and the root corresponds to the entire set. Each edge in the dendrogram represents an inclusion relationship (see Figure   for illustration).

This paper develops a new method for hierarchical clustering based on a generative dendritic cluster model. The objects are viewed as being generated through a tree structured refinement process. In certain problems, this generative model naturally captures the physical mechanisms responsible for relationships among objects, for example, in genetic studies and network topology identification. The latter problem is examined in detail in this paper to illustrate the new

[*] This work was partially sponsored by the National Science Foundation, grant nos. MIP-9701692 and ANI-0099148, the Army Research Office, grant no. DAAD19-99-1-0349 and the Office of Naval Research, grant no. N00014-00-1-0390.

A. Rangarajan et al. (Eds.): EMMCVPR 2003, LNCS 2683, pp. 113–   , 2003.
© Springer-Verlag Berlin Heidelberg 2003

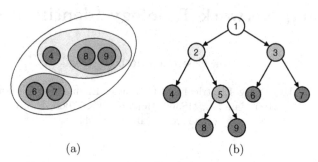

(a)   (b)

Fig. 1. (a) Example of an hierarchical clustering, (b) corresponding binary tree representation

clustering method. In general, the generative model is not representative of actual physical mechanisms, but it nonetheless provides a means for dealing with errors in the similarity matrix $\mathbf{X}$ and simultaneously promotes two desirable features in clustering: intra-class similarity and inter-class dissimilarity.

The new clustering method is based on a maximum likelihood framework. We assume that the empirical similarity matrix $\mathbf{X}$ is related to an ideal (or "true") similarity matrix γ through a probability density function that describes the possible errors or distortions in $\mathbf{X}$. That is, $\mathbf{X} \sim p(\mathbf{x}|\gamma)$. As a simple example, $p(\mathbf{x}|\gamma)$ might be a Gaussian density with mean γ and diagonal covariance σ^2, in which case γ is the mean of the density and $\mathbf{X}$ can be regarded as a "noisy" version of γ. In general, $\mathbf{X}$ may be related to γ in a much more complicated manner. The similarity matrix γ satisfies a dendritic structure, but is otherwise unknown. The likelihood is also a function of the unknown dendritic tree $\mathcal{T}$, governing the structure of γ, and which is our main object of interest. We present deterministic and Monte Carlo approaches to this problem.

Hierarchical clustering is a widely used approach and has a long history [, , , ,] and is especially popular for document clustering [, , ,]. Much of the work in hierarchical clustering research revolves around deriving of useful linkage metrics from the similarity matrix $\mathbf{X}$. Linkage metrics embody the notions of closeness or connectedness in the clustering process and thus significantly impact performance. In our model-based approach this issue is less arbitrary since the linkage metrics are induced from the assigned probability density $p(\mathbf{x}|\gamma, \mathcal{T})$. Other model-based approaches have been used for hierarchical clustering in the past [, , ,]. Such methods usually model the clusters directly, as Gaussian components for example. The cluster models induce a distance measure. The work of Banfield and Raftery [ ] is representative of this strategy. In contrast, our approach is based on a generative model only for the similarity matrix $\mathbf{X}$ rather than the objects in the clusters. This allows us to express possible errors or uncertainties in our similarity measures in a simple manner. We are not aware of previous work that has adopted this approach. Moreover, in certain problems such a formulation is physically motivated and more natural than devising models for the individual classes.

This paper is organized as follows: In Section   and   introduces the problem and the likelihood framework. Section   provides some important characterizations and key properties of our framework. In Section   two algorithms seeking the solution of our problem are introduced; one more deterministic and greedy in nature, and the other based on a random search technique. In Section   we present a practical and relevant application of the concept and algorithms introduced previously. Finally in Section   we present some concluding remarks.

2   Problem Statement

We formulate the hierarchical clustering problem as a tree estimation. As pointed out before each node in the tree corresponds to one cluster. An example is depicted in Figure . In our formulation we focus mainly on the tree representation.

Let $T = (V, L)$ denote a rooted tree with nodes V and directed links L (we consider a strongly acyclic tree, that is, if we disregard the direction of the edges the graph is still acyclic). Denote the root node by 1. Denote by R the leaf nodes. Each leaf node corresponds to one object in the input set R, and the root node corresponds to a cluster encompassing all input elements. For example, in Figure , $R = \{4, 6, 7, 8, 9\}$.

Every node has at least two descendants, apart from the leaf nodes, which have none. If all internal nodes have exactly two descendants then the tree is called binary. For each node $i \in V$ let $f(i)$ denote the parent of i, e.g. $f(8) = 5$. We can identify each link with the corresponding end node, i.e., $(f(i), i) \sim i$, $(f(i), i) \in L$. Denote by $\mathcal{P}_i$ the (unique) path from the source node to i, e.g., $\mathcal{P}_8 = \{1, 2, 5, 8\}$. Let $a(i, j)$, $i, j \in V$, denote the nearest ancestor of the pair of nodes (i, j), e.g., $a(4, 9) = 2$. We define also $d(i)$, $i \in V$, as the set of children nodes of i, e.g. $d(3) = \{6, 7\}$.

For a given node k we denote by $R(k)$ the subset of leafs R with k as an ancestor. This set corresponds to the elements in the cluster represented by node k. For example node 2 represents the cluster consisting of elements $\{4, 8, 9\}$ of R. We define $T(k)$ as the subtree of T rooted at $f(k)$ with leafs $R(k)$.

For each pair of input elements we can consider a similarity metric. This value reflects how similar (with respect to some characteristics) are the two objects (the larger the value, the more similar they are). Let the input elements be $i, j \in R$ and denote by γ_{ij} the corresponding pairwise similarity. Note that this is a theoretical quantity, and it is not directly observable (we address this issue in the next section).

In hierarchical clustering one would like to aggregate clusters such that the inter-cluster similarity is roughly the same. For example, for the clustering in Figure , γ_{46} and γ_{47} are, ideally, equal. However, we stress that this ideal condition is not generally met by the measurable counterparts x_{46} and x_{47}.

We are going to enforce this property on our generative model. Formally, consider an arbitrary tree $T = (V, L)$. For each node in the tree we associate a metric value $\gamma_k \in \mathbb{R}$, $k \in V$. This metric value provides a measure of the similarity of the elements in $R(k)$. For each pair of input elements $i, j \in R$ we require the pairwise metric value γ_{ij} to be the metric value of the nearest ancestor, that is $\gamma_{ij} \equiv \gamma_{a(i,j)}$. The value of γ_{ij} can be regarded as a measure of the extent of the shared portion of the paths to i and j.

Notice that the tree structure imposes restrictions on γ_{ij}; for example, if two different pairs of nodes have the same shared paths then their similarity values must be the same, e.g. consider the tree in Figure ; The pairs of nodes $(6, 8)$ and $(4, 7)$ have the same shared paths, thus $\gamma_{68} = \gamma_{47}$.

Define the matrix $\gamma = (\gamma_{ij} : i, j \in R)$. According to the discussion above, in order for γ to be compatible with the tree structure it must belong to the set

$$\Gamma(\mathcal{T}) = \{\gamma : \gamma_{ij} = \gamma_{kl} \text{ if } a(i, j) = a(k, l), \forall i, j, k, l \in R\} . \tag{1}$$

To ensure identifiability of the tree $\mathcal{T}$ (that is, to ensure we can fully recover the tree given the set of pairwise metrics) we require the metrics γ to satisfy the

Monotonicity Property: Let $i, j \in V \setminus R$ be any two nodes and let $\mathcal{P}_i$, $\mathcal{P}_j$ denote the paths from the root to i and j respectively . If $\mathcal{P}_i$ is a proper subpath of $\mathcal{P}_j$ then $\gamma_i < \gamma_j$.

Knowledge of the metric values for each pair of elements of R and above monotonicity property are sufficient for identification of the underlying topology. For example, referring to Figure , the metric γ_{89} will be greater than γ_{i9} for all $i \in R \setminus \{8, 9\}$, revealing that nodes 8 and 9 have a common parent in the tree. The property can be exploited in this manner to devise simple and effective bottom-up agglomerative algorithm that identifies the dendritic tree [,].

For a given tree $\mathcal{T}$, the set of all metrics satisfying the monotonicity property is defined as

$$\mathcal{G}(\mathcal{T}) = \{\gamma \in \Gamma(\mathcal{T}) : \gamma_{f(k)} < \gamma_k, \ \forall k \in V \setminus \{1, R\}\} . \tag{2}$$

3   Likelihood Formulation

Recall that $\mathbf{X}$ denotes the empirical similarity matrix. These are the measurements we have access to, conveying information about γ and $\mathcal{T}$. We consider these similarities to be imperfect, possibly contaminated with errors or only crude reflections of the true similarities between objects. We regard $\mathbf{X}$ as being a realization of a random variable parameterized by γ and $\mathcal{T}$.

For a given unknown tree $\mathcal{T}$ let $\mathbf{X} \equiv \{X_{ij} : i, j \in R, \ i \neq j\}$, where each X_{ij} is a random variable parameterized by $\gamma \equiv (\gamma_{ij}) \in \Gamma(\mathcal{T})$. Let $p(\mathbf{x}|\gamma)$ denote the probability density function of $\mathbf{X}$, parameterized by $\gamma \in \Gamma(\mathcal{T})$, with respect to some dominating measure. A sample $\mathbf{x} \equiv \{x_{ij} : i, j \in R, \ i \neq j\}$ of $\mathbf{X}$ is observed. Let $\gamma \in \mathcal{G}(\mathcal{T})$; When $p(\mathbf{x}|\gamma)$ is viewed as a function of $\mathcal{T}$ and γ it is called the likelihood of $\mathcal{T}$ and γ. The maximum likelihood tree estimate is given by

$$\mathcal{T}^* = \arg\max_{\mathcal{T} \in \mathcal{F}} \sup_{\gamma \in \mathcal{G}(\mathcal{T})} p(\mathbf{x}|\gamma) , \tag{3}$$

where $\mathcal{F}$ denotes the *forest* of all possible trees with leafs R. If the maximizer of the above expression is not unique define T^* as one of the possible maximizers.

In many situations we are not directly interested in $\widehat{\gamma}(\mathbf{x})$, an estimate of γ from the measurements. Hence we can regard γ as nuisance parameters. In that case ( ) can be interpreted as a maximization of the profile likelihood [ ]

$$\mathcal{L}(\mathbf{x}|T) \equiv \sup_{\gamma \in \mathcal{G}(T)} p(\mathbf{x}|\gamma) \; . \tag{4}$$

The solution of ( ) is referred to as the Maximum Likelihood Tree (MLT).

Consider now some more structure in the log-likelihood $\log p(\mathbf{x}|\gamma)$: Assume the random variables X_{ij} are independent and have densities $p(x_{ij}|\gamma_{ij})$, $i, j \in R$, $i \neq j$, with respect to a common dominating measure. Let $f_{ij}(x_{ij}|\gamma_{ij}) = \log p(x_{ij}|\gamma_{ij})$. Assume that $f_{ij}(x_{ij}|\gamma_{ij})$ is a strictly concave functional of γ_{ij} having a maximizer in $\mathbb{R}$ (note that the maximizer is unique since the function is strictly concave). The log-likelihood is hence

$$\log p(\mathbf{x}|\gamma) = \sum_{i \in R} \sum_{j \in R \setminus \{i\}} f_{ij}(x_{ij}|\gamma_{ij}) \; . \tag{5}$$

Notice that, although parameterized by the a common parameter γ_{ij}, the densities f_{ij} and f_{ji} are not necessarily the same (as it is the case in the example in Section), so the two measurements x_{ij} and x_{ji} are different, and convey different information.

4   Characterization of the Maximum Likelihood Structure

The optimization problem in ( ) is quite formidable. We are not aware of any method for computation of the global maximum except by a brute force examination of each tree in the forest. Consider a tree with N leafs. A very loose lower bound on the size of the forest $\mathcal{F}$ is $N!/2$. For example, if $N = 10$ then there are more than 1.8×10^6 trees in the forest. This explosion of the search space precludes the brute force approach in all but very small forests. Moreover, the computation of the profile likelihood ( ) is non-trivial because it involves a constrained optimization over $\mathcal{G}(T)$. Using the model ( ) we have that $p(\mathbf{x}|\gamma)$ is a continuous function of γ and hence we can rewrite the profile likelihood as

$$\mathcal{L}(\mathbf{x}|T) \equiv \max_{\gamma \in \overline{\mathcal{G}(T)}} p(\mathbf{x}|\gamma) \; , \tag{6}$$

where $\overline{\mathcal{G}(T)}$ denotes the closure of the set $\mathcal{G}(T)$. Hence the profile likelihood can be computed solving this constrained optimization problem.

The following results establish some key properties for this problem.

Lemma 1. *Let T be an arbitrary tree. The solution of*

$$\widehat{\gamma} = \arg \max_{\gamma \in \mathbf{\Gamma}(T)} p(\mathbf{x}|\gamma)$$

is unique and given by

$$\widehat{\gamma}_{ij} = \arg\max_{\gamma \in \mathbb{R}} \sum_{k,l \in R : a(k,l)=a(i,j)} f_{kl}(x_{kl}|\gamma) . \tag{7}$$

This lemma, whose proof is elementary, characterizes a modified version of the profile likelihood ( ) (this version of the profile likelihood is "unconstrained", that is, the optimization is over $\varGamma(\mathcal{T})$ instead of $\mathcal{G}(\mathcal{T})$). The evaluation of this version of the profile likelihood for a given tree is very simple.

The theorem below (proved in Section) establishes a key property that leads to some important characterizations of the trees candidate to be the MLT and allow us to use the above lemma to compute the profile likelihood.

Theorem 1. *Let* $\log p(\mathbf{x}|\gamma)$ *be given by ( ) and* $\widetilde{\mathcal{T}}$ *be a tree such that*

$$\max_{\gamma' \in \varGamma(\widetilde{\mathcal{T}})} p(\mathbf{x}|\gamma') > \max_{\gamma' \in \mathcal{G}(\widetilde{\mathcal{T}})} p(\mathbf{x}|\gamma') . \tag{8}$$

Then there exists another tree $(\mathcal{T}, \gamma)$, $\gamma \in \mathcal{G}(\mathcal{T})$, *satisfying the monotonicity property, such that*

$$p(\mathbf{x}|\gamma) > \max_{\gamma' \in \mathcal{G}(\widetilde{\mathcal{T}})} p(\mathbf{x}|\gamma') . \tag{9}$$

In particular, if $\mathcal{T}^*$ *is the solution to ( ), i.e., the MLT, we have*

$$\arg\max_{\gamma' \in \varGamma(\mathcal{T}^*)} p(\mathbf{x}|\gamma') = \arg\max_{\gamma' \in \mathcal{G}(\mathcal{T}^*)} p(\mathbf{x}|\gamma') . \tag{10}$$

Remark 1: Consider a arbitrary tree $\widetilde{\mathcal{T}}$. Suppose that the maximum of $p(\mathbf{x}|\gamma)$ is attained for $\gamma \in \varGamma(\widetilde{\mathcal{T}}) \setminus \overline{\mathcal{G}(\widetilde{\mathcal{T}})}$, that is, expression ( ) holds. The theorem says that in that case we can construct another tree $(\mathcal{T}, \gamma)$ from $\widetilde{\mathcal{T}}$ such that it yields a higher likelihood than any tree $(\widetilde{\mathcal{T}}, \gamma)$, $\gamma \in \mathcal{G}(\widetilde{\mathcal{T}})$. Consequently $\widetilde{\mathcal{T}}$ cannot be the maximum likelihood tree, proving ( ).

Remark 2: The second part of the theorem ( ) shows that it is unnecessary to perform the "constrained" optimization over $\mathcal{G}(\mathcal{T})$. For each tree, we can compute the "unconstrained" optimization (over $\varGamma(\mathcal{T})$), using Lemma , and simply check if the resulting maximizer lies in the set $\overline{\mathcal{G}(\mathcal{T})}$.

Define the set of trees

$$\mathcal{F}' = \left\{ \mathcal{T} \in \mathcal{F} : \arg\max_{\gamma \in \varGamma(\mathcal{T})} \log p(\mathbf{x}|\gamma) \in \overline{\mathcal{G}(\mathcal{T})} \right\} .$$

Note that the maximum likelihood tree belongs to this set, i.e., $\mathcal{T}^* \in \mathcal{F}'$.

Remark 3: From the proof technique (in Section) we also note that we can consider only binary trees. For any non-binary tree we can construct a corresponding binary tree yielding the same likelihood value, obtained from the former adding links with metric identical to the one of the parent link.

5   Hierarchical Clustering Algorithms

In this section we present two algorithms intended to solve (at least approximately) the problem ( ). Hierarchical clustering algorithms generally belong to one of two types: bottom-up, agglomerative constructions or top-down divisive methods. Our probabilistic model for the similarity matrix allows us to develop a novel agglomerative algorithm based on the likelihood function. Furthermore, by viewing the (profile) likelihood function as a discrete probability mass function, we also devise a Metropolis-Hastings search strategy that circumvents the greedy search strategy associated with agglomerative and divisive algorithms.

5.1   Bottom-Up Agglomerative Approach

In *Remark 2* above we observed that we can greatly simplify the task of evaluating the profile likelihood for trees belonging to $\mathcal{F}'$, and we know that the MLT, ultimately what we want to determine, belongs to that set. Nevertheless a brute force examination of each tree in $\mathcal{F}'$ is still unfeasible.

Given the pairwise similarities γ characterizing the input set, it is possible to reconstruct the dendritic tree using a simple agglomerative bottom-up procedure, following the same conceptual framework as many hierarchical clustering methods [,]. The following result ensures that, for a similarity matrix γ satisfying the monotonicity property, the set of pairwise similarities for a given tree completely determines the tree. In fact, there is only one such tree.

Proposition 1. *Let $\mathcal{T}$ be a tree topology with object set R. Let $\{\gamma_{ij}\}$ be the set of pairwise similarities, corresponding to a monotonic metric on $\mathcal{T}$. Then $\mathcal{T}$ is the only tree with pairwise similarities $\{\gamma_{ij}\}$ satisfying the monotonicity property. That is*

$$\gamma \in \mathcal{G}(\mathcal{T}), \quad and \quad \gamma \not\subseteq \mathcal{G}(\mathcal{T}'), \ \forall \ \mathcal{T}' \neq \mathcal{T} .$$

Due to space limitations the proof of the proposition is omitted. Recall that, in most practical scenarios, we only have access to the measurements $\mathbf{x}$, conveying information about γ (and hence about $\mathcal{T}$). In this case we can still develop a bottom-up agglomerative clustering algorithm to estimate the true dendrogram.

We restrict ourselves to binary trees. Note that for any non-binary clustering tree there exists an equivalent binary tree (in the sense that there is a binary tree that contains all clusters in the non-binary tree and attains the same likelihood value as the non-binary tree; i.e., there are extra, unnecessary branches in the binary tree). The binary restriction leads to a particularly simple clustering algorithm as follows. Consider the estimates of the pairwise similarities for each pair of leaf nodes, given by

$$\widehat{\gamma}_{ij} = \arg\max_{\gamma \in \mathbb{R}} \left(f_{ij}(x_{ij}|\gamma) + f_{ji}(x_{ji}|\gamma) \right), \ i,j \in R, \ i \neq j .$$

One expects that the above estimated pairwise similarities are reasonably close to the true similarities γ, with the differences being due to measurement noise and limitations of the measurement procedure.

1. **Input:** Set of input nodes R, likelihood functions $\{f_{ij}\}$.
2. **Initialization:** $R' := R$, $V = R$, $S_r = \{r\}, \forall r \in R$, and $\widehat{\gamma}_{ij} = \arg\max_{\gamma \in \mathbb{R}} (f_{ij}(x_{ij}|\gamma) + f_{ji}(x_{ji}|\gamma))$.
3. Find the a pair of nodes $i, j \in R'$ such that

$$\widehat{\gamma}_{ij} \geq \widehat{\gamma}_{kl}, \ \forall k, l \in R' .$$

4. Denote by k the new node, the inferred parent of the nodes i, j. Set $V := V \cup \{k\}$, $R' := R' \cup \{k\} \setminus \{i, j\}$ and $S_k = \bigcup_{r \in S} S_r$. Set also $f(i) := k$; $f(j) := k$. Define

$$\widehat{\gamma}_{kl} = \widehat{\gamma}_{lk} \equiv \arg\max_{\gamma \in \mathbb{R}} \sum_{r \in S_k} f_{rl}(x_{rl}|\gamma) + f_{lr}(x_{lr}|\gamma) , \quad \text{where } l \in R' \setminus \{k\} .$$

5. If $|R'| > 1$ go back to 3. Otherwise set Root $\equiv k$.
6. **Output:** The node set V and the parent function $f : V \setminus \{\text{Root}\} \to V$, defining a unique tree. Also the set of similarity estimates $\widehat{\gamma}$, if desired.

Fig. 2. Agglomerative Likelihood Tree (ALT) algorithm

Consider the pair of leaf nodes such that $\widehat{\gamma}_{ij}$ is greatest, that is

$$\widehat{\gamma}_{ij} \geq \widehat{\gamma}_{kl}, \ \forall k, l \in R' .$$

We infer that i and j are the most similar leaf nodes, and so they must have a common parent in the dendrogram. Denote their parent node by k. In other words, we are constructing the cluster $S_k = \{i, j\}$ and node k in the dendrogram represents that cluster.

Assuming that our decision is correct then the tree structure imposes that $a(i, l) = a(j, l)$ for all $l \notin \{i, j\}$. Hence we can update our pairwise similarity estimates for pairs involving i and j, using Lemma . Furthermore, since $\widehat{\gamma}_{il} = \widehat{\gamma}_{jl}$ for any $l \notin \{i, j\}$, we can just add node k as a new leaf node, and remove i and j from the leafs set. Define the new leaf set $R' = R \bigcup \{k\} \setminus \{i, j\}$. We just need to define pairwise similarity estimates for pairs involving the new node k:

$$\widehat{\gamma}_{kl} = \widehat{\gamma}_{lk} \equiv \arg\max_{\gamma \in \mathbb{R}} \sum_{r \in S_k} f_{rl}(x_{rl}|\gamma) + f_{lr}(x_{lr}|\gamma) , \quad \text{where } l \in R' \setminus \{k\} .$$

This procedure is iterated until there is only one element left in R'. The algorithm is outlined in Figure .

Notice that the number of elements of R' is decreased by one at each step of the algorithm, guaranteeing the algorithm to stop. The algorithm structure ensures that the obtained tree and similarity estimates $\widehat{\gamma}$ satisfy the monotonicity property.

As pointed out before one expects the estimated pairwise similarity values $\widehat{\gamma}$ to be close to the true similarities γ. We develop those notions next. Define

$$\gamma_{ij}(\mathbf{x}) = \arg\max_{\gamma \in \mathbb{R}} f_{ij}(x_{ij}|\gamma) + f_{ji}(x_{ji}|\gamma) \, .$$

Given the measurements $\mathbf{x}$, $\gamma_{ij}(\mathbf{x})$ is the maximum likelihood estimate of the pairwise similarities γ_{ij}. In various scenarios we can increase the accuracy of $\gamma_{ij}(\mathbf{x})$ by considering more elaborate similarity measurements, or considering multiple (roughly independent) measurements. We address here the later case.

Assume that $\mathbf{X}$ corresponds to $n \in \mathbb{N}$ measurements for each input pair and that $\gamma_{ij}(\mathbf{X})$ converges in probability to γ_{ij} as n tends to infinity. It can be shown that, for an underlying "true" binary tree $\mathcal{T}$, the ALT algorithm is consistent, that is, if $\widehat{\mathcal{T}}(\mathbf{X})$ is the tree obtained by the ALT algorithm then $\lim_{n\to\infty} \Pr(\mathcal{T} = \widehat{\mathcal{T}}(\mathbf{X})) = 1$. Hence, the ALT algorithm perfectly reconstructs the original binary tree, provided that one can estimate the similarity values with enough accuracy. Also can be shown that, as n grows, this is the only tree in $\mathcal{F}'$, that is $\lim_{n\to\infty} \Pr(\mathcal{F}' = \{\mathcal{T}\}) = 1$. From this we conclude the following, important result:

Proposition 2. *The MLT is a consistent estimator of the true dendritic tree, for binary trees. That is, if $\mathcal{T}^*$ denotes the MLT then $\lim_{n\to\infty} \Pr(\mathcal{T} = \mathcal{T}^*) = 1$.*

Proof. The proof of this result is elementary, since the maximum likelihood tree belongs to $\mathcal{F}'$ and, as n increases the probability of $\mathcal{F}'$ having only the tree $\mathcal{T}$ converges to one.

Although we formulated this results in terms of the number of measurements per individual pair, the results are also applicable with more generality where the limits are taken with respect to some process that increases the accuracy of our similarity measures.

5.2   Markov Chain Monte Carlo Method

Although the ALT algorithm is a consistent estimator of the true dendrogram, it is essentially greedy, based on local decisions over the pairwise similarities. Unlike the ALT, the MLT estimator takes a global approach, seeking for the best (in a maximum likelihood sense) tree. The price to pay is that we now must search over the entire forest $\mathcal{F}$. In this section we propose a random search technique to efficiently search the forest of trees.

Consider the profile likelihood $\mathcal{L}(\mathbf{x}|\mathcal{T})$, as defined in ( ). Note that the maximum likelihood tree is the tree that maximizes $\mathcal{L}(\mathbf{x}|\mathcal{T})$. For a fixed measurement $\mathbf{x}$ we can regard the profile likelihood $\mathcal{L}(\mathbf{x}|\mathcal{T})$ as a discrete distribution over $\mathcal{F}$ (up to a normalizing factor). Then one way of searching the set $\mathcal{F}$ is to sample it according to this distribution [ ]. The more likely trees are going to be sampled more often than the less likely trees, making the search more efficient than drawing trees drawing trees uniformly at random from $\mathcal{F}'$.

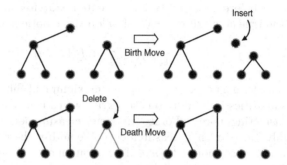

Fig. 3. The birth-step and death-step moves illustrated: The birth-step selects a node with more than two children, chooses two of these children, and inserts an extra node as the new parent of these children. The death step chooses a node with two children, and deletes that node

The evaluation of the profile likelihood ( ) is still complicated, since it involves a constrained optimization over $\mathcal{G}(\mathcal{T})$. As we observed in Section   the MLT belongs to the set of feasible trees $\mathcal{F}'$. For trees in $\mathcal{F}'$ one can compute the profile likelihood very easily using Lemma . Also, given a tree, one can easily verify if that tree belongs to $\mathcal{F}'$ or not: For a given tree compute the "unconstrained" optimization (over $\overline{\Gamma(\mathcal{T})}$), using Lemma , and check if the resulting maximizer lies in the set $\overline{\mathcal{G}(\mathcal{T})}$. If so the tree lies in $\mathcal{F}'$. Define

$$\mathcal{L}'(\mathbf{x}|\mathcal{T}) = \begin{cases} \mathcal{L}(\mathbf{x}|\mathcal{T}) & \text{if } \mathcal{T} \in \mathcal{F}' \\ 0 & \text{otherwise} \end{cases} . \tag{11}$$

The above expression can be evaluated much faster than ( ). Again, for a fixed measurement $\mathbf{x}$ we can regard $\mathcal{L}'(\mathbf{x}|\mathcal{T})$ as a discrete distribution over $\mathcal{F}'$ (up to a normalizing factor). We can search the set $\mathcal{F}'$ by sampling it according to this distribution. One way of performing this task is to use the Metropolis-Hastings algorithm. For this we need to construct a irreducible Markov chain with state space $\mathcal{F}$ (note that in this case the state space is finite), so each state corresponds to a tree. We allow only certain transitions (equivalently, some transitions have probability 0). For a given state (a tree) $s_i \in \mathcal{F}$ we can move to another state (tree) using "birth moves" and "death moves" as illustrated in Figure .

For a given state $s_i \in \mathcal{F}$ there are n_{s_i} allowed transitions (both deaths and births). This number, denoted n_{s_i}, can be easily determined by simple enumeration of the possibilities. The transition matrix for this chain is

$$q_{\mathcal{T},\mathcal{T}'} = \Pr(s_{i+1} = \mathcal{T}'|s_i = \mathcal{T})$$
$$= \begin{cases} 0 & \text{if } \mathcal{T}' \text{ is not within one move from } \mathcal{T} \\ \frac{1}{n_{\mathcal{T}}} & \text{otherwise} \end{cases} . \tag{12}$$

Let $\{s_i : i \in \mathbb{N}\}$ be the chain satisfying the Markov condition ( ). It can be easily shown that the chain $\{s_i\}$ is irreducible, that is, with positive probability we can reach an arbitrary tree in a finite number of steps (regardless of the choice of tree where we start).

Using a generalization of the Metropolis algorithm due to Hastings [ ] we construct another Markov Chain, whose unique limit distribution (and also unique stationary distribution) is precisely $\mathcal{L}'(\mathbf{x}|\mathcal{T})$. Thus if we sample from this chain for a sufficiently large period of time, the observed states will be samples of the distribution $\mathcal{L}'(\mathbf{x}|\mathcal{T})$, regardless of the initial state.

The new chain can be constructed in a two-stage fashion. Define the probability of acceptance $\alpha_{\mathcal{T},\mathcal{T}'}$

$$\alpha_{\mathcal{T},\mathcal{T}'} = \begin{cases} \min\left\{ \frac{\mathcal{L}'(\mathbf{x}|\mathcal{T}')\cdot q_{\mathcal{T}',\mathcal{T}}}{\mathcal{L}'(\mathbf{x}|\mathcal{T})\cdot q_{\mathcal{T},\mathcal{T}'}}, 1 \right\} & \text{if } \mathcal{L}'(\mathbf{x}|\mathcal{T}) \cdot q_{\mathcal{T},\mathcal{T}'} > 0 \\ 0 & \text{otherwise} \end{cases}.$$

For a given state $\mathcal{T} \in \mathcal{F}'$ we randomly choose the possible next state according to $q_{\mathcal{T},\mathcal{T}'}$, and accept that transition with probability $\alpha_{\mathcal{T},\mathcal{T}'}$. This gives rise to the chain

$$p_{\mathcal{T},\mathcal{T}'} = \begin{cases} \alpha'_{\mathcal{T},\mathcal{T}'} q_{\mathcal{T},\mathcal{T}'} & \text{if } \mathcal{T} \neq \mathcal{T}' \\ 1 - \sum_{\mathcal{T}'' \neq \mathcal{T}} \alpha'_{\mathcal{T},\mathcal{T}''} q_{\mathcal{T},\mathcal{T}''} & \text{if } \mathcal{T} = \mathcal{T}' \end{cases}.$$

It can be easily shown that the resulting chain (over $\mathcal{F}'$) is still irreducible, and thus it has a unique limit distribution ( ). To get our (approximate) solution of ( ) we simulate the above chain and recall the state with largest likelihood visited, the longer the chain is simulated the higher is the chance of visiting the MLT at least one time.

Although theoretically the starting point (initial state) of the chain is not important, provided that the chain is simulated from long enough, starting at a reasonable point can help the chain to converge more rapidly. Starting the chain simulation from the tree obtained using the ALT algorithm seems to be a reasonable decision, since this is a consistent estimator, and so one expects the resulting tree to be "close" (in terms of the number of moves) to the actual MLT tree. Different techniques can be used to improve the search, like starting several chains at a set of different trees in parallel [ ].

6   Network Topology Identification

In this Section we present a practical example that illustrates the use of the above framework. This is not intended to be an experimental characterization techniques developed in the paper.

Consider a network, where a sender node transmits information packets to a set of receivers denoted by R. The receivers are, in this case, the usual "objects" to be classified. Assume that the routes from the sender to the receivers are fixed. The physical network topology is essentially a graph where each node corresponds to a physical device (e.g. router, switch, terminal, etc...) and the links correspond to the connections between these.

The problem we address is the identification of the network topology based on end-to-end measurements, this is a practical problem relevant in the networking community [, ,]. The fact that we allow only end-to-end measurements prevents us from utilizing internal network device information, and force us to rely only on the traffic and queueing characteristics. With this limited information, it is only possible to identify the so-called "logical topology" defined by the branching points between paths to different receivers. This corresponds to a tree-structured topology with the sender at the root and the receivers at the leaves, as depicted in Figure . The tree topology is effectively a hierarchical clustering of the receivers.

We define a similarity metric γ_{ij}, associated with each pair of receivers $i, j \in R$. The value of γ_{ij} is related to the extent of the shared portion of the paths to i and j, and satisfies the monotonicity property. We can not measure the pairwise metrics directly, so we estimate them performing measurements in the network. In most situations one sends probes from the source to the receivers that allow us to estimate γ_{ij}.

In earlier work we proposed a metric based on delay differences [ ]. The delay difference measurements provide (noisy) versions of a metric related to the number of shared queues in the paths to two receivers. The measurements $\{x_{ij}\}$ are the empirical means of repeated delay difference measurements. Under reasonable assumptions the measurements are statistically independent and, according to the Central Limit Theorem, the distribution of each empirical mean tends to a Gaussian. This motivates the following (approximate) model:

$$x_{ij} \sim \mathcal{N}(\gamma_{ij}, \sigma_{ij}^2 / n_{ij}), \tag{13}$$

where σ_{ij}^2 is sample variance of the n_{ij} measurements associated with empirical mean x_{ij}, and $\mathcal{N}(\gamma, \sigma^2)$ denotes the Gaussian density with mean γ and variance σ^2. The measurements for different pairs of receivers are also independent.

Note that, using the models describe above, we are in the scenario described in Section :

$$f_{ij}(x_{ij}, \sigma_{ij} | \gamma_{ij}) = -\frac{(x_{ij} - \gamma_{ij})^2}{2\sigma_{ij}^2} + C_{ij} , \tag{14}$$

where C_{ij} is a normalizing constant, and the densities are taken with respect to the Lebesgue measure. We can then apply the algorithms developed before to estimate the network topology. Furthermore the model ( ) has some desirable properties, namely, it is closed under summation:

$$f(x_{ij}, \sigma_{ij}^2 | \gamma) + f_{kl}(x_{kl}, \sigma_{kl}^2 | \gamma) = -\frac{\left(\left(\frac{x_{ij}}{\sigma_{ij}^2} + \frac{x_{kl}}{\sigma_{kl}^2}\right) / \left(\frac{1}{\sigma_{ij}^2} + \frac{1}{\sigma_{kl}^2}\right) - \gamma\right)^2}{2\left(\frac{1}{\sigma_{ij}^2} + \frac{1}{\sigma_{kl}^2}\right)} + C .$$

This makes the computations arising from Lemma very simple.

We conducted Internet experiments that demonstrate the use of the techniques described before. In this case we had also access to a partial topology map of the network, obtained using a tool (called *traceroute*) relying on network device information. This map is expected to be close to the real network topology. In Figure we depict the topology obtained using *traceroute* and the

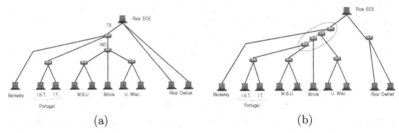

Fig. 4. (a) The topology of the network used for Internet experiments, obtained using *traceroute*. (b) Estimated topology using the ALT algorithm. The signaled links have link-parameter values $\gamma_k - \gamma_{f(k)}$ one order of magnitude smaller than all the other links. Those links can be collapsed, that is, the three devices inside the circle can be identified as one unique device

topology obtained solely from end-to-end measurements, using the algorithms described in Section . As one can observe, the two topologies are similar (apart from some artifacts do to the binary topology assumption). See [ ] for details.

7   Final Remarks

In this paper we develop a new framework for hierarchical clustering based on a generative dendritic cluster model. We present two clustering algorithms on top of this framework. The ALT algorithm has low complexity, and is essentially an agglomerative hierarchical clustering algorithm, hence greedy. The second algorithm presented overcomes the problems of the greedy nature of the ALT by performing a random (but informed) search on the space of possible clusterings.

The framework presented can be also extended to a maximum penalized likelihood approach. For example, if we penalize the complexity of the dendritic tree with a penalty based on the number of internal nodes, a modified version of Theorem   still applies. This allows for more conservative clustering, yielding non-binary trees.

The framework is very well suited to problems like the network topology identification, wherein the generative model reflects the physical mechanisms involved. Ongoing research is aimed at assessing the advantages and disadvantages of the framework in more general settings.

Acknowledgements

The authors thanks Mark Coates for many helpful discussions and suggestions.

8   Proof of Theorem

We start this section with a simple lemma characterizing the sum of strictly concave functions.

Lemma 2. *Let* $i \in \{1,\ldots,n\}$ *and* $f_i(\cdot)$ *be strictly concave functions with (unique) maximizers* $x_i \in \mathbb{R}$. *Let*

$$g(x) = \sum_{i=1}^{n} f_i(x) .$$

Define $x_{\max} = \max_i x_i$ *and* $x_{\min} = \min_i x_i$. *The function* $g(x)$ *is strictly concave, has a unique maximizer* $\widehat{x} = \arg\max_{x \in \mathbb{R}} g(x)$ *and, if* $x_{\max} \neq x_{\min}$ *then*

$$x_{\min} < \widehat{x} < x_{\max} . \tag{15}$$

The proof of the lemma is simple, and therefore omitted. We are now ready to prove the Theorem. The proof is done by construction. Given a tree $\widetilde{T}$ satisfying ( ) we construct a tree T satisfying ( ).

Let $\widetilde{T}$ be a tree satisfying ( ). Let

$$\widetilde{\gamma} = \arg\max_{\gamma' \in \mathcal{G}(\widetilde{T})} \log p(\mathbf{x}|\gamma') \quad \text{and} \quad \widetilde{\gamma}_{\text{unconst}} = \arg\max_{\gamma' \in \mathbf{\Gamma}(\widetilde{T})} \log p(\mathbf{x}|\gamma') .$$

Note that $\mathbf{\Gamma}(\widetilde{T}) \subseteq \overline{\mathcal{G}(\widetilde{T})}$ and note also that $\mathcal{G}(\widetilde{T})$ is an open set. By concavity of the log likelihood we have

$$\log p(\mathbf{x}|(1-\lambda)\widetilde{\gamma} + \lambda\widetilde{\gamma}_{\text{unconst}}) > (1-\lambda)\log p(\mathbf{x}|\widetilde{\gamma}) + \lambda\log p(\mathbf{x}|\widetilde{\gamma}_{\text{unconst}})$$
$$\geq \log p(\mathbf{x}|\widetilde{\gamma}), \quad \lambda \in (0,1) .$$

Thus, if $\widetilde{\gamma} \in \mathcal{G}(\widetilde{T})$ then choosing a small $\lambda > 0$ we get another point in $\mathcal{G}(\widetilde{T})$ yielding a higher log likelihood, a contradiction, thus

$$\widetilde{\gamma} \in \partial\mathcal{G}(\widetilde{T}) , \tag{16}$$

where ∂ denotes the boundary of a set.

The fact that ( ) holds indicates that there are links l such that $\widetilde{\gamma}_l = \widetilde{\gamma}_{f(l)}$. Consider now the tree obtained collapsing all such links and keeping the value of the remaining link-level parameters unchanged. Denote tree and corresponding metric values by T' and γ' respectively (see Figure   (a)(b)).

Note that the parameters γ' satisfy the constrains ( ), and that (T',γ') yields the same log likelihood value as $(\widetilde{T},\widetilde{\gamma})$, that is $\log p(\mathbf{x}|\widetilde{\gamma},\widetilde{T}) = \log p(\mathbf{x}|\gamma',T')$. By our construction we see that $\gamma' \in \mathcal{G}(T')$. We then conclude that

$$\gamma' = \arg\max_{\gamma \in \mathbf{\Gamma}(T')} \log p(\mathbf{x}|\gamma) . \tag{17}$$

To see this suppose that ( ) does not hold. Then, by the same argument used in the beginning of the proof (but now applied to T' instead of $\widetilde{T}$) we must have $\gamma' \in \partial\mathcal{G}(T')$, a contradiction. Note that, according to Lemma , γ' satisfies ( ).

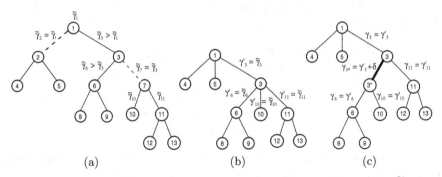

Fig. 5. Trees illustrating the proof of Theorem   (a) Original tree $(\widetilde{T}, \widetilde{\gamma})$ (b) Collapsed tree (T', γ') (c) Constructed tree (T, γ)

The rest of the proof entails by constructing another tree by adding links to T', such that ( ) holds.

Consider a node k of T' such that k has more than two descendants (such a node must exist because we pruned at least one link from $\widetilde{T}$). Define

$$g_{ij}(\gamma) = \sum_{m \in R(i)} \sum_{n \in R(j)} f_{mn}(x_{mn}|\gamma) + f_{nm}(x_{nm}|\gamma), \quad i, j \in d(k), \ i \neq j \,,$$

and

$$\beta_{ij} = \arg\max_{\gamma \in \mathbb{R}} g_{ij}(\gamma), \quad i, j \in d(k), \ i \neq j \,.$$

From Lemma   we know that

$$\gamma'_k = \arg\max_{\gamma \in \mathbb{R}} \sum_{i,j \in d(k), \ i \neq j} g_{ij}(\gamma) \,.$$

Case 1: Suppose now that not all the values β_{ij} are the same, then there exist a pair of nodes $o, p \in d(k)$ such that $\beta_{op} \geq \beta_{ij}$, for all $i, j \in d(k)$. From Lemma we conclude that $\beta_{op} \neq \gamma'_k$ (since $\min_{i,j} \beta_{ij} < \gamma'_k < \max_{i,j} \beta_{ij}$). Using the chosen pair (o, p), we construct a new tree T (refer to Figure (c)) adding an extra node k^* and the link (k, k^*). Node k^* has children o and p. Loosely speaking we are pulling the pair of nodes o and p down, adding a new node k^*. The parameter values for this new tree, denoted by γ, are adjusted such that $\gamma_{k^*} = \gamma'_k + \delta$, $\delta > 0$. All the other metric values remain the same. Note that $\delta > 0$, but small enough so that the tree (T, γ) still satisfies the constraints ( ).

The log likelihood of (T, γ) is identical of the one from $(\widetilde{T}, \widetilde{\gamma})$, except for the term involving γ_{k^*}. Thus

$$
\begin{aligned}
\log p(\mathbf{x}|\gamma) - \log p(\mathbf{x}|\gamma') &= g_{op}(\gamma_k^*) - g_{op}(\gamma_k') \\
&= g_{op}(\gamma_k' + \delta) - g_{op}(\gamma_k') \\
&= g_{op}((1 - \lambda)\gamma_k' + \lambda\beta_{op}) - g_{op}(\gamma_k') \\
&> (1 - \lambda)g_{op}(\gamma_k') + \lambda g_{op}(\beta_{op}) - g_{op}(\gamma_k') \\
&= \lambda(g_{op}(\beta_{op}) - g_{op}(\gamma_k')) > 0 \, ,
\end{aligned}
$$

where we take $\lambda = \delta/(\beta_{op} - \gamma_k')$. The last inequality follows from uniqueness of the maximizer of g_{op} and $\beta_{op} \neq \gamma_k'$.

In conclusion, for δ small enough, we have $\log p(\mathbf{x}|\gamma) > \log p(\mathbf{x}|\gamma')$, and hence

$$
\log p(\mathbf{x}|\gamma) > \log p(\mathbf{x}|\widetilde{\gamma}) \tag{18}
$$

Case 2: In this case we have that all values β_{ij}, $i, j \in d(k)$ are the same. Thus, $\gamma_k' = \beta_{ij}$ for all $i, j \in d(k)$. Like in case 1, we construct another tree T by adding an extra node k^* and the link (k, k^*), such that node k^* has children o and p. The parameter values for this new tree, denoted by γ, are adjusted such that $\gamma_{k^*} = \gamma_k'$. All the other metric values remain the same. From Lemma   we observe that γ is the maximizer over $\boldsymbol{\Gamma}(T)$ of $\log p(\mathbf{x}|\gamma)$. Hence

$$
\log p(\mathbf{x}|\gamma, T) = \log p(\mathbf{x}|\widetilde{\gamma}, \widetilde{T}) \, .
$$

Suppose that all nodes with more than two descendants correspond to case 2, then we could add to T' all the links we removed (when we constructed T' from $\widetilde{T}$), and obtain the original tree $\widetilde{T}$, but in this case

$$
\max_{\gamma' \in \boldsymbol{\Gamma}(\widetilde{T})} \log p(\mathbf{x}|\gamma') = \max_{\gamma' \in \mathcal{G}(\widetilde{T})} \log p(\mathbf{x}|\gamma') \, ,
$$

a contradiction. Hence at least one node of T' corresponds to case 1, and so ( ) holds, proving the result. The second part follows from *Remark 1*.

References

[1] Fasulo, D.: An analysis of recent work on clustering algorithms. Technical Report # 01-03-02, Department of Computer Science and Engineering, University of Washington (1999)   ,   ,

[2] Jain, A.K., Murty, M.N., Flynn, P.J.: Data clustering: a review. ACM Computing Surveys 31 (1999) 264-323

[3] Fisher, D.: Iterative optimization and simplification of hierarchical clusterings. Journal of Artificial Intelligence Research 4 (1996) 147-180

[4] Murtagh, F.: A survey of recent advances in hierarchical clustering algorithms. The Computer Journal 26 (1983)   ,   ,

[5] Banfield, J.D., Raftery, A.E.: Model-based gaussian and non-gaussian clustering. Biometrics 49 (1993) 803-821

[6] Willet, P.: Recent trends in hierarchical document clustering: a critical review. Information Processing and Management 24 (1988) 577-597

[7] Voorhees, E.M.: Implementing agglomerative hierarchical clustering algorithms for use in document retrieval. Information Processing and Management 22 (1986) 465-476

[8] El-Hamdouchi, A., Willet, P.: Hierarchic document clustering using ward's method. In: proceedings of the Ninth Annual International ACM SIGIR Conference on Research and Development in Information Retrieval. (1986)

[9] Zhang, T., Ramakrishnan, R., Livny, M.: BIRCH: an efficient data clustering method for very large databases. In: ACM SIGMOD International Conference on Management of Data, Montreal, Canada (1996) 103-114

[10] Hofmann, T.: Unsupervised learning by probabilistic latent semantic analysis. Machine Learning 42 (2001) 177-196

[11] Fraley, C.: Algorithms for model-based gaussian hierarchical clustering. SIAM Journal on Scientific Computing 20 (1998) 270-281

[12] Vaithyanathan, S., Dom, B.: Model-based hierarchical clustering. In: Proceedings of the Sixteenth Conference on Uncertainty in Artificial Intelligence, Stanford University; Stanford, CA. (2000)

[13] Kamvar, S.D., Klein, D., Manning, C.D.: Interpreting and extending classical agglomerative clustering algorithms using a model-based approach. In: International Conference on Machine Learning (ICML). (2002)

[14] Berger, J.O., Liseo, B., Wolpert, R.L.: Integrated likelihood methods for eliminating nuisance parameters. Statistical Science 14 (1999) 1-28

[15] Tanner, M.A.: Tools for Statistical Inference - Methods for the Exploration of Posterior Distributions and Likelihood Functions. Springer Verlag Series in Statistics (1996)   ,

[16] Hastings, W.: Monte Carlo sampling methods using Markov chains and their applications. Biometrika 57 (1970) 97-109

[17] Ratnasamy, S., McCanne, S.: Inference of multicast routing trees and bottleneck bandwidths using end-to-end measurements. In: Proceedings of IEEE INFOCOM 1999, New York, NY (1999)

[18] Duffield, N., Horowitz, J., Presti, F.L., Towsley, D.: Multicast topology inference from end-to-end measurements. In: ITC Seminar on IP Traffic, Measurement and Modelling, Monterey, CA (2000)

[19] Castro, R., Coates, M., Gadhiok, M., King, R., Nowak, R., Rombokas, E., Tsang, Y.: Maximum likelihood network topology identification from edge-based unicast measurements. Technical Report TREE0107, Department of Electrical and Computer Engineering, Rice University (2001)   ,

Learning Mixtures of Tree-Unions
by Minimizing Description Length

Andrea Torsello and Edwin R. Hancock

Dept. of Computer Science, University of York
Heslington, York, YO10 5DD, UK
atorsell@cs.york.ac.uk

Abstract. This paper focuses on how to perform the unsupervised
learning of tree structures in an information theoretic setting. The approach is a purely structural one and is designed to work with representations where the correspondences between nodes are not given, but
must be inferred from the structure. This is in contrast with other structural learning algorithms where the node-correspondences are assumed
to be known. The learning process fits a mixture of structural models to
a set of samples using a minimum description length formulation. The
method extracts both a structural archetype that desribes the observed
structural variation, and the node-correspondences that map nodes from
trees in the sample set to nodes in the structural model. We use the
algorithm to classify a set of shapes based on their shock graphs.

1   Introduction

Graph-based representations [ ] have been used with considerable success in
computer vision in the abstraction and recognition of object shape and scene
structure. Concrete examples include the use of shock graphs to represent shape-
skeletons [,], the use of trees to represent articulated objects [, ,] and
the use of aspect graphs for 3D object representation [ ]. The attractive feature of structural representations is that they concisely capture the relational
arrangement of object primitives, in a manner which can be invariant to changes
in object viewpoint. However, despite the many advantages and attractive features of graph representations, the methodology available for learning structural
representations from sets of training examples is relatively limited. As a result,
the process of constructing shape-spaces which capture the modes of structural
variation for sets of graphs has proved to be elusive. Hence, geometric representations of shape such as point distribution models [,], have proved to be
more amenable when variable sets of shapes must be analyzed.

Recently there has been considerable interest in learning structural representations from samples of training data, in particular in the context of Bayesian
networks [,], mixtures of tree-classifiers [ ], or general relational models [ ].
The idea is to associate random variables with the nodes of the structure and to
use a structural learning process infer the stochastic dependency between these

A. Rangarajan et al. (Eds.): EMMCVPR 2003, LNCS 2683, pp. 130–   , 2003.
© Springer-Verlag Berlin Heidelberg 2003

variables. Although these approaches provide a powerful way to infer the relations between the observable quantities of the model under examination, they rely on the availability of correspondence information for the nodes of the different structures used in learning. However, in many cases the identity of the nodes and their correspondences across samples of training data are not to hand, Instead, the correspondences must be recovered using a graph matching technique during the learning process. Hence, there is a chicken and egg problem in structural learning. Before the structural model can be learned, the correspondences with it must be available, and yet the model itself must be to hand to locate correspondences.

The aim in this paper is to develop a framework for the unsupervised learning of generative models of tree-structures from sets of examples. We pose the problem as that of learning a union structure from the set of examples with hidden or unknown correspondences. The structure is constructed through a set of edit operations. Associated with each node of the structure is a random variable which represents the probability of the node. There are hence three quantities that must be estimated. The first of these are the correspondences between the nodes in training examples and the estimated union structure. Secondly, there is the union structure itself. Finally, there are the node probabilities.

We cast the estimation of these three quantities in an information theoretic setting. The problem is that of learning a mixture of trees to represent the classes of tree present in the training data. We use as our information criterion the description length for the union structure and its associated node probabilities given correspondences with the set of training examples [ ]. An important contribution is to demonstrate that the description length is related to the edit distance between the union structure and the training examples. From our analysis it follows that the edit costs are directly related to the entropy associated with the node probabilities. We perform three sets of updates. First, correspondences are located so as to minimize the edit distance. Secondly, the union structure is edited to minimize the description length. Thirdly, we make maximum likelihood estimates of the node probabilities. It is important to note that the union model underpinning our method assumes node independence on the training samples. Using a mixture of unions we condition this independence on the class. This conditional independence assumption, while often unrealistic, is at the basis of the naive Bayes model [ ] which has proven to be robust and effective for a wide range of classification problems.

We apply the resulting framework to the problem of learning a generative model for sets of shock trees. The shock tree is an abstraction of 2D shape which is obtained by assigning labels to the branches of the Blum skeleton for the object boundary. [ ]. The shock labels are related to the differential structure of the object boundary. They distinguish whether the radius of the bitangent circle to the object boundary is increasing, decreasing, constant, locally maximum or locally minimum. The shock-graph is hence a tree-like characterization of the differential structure of the boundaries of 2D shapes, where nodes represent sections of the morphological skeleton of the shape and edges represent their adjacency relations. Changes in shape give rise to structural variations in the shock tree. By fitting our mixture of tree-unions to sets of shock trees we are able to construct a shape-space for the set of examples. We both learn shape classes present in the training data, and construct a shape space for each class. To construct the shape-space, we develop our previously published work where the node frequencies are used as the components of a pattern-vector [ ]. Here, we construct a generative model and the node probabilities for each union-structure are used as the components of the pattern vectors in shape-space. Moreover, we can potentially sample example trees from the generative model learned in this way.

Hence we make a number of contributions. There have been a previous attempts to learn trees and mixtures of trees, and to apply these methods to vision For instance Meilla [ ] has developed a probabilistic framework for learning mixtures of trees. Our work develops these theoretical ideas by establishing the link between description length and tree edit distance. From an applications perspective, there have been several attempts to use tree representations in vision. As a concrete example, Liu and Gieger [ ] have used free trees to represent articulated objects. The FORMS system of Zhu and Yuille [ ] also uses tree representations. Ioffe and Forsyth [ ] have used related ideas of model walking people using mixtures of trees. Our work provides a means of learning tree representations that can be used to construct shape-spaces for such applications.

Finally, from the perspective of shock-tree analysis we also provide a number of concrete contributions. Any attempt to learn the modes of structural variation linked to a shape has to deal with the lack of prior knowledge about the correspondences between skeletal components belonging to different sample training shapes. Graph-matching allows the explicit pairwise comparison of graphical representations. For example [, ,] use edit distance to extract the node correspondences and provide a measure of dissimilarity between structures. Furthermore, in [ ] we use a pairwise clustering algorithm to classify the shapes based on the edit distance between their shock-graphs. These approaches, while effective, give no insight into the generative model which gives rise to the observed distribution of shock-trees for a particular shape. Furthermore, the notion of distance that pairwise comparison approaches rely on is purely geometrical and it does not differentiate between shape elements that present a great variation among the training samples and elements that are virtually invariant. Recently there have been some attempts to extend the graph matching approach to take into account a set of sample training structures. In [ ] the authors use the mean graph as a representative of the training samples, while [ ] introduces the tree-union as a model of the structural variability present in a set of trees. An important advantage that the union approach has over the mean graph is that it represents explicitly how the training samples vary as well as what their common features. The generative tree model that we are proposing is obtained using the tree-union as the structural archetype for every tree in the distribution. Following this approach, we pose the shape classification problem as one of unsupervised learning of a mixture model, where each element of the mixture is a tree-union which represents the intrinsic structural variations in a shape class.

The outline of this paper is as follows. In Section 2 we describe the generative tree model that underpins our graph-clustering method. This focuses on details of the tree-union, and structure in terms of order-relations, and the maximum likelihood framework for node probability estimation. Section 3 extends the framework to mixtures of tree-unions. Here we show how the problem of selecting the mixture of trees may be posed as a process of minimizing a description length criterion. Section 4 turns to details of how the description length criterion may be minimized. This is realized by commencing with an over-specific model in which there is a mixture component per data sample. We then merge pairs of trees so as to maximize the gain in description length advantage. In Section 5, we explore the relationship between the change in description length gained through tree merge operations and the corresponding tree edit distance. Here we show that the edit costs are related to the node entropies (and hence the node probabilities). This demonstrates that we effectively have a means by which tree edit costs may be learned. In Section 6 we provide experiments which demonstrates the utility of our method for the problem of clustering shock trees. Finally, Section 7 offers some conclusions and directions for future work.

2   Generative Tree Model

Consider the set or sample of trees $\mathcal{D} = \{t_1, t_2, \ldots, t_n\}$. Our aim in this paper is to cluster these trees, i.e. to perform unsupervised learning of the class structure of the sample. We pose this problem as that of learning a generative model for the distribution of trees in a pattern space. The distribution of trees in the pattern space is modeled using a mixture model. Each class or cluster of trees is represented by a separate generative model. In other words, the components of the mixture model must be capable of capturing the structural variations for the sample trees which belong to a separate class using a probability distribution.

The set of tree-models constituting the mixture model is denoted by $\mathcal{H} = \{\mathcal{T}_1, \mathcal{T}_2, \ldots, \mathcal{T}_k\}$. Each tree model $\mathcal{T}$ is a structural archetype derived from the tree-union over the set of trees constituting a class. Associated with the archetype is a probability distribution which captures the variations in tree structure within the class. Hence, the learning process involves estimating the union structure and the parameters of the associated probability distribution for the class model $\mathcal{T}$. As a prerequisite, we require the set of node correspondences $\mathcal{C}$ between sample trees and the union tree for each class.

The learning process is cast into an information theoretic setting and the estimation of the required class models is effected using optimization methods. The quantity to be optimized is the description length for the sample-data set $\mathcal{D}$. The parameters to be optimized include the structural archetype of the model $\mathcal{T}$ as well as the node correspondences $\mathcal{C}$ between samples and the archetype. Hence, the inter-sample node correspondences are not assumed to be known a priori. Since the correspondences are uncertain, we must solve two interdependent optimization problems. These are the optimization of the union structure given a set of correspondences, and the optimization of the correspondences given the tree structure. These dual optimization steps are approximated by greedily merging similar tree-models.

The basic ingredients of our structural learning approach are:

1. A structural model of tree variation.
2. A probability distribution on the said model.
3. A structural optimization algorithm that allows us to merge two structural models in a way that minimizes the description length.

In prior work, we have described how tree unions can be used as structural models for samples of trees [ ]. However, the union is constructed so as to minimize tree-edit distance. Here we intend to use the union structure as a class model. However, we extend the idea in two important ways. First, we pose the recovery of the union tree in an information theoretic setting. Second, we aim to characterize uncertainties in the structure by assigning probabilities to nodes. Hence, the structural model is provided by the tree-union of the set of samples assigned to a mixture component, while the frequencies with which nodes from the sample set are mapped to nodes in the model provide the probability distribution. By adopting this information theoretic approach we demonstrate that the tree-edit distance, and hence the costs for the edit operations used to merge trees, are related to the entropies associated with the node probabilities. As a result, we provide a framework in which tree edit distances are learned. This has been a longstanding problem since Fu and his co-workers introduced the idea of edit distance in the early 1980's [,].

The basis of the proposed structural learning approach is a generative model of trees which allows us to assign a probability distribution to a sample of hierarchical trees. A hierarchical tree t is defined by a set of nodes $\mathcal{N}^t$ and a tree-order relation $\mathcal{O}^t \subset \mathcal{N}^t \times \mathcal{N}^t$ between the nodes. A tree-order relation $\mathcal{O}^t$ is an order relation with the added constraint that if $(x, y) \in \mathcal{O}^t$ and $(z, y) \in \mathcal{O}^t$, then either $(x, z) \in \mathcal{O}^t$ or $(z, x) \in \mathcal{O}^t$. A node b is said to be a *descendent* of a, or $a \rightsquigarrow b$, if $(a, b) \in \mathcal{O}^t$, furthermore, b descendent of a is also a *child* of a if there is no node x such that $a \rightsquigarrow x$ and $x \rightsquigarrow b$, that is there is non node between a and b in the tree-order.

Given this definition, we can construct a generative model for a class of trees $\mathcal{D}_c \subset \mathcal{D}$. This model $\mathcal{T} = T = (\mathcal{N}, \mathcal{O}, \Theta)$ is an instance of a set of nodes $\mathcal{N}$. Associated with the set of nodes is a tree order relation $\mathcal{O} \subset \mathcal{N} \times \mathcal{N}$ and a set $\Theta = \{\theta^i, i \in \mathcal{N}\}$ of sampling probabilities θ^i for each node $i \in \mathcal{N}$.

A sample from this model is a hierarchical tree $t = (\mathcal{N}^t, \mathcal{O}^t)$ with node set $\mathcal{N}^t \subset \mathcal{N}$ and a node hierarchy $\mathcal{O}^t$ that is the restriction to $\mathcal{N}^t$ of $\mathcal{O}$.

The probability of observing the sample tree t given the model tree $\mathcal{T}$ is $P\{t|\mathcal{T}\} = \prod_{i \in \mathcal{N}^t} \theta^i \prod_{j \in (\mathcal{N} \setminus \mathcal{N}^t)} (1 - \theta^j)$. The model underpinning this probability distribution is as follows. First, we assume that the set of nodes $\mathcal{N}$ for the union structure $\mathcal{T}$ spans all the nodes that might be encountered in the set of sample trees. Second, we assume that the sampling error acts only on nodes, while the hierarchical relations are always sampled correctly. That is, if nodes i and j

satisfy the relation $i \mathcal{O} j$, node i will be an anchestor of node j in each tree-sample that has both nodes. This assumption implies that two nodes will always satisfy the same hierarchical relation whenever they are both present in a sample tree. A consequences of this assumptions is that the structure of a sample tree is completely determined by restricting the order relation of the model $\mathcal{O}$ to the nodes observed in the sample tree. Hence, the links in the sampled tree can be seen as the minimal representation of the order relation between the nodes. The sampling process is equivalent to the application of a set of node removal operations to the archetypical structure $\mathcal{T} = (\mathcal{N}, \mathcal{O}, \Theta)$, which makes the archetype a union of the set of all possible tree samples.

The definition of the structural distribution assumes that we know the correspondences between the nodes in the sample tree t and the nodes in the class-model $\mathcal{T}$. When obtaining a sample from the generative model this assumption obviously holds. However, given a tree t, the probability that this tree is a sample from the class model $\mathcal{T}$ depends on the tree, the model, but also on the way we map the nodes of the tree to the corresponding nodes of the model. To capture this correspondence problem, we define a map $\mathcal{C} : \mathcal{N}^t \to \mathcal{N}$ from the set $\mathcal{N}^t$ of the nodes of t, to the nodes of the model.

The mapping induces a sample-correspondence for each node $i \in \mathcal{N}$. The correspondence probability for the node i is

$$\phi(i|t, \mathcal{T}, \mathcal{C}) = \begin{cases} \theta^i & \text{if } \exists j \in \mathcal{N}^t | \mathcal{C}(j) = i \\ 1 - \theta^i & \text{otherwise.} \end{cases}$$

while the probability of sampling the tree t from the model $\mathcal{T}$ given the set of correspondences $\mathcal{C}$ is

$$\Phi(t|\mathcal{T}, \mathcal{C}) = \begin{cases} \prod_{i \in \mathcal{N}} \phi(i|t, \mathcal{T}, \mathcal{C}) & \text{if } \forall v, w \in \mathcal{N}^t, v \rightsquigarrow w \iff \mathcal{C}(v) \rightsquigarrow \mathcal{C}(w) \\ 0 & \text{otherwise.} \end{cases}$$

Given a set $\mathcal{D} = \{t_1, t_2, \ldots, t_n\}$ of sample trees, we would like to estimate the tree model $\mathcal{T}$ that generated the samples, and the mapping $\mathcal{M}$ from the nodes of the sample trees to the nodes of the tree model. Here we use a maximum likelihood method to estimate the parameters. The log-likelihood of the sample data $\mathcal{D}$ given the tree-union model $\mathcal{T}$ and the correspondence mapping function $\mathcal{C}$ is $\mathcal{L}(\mathcal{D}|\mathcal{T}, \mathcal{C}) = \sum_{t \in \mathcal{D}} \log [\Phi(t|\mathcal{T}, \mathcal{C})]$. Our aims is to optimize the log-likelihood with respect to two variables: the correspondence map $\mathcal{C}$ and the tree union model $\mathcal{T}$. These variables, though, are not independent. The reason for this is that they both depend on the node-set $\mathcal{N}$. However, the dependency to the node-set can be lifted. The value of the log-likelihood function does not depend on the actual number of nodes because nodes with no associated samples will have correspondence probability $\phi(i|t, \mathcal{T}, \mathcal{C}) = 1$. Hence, the dependency to the node-set can be lifted by simply assuming that the node set is $Im(\mathcal{C})$, the image of the correspondence map. With this simplification, the remaining variables are: the order relation $\mathcal{O}$, the set of sampling probabilities Θ, and the map $\mathcal{C}$.

Given $\mathcal{C}$, it is easy to maximize with respect to the remaining two sets of variables. log-likelihood function is maximized by any order relation $\mathcal{O}$ that is consistent with the hierarchies for the sample trees (if any exists). Let $n_i(\mathcal{C})$ be the number of trees $t \in \mathcal{D}$ such that $\exists j | \mathcal{C}(j) = i$, that is there is a node that maps to i. Furthermore, let $m = \#\mathcal{D}$ be the number of trees in the data set, then the sampling probability θ^i for the node i that maximizes the likelihood function is $\hat{\theta}^i = \frac{n_i(\mathcal{C})}{m}$. When the optimal sampling probabilities are substituted into the log-likelihood, we have that

$$\hat{\mathcal{L}}(\mathcal{D}|\mathcal{C}) = \sum_{i \in \mathcal{N}} m \left[\frac{n_i(\mathcal{C})}{m} \log \left(\frac{n_i(\mathcal{C})}{m} \right) + \left(1 - \frac{n_i(\mathcal{C})}{m} \right) \log \left(1 - \frac{n_i(\mathcal{C})}{m} \right) \right] =$$

$$- \sum_{i \in \mathcal{N}} m I(\hat{\theta}^i), \quad (1)$$

where $I(\hat{\theta}^i) = - \left[\hat{\theta}^i \log(\hat{\theta}^i) + (1 - \hat{\theta}^i) \log(1 - \hat{\theta}^i) \right]$ is the entropy of the sampling distribution for node i. This equation holds assuming that there exists an order relation that is respected by every hierarchical tree in the sample set $\mathcal{D}$. If this is not the case then the log-likelihood function takes on the value $-\infty$.

The structural component of the model is a tree union constructed from the trees in the sample $\mathcal{D}$ so as to maximize the likelihood function.In our previous work [ ]. we have shown how the union tree may be constructed so that every tree in the sample set $\mathcal{D}$ may be obtained from it by using node removal operations alone. Hence every node in the tree sample is represented in the union structure. Moreover, the order-relations in the union structure are all preserved by pairs of nodes in the tree-samples in $\mathcal{D}$.

3   Mixture Model

A single tree-union may be used to represent a distribution of trees that belong to a single class $\mathcal{D}_c$. Defining characteristic of the class is tha fact that the nodes present in the sample trees satisfy a single order relation $\mathcal{O}_c$. However, the sample set $\mathcal{D}$ may have a more complex class structure and it may be necessary to describe it using multiple tree unions. Under these conditions the unsupervised learning process must allow for the multiple classes, and we represent the distribution sample trees using a mixture model over separate union structures. Let the set of union structures be denoted by $\mathcal{H} = \{\mathcal{T}_1, \mathcal{T}_2, \ldots, \mathcal{T}_c, \ldots, \mathcal{T}_k\}$, and let the corresponding mixing proportions be represented by the vector $\bar{\alpha} = (\alpha_1, \alpha_2, \ldots, \alpha_c, \ldots, \alpha_k)$. The mixture model for the distribution of sample trees is

$$P(t|\mathcal{H}, \mathcal{C}) = \sum_{c=1}^{k} \alpha_c \Phi(t|\mathcal{T}_c, \mathcal{C}).$$

where z_c^t is an indicator variable, that is 1 if tree t belongs to the mixture component c, and 0 otherwise. The log-likelihood function for the mixture model over the sample-set $\mathcal{D}$ is:

$$\mathcal{L}(\mathcal{D}|\mathcal{H}, \mathcal{C}, \bar{z}) = \sum_{t \in \mathcal{D}} \sum_{c=1}^{k} \left[\ln \alpha_c + z_c^t \ln \Phi(t|\mathcal{T}_c, \mathcal{C}) \right],$$

It is well known that the maximum likelihood criterion cannot be directly used to estimate the number of mixture components, since the maximum of the likelihood function is a monotonic function on the number of components. In order to overcome this problem we use use the Minimum Description Length (MDL) principle. The MDL principle [ ] asserts that the model that best describes a set of data is that which minimizes the combined cost of encoding the model and the error between the model and the data.

Our model is prescribed by the the vector of mixing proportions $\bar{\alpha}$ and the set of union structures $\mathcal{H} = \{\mathcal{T}_1, \ldots, \mathcal{T}_c, \ldots, \mathcal{T}_k\}$. The union structure $\mathcal{T}_c = \{\mathcal{N}_c, \mathcal{O}_c, \Theta_c\}$ for the mixture component indexed c consists of a set of nodes $\mathcal{N}_c$, a set of order relations $\mathcal{O}_c$ and a set of node probabilities $\Theta_c = \{\theta_c^i, i \in \mathcal{N}_c\}$, where θ_c^i is the probability for the node i in the union-tree indexed c. To describe or encode the fit of the model to the data, for each tree sample t we use the indicator variables z_c^t which indicates from which tree model the sample was drawn. Additionally, for each node in the model, we need to describe or encode whether or not the node was present in the sample.

By virtue of Shannon theorem, the cost incurred describing or encoding the model $\mathcal{H}$ is $-\log[P(\mathcal{H})]$, while the cost of describing data $\mathcal{D}$ using that model is $-\log[P(\mathcal{D}|\mathcal{H})]$. Making the dependence on the correspondences $\mathcal{C}$ explicit, we have: $LL(\mathcal{D}|\mathcal{H}) = -\mathcal{L}(\mathcal{D}|\mathcal{H}, \mathcal{C})$. Asymptotically the cost of describing the vector of mixing components $\bar{\alpha}$ and the set of indicator variables $\bar{z} = \{z_c^T, t \in \mathcal{D}, c = 1, \ldots, k\}$ is bounded by $nI(\bar{\alpha})$, where n is the number of samples in $\mathcal{D}$ and $I(\bar{\alpha}) = -\sum_{c=1}^k \alpha_c \log(\alpha_c)$ is the entropy of the mixture distribution $\bar{\alpha}$. The cost of describing the structure of a union model is proportional to the number of nodes contained within it, while the cost of describing the sampling probability θ_c^i of node i for model c and the existence of this node in each of the $n\alpha_c$ samples generated by union c is asymptotically equal to $n\alpha_c I(\theta_c^i)$. Here $I(\theta_c^i) = -\theta_c^i \log(\theta_c^i) - (1 - \theta_c^i) \log(1 - \theta_c^i)$ is the entropy associated with the node sampling probability. Hence, given a model $\mathcal{H}$ consisting of k tree-unions, where the component $\mathcal{T}_c$ has d_c nodes and a mixing proportion α_c, the description length for the model, conditional on the set of correspondences is $\mathcal{C}$ is:

$$LL(\mathcal{D}|\mathcal{H}, \mathcal{C}) = nI(\bar{\alpha}) + \sum_{c=1}^{k} \sum_{i=1}^{d_c} \left[n\alpha_c I(\theta_c^i) + l \right]. \qquad (2)$$

where l is the description length per node of the tree-union structure, which we set to 1. Given that $p_c^i = \{j \in \mathcal{N}^t | t \in \mathcal{D}, \mathcal{C}(j) = i\}$ is the set of nodes from sample trees in $\mathcal{D}$ mapped by $\mathcal{C}$ to node i of model c, the node probability θ_c^i is estimated using $\hat{\theta}_c^i = \frac{\#p_c^i}{d_c}$.

4   Learning the Mixture

Finding the global minimum of the description length is an intractable combinatorial problem. Hence, we resort to a local search technique. A widely used method for minimizing the description length of a mixture model is to use the

Expectation-Maximization algorithm. Unfortunately, the complexity of the maximization step for our union-tree model grows dramatically with the number of trees in the union. The problem arises from the fact that the membership indicators admit the possibility that each union can potentially include every sample-tree.

We have adopted a different approach which allows us to limit the complexity of the maximization step. The approach we have used is as follows.

– Commence with an overly-specific model. We use a structural model per sample-tree, where each model is equiprobable and structurally identical to the respective sample-tree, and each node has sample probability 1.
– Iteratively generalize the model by merging pairs of tree-unions. The candidates for merging are chosen so that they maximally decrease the description length.
– The algorithm stops when there are no merges remaining that can decrease the description length.

This algorithm bears some resemblance with the spanning tree clustering algorithm [ ]. Both algorithms iteratively merge samples or clusters that satisfy a minimum distance or maximum similarity criterion. The main difference is that, in our algorithm, the similarity matrix is cannot be assumed fixed as is the case with the spanning tree algorithm. Rather, it changes after each merge to reflect the changes in the joint model. This change in the distance matrix will limit the amount of chaining allowed in the clusters. This is due to the fact that the models describing the two clusters that are merged are substituted by a single model. This new model must be able to describe the variation present in both clusters, hence, its mean must be placed in model-space somewere between the means of two models. This implies that the distance to the remaining cluster must vary. Regardless of these differences, the algorithm is still guaranteed to converge to a local minimum with at most a linear number of merges.

The main requirement of our description length minimization algorithm is that we can optimally merge two tree models. That is that we can find a structure from which it is possible to sample every tree previously assigned to the two models. From equation   we see that the description length is linear with respect to the contribution from each component of the mixture. In fact, writing the description cost of component c as $LL_c(\mathcal{D}|\mathcal{T}_c, \mathcal{C}) = \sum_{j=1}^{dc} \left[na_c I(\theta_c^j) + l \right]$, where na_c is the number of data samples assigned to the component indexed c, the description cost becomes: $LL(\mathcal{D}|\hat{T}, \mathcal{C}) = nI(\alpha) + \sum_{c=1}^{k} LL_c(\mathcal{D}|\mathcal{T}_c, \mathcal{C})$. Furthermore, the description length per component $LL_c(\mathcal{D}|\mathcal{T}_c, \mathcal{C})$ is linear in the number of model nodes. This allows us to pose the minimization of the description length as a linear optimization problem with a combinatorial constraint. In particular, as will be shown in the next section, we can pose the model-merging problem as an instance of a particular minimum edit-distance problem.

Given two tree models $\mathcal{T}_1$ and $\mathcal{T}_2$, we wish to construct a union $\hat{T}$ whose structure respects the hierarchical constraints present in both $\mathcal{T}_1$ and $\mathcal{T}_2$, and that also minimizes the quantity $LL(\hat{T})$. Since the trees $\mathcal{T}_1$ and $\mathcal{T}_2$ already assign node correspondences $\mathcal{C}_1$ and $\mathcal{C}_2$ from the data samples to the model, we can simply find a map $\mathcal{M}$ from the nodes in T_1 and T_2 to $\hat{T}$ and transitively extend the correspondences from the samples to the final model $\hat{T}$ in such a way that $\hat{C}(v) = \hat{C}(w) \Leftrightarrow w = \mathcal{M}(v)$.

Reduced to the merge of two structures, the correspondence problem is reduced to finding the set of nodes in T_1 and T_2 that are in common. Starting with the two structures, we merge the sets of nodes that would reduce the description length by the largest amount while still satisfying the hierarchical constraint. That is we merge nodes v and w of T_1 with node v' and w' of T_2 respectively if and only if $v \rightsquigarrow w \Leftrightarrow v' \rightsquigarrow w'$, where $a \rightsquigarrow b$ indicates that a is an ancestor of b.

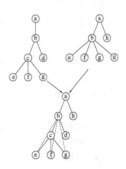

Fig. 1. Merging two trees

Let n_1 and n_2 be the number of tree samples from $\mathcal{D}$ that are respectively assigned to T_1 and T_2. Further let p_v and $p_{v'}$ be the number of times the nodes v and v' in T_1 and T_2 are respectively in correspondence with nodes of trees in the data sample $\mathcal{D}$. The sampling probabilities for the two nodes, if they are not merged, are $\theta v = \frac{p_v}{n_1+n_2}$ and $\theta v' = \frac{p'_v}{n_1+n_2}$ respectively, while the sampling probability of the merged node is $\theta vv' = \frac{p_v + p_{v'}}{n_1+n_2}$. Hence, the description length advantage obtained by merging the nodes v and v' is:

$$\mathcal{A}(v, v') = (n_1 + n_2) \left[I(\theta v) + I(\theta v') - I(\theta vv') \right] + l. \tag{3}$$

This implies that the set of merges $\mathcal{M}$ that minimizes the description length of the combined model maximizes the advantage function

$$\mathcal{A}(\mathcal{M}) = \sum_{(v,v') \in \mathcal{M}} \mathcal{A}(v, v') = \sum_{(v,v') \in \mathcal{M}} \left[(n_1 + n_2) \left[I(\theta v) + I(\theta v') - I(\theta vv') \right] + l \right]. \tag{4}$$

Assuming that the class archetypes T_1 and T_2 are trees, finding the set of nodes to be merged can be transformed into a tree-edit distance problem. That is, assigning particular costs to node removal and matching operations, the set of correspondences that minimize the edit distance between the archetypes of T_1 and T_2 also maximizes the advantage of the merged model. The costs that allowed the problem to be posed as an edit distance problem are $r_v = (n_1 + n_2)I(\theta v) + l$ for the removal of node v, and $m_{vv'} = (n_1 + n_2)I(\theta vv') + l$ for matching node v with node v'. In the next section, we will discuss this relationship in more detail.

At the end of the node merging operation we are left with a set of nodes that respects the original partial order defined by all the hierarchies in the sample-trees. We initialize our algorithm by calculating the description length of a model in which there is a mixing component per tree-sample in $\mathcal{D}$. The description length is given by $-\log(n) + l\sum_{t \in \mathcal{D}} \#\mathcal{N}^t$, where $n = \#\mathcal{D}$ is the number of samples and $\#\mathcal{N}^t$ is the number of nodes in the tree-sample t. For each pair of initial mixture components we calculate the union and the description length of the merged structure. From the set of potential merges, we can identify the one which reduces the description cost by the greatest amount. The mixing proportion for this optimal merge is equal to the sum of the proportions of the individual unions. At this point we calculate the union and description cost obtained merging the newly obtained model with each of the remaining components, and we iterate the algorithm until no more merges that reduce the description length can be found.

5   Tree Edit-Distance

As noted in earlier, the description length advantage is related to the edit distance between tree structures. This is an important observation. One of the difficulties with graph edit distance [,] is that there is no methodology for assigning costs to edit operations. By contrast, in the work reported in this paper the description length change associated with tree merge operations are determined by the node probabilities, and these in turn may be estimated from the available sample of trees. Hence by establishing a link between tree edit distance and description length, we provide a means by which edit costs may be estimated.

Hence, in this section we review the computation of tree edit-distance developed in our previous work [ ]. In particular, we describe how tree edit distance may be used to estimate node-correspondences, and give an overview of the algorithm we use to approximate the computation of tree edit distance.

The idea behind edit distance is that it is possible to identify a set of basic edit operations on nodes and edges of a structure, and to associate with these operations a cost. The edit-distance is found by searching for the sequence of edit operations that will make the two graphs isomorphic with one-another and which have minimum cost. The optimal sequence can be found using only structure reducing operations. This can be explained by the fact that we can transform node insertions in one tree into node removals in the other. This means that the edit distance between two trees is completely determined by the subset of residual nodes left after the optimal removal sequence, or, equivalently, by the nodes that are in correspondence. This means that the constraints posed by the edit-distance framework on the set of matching nodes are equivalent to those required to merge nodes on the model archetypes. Namely, that they preserve the hierarchy present in the two original structures.

The edit-distance between two trees t and t' can be defined in terms of the matching nodes:

$$D(t, t') = \sum_{i \notin \mathrm{Dom}(\mathcal{M})} r_i + \sum_{j \notin \mathrm{Im}(\mathcal{M})} r_j + \sum_{<i,j> \in \mathcal{M}} m_{ij}. \tag{5}$$

Here r_i and r_j are the costs of removing i and j respectively, $\mathcal{M}$ is the set of pairs of nodes from t and t' that match, $m_{i,j}$ is the cost of matching i to j, and $\mathrm{Dom}(\mathcal{M})$ and $\mathrm{Im}(\mathcal{M})$ are the domain and image of the relation $\mathcal{M}$. Letting $\mathcal{N}^t$

be the set of nodes of tree t, the distance can be rewritten as

$$D(t,t') = \sum_{u \in \mathcal{N}^t} r_u + \sum_{v \in \mathcal{N}^{t'}} r_v + \sum_{(u,v) \in \mathcal{M}} (m_{uv} - r_u - r_v).$$

Hence the distance is minimized by the set of correspondences that maximizes the utility $\mathcal{U}(\mathcal{M}) = \sum_{(u,v) \in \mathcal{M}} (r_u + r_v - m_{uv})$.

Setting $r_u = (n_1 + n_2)I(\theta u) + l$, $r_v = (n_1 + n_2)I(\theta v) + l$, and $m_{uv} = (n_1 + n_2)I(\theta uv) + l$, we have

$$\mathcal{U}(\mathcal{M}) = \sum_{(u,v) \in \mathcal{M}} [(n_1 + n_2)(I(\theta u) + I(\theta v) - I(\theta uv)) + l], \tag{6}$$

which is equal to the advantage in description length in ( ). Since the combinatorial problem underlying both edit-distance and model merge share the same hierarchical constraints and objective function, the solution to one problem can be derived from the solution to the other. In particular the set of common nodes obtained through the edit-distance approach is equal to the set of nodes to be merged to optimally merge the tree-models.

To find the set correspondences that minimizes the edit distance between two trees we make use of two results presented in [ ]. We call $\Omega(t)$ the closure of tree t, $E_i(t)$ the edit operation that removes node i from t and $\mathcal{E}_i(\Omega(t))$ the equivalent edit operation that removes i from the closure. The first result is that edit and closure operations commute: $\mathcal{E}_i(\Omega(t)) = \Omega(E_i(t))$. For the second result we need some more definitions: We call a subtree s of $\Omega(t)$ *obtainable* if for each node i of s if there cannot be two children a and b so that (a,b) is in $\Omega(t)$. In other words, for s to be obtainable, there cannot be a path in t connecting two nodes that are siblings in s. We can, now, introduce the following:

Theorem 1. *A tree $\hat{t}$ can be generated from a tree t with a sequence of node removal operations if and only if $\hat{t}$ is an obtainable subtree of the directed acyclic graph $\Omega(t)$.*

By virtue of the theorem above, the node correspondences yielding the minimum edit distance between trees t and t' form an obtainable subtree of both $\Omega(t)$ and $\Omega(t')$, hence we reduce the problem to the search for a common substructure that maximizes the utility: the maximum common obtainable subtree (MCOS). That is, Let O be the set of matches that satisfy the obtainability constraint, the node correspondence that minimized the edit distance is $\mathcal{M}^* = \text{argmax}_{\mathcal{M} \in O} \mathcal{U}(\mathcal{M})$.

The solution to this problem is obtained by looking for the best matches at the leaves of the two trees, and by then propagating them upwards towards the roots. Let us assume that we know the utility of the best match rooted at every descendent of nodes i and j of t and t' respectively. To propagate the matches to i and j we need to find the set of siblings with greatest total utility. This problem can be transformed into a maximum weighted clique problem on a derived structure and then approximated using a heuristical algorithm. When

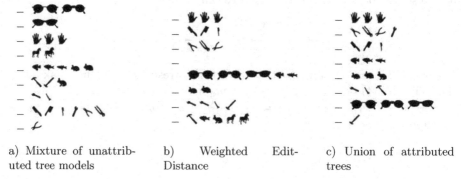

| a) Mixture of unattributed tree models | b) Weighted Edit-Distance | c) Union of attributed trees |

Fig. 2. Clusters extracted with a purely-structural mixture of trees approach versus pairwise clustering of attributed distances obtained with edit distance and tree union

the matches have been propagated to all the pairs of nodes drawn from t and t', the set of matches associated with the maximum utility give the solution to the maximum common obtainable subtree problem, and hence the edit-distance. We refer to [ ] for a detailed explanation of the approach.

6   Experimental Results

We evaluate the approach on the problem of shock tree matching. The idea behind the shock formulation of shape is to evolve the boundary of an object to a canonical skeletal form using the eikonal equation. The skeleton represents the singularities (shocks) in the curve evolution, where inward moving boundaries collide. Once the skeleton is to hand, the next step is to devise ways of using it to characterize the shape of the original boundary. Here we follow Zucker, Siddiqi, and others, by labeling points on the skeleton using so-called shock-classes [ ]. According to this taxonomy of local differential structure, there are different classes associated with behavior of the radius of the maximal circle bitangent to the boundary. The so-called shocks distinguish between the cases where the local maximal circle has maximum radius, minimum radius, constant radius or a radius which is strictly increasing or decreasing. We abstract the skeletons as trees in which the level in the tree is determined by their time of formation [ ]. The later the time of formation, and hence their proximity to the center of the shape, the higher the shock in the hierarchy.

In order to asses the quality of the method we compare clusters defined by the components of the mixture with those obtained with other two graph-clustering algorithms. The first graph-clustering method we compare to, is the one described in [,]. This method extracts the clusters by applying a pairwise clustering algorithm to the matrix of edit-distances between the graphs. The second method extracts the clusters by applying the same pairwise clustering algorithm to a different distance matrix, namely the distance obtained from the embedding space defined by a single tree-union that encompasses every shape [ ]. In our experiments the data clustered with the mixture of tree-unions approach use only structural information to characterize the shapes. On the other hand the cluster extracted using edit-distance and tree-union are based on data enhanced with geometrical information linked to the nodes of the trees.

Figure shows the clusters extracted on a database of 25 shapes. The first column shows the clusters extracted through the mixture of trees approach on purely structural representation of shape. The second column displays the cluster extracted from the weighted edit-distances of shock-trees enhanced with geometrical information. The geometric information added to the nodes is the proportion of the border length that genetated the skeletal branch associated with

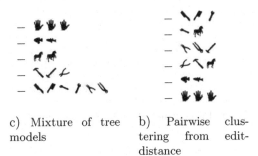

c) Mixture of tree models

b) Pairwise clustering from edit-distance

Fig. 3. Clusters obtained from non-attributed edit-distance and mixture of trees

the node. The third and last column shows the clusters extracted from the distances obtained by embedding the the geometrically-enhanced shock-trees in a single tree-union. While there is some merge and leakage, the cluster extracted with the mixture of trees method compare favorably with those obtained using the other two clustering algorithm, even where these are based on data enhanced with geometrical information. The second to last cluster extracted by the mixture of trees approach deserves some explanation: the structure of the shock-trees of the tools in the cluster is identical. Hence the model, which uses only structural infoprmation, correctly clusters the shock-trees toghether. To overcome this problem we need to provide more information than just the shock structure. The geometrical information allows the other methods to distinguish between wrenches, brushes and pliers.

Figure compares the results of graph clustering performed on purely structural information only. Here the clusters obtained through the mixture of tree-unions approach (left)is compared with those extracted by pairwise clustering of unweighted edit-distance (right)[ ]. No geometrical information used to aid the edit-distance-based clustering process. These results suggest that the mixture of tree-unions method outperforms pairwise clustering of edit-distance on purely structural data.

6.1   Synthetic Data

To augment these real world experiments, we have fitted the model on synthetic data. The aim of the experiments is to characterize the sensitivity of the classification approach to class merge. To meet this goal we have randomly generated

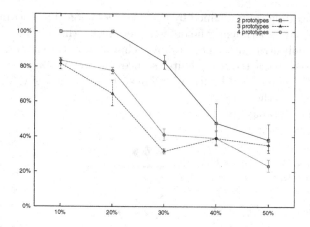

Fig. 4. Percentage of correct classifications under increasing structural noise

some prototype trees and, from each tree, we generated structurally perturbed copies. The procedure for generating the random trees was as follows: we commence with an empty tree (i.e. one with no nodes) and we iteratively add the required number of nodes. At each iteration nodes are added as children of one of the existing nodes. The parents are randomly selected with uniform probability from among the existing nodes. The trees are perturbed by randomly adding the required amount of nodes.

In our experiments we fit samples generated from an increasing number of prototypes and subject to an increasing amount of structural perturbation. We tested the classification performance on samples dawn from 2, 3, and 4 prototypes of 10 nodes each. The amount of noise is increased from an initial 10% of the total number of nodes to a maximum of 50%. Figure   plots the fraction of pairs of trees that are correctly classified as belonging to the same or different clusters as the noise is increased. From these experiment we can see that the approach works well with compact and well separated classes. The algorithm presents a sudden drop in performance when the structural variability of the class reaches 40% of the total number of nodes of the prototypes. Furthermore, when more prototypes are used, the distance between the clusters is smaller and, consequently the classes are harder to separate.

7   Conclusions

This paper presented a novel algorithm to learn a generative model of tree structures. The approach uses the the Tree-Union as the structural archetype for every tree in the distribution and fits a mixture of these structural models using a minimal description length formulation. In a set of experiments we apply the algorithm to the problem of unsupervised classification of shape using the shock-graphs. The results of these experiments are very encouraging, showing that the algorithm,although purely structural, compares favorably with pairwise classification approaches on attributed shock-graph. We are convinced that the results can be further improved by extending the model to take into account node-attributes.

References

[1] H. G. Barrow and R. M. Burstall, Subgraph isomorphism, matching relational structures and maximal cliques, *Inf. Proc. Letters*, Vol. 4, pp.83, 84, 1976.

[2] S. J. Dickinson, A. P. Pentlan, and A. Rosenfeld, 3-D shape recovery using distributed aspect matching, *PAMI*, Vol. 14(2), pp. 174-198, 1992.

[3] M. A. Eshera and K-S Fu, An image understanding system using attributed symbolic representation and inexact graph-matching, *PAMI*, Vol 8, pp. 604-618, 1986.
,

[4] N. Friedman and D. Koller, Being Bayesian about Network Structure, *Machine Learning*, to appear, 2002

[5] L. Getoor et al., Learning Probabilistic models of relational structure, in *8th Int. Conf. on Machine Learning*, 2001.

[6] D. Heckerman, D. Geiger, and D. M. Chickering, Learning Bayesian networks: the combination of knowledge and statistical data, *Machine Learning*, Vol. 20(3), pp. 197-243, 1995.

[7] T. Heap and D. Hogg, Wormholes in shape space: tracking through discontinuous changes in shape, in *ICCV*, pp. 344-349, 1998.

[8] Ioffe, S. and Forsyth, D. A., Human Tracking with Mixtures of Trees, *ICCV*, Vol. I, pp. 690-695, 2001.   ,

[9] X. Jiang, A. Muenger, and H. Bunke, Computing the generalized mean of a set of graphs, in *Workshop on Graph-based Representations, GbR'99*, pp 115-124, 2000.

[10] S. C. Johnson, Hierarchical clustering schemes, *Psychometrika*, Vol. 32(3), 1967.

[11] B. B. Kimia, A. R. Tannenbaum, and S. W. Zucker, Shapes, shocks, and deformations I, *International Journal of Computer Vision*, Vol. 15, pp. 189-224, 1995.

[12] P. Langley, W. Iba, and K. Thompson, An analysis of Bayesian classifiers, in *AAAI*, pp. 223-228, 1992

[13] Liu, T. and Geiger, D. , Approximate Tree Matching and Shape Similarity, *ICCV*, pp. 456-462, 1999.   ,

[14] B. Luo, et al., A probabilistic framework for graph clustering, in *CVPR*, pp. 912-919, 2001.   ,

[15] M. Meilă. *Learning with Mixtures of Trees.* PhD thesis, MIT, 1999.   ,

[16] J. Riassen, Stochastic complexity and modeling, *Annals of Statistics*, Vol. 14, pp. 1080-1100, 1986.   ,

[17] A. Sanfeliu and K. S. Fu. A distance measure between attributed relational graphs fro pattern recognition. *IEEE Transactions on Systems, Man and Cybernetics*, 13:353–362, 1983.   ,

[18] S. Sclaroff and A. P. Pentland, Modal matching for correspondence and recognition, *PAMI*, Vol. 17, pp. 545-661, 1995.

[19] A. Shokoufandeh, S. J. Dickinson, K. Siddiqi, and S. W. Zucker, Indexing using a spectral encoding of topological structure, in *CVPR*, 1999.

[20] K. Siddiqi et al., Shock graphs and shape matching, *Int. J. of Comp. Vision*, Vol. 35, 1999.   ,

[21] T. Sebastian, P. Klein, and B. Kimia, Recognition of shapes by editing shock graphs, in *ICCV*, Vol. I, pp. 755-762, 2001.

[22] A. Torsello and E. R. Hancock, Efficiently computing weighted tree edit distance using relaxation labeling, in *EMMCVPR*, LNCS 2134, pp. 438-453, 2001.   ,
      ,   ,   ,

[23] A. Torsello and E. R. Hancock, Matching and embedding through edit-union of trees, in *ECCV*, LNCS 2352, pp. 822-836, 2002.   ,   ,   ,

[24] Zhu, S. C. and Yuille, A. L., FORMS: A Flexible Object Recognition and Modelling System, *IJCV*, Vol. 20(3), pp. 187-212, 1996.   ,

Image Registration and Segmentation by Maximizing the Jensen-Rényi Divergence

A. Ben Hamza and Hamid Krim

Department of Electrical and Computer Engineering
North Carolina State University
Raleigh NC 27695, USA

Abstract. Information theoretic measures provide quantitative entropic divergences between two probability distributions or data sets. In this paper, we analyze the theoretical properties of the Jensen-Rényi divergence which is defined between any arbitrary number of probability distributions. Using the theory of majorization, we derive its maximum value, and also some performance upper bounds in terms of the Bayes risk and the asymptotic error of the nearest neighbor classifier. To gain further insight into the robustness and the application of the Jensen-Rényi divergence measure in imaging, we provide substantial numerical experiments to show the power of this entopic measure in image registration and segmentation.

1 Introduction

Information-theoretic divergence measures [ ] have been successfully applied in many areas including but not limited to statistical pattern recognition, neural networks, signal/image processing, speech processing, graph theory and computer vision. Kulback-Liebler (or directed) divergence, one of Shannon's entropy-based measures, has had success in many applications including indexing and image retrieval [ ]. A generalization of the directed divergence is the so-called α-divergence based on Rényi entropy [,]. The α-divergence measure has been applied in image registration/alignment as well as a variety of other problems [ ]. Another entropy-based measure is called the Jensen-Shannon divergence [ ]. This similarity measure may be defined between any number of probability distributions. Due to this generalization, the Jensen-Shannon divergence may be used as a coherence measure between any number of distributions and may be applied to a variety of signal/image processing and computer vision applications including image edge detection [ ] and segmentation of DNA sequences into homogenous domains [ ].

Inspired by the successful application of the mutual information measure [,], and looking to address its limitations in often difficult imagery, we recently proposed an information-theoretic approach to ISAR image registration [ ]. The objective of the proposed technique was to estimate the target motion during the imaging time, and was accomplished using a generalized Rényi's entropy-based similarity measure called the Jensen-Rényi divergence [,]. This divergence in fact measures the statistical dependence between an arbitrary number

A. Rangarajan et al. (Eds.): EMMCVPR 2003, LNCS 2683, pp. 147–   , 2003.

of consecutive ISAR image frames, which would be maximal if the images were geometrically aligned. In contrast to when using the mutual information [,], one is able through the Jensen-Rényi divergence to adjust the weights, and also the exponential order of Rényi entropy to control the measurement sensitivity of the joint histogram, that is the relative contributions of the histograms together with their order [ ]. This flexibility ultimately results in a better registration accuracy. The most fundamental and appealing characteristics of this divergence measure are its convexity and symmetry. In addition to its generality in involving an arbitrary number of probability distributions with possibly different weights, the Jensen-Rényi divergence measure enjoys appealing mathematical properties such as convexity and symmetry affording a great flexibility in a number of applications.

In this paper, we investigate some of the theoretical properties of the Jensen-Rényi divergence as well as their implications. In particular, we derive its upper bounds, which are very useful for normalization purposes. Using the theory of majorization [ ], we derive the maximum value of this divergence measure. Furthermore, we derive its performance bounds in terms of the Bayes risk and the asymptotic error of the nearest neighbor classifier within the statistical pattern recognition framework [ ].

The remainder of the this paper is organized as follows. In the next section, we briefly recall some facts about Rényi entropy prior to introducing the Jensen-Rényi divergence. Section 3 is devoted to the theoretical properties of this divergence measure. Subject to some conditions, its convexity is subsequently established. Next, by exploiting these properties, the maximum value of the Jensen-Rényi divergence is derived based on the theory of majorization. Then, we derive the maximum value of the Jensen-Rényi divergence for a weighted distribution, followed by a discussion on its application in parametric classification with context of statistical pattern recognition, and some performance upper bounds are also derived. And finally in section 4, some experimental results are provided to show the much improved performance of the Jensen-Rényi divergence in image registration and segmentation.

2   Jensen-Rényi Divergence Measure

Let $k \in \mathbb{N}$ and $X = \{x_1, x_2, \ldots, x_k\}$ be a finite set with a probability distribution $\boldsymbol{p} = (p_1, p_2, \ldots, p_k)$, i.e. $\sum_{j=1}^{k} p_j = 1$ and $p_j = P(X = x_j) \geq 0$, where $P(\cdot)$ denotes the probability.

Shannon's entropy is defined as $H(\boldsymbol{p}) = -\sum_{j=1}^{k} p_j \log(p_j)$, and it is a measure of uncertainty, dispersion, information, and randomness. The maximum uncertainty or equivalently minimum information is achieved by the uniform distribution. Hence, we can think of the entropy as a measure of uniformity of a probability distribution. Consequently, when uncertainty is higher it becomes more difficult to predict the outcome of a draw from a probability distribution.

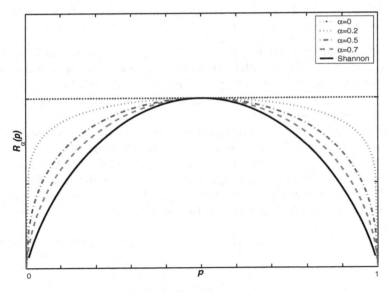

Fig. 1. Rényi's entropy

A generalization of Shannon entropy is Rényi entropy [ ] given by

$$R_\alpha(\boldsymbol{p}) = \frac{1}{1-\alpha} \log \sum_{j=1}^{k} p_j^\alpha, \quad \alpha \in (0,1) \cup (1,\infty). \tag{1}$$

For $\alpha > 1$, the Rényi entropy is neither concave nor convex.

For $\alpha \in (0,1)$, it is easy to see that Rényi entropy is concave, and tends to Shannon entropy $H(\boldsymbol{p})$ as $\alpha \to 1$. One may easily verify that R_α is a non-increasing function of α, and hence

$$R_\alpha(\boldsymbol{p}) \geq H(\boldsymbol{p}), \quad \forall \alpha \in (0,1). \tag{2}$$

When $\alpha \to 0$, Rényi entropy is equal to the logarithm of the cardinality of the set $\{j \in [1,k] : p_j > 0\}$.

Fig.   depicts Rényi entropy for a Bernoulli distribution $\boldsymbol{p} = (p, 1-p)$, with different values of the parameter α. As illustrated in Fig.   , the measure of uncertainty is at a minimum when Shannon entropy is used, and it increases as the parameter α decreases. Rényi entropy attains a maximum uncertainty when its exponential order α is equal to zero.

Definition 1. *Let* $\boldsymbol{p}_1, \boldsymbol{p}_2, \ldots, \boldsymbol{p}_n$ *be* n *probability distributions. The Jensen-Rényi divergence is defined as*

$$JR_\alpha^\omega(\boldsymbol{p}_1, \ldots, \boldsymbol{p}_n) = R_\alpha \left(\sum_{i=1}^{n} \omega_i \boldsymbol{p}_i \right) - \sum_{i=1}^{n} \omega_i R_\alpha(\boldsymbol{p}_i),$$

where $R_\alpha(\boldsymbol{p})$ is Rényi's entropy, and $\boldsymbol{\omega} = (\omega_1, \omega_2, \ldots, \omega_n)$ be a weight vector such that $\sum_{i=1}^n \omega_i = 1$ and $\omega_i \geq 0$.

Using the Jensen inequality, it is easy to check that the Jensen-Rényi divergence is nonnegative for $\alpha \in (0, 1)$. It is also symmetric and vanishes if and only if the probability distributions $\boldsymbol{p}_1, \boldsymbol{p}_2, \ldots, \boldsymbol{p}_n$ are equal, for all $\alpha > 0$.

Note that the Jensen-Shannon divergence [ ] is a limiting case of the Jensen-Rényi divergence when $\alpha \to 1$.

Unlike other entropy-based divergence measures such as the Kullback-Leibler divergence, the Jensen-Rényi divergence has the advantage of being symmetric and generalizable to any arbitrary number of probability distributions or data sets, with a possibility of assigning weights to these distributions. Fig. shows three-dimensional representations and contour plots of the Jensen-Rényi divergence with equal weights between two Bernoulli distributions for $\alpha \in (0, 1)$ and also for $\alpha \in (1, \infty)$.

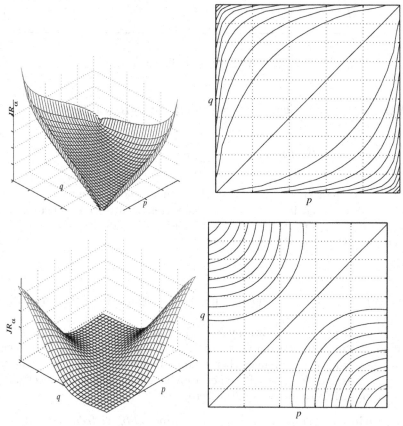

Fig. 2. 3D and contour plots of Jensen-Rényi divergence with equal weights. Top: $\alpha \in (0, 1)$. Bottom: $\alpha > 1$

In the sequel, we will restrict $\alpha \in (0,1)$, unless specified otherwise, and will use a base 2 for the logarithm, i.e., the measurement unit is in *bits*.

3   Properties of the Jensen-Rényi Divergence

The following result establishes the convexity of the Jensen-Rényi divergence of a set of probability distributions.

Proposition 1. *For $\alpha \in (0,1)$, the Jensen-Rényi divergence JR_α^ω is a convex function of $p_1, p_2, \ldots, p_n$.*

In addition to its convexity property, the Jensen-Rényi divergence is shown to be an adapted measure of disparity among n probability distributions as follows.

Proposition 2. *The Jensen-Rényi divergence achieves its maximum value when $p_1, p_2, \ldots, p_n$ are degenerate distributions, that is $p_i = (\delta_{ij})$, where $\delta_{ij} = 1$ if $i = j$ and 0 otherwise.*

3.1   Maximum Value of the Jensen-Rényi Divergence

Since the Jensen-Rényi divergence is a convex function of $p_1, \ldots, p_n$, it achieves its maximum value when the Rényi entropy function of the ω-weighted average of degenerate probability distributions, achieves its maximum value as well.

Assigning weights ω_i to the degenerate distributions $\Delta_1, \Delta_2, \ldots, \Delta_n$, where $\Delta_i = (\delta_{ij})_{1 \leq j \leq k}$, the following upper bound

$$JR_\alpha^\omega \leq R_\alpha \left(\sum_{i=1}^n \omega_i \Delta_i \right), \tag{3}$$

which easily falls out of the Jensen-Rényi divergence, may be used as a starting point. Without loss of generality, consider the Jensen-Rényi divergence with equal weights $\omega_i = 1/n$ for all i, and denote it simply by JR_α, to write

$$JR_\alpha \leq R_\alpha \left(\sum_{i=1}^n (\Delta_i/n) \right)$$

$$= \frac{1}{1-\alpha} \log \sum_{j=1}^k \left(\sum_{i=1}^n (\delta_{ij}/n) \right)^\alpha$$

$$= R_\alpha(a) + \frac{\alpha}{\alpha - 1} \log(n), \tag{4}$$

where

$$a = (a_1, a_2, \ldots, a_k) \quad \text{such that} \quad a_j = \sum_{i=1}^n \delta_{ij}. \tag{5}$$

Since $\mathbf{\Delta}_1, \mathbf{\Delta}_2, \ldots, \mathbf{\Delta}_n$ are degenerate distributions, it follows that $\sum_{j=1}^{k} a_j = n$. From ( ), it is clear that the maximum value of JR_α is also a maximum value of $R_\alpha(\mathbf{a})$.

In order to maximize $R_\alpha(\mathbf{a})$, the concept of majorization will be used [ ]. Let $(x_{[1]}, x_{[2]}, \ldots, x_{[k]})$ denote the non-increasing arrangement of the components of a vector $\mathbf{x} = (x_1, x_2, \ldots, x_k)$.

Definition 2. *Let $\mathbf{a}$ and $\mathbf{b} \in \mathbb{N}^k$. $\mathbf{a}$ is said to be majorized by $\mathbf{b}$, written $\mathbf{a} \prec \mathbf{b}$, if*

$$\begin{cases} \sum_{j=1}^{k} a_{[j]} = \sum_{j=1}^{k} b_{[j]} \\ \sum_{j=1}^{\ell} a_{[j]} \leq \sum_{j=1}^{\ell} b_{[j]}, \quad \ell = 1, 2, \ldots, k-1. \end{cases}$$

Since R_α is Schur-concave function, it follows that $R_\alpha(\mathbf{a}) \geq R_\alpha(\mathbf{b})$ whenever $\mathbf{a} \prec \mathbf{b}$.

The following result establishes the maximum value of the Jensen-Rényi divergence.

Proposition 3. *Let $\mathbf{p}_1, \ldots, \mathbf{p}_n$ be n probability distributions. If $n \equiv r \pmod{k}$, $0 \leq r < k$, then*

$$JR_\alpha \leq \frac{1}{1-\alpha} \log \left(\frac{(k-r)q^\alpha + r(q+1)^\alpha}{(qk+r)^\alpha} \right), \tag{6}$$

where $q = (n-r)/k$, and $\alpha \in (0,1)$.

Proof. It is clear that the vector

$$\mathbf{g} = (\overbrace{q+1, \ldots, q+1}^{r}, \overbrace{q, \ldots, q}^{k-r})$$

is majorized by the vector $\mathbf{a}$ defined in ( ). Therefore, $R_\alpha(\mathbf{a}) \leq R_\alpha(\mathbf{g})$. This completes the proof using ( ). $\square$

Corollary 1. *If $n \equiv 0 \pmod{k}$, then*

$$JR_\alpha(\mathbf{p}_1, \mathbf{p}_2, \ldots, \mathbf{p}_n) \leq \log(k),$$

where k is the number of components of each probability distribution.

3.2   Jensen-Rényi Divergence and Mixture Models

Mixture probability distributions provide a multimodal distribution that model the data with greater flexibility and effectiveness. These mixture models have been applied to a number of areas including unsupervised learning [ ], and computer vision applications such as detection and object tracking [ ]. It is therefore of great interest to evaluate the Jensen-Rényi divergence between two probability distributions $\mathbf{p}$ and $\mathbf{q}$ with weights $\{\lambda, 1-\lambda\}$, where $\lambda \in [0,1]$.

If we denote by r the weighted probability distribution defined by

$$r = (1 - \lambda/2)p + (\lambda/2)q,$$

then the Jensen-Rényi divergence can be expressed as a function of λ as follows

$$JR_\alpha(\lambda) = R_\alpha(r) - \frac{R_\alpha((1 - \lambda)p + \lambda q) + R_\alpha(p)}{2}.$$

Proposition 4. *The Jensen-Rényi divergence $JR_\alpha(\lambda)$ achieves its maximum value when $\lambda = 1$.*

Proof. Let $p = (p_i)_{i=1}^k$ and $q = (q_i)_{i=1}^k$ be two distinct probability distributions. The Jensen-Rényi divergence can then be written as

$$JR_\alpha(\lambda) = \frac{1}{1-\alpha} \log \sum_{i=1}^k \left(p_i + \frac{\lambda}{2}(q_i - p_i) \right)^\alpha$$
$$- \frac{1}{2(1-\alpha)} \left(\log \sum_{i=1}^k (p_i + \lambda(q_i - p_i))^\alpha + \log \sum_{i=1}^k p_i^\alpha \right).$$

Using calculus, we can show that $\lambda = 0$ is a singular point of the Jensen-Rényi divergence $JR_\alpha(\lambda)$, i.e. the first derivative $JR'_\alpha(\lambda)$ vanishes at $\lambda = 0$. Furthermore, it can be verified that the second derivative $JR''_\alpha(\lambda)$ is always positive. Hence, the first derivative $JR'_\alpha(\lambda)$ is an increasing function of λ, and therefore $JR'_\alpha(\lambda) \geq 0$ for all $\lambda \in [0, 1]$. Consequently, $JR_\alpha(\lambda)$ is an increasing function of λ. This concludes the proof.   □

Fig.   depicts the Jensen-Rényi divergence as a function of λ when $p = (.35, .12, .53)$, $q = (.25, .34, .41)$ and $\alpha = 0.6$.

3.3   Jensen–Rényi Divergence: Performance Bounds

In this subsection, performance bounds of the Jensen-Rényi divergence in terms of the Bayes error and also of the asymptotic error of the nearest-neighbor (NN) classifier are derived.

Let $C = \{c_1, c_2, \ldots, c_n\}$ be a set of n classes. By a classifier we mean a function $f : X \to C$ that classifies a given feature vector (pattern) $x \in X$ to the class $c = f(x)$. It is well known that the classifier that minimizes the error probability $P(f(X) \neq C)$ is the result of the Bayes classifier with an error L_B written in discrete form as $L_B = \inf_{f:X \to C} P\{f(X) \neq C\} = 1 - \sum_{j=1}^k \max_{1 \leq i \leq n}\{\omega_i p_{ij}\}$, where $\omega_i = P(C = c_i)$ are the class probabilities, and $p_{ij} = P(X = x_j | C = c_i)$ are the class-conditional probabilities. Denote by $\omega = \{\omega_i\}_{1 \leq i \leq n}$, and $p_i = (p_{ij})_{1 \leq j \leq k}$, $\forall i = 1, \ldots, n$.

Proposition 5. *The Jensen-Rényi divergence is upper bounded by*

$$JR_\alpha^\omega(p_1, p_2, \ldots, p_n) \leq R_\alpha(\omega) - 2L_B, \tag{7}$$

where $R_\alpha(\omega) = R_\alpha(C)$, and $\alpha \in (0, 1)$.

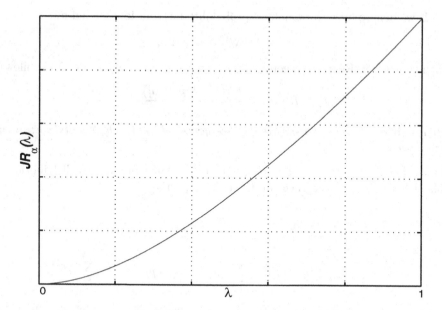

Fig. 3. Jensen-Rényi divergence as a function of λ

Proof. It follows from the definition of the Jensen-Rényi divergence that

$$R_\alpha(C) - JR_\alpha^\omega(p_1, p_2, \ldots, p_n) = R_\alpha(C|X).$$

It can be shown that $H(C|X) \geq 2L_B$ (see [ ]), therefore Eq. ( ) implies $R_\alpha(C|X) \geq 2L_B$. This completes the proof. $\square$

A method that provides an estimate for the Bayes error without requiring knowledge of the underlying class distributions is based on the NN classifier which assigns a test pattern to the class of its closest pattern according to some metric [ ]. For n sufficiently large, the following result relating the Bayes error L_B and the asymptotic error L_{NN} of the NN classifier holds [ ]

$$\frac{n-1}{n}\left(1 - \sqrt{1 - \frac{n}{n-1}L_{NN}}\right) \leq L_B \leq L_{NN}. \tag{8}$$

Using ( ), the following inequality is deduced

$$JR_\alpha^\omega \leq R_\alpha(\omega) - \frac{2(n-1)}{n}\left(1 - \sqrt{1 - \frac{n}{n-1}L_{NN}}\right).$$

4   Imaging Applications of the Jensen-Rényi Divergence

4.1   Image Registration

Image registration is an important problem in computer vision [ ], remote sensing data processing [ ] and medical image analysis [ ]. The goal of image registration is to find a spatial transformation such that a similarity metric between two or more images taken at different times, from different sensors, or from different viewpoints achieves its maximum.

Given two images $f_1, f_2 : \Omega \subset \mathbb{R}^2 \to \mathbb{R}$, where Ω is a bounded set (usually a rectangle), the goal of image registration in the context of the Jensen-Rényi divergence is to find the spatial transformation parameters $(\ell^*, \theta^*, \gamma^*)$ such that

$$(\ell^*, \theta^*, \gamma^*) = \arg \max_{(\ell, \theta, \gamma)} JR_\alpha^\omega (f_1, \mathcal{T}_{(\ell, \theta, \gamma)} f_2) = \arg \max_{(\ell, \theta, \gamma)} JR_\alpha^\omega (\boldsymbol{p}_1, \ldots, \boldsymbol{p}_n), \quad (9)$$

where $\boldsymbol{p}_i = \boldsymbol{p}_i(f_1, \mathcal{T}_{(\ell, \theta, \gamma)} f_2)$, and $\mathcal{T}$ is a Euclidean transformation with translational parameter $\ell = (\ell_x, \ell_y)$, a rotational angle θ and a scaling factor γ.

Denote $\mathcal{X} = \{x_1, x_2, \ldots, x_n\}$ and $\mathcal{Y} = \{y_1, y_2, \ldots, y_n\}$ the sets of pixel intensity values of f_1 and $\mathcal{T}_{(\ell, \theta, \gamma)} f_2$ respectively, and let X, Y be two random variables taking values in $\mathcal{X}$ and $\mathcal{Y}$. $\boldsymbol{p}_i(f_1, \mathcal{T}_{(\ell, \theta, \gamma)} f_2) = (p_{ij})_{1 \leq j \leq n}$ is defined as

$$p_{ij} = P(Y = y_j | X = x_i), \quad j = 1, 2, \ldots, n$$

which is the conditional probability of $\mathcal{T}_{(\ell, \theta, \gamma)} f_2$ given f_1 for the corresponding pixel pairs. Here the Jensen-Rényi divergence acts as a similarity measure between images. If the two images are exactly matched, then $\boldsymbol{p}_i = (\delta_{ij})_{1 \leq j \leq n}$, $i = 1, \ldots, n$. Since $\boldsymbol{p}_i$'s are degenerate distributions, it follows from Proposition 2 that the Jensen-Rényi divergence is maximized for a fixed α and ω.

Fig. (1)- (2) show two brain MRT images in which the misalignment is an Euclidean rotation. The conditional probability distributions $\{\boldsymbol{p}_i\}$ are crisp, as in Fig. (3), when the two images are aligned, and dispersed, as in Fig. (4), when they are not matched.

It is worth noting that the maximization of the Jensen-Rényi divergence holds for any α and ω such that $0 \leq \alpha \leq 1$ and $\omega_i \geq 0$, $\sum_i \omega_i = 1$. If we take $\alpha = 1$ and $\omega_i = P(X = x_i)$ then, by Proposition 1, the Jensen-Rényi divergence is reduced to the Shannon mutual information. Indeed, the Jensen-Rényi divergence measure provides a more general framework for the image registration problem. If the two images f_1 and $\mathcal{T}_{(\ell, \theta, \gamma)} f_2$ are matched, the Jensen-Rényi divergence is maximized for any valid weight. Assigning $\omega_i = P(X = x_i)$ is not always a good choice. Fig.   shows the registration results of the two brain images in Fig.   using the mutual information and the Jensen-Rényi divergence of $\alpha = 1$ and uniform weights. The peak at the matching point generated by the Jensen-Rényi divergence is clearly much higher than the peak by the mutual information. $\omega_i = P(X = x_i)$ gives the background pixels the largest weights.

In the presence of noise, the matching in background is corrupted. Mutual information may fail to identify the registration point. This phenomenon is

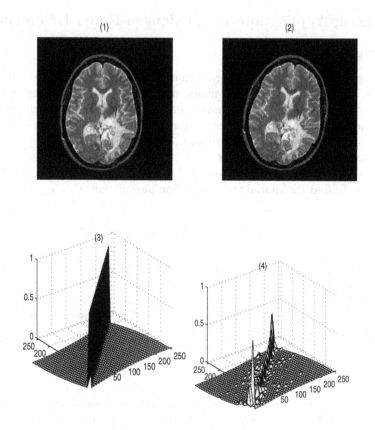

Fig. 4. Conditional probability distributions

demonstrated in Fig.   which demonstrates the registration results by mutual information and by the Jensen-Rényi divergence, in the presence of the noise. $SNR = 1.92dB$. For the Jensen-Rényi divergence, the parameters used are $\alpha = 1$ and $\omega_i = 1/n$. The following result establishes the optimality of the uniform weights for image registration in the context of the Jensen-Rényi divergence.

Proposition 6. *Let β be an n-dimensional uniform weight vector, and ω be any n-dimensional vector such that $\omega_i \geq 0$, $\sum_{i=1}^{n} \omega_i = 1$. If the misalignment between f_1 and f_2 can be modeled by a spatial transformation T^*, then the following inequality holds*

$$JR_\alpha^\beta(\boldsymbol{p}_1, \ldots, \boldsymbol{p}_n) \geq JR_\alpha^\omega(\boldsymbol{p}_1, \ldots, \boldsymbol{p}_n), \quad \forall \alpha \in [0, 1], \tag{10}$$

where $\boldsymbol{p}_i = \boldsymbol{p}_i(f_1, T^* f_2), i = 1, \ldots, n$.

Proof. When f_1 and f_2 are aligned by the spatial transformation T^*, then $\boldsymbol{p}_i = \boldsymbol{\Delta}_i$, and hence $JR_\alpha^\omega(\cdot)$ becomes

$$JR_\alpha^\omega(\boldsymbol{p}_1(f_1, T^* f_2), \ldots, \boldsymbol{p}_n(f_1, T^* f_2)) = R_\alpha(\boldsymbol{\omega}).$$

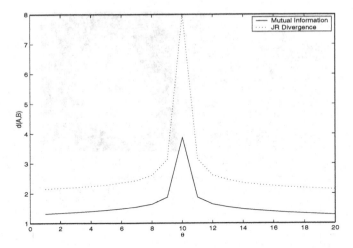

Fig. 5. Mutual information vs. Jensen-Rényi divergence of uniform weights

Since $\beta \prec \omega$ and $R_\alpha(\cdot)$ is Schur-concave, it follows that $R_\alpha(\beta) \geq R_\alpha(\omega)$. This completes the proof. $\square$

After assigning uniform weights to the various distributions in the Jensen-Rényi divergence, a free parameter α, which is directly related to the measurement sensitivity, remains to be selected. In the image registration problem, one desires a sharp and distinguishable peak at the matching point. The sharpness of the Jensen-Rényi divergence can be characterized by the maximal value as well as the width of the peak. The sharpest peak is clearly a Dirac function. The following proposition establishes that the maximal value of the Jensen-Rényi divergence is independent of α if the two images are aligned, and $\alpha = 0$ yields the sharpest peak, a Dirac function. The next result follows from Proposition 3.

Proposition 7. *Let β be a uniform weight vector. If the misalignment between f_1 and f_2 can be modeled by a spatial transformation T^*, then for all $\alpha \in [0, 1]$*

$$JR_\alpha^\beta(\boldsymbol{p}_1(f_1, T^*f_2), \dots, \boldsymbol{p}_n(f_1, T^*f_2)) = \log(n). \tag{11}$$

In particular for $\alpha = 0$, we have $JR_\alpha^\beta(\boldsymbol{p}_1, \dots, \boldsymbol{p}_n) = 0$, for any probability distribution $\boldsymbol{p}_i$. In addition, we have

$$JR_\alpha^\beta(\boldsymbol{p}_1, \dots, \boldsymbol{p}_n) = \log(n) \quad \textit{if and only if} \quad \boldsymbol{p}_i = \boldsymbol{\Delta}_i.$$

Fig. (1) demonstrates the registration results of the two brain images in Fig. with the choice of different α. In this case, $\alpha = 0$ is the best choice and would

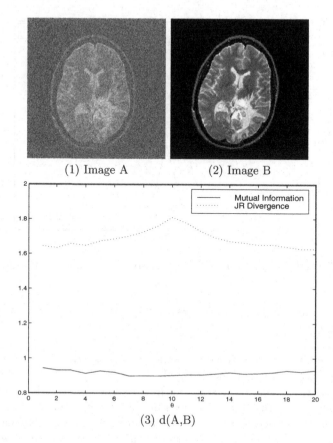

(1) Image A   (2) Image B

(3) d(A,B)

Fig. 6. Registration result in the presence of the noise. $SNR = 1.92dB$. For the Jensen-Rényi divergence, $\alpha = 1$ and $\omega_i = 1/n$ is used

generate a Dirac function with a peak at the matching point, as illustrated in Fig. (2).

If there exists local variation between f_1 and f_2, or, if the registration of the two images is in the presence of noise, then an exact alignment $\mathcal{T}^*$ may not be found. The conditional probability distribution $\boldsymbol{p}_i(f_1, \mathcal{T}^* f_2)$ is no longer a degenerate distribution in this case. The next result establishes that taking $\alpha = 1$ would provide a higher peak than any other choice of α for the non-ideal alignment.

Proposition 8. *Let* $\boldsymbol{p}_i = \boldsymbol{\Delta}_i + \delta\boldsymbol{p}_i$, $i = 1, 2, \ldots, n$, *where* $\delta\boldsymbol{p}_i = (\delta p_{ij})_{1 \leq j \leq n}$ *is a real distortion vector such that* $p_{ij} \geq 0$, $\sum_{j=1}^{n} \delta p_{ij} = 0$ *and* $\sum_{i=1}^{n} \delta p_{ij} = 0$. *Let* $\boldsymbol{\omega}$ *be a weight vector, then for all* $\alpha \in [0, 1]$, *we have*

$$JR_{\alpha=1}^{\omega}(\boldsymbol{p}_1, \boldsymbol{p}_2, \ldots, \boldsymbol{p}_n) \geq JR_{\alpha}^{\omega}(\boldsymbol{p}_1, \boldsymbol{p}_2, \ldots, \boldsymbol{p}_n). \tag{12}$$

Proof. Eq. (2) yields

$$\sum_{i=1}^{n} \omega_i H(\boldsymbol{p}_i) \leq \sum_{i=1}^{n} \omega_i R_\alpha(\boldsymbol{p}_i), \quad \forall \alpha \in (0,1). \tag{13}$$

Since $\sum_{j=1}^{n} \delta p_{ij} = 0$, $\sum_{i=1}^{n} \delta p_{ij} = 0$, and the Rényi entropy for $\alpha = 1$ is the Shannon entropy, the inequality ( ) is equivalent to the inequality ( ).   □

It is worth pointing out that the Jensen-Rényi divergence is not equivalent to mutual information by setting $\alpha = 1$. The equivalence holds only if $\alpha = 1$ and $\omega_i = P(X = x_i)$.

Discussion: The parameter α of the Jensen-Rényi divergence plays a role of scaling factor to adjust registration peaks, and the location of registration point is independent of α. In real world applications, there is a trade off between optimality and practicality in choosing α. If one can model the misalignment between f_1 and f_2 completely and accurately, $\alpha = 0$ would correspond to the best choice since it generates a Dirac function at the matching point. It is, however, also the least robust selection, as it tends to make all the $\boldsymbol{p}_i's$ the same as the uniform distribution, if $\boldsymbol{p}_i$ is not degenerate distribution and $p_{ij} > 0$, then the Jensen-Rényi divergence would be zero for the whole transformation parameter space as in case where the adapted transformation group can not accurately model the relationship between f_1 and f_2. On the other hand, $\alpha = 1$ is the most robust choice, in spite of also resulting in the least sharp peak. The choice of α therefore depends largely on the accuracy of the invoked model and on the specific application as well as the available computational resource. We further showed that $\omega_i = 1/n$ is optimal, thus the best choice for non-ideal image

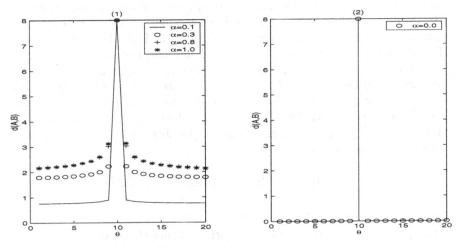

Fig. 7. Effect of the order α in image registration

registration in the context of the Jensen-Rényi divergence is $\{\alpha = 1, \omega = 1/n\}$, in comparison with mutual information based methods, in which the parameters are set to $\{\alpha = 1, \omega = P(X = x_i)\}$. Fig.   depicts the effect of the parameter α in image registration.

4.2   Image Segmentation

Edge detection is a fundamental problem in image processing. The use of the Jensen-Rényi divergence in image segmentation can be formulated as follows: an image sliding window W is split into two equal and adjacent subwindows W_1 and W_2. For each position of the sliding window, the histograms p_1 and p_2 of the subwindows W_1 and W_2 are computed, as well as the Jensen-Rényi divergence between p_1 and p_2. We repeat this procedure for several orientations of the sliding window to ensure detection in all directions, and we then select the maximum divergence at each pixel of a given image. Consequently, we construct a divergence mapping matrix where the largest values in linear neighborhoods are identified. These largest pixel values correspond to edge points. It is worth noting that the window W can be split into any finite number of equal and adjacent subwindows since the Jensen-Rényi divergence is defined between any number of probability distributions. In the simulations we consider without loss of generality the Jensen-Rényi divergence between the histograms of two equal and adjacent subwindows which form the entire sliding window. To illustrate the behavior of the Jensen-Rényi divergence, consider an image which consists of two regions A and B with respective histograms p_a and p_b, the former at the left and the latter at the right, with a vertical boundary between them as shown in Fig.   . The window W slides from left to right, so that it passes gradually from the region A to the region B. Under a hypothesis of statistical homogeneity, the histograms p_1 and p_2 are constant and equal when W is located in the same region, thus the Jensen-Rényi divergence between p_1 and p_2 vanishes. If the sliding window is located over an edge, one of the two subwindows will participate in the two regions. Without loss of generality, we consider a subwindow W_2. Again under the hypothesis of homogeneity, the parts of W_2 located in the regions A and B have partial histograms p_a and p_b, with weights proportional to the sizes of the subregions $A \cap W_2$ and $B \cap W_2$, respectively. More precisely, if $\lambda \in [0, 1]$ represents the fraction of W_2 included in the region B, then $p_2 = (1 - \lambda)p_a + \lambda p_b$, giving rise, consequently, to a histogram which varies with respect to the position of W. Since the subwindow W_1 is located in the region A, then $p_1 = p_a$ and therefore $p = (1 - \lambda/2)p_a + (\lambda/2)p_b$. The corresponding Jensen-Rényi divergence can then be expressed as a function of λ

$$JR_\alpha(\lambda) = R_\alpha(p) - \frac{R_\alpha((1 - \lambda)p_a + \lambda p_b) + R_\alpha(p_a)}{2},$$

where $p = (1 - \lambda/2)p_a + (\lambda/2)p_b$, and $\alpha \in (0, 1)$.

The performance of the proposed algorithm using the Jensen-Rényi divergence for various values of α is illustrated in Fig.   . We consider this application

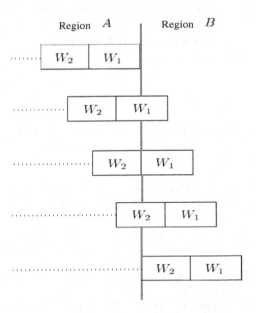

Fig. 8. Vertical Edge

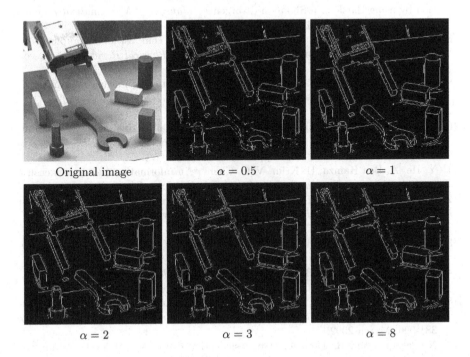

Fig. 9. Edge detection results using Jensen-Rényi divergence for various values of α

on image segmentation to be a preliminary investigation. An important issue for further research in this direction is development of robust edge linking algorithms to be included in conjunction with the image edge detection based on the Jensen-Rényi divergence measure.

References

[1] S. Ali and S. Silvey, "A general class of coefficients of divergence of one distribution from another," *J. Roy. Soc.*, vol. 28, pp. 131-142, 1966.

[2] S. Kullback and R. Liebler, "On information and sufficiency," *Ann. Math. Statist.*, vol. 22, pp. 79-86, 1951.

[3] R. Stoica, J. Zerubia, and J. M. Francos, "Image retrieval and indexing: A hierarchical approach in computing the distance between textured images" *IEEE Int. Conf. on Image Processing*, Chicago, 1998.

[4] A. O. Hero, B. Ma, O. Michel and J. Gorman, "Applications of entropic spanning graphs," *IEEE Signal Processing Magazine*, vol. 19, no. 5, pp. 85-95, Sept. 2002.

[5] A. Rényi, *On Measures of Entropy and Information*, Selected Papers of Alfréd Rényi, vol.2, pp. 525-580, 1961.   ,

[6] J. Lin, "Divergence Measures Based on the Shannon Entropy," *IEEE Trans. Information Theory*, vol. 37, no. 1, pp. 145-151, 1991.   ,

[7] J. F. Gomez, J. Martinez, A. M. Robles, and R. Roman, "An analysis of edge detection by using the Jensen-Shannon divergence," *Journal of Mathematical Imaging and Vision*, vol. 13, no. 1, pp. 35-56, Aug. 2000.

[8] R. Roman, P. Bernaola, and J. L. Oliver, "Sequence compositional complexity of DNA through an entropic segmentation method," *Physical Review Letters*, vol. 80, no. 6, pp. 1344-1347, Feb. 1998.

[9] P. Viola and W. M. Wells, "Alignment by maximization of mutual information," *International Journal of Computer Vision*, vol. 24, no. 2, pp. 173-154, 1997.   ,

[10] F. Maes, A. Collignon, D. Vandermeulen, G. Marchal, P. Suetens, "Multimodality image registration by maximization of mutual information," *IEEE Trans. on Medical Imaging*, vol. 16, no. 2, pp. 187-198, 1098.   ,

[11] Y. He, A. Ben Hamza, H. Krim, V. C. Chen, "An information theoretic measure for ISAR imagery focusing," *Proc. SPIE*, vol. 4116, San Diego, 2000.

[12] Y. He, A. Ben Hamza, H. Krim, "A generalized divergence measure for robust image registration," *IEEE Trans. Signal Processing*, vol. 51, no. 5, May 2003.   ,

[13] A. W. Marshall and I. Olkin, *Inequalities: Theory of Majorization and Its Applications*, Academic Press, 1979.   ,

[14] L. Devroye, L. Gyorfi, G. Lugosi, *A probabilistic theory of pattern recognition*, New York, Springer, 1996.

[15] M. A. Figueiredo and A. K. Jain, "Unsupervised learning of finite mixture models," *IEEE Trans. on pattern analysis and machine intelligence*, vol. 24, no. 3, pp. 381-396, March 2002.

[16] N. Paragios and R. Deriche, "Geodesic active contours and level sets for the detection and tracking of moving objects," *IEEE Trans. on pattern analysis and machine intelligence*, vol. 22, no. 3, pp. 266-280, March 2000.

[17] M. Hellman and J. Raviv, "Probability of error, equivocation, and the Chernoff bound," *IEEE Trans. Information Theory*, vol. 16, pp. 368-372, 1970.

[18] T. M. Cover and P. E. Hart, "Nearest neighbor pattern classification," *IEEE Trans. Inform. Theory*, vol. 13, pp. 21-27, January 1967.

[19] R. Katuri and R. C. Jain, *Computer Vision: Principles*, IEEE Comnputer Society Press, Los Alamitos, CA, 1991.

[20] J. R. Jensen, *Introductory digital image processing: a remote sensing perspective*, 2nd edition, Prentice Hall, Upper Saddle River, NJ, 1996.

[21] P. A. Van den Elsen, E. J. D. Pol, M. A. Viergever, "Medical image matching-a review with classification," *IEEE Engineering in Medicine and Biology Magazine*, vol. 12, no. 1, pp. 26-39, March 1993.

Asymptotic Characterization
of Log-Likelihood Maximization Based
Algorithms and Applications

Doron Blatt and Alfred Hero

Department of Electrical Engineering and Computer Science
University of Michigan, Ann Arbor, MI
dblatt@umich.edu, hero@eecs.umich.edu

Abstract. The asymptotic distribution of estimates that are based on a sub-optimal search for the maximum of the log-likelihood function is considered. In particular, estimation schemes that are based on a two-stage approach, in which an initial estimate is used as the starting point of a subsequent local maximization, are analyzed. We show that asymptotically the local estimates follow a Gaussian mixture distribution, where the mixture components correspond to the modes of the likelihood function. The analysis is relevant for cases where the log-likelihood function is known to have local maxima in addition to the global maximum, and there is no available method that is guaranteed to provide an estimate within the attraction region of the global maximum. Two applications of the analytic results are offered. The first application is an algorithm for finding the maximum likelihood estimator. The algorithm is best suited for scenarios in which the likelihood equations do not have a closed form solution, the iterative search is computationally cumbersome and highly dependent on the data length, and there is a risk of convergence to a local maximum. The second application is a scheme for aggregation of local estimates, e.g. generated by a network of sensors, at a fusion center. This scheme provides the means to intelligently combine estimates from remote sensors, where bandwidth constraints do not allow access to the complete set of data. The result on the asymptotic distribution is validated and the performance of the proposed algorithms is evaluated by computer simulations.

Keywords – Maximum likelihood, mixture models, clustering, sensor networks, data fusion.

1   Introduction

The maximum likelihood (ML) estimation method introduced by Fisher [ ] is one of the standard tools of statistics. Among its appealing properties are consistency and asymptotic efficiency [ ]. Furthermore, its asymptotic Gaussian distribution makes the asymptotic performance analysis tractable [ ]. However, one drawback of this method is the fact that the associated likelihood equations

A. Rangarajan et al. (Eds.): EMMCVPR 2003, LNCS 2683, pp. 164–   , 2003.
© Springer-Verlag Berlin Heidelberg 2003

required for the derivation of the estimator rarely have a closed form analytic solution. Therefore, suboptimal iterative maximization procedures are used. In many cases, the performance of these methods depends on the starting point. In particular, if the likelihood function of a specific statistical model does not have a known strictly convex property and there is no available method that is guaranteed to provide a starting point within the attraction region of the global maximum, then there is a risk of convergence to a local maximum, which leads to large-scale estimation errors.

The first part of this paper considers the asymptotic distribution of estimates that are based on a sub-optimal search for the ML estimate. In particular, estimators that are based on a two-stage approach, in which an initial estimate is used as the starting point of a subsequent iterative search that converges to a maximum point, are analyzed and shown to be asymptotically Gaussian mixture distributed. The results are linked to previous results by Huber [ ], White [ ], and Gan and Jiang [ ] as explained in detail below.

In the second part of the paper, two applications of the analytical results are presented. The first is an algorithm for finding the ML estimate. The algorithm is best suited for scenarios in which the likelihood equations do not have a closed form solution, the iterative search is computationally cumbersome and highly dependent on the data length, and there is a risk of convergence to a local maximum. The algorithm is performed in two stages. In the first stage, the data are divided into sub-blocks in order to reduce the computational burden, and local estimates are computed from each block. The second stage involves clustering of these local estimates using a finite Gaussian mixture model, which is a classic problem in statistical pattern recognition (e.g. [ ], [ ], and references therein.) The second application arises in distributed sensor networks. In particular, consider a case where a large number of sensors are distributed in order to perform an estimation task. Due to power and bandwidth constraints the sensors do not transmit the complete data but rather only a suboptimal estimate. As will be shown, the analytical results provide the means for combining these sub-optimal estimates into a final estimate.

2   Problem Formulation

The independent random vectors $\mathbf{y}_n$, $n = 1, \ldots, N$ have a common probability density function (p.d.f.) $f(\mathbf{y}; \boldsymbol{\theta})$, which is known up to a vector of parameters $\boldsymbol{\theta} = [\theta_1 \theta_2 \ldots \theta_K]^T \in \boldsymbol{\Theta}$. The unknown true parameter vector will be denoted by $\boldsymbol{\theta}^0$. The log-likelihood of the measurements under $f(\mathbf{y}; \boldsymbol{\theta})$ is

$$L_N(\mathbf{Y}; \boldsymbol{\theta}) = \sum_{n=1}^{N} \ln f(\mathbf{y}_n; \boldsymbol{\theta}) \ , \tag{1}$$

where $\mathbf{Y} = [\mathbf{y}_1 \, \mathbf{y}_2 \, \ldots \, \mathbf{y}_N]$. The ML estimator (MLE) for $\boldsymbol{\theta}$, which will be denoted by $\widehat{\boldsymbol{\theta}}_N$ is

$$\widehat{\boldsymbol{\theta}}_N = \arg \max_{\boldsymbol{\theta}} L_N(\mathbf{Y}; \boldsymbol{\theta}) \ . \tag{2}$$

In many cases, the above maximization problem does not have an analytical solution, and a sub-optimal maximization technique is used. One possible method
could be the following. First, a sub-optimal algorithm generates a rough estimate
for $\boldsymbol{\theta}$. Then, this rough estimate is used as the starting point of an iterative algorithm, which searches for the maximum of the log-likelihood function. Among
those are the standard maximum search algorithms, such as the steepest ascent
method, Newton's algorithm, the Nelder-Mead method, and the statistically derived expectation maximization algorithm [ ] and its variations. This class of
methods will be referred to as two-stage methods, and the resulting estimator
will be denoted by $\tilde{\boldsymbol{\theta}}_N$. If the starting point of the search algorithm is within
the attraction region of the global maximum (with respect to the specific search-
ing technique), then this approach leads to the MLE. However, if the likelihood
function has more than one maximum and if the staring point is not within the
attraction region of the global maximum, then the algorithm will converge to
a local maximum resulting in a large-scale estimation error. In the next section,
the asymptotic p.d.f. of $\tilde{\boldsymbol{\theta}}_N$ is derived. The derivation is performed using conditional distributions, where the conditioning is on the location of the initial
estimator in $\boldsymbol{\Theta}$.

3   Asymptotic Analysis

The maximization of $L_N(\mathbf{Y}; \boldsymbol{\theta})$ is identical to the maximization of $\frac{1}{N} L_N(\mathbf{Y}; \boldsymbol{\theta})$,
which, due to the law of large numbers, converges almost surely (a.s.) to the
ambiguity function

$$\frac{1}{N} \sum_{n=1}^{N} \ln f(\mathbf{y}_n; \boldsymbol{\theta}) \to \mathrm{E}_{\boldsymbol{\theta}^0} \left\{ \ln f(\mathbf{y}; \boldsymbol{\theta}) \right\} \quad \text{a.s.}$$

$$= \int_{\mathcal{y}} \ln \left(f(\mathbf{y}; \boldsymbol{\theta}) \right) f(\mathbf{y}; \boldsymbol{\theta}^0) d\mathbf{y} \overset{\triangle}{=} g(\boldsymbol{\theta}^0, \boldsymbol{\theta}) , \tag{3}$$

where $\mathrm{E}_{\boldsymbol{\theta}^0} \{\cdot\}$ denotes the statistical expectation with respect to the true pa-
rameter $\boldsymbol{\theta}^0$, and $\mathrm{E}_{\boldsymbol{\theta}^0} \{\ln f(\mathbf{y}; \boldsymbol{\theta})\}$ is assumed to be finite for all $\boldsymbol{\theta} \in \boldsymbol{\Theta}$. Therefore,
asymptotically, the two-stage method will result in an estimate which is in the
vicinity of one of the local maxima of the ambiguity function. The ambiguity
function has its global maximum at the true parameter $\boldsymbol{\theta}^0$ [ ], and it is assumed
to have a number of local maxima in $\boldsymbol{\Theta}$ at points which will be denoted by
$\boldsymbol{\theta}^m$, $m = 1, \ldots, M$. All the local maxima satisfy

$$\left. \frac{\partial g(\boldsymbol{\theta}^0, \boldsymbol{\theta})}{\partial \theta_k} \right|_{\boldsymbol{\theta} = \boldsymbol{\theta}^m} = 0, \quad m = 0, \ldots, M, \quad k = 0, \ldots, K , \tag{4}$$

by definition, and we assume that

$$\frac{\partial \mathrm{E}_{\boldsymbol{\theta}^0} \{\ln f(\mathbf{y}; \boldsymbol{\theta})\}}{\partial \boldsymbol{\theta}} = \mathrm{E}_{\boldsymbol{\theta}^0} \left\{ \frac{\partial \ln f(\mathbf{y}; \boldsymbol{\theta})}{\partial \boldsymbol{\theta}} \right\} \tag{5}$$

for all $\boldsymbol{\theta} \in \boldsymbol{\Theta}$.

The computation of the asymptotic p.d.f. is done using conditional probability density functions. The conditioning is on the event that the initial estimate is within the attraction region of the m'th maxima, which will be denoted by Θ^m, i.e.

$$f(\widetilde{\boldsymbol{\theta}}_N) = \sum_{m=0}^{M} f(\widetilde{\boldsymbol{\theta}}_N|\boldsymbol{\Theta}^m)\mathbb{P}(\boldsymbol{\Theta}^m) \ , \tag{6}$$

where $f(\widetilde{\boldsymbol{\theta}}_N)$ is the distribution of $\widetilde{\boldsymbol{\theta}}_N$, $f(\widetilde{\boldsymbol{\theta}}_N|\boldsymbol{\Theta}^m)$ is the distribution of $\widetilde{\boldsymbol{\theta}}_N$ given that the initial estimate was in $\boldsymbol{\Theta}^m$, and $\mathbb{P}(\boldsymbol{\Theta}^m)$ is the probability that the initial estimate was in $\boldsymbol{\Theta}^m$. The prior probabilities $\mathbb{P}(\boldsymbol{\Theta}^m)$ are assumed to be known in advance and can be found by empirical analysis of the initial estimator. These probabilities do not play a key role in the derivation or the applications discussed in the sequel. Here we implicitly assume that the entire space $\boldsymbol{\Theta}$ can be divided into disjoint subsets $\boldsymbol{\Theta}^m$, each of which is the attraction region of one of the maxima of $g(\boldsymbol{\theta}^0, \boldsymbol{\theta})$, and that $\bigcup_{m=0}^{M} \boldsymbol{\Theta}^m = \boldsymbol{\Theta}$. ~

For large N, given that the initial estimate is in $\boldsymbol{\Theta}^m$, $\widetilde{\boldsymbol{\theta}}_N$ is assumed to be in the close vicinity of $\boldsymbol{\theta}^m$, and the asymptotic conditional p.d.f. can be found using an analysis similar to that presented in [ ] for the standard MLE and similar to Huber's derivation of the asymptotic p.d.f. of M-estimators [ ]. The regularity conditions on $L_N(\mathbf{Y}; \boldsymbol{\theta})$, which are needed for the derivation, are summarized in [ ], and will be recalled during the derivation. One major difference of the present derivation from these other methods is that the Taylor expansion is performed around $\boldsymbol{\theta}^m$, which is not necessarily the true parameter, nor is it the global maximum (or minimum) of the target function. In order to give a self-contained treatment, we give the complete derivation for the case of a scalar parameter. For the case of a vector of parameters, we only state the final result.

3.1   Scalar Parameter Case

From the mean value theorem we have

$$\left.\frac{\partial L_N(\mathbf{Y}; \theta)}{\partial \theta}\right|_{\theta=\widetilde{\theta}_N} = \left.\frac{\partial L_N(\mathbf{Y}; \theta)}{\partial \theta}\right|_{\theta=\theta^m} + \left.\frac{\partial^2 L_N(\mathbf{Y}; \theta)}{\partial^2 \theta}\right|_{\theta=\bar{\theta}} (\widetilde{\theta}_N - \theta^m) \ , \tag{7}$$

where $\theta^m < \bar{\theta} < \widetilde{\theta}_N$, assuming that the derivatives exist and are finite. Since $\widetilde{\theta}_N$ is a local maximum of the log-likelihood function, we have

$$\left.\frac{\partial L_N(\mathbf{Y}; \theta)}{\partial \theta}\right|_{\theta=\widetilde{\theta}_N} = 0 \ . \tag{8}$$

Therefore,

$$\sqrt{N}(\widetilde{\theta}_N - \theta^m) = \frac{\frac{1}{\sqrt{N}}\left.\frac{\partial L_N(\mathbf{Y};\theta)}{\partial \theta}\right|_{\theta=\theta^m}}{-\frac{1}{N}\left.\frac{\partial^2 L_N(\mathbf{Y};\theta)}{\partial^2 \theta}\right|_{\theta=\bar{\theta}}} \ . \tag{9}$$

---

[1] The dependency on the true parameter $\boldsymbol{\theta}^0$ has been omitted in order to simplify the notation.

Next, $\frac{\partial^2 L_N(\mathbf{Y};\theta)}{\partial^2 \theta}$ in the denominator is written explicitly

$$\frac{1}{N} \left.\frac{\partial^2 L_N(\mathbf{Y};\theta)}{\partial^2 \theta}\right|_{\theta=\bar{\theta}} = \frac{1}{N} \sum_{n=1}^{N} \left.\frac{\partial^2 \log f(\mathbf{y}_n;\theta)}{\partial\theta^2}\right|_{\theta=\bar{\theta}} . \tag{10}$$

Since $\theta^m < \bar{\theta} < \widetilde{\theta}_N$ and $\widetilde{\theta}_N \to \theta^m$ as $N \to \infty$ a.s., we must have $\bar{\theta} \to \theta^m$ as $N \to \infty$ a.s.. Hence

$$\frac{1}{N} \left.\frac{\partial^2 L_N(\mathbf{Y};\theta)}{\partial^2 \theta}\right|_{\theta=\bar{\theta}} \to \mathrm{E}_{\boldsymbol{\theta}^0}\left\{ \left.\frac{\partial^2 \log f(\mathbf{y}_n;\theta)}{\partial\theta^2}\right|_{\theta=\theta^m}\right\} \quad \text{a.s.}$$
$$\overset{\triangle}{=} A(\theta^m) , \tag{11}$$

due to the law of large numbers, where $\mathrm{E}_{\boldsymbol{\theta}^0}\left\{ \left.\frac{\partial^2 \log f(\mathbf{y}_n;\theta)}{\partial\theta^2}\right|_{\theta=\theta^m}\right\}$ is assumed to be finite. In order to evaluate the numerator of ( ), the following random variables are defined

$$x_n = \left.\frac{\partial \ln f(\mathbf{y}_n;\theta)}{\partial\theta}\right|_{\theta=\theta^m} \quad n = 1,\ldots,N . \tag{12}$$

Since the $\mathbf{y}_n$'s are independent and identically distributed, so are the x_n's. Therefore, by the Central Limit Theorem, the p.d.f. of the numerator of ( ) will converge to a Gaussian p.d.f. with mean

$$\mathrm{E}_{\boldsymbol{\theta}^0}\left\{ \frac{1}{\sqrt{N}} \sum_{n=1}^{N} \left.\frac{\partial \log f(\mathbf{y}_n;\theta)}{\partial\theta}\right|_{\theta=\theta^m}\right\} = 0 \tag{13}$$

and variance

$$\mathrm{E}_{\boldsymbol{\theta}^0}\left\{ \left(\frac{1}{\sqrt{N}} \sum_{n=1}^{N} \left.\frac{\partial \log f(\mathbf{y}_n;\theta)}{\partial\theta}\right|_{\theta=\theta^m}\right)^2\right\} = \mathrm{E}_{\boldsymbol{\theta}^0}\left\{ \left(\left.\frac{\partial \log f(\mathbf{y}_n;\theta)}{\partial\theta}\right|_{\theta=\theta^m}\right)^2\right\}$$
$$\overset{\triangle}{=} B(\theta^m) , \tag{14}$$

where we assume that $B(\theta^m)$ is finite. Next, Slutsky's theorem [ ] is invoked. The theorem says that if x_n converges in distribution to x and z_n converges in probability to a constant c than x_n/z_n converges in distribution to x/c. Therefore, we arrive at the following result

$$\sqrt{N}(\widetilde{\theta}_N - \theta^m) \overset{a}{\sim} N\left(0, \frac{B(\theta^m)}{A^2(\theta^m)}\right) \tag{15}$$

or, equivalently,

$$\widetilde{\theta}_N \overset{a}{\sim} N\left(\theta^m, \frac{B(\theta^m)}{NA^2(\theta^m)}\right) , \tag{16}$$

where $\overset{a}{\sim}$ denotes convergence in distribution. In the case where θ^m is the true parameter θ^0, we obtain the standard asymptotic Gaussian distribution of the MLE

$$\widetilde{\theta}_N \overset{a}{\sim} N\left(\theta^0, I^{-1}(\theta^0)\right) , \tag{17}$$

where $I(\theta^0) = NA(\theta^0)$ is the Fisher Information (FI) of the measurements. However, it should be noted that in the general case $A(\theta^m) \neq -B(\theta^m)$.

In summary, the conditional p.d.f. $f(\hat{\theta}_N|\Theta^m)$ is asymptotically Gaussian with mean θ^m and variance $\frac{B(\theta^m)}{NA^2(\theta^m)}$, which equals $I^{-1}(\theta^0)$ only in the case where $m = 0$. Using this result, we can state that the asymptotic distribution of $\tilde{\theta}_N$ in ( ) is a Gaussian mixture with weights $\mathbb{P}(\Theta^m)$, $m = 0, \ldots, M$, which depend on the p.d.f. of the initial estimator.

3.2 Generalization to a Vector of Parameters

In the case of a vector of parameters, the conditional p.d.f. $f(\tilde{\theta}_N|\Theta^m)$ is asymptotically multivariate Gaussian with vector mean θ^m and covariance matrix

$$\mathbf{C}_m \triangleq \mathrm{Cov}_{\theta^0}(\tilde{\theta}_N) = \frac{1}{N}\mathbf{A}^{-1}(\theta^m)\mathbf{B}(\theta^m)\mathbf{A}^{-1}(\theta^m) \ , \tag{18}$$

which equals $\frac{1}{N}\mathbf{I}^{-1}(\theta^0)$ - the Fisher Information Matrix (FIM) - in the case where $m = 0$, i.e. θ^m is the global maximum. The kl elements of the matrices $\mathbf{A}(\theta)$ and $\mathbf{B}(\theta)$ are given by

$$\{\mathbf{A}(\theta)\}_{kl} = \mathrm{E}_{\theta^0}\left\{ \frac{\partial^2 \log f(\mathbf{y}_n;\theta)}{\partial\theta_k\partial\theta_l} \right\} \ , \tag{19}$$

and

$$\{\mathbf{B}(\theta)\}_{kl} = \mathrm{E}_{\theta^0}\left\{ \frac{\partial \log f(\mathbf{y}_n;\theta)}{\partial\theta_k} \frac{\partial \log f(\mathbf{y}_n;\theta)}{\partial\theta_l} \right\} \ . \tag{20}$$

Therefore the asymptotic p.d.f. of $\tilde{\theta}_N$ is a multivariate Gaussian mixture.

The result ( ) on the asymptotic conditional p.d.f. coincides with results reported in [ ] in the context of misspecified models. Indeed, under the assumption $\tilde{\theta}_N \in \Theta^m$, $m \neq 0$, the estimation problem can be viewed as a misspecified model. The family of distributions is correct but the domain of θ does not contain the true parameter. In addition, the conditional p.d.f. $f(\tilde{\theta}_N|\Theta^m)$ can be found from Huber's work on M-estimators [ ] by taking the target function that is minimized to be the negation of the log-likelihood function restricted to the attraction region of the specific local maximum.

The covariance ( ) being equal to the inverse FIM is a necessary but not sufficient condition for θ^m to be the global maximum. In particular, it is possible to construct a special parametric model in which $\mathbf{A}(\theta^m)$ equals $-\mathbf{B}(\theta^m)$ for θ^m which is not the global maximum [ ].

The following proposition summarizes the result presented in this section.

Proposition 1. *Under the assumptions made above, an estimator $\tilde{\theta}_N$ asymptotically follows a Gaussian mixture distribution with mean vectors θ^m and covariance matrices $\mathbf{C}_m$ specified in ( ), i.e.*

$$f_{\tilde{\theta}_N}(\mathbf{t};\theta^0) \rightarrow \sum_{m=0}^{M} \frac{\mathbb{P}(\Theta^m)}{(2\pi)^{K/2}\sqrt{|\mathbf{C}_m|}} \exp\left\{ -\frac{1}{2}(\mathbf{t} - \theta^m)^T\mathbf{C}_m^{-1}(\mathbf{t} - \theta^m) \right\}$$

$$\text{as } N \rightarrow \infty, \quad \forall \mathbf{t} \in \Theta \ .$$

4   Applications

4.1   An Algorithm for Finding the MLE Based on the Asymptotic Distribution Result

In the present section, we propose an algorithm for finding the MLE that exploits the asymptotic results of the last section. As mentioned above, the algorithm was designed for scenarios in which the likelihood equations do not have a closed form solution, and, therefore, one must rely on iterative search over Θ to find the MLE. If, in addition, the iterative search becomes computationally cumbersome for large data length, it might be impossible to perform the search algorithm on the log-likelihood function of the entire data set. In such cases, one can divide the complete data set into sub-blocks and find an estimator for each sub-block. These estimators will be referred to as sub-estimators. If the ambiguity function has one global maximum, then the average of the sub-estimators will closely approximate the MLE. However, if the ambiguity function has local maxima in addition to the global maximum, then some of the sub-estimators might converge to those local maxima and contribute large errors to the sub-estimators' average. A possible solution to this problem could be to cluster the sub-estimators and to choose the cluster whose members have the largest average log-likelihood value. However, if the dimension of the parameter vector is large and the local maxima of the ambiguity function are close to each other in Θ, the clustering problem becomes numerically intractable as well. Furthermore, as will be shown later, two remote local maxima might have nearly identical log-likelihood values. In such a case, the hight of the likelihood is not reliable for discriminating local from global maxima.

Therefore, we resort to a solution that circumvents the clustering requirement. To this end, we first employ the component-wise EM for mixtures (CEM) algorithm proposed by Figueiredo and Jain in [ ]. Recall that according to the asymptotic result presented in the previous section, if the length of each data sub-block is large enough, the sub-estimators are random variables drawn from a Gaussian mixture distribution with means equal to the locations of the local maxima of the ambiguity function and covariance matrices as specified by ( ). Therefore, the CEM can be used to estimate these mean and covariance parameters. The estimated means serve as candidates for the final estimate, and the estimated covariance matrices provide the means for discerning the global maximum using the procedure described below.

As can be seen from the derivation in Sec. , at the global maximum the covariance matrix of the estimates equals the inverse of the FIM. Therefore, in order to decide which local maxima are close to the global maximum, we can compare the estimated covariance matrices to the inverse of the FIM computed by an analytical or a numerical calculation, and choose the one having the best fit to this inverse FIM.

In order to explicitly state the algorithm, recall the statistical setting of our problem. The independent random vectors $\mathbf{y}_n$, $n = 1, \ldots, N$ have a common p.d.f. $f(\mathbf{y}; \boldsymbol{\theta})$, which is known up to the parameter vector $\boldsymbol{\theta}$ that is to be estimated. The algorithm is as follows:

1. Divide the entire data set into L sub-blocks of length N_s.
2. Find an estimator, which is a maximum of the log-likelihood of each of the sub-blocks, $\widehat{\boldsymbol{\theta}}^l_{N_s}; l = 1, \ldots, L$, by some local optimization algorithm .
3. Run the CEM algorithm on $\widehat{\boldsymbol{\theta}}^l_{N_s}; l = 1, \ldots, L$ to find the estimated means and covariance matrices of the Gaussian mixture model.
4. Compute either analytically or numerically the inverse of the FIM at each of the estimated means of the Gaussian mixture.
5. Choose the final estimate $\widehat{\boldsymbol{\theta}}_{final}$ to be the mean of the cluster that has the best fit between its estimated covariance and the inverse of the FIM evaluated at its mean (in the Forbenius norm sense, for example).

As for choosing the length N_s of the data sub-block, we will see in the simulations described below that the choice of N_s in the range of $\sqrt{N}$ gives the best results. Furthermore, since the covariance matrices of the clusters are known to be close to the inverse of the FIM, we use the FIM to initialize the CEM algorithm. Next, we present simulation results that validate the asymptotic p.d.f. stated in Prop. and present a study of the performance of the proposed estimator.

4.2   Estimating Cauchy Parameters on a Non-linear Manifold

Consider the following estimation problem, which is related to the estimation of a parameter, e.g. an image or a shape, embedded in a non-linear smooth manifold. The data are independent random vectors $\mathbf{y}_1, \mathbf{y}_2, \ldots, \mathbf{y}_N$ each of which is composed of three independent Cauchy random variables, with parameter $\alpha = 1$ and mode (median)

$$\boldsymbol{\mu}(\theta) = \begin{bmatrix} \mu_1(\theta) \\ \mu_2(\theta) \\ \mu_3(\theta) \end{bmatrix} = \begin{bmatrix} \theta \\ \theta \sin(\theta) \\ \theta \cos(\theta) \end{bmatrix}, \tag{21}$$

i.e.,

$$f(y_i; \theta) = \frac{1/\pi}{1 + (y_i - \mu_i(\theta))^2}, \quad i = 1, 2, 3 . \tag{22}$$

These data can be considered as noisy measurements in $\mathbb{R}^3$ of the mode of the Cauchy density, which is constrained to lie on the manifold (a spiral) defined by ( ). Since there exists no finite dimensional sufficient statistic for the mode of the Cauchy density, the complexity of the estimation problem increases in the number of samples. The ambiguity function associated with this estimation problem is depicted in Fig.   for different values of the true parameter θ^0, and a cross section is presented in Fig.   for $\theta^0 = 5$ - the value used in our simulations. Numerical calculations showed that the ambiguity function has two

---

[2] We assume that $\mathbb{P}(\boldsymbol{\Theta}^0) > 0$.

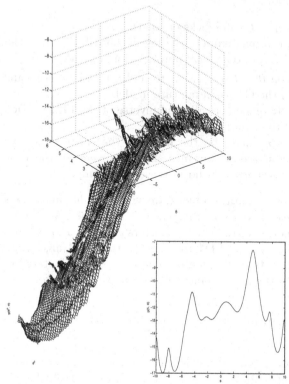

(a) The ambiguity function for differ- (b) Cross section of the ambiguity
ent values of θ^0.   function at $\theta^0 = 5$.

Fig. 1. Multi-modal ambiguity function

maxima in this region. One is the true parameter $\theta^0 = 5$ and another local
maximum at $\theta^1 = 0.82$. Further analysis revealed that the regions of attraction
associated with these modes are the open intervals $\Theta^0 = (2.56, 6)$ and $\Theta^1 =
(0, 2.56)$, respectively. In addition, the analytical result ( ) predicts that in
cases where the search algorithm converges to θ^0, the estimate will be Gaussian
with mean θ^0 and variance $\frac{B(\theta^0)}{NA^2(\theta^0)} = \frac{1}{NA(\theta^0)} = \frac{0.074}{N}$, and in cases where the
search algorithm converges to θ^1, the estimate will be Gaussian with mean θ^1 and
variance $\frac{B(\theta^1)}{NA^2(\theta^1)} = \frac{0.31}{N}$. Since the initial estimate is uniformly distributed, it is
easily found that $\mathbb{P}(\Theta^0) = 0.57$ and $\mathbb{P}(\Theta^1) = 0.43$. In practice, these values are
estimated by the CEM algorithm, even though they play no role in determining
the final estimate.

In our simulations, $N = 200$ and the local optimization algorithm is Matlab's
routine 'fminsearch', which implements the Nelder-Mead algorithm on the log-
likelihood function. The starting point for the algorithm is chosen randomly
in the interval $[0, 6]$. 1000 Monte Carlo trials showed good agreement with the
analytical predictions ( ). In order to verify the Gaussian mixture distribution
of the estimates, they were divided into two groups, one contained the estimates
that were around θ^0 and the second contained the estimates around θ^1. Then,
the two groups were centralized according to the predicted mean, divided by
the predicted standard deviation, and compared against the standard Gaussian
distribution. The resulting Q-Q plots are depicted in Figs.   and   .

Next, the performance of this algorithm was examined. The entire data record
was divided into sub-blocks for several choices of block lengths. The CEM was
used to find the estimated number of clusters, their means, and variances. The
variance of each cluster was compared to the inverse of the Fisher information

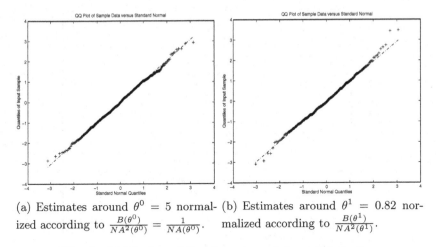

(a) Estimates around $\theta^0 = 5$ normalized according to $\frac{B(\theta^0)}{NA^2(\theta^0)} = \frac{1}{NA(\theta^0)}$.

(b) Estimates around $\theta^1 = 0.82$ normalized according to $\frac{B(\theta^1)}{NA^2(\theta^1)}$.

Fig. 2. Validation of the Gaussian mixture distribution

at the mean of each cluster. The Fisher information for this statistical problem can be found analytically to be $I(\theta) = \frac{2+\theta^2}{2\alpha^2}$. The final estimate was the mean of the cluster that its variance was closer to the inverse of $I(\theta)$ evaluated at the mean.

The probability of deciding on the wrong maximum, which will be referred to as the probability of large error, and the small error performance in cases where the decision was correct were estimated using 500 Monte Carlo trials. As expected, the small error performance improved as the number of samples in each sub-block increases. However, the probability of a large scale error has a minimum point with respect to the sub-block length as seen in Fig. . Thus, there is an optimum sub-block length for minimizing the influence of large errors. An intuitive explanation of this phenomenon is the following. When the sub-block size is too large, the Gaussian mixture approximation is good but the number of samples available for the CEM estimation is small, resulting in poor covariance estimation which leads to estimation errors. On the other hand, when the number of sub-blocks is large the amount of data available to the CEM algorithm is large. However, since the number of samples at each sub-block is small, the data are far from being distributed as a Gaussian mixture, and the variance of the estimator around the true parameter no longer equals the inverse of the Fisher information, which again results in estimation errors.

4.3   Aggregation of Estimates from Remote Sensors

The present section, addresses a scenario in which the division of the entire data sample into sub-blocks is imposed by the system design. Consider the following distributed processing problem. A large number of low power sensors are geographically distributed in order to perform an estimation task. Each of

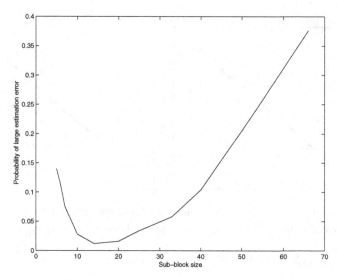

Fig. 3. Influence of sub-block length on the probability of large error. Note that the optimal block length is $\sqrt{N}$, where here $N = 200$

these sensors collects data generated independently by a common parametric model $f(\mathbf{y}; \boldsymbol{\theta})$, which has a multi-modal ambiguity function. Due to power and bandwidth constraints, the sensors do not transmit the complete data to the central processing unit, but rather each performs a suboptimal local search on the log-likelihood function and transmits only its local estimate. The question then arises as to how to treat the large number of estimates, some of which may correspond to successful convergence to the global maximum and some to erroneous local maxima.

Again, the analytical result stated in Prop.   provides the means to find a global estimate through a well-posed Gaussian mixture problem. The data available for the central processing unit are the local estimates delivered by the individual sensors. The theory in Sec.   asserts that these are drawn from a Gaussian Mixture model. Furthermore, the cluster corresponding to estimates which are close to the global maximum has the property that its covariance matrix is close to the inverse of the FIM evaluated at mean of this cluster of estimates. As in the previous application, this property will be used to find the final estimate.

Simulation Results. We generate 2D sensors data from the following Gaussian mixture density

$$f(\mathbf{y}; \boldsymbol{\theta}) = \sum_{j=1}^{2} \alpha_j f(\mathbf{y}; \boldsymbol{\mu}_j) \ , \tag{23}$$

where $f(\mathbf{y}; \boldsymbol{\mu}_j)$ is the bivariate Gaussian density

$$f(\mathbf{y}; \boldsymbol{\mu}_j) = \frac{1}{2\pi\sqrt{|\mathbf{C}_j|}} \exp\left\{-\frac{1}{2}(\mathbf{y} - \boldsymbol{\mu}_j)^T \mathbf{C}_j^{-1}(\mathbf{y} - \boldsymbol{\mu}_j)\right\} , \qquad (24)$$

and where $\mathbf{y} = [y_1\ y_2]^T$. Note that the Gaussian mixture model of the new data ( ) has nothing to do with the Gaussian mixture model which is an asymptotic distribution for the local estimates $\widehat{\boldsymbol{\theta}}_N^l$; $l = 1, \dots, L$. The parameters vector $\boldsymbol{\theta}$ contains the two vector means $\boldsymbol{\mu}_j = [\mu_{j1}\ \mu_{j2}]^T$; $j = 1, 2$ in the following order

$$\boldsymbol{\theta} = \begin{bmatrix} \mu_{11} \\ \mu_{12} \\ \mu_{21} \\ \mu_{22} \end{bmatrix}. \qquad (25)$$

The entries of the covariance matrices $\mathbf{C}_j$; $j = 1, 2$ associated with each of the components and the mixing probabilities α_1 and α_2 are assumed known. This is a simple model corresponding to a network of L 2D position estimating sensors.

Each sensor estimates $\boldsymbol{\theta}$ from $N = 50$ samples. The true values for the location parameters to be estimated were chosen to be

$$\boldsymbol{\theta}^0 = \begin{bmatrix} 1 \\ 2 \\ 2 \\ 1 \end{bmatrix}. \qquad (26)$$

The remaining known parameters were chosen to be

$$\mathbf{C}_1 = \mathbf{C}_2 = \begin{bmatrix} 0.2 & 0 \\ 0 & 0.2 \end{bmatrix} \qquad (27)$$

and

$$\alpha_1 = 0.4; \qquad \alpha_2 = 0.6 . \qquad (28)$$

The vector means are known a-priori to lie in the rectangle $\boldsymbol{\Theta} = \{[0, 3] \times [0, 3]\}$. Typical sensor data, generated according to the above model ( ) are presented in Fig. . The two circles correspond to the two components.

Each sensor uses the following algorithm to find an estimate. A point is generated randomly, according to a uniform distribution on the given rectangle $\boldsymbol{\Theta}$. Then this point is used as the starting point of a local search for a maximum of the log-likelihood function of the measurement. In our simulation, we used the Matlab routine 'fminsearch' which applies the Nelder-Mead algorithm to maximize the local log-likelihood function $L_N(\mathbf{Y}; \boldsymbol{\theta})$ with respect to the unknown parameters $\boldsymbol{\theta}$. Denote the estimate from the l'th sensor by $\widehat{\boldsymbol{\theta}}_N^l$.

We have found that the ambiguity function has two maxima in $\boldsymbol{\Theta}$. One maximum is at the true parameters vector $\boldsymbol{\theta}^0$ and the second maximum

$$\boldsymbol{\theta}^1 = \begin{bmatrix} 2.05 \\ 0.95 \\ 1.08 \\ 1.92 \end{bmatrix} \qquad (29)$$

corresponds to the reversed model, i.e., switching between the two components. Therefore, the estimates $\widehat{\boldsymbol{\theta}}_N^l$; $l = 1, \ldots, L$ available at the processing unit can be seen as samples drawn from a two component multi-variate (4-dimensional) Gaussian mixture, where the vector means of the two components are the locations of the two maxima of the ambiguity function in the parameters space and the covariance matrices are as presented in ( ). The 4-dimensional estimates generated by $L = 200$ sensors are presented in the Figs.   and   . Each sub-figure corresponds to two parameters. In each figure, the circled cluster correspond to estimates that are close to the global maximum and the second cluster corresponds to estimates that are close to the local maximum.

An intuitive approach for clustering the two groups of estimates could be to use the actual values of the log-likelihood at the point of convergence, which could be transmitted in addition to the estimates to the central processing unit. However, since the mixing probabilities $\{\alpha_1, \alpha_2\}$ are close to $\{1/2, 1/2\}$, the two components are similar and the value of the log-likelihood function at the global and local maxima are nearly identical. This phenomenon renders impossible the discrimination between 'good' estimates (global maximum) and erroneous ones (local maximum), using only the log-likelihood function values. In Fig.   a histogram of the negative log-likelihood function values $\ln f(\mathbf{Y}; \widehat{\boldsymbol{\theta}}_N^l)$; $l = 1, \ldots, L$ from one simulation is presented. It is not clear from this histogram that there are two separable components.

In contrast, we can reliably discriminate between the two local maxima based on the curvature of the parametric model at each local maxima. As was shown in Sec.   , the covariance matrices of the two components of estimates are directly related to the curvature of the ambiguity function at the two maxima, and at

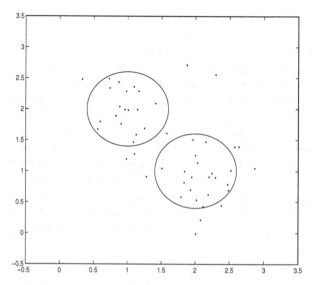

Fig. 4. Measured data for a single sensor

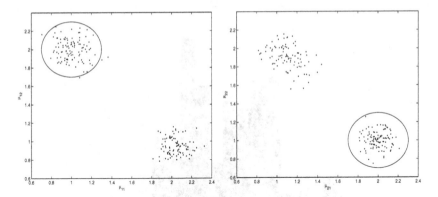

Fig. 5. Estimates $\widehat{\theta}_N^l$; $l = 1, \ldots, L$ generated by $L = 200$ sensors

the global maximum equal the inverse of the FIM. Therefore, the algorithm proposed in Sec. can be applied.

First the number of components, the mean vectors and the covariance matrices, of the estimates are estimated using the CEM algorithm. The estimated mean vectors serve as candidates for the final estimate and the estimated covariance matrices provides the means to find the component that corresponds to the global maximum. More explicitly, for each component the distance between the estimated covariance and the inverse of the FIM calculated at the point of the mean is computed. In our simulation, the Frobenius norm of the difference matrix was used as the distance measure. Finally, the mean of the component with the smallest norm is chosen as the final estimate. Since the 4×4 dimensional FIM cannot be computed analytically, it is computed by numerical integration and then inverted. The kl entry of the FIM is found by numerically calculating the following integral

$$\mathrm{FIM}_{kl} = \int_{-\infty}^{\infty} \frac{\partial \log f(\mathbf{y}; \boldsymbol{\theta})}{\partial \theta_k} \frac{\partial \log f(\mathbf{y}; \boldsymbol{\theta})}{\partial \theta_l} f(\mathbf{y}; \boldsymbol{\theta}) \mathrm{d}\mathbf{y} , \qquad (30)$$

where the estimated mean of the candidate component is plugged-in for the unknown parameters.

The algorithm was tested in the above setting for several possible numbers of sensors L in order to evaluate two aspects of its performance. The first is the probability of detecting the global maximum. The second is the small-scale estimation errors when the global maximum is detected correctly. The algorithm was run 100 times for $L = 50, 100, 150$ and 200 sensors. In the case of $L = 50$ sensors, there were 6 cases of erroneous decisions. For systems of $100, 150$, and 200 sensors there was 100 percent success, i.e. the algorithm always detected the correct maximum. The fact that the estimated covariance matrix of the two components is small, which is usually the case when the number of samples at each sensor is sufficiently large, contributed to the success of the CEM stage.

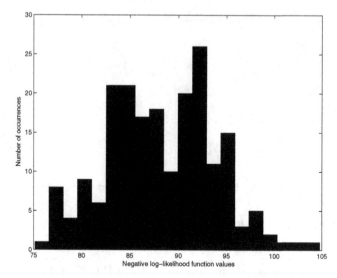

Fig. 6. Histogram of the log-likelihood function values $\ln f(\mathbf{Y}; \widehat{\theta}_N^l)$; $l = 1, \ldots, L$ obtained from estimates $\widehat{\theta}_N^l$; $l = 1, \ldots, L$ generated by $L = 200$ sensors

The small-scale estimation errors in cases where the global maximum was detected correctly, were compared to the performance of a clairvoyant estimator which knows which local estimates are close to the global max. This clairvoyant estimator averages only those estimates that close to the global maximum. The performances of the CEM estimator and the clairvoyant estimator are identical.

5   Concluding Remarks

The work presented in this paper is closely related to the work of White [ ] on misspecified models and to the work of Gan and Jiang [ ] on the problem of local maxima. Given a ML estimate, White proposed a test to detect a misspecified model. Given a local maximizer of the log-likelihood function, Gan and Jiang offered the same test in order to detect a scenario of convergence to a local maximum. This test is based on the observation that the two ways to estimate the FIM from the data given the estimated parameters, i.e., the Hessian form and the outer product form, converge to the same value in the case of a global maximum in a correctly specified model. The test statistic, which is the difference between those two estimators of the FIM, was shown to be asymptotically Gaussian distributed. However, as mentioned in [ ], the convergence of the test statistic to its asymptotic distribution is slow and the test suffers from over rejection in a moderate number of samples. Therefore, this test could not be used to determine whether or not the sub-estimates of the algorithm proposed in Sec. are related to a global maximum. Furthermore, this test requires access to the data and therefore, could not be used in the estimates fusion problem, discussed in Sec.   .

In contrast, the present paper considers cases in which the complete data are divided into sub-blocks, either due to computational burden or due to the system design. This data partitioning gives direct access to the estimated covariance matrix of the sub-estimates, which can then be compared to the calculated FIM. This procedure has considerably better performance and does not require re-processing the complete data.

Acknowledgement

This work was partially supported by a Dept. of EECS at the University of Michigan Fellowship and DARPA-MURI Grant Number DAAD19-02-1-0262.

References

[1] R. A. Fisher. On the mathematical foundation of theoretical statistics. *Phil. Trans. Roy. Soc. London*, 222:309–368, 1922.

[2] P. J. Huber. *Robust Statistics*. John Wiley & Sons, 1981.   ,   ,

[3] P. J. Huber. The behavior of maximum likelihood estimates under nonstandard conditions. *Proceedings of the Fifth Berkeley Symposium in Mathematical Statistics and Probability*, 1967.   ,

[4] H. White. Maximum likelihood estimation of misspecified models. *Econometrica*, 50(1):1–26, Jan 1982.   ,   ,

[5] L. Gan and J. Jiang. A test for global maximum. *Journal of the American Statistical Association*, 94(447):847–854, Sep 1999.   ,   ,

[6] A. K. Jain, R. Duin, and J. Mao. Statistical pattern recognition: A review. *IEEE Trans. Pattern Analysis and Machine Intelligence*, 22(1):4–38, Jan 2000.

[7] M. A. T. Figueiredo and A. K. Jain. Unsupervised learning of finite mixute models. *IEEE Trans on Pattern Anal and Machine Intelligence*, 24:381–396, March 2002.

[8] A. P. Dempster, N. M. Laird, and D. B. Rubin. Maximum likelihood from incomplete data using the em algorithm. *Ann. Roy. Statist. Soc.*, 39:1–38, Dec 1977.

[9] A. Wald. Note on the consistency of the maximum likelihood estimate. *Annals of Mathematical Statistics*, 60:595–603, Dec 1949.

[10] S. M. Kay. *Fundamentals of Statistical Signal Processing - Estimation Theory*. Prentice Hall, 1993.

[11] P. J. Bickel and K. A. Doksum. *Mathematical Statistics*. Holden-Day, San Francisco, 1977.

Maximum Entropy Models for Skin Detection

Bruno Jedynak[1], Huicheng Zheng[2], and Mohamed Daoudi[2]

[1] Laboratoire de Mathématiques appliquées, USTL, Bât M2
59655 Villeneuve d'Ascq, France
jedynak@univ-lille1.fr
http://univ-lille1.fr/labo-stat-proba/jedynak.html
[2] MIIRE Group, Enic Telecom Lille 1
Cité Scientifique, Rue G.Marconi 59655 Villeneuve d'Ascq, France
{daoudi,zheng}@enic.fr
http://www-rech.enic.fr/miire/

Abstract. We consider a sequence of three models for skin detection built from a large collection of labelled images. Each model is a maximum entropy model with respect to constraints concerning marginal distributions. Our models are nested. The first model, called the baseline model is well known from practitioners. Pixels are considered independent. Performance, measured by the ROC curve on the Compaq Database is impressive for such a simple model. However, single image examination reveals very irregular results. The second model is a Hidden Markov Model which includes constraints that force smoothness of the solution. The ROC curve obtained shows better performance than the baseline model. Finally, color gradient is included. Thanks to Bethe tree approximation, we obtain a simple analytical expression for the coefficients of the associated maximum entropy model. Performance, compared with previous model is once more improved.

1   Introduction

1.1   Skin Detection

Skin detection   consists in detecting human skin pixels from an image. The system output is a binary image defined on the same pixel grid as the input image.

Skin detection plays an important role in various applications such as face detection [ ], searching and filtering image content on the web [ ][ ]. Research has been performed on the detection of human skin pixels in color images and on the discrimination between skin pixels and "non-skin" pixels by use of various statistical color models. Some researchers have used skin color models such as Gaussian, Gaussian mixture or histograms [ ] [ ]. In most experiments, skin pixels are acquired from a limited number of people under a limited range of lighting conditions.

---

[1] This work is partially supported by European Community IAP 2117/27572-POESIA www.poesia-filter.org.

Unfortunately, the illumination conditions are often unknown in an arbitrary image, so the variation in skin colors is much less constrained in practice. This is particularly true for web images captured under a wide variety of conditions. However, given a large collection of labeled training pixels including all human skin (Caucasians, Africans, Asians) we can still model the distribution of skin and non-skin colors in the color space. Recently, in [ ], the authors proposed to estimate the distribution of skin and non-skin color using labeled training data. The comparison of histogram models and Gaussian mixture density models estimated with EM algorithm was analyzed for the standard 24-bit RGB color space. The histogram models were found to be slightly superior to Gaussian mixture models in terms of skin pixel classification performance.

A skin detection system is never perfect and different users use different criteria for evaluation. General appearance of the skin-zones detected, or other global criteria might be important for further processing. For quantitative evaluation, we will use false positive rate and detection rate. False positive rate is the proportion of non-skin pixels classified as skin and detection rate is the proportion of skin pixels classified as skin. The user might wish to combine these two indicators his own way depending on the kind of error he is more willing to afford. Hence we propose a system where the output is not binary but a floating number between zero and one, the larger the value, the larger the belief for a skin pixel. The user can then apply a threshold to obtain a binary image. Error rates for all possible thresholding are summarized in the Receiver Operating Characteristic (ROC) curve.

We have in our hands the Compaq Database [ ]. It is a catalog of almost twenty thousand images. Each of them is manually segmented such that the skin pixels are labelled. Our goal in this paper is to explore different ways in which this set of data can be used to perform skin detection on new images. We will use Markov random field approach [ ] [ ] combined with Maximum Entropy Modeling [ ] [ ], referred to as MaxEnt.

1.2   Methodology

Maximum Entropy Modeling (MaxEnt) is a method for inferring models from a data set. See [ ] for the underlying philosophy. It works as follows: 1) choose relevant features 2) compute their histograms on the training set 3) write down the maximum entropy model within the ones that have the feature histograms as observed on the training set 4) estimate the parameters of the model 5) use the model for classification. This plan has been successfully completed for several tasks related to speech recognition and language processing. When working with images, the graph underlying the model is the pixel lattice. It has many nodes and many loops. Task 4) is much more difficult. A break through appeared with the work in [ ] on texture simulation where 1) 2) 3) 4) was performed for images and 5) replaced by simulation.

We adapt this methodology to skin detection as follows: in 1) we specialize in colors and skinness for one pixel and two adjacent pixels. In 2) we compute the histogram of these features in the Compaq manually segmented database. Models for 3) are then easily obtained. In 4) we use the Beth tree approximation, see [ ]. It consists in approximating locally the pixel lattice by a tree. The parameters of the MaxEnt models are then expressed analytically as functions of the histograms of the features. This is a particularity of our features. In 5) we use the Gibbs sampler algorithm for inferring the probability for skin at each pixel location.

The rest of this paper is organized as follows: After setting up the notations in section   , we present in section   a very simple and crude model that we refer to as the baseline model. This model is commonly used by practitioners. In section   , we present a hidden Markov Random Field model that takes into account the spatial regularity of skin and non-skin regions. A novel method for parameter estimation is explored. In section   , we examine models that take into account joint color and skinness distribution for nearby pixels. Finally, in Section   we present concluding remarks.

2   Notations

Let's fix the notations. The set of pixels of an image is S. The color of a pixel $s \in S$ is x_s. It is a 3 dimensional vector, each component being usually coded on one octet. We notate $C = \{0, \ldots, 255\}^3$. The "skinness" of a pixel s, is y_s with $y_s = 1$ if s is a skin pixel and $y_s = 0$ if not. The color image, which is the vector of color pixels, is x and the binary image made up of the y_s's is notated y.

Let's assume for a moment that we knew the joint probability distribution $p(x, y)$ of the vector (x, y), then Bayesian analysis tells us that, whatever cost function the user might think of, all that is needed is the posterior distribution $p(y|x)$. From the user's point of view, the useful information is contained in the one pixel marginal of the posterior, that is, for each pixel, the quantity $p(y_s = 1|x)$, quantifying the belief for skinness at pixel s given the full color image.

In practice the model $p(x, y)$ is unknown. Instead, we have the Compaq Database. It is a collection of samples

$$\{(x^{(1)}, y^{(1)}), \ldots, (x^{(n)}, y^{(n)})\}$$

where for each $1 \leq i \leq n = 18,696$, $x^{(i)}$ is a color image and $y^{(i)}$ is the associated binary skinness image. We assume that the samples are independent of each other with distribution $p(x, y)$. The collection of samples is referred later as the training data. Probabilities are estimated by using classical empirical estimators and are denoted with the letter q.

In what follows, we build models for the joint probability distribution of color and skinness image using maximum entropy modeling.

3   Baseline Model

3.1   Defining the Model

First, we build a model that respects the one pixel marginal observed in the Compaq Database. That is, consider the set of probability distributions (pd)

$p(x, y)$ that verify:

$$C_0 : \forall s \in S, \forall x_s \in C, \forall y_s \in \{0, 1\}, p(x_s, y_s) = q(x_s, y_s) \tag{1}$$

In ( ), the quantity on the right side of the equal sign is the proportion of pixels with color x_s and label y_s in the training data. Remark that all the pd's in C_0 have their single pixel marginals $p(x_s, y_s)$ that doesn't depend on the location s. The MaxEnt solution under C_0 is the independent model:

$$p(x, y) = \prod_{s \in S} q(x_s, y_s) \tag{2}$$

The proof is postponed in Appendix . Using Bayes formulae, one then obtains:

$$p(y|x) = \prod_{s \in S} q(y_s | x_s) \tag{3}$$

We call the model in ( ) the baseline model. It is the most commonly used model in the literature [ ] [ ].

3.2   Experiments

Each term of the product on the right side of ( ) can be computed using probabilities estimated on the training data as follows using Bayes formula:

$$q(y_s | x_s) = \frac{1}{q(x_s)} q(x_s | y_s) q(y_s) \tag{4}$$

with

$$q(x_s) = \sum_{y_s = 0}^{1} q(x_s | y_s) q(y_s)$$

Evaluation of the quantities in ( ) is based on two 3-dimension histograms, $q(x_s | y_s = 1)$ and $q(x_s | y_s = 0)$ describing the one pixel color skin regions and non-skin regions respectively. Several authors have tried to get a parametric expression for these histograms as a mixture of Gaussian distribution [ ] [ ]. Our experience is that the Compaq Database is large enough so that crude histograms made with 512 color value per bin uniformly distributed do not over-fit. Each histogram is then made of 32^3 bins. The ROC curve for this model is presented in figure . Experiments for this model, as well as for the other ones were made using the following protocol. The Compaq database contains about 18,696 photographs. It was split into two almost equal parts randomly. The first part, containing nearly two billion pixels was used as training data while the other one, the test set, was let aside for ROC curve computation. In Figure , first column displays test images. The second column displays grey level images. The grey-level is proportional to the quantity $p(y_s = 1|x)$ evaluated with the Baseline model. On the top image, skin pixels are not detected, especially on the neck of the rightmost person. On the bottom image, we notice many false positives. Figure   show ROC curves computed from 100 images (around 10 millions pixels), randomly extracted from the test set. The Baseline model (with crosses) permit to detect more than 80% of the skin pixels with less than 10% of false positive rate.

4   Hidden Markov Model

4.1   Defining the Model

The baseline model is certainly too loose and one might hope to get better detection results by constraining it to a model that takes into account the fact that skin zones are not purely random but are made of large regions with regular shapes. Hence, we fix the marginals of y for all the neighboring pixels couples. We use 4-neighbor system for simplicity in all that follows. For 2 neighboring pixels s and t, the expected proportion of times that we observe $(y_s = 0, y_t = 0)$, and $(y_s = 1, y_t = 1)$ should be respectively $q(0, 0)$ and $q(1, 1)$, the corresponding quantities measured on the training set. We assume that the model is isotropic, aggregating the cases where s and t are in vertical position to the cases where s and t are in horizontal position. Hence let us define the following constraints:

$$\mathcal{D} : \forall < s, t > \in S \times S, \, p(y_s = 0, y_t = 0) = q(0, 0) \text{ and} \\ p(y_s = 1, y_t = 1) = q(1, 1) \tag{5}$$

where $< s, t >$ defines a couple of neighbor pixels.

The MaxEnt model under $\mathcal{C}_0 \cap \mathcal{D}$ is then the following Gibbs distribution:

$$p(x, y) \approx \prod_{s \in S} q(x_s | y_s) \exp[\sum_{<s,t>} (a_0(1 - y_s)(1 - y_t) + a_1 y_s y_t)] \tag{6}$$

Here and thereafter, the sign $\approx$ means equality up to a function that might depend on x but not on y. a_0 and a_1 are constant that must be set up such that the constraints are satisfied. The proof is in Appendix   . From ( ) one then obtains the following Hidden Markov Model (HMM):

$$p(y | x) \approx \prod_{s \in S} q(x_s | y_s) p(y) \tag{7}$$

with

$$p(y) = \frac{1}{Z(a_0, a_1)} \exp[\sum_{<s,t>} (a_0(1 - y_s)(1 - y_t) + a_1 y_s y_t)] \tag{8}$$

where $Z(a_0, a_1)$ is a normalization function also known in statistical mechanics as the partition function.

The model in equation ( ) is well known, see [ ] and [ ]. Remark that for any $< s, t >$, the pd in ( ) verifies $p(y_s = 1, y_t = 0) = p(y_t = 0, y_s = 1)$ which is a welcome invariance property.

4.2   Parameter Estimation

Parameter estimation in the context of MaxEnt is still an active research subject, especially in situations where even the likelihood function cannot be computed for a given value of the parameters. This is the case here since the partition function cannot be evaluated even for very small size images. One line of research consists in approximating the model in order to obtain a formula where the partition function no longer appears: Pseudo-likelihood [ ] [ ], mean field methods [ ] [ ], as well as Bethe Trees models [ ] are among them. Another possibility is to use stochastic gradient as in [ ]. Here we explore a related method based on the concept of Julesz ensembles defined in [ ]. We learn from this work that one can sample an image from the model defined in ( ) without knowing the parameters a_0 and a_1. This is true only in the asymptotic of an infinite image but we will apply the result for a large image, say 512x512 pixels. In a second step, we use this sample image in order to estimate the parameters a_0 and a_1. This is done using the quantity $p(y_s = 1|y_{(s)})$ which is the probability to observe the label 1 at pixel s given all the other values y_t, for $t \in S$ and $t \neq s$. For the model in ( ), this quantity can be easily analytically computed as

$$p(y_s = 1|y_{(s)}) = \phi((a_1 + a_0)n_s(1) - 4a_0) \qquad (9)$$

where $\phi(x) = (1 + e^{-x})^{-1}$ is the sigmoïd (also known as logistic) function and $n_s(1)$ is the number of neighbors of s that take the label 1. This sum can take only five different values. For each one, the quantity $p(y_s = 1|y_{(s)})$ can be estimated from the sample image, leading to five linearly independent equations from which parameters a_0 and a_1 can be estimated. Now, returning to how to obtain a sample from the model in ( ). The key idea which originated in statistical physics [ ], is that the MaxEnt model we are looking for is, in an appropriate asymptotic meaning, the uniform distribution over the set of images that respect the constraints $\mathcal{D}$. Now, in the absence of phase transition, sampling from this set can be achieved numerically using simulated annealing, see [ ].

4.3   Experiments

Figure shows a 512×512 sample of the prior model defined in equation ( ). One can qualitatively appreciate how well it models skin regions. Notice that vertical and horizontal borders are preferred. This is a bias of the neighborhood system. Choosing 8 neighbors could improve it at the expense of computational load. The quantities $Pr(Y_s = y_s, Y_t = y_t)$, for neighboring pixels s and t are presented in figure , first, as estimated from the training set, and secondly, as estimated from the image in the same figure. The constraints are nearly respected. Parameter estimation from the image in figure leads to the numerical values: $a_0 = 3.76$ and $a_1 = 3.94$.

For a new image x, skin detection requires to compute for each pixel the quantity $p(y_s|x)$. We use Markov Chain Monte Carlo. We generate, using the Gibbs sampler algorithm [ ], a sequence of label images

$$y^1, y^2, \ldots, y^{n_1}, \ldots, y^{n_2}$$

	database values	image values
$Pr(Y_s = 0, Y_t = 0)$	0.828	0.827991
$Pr(Y_s = 1, Y_t = 1)$	0.159	0.151646

Fig. 1. Top: a sample image from the prior distribution used in the Hidden Markov Model. **Bottom:** probabilities estimated from the training set and from the image on the top

with stationary distribution ( ). Then, we estimate the quantity $p(y_s|x)$ by the empirical mean

$$\frac{1}{n2 - n1} \sum_{j=n_1+1}^{n_2} y_s^{(j)}$$

Our working parameters are $n_1 = 1$ and $n_2 = 100$. Two output images are presented in Figure . It compares favorably with the Baseline model. The ROC curve in Figure indicates a drop of about 1% in false positive for the same detection rate as the Baseline model.

5   First Order Model

5.1   Defining the Model

The baseline model was built in order to mimic the one pixel marginal of the joint distribution of color and skinness as observed on the database. Then, in building the HMM model we added constraints on the prior skinness distribution in order to smooth the model. Now, we constrain once more the MaxEnt model by imposing the two-pixel marginal that is $p(x_s, x_t, y_s, y_t)$, for 4-neighbor s and t, to match those observed in the training data. Hence we define the following constraints:

$$\mathcal{C}_1 : \forall < s, t > \in S \times S, \forall x_s \in C, \forall x_t \in C, \forall y_s \in \{0, 1\}, \forall y_t \in \{0, 1\},$$
$$p(x_s, x_t, y_s, y_t) = q(x_s, x_t, y_s, y_t) \tag{10}$$

The quantity $q(x_s, x_t, y_s, y_t)$ is the expected proportion of times we observe the values (x_s, x_t, y_s, y_t) for a couple of neighboring pixels, regardless of the orientation of the pixels s and t in the training set.

Clearly, $\mathcal{C}_1 \subset (\mathcal{C}_0 \cap \mathcal{D}) \subset \mathcal{C}_0$. The solution to the MaxEnt problem under $\mathcal{C}_1$ is then, see Appendix , the following Gibbs distribution:

$$p(x,y) \approx \exp[\sum_{<s,t>} \lambda(x_s, x_t, y_s, y_t)] \tag{11}$$

where $\lambda(s, t, x_s, x_t, y_s, y_t)$ are parameters that should be set up to satisfy the constraints. From ( ), one gets

$$p(y|x) \approx \exp[\sum_{<s,t>} \lambda(x_s, x_t, y_s, y_t)] \tag{12}$$

Assuming that one color can take 256^3 values, the total number of parameters is $256^3 \times 256^3 \times 2 \times 2$. The previously mentioned parameter estimation methods clearly do not apply. In [ ], the authors present a tree approximation to the pixel grid, called "Bethe tree", after the physicist H.A. Bethe who used trees in statistical mechanics problems. Bethe trees permit us to compute analytically an approximation of the parameters in the model ( ) and consequently in ( ) as we shall see now.

5.2   Parameter Estimation and Bethe Tree Approximation

Bethe tree have been introduced in computer vision as a way of approximating estimators in Markov Random Field models in [ ]. We shall revisit this work in connection with maximum entropy models. The key idea is to provide a tree that approximates locally the pixel lattice. More precisely, for each pixel s, we consider a sequence of trees $T_1^{(s)}, T_2^{(s)}, \ldots$ of increasing depth. The construction is as follow: the root node of the tree is associated with s. For each neighbor t of s in the pixel-graph, a child node indexed by t is added to the root node. This defines $T_1^{(s)}$. Subsequently, for each u, neighbor of a neighbor of s, (excluding s itself), a grandchild node indexed by u is added to the appropriate child node. This defines $T_2^{(s)}$, and so on, see [ ] for a detailed account. An important remark is that a single pixel might lead to several different nodes in the tree! For example $T_2^{(s)}$ is built with s, the neighbors of s and the neighbors of these. Using 4-neighbors, and assuming that s is not in the border of the image, this makes up 13 pixels, but the associated tree has 17 nodes, 4 pixels being replicated twice each, see figure .

Let us consider the following model

$$p(x,y) \approx \exp H(x;y) \text{ with}$$
$$H(x;y) = \sum_{<s,t>} \log q(x_s, x_t, y_s, y_t) - n(s) \sum_{s \in \mathring{S}} \log q(x_s, y_s) \tag{13}$$

where $n(s)$ is the number of neighbors of s and $\mathring{S}$ is the set of interior pixels of S, that is the ones that have exactly four neighbors. First, remark that the model in ( ) is a special case of model in ( ). Second, under the Beth tree approximation, with arbitrarily finite depth, the model in ( ) satisfies the constraints.

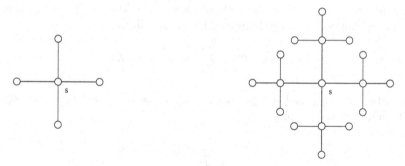

Fig. 2. Left: a Bethe tree of depth 1 rooted at s. **Right:** a Bethe tree of depth 2 rooted at s

Indeed, this is a particular case of a more general result, see [ ], saying that any pairwise MRF defined on a tree graph can be written as a function of it's marginal distributions as in ( ). We can then conclude that under the Bethe Tree approximation, ( ) is the MaxEnt solution for C_1 .

Now, let us see how in practice one can use the model in ( ). As for the HMM model, the objective is to obtain simulations using the Gibbs sampler algorithm. This requires to compute the conditional distribution of a label y_s given all the other labels and the image of the colors x. For $s \in \overset{\circ}{S}$, we obtain

$$p(y_s = 1|y_{(s)}, x) = \phi(U(x; y)) \text{ with}$$

$$U(x; y) \quad = \sum_{t \in \mathcal{V}(s)} \log \frac{q(y_s=1, y_t|x_s, x_t)}{q(y_s=0, y_t|x_s, x_t)} - n(s) \log \frac{q(y_s=1|x_s)}{q(y_s=0|x_s)}$$

(14)

Where ϕ is the logistic function and $\mathcal{V}(s)$ are the neighbors of s.

5.3 Experiments

Now let's see how each term in ( ) can be evaluated. First,

$$\frac{q(y_s = 1|x_s)}{q(y_s = 0|x_s)} = \frac{q(x_s|y_s = 1)}{q(x_s|y_s = 0)} \frac{q(y_s = 1)}{q(y_s = 0)}$$

(15)

and the quantities on the right side of ( ) are easily obtained from the database as before. Second,

$$\frac{q(y_s = 1, y_t|x_s, x_t)}{q(y_s = 0, y_t|x_s, x_t)} = \frac{q(x_s, x_t|y_s = 1, y_t)}{q(x_s, x_t|y_s = 0, y_t)} \frac{q(y_s = 1, y_t)}{q(y_s = 0, y_t)}$$

(16)

Now the quantities on the right side of ( ) involving the color values cannot be directly extracted from the database without drastic over-fitting since the histogram involved have a support of dimension six. Hence some kind of dimension reduction is needed.

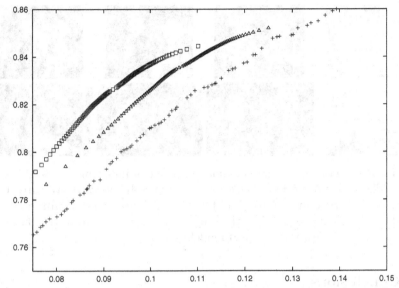

Fig. 3. Receiver Operating Characteristics (ROC) curve for each model. x-axis is the false positive rate, y-axis is the detection rate. Baseline model is shown with crosses, HMM model with triangles, while the first order model is shown with squares

One natural solution is to assume conditional independence, that is

$$\frac{q(x_s, x_t | y_s = 1, y_t)}{q(x_s, x_t | y_s = 0, y_t)} = \frac{q(x_s | y_s = 1)}{q(x_s | y_s = 0)} \quad (17)$$

The obtained model is then a HMM model, as in equation ( ). Hence, Bethe tree method gives another way to estimate parameters a_0 and a_1. Obtained values are $a_0 = 3.94$ and $a_1 = 4$, which are close to the values obtained in section .

A more promising dimension reduction procedure is the following approximation:

$$q(x_s, x_t | y_s, y_t) \sim q(x_s | y_s) q(x_t - x_s | y_s, y_t) \quad (18)$$

That is, we assume that the color gradient at s, measured by the quantity $x_t - x_s$, is, given the labels at s and t, independent of the actual color x_s. Evaluation of the right side of the sign $\sim$ requires to compute 6 histograms with a support of dimension 3 only. We use 32^3 bins of 512 colors each.

Experiments with this model are presented in figures   and . The setup is the same as for the HMM model. In figure , one can visually appreciate the improvement in localization of the skin zones compared to the HMM model. Bulk results in the ROC curve of Figure   show a slight improvement of performance too.

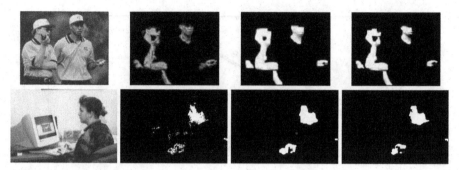

Fig. 4. First column: original color images. The image on top is 225 × 180 pixels. The image on the bottom is 541 × 361 pixels. **Second column:** Baseline model. **Third column:** hidden Markov model. **Fourth column:** first order model. In the computed images, the grey level is proportional to the skin probability evaluated with the specified model

6   Conclusions

We have considered a sequence of three models for skin detection built from a large collection of labelled images. For a given color image, such a model puts weight on binary images defined on the same pixel grid. Each model is a maximum entropy model with respect to constraints. These constraints concern marginal distributions. Our models are nested. The first model, called the baseline model is well known from practitioners. Pixels are considered as independent. Performance, measured by the ROC curve on the Compaq database is impressive for such a simple model. However, single image examination reveals very irregular results. The second model is a Hidden Markov Model. It includes constraints that force smoothness of the solution. The ROC curve obtained shows better performance than the baseline model. Finally, color gradient is included in the set of constraints. Thanks to Bethe tree approximation, we obtain a simple analytical expression for the coefficients of the associated MaxEnt model. Performance, compared with previous model is once more improved.

For many applications involving skin detection as an intermediate stage, processing time is of major importance. In future work we plan to replace the stochastic sampling algorithm by a deterministic scheme as Mean Field method [ ] or Belief Propagation [ ] method in order to meet the required time constraints.

References

[1] M. J. Jones and James M. Rehg, Statistical Color Models with Application to Skin Detection, Compaq, 1998, CRL 98/11   ,
[2] C. Wu and Peter C. Doerschuk, Tree Approximations to Markov Random Fields, IEEE Transactions on PAMI, 1995, Vol. 17,4, pp. 391-402   ,   ,

[3] L. M. Bergasa and M. Mazo. and A. Gardel and M. A. Sotelo and L. Bo-
     quete, Unsupervised and adapative Gaussian skin-color model,Image and Vision
     Computing,2000,18,987-1003
[4] M. J. Jones and J. M. Rehg,Statistical color models with application to skin de-
     tection,Computer Vision and Pattern Recognition, 274-280,1999   ,
[5] J.-C. Terrillon and M. N. Shirazi and H. Fukamachi and S. Akamatsu,Comparative
     Performance of Different Skin Chrominance Models and Chrominance Spaces for
     the Automatic Detection of Human Faces in Color Images, Fourth International
     Conference On Automatic Face and gesture Recognition, 54-61, 2000   ,
[6] J.-C. Terrillon and M. David and S. Akamatsu, Automatic Detection of Human
     Faces in Natural Scene Images by Use of a Skin Color Model and of Inavariant
     Moments, IEEE Third International Conference on Automatic Face and gesture
     Recognition,112-117, 1998   ,
[7] J. Z. Wang and Jia Li and Gio Wiederhold and Oscar Firschein, System for Screen-
     ing Objectionable Images, Images, Computer Communications Journal, 1998
[8] J. Z. Wang and Jia Li and Gio Wiederhold and Oscar Firschein, Classifying ob-
     jectionable websites based on image content, Notes in Computer Science, Special
     issue on iteractive distributed multimedia systems and telecommunication ser-
     vices, 1998, 21/15, 113-124
[9] L.Y. Estimation and annealing for Gibbsian fields, Annales de l'Institut Henry
     Poincare, Section B, Calcul des Probabilités et Statistique,1998, 24, 269-294
[10] S. Geman and D. Geman,Stochastic relaxation, Gibbs distributions, and the
     Bayesian Restoration of Images, IEEE Transactions on PAMI, 1984, 6, 721-741

[11] J. Besag, On the Statistical Analysis of Dirty Pictures, Journal of the Royal
     Statistical Society, B 1986, 48,3 259-302
[12] J. Zhang, The mean field theory in EM procedure for Markov Random Fields
     IEEE Transactions on Signal Processing, 1992 40,10, 2570-2583, October   ,

[13] E. T.Jaynes, Information Theory and Statistical Mechanics, Physical Review,
     1957, 106, 620-630   ,
[14] Y. N. Wu and S. C. Zhu and X. W. Liu, Equivalence of Julesz Ensemble and
     FRAME models, International Journal of Computer Vision, 200038,3, 247-265,
     July
[15] G. Winkler, Image Analysis, Random Fields and Dynamic Monte Carlo Methods,
     Springer-Verlag,1995   ,   ,
[16] J. W. Gibbs, Elementary Principles of Statistical Mechanics, Yale University
     Press, 1902
[17] A. Martin-Lof, The Equivalence of Ensembles and Gibbs'Phase Rule for Classical
     Lattice-Systems, Journal of Statistical Phisics,1979, 20, 557–569,
[18] R. Chellappa and A. Jain,Markov Random Fields: Theory and Applica-
     tions,Academic Press, 1996   ,
[19] Cover and Thomas, Elements of Information Theory, Wiley, 1991
[20] F. Divino and A. Frigessi, Penalized pseudolikelihood inference in spatial interac-
     tion models Scandinavian Journal of Statistics 27, 3, 2000, pp. 445–458
[21] S. C. Zhu and Yingnian Wu and David Mumford,Filters, Random Fields and
     Maximum ,International Journal of Computer Vision, 1998, 27, 2, 107–126
[22] G. Celeux and F. Forbes and N. Peyrard, EM Procedures Using Mean Field-Like
     Approximations for Markov Model-Based Image Segmentation,Pattern Recogni-
     tion, Vol. 36, 1, 2002

[23] B. Jedynak and H. Zheng and M. Daoudi and D. Barret, Maximum Entropy Models for Skin Detection,Université des Sciences et Technologies de Lille, France, 2002, publication IRMA, Volume 57, number XIII.

[24] J.S. Yedida, W.T. Freeman and Y. Weiss, Understanding Belief Propagation and its Generalisations, Mitsubitch Electric Rsearch Laboratories, TR-2001-22, January 2002.

[25] J. Pearl, Probabilistic Reasoning in intelligent systems : networks of plausible inference, Morgan Kaufmann, 1988.

A   Appendix

Here we shall derive a MaxEnt solution for the joint distribution $p(x, y)$ under the constraints $\mathcal{C}_0$. See ( ).

Remark that the constraints in ( ) are expectations with respect to p. Indeed,

$$p(x_s, y_s) = E_p[\delta_{x_s}(X_s)\delta_{y_s}(Y_s)] \tag{19}$$

with

$$\delta_a(b) = \begin{cases} 1 \text{ if } a = b \\ 0 \text{ if } a \neq b \end{cases}$$

Then, following Jaynes' argument [ ], the MaxEnt solution under $\mathcal{C}_0$ is unique if it exists, and can be obtained using Lagrange multipliers. One gets:

$$p(x, y) = \exp(\lambda_0 + \sum_{s \in S} \lambda(s, x_s, y_s)) \tag{20}$$

where the parameters λ should be set up such that the constraints are satisfied. Now if

$$\forall x_s \in C, \forall y_s \in \{0, 1\}, q(x_s, y_s) > 0 \tag{21}$$

then one can choose

$$\lambda_0 = 0 \text{ and } \lambda(s, x_s, y_s) = \log q(x_s, y_s) \tag{22}$$

which leads to the unique solution of the MaxEnt problem:

$$p(x, y) = \prod_{s \in S} q(x_s, y_s) \tag{23}$$

Condition in ( ) is saying that there is no empty bin in the empirical joint histogram $q(x_s, y_s)$. This will be our case. MaxEnt solutions still exist when ( ) is not verified.

Here we shall obtain a MaxEnt solution for the joint distribution $p(x, y)$ under $\mathcal{C}_0 \cap \mathcal{D}$, see ( ) and ( ).

As for $\mathcal{C}_0$, the constraints in $\mathcal{D}$ are expectations. Indeed,

$$\forall y_s \in \{0, 1\}, \forall y_t \in \{0, 1\}, p(y_s, y_t) = E_p[\delta_{y_s}(Y_s)\delta_{y_t}(Y_t)] \tag{24}$$

Using once more Lagrange multipliers, one obtains that the MaxEnt solution, if it exists, is

$$
\begin{aligned}
p(x,y) &= \exp H(x,y,\lambda_0,\lambda_1,\lambda_2,\lambda_3) \text{ with}\\
H(x,y,\lambda_0,\lambda_1,\lambda_2,\lambda_3) &= \lambda_0 + \sum_{s\in S}\lambda_1(s,x_s,y_s)+\\
&\quad \sum_{<s,t>\in S\times S}\lambda_2(s,t)(1-y_s)(1-y_t)+\\
&\quad \sum_{<s,t>\in S\times S}\lambda_3(s,t)y_s y_t]
\end{aligned}
\tag{25}
$$

where $< s,t >$ is a couple of 4-neighbors pixels and $\lambda_0,\ \lambda_1,\ \lambda_2,\ \lambda_3$ define parameters that should be set up such that the constraints are satisfied. Starting from ( ), remark that

$$
p(x_s,y_s) = \sum_{x_t;t\in S,t\neq s}\ \sum_{y_t;t\in S,t\neq s} p(x,y) = \exp[\lambda_0 + \lambda_1(s,x_s,y_s)]g(s,y_s) \tag{26}
$$

with $g(s,y_s)$ a function that doesn't depend on x_s. Now,

$$
p(y_s) = \sum_{x_s}p(x_s,y_s) = \exp[\lambda_0]g(s,y_s)\sum_{x_s}\exp[\lambda_1(s,x_s,y_s)] \tag{27}
$$

hence

$$
p(x_s|y_s) = \frac{p(x_s,y_s)}{p(y_s)} = \frac{\exp[\lambda_1(s,x_s,y_s)]}{\sum_{x_s}\exp[\lambda_1(s,x_s,y_s)]} \tag{28}
$$

Since $p(x,y)$ lies in $\mathcal{C}_0$, it verifies: $p(x_s|y_s) = q(x_s|y_s)$. Assuming positivity ( ), we can choose

$$
\lambda_1(s,x_s,y_s) = \log q(x_s|y_s) \tag{29}
$$

Now, constraints in $\mathcal{D}$, see ( ), do not depend on the location $< s,t >$. Hence, one can reduce to translation invariant models as in ( ).

Constraints in $\mathcal{C}_1$, see ( ) are also expectations. Indeed,

$$
p(x_s,x_t,y_s,y_t) = E_p[\delta_{(x_s)}(X_s)\delta_{(x_t)}(X_t)\delta_{(y_s)}(Y_s)\delta_{(y_t)}(Y_t)] \tag{30}
$$

Using Lagrange multipliers, one obtains ( ).

Hierarchical Annealing
for Random Image Synthesis*

Simon K. Alexander[1], Paul Fieguth[2], and Edward R. Vrscay[1]

[1] Department of Applied Mathematics
University of Waterloo, Waterloo, Ontario, Canada, N2L-3G1
{sk2alexa,ervrscay}@uwaterloo.ca
ph: (519) 888-4567 Ext. 5455 fax: (519) 746-4319
[2] Department of Systems Design Engineering
University of Waterloo, Waterloo, Ontario, Canada, N2L-3G1
pfieguth@ocho.uwaterloo.ca

Abstract. Simulated annealing has been applied to a wide variety of problems in image processing and synthesis. However, particularly in scientific applications, the computational complexity of annealing may constrain its effectiveness, in that the demand for very high resolution samples or even three-dimensional data may result in huge configuration spaces. In this paper a method of hierarchical simulated annealing is introduced, which can lead to large gains in computational complexity for suitable models. As an example, the approach is applied to the synthesis of binary porous media images.

1 Introduction

In this work we are motivated by challenges in scientific imaging, in particular, by the demand for the random synthesis of very high resolution 2D images or 3D cubes. Our interest in this field is driven by studies in binary porous media, possessing solid-gas or solid-fluid distributions, two examples of which are shown in Fig. . Although these have been simulated extensively (stochastic geometry [,], annealing methods [,]) computational issues are at the heart of further research progress: Larger 2D and 3D simulations are required to validate scientific models on ever smaller scales. Thus our goal is efficient synthesis or sampling of huge random images of this type.

It is important the recognize the distinction between the superficially similar problems of random synthesis, considered here, and the much more common problem of image estimation. The problem of estimation involves finding that particular, normally unique, image which *optimizes* some criterion (with respect

---

* This research was supported in part by the Natural Sciences and Engineering Council of Canada (NSERC).in the form of grants (P.F. and E.R.V) and a Postgraduate Scholarship (S.K.A). We also wish to thank M. Ioannidis, Dept. of Chemical Engineering University of Waterloo for providing sample porous media images, and interesting discussions.

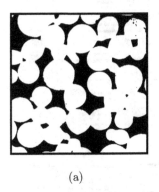

(a)   (b)

Fig. 1. Binary image (a) of packed glass spheres (common test data for porous media applications) and (b) a rock sample

to some model and measurements), an inherently deterministic problem. In contrast, the synthesis of appropriate images by sampling is an inherently stochastic problem, the selection of random samples from a statistical distribution. The distinction between the two is illustrated in Fig. . Although *many* approaches have been developed for optimization (including closed-form solvers, linear systems, and a huge variety of ad-hoc methods), the sampling problem is much more subtle.

As opposed to relatively well-conditioned problems involving densely-measured images, such as image denoising and segmentation, our interests involve the sampling of random images subject to prior constraints and sparsely sampled measurements, normally a very difficult and poorly-conditioned problem. Applying annealing approaches to such numerical stiffness typically requires huge numbers of iterations and vast computational requirements.

There is one approach, however, which blurs the distinction between sampling and estimation, and which may hold the key to an efficient sampler. The method of simulated annealing (SA) (described in §) has been widely used for common imaging processing tasks, such estimation from noisy images [,], image segmentation [, ,], and image synthesis [,]. It is a promising approach in many imaging applications, in that it can accommodate a wide variety of assumptions and prior image models, even nonlinear ones. Estimation effectively becomes a limiting case of random sampling, in the limit where only the most probable samples are accepted. The well-known problem, however, is that SA is exceptionally slow.

To be sure, a wide variety of accelerated annealing methods have been proposed, many promising ones based on various hierarchical approaches [, , ,]. The basic premise, as with related methods such as multigrid [, ,], is that the problem is greatly accelerated by addressing long-range phenomena and dependencies on a coarse-scale, leaving only more local phenomena to be ad-

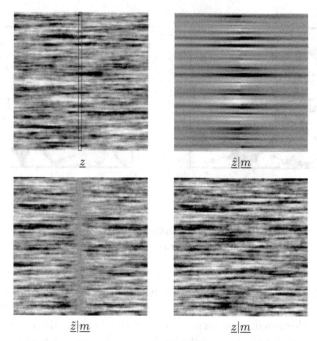

z

$\hat{z}|\underline{m}$

$\tilde{z}|\underline{m}$

$z|\underline{m}$

Fig. 2. A comparison of estimation and posterior sampling: the top left panel shows an anisotropic wood-grain texture and the measured central column $\underline{m}$. The estimates $\hat{z}|\underline{m}$ clearly reveal the pattern of the measurements, and bears little resemblance to the original texture. The bottom panels show the sampled posterior estimation error $\tilde{z}|\underline{m}$, in which a low-variance zero-mean band can be seen where the estimates are good. Finally the posterior sample $z|\underline{m}$ shows the random texture, consistent with both the measurements and the prior statistics

dressed on finer scales. It would appear, then, that the success of these methods should lead to the desired large-scale sampling. Unfortunately, this appearance is misleading, and underlies our whole research objective.

In particular, virtually every method of accelerated annealing has been aimed at problems of estimation/optimization, such as image classification [ ], segmentation [, ,], and image restoration [, ,]. In *each* of these cases the finest scale is *densely* measured (the image to be analyzed), strongly constraining the problem, thus both the passing of long-range information and the constraints imposed by a prior model are relied upon relatively weakly in arriving at a solution. That is, the hierarchical framework can be relatively heuristic and approximate and still produce excellent estimates. In sharp contrast, random sampling proceeds from a blank slate — all long-range structure has to be synthesized explicitly, based on the constraints of the prior model, which therefore needs to be implemented and followed faithfully.

Secondly, the strong conditioning of an estimation problem implies that coarse-scale convergence is fairly robust, making it possible to avoid annealing at all but the finest scale [ ]; thus the coarse scales can be managed by fast, deterministic methods such as *iterated conditional mode* (ICM). Again, in distinct contrast, any hierarchical approach to random sampling will require proper sampling on each scale, which furthermore raises subtle issues of how to move from scale to scale and the range of temperatures over which to anneal.

In order to address these difficulties in a hierarchical framework we are motivated by the renormalization group theory approaches originating in statistical mechanics [ ], which suggests that temperature and scale are related. Intuitively, at a particular scale and temperature, structures from coarser scales are 'slushy' (i.e., relatively frozen for some length of time) while at finer scales are a 'boiling froth' (i.e., highly variable). Hence both the coarser and finer scales can, to some extent, be ignored while the structure at the given scale is developing. To be sure, other renormalization-motivated approaches have been proposed for image modelling in applications such as restoration [ ] and vision [ ], however both of these are subject to the limitations of estimation-based approaches, as discussed earlier.

From the preceding discussion, we see how the application of hierarchical sampling represents a significant departure from existing methods, and yet represents a significant problem in scientific modeling and analysis. In this work, we will discuss how the reduction in the size of configuration space represented by subsampling (e.g. renormalization) can be used to reduce computation cost, concentrating on the potential gains for the computationally expensive applications of image synthesis.

This paper seeks to initiate discussion of methods to improve the computational cost of sampling by working in a multiscale/hierarchical framework. One method to do this is to use a simulated annealing approach, recast in a hierarchy of coarse-grained approximations to the configuration space. In the following sections, we discuss the algorithms involved, the construction of energy functions to describe appropriate Gibbs random fields, and the resulting image samples.

2   Simulated Annealing

2.1   Background

In this work we are interested in Markov Chain Monte-Carlo (MCMC) sampling methods [,]. MCMC methods are used to draw samples from Gibbs random field — that is, a random field whose probability distribution π is written in terms of an energy function $\mathcal{E}(x)$ weighted by inverse temperature $\beta = 1/T$:

$$\pi_\beta(x) = \frac{e^{-\beta\mathcal{E}(x)}}{Z_\beta} \ . \tag{1}$$

Note that the normalizing *partition function* Z_β, which is particularly difficult to calculate for most problems, is not needed by the sampling algorithms under consideration (e.g. Metropolis[ ] and Gibbs[ ] samplers), which is one of the primary benefits of MCMC methods.

Algorithm 1 Simulated Annealing

$n \Leftarrow 0$
while $\mathcal{E}(x)$ not converged **do**
   $\beta \Leftarrow 1/T_n$
   $x \Leftarrow$ sample $\pi_\beta(x)$ \{ draw a sample from π_β\}
   $n \Leftarrow n + 1$
end while

The simulated annealing (or stochastic relaxation [ ]) algorithm is as follows:
Here $\{T_k\}$ describes a general *cooling schedule*, a sequence of (eventually) decreasing temperature values with

$$T_k > 0 \qquad \forall k \ , \tag{2}$$

$$\lim_{k \to \infty} T_k = 0 \ . \tag{3}$$

We note, however, that convergence to a global minimum (i.e. global optimization of the energy function) is guaranteed [ ] only for impractically slow logarithmic cooling satisfying

$$T_k \geq \frac{A}{\log{(k+1)}} \ , \tag{4}$$

where A is some model-dependent constant. Determining the minimal value
of A is not straightforward [ ]. Furthermore, it can be shown that for appropriate sampling algorithms, if the energy function has multiple global minima,
the algorithm will sample uniformly from these minima (independent of initial
states) [,]. This property will be employed in § to draw samples from a large
class of images.

There are thus two basic considerations for the computational cost of this
class of algorithms:

1. The process of drawing samples (the MCMC algorithm);
2. The cooling schedule of the annealing.

We maintain that these two issues are orthogonal; that is, that they can be separately addressed, and that gains from accelerated cooling [ ] can be applied
more or less equally to both regular and multiscale annealing. Additionally, extensive research into improving the performance of MCMC samplers has not
resulted in general improvements, although special conditions can result in improved convergence [,].

Therefore the focus of this paper is to reduce the computational cost of annealing by restructuring the process to take advantage of sampling on smaller
lattices where possible. We will construct a hierarchy of coarse-grainings of the
configuration space, in order to allow fast convergence of lower frequency components, as discussed in the following section.

If we consider the cost of individual site updates to be fixed (true for a large
class of models), then the computational cost of drawing samples is driven by

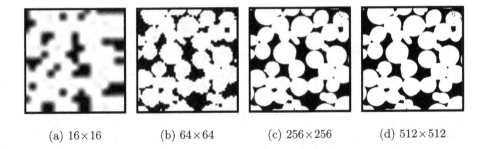

(a) 16×16   (b) 64×64   (c) 256×256   (d) 512×512

Fig. 3. A porous medium image viewed at several resolutions: How do local and non-local features scale and map across resolutions?

the rate of convergence of the Markov chain, which increases with the size of the domain, as does the number of pixels. For large domains, the number of iterations can scale to huge proportions.

It is this last aspect, the scaling of computational cost with domain size, that we will leverage to reduce total computational cost. The key proposal is that by annealing in a multiscale hierarchy, the computational cost of annealing is greatly reduced.

2.2   Multiscale Annealing

The purpose of this approach is to take advantage of the lower complexity at higher levels in the hierarchy, and to have these higher levels precondition, in a sense, or simplify the task at the lower levels.

Our proposal is to apply the central idea of renormalization group theory to accelerate computationally burdensome annealing in scientific applications. This approach is distinct from existing research on hierarchical structures and accelerated annealing such as "multi-temperature annealing" [ ] which constructs a hierarchical Markov random field model with scale dependent cooling, but where the Markov model explicitly couples together adjacent scales. In contrast, we treat each scale as a single image, only mapping the coarse configuration onto the finer lattice, i.e. always in the direction of increasing resolution.

As we work down a hierarchy from coarsest to finest resolution, the question then is to determine what image features are preserved (or lost) across rescaling. At any particular level in this multiscale hierarchy, what image features are represented? How may we anneal in such a way that certain features of interest are represented at the current level and can be meaningfully mapped to the the next finer level? Figure   illustrates this view.

The key insight that we bring from renormalization methods is that the effective temperature for a given feature size is scale dependent. In particular, for some temperature at some intermediate scale, coarser scales are cold (meaning

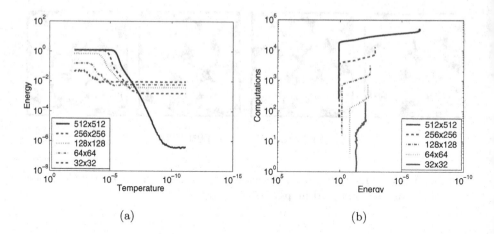

(a)   (b)

Fig. 4. Annealing to convergence at several resolutions. (a) Effective temperature shifts for convergence are evident. Note that the energy axis represents the energy as measured at finest resolution, regardless of the resolution.(b) Computations normalized to cost of 32×32 pixel flips

that the large, coarse features are 'frozen'), and finer scales are hot (meaning that the tiny features, not resolved at the intermediate scale, are still in a state of flux). What this implies is that we are able to concentrate on one intermediate scale at a time. To illustrate this approach, Figs.   and   illustrate the convergence process at several scales (empirical curves based on the model in §   ), plotting the energy (that is, the convergence) versus both temperature and computational cost. We note the following:

- Each curve is characterized by a rapid drop in energy, followed by convergence.
- The computational cost of a single sweep at fine levels can be high relative to the total cost of convergence at a coarse level.
- The finer the scale, the better the ultimate convergence.
- Some features of these plots are model dependent; the large difference between minimal energy at finest resolution and all the other resolutions is an artifact of the sensitivity of the model to blocks (i.e. from supersampling coarser resolutions) in the high resolution image. This is not a measure of distance in configuration space.

From which it follows that, in general, we want to be working on the coarsest, unconverged scale.

The benefit of this approach stems from two observations. First, the size of the coarse domains is small, allowing rapid sampling. Second, and much more significant: At an intermediate scale the algorithm needs to be iterated only enough to allow relatively local structure to converge, since the larger structures

---

Algorithm 2 Multiscale Annealing

$k \Leftarrow 0$
for $s = S$ to 0 **do**
   while $\mathcal{E}_s(X_s)$ not converged **do**
      $\beta \Leftarrow 1/T_k$
      $X_s \Leftarrow$ sample π_β { draw a sample from π_β }
      $k \Leftarrow k + 1$
   end while
   $X_{s-1} \Leftarrow M_s(X_s)$ {map to next finer resolution}
end for

---

already converged at coarser scales. Our goal, then, is to work in a decimated configuration space (at less computational cost) for sufficient time and then map onto the next larger space and to continue annealing. Clearly this idea may be applied hierarchically, leading to a succession of coarse-grained configuration spaces. If we consider the Gibbs field X at the target resolution, we can denote a hierarchy $\{X_s\}_{s=0}^{S}$ of coarse-grainings of the configuration space where each increase in level represents decimation by a factor of two (and where X_0 is finest resolution). We note that this is not the only possible renormalization map [ ].

Annealing with too low an initial temperature (not enough energy) approaches a greedy algorithm, prone to finding local minima. On the other hand, too much energy may destroy the larger structures passed down from coarser scales. Since the above holds true at any level in the hierarchy, clearly there is a delicate balance in achieving computational gains while retaining good optimization performance.

An analysis of interactions between the cooling schedule of the annealing, the mappings in the annealing hierarchy, and the convergence of the stochastic sampler is not straightforward. At present, we rely on heuristic rules to determine the cooling and mapping schedule. Future work will concentrate on an analysis of this process. It is worth noting that since we employ a single cooling schedule across the entire hierarchy, the 'shape' of this schedule will strongly effect overall computational costs. From a computational point of view, the more time spent in the coarser levels of the hierarchy the better. Of course this must be balanced against the effects of the cooling schedule on convergence.

The model presented in the next section uses the following heuristic. At each higher level in the hierarchy, the energy function can be viewed as an approximation for the energy function at the final resolution, denoted as $\mathcal{E}_s$. Denote the mapping operator (coarse to fine) from one level to the next as $M_s :$ $X_s \rightarrow X_{s-1}$. Multiscale annealing is performed as shown in Algorithm .

While in no sense is this heuristic considered to be "optimal", in the next section it is applied to a simple model and shown to be effective.

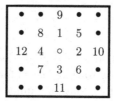

$$
\begin{array}{ccccc}
\bullet & 4 & 3 & 4 & \bullet \\
4 & 2 & 1 & 2 & 4 \\
3 & 1 & \circ & 1 & 3 \\
4 & 2 & 1 & 2 & 4 \\
\bullet & 4 & 3 & 4 & \bullet
\end{array}
$$

Fig. 5. Neighbourhoods up to 4th order

$$
\begin{array}{ccccc}
\bullet & \bullet & 9 & \bullet & \bullet \\
\bullet & 8 & 1 & 5 & \bullet \\
12 & 4 & \circ & 2 & 10 \\
\bullet & 7 & 3 & 6 & \bullet \\
\bullet & \bullet & 11 & \bullet & \bullet
\end{array}
$$

Fig. 6. Bit indices for a 3rd-order neighbourhood defining the mapping $\mathcal{F}$

3   A Simple Model for Synthesizing Porous Media

We have intentionally chosen a simplistic model in order minimize computational cost, as well as model parameters and clutter in order to interpret the results more easily. In particular we will work with binary images, which have the advantage of smaller configuration spaces (compared to non-binary images of the same size) while still being important for many application areas. Henceforth the two pixel states will be referred to as *white* (1) and *black* (0).

We consider local neighbourhoods of fairly small order. Using a common notation, neighbourhoods are determined by increasing Euclidean distance from the current pixel. The $k + 1^{\text{th}}$ order neighbourhood contains all of the pixels in the kth order neighbourhood, and so on. Figure   illustrates the first four neighbourhoods.

We denote the neighbourhood (of some fixed order) of a pixel as $\mathcal{N}$, and let b denote the size of the neighbourhood (i.e the number of pixels). Since each pixel is binary, the size of the set of all possible configurations within a neighbourhood is 2^b. For reasonably small order, it is computationally feasible to count the instances of each local configuration in an image.

For this purpose, there is a natural bijective mapping constructed by labelling each pixel in the neighbourhood uniquely from 1 to b, and treating the mth pixel state as the state of the mth bit in a b bit binary representation of an integer in $0 \ldots 2^b - 1$. For example with 3rd-order neighbourhoods there are 12 pixel locations. Figure   shows one possible indexing scheme forming a map onto $0 \ldots 4095$. Under such an indexing scheme, each location in the image has, via the neighbourhood structure, a mapping:

$$
\mathcal{F}_{i,j} : X_{i,j} \to 0 \ldots 2^b - 1 \ . \tag{5}
$$

Given this indexing of local configurations, one possible approach is to consider, for some class of bitmap images, the global distribution of local configurations. Designate target probability mass functions (pmfs) for the two cases of white central pixel and black central pixel as the following:

$$p_w^s[n], \ p_b^s[n], \qquad n = 0 \ldots N-1 \ , \tag{6}$$

Where $N = 2^b$.

Figure   shows several such pmfs for the packed spheres data (Fig.   ), demonstrating the difference in mass distribution at several different resolutions. For any given image (i.e configuration) the pmf may be approximated by a histogram:

$$h_x^w[n], \ h_x^b[n], \qquad n = 0 \ldots N-1 \ , \tag{7}$$

with total counts C_x^w, C_x^b, respectively. Thus the sample probability of configuration k for a white central pixel is $\frac{h_x^w[k]}{C_x^w}$. These sample statistics can be efficiently maintained while performing stochastic sampling.

Given the above, one possible energy function (used in ( )) at level s is a weighted sum of errors with respect to the target pmf at level s in the hierarchy:

$$\mathcal{E}_s(x) = \sum_{n=0}^{N-1} \left[\alpha_n^s \left(p_w^s[n] - \frac{h_x^w[n]}{C_x^w} \right)^2 + \beta_n^s \left(p_b^s[n] - \frac{h_x^b[n]}{C_x^b} \right)^2 \right] \ . \tag{8}$$

At each level in the hierarchy, the target pmfs define a new energy function. This can, however, be viewed as an approximation to the energy function at the final resolution.

More complicated energy functions may be proposed to allow more sophisticated modelling of particular image classes. In particular, nonlocal terms may be needed to accurately reflect image morphology. These considerations, while interesting, are separate from the issues surrounding hierarchical annealing proposed here. Additionally, the best choice of distance metric (or for that matter, including a non-metric such as the Kullback-Leibler distance) is not clear for this process. No claim of optimality is made the example given in ( ).

3.1   Implementation

In this experiment, target pmfs were measured as the mean of sample distributions from sets (50 − 100 images) of training data. Weights in ( ) are taken as 1 for this experiment, but need not be in general. The pmfs shown in Fig. correspond to the resolutions shown in Fig   , illustrating how mass distribution in the pmf varies with scale. This approach allows a very simple training of our model.

Samples were drawn from the models using a Metropolis [ ] sampler with random site location. In all cases annealing was performed using a geometric cooling schedule [ ]:

$$T_k = \alpha^k T_0 \qquad 0 < \alpha < 1 \ . \tag{9}$$

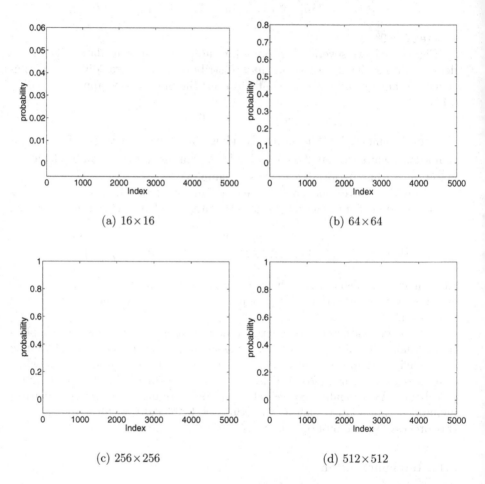

(a) 16×16

(b) 64×64

(c) 256×256

(d) 512×512

Fig. 7. Target pmfs at several resolutions. These particular pmfs are the sample mean distributions given a white central pixel at various resolutions for a set of packed glass spheres, see Fig. . The mass of the distribution is mostly located at homogeneous white neighbourhoods at the finest resolution (index 4095 corresponds to all white pixels). At low resolutions, the mass distribution exhibits a more interesting structure

In the experimental data presented here, the cooling parameter was taken as $\alpha = 0.9$. This parameter could, of course, be tuned to particular applications. As previously discussed, issues of 'optimal' cooling are considered to distract from the purpose of illustrating hierarchical annealing. Improvements may be made with analysis of particular models and cooling characteristics.

The heuristic rules discussed in §   were used to define progression through the hierarchy while annealing. In these experiments such an approach proved capable of reaching globally minimal energy states. It is expected that work with more complex energy functions (and therefore more expensive to compute) would reveal limitations for this simple heuristic and present directions for more sophisticated approaches.

It is worth noting that, by construction, ( ) does not allow for zero energy states in general. The size of the image domain will constrain the quantization, or step size, of the histogram approximations to the target probability mass functions. Hence in the general case for each non-zero value in the target pmf we can expect an error on the order of the inverse of the number of pixels. If we denote the number of pixels in an image domain D as $|D|$, and take b as the number of bits in the mapping ( ) then we may estimate the minimal energy as

$$\mathcal{E}^2_{\min} \approx 2^b \frac{1}{2} \frac{1}{|D|^2} \ . \tag{10}$$

4 Results

The results that follow are demonstrative of typical runs of the hierarchical annealing method presented in this paper. Two training data sets were used, one of a pack of glass beads, the other, natural rock.

Figure   shows a plot of computational cost vs. energy. This graph is identical to the one given in Fig   with the addition of a curve for the hierarchical annealing. Here, as previously, the energy for all curves is measured in the finest resolution lattice (the convergence in higher levels is governed by the energy function at that level, of course) in order to make comparison possible. This plot clearly demonstrates the computational advantages of the approach. Additionally, it is shown that both methods converge to a minimal energy. As noted above the histogram quantization does not allow zero energy configurations.

Figure , similarly, contains the data of Fig.   along with the hierarchical annealing values for comparison purposes. This figure demonstrates how the annealing schedule for a hierarchical annealing compares to 'flat' annealing at the highest resolution 512×512. Initial convergence is slower (relative to temperature) as the hierarchical method roughly follows the profile of coarser resolution curves. After mapping to the highest resolution, extremely fast convergence shows the 'preconditioning' effect of the method.

Figure   shows examples of synthetic images resulting from this algorithm, along with representative samples of the training data used to define target pmfs for both cases.

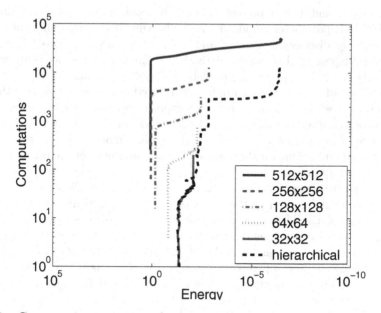

Fig. 8. Computation vs. energy for hierarchical and 'flat' annealing. Geometric cooling schedule with $\alpha = 0.9$. The target resolution is 512×512, and the hierarchy has 5 levels, with the coarsest level ($s = 4$) being 32×32. The two approaches converge to a similar minimal energy, however the hierarchical approach converges much more quickly. The repeated convergence/saturation of the energy is visible in the hierarchical curve, preceding shifts to the next scale

These images serve to demonstrate the capabilities (and limitations) of our simple model. Locally, the agreement seems qualitatively quite good; in terms of smooth edges, homogeneous regions, etc. Unsurprisingly, larger scale morphological features of the training data are *not* captured by our simple local model.

Computation times are very reasonable. The 512×512 samples shown here were generated in a few minutes on a 1Ghz PC workstation. By comparison, the synthesis of much smaller images has been reported to take on the order of 20–30 hours on an RS6000 workstation, by another stochastic relaxation approach [ ].

5   Conclusions

This paper has described a method of hierarchical annealing that can result in large computational gains for appropriate models. A simple model for binary porous media images was presented to demonstrate its effectiveness. The heuristic approach to multiscale annealing given here is supported somewhat by these simple experiments, but may prove to be naïve when generalizing to more complicated models. Future work must be performed with an aim to analyze

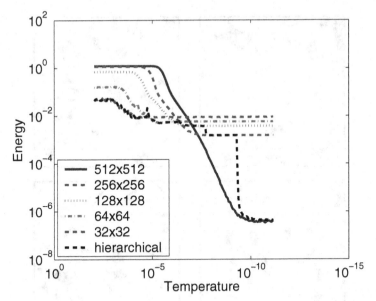

Fig. 9. Comparison of hierarchical annealing method with (flat) annealing at several resolutions. Hierarchical annealing results in highly accelerated convergence after mapping to the highest resolution

the complicated interaction between sampling, annealing, and refinement in the hierarchy.

Thus there are several directions open to future work in developing this approach. Of primary importance is analysis of the process for mapping to finer resolutions in the hierarchy. Other interesting questions abound; for example, convergence issues for the Markov chain samplers and relation to grid size, cooling schedule improvement, and introducing more complicated models as mentioned previously.

As illustrated in the previous section, the simplicity of this model restricts the class of appropriate images for direct application. It is interesting to consider the local features that are captured by this simple model, as well as the morphological differences that lie beyond the representation capability of the model.

Simple extensions to more complex models involving some non-local attributes such as chord-length [ ] could prove to be quite effective, while still very computationally tractable. Extension to 3D data should be straightforward in principle, and yield even greater computational savings than seen in 2D.

In addition to refining this method, other applications are of interest. Constraining synthesis with particular data is one possibility, and could be extended to 3D reconstruction from 2D data.

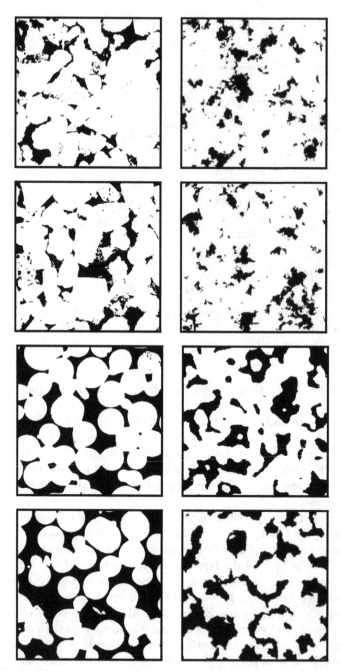

Fig. 10. Imaged (left column) and synthetic (right column) binary porous media images for two data sets; sandstone (top four) and packed glass spheres (bottom four)

References

[1] J. Besag, P. Green, D. Higdon, and K. Mengersen, *Bayesian computation and stochastic systems (with discussion)*, Statistical Science **10** (1995), 3–66.

[2] C. Bouman and M. Shapiro, *A multiscale random field model for Bayesian image segmentation*, IEEE Image Processing **3** (1994), no. 2, 162–177.

[3] Charles Bouman and Bede Liu, *Multiple resolution segmentation of textured images*, IEEE Transactions on Pattern Analysis and Machine Intelligence **13** (1991), no. 2, 99–113.

[4] J. Bramble, *Multigrid method*, John Wiley & Sons, 1993.

[5] Pierre Brémaud, *Markov chains: Gibbs fields, monte carlo simulation, and queues*, Springer, 1998.

[6] Davi Geiger and João E. Kogler Jr., *Scaling images and image features via the renormalization group*, Proceedings IEEE CVPR '93 (New York), June 1993.

[7] S. Geman and D. Geman, *Stochastic relaxation, Gibbs distributions, and the Bayesian restoration of images*, IEEE Transactions on Pattern Analysis and Machine Intelligence **6** (1984), 721–741.   ,   ,   ,

[8] B. Gidas, *Nonstationary markov chains and convergence of the annealing algorithm*, Journal of Statistical Physics **39** (1985), 73–131.   ,

[9] Basilis Gidas, *A renormalization group approach to image processing problems*, IEEE Transactions on Pattern Analysis and Machine Intelligence **11** (1989), no. 2, 164–180.   ,   ,

[10] W. Hackbusch, *Multigrid methods and applications*, Computational Mathematics, vol. 4, Springer Verlag, 1985.

[11] F. Heitz, P. Perez, and P. Bouthemy, *Multiscale minimization of global energy functions in some visual recovery problems*, Computer Vision, Graphics, and Image Processing. Image Understanding **59** (1994), no. 1, 125–134.

[12] Zoltan Kato, Marc Berthod, and Josiane Zerubia, *A hierarchical Markov random field model and multitemperature annealing for parallel image classification*, Graphical Models and Image Processing **58** (1996), no. 1, 18–37.

[13] Z. Liang, M. A. Ioannidis, and I Chatzis, *Reconstruction of 3d porous media using simulated annealing*, Computational Methods in Water Resources XIII (Balkema, Rotterdam) (Bentley et al., ed.), 2000.

[14] M. Luettgen, W. Karl, A. Willsky, and R. Tenney, *Multiscale representations of Markov random fields*, IEEE Transactions on Signal Processing **41** (1993), no. 12, 3377–3395.

[15] S. McCormick, *Multigrid methods*, SIAM, Philadelphia, 1987.

[16] N. Metropolis, A. W. Rosenbluth, M. N. Rosenbluth, A. H Teller, and E. Teller, *Equation of state calculations by fast computing machines*, Journal of Chemical Physics **21** (1953), 1087–1092.   ,

[17] R. Paget and I. D. Longstaff, *Texture synthesis via a noncausal nonparametric multiscale markov random field*, IEEE Transactions on Image Processing **7** (1998), no. 6, 925–931.

[18] Jan Puzicha and Joachim M. Buhmann, *Multiscale annealing for grouping and unsupervised texture segmentation*, Computer Vision and Image Understanding: CVIU **76** (1999), no. 3, 213–230.   ,

[19] Dietrich Stoyan, Wilfrid S. Kendall, and Joseph Mecke, *Stochastic geometry and its applications*, 2 ed., J. Wiley, 1996.

[20] Dietrich Stoyan and Helga Stoyan, *Fractals, random shapes and point fields: Methods of geometrical statistics*, J. Wiley, 1994.

[21] R. H. Swendson and J. S. Wang, *Nonuniversal critical dynamics in monte carlo simulations*, Physical Review Letters **58** (1987), 86–88.

[22] H. Szu and R. Hartley, *Fast simulated annealing*, Physics Letters A **122** (1987), 157–162.   ,

[23] M. S. Talukdar, O. Torsaeter, and M. A. Ionnidis, *Stochastic recontruction of particulate media from two-dimensional images*, Journal of Colloid and Interface Science **248** (2002), 419–428.   ,   ,   ,

[24] K. Wilson and J. Kogut, *The renormalization group and the ϵ-expansion*, Phys. Rep. **C12** (1974), 75–200.

[25] J. Zerubia, Z. Kato, and M. Berthod, *Multi-temperature annealing: a new approach for the energy-minimization of hierarchical markov random field models*, Proceedings of the 12th IAPR International Conference on Pattern Recognition (Jerusalem, Israel), vol. 1, 1994.   ,   ,

On Solutions to Multivariate Maximum α-Entropy Problems

Jose Costa[1], Alfred Hero[1], and Christophe Vignat[2]

[1] Department of Electrical Engineering and Computer Science
University of Michigan, Ann Arbor, MI 48109-2122, USA
`jcosta@umich.edu,hero@eecs.umich.edu`
[2] Laboratoire Systèmes de Communications
Université Marne la Vallée, France
`vignat@univ-mlv.fr`

Abstract. Entropy has been widely employed as an optimization function for problems in computer vision and pattern recognition. To gain insight into such methods it is important to characterize the behavior of the maximum-entropy probability distributions that result from the entropy optimization. The aim of this paper is to establish properties of multivariate distributions maximizing entropy for a general class of entropy functions, called Rényi's α-entropy, under a covariance constraint. First we show that these entropy-maximizing distributions exhibit interesting properties, such as spherical invariance, and have a stochastic Gaussian-Gamma mixture representation. We then turn to the question of stability of the class of entropy-maximizing distributions under addition.

1 Introduction

Entropy has been widely employed as an optimization function for problems in computer vision, communications, clustering, and pattern recognition; see [, , , , ,] for representative examples. In particular, entropy maximization/minimization methods have found natural application in areas where an entropy or information divergence can be used as a discriminant of the data. These include: texture classification, feature clustering, image indexing or image registration, which are all core problems in areas such as geographical information systems, medical information processing, multi-sensor fusion and image content based retrieval. For example, the mutual information method of image registration (see [ ] and references therein) searches through a set of coordinate transformations to find the one that minimizes the α-entropy of the joint feature distribution of the two images. In a similar way, a statistical image retrieval algorithm ([ ]) searches trough a database of images to choose the image whose feature distribution is the closest to the query image in a minimum information divergence sense. Thus, studying the entropy maximizing distributions is important for understanding the advantages and limitations of such entropy maximization methods.

A. Rangarajan et al. (Eds.): EMMCVPR 2003, LNCS 2683, pp. 211–   , 2003.
© Springer-Verlag Berlin Heidelberg 2003

The Rényi α-entropy [ ] is a generalization of the Shannon entropy and is defined as follows:

$$S_\alpha(f) = \frac{1}{1-\alpha} \log \int_{\mathbb{R}^n} f^\alpha(\mathbf{x}) \, d\mathbf{x} , \tag{1}$$

where f is the multivariate probability density of the n-dimensional random variable $\mathbf{X}$, and α is a real positive parameter. It can be easily shown that, as $\alpha \to 1$, the α-entropy S_α converges to the well known Shannon entropy:

$$S_1(f) \stackrel{\Delta}{=} \lim_{\alpha \to 1} S_\alpha(f) = - \int_{\mathbb{R}^n} f(\mathbf{x}) \log f(\mathbf{x}) \, d\mathbf{x} . \tag{2}$$

It is well-known that among all multivariate continuous distributions, the classical Gaussian distribution maximizes the Shannon entropy under a covariance (power) constraint. The question addressed in this paper is the characterization of the maximizing distribution of the Rényi entropy under the same covariance constraint.

The remainder of this paper is organized as follows. In Section 2, we show that the multivariate Student-t ($\alpha < 1$) and Student-r ($\alpha > 1$) densities are the maximum entropy distributions under a covariance constraint for different ranges of the parameter α. We then show that these distributions are elliptically invariant, which will allow a representation in terms of Gaussian scale mixtures. In addition, we give an alternative characterization for the maximum entropy distributions in terms of the Shannon entropy and a logarithmic constraint. In Section 3, we address the question of stability of the class of entropy-maximizing distributions under addition.

2   The Multivariate α-Entropy Maximizing Distribution

Rényi-entropy maximizing distributions have been studied for the restricted case of $\alpha > 1$, by Moriguti in the scalar case [ ] and by Kapur [ ] in the multivariate case. The case of $\alpha \in [0,1]$ is of special interest since, in this region, the Rényi-entropy generalizes easily to Rényi-divergence via measure transformation [ ].

Throughout, $\mathbf{X}$ will denote an n-dimensional real random vector with covariance matrix $\mathbf{K} = E(\mathbf{X}-\mu_{\mathbf{X}})(\mathbf{X}-\mu_{\mathbf{X}})^T$. In what follows, we consider, without loss of generality, the centered case $\mu_{\mathbf{X}} = E\mathbf{X} = 0$. Define next the following constants:

$$m = \begin{cases} n + \frac{2}{\alpha-1} & \text{if } \alpha > 1 \\ \frac{2}{1-\alpha} - n & \text{if } \alpha < 1 \end{cases}, \qquad \mathbf{C}_\alpha = \begin{cases} (m+2)\mathbf{K} & \text{if } \alpha > 1 \\ (m-2)\mathbf{K} & \text{if } \alpha < 1 \end{cases},$$

and

$$A_\alpha = \begin{cases} \dfrac{1}{|\pi \mathbf{C}_\alpha|^{\frac{1}{2}}} \dfrac{\Gamma(\frac{m}{2}+1)}{\Gamma(\frac{m-n}{2}+1)} & \text{if } \alpha > 1 \\[2ex] \dfrac{1}{|\pi \mathbf{C}_\alpha|^{\frac{1}{2}}} \dfrac{\Gamma(\frac{m+n}{2})}{\Gamma(\frac{m}{2})} & \text{if } \frac{n}{n+2} < \alpha < 1 \end{cases},$$

and the following sets

$$\Omega_\alpha = \begin{cases} \{\mathbf{x} \in \mathbb{R}^n : \mathbf{x}^T \mathbf{C}_\alpha^{-1} \mathbf{x} \le 1\} & \text{if } \alpha > 1 \\ \mathbb{R}^n & \text{if } \frac{n}{n+2} < \alpha < 1 \end{cases}.$$

Define the $n-$variate probability density f_α as follows:

– if $\alpha > 1$

$$f_\alpha(\mathbf{x}) = \begin{cases} A_\alpha \left(1 - \mathbf{x}^T \mathbf{C}_\alpha^{-1} \mathbf{x}\right)^{\frac{1}{\alpha-1}} & \text{if } \mathbf{x} \in \Omega_\alpha \\ 0 & \text{otherwise} \end{cases} \tag{3}$$

– if $\frac{n}{n+2} < \alpha < 1$

$$f_\alpha(\mathbf{x}) = A_\alpha \left(1 + \mathbf{x}^T \mathbf{C}_\alpha^{-1} \mathbf{x}\right)^{\frac{1}{\alpha-1}} \quad \forall \mathbf{x} \in \mathbb{R}^n \tag{4}$$

The following theorem provides a general description of the $\alpha-$entropy maximizing densities.

Theorem 1. *For any probability density f with covariance matrix $\mathbf{K}$ and $\alpha > \frac{n}{n+2}$,*

$$S_\alpha(f) \le S_\alpha(f_\alpha) ,$$

with equality if and only if $f = f_\alpha$ almost everywhere.

Note that Theorem implies that the entropy $S_\alpha(f)$ has a unique maximizer f_α. We also point out that, when $0 < \alpha \le \frac{n}{n+2}$, f_α has infinite covariance and so the covariance constraint cannot be met.

We prove this theorem by introducing a new divergence measure and adopting an information theoretic approach similar to that used by [, Theorem 6.9.5] to prove that the Gaussian distribution maximizes Shannon entropy.

Consider the following non-symmetric directed divergence measure

$$D_\alpha(f\|g) = \text{sign}(\alpha - 1) \int_{\mathbb{R}_n} \left(\frac{f^\alpha}{\alpha} + \frac{\alpha-1}{\alpha} g^\alpha - f g^{\alpha-1} \right) \tag{5}$$

The general theory of directed divergence measures is discussed in [ ] and [ ]. Convexity of D_α gives the following positivity property: for any two probability densities f and g, we have

$$D_\alpha(f\|g) \ge 0$$

with equality if and only if $f = g$ a.e.

Lemma 1. *For any $n-$variate probability density f with covariance matrix $\mathbf{K}$,*

$$\int_{\mathbb{R}_n} f f_\alpha^{\alpha-1} \ge \int_{\mathbb{R}_n} f_\alpha , \tag{6}$$

with equality iff $\text{supp}(f) \subseteq \Omega_\alpha$.

Proof. Suppose for example $\alpha > 1$. Then

$$\int_{\mathbb{R}_n} f f_\alpha^{\alpha-1} = \int_{\Omega_\alpha} f(\mathbf{x}) A_\alpha^{\alpha-1} \left(1 - \mathbf{x}^T \mathbf{C}_\alpha^{-1} \mathbf{x}\right) d\mathbf{x}$$

$$\ge \int_{\mathbb{R}_n} f(\mathbf{x}) A_\alpha^{\alpha-1} \left(1 - \mathbf{x}^T \mathbf{C}_\alpha^{-1} \mathbf{x}\right) d\mathbf{x} ,$$

with equality iff $\mathrm{supp}(f) \subseteq \Omega_\alpha$. But, as f and f_α have the same covariance matrix,

$$\int_{\mathbb{R}_n} \mathbf{x}^T \mathbf{C}_\alpha^{-1} \mathbf{x} f(\mathbf{x})\, d\mathbf{x} = \int_{\mathbb{R}_n} \mathbf{x}^T \mathbf{C}_\alpha^{-1} \mathbf{x} f_\alpha(\mathbf{x})\, d\mathbf{x} ,$$

which implies

$$\int_{\mathbb{R}_n} f f_\alpha^{\alpha-1} \geq \int_{\mathbb{R}_n} f_\alpha A_\alpha^{\alpha-1} \left(1 - \mathbf{x}^T \mathbf{C}_\alpha^{-1} \mathbf{x}\right) d\mathbf{x} = \int_{\mathbb{R}_n} f_\alpha^\alpha .$$

The proof is similar in the case $\alpha < 1$. ☐

We can now deduce the extremal property of the density f_α.

Proof (of Theorem   ). Suppose, for example, $\alpha > 1$. Then, by Lemma   and positivity of D_α,

$$0 \leq D_\alpha(f \| f_\alpha) \leq \int_{\mathbb{R}_n} \left(\frac{f^\alpha}{\alpha} + \frac{\alpha-1}{\alpha} f_\alpha^\alpha - f_\alpha^\alpha\right) = \frac{1}{\alpha} \int_{\mathbb{R}_n} (f^\alpha - f_\alpha^\alpha) .$$

Theorem   now follows. The proof is similar for $\alpha < 1$. ☐

Although the case $\alpha = 1$ was not explicitly addressed above, it can easily be shown that f_α converges pointwise to the density of $\mathcal{N}(0, \mathbf{K})$ when $\alpha \to 1$. Likewise, the corresponding entropies also converge to the Shannon entropy, thus extending, by continuity, Theorem   to the well known case of $\alpha = 1$.

Definition 1. *A distribution is called elliptically invariant if it has the form*

$$p_\mathbf{X}(\mathbf{x}) = \phi_\mathbf{X}\left(\mathbf{x}^T \mathbf{C}^{-1} \mathbf{x}\right) \tag{7}$$

for some function $\phi_\mathbf{X} : \mathbb{R}^+ \to \mathbb{R}^+$ and some positive definite matrix $\mathbf{C}$, called the characteristic matrix.

It is easily seen that f_α, defined by equations ( ) and ( ), is an elliptically invariant density. A consequence of this elliptical invariance property is that if $\mathbf{X}$ is a random vector with density f_α, $\alpha < 1$, then it can be represented as a Gaussian scale mixture [ ]: $\mathbf{X} = A\mathbf{N}$, where A is a Gamma random variable with shape parameter $\frac{m}{2} = \frac{1}{1-\alpha} - \frac{n}{2}$ and scale parameter 2, i.e., $A \sim \Gamma(\frac{m}{2}, 2)$. When $m = \frac{2}{1-\alpha} - n$ is a positive integer, A can be represented as a Chi-square random variable with m degrees of freedom. $\mathbf{N}$ is a n-variate Gaussian random vector, independent of A, with covariance matrix $\mathbf{C}_\alpha$. For more details see [ ]. Equivalently, $\mathbf{X}$ can be rewritten as

$$\mathbf{X} = \frac{\mathbf{C}_\alpha^{\frac{1}{2}} \mathbf{N}_0}{\sqrt{\sum_{i=1}^m N_i^2}} , \tag{8}$$

where $\mathbf{N}_0$ is a zero mean Gaussian random vector with identity covariance matrix $\mathbf{I}_n$. As

$$\frac{\mathbf{C}_\alpha^{\frac{1}{2}}}{\sqrt{\sum_{i=1}^m N_i^2}} = \frac{\mathbf{K}^{\frac{1}{2}}}{\sqrt{\frac{1}{m-2} \sum_{i=1}^m N_i^2}}$$

converges a.s. to the constant matrix $\mathbf{K}^{\frac{1}{2}}$ when $m \to +\infty$ (i.e. $\alpha \to 1$), it is evident that, by Slutzky's theorem, $\mathbf{X}$ converges in distribution to a Gaussian random vector.

Although the Gaussian scale mixture representation does not hold in the case $\alpha > 1$, we can extend the stochastic representation based on the existence of a natural bijection between the cases $\alpha < 1$ and $\alpha > 1$. This gives the following proposition:

Proposition 1. *If* $\mathbf{X}$ *is an* $n-$*variate random vector distributed according to* f_α *with* $\alpha > 1$, *and if* m, *defined as*

$$\alpha = \frac{m+n}{m+n-2} , \tag{9}$$

is an integer not equal to zero, then $\mathbf{X}$ *has the representation*

$$\mathbf{X}_\alpha = \mathbf{C}_\alpha^{\frac{1}{2}} \frac{\mathbf{N}}{\sqrt{\|\mathbf{N}\|_2^2 + N_1^2 + \cdots + N_m^2}} , \tag{10}$$

where $\{N_i\}_{1 \leq i \leq m}$ *are Gaussian* $\mathcal{N}(0,1)$ *mutually independent, and independent of* $\mathbf{N}$ *which is Gaussian* $\mathcal{N}(0, \mathbf{I}_n)$.

We remark here that the denominator in ( ) is a chi random variable with $m+n$ degrees of freedom which, contrarily to the case $\alpha < 1$, is not independent of the numerator. Using these stochastic representations, random samples from f_α with integer degrees of freedom can be easily implemented with a Gaussian random number generator and a squarer.

Characteristic Function The characteristic function φ_α of f_α can be deduced from the following formula [ ]:

$$\varphi_\alpha(\mathbf{u}) = \mathcal{L}\left[w^{-2} f_W\left(w^{-1}\right)\right]_{s=\mathbf{u}^T \mathbf{C}_\alpha \mathbf{u}} ,$$

where $\mathcal{L}$ denotes the Laplace transform.

(a) – Case $\alpha < 1$. From [ ],

$$\mathcal{L}\left[w^{-2} f_W\left(w^{-1}\right)\right] = \frac{2^{1-\frac{m}{2}}}{\Gamma\left(\frac{m}{2}\right)} s^{\frac{m}{2}} K_{\frac{m}{2}}(s) .$$

The characteristic function of the Rényi distribution can then be written as

$$\varphi_\alpha(\mathbf{u}) = \frac{2^{1-\frac{m}{2}}}{\Gamma\left(\frac{m}{2}\right)} \left(\mathbf{u}^T \mathbf{C}_\alpha \mathbf{u}\right)^{\frac{m}{2}} K_{\frac{m}{2}}\left(\mathbf{u}^T \mathbf{C}_\alpha \mathbf{u}\right) , \tag{11}$$

where $K_{\frac{m}{2}}$ denotes the modified Bessel function of the second kind.

(b) – Case $\alpha > 1$. Although the preceding technique does not apply in the case $\alpha > 1$, a direct computation yields the characteristic function in this case as

$$\varphi_\alpha\left(\mathbf{u}\right) = 2^{\frac{m}{2}}\Gamma\left(\frac{m}{2}+1\right)\left(\mathbf{u}^T\mathbf{C}_\alpha\mathbf{u}\right)^{-\frac{m}{2}}J_{\frac{m}{2}}\left(\mathbf{u}^T\mathbf{C}_\alpha\mathbf{u}\right), \qquad (12)$$

where $J_{\frac{m}{2}}$ denotes the Bessel function of the first kind.

We remark that both families of characteristic functions ( ) and ( ) are normalized in such a way that

$$\varphi_\alpha\left(\mathbf{u}\right) = 1 + O\left(\left(\mathbf{u}^T\mathbf{C}_\alpha\mathbf{u}\right)^2\right).$$

Moreover, it can be checked that, as $\alpha \to 1$, these functions converge pointwise to the classical Gaussian characteristic function.

2.1   An Alternative Entropic Characterization

The Rényi-entropy maximizing distribution can be characterized as a Shannon entropy maximizer under a logarithmic constraint: this property was first derived by Kapur in his seminal paper [ ]. It was remarked also by Zografos [ ] in the multivariate case, but not connected to the Rényi entropy. We state here an extension of Kapur's main result to the correlated case. This result can be proven using the stochastic representation (see [ ] for details).

Theorem 2. f_α *with* $\alpha < 1$ *(resp.* $\alpha > 1$*) and characteristic matrix* $\mathbf{C}_\alpha$ *is the solution of the following optimization problem*

$$f_\alpha = \arg\max_f S_1\left(f\right)$$

under constraint

$$\int \log\left(1 + \mathbf{x}^T\mathbf{C}_\alpha^{-1}\mathbf{x}\right)f\left(\mathbf{x}\right)d\mathbf{x} = \psi\left(\frac{m+n}{2}\right) - \psi\left(\frac{m}{2}\right) \qquad (13)$$

$\left(\text{resp.} \int \log\left(1 - \mathbf{x}^T\mathbf{C}_\alpha^{-1}\mathbf{x}\right)f\left(\mathbf{x}\right)d\mathbf{x} = \psi\left(\frac{m}{2}\right) - \psi\left(\frac{m+n}{2}\right)\right)$, *where* $\psi(m) = \frac{\Gamma'(m)}{\Gamma(m)}$ *is the digamma function.*

We make the following observations. Firstly, the constraint in this multivariate optimization problem is real-valued, and its value is independent of the characteristic matrix $\mathbf{C}_\alpha$. Secondly, as the logarithmic moment $E\log\left(1 + \mathbf{X}^T\mathbf{C}_\alpha^{-1}\mathbf{X}\right)$ exists for all $\alpha > 0$, the distributions f_α as defined by ( ) are solutions of the logarithmic constrained maximum Shannon entropy problem even in the case $\alpha < \frac{n}{n+2}$. However, in this case the covariance matrix does not exist and therefore the matrix $\mathbf{C}_\alpha$ can not be interpreted as a covariance matrix.

3   Convolution of Entropy Maximizing Distributions

We first discuss the issue of renormalization as presented by Mendes et al. [ ]. Then we address the issue of stability under the addition operation.

3.1   Renormalizability of f_α

Mendes and Tsallis ([ ]) have shown that Rényi distributions have the important property of "renormalizability", but contrarily to the Gaussian case, they
are not "factorizable". f_α has the renormalizability property when

$$\int_{-\infty}^{+\infty} f_\alpha(x_1, x_2)\, dx_2 = f_{\alpha'}(x_1)$$

for some α'. In statistical terms, this expresses the fact that the 2$-$dimensional
distributions remain of the same type after marginalization. Using the elliptical
invariance property, we provide here a much more general result, as stated by
the following theorem.

Theorem 3. *Let* $\mathbf{X}^T = \begin{bmatrix} \mathbf{X}_1^T, \mathbf{X}_2^T \end{bmatrix}$ *(dim* $\mathbf{X}_i = n_i, n_1 + n_2 = n$*) be a ran-*
dom vector distributed according to f_α *with characteristic matrix* $\mathbf{C} =$
$[\mathbf{C}_{11}, \mathbf{C}_{12}; \mathbf{C}_{21}, \mathbf{C}_{22}]$ *(dim* $\mathbf{C}_{ij} = n_i \times n_j$*). Then the marginal density of vector*
$\mathbf{X}_i$ *(*$i = 1, 2$*) is* f_{α_i}*, with index* α_i *such that*

$$\frac{1}{1-\alpha_i} = \frac{1}{1-\alpha} - \frac{n_i}{2} \ ,$$

and characteristic matrix $\mathbf{C}_{ii}$.

Proof. Suppose first $\alpha < 1$ and consider the stochastic representation

$$\mathbf{X} = \mathbf{C}^{\frac{1}{2}} \frac{\begin{bmatrix} \mathbf{N}_1^T, \mathbf{N}_2^T \end{bmatrix}^T}{\chi_m} \ ,$$

where $\begin{bmatrix} \mathbf{N}_1^T, \mathbf{N}_2^T \end{bmatrix}$ is a Gaussian vector with identity covariance and partitioned
similarly to $\mathbf{X}$. Then the stochastic representation of $\mathbf{X}_i$ is

$$\mathbf{X}_i = \frac{\tilde{\mathbf{N}}_i}{\chi_m}$$

for some n_i-variate Gaussian vector $\tilde{\mathbf{N}}_i$ so that the indices α and α_i are characterized by

$$\alpha = \frac{m+n-2}{m+n}, \qquad \alpha_i = \frac{m+n_i-2}{m+n_i} \ .$$

Hence

$$\frac{1}{1-\alpha_i} = \frac{1}{1-\alpha} - \frac{n_i}{2} \ .$$

The characteristic matrix of $\mathbf{X}_i$ can be deduced by remarking that $\mathbf{X}_i$ can be
expressed as

$$\mathbf{X}_i = \mathbf{H}\mathbf{X} \ ,$$

where $\mathbf{H}$ is a $n_i \times n$ matrix whose $i-th$ block is the $n_i \times n_i$ identity matrix so
that the characteristic matrix of $\mathbf{X}_i$ writes (see [, corollary 3.2])

$$\mathbf{H}\mathbf{C}\mathbf{H}^T = \mathbf{C}_{ii} \ .$$

The case $\alpha > 1$ follows accordingly.   □

Thus the renormalization property, as observed in [   ], is nothing but a consequence of the elliptical invariance property, which is itself induced by the orthogonal invariance of both the Rényi entropy and the covariance constraint.

3.2   Stability of Rényi Distributions

It is well known that the Gaussian distributions are stable in the sense that the sum of two Gaussian random vectors is also Gaussian, although with possibly different means and variances. An interesting question is the stability of the class of Rényi-entropy maximizing distributions defined as the set of all densities f_α of the form ( )-( ) for some $\alpha \in (0,1]$ and some positive definite characteristic matrix $\mathbf{C}_\alpha$. In the following, we characterize the conditions under which stability of the Rényi-entropy maximizing distributions is ensured, and link this feature with their elliptical invariance property, distinguishing between three important cases: the Rényi mutually dependent case, the mutually independent case and the special case of odd degrees of freedom. For proofs of these results see the referenced articles or [   ].

Mutually Dependent Case

Theorem 4 ([ ]). *If $\mathbf{X}_1$ and $\mathbf{X}_2$ are n_1 and n_2-variate vectors mutually distributed according to a Rényi-entropy maximizing density f_α with index α and characteristic matrix $\mathbf{C}_\alpha$, and if $\mathbf{H}$ is a $n' \times n$ matrix with $n = n_1 + n_2$, then the n'-variate vector*

$$\mathbf{Z} = \mathbf{H} \begin{bmatrix} \mathbf{X}_1 \\ \mathbf{X}_2 \end{bmatrix}$$

is distributed according to a Rényi-entropy maximizing density $f_{\alpha'}$ with index α' and characteristic matrix $\mathbf{C}_{\alpha'}$ such that

$$\mathbf{C}_{\alpha'} = \mathbf{H}\mathbf{C}_\alpha\mathbf{H}^T \ ,$$
$$\frac{1}{1-\alpha'} = \frac{1}{1-\alpha} + \frac{n'-n}{2} \ .$$

Independent Rényi-Entropy Maximizing Random Variables

Theorem 5 ([ ]). *If X and Y are two scalar i.i.d. random variables with density f_α, then $Z = X + Y$ has a density which is **nearly** equal to $f_{\alpha'}$, with index α' such that*

$$\alpha' = 2 - (2-\alpha)\left(1 - 4\frac{\alpha(\alpha-1)}{(3\alpha-5)(\alpha+3)}\right) \ . \tag{14}$$

The relative mean square error of this approximation is numerically bounded by 10^{-5}.

Relation ( ) was obtained in [ ] by evaluating all derivatives up to order 5 at point 0 of the distribution of $X + Y$ and showing that they are nearly identical (up to numerical precision of the simulations) to those of a Rényi-entropy maximizing distribution $f_{\alpha'}$ with the given parameter α'. In the case where m is an odd integer stronger results can be established. For economy of notation, we define, for m a positive integer,

$$f^{(m)} = f_\alpha , \quad \alpha = \frac{m + n - 2}{m + n} . \tag{15}$$

The first original result we state now is an extension to the multivariate case of the classical one-dimensional result, for which a rich literature already exists (see for example [ ],[ ]).

Theorem 6. *Suppose that* $\mathbf{X}$ *and* $\mathbf{Y}$ *are two independent n-variate random vectors with densities* $f^{(m_{\mathbf{X}})}$ *and* $f^{(m_{\mathbf{Y}})}$, *respectively, and characteristic matrices* $\mathbf{C_X} = \mathbf{C_Y} = \mathbf{I}_n$, *with* **odd** *degrees of freedom* $m_{\mathbf{X}}$ *and* $m_{\mathbf{Y}}$. *Then, for* $0 \leq \beta \leq 1$, *the distribution of* $\mathbf{Z} = \beta \mathbf{X} + (1 - \beta) \mathbf{Y}$ *is*

$$p_{\mathbf{Z}} (\mathbf{z}) = \sum_{k=0}^{k_{\mathbf{Z}}} \alpha_k f^{(2k+1)} (\mathbf{z}) , \tag{16}$$

where $k_{\mathbf{Z}} \leq \frac{m_{\mathbf{X}} + m_{\mathbf{Y}}}{2} - 1$.

Proof. Denote $k_{\mathbf{X}} \in \mathbb{N}$ such that, by hypothesis, $m_{\mathbf{X}} = 2k_{\mathbf{X}} + 1$, and $k_{\mathbf{Y}}$ accordingly. The characteristic function of $\mathbf{X}$ in this special case writes

$$\phi_{\mathbf{X}} (\mathbf{u}) = e^{-\|\mathbf{u}\|} Q_{k_{\mathbf{X}}} (\|\mathbf{u}\|) ,$$

where $\|\mathbf{u}\| = \sqrt{\mathbf{u}^T \mathbf{u}}$ and $Q_{k_{\mathbf{X}}}$ is a polynomial of degree $d(Q_{k_{\mathbf{X}}}) = k_{\mathbf{X}}$. By the independence assumption, the characteristic function of $\mathbf{Z}$ writes

$$\begin{aligned}\phi_{\mathbf{Z}} (\mathbf{u}) &= \phi_{\mathbf{X}} (\beta \mathbf{u}) \phi_{\mathbf{Y}} ((1 - \beta) \mathbf{u}) \\ &= e^{-|\beta| \|\mathbf{u}\|} Q_{k_{\mathbf{X}}} (\beta \|\mathbf{u}\|) e^{-|1 - \beta| \|\mathbf{u}\|} Q_{k_{\mathbf{Y}}} ((1 - \beta) \|\mathbf{u}\|) \\ &= e^{-\|\mathbf{u}\|} Q_{k_{\mathbf{X}}} (\beta \|\mathbf{u}\|) Q_{k_{\mathbf{Y}}} ((1 - \beta) \|\mathbf{u}\|) .\end{aligned}$$

As each polynomial Q_k has exactly degree k, the set of polynomials $\{Q_l\}_{0 \leq k \leq k_{\mathbf{Z}}}$ is a basis of the linear space of polynomials with degree lower or equal to $k_{\mathbf{X}} + k_{\mathbf{Y}}$: thus, $Q_{k_{\mathbf{X}}} (\beta \|\mathbf{u}\|) Q_{k_{\mathbf{Y}}} ((1 - \beta) \|\mathbf{u}\|)$, itself a polynomial of degree $k_{\mathbf{Z}} \leq k_{\mathbf{X}} + k_{\mathbf{Y}} = \frac{m_{\mathbf{X}} + m_{\mathbf{Y}}}{2} - 1$, can be expressed in a unique way in this basis. Consequently, there exists a unique set $\{\alpha_k\}_{0 \leq k \leq k_{\mathbf{Z}}}$ of real numbers such that

$$Q_{k_{\mathbf{X}}} (\beta \|\mathbf{u}\|) Q_{k_{\mathbf{Y}}} ((1 - \beta) \|\mathbf{u}\|) = \sum_{k=0}^{k_{\mathbf{Z}}} Q_k (\|\mathbf{u}\|)$$

and

$$\phi_{\mathbf{Z}} (\mathbf{u}) = e^{-\|\mathbf{u}\|} \sum_{k=0}^{k_{\mathbf{Z}}} \alpha_k Q_k (\|\mathbf{u}\|) .$$

Result ( ) now follows by inverse Fourier transform. Note that coefficients $\{\alpha_k\}$ depend on β. ☐

This result can be restated as follows: the distribution of a convex linear combination of independent Rényi-entropy maximizing random variables with odd degrees of freedom is distributed according to a **discrete scale mixture** of Rényi-entropy maximizing distributions with odd degrees of freedom. However, although the fact that

$$\sum_{k=0}^{k_{\mathbf{Z}}} \alpha_k = 1$$

holds trivially by integrating relation ( ) over $\mathbb{R}^n$, the positiveness of the coefficients α_k has, to our best knowledge, never proved in the literature. We are currently working on this conjecture, for which numerical simulations have confirmed the positivity of α_k's for a large number of special cases.

A Second Result: An Information Projection Property

The second result that we propose in this context allows us to characterize the projection of the Rényi entropy maximizing distribution onto a convolution of $f^{(m')}$'s with odd degrees of freedom.

Theorem 7. *Consider* $\mathbf{X}$ *and* $\mathbf{Y}$ *two independent n-variate random vectors following densities* $f^{(m_{\mathbf{X}})}$ *and* $f^{(m_{\mathbf{Y}})}$, *respectively, with characteristic matrices* $\mathbf{C_X} = \mathbf{C_Y} = \mathbf{I}_n$ *and* **odd** *degrees of freedom* $m_{\mathbf{X}}$ *and* $m_{\mathbf{Y}}$. *Let* $\mathbf{Z} = \frac{1}{2}(\mathbf{X} + \mathbf{Y})$. *Then, the Rényi distribution which is the closest to the distribution of* $\mathbf{Z}$ *in the sense of the Kullback-Leibler divergence has* m' *degrees of freedom such that*

$$w_n(m') = E w_n[M] , \tag{17}$$

where,

− *function* w_n *is defined as*

$$w_n(m) = \psi\left(\frac{m+n}{2}\right) - \psi\left(\frac{m}{2}\right) ;$$

− *the random variable* M *is distributed according to*

$$\Pr\{M = 2k+1\} = \alpha_k , \tag{18}$$

where coefficients α_k *are defined by* ( ) *for* $\beta = \frac{1}{2}$.

Moreover, condition ( ) *is equivalent to*

$$E_{f^{(m')}} \log\left(1 + \mathbf{x}^T\mathbf{x}\right) = E_{f_{\mathbf{Z}}} \log\left(1 + \mathbf{x}^T\mathbf{x}\right) .$$

Proof. The Kullback-Leibler distance between the distribution p_Z of Z and a Rényi distribution $f^{(m')}$ with parameter m' is given by

$$D\left(p_Z || f^{(m')}\right) = \int p_Z \log \frac{p_Z}{f^{(m')}}$$

$$= -S_1\left(p_Z\right) - \int p_Z \log f^{(m')} .$$

Distribution p_Z takes the form

$$p_Z\left(\mathbf{z}\right) = \sum_{k=0}^{k_Z} \alpha_k f^{(2k+1)}\left(\mathbf{z}\right) ,$$

with $k_Z = \frac{m_X + m_Y}{2} - 1$. Finding the optimal value of m' is thus equivalent to maximizing the integral $\int p_Z \log f^{(m')}$ that can be explicitly computed using a result obtained by Zografos [ ]: if $\mathbf{X} \sim f_m$ then

$$E \log\left(1 + \mathbf{X}^T \mathbf{X}\right) = w_n\left(m\right) \overset{\Delta}{=} \psi\left(\frac{m+n}{2}\right) - \psi\left(\frac{m}{2}\right) .$$

Thus

$$\int p_Z \log f^{(m')} = \int \sum_{k=0}^{m_Z} \alpha_k f^{(2k+1)}\left(\mathbf{z}\right) \log f^{(m')}\left(\mathbf{z}\right) d\mathbf{z}$$

$$= \sum_{k=0}^{m_Z} \alpha_k \int f^{(2k+1)} \log A_{\alpha'}\left(1 + \mathbf{z}^T \mathbf{z}\right)^{-\frac{m'+n}{2}} d\mathbf{z}$$

$$= \sum_{k=0}^{m_Z} \alpha_k \log A_{\alpha'} - \frac{m'+n}{2} \sum_{k=0}^{m_Z} \alpha_k E_{f^{(2k+1)}}\left(1 + \mathbf{Z}^T \mathbf{Z}\right)$$

$$= \log \frac{\Gamma\left(\frac{m'+n}{2}\right)}{\Gamma\left(\frac{1}{2}\right) \Gamma\left(\frac{m'}{2}\right)} - \frac{m'+n}{2} \sum_{k=0}^{m_Z} \alpha_k w_n\left(2k+1\right) .$$

Taking the derivative and equating to zero yields

$$w_n\left(m'\right) = E w_n\left(M\right) ,$$

where M is distributed according to ( ). The fact that m' corresponds to a maximum of the considered integral (and thus to a minimum of the Kullback-Leibler distance) is a direct consequence of the negativity of the second derivative of ψ, together with

$$\psi'(\frac{m'+n}{2}) - \psi'(\frac{m'}{2}) = \frac{\partial^2}{\partial m'^2} \int p_Z \log f^{(m')} .$$

---

[1] Function $w_n\left(m\right)$ is denoted as $w_2\left(m, n\right)$ in [ ].

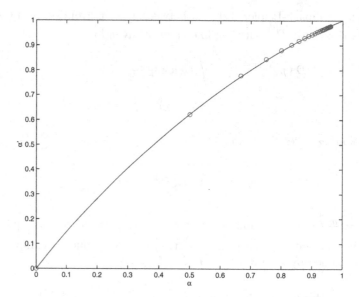

Fig. 1. Equation ( ) (*solid line*) and the solutions of equation ( ) (*circles*). See text for explanation

Finally, computing

$$E_{f(m')} \log\left(1 + \mathbf{Z}^T\mathbf{Z}\right) = w_n\left(m'\right)$$

$$= \sum_{k=0}^{m_Z} \alpha_k w_n\left(2k + 1\right)$$

$$= \sum_{k=0}^{m_Z} \alpha_k E_{f(2k+1)} \log\left(1 + \mathbf{Z}^T\mathbf{Z}\right)$$

$$= E_{f_Z} \log\left(1 + \mathbf{Z}^T\mathbf{Z}\right)$$

yields the final result.   □

    Equation ( ) defining variable m' in terms of dimension n and degrees of freedom m does not seem to have any closed-form solution. However, it can be solved numerically : Fig. represents the resulting values of α' as a function of α, when m takes all odd values from 1 to 51 (circles); moreover, the superimposed solid line curve shows α' as a function of α as defined by ( ) in the approach by Oliveira et al [ ]. This curve shows a very accurate agreement between our results and Oliveira's results.

---

[2] Note that in the case $m = 1$, the solution is obviously $m' = 1$ since the Cauchy distributions are stable.

Table 1. m' as a function of m

$m =$	3	5	9	11	21	51
$n = 1$	4.2646	8.0962	16.026	20.017	40.004	100.0
$n = 2$	4.2857	8.1116	16.047	20.021	40.005	100.0
$n = 5$	4.318	8.1406	16.032	20.031	40.008	100.0

Moreover, by inspecting the numerical solutions m' of equation ( ) for different values of m and n, as depicted in Table , we propose an approximation rule called the "$m' = 2m - 2$" rule.

Proposition 2. *Given m and n, the solution m' of ( ) can be approximated, for m sufficiently large, as:*

$$m' \simeq 2m - 2 \; ,$$

or, equivalently $\left(as\ \alpha = \frac{m+n-2}{m+n} \right)$

$$\alpha' \simeq \frac{(4+n)\,\alpha - n}{(2+n)\,\alpha - (n-2)} \; .$$

We note that this approximation is all the more accurate when α is near 1, and it is in agreement with the approximation provided by Oliveira et al.

A Third Result: Almost Additivity Unfortunately, a closed form expression for the distance between p_Z and $f^{(m')}$ is difficult to derive. The following theorem, however, allows us to derive an upper bound on this distance.

Theorem 8. *The distribution of the form $f^{(m')}$ closest to p_Z satisfies the orthogonality property*

$$D\left(f^{(m')} \| p_Z \right) = S_1\left(f^{(m')} \right) - S_1\left(p_Z \right) \; . \tag{19}$$

Moreover, the corresponding minimum Kullback-Leibler distance can be bounded as follows:

$$D\left(f^{(m')} \| p_Z \right) \leq S_1\left(f^{(m')} \right) - S_1\left(f^{(m)} \right) + \frac{1}{2}\log 2 \; . \tag{20}$$

Proof. Remarking that

$$\int p_Z \log f^{(m')} = \log A_{\alpha'} - \frac{m'+n}{2} \sum_{k=0}^{m_Z} \alpha_k w_n\,(2k+1)$$

$$= \log A_{\alpha'} - \frac{m'+n}{2} w_n\,(m') \; ,$$

we deduce

$$D\left(p_{\mathbf{Z}}||f^{(m')}\right) = -S_1\left(p_Z\right) - \int p_{\mathbf{Z}} \log f^{(m')}$$

$$= S_1\left(f^{(m')}\right) - S_1\left(p_Z\right) .$$

Let us now consider

$$S_1\left(p_{\mathbf{Z}}\right) = S_1\left(p_{\frac{\mathbf{X+Y}}{2}}\right) = S_1\left(p_{\mathbf{X+Y}}\right) - \log 2 .$$

A classical inequality on the Shannon entropy of the sum of independent random variables is the so called entropy power inequality [ ]:

$$S_1\left(p_{\mathbf{X+Y}}\right) \geq S_1\left(p_{\tilde{\mathbf{X}}+\tilde{\mathbf{Y}}}\right) , \tag{21}$$

where $\tilde{\mathbf{X}}$ and $\tilde{\mathbf{Y}}$ are independent Gaussian random variables such that

$$S_1\left(p_{\tilde{\mathbf{X}}}\right) = S_1\left(p_{\mathbf{X}}\right) \text{ and } S_1\left(p_{\tilde{\mathbf{Y}}}\right) = S_1\left(p_{\mathbf{Y}}\right) .$$

These constraints are equivalent to

$$\sigma_{\tilde{\mathbf{X}}} = \sigma_{\tilde{\mathbf{Y}}} = \frac{\exp\left(\frac{m+n}{2} w_n\left(m\right)\right)}{A_\alpha \sqrt{2\pi e}} ,$$

so that

$$S_1\left(p_{\tilde{\mathbf{X}}+\tilde{\mathbf{Y}}}\right) = \frac{1}{2} \log\left(2\pi e 2\sigma_{\tilde{\mathbf{X}}}\right)$$

$$= S_1\left(f^{(m)}\right) + \frac{1}{2} \log 2 .$$

$\square$

Let us remark that, as m grows, the Shannon inequality ( ) and the bound expressed by ( ) become tighter.

For the sake of comparison, it is more convenient to consider a **relative Kullback-Leibler distance** defined as

$$D_{rel}\left(f^{(m')}||p_Z\right) = \left|\frac{S_1\left(f^{(m')}\right) - S_1\left(p_Z\right)}{S_1\left(f^{(m')}\right)}\right| , \tag{22}$$

so that the computed upper bound is now defined by

$$D_{rel}\left(f^{(m')}||p_Z\right) \leq \left|\frac{S_1\left(f^{(m')}\right) - S_1\left(f^{(m)}\right) + \frac{1}{2}\log 2}{S_1\left(f^{(m')}\right)}\right| . \tag{23}$$

In Table , we present, for $n = 1$ and several values of m, the values of the relative upper bound as defined by the right hand side of ( ). Moreover, we

Table 2. Relative Kullback-Leibler distance, upper bound and numerical approximation

$m =$	3	5	7	9	11	13	15	21	25	31
$D_{rel}(f^{(m')}\|p_Z)\times 10^4$	9.176	5.931	3.501	148.7	1.875	1.407	0.516	0.028	0.042	0.031
bound ( )$\times 10^4$	660	480	476	783	1718	2 75	1 25	33.18	18.75	9.82

give an approximated numerical value of the true relative distance as defined by
( ).

Inspection of the numerical values of $D_{rel}(f^{(m')}\|p_Z)$ as a function of m shows that the approximation of p_Z by $f^{(m')}$ holds up to a relative error bounded by 0.1%, which is decreasing a function of m, for $m \geq 11$. The bound ( ) is weaker but has the advantage of being in closed form.

4 Conclusion

In this paper, we have provided a complete characterization of the α−entropy maximizers under covariance constraints for multivariate densities. Elliptical invariance and a Gaussian mixture representation where established and the issue of stability of the entropy-maximizing densities was addressed. Applications of these results to pattern recognition, inverse problems, communications, and independent components analysis are currently being pursued.

Acknowledgments

This work was partially supported by Fundação para a Ciência e Tecnologia under the project SFRH/BD/2778/2000, a Dept. EECS UM Fellowship, and DARPA-MURI Grant Number DAAD19-02-1-0262.

References

[1] M. Abramowitz and I. Stegun. *Handbook of mathematical functions with formulas, graphs, and mathematical tables*, volume 55 of *Applied Mathematics Series*. U.S. Govt. Print. Off., 1964.

[2] K. C. Chu. Estimation and decision for linear systems with elliptical random processes. *IEEE Trans. on Automatic Control*, 18:499–505, 1973.   ,   ,

[3] T.M. Cover and J.A. Thomas. *Elements of Information Theory*. Wiley, New York, 1987.   ,

[4] I. Csiszár. Information-type measures of difference of probability distributions and indirect observations. *Studia Sci. Math. Hungar.*, 2:299–318, 1967.

[5] W. Feller. *An introduction to probability theory and its applications*, volume I. John Wiley & Sons, Inc., third edition, 1968.

[6] D. Geman and B. Jedynak. An active testing model for tracking roads in satellite images. *IEEE Trans. on Pattern Anal. and Machine Intell.*, 1:10–17, 1996.

[7] G. T. Gullberg and B. M. W. Tsui. Maximum entropy reconstruction with constraints: Iterative algorithms for solving the primal and dual programs. In C. N. de Graaf and M. A. Viergever, editors, *Information Processing in Medical Imaging*, chapter 23. Plenum Press, New York and London, 1988.

[8] H. Heemuchwala, A. O. Hero, and P. Carson. Image registration using entropy measures and entropic graphs. *To appear in European Journal of Signal Processing, Special Issue on Content-based Visual Information Retrieval*, Dec. 2003.

[9] A.O. Hero, B. Ma, O. Michel, and J. Gorman. Applications of entropic spanning graphs. *IEEE Signal Processing Magazine*, 19(5):85–95, Oct. 2002.   ,

[10] J. N. Kapur. Generalised Cauchy and Student's distributions as maximum-entropy distributions. *Proc. Nat. Acad. Sci. India Sect. A*, 58(2):235–246, 1988.
        ,

[11] R. J. McEliece, E. R. Rodemich, and L. Swanson. An entropy maximization problem related to optical communication. *IEEE Trans. on Inform. Theory*, 32:322–325, March 1986.

[12] R. S. Mendes and C. Tsallis. Renormalization group approach to nonextensive statistical mechanics. *Phys. Lett. A*, 285(5-6):273–278, 2001.   ,   ,

[13] M. I. Miller and D. L. Snyder. The role of likelihood and entropy in incomplete-data problems: applications to estimating point-process intensities and Toeplitz constrained covariances. *IEEE Proceedings*, 75(7):892–907, July 1987.

[14] S. Moriguti. A lower bound for a probability moment of any absolutely continuous distribution with finite variance. *Ann. Math. Statistics*, 23:286–289, 1952.

[15] F.A. Oliveira, B.A. Mello, and I.M. Xavier Jr. Scaling transformation of random walk distributions in a lattice. *Physical Review. E*, 61(6, Part B):7200–7203, June 2000.   ,   ,

[16] A. Rényi. On measures of entropy and information. In *Proc. 4th Berkeley Symp. Math. Stat. and Prob.*, volume 1, pages 547–561, 1961.

[17] S. D. Silvey S. M. Ali. A general class of coefficients of divergence of one distribution from another. *J. Roy. Statist. Soc. Ser. B*, 28:131–142, 1966.

[18] C. Vignat, J. Costa, and A. Hero. Characterization of the multivariate distributions maximazing Tsallis entropy under covariance constraint. Technical report, January 2003.   ,   ,

[19] G.A. Walker and J.G. Saw. The distribution of linear combinations of *t*-variables. *J. Amer. Statist. Assoc.*, 73(364):876–878, 1978.

[20] V. Witkovsky. On the exact computation of the density and of the quantiles of linear combinations of t and F random variables. *J. Statist. Plann. Inference*, 94(1):1–13, 2001.

[21] K. Zografos. On maximum entropy characterization of Pearson's type II and VII multivariate distributions. *Journal of Multivariate Analysis*, 71(1):67–75, 1999.
        ,

Semi-supervised Image Segmentation
by Parametric Distributional Clustering

Lothar Hermes and Joachim M. Buhmann

Rheinische Friedrich-Wilhelms-Universität
Institut für Informatik III, Römerstr. 164
53117 Bonn, Germany
{hermes,jb}@iai.uni-bonn.de
tel: (+49) 228 / 73-4102
fax: (+49) 228 / 73-4382

Abstract. The problem of semi-supervised image segmentation is frequently posed e.g. in remote sensing applications. In this setting, one aims at finding a decomposition of a given image into its constituent regions, which are typically assumed to have homogeneously distributed pixel values. In addition, it is requested that these regions can be equipped with some semantics, i.e. that they can be matched to particular land cover classes. For this purpose, class labels are provided for a small subset of the image data. The demand that the image segmentation respects those class labels implies that the segmentation algorithm should be posed as a constrained optimization problem.
We extend the Parametric Distributional Clustering (PDC) algorithm to fit into this learning framework. The resulting optimization problem is solved by constrained Deterministic Annealing. The approach is illustrated for both artificial data and real-world synthetic aperture radar (SAR) imagery.

Keywords: image segmentation, distributional clustering, semi-supervised learning

1 Introduction

Unsupervised clustering methods are often used as an initial module of complex recognition systems. In remote sensing, for example, it is a very common strategy to compute an unsupervised segmentation of the image in a first step. Afterwards, the segments form the basic entities which are analyzed by supervised algorithms to produce the intended class output (e.g. land cover information). The supervised algorithms are trained with additional ground truth data (class labels), that the unsupervised preprocessing steps are typically deprived of.

This separation between unsupervised and supervised data analysis can obviously have undesirable side-effects. We, therefore, argue that the initial clustering algorithm should be given access to the class labels as well, so that it can adapt its solution to the structure the user intends to detect. The approach presented in

A. Rangarajan et al. (Eds.): EMMCVPR 2003, LNCS 2683, pp. 229–   , 2003.
© Springer-Verlag Berlin Heidelberg 2003

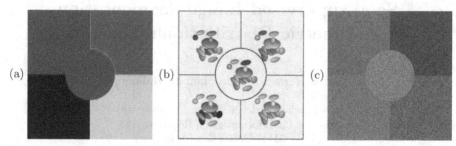

Fig. 1. The assumed image formation process: (a) Cluster labels are assigned to each image site. (b) Color values are then sampled from cluster-specific mixture distributions. They are defined by combining Gaussian distributions in the RGB color space, which are visualized by colored ellipsoids here. The color saturation indicates the mixture weights. (c) Due to the assumption that all sites are statistically independent, there is no spatial structure inside the segments of the sampled image

this paper implements this idea for Parametric Distributional Clustering (PDC). PDC describes histogram datasets as the statistical realization of a mixture of Gaussian mixture models [ ]. We extend the corresponding generative model by the natural assumption that the class labels are sampled from conditional probability distributions, which depend only on the individual clusters. This assumption also supports the formation of *multiple-cluster classes*, i.e. classes which are represented by more than one cluster. By applying the Maximum Likelihood framework, it can be shown that the cost function of the original PDC model has to be augmented by an additional penalty term. This penalty term measures the conditional entropy of class labels given cluster assignments and, therefore, enforces a strong correlation between clusters and classes. The resulting optimization problem is solved by a constrained variant of Deterministic Annealing (DA), which couples the weighting of the penalty term to a computational temperature.

The following section summarizes the basic PDC model. In its original form, PDC is acting on the pure color data, and it does not use any additional class label information to segment an image. Section   presents the extension to the semi-supervised case.

2   Parametric Distributional Clustering

The PDC approach assumes that the image formation process is a combination of two subsequent stages, i.e. the corresponding graphical model is a linear chain.

Let the image be structured according to a site grid Ω. At each site $o_i \in \Omega$ on this grid, one measures a finite set of observations, which are summarized by $\mathcal{X}_i$. In our particular application, $\mathcal{X}_i$ contains the color values of all pixels in a small neighborhood around site o_i. It is assumed that all the observations affiliated with site o_i are statistically independent of the other sites o_j, $j \neq i$. In the following, we describe the two random processes from which the observed pixel values $\mathcal{X}_i$ supposedly have emerged.

The first process assigns a cluster label to each site $o_i \in \Omega$ (Fig.   a). It is assumed that there is a total of k different clusters, which represent the entire distribution of color values in the given image. The probability that a randomly selected site i is part of cluster $\nu \in \{1, \ldots, k\}$ is denoted by p_ν. Once all cluster assignments have been chosen, it is possible to construct a deterministic function which maps each site to its corresponding segment index. This function is represented by a boolean matrix $\mathbf{M} = (M)_{i\nu}$. $M_{i\nu}$ equals one if site i is assigned to cluster ν. Otherwise, $M_{i\nu}$ is set to zero.

The second random process actually samples the image data. Each cluster ν is characterized by a specific probability distribution $p(\mathbf{x}|\nu)$, according to which it generates features (Fig.   b). Sampling the image data is essentially regarded as a Markovian process: once the cluster membership of a site o_i has been fixed, the color distribution in its neighborhood does no longer depend on the site itself, but it is solely determined by the cluster that o_i belongs to. The distributions $p(\mathbf{x}|\nu)$ are represented by Gaussian mixture models

$$p(\mathbf{x}|\nu) = \sum_{\alpha=1}^{l} p_{\alpha|\nu} \mathcal{N}(\mathbf{x}|\boldsymbol{\mu}_\alpha, \boldsymbol{\Sigma}_\alpha) \ . \tag{1}$$

Consequently, the cluster-specific distributions $p(\mathbf{x}|\nu)$ differ with respect to their mixture weights $p_{\alpha|\nu}$ only, whereas the underlying Gaussian distributions $\mathcal{N}(\mathbf{x}|\boldsymbol{\mu}_\alpha, \boldsymbol{\Sigma}_\alpha)$ are identical for each cluster ν ($1 \leq \alpha \leq l$, $1 \leq \nu \leq k$).

Although the generative model principally supports a continuous color space (i.e. the colors are sampled from $\mathbb{R}^d$, where d is the number of channels), the observed colors will in practice be located on a discrete grid in this color space. This discretization is equivalent to introducing intervals or *bins* $I_j \subset \mathbb{R}^d$, so that each color value inside the bin I_j is mapped onto the a single prototype with index j. In consequence, the color information around site o_i can be summarized by a histogram $\mathbf{n}_i = (n_{i1}, \ldots, n_{im})$, where n_{ij} denotes the number of occurrences that a color value from bin I_j appears in the set $\mathcal{X}_i$.

The natural cost function for the described generative model is the negative log-likelihood function

$$H^{\mathrm{PDC}} = -\sum_{i=1}^{n} \sum_{\nu=1}^{k} M_{i\nu} \left[\log p_\nu + \sum_{j=1}^{m} n_{ij} \log \left(\sum_{\alpha=1}^{l} p_{\alpha|\nu} G_\alpha(j) \right) \right] , \tag{2}$$

where

$$G_\alpha(j) = \int_{I_j} \mathcal{N}(\mathbf{x}|\boldsymbol{\mu}_\alpha, \boldsymbol{\Sigma}_\alpha) \, d\mathbf{x} \tag{3}$$

is the probability mass of the Gaussian prototype with index α inside bin I_j. H^{PDC} can also be shown to be the expected codelength of a two-part code, which

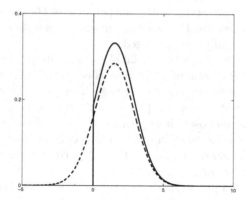

Fig. 2. Constructing a rectified Gaussian distribution. The original probability density function (dashed line) is set to zero outside the data domain. It is then rescaled, so that it integrates to one again (solid line)

first encodes the cluster assignments for each site, and then, based on those cluster assignments, encodes the individual color values (resp. their corresponding bin indices). An mathematically equivalent cost function is obtained by applying the *Information Bottleneck* principle [ ], as has been shown in [ ].

One might argue that the probability density functions $\mathcal{N}(\mathbf{x}|\boldsymbol{\mu}_\alpha, \boldsymbol{\Sigma}_\alpha)$ have an infinite support, whereas the actual color values are always restricted to finite intervals. In order to avoid that the Gaussian prototypes spend parts of their probability mass on color values which will never occur in reality, they can be replaced by *rectified Gaussians* [ ]. Applying rectified Gaussians instead of conventional Gaussian prototypes can occasionally be advantageous, e.g. if an input image contains many color values which are located at the outer boundary of the RGB color cube (Fig.). In practice, this means that the variables $G_\alpha(j)$ introduced in Eq. ( ) have to be replaced by integrals $\widetilde{G}_\alpha(j)$ of rectified Gaussian distributions.

The inherent difficulty of assignment problems like the one defined above is caused by the fact that they involve both latent assignment variables $\mathbf{M}$ and unknown model parameters $\boldsymbol{\Theta}$. Typically it will be straight forward to determine the model parameters if the true cluster assignments are known. Vice versa, knowing the true model parameters significantly facilitates the estimation of the cluster assignments. But since the correct values of neither of both are known in advance, solving the assignment problem means operating in the joint configuration space of $\mathbf{M}$ and $\boldsymbol{\Theta}$, which typically leads to $\mathcal{NP}$ hard problems.

Deterministic Annealing (DA) is an efficient continuation method for Simulated Annealing (SA), which is a classical strategy to solve assignment problems in a robust fashion [ ]. DA makes use of the fact that, if one fixes the computational temperature at a particular value T, the sampling process used in SA will converge towards the *Gibbs distribution* for temperature T. The Gibbs distribution can be shown to minimize the so-called *free energy* $\mathcal{F}$, which is given by

$$\mathcal{F} = \mathrm{E}\,[H] - T \cdot S \,. \tag{4}$$

In the equation above, H denotes the cost function of the clustering model, and S is the entropy of the cluster assignments. Instead of sampling solutions from the Gibbs distribution (which is usually done by a Markov process formed by single-site updates), the general paradigm of DA is to directly compute this distribution (resp. its parameters). It can be shown that the Gibbs distribution factorizes for any cost function which can be written as a single sum over the sites [ ]. In consequence, the Gibbs distribution can be written as a product of assignment probabilities $q_{i\nu} = \mathrm{E}[M_{i\nu}]$, where the expectation is taken w.r.t. the Gibbs distribution. Therefore, the discrete optimization problem of choosing the best assignment matrix $\mathbf{M}$ is transformed into the continuous optimization problem of estimating the assignment probabilities $q_{i\nu}$, $1 \le i \le n$, $1 \le \nu \le k$. It is solved by an iterative optimization process, which alternates between updating the probabilities $q_{i\nu}$ and re-estimating the model parameters $\boldsymbol{\Theta}$, respectively. If the computational temperature T is fixed to one, this update scheme is equivalent to the well-known EM algorithm [ ].

In the E-step, the alternating optimization scheme updates the estimates $q_{i\nu} = \mathrm{E}[M_{i\nu}]$, $1 \le i \le n$, $1 \le \nu \le k$. It can be shown that the variables $q_{i\nu}$ have to satisfy the stationary equations

$$q_{i\nu} = \frac{\exp\left(-\beta h_{i\nu}\right)}{\sum_{\tau \le k} \exp\left(-\beta h_{i\tau}\right)} \,, \tag{5}$$

where $h_{i\nu}$ are the expected costs of assigning site i to cluster ν, and $\beta = 1/T$ is the inverse computational temperature (for a formal proof, see e.g. [ ]). For the cost function H^{PDC} introduced in Eq. ( ), the *mean fields* $h_{i\nu}$ are given by

$$h_{i\nu} = -\log p_\nu - \sum_{j=1}^{m} n_{ij} \log\left(\sum_{\alpha=1}^{l} p_{\alpha|\nu} \tilde{G}_\alpha\,(j)\right) \,. \tag{6}$$

Therefore, the E-step of the EM scheme consists of a single sweep through all sites o_i, in which the assignment probabilities $q_{i\nu}$ are re-estimated according to ( ) and ( ).

In the M-step, the algorithm updates the free model parameters $\boldsymbol{\Theta}$ according to the current estimates for $q_{i\nu}$. The set $\boldsymbol{\Theta}$ contains the cluster probabilities p_ν, the mixture weights $p_{\alpha|\nu}$, and the means $\boldsymbol{\mu}_\alpha$. The covariance matrices $\boldsymbol{\Sigma}_\alpha$ are excluded from $\boldsymbol{\Theta}$ to keep the number of free parameters small. In practice, they are computed in advance by fitting a conventional Gaussian mixture model to the image data.

The necessary optimality condition for the cluster probabilities p_ν implies

$$p_\nu = \frac{1}{n} \sum_{i=1}^{n} q_{i\nu} \,, \quad \nu = 1, \ldots, k \,. \tag{7}$$

To optimize the parameters $p_{\alpha|\nu}$, we repeatedly select two Gaussian components α_1 and α_2. Keeping $p_{\gamma|\nu}$ fixed for $\gamma \notin \{\alpha_1, \alpha_2\}$, $p_{\alpha_2|\nu}$ is directly coupled to $p_{\alpha_1|\nu}$,

$$p_{\alpha_2|\nu} = 1 - \sum_{\gamma \notin \{\alpha_1, \alpha_2\}} p_{\gamma|\nu} - p_{\alpha_1|\nu} , \tag{8}$$

so that only one free parameter $(p_{\alpha_1|\nu})$ remains. By introducing auxiliary variables

$$c_{\nu j} := \sum_{i=1}^{n} q_{i\nu} n_{ij} \quad \text{and} \quad w_{\nu j} := \sum_{\alpha=1}^{l} p_{\alpha|\nu} \widetilde{G}_{\alpha}(j) , \tag{9}$$

one obtains

$$\frac{\partial}{\partial p_{\alpha_1|\nu}} \mathcal{F}\left(p_{\alpha_1|\nu}, p_{\alpha_2|\nu}\right) = -\sum_{j=1}^{m} c_{\nu j} \frac{\widetilde{G}_{\alpha_1}(j) - \widetilde{G}_{\alpha_2}(j)}{w_{\nu j}} \tag{10}$$

and

$$\frac{\partial^2}{\partial p_{\alpha_1|\nu}^2} \mathcal{F}\left(p_{\alpha_1|\nu}, p_{\alpha_2|\nu}\right) = \sum_{j=1}^{m} c_{\nu j} \frac{\left(\widetilde{G}_{\alpha_1}(j) - \widetilde{G}_{\alpha_2}(j)\right)^2}{w_{\nu j}^2} \geq 0 . \tag{11}$$

The joint optimization of $p_{\alpha_1|\nu}$ and $p_{\alpha_2|\nu}$, therefore, amounts to solving a one-dimensional convex optimization problem, which can be achieved by interval bisection.

The adaptation of the means $\boldsymbol{\mu}_\alpha$, $1 \leq \alpha \leq l$ is slightly more involved. In our implementation, they are initialized by fitting a conventional Gaussian mixture model to the image data. In each subsequent M-step, their position can be adapted by a Newton descent in $E[H^{\mathrm{PDC}}]$.

3   Incorporating Side Knowledge

In its original form presented so far, the PDC model can be classified as an *unsupervised learning* approach. It describes the structure of a given dataset by specifying clusters in it, but those clusters solely reflect the similarities between data items, and they can not necessarily be mapped to semantic entities. In contrast, *supervised learning* approaches require explicit training data sets, in which each element is equipped with a class label (in our terminology, this setting is, therefore, called a *classification* problem as opposed to the unsupervised *clustering* problem). By fitting a parametric labelling function to the training set, classification algorithms are, therefore, able to analyze particular characteristics of the data which have implicitly been specified by the choice of the class labels in the training data set. So the class labels used in the classification setting offer a convenient means to encode what kind of information the user is actually interested in. In contrast, the unsupervised setting requires it to explicitly specify the relevant information by the choice of the cost function (the Information Bottleneck approach [ ] offering a formal framework for this task).

If there is no obvious way to express the relevant information in terms of the input data (which is often the case for applications with practical relevance), a general-purpose approach like support vector machines (i.e. *classification* instead of *clustering*) is usually the more promising way to solve the learning problem.

Yet supervised learning algorithms have their typical disadvantages. The need to supply a sufficiently large training data set equipped with reliable class label information often poses insolvable problems. For instance, in remote sensing applications the need for class labels usually means that one has to conduct large-scale ground truth campaigns. Typically the costs for a ground truth campaign exceed the costs for the raw satellite data by far, so that there is a strong economic pressure to curtail the required amount of ground truth data as much as possible.

In fact, the situation of coping with insufficient ground truth information while, at the same time, facing an abundant amount of unlabeled data is quite common in various application domains. This is why *semi-supervised learning approaches* have recently found increasing interest in the machine learning community [ ] [ ]. The basic intention behind semi-supervised learning is to bridge the gap between supervised and unsupervised learning. Often it is regarded as a conceptual refinement of the standard classification problem, i.e. one supplements the labeled training data by additional unlabeled data, which may contain important information about the data source and, therefore, might be useful to reduce the misclassification rate [ ]. Likewise, semi-supervised learning can be regarded from a clustering point of view: given a large set of unlabeled data which need to be analyzed, some of the data items are equipped with class labels to give the clustering process an additional guidance. So the class labels are used to specify what kind of structure is expected to be found. If two items have different class labels, then this information indicates that they are known to be generated by different sources, which should of course have implications for their cluster assignments.

This section presents a variant of the PDC model which implements the latter view. The original model is supplemented by a set of assignment variables which provide class label information for a subset of the training data. It is important to note here that these new assignment variables introduce an additional level of abstraction. The class labels encode some information about the image semantics that the user is interested in (e.g. land cover types, if the model is applied to remote sensing applications), whereas the clusters refer to locally measured color statistics. So there does not have to be a 1:1 match from classes to clusters. In fact, there may be clusters which can not be matched to any semantic class because of insufficient ground truth information, or there may be classes which are represented by more than one cluster.

Let us assume that the additional class label information is provided as a Boolean matrix $\mathbf{C} = (C)_{i\rho}$ with $C_{i\rho} \in \mathbb{B}^{n \times \kappa}$. $C_{i\rho} = 1$ indicates that all observations at site i are known to belong to class ρ. In consequence, each row of $\mathbf{C}$ must satisfy the uniqueness constraint $\sum_{\rho=1}^{\kappa} C_{i\rho} \leq 1$, i.e. a site o_i can not belong to

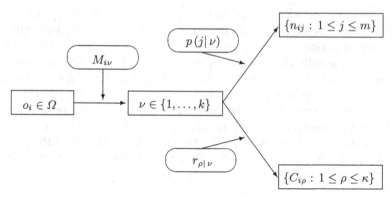

Fig. 3. Extending the PDC model to semi-supervised learning

more than one class. If all entries of row i equal zero, i.e. $\sum_{\rho=1}^{\kappa} C_{i\rho} = 0$, then no ground-truth information is available for site o_i.

The generative model which incorporates the class labels is shown in Fig. . As in the original PDC model, it is assumed that each site o_i belongs to a cluster ν, and that the measured color values have been sampled from the Gaussian mixture distribution $p(\mathbf{x}|\nu) = \sum_{\alpha=1}^{l} p_{\alpha|\nu} \mathcal{N}(\mathbf{x}|\boldsymbol{\mu}_\alpha, \boldsymbol{\Sigma}_\alpha)$ which is a characteristic of that cluster. However, in contrast to the original graphical model, the model depicted in Fig. is equipped with an additional branch that points to the class assignment variables $C_{i\rho}$. This additional branch symbolizes the assumption that all observations at site o_i have identical class labels, which are drawn i.i.d. according to the conditional probabilities $r_{\rho|\nu}$, $1 \leq \rho \leq \kappa$. In particular, it is assumed that the color values and the class labels are sampled independently of each other, i.e. the histogram $\{n_{ij} : 1 \leq j \leq m\}$ and the assignment vector $(C_{i1}, \ldots, C_\kappa)$ are statistically independent random variables given the cluster index ν. Land cover classification is a typical example where this assumption should hold. A land cover class like *forest* will usually be represented by a couple of autonomously detected clusters which are related to different tree species. So the membership to a cluster (*oaks*) provides all necessary information to infer the class label (*forest*) and the expected histogram (*a certain color distribution in the green part of the spectrum*).

In consequence, the set $\boldsymbol{\Theta} = \{p_\nu, p_{\alpha|\nu}, \boldsymbol{\mu}_\alpha : 1 \leq \alpha \leq l, 1 \leq \nu \leq k\}$ has to be enlarged to include the additional free parameters $r_{\rho|\nu}$, $1 \leq \nu \leq k$, $1 \leq \rho \leq \kappa$. $r_{\rho|\nu}$ captures the probability that a site which belongs to cluster ν carries the class label ρ. The estimation of those probabilities can easily be incorporated into the M-step of the EM update scheme, as will be described later.

On the assumption that the class label of site o_i and the observed histogram $\mathbf{n}_i$ are statistically independent given the membership to a certain cluster ν, the complete data likelihood function $p(\mathcal{X}, \mathbf{M}, \mathbf{C}|\boldsymbol{\Theta})$ reads

$$p(\mathcal{X}, \mathbf{M}, \mathbf{C}|\boldsymbol{\Theta}) = \prod_{i=1}^{n} \prod_{\nu=1}^{k} [p_\nu \cdot p(\mathbf{n}_i|\nu, \boldsymbol{\Theta}) \cdot p(C_{i1}, \ldots, C_{i\kappa}|\nu, \boldsymbol{\Theta})]^{M_{i\nu}} , \quad (12)$$

where p_ν is again the probability that a randomly chosen site belongs to cluster ν, and $p\,(\mathbf{n}_i|\,\nu,\boldsymbol{\Theta})$ and $p\,(C_{i1},\dots,C_{i\kappa}|\,\nu,\boldsymbol{\Theta})$ are the likelihoods of the histogram $\mathbf{n}_i$ and the label vector $(C_{i1},\dots,C_{i\kappa})$, respectively. $p\,(\mathbf{n}_i|\,\nu,\boldsymbol{\Theta})$ is given by

$$p\,(\mathbf{n}_i|\,\nu,\boldsymbol{\Theta}) = \prod_{j=1}^{m}\left(\sum_{\alpha=1}^{l}p_{\alpha|\,\nu}G_\alpha\,(j)\right)^{n_{ij}}. \tag{13}$$

The likelihood of the class label vector $(C_{i1},\dots,C_{i\kappa})$ reads

$$p\,(C_{i1},\dots,C_{i\kappa}|\,\nu,\boldsymbol{\Theta}) = \prod_{\rho=1}^{\kappa}\left(r_{\rho|\,\nu}\right)^{C_{i\rho}\cdot\sum_{j\leq m}n_{ij}}, \tag{14}$$

since we have assumed that the class label associated with site o_i has independently been drawn for all observations $\mathcal{X}_i$ made for this site ($\sum_{j\leq m}n_{ij}$ observations in total). Hence we have the following negative complete-data log-likelihood function:

$$\mathcal{L}\,(\boldsymbol{\Theta}|\,\mathcal{X},\mathbf{M},\mathbf{C}) = -\sum_{i=1}^{n}\sum_{\nu=1}^{k}M_{i\nu}\left[\log p_\nu + \sum_{j=1}^{m}n_{ij}\log\left(\sum_{\alpha=1}^{l}p_{\alpha|\,\nu}G_\alpha\,(j)\right)\right]$$
$$-\sum_{i=1}^{n}\sum_{\nu=1}^{k}M_{i\nu}\left[\sum_{j=1}^{m}n_{ij}\sum_{\rho=1}^{\kappa}C_{i\rho}\log r_{\rho|\,\nu}\right]. \tag{15}$$

Due to the assumed statistical independence between class labels and color values given the cluster assignments, the function above is a sum of two essential parts. The first part is the original PDC cost function, which has been introduced in Sect. . It exerts a data driven force, i.e. it encourages clusters with homogeneous color statistics. The second part incorporates the ground truth knowledge. It takes the role of a penalty term which measures the conditional entropy of class labels given the cluster assignments. If $C_{i\rho} = 0 \;\forall i \in \{1,\dots,n\}$, $\rho \in \{1,\dots,\kappa\}$, i.e. if no ground truth data is available at all, then the negative log-likelihood (Eq.) reduces to the original PDC cost function H^{PDC} again.

The additional penalty term in Eq. ( ) essentially imposes the constraint that any cluster ν should be associated with at most one class ρ. If this constraint is met, the penalty term will become zero, because in this case one can specify a function which maps clusters to class labels, and thus the corresponding conditional entropy vanishes. If the constraint is violated, the penalty term will take a positive value, which is the larger the more randomness is measured in the interplay between cluster assignments and class labels.

Although the penalty term thus implements the desired coupling between clusters and classes, it may counteract the general optimization strategy of Deterministic Annealing (DA). In fact, DA is so robust because it temporarily encourages a high level of randomness in the cluster assignments $\mathbf{M}$. Random cluster assignments correspond to high entropy values S, so that at high temperatures T the most random state is always the one with the smallest free energy $\mathcal{F} = \mathrm{E}\,[H] - T \cdot S$. However, the penalty term in Eq. ( ) implements the opposite goal: it impedes random cluster assignments, if they do not fit to the observed class labels. In consequence, the optimization procedure becomes more likely to get trapped in local minima, which usually results in sub-optimal clustering solutions.

A similar problem has previously been discussed by Geman et al. [ ] for Simulated Annealing. We follow the general idea there to couple the strength of the regularization with the computational temperature T. At high temperatures T, the regularization term is given a small weight, so that the class labels influence the cluster assignments only weakly. While cooling down the system from the initial temperature $T^{\oplus}$ to the final temperature $T^{\ominus}$, $T^{\oplus} > T^{\ominus} > 0$, the weight is monotonously increased until arriving at $\sum_{j=1}^{m} n_{ij}$ for $T = T^{\ominus}$.

To accomodate typical learning scenarios in which the available ground truth information is very scarce, it can furthermore be helpful to supplement labeled objects by a control parameter $\xi \in \mathbb{N}$ which will be called their *multiplicity*. The multiplicity ξ can be used to give the labeled objects an additional weight over the unlabeled ones. Setting $\xi = 2$ is equivalent to inserting each labeled example twice into the training data set. Setting $\xi = 1$ means that labeled and unlabeled samples are given exactly the same weight.

In summary, we obtain the temperature-controled cost function

$$H^{\mathrm{SPDC}}\,(T) = -\sum_{i=1}^{n} \xi^{\sum_{\rho \leq \kappa} C_{i\rho}} \sum_{\nu=1}^{k} M_{i\nu} \left[\log p_{\nu} + \sum_{j=1}^{m} n_{ij} \log \left(\sum_{\alpha=1}^{l} p_{\alpha|\nu} G_{\alpha}\,(j) \right) \right]$$
$$- \sum_{i=1}^{n} \xi^{\sum_{\rho \leq \kappa} C_{i\rho}} \sum_{\nu=1}^{k} M_{i\nu} \left[\zeta\,(T) \sum_{\rho=1}^{\kappa} C_{i\rho} \log r_{\rho|\nu} \right], \qquad (16)$$

where the weight

$$\zeta\,(T) := \frac{T^{\oplus} - T}{T^{\oplus} - T^{\ominus}} \sum_{j=1}^{m} n_{ij} \qquad (17)$$

couples the penalty term to the computational temperature T. By the choice of $\zeta\,(T)$, it is possible to preserve the smoothing effect of the annealing, but it is also made sure that the optimization process finally employs the correct weight $(\sum_{j=1}^{m} n_{ij})$ suggested in Eq. ( ).

In Sect. , the partial costs $h_{i\nu}$ of attributing site o_i to cluster ν have been computed for the original PDC model (Eq.). If one adds the cost term which is induced by the ground truth information about class labels, one arrives at modified partial costs

$$\tilde{h}_{i\nu} = h_{i\nu} - \zeta\,(T) \sum_{\rho=1}^{\kappa} C_{i\rho} \log r_{\rho|\nu} . \qquad (18)$$

In consequence, the rule to update the assignment probabilities $q_{i\nu} = \langle M_{i\nu} \rangle$ has to be changed to

$$q_{i\nu} = \frac{\exp\left(-\beta \tilde{h}_{i\nu}\right)}{\sum_{\tau \leq k} \exp\left(-\beta \tilde{h}_{i\tau}\right)}, \tag{19}$$

where $\beta = 1/T$ is again the inverse computational temperature. Therefore, the incorporation of class label information into the generative model can be implemented by a slight modification of the E-step.

The M-step equations presented in Sect.   remain completely unaffected by the modification of the generative model if one chooses the multiplicity $\xi = 1$. This fact is due to the statistical independence of class labels $C_{i\rho}$ and measurements n_{ij} given the cluster information (ν, Θ), i.e. the class labels $\mathbf{C}$ do not directly interfere with the estimation of the original model parameters. In practical applications, the fraction of labeled sites is usually rather small, though, so that it often makes sense to increase their influence by choosing $\xi > 1$. As introduced above, this decision is equivalent to replacing any labeled site o_i by a virtual set of ξ independent sites with identical color and label information. For the cost function $H^{\mathrm{SPDC}}(T)$, it has the effect that the partial costs of labeled sites o_i satisfying $\sum_{\rho \leq \kappa} C_{i\rho} = 1$ are weighted by the factor ξ, whereas the contributions of unlabeled sites ($\sum_{\rho \leq \kappa} C_{i\rho} = 0$) remain unchanged. In consequence, the stationary equations for the M-step parameters are slightly different between the original PDC model and its augmented variant: wherever the assignment probability $q_{i\nu}$ appears in the original update formulas for p_ν, $p_{\alpha|\nu}$, and $\boldsymbol{\mu}_\alpha$, it has to be replaced by

$$\tilde{q}_{i\nu} = \xi^{\sum_{\rho \leq \kappa} C_{i\rho}} q_{i\nu} \tag{20}$$

to obtain the corresponding formula for semi-supervised PDC. This finding can be verified by recomputing the derivatives in Sect.   for the modified cost function $H^{\mathrm{SPDC}}(T)$. The update equations for the new parameters $r_{\rho|\nu}$ are obtained as usual by setting up the necessary optimality condition

$$\frac{\partial}{\partial r_{\rho|\nu}} \left(\mathcal{F} + \lambda_\nu \cdot \sum_{\rho'=1}^{\kappa} r_{\rho'|\nu} \right) = 0 , \tag{21}$$

in which $\lambda_\nu > 0$ is a Langrange parameter for the constraint that the probability estimates $r_{\rho|\nu}$, $1 \leq \rho \leq \kappa$, must sum to one. Expanding $\mathcal{F} = \mathrm{E}\left[H^{\mathrm{SPDC}}\right] - TS$, one obtains

$$r_{\rho|\nu} \propto \sum_{i=1}^{n} \xi^{\sum_{\rho \leq \kappa} C_{i\rho}} \zeta(T) \cdot q_{i\nu} C_{i\nu} . \tag{22}$$

Therefore, the necessary modifications of the M-step remain moderately small, too. In essence, one has to introduce different weights for labeled and unlabeled samples, and to include the update equations ( ).

4 Experiments

The PDC model describes images as the result of a stochastic sampling process, in which each random source is a mixture of multivariate Gaussian distributions. Provided that the number of Gaussian prototypes is allowed to approach infinity, mixtures of Gaussians form universal function approximators [ ]. Therefore, the model is applicable to a wide range of possible data sources.

In this paper, we first illustrate its general principle on synthetic data sampled from Gaussian mixture models. Afterwards, we describe an application to synthetic aperture radar (SAR) imagery. Due to its typically strong noise contamination, SAR imagery is particularly suitable to study the robustness of segmentation approaches.

For the experiment shown in Fig. , a synthetic RGB image was generated by sampling color values from five different Gaussian mixture models, thereby following the assumed image formation process sketched in Fig. . The sampled image is shown in Fig. (a). If one trains a conventional PDC model for this image without using any side information, then the brownish upper part of the image is first separated from the blueish lower part (Fig. c). When introducing additional clusters, the trained PDC model successively identifies sub-clusters (Fig. e, g), until the original five clusters are found in Fig. (i). In contrast, if one introduces three labeled image patches as illustrated in Fig. (c), the PDC model first defines clusters which are consistent with the class label information (Fig. d, f). The semi-supervised segmentation result based on three clusters reveals a couple of wrong assignments in the lower left image quadrant (Fig. f). The wrong assignments are caused by the antagonism of the class label information to the measured color histograms. The provided class labels force the model to split the lower left quadrant and the center of the image into different clusters. The color distributions in those two regions are quite similar, though. From that point of view, the lower left quadrant should rather be segregated from the upper left quadrant first (in fact, as shown in Fig. (i), the lower left quadrant and the center of the image are the last ones to be separated if the model is trained in an unsupervised fashion). The contradiction is alleviated when allowing an additional fourth cluster in Fig. (h). Since the model decides to split the left side of the image into an upper and a lower part, the left lower quadrant is now represented by a cluster of its own. The color distribution of this cluster is no longer diluted by the color histogram of the left upper quadrant, so that it can be discriminated more easily from the color distribution of the center part of the image. In consequence, the wrong assignments dissappear in Fig. (h). If the model complexity is extended to five clusters (Fig. j), essentially the same solution is obtained as in the unsupervised case, i.e. the true cluster structure is correctly found. So the additional class labels can be used to guide the clustering process, and to force the model to distinguish image structures which are relevant for the user. Provided that the model is equipped with sufficiently many degrees of freedom, it can autonomously detect additional clusters in the data, and it can map them to the individual classes.

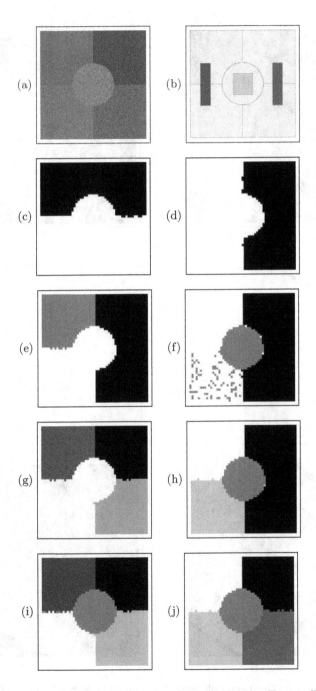

Fig. 4. (a) Synthetic RGB image generated according to Fig.   . (b) Additional class label image (true segment boundaries indicated by dashed lines). Left column below (a): PDC segmentation without class labels (number of clusters varied between 2 and 5). Right column below (b): Corresponding results when using class labels

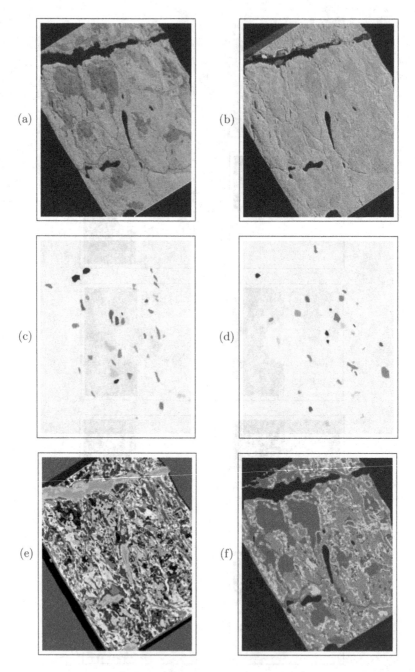

Fig. 5. Semi-supervised sementation of a polarimetric SAR image (L-band and X-band). (a), (b) Color composites of the L-band data and the X-band data, respectively. (c) Patches with class-label information for training and (d) for performance evaluation. (e) Cluster assignments and (f) class assignments generated by the PDC model

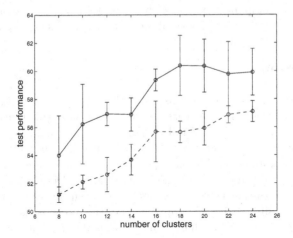

Fig. 6. Test performance of semi-supervised (solid line) and unsupervised (dashed line) PDC for different numbers of clusters. Error bars indicate standard deviations

Fig.   illustrates that the model can also be applied to SAR imagery. The image which has been gathered for a forestry application in Finland is composed of polarimetric L-band and X-band data (Fig.   (a) and (b), respectively). Some patches with known ground truth data have been selected for training and testing, as shown in Fig.   (c) and (d). The eight ground truth classes essentially correspond to several types of coniferous forest, which have different proportions of pines and spruces. Fig.   (e) shows a segmentation result with $k = 32$ different clusters. For the same segmentation result, Fig.   (f) depicts the corresponding class labels. A narrow band in this image is depicted in black, which encodes the doubt class, i.e. the corresponding segments could not be mapped to any class label. In fact, since the outer boundaries of the L-band and the X-band image do not match exactly, the corresponding areas in the original image have color statistics which do not appear in the training data. Therefore, the augmented PDC model decides to spend a single cluster ν to describe this image part, and not to map this cluster to any class label (i.e. $r_{\rho\mid\nu} = 0 \; \forall\, 1 \le \rho \le \kappa$).

Fig   depicts the test performance of semi-supervised PDC as a function of k. It is compared to the standard case, in which majority voting is used to assign a class label to each cluster after unsupervised clustering. Each experiment was performed several times by randomly selecting around 240 labeled and 8000 unlabeled pixels from the training data. Semi-supervised PDC significantly outperforms the standard variant, because it can tailor the clusters to achieve the desired class separation. When increasing k, the performance of the unsupervised PDC is improved because small clusters have a better chance to be matched to a unique semantic class. The semi-supervised PDC model also benefits from large k, because compound classes with inhomogeneous color distributions can then be represented by sets of several more homogeneous clusters.

5 Conclusion

We have presented a generic extension of the PDC model to fit into a semi-supervised segmentation framework. Semi-supervised segmentation applies to the case when a vast amount of unlabelled and only a small amount of labeled pixels are available. By integrating class labels into the generative model and by following the Maximum Likelihood approach, we obtain a constrained optimization problem which can e.g. be solved by a variant of Deterministic Annealing.

The general intuition behind the model has been illustrated on a synthetic data set. One possible real-world application of the model is the segmentation of remote sensing imagery, which has been demonstrated for polarimetric synthetic aperture radar data.

Acknowledgement

This work has been made possible through a research grant from Infoterra GmbH. L. Hermes was supported by a Marie-Curie fellowship of the European Union during a research visit at the Ariana group headed by J. Zerubia (IMAVIS project). The depicted remote sensing imagery have been used by courtesy of the German Aerospace Center (DLR). Additional images for model evaluation have been provided by the Centre National d'Études Spatiales (CNES).

References

[1] Vittorio Castelli and Thomas M. Cover. On the exponential value of labeled samples. *Pattern Recognition Letters*, 16(1):105–111, January 1995.

[2] Ayhan Demiriz and Kristin P. Bennett. Optimization approaches to semi-supervised learning. In M. C. Ferris, O. L. Mangasarian, and J. S. Pang, editors, *Applications and Algorithms of Complementarity*. Kluwer, 2000.

[3] Richard O. Duda, Peter E. Hart, and David G. Stork. *Pattern Classification*. John Wiley & Sons, 2nd ed. edition, 2000.

[4] Donald Geman, Stuart Geman, Christine Graffigne, and Ping Dong. Boundary detection by constrained optimization. *IEEE Transactions on Pattern Analysis and Machine Intelligence*, 12(7):609–628, July 1990.

[5] Lothar Hermes, Thomas Zöller, and Joachim M. Buhmann. Parametric distributional clustering for image segmentation. In *Computer Vision - ECCV '02*, volume 2352 of *LNCS*, pages 577–591. Springer, 2002.   ,

[6] Scott Kirkpatrick, C. D. Gelatt, and M. P. Vecchi. Optimization by simulated annealing. *Science*, 220(4598):671–680, 1983.

[7] Tom M. Mitchell. The role of unlabeled data in supervised learning. In *Proc. of the Sixth International Colloquium on Cognitive Science (ICCS'99)*, San Sebastian, 1999.

[8] Radford M. Neal and Geoffrey E. Hinton. A view of the EM algorithm that justifies incremental, sparse, and other variants. In Michael I. Jordan, editor, *Learning in Graphical Models*, volume 89 of *NATO Science Series*, pages 355–368. Kluwer Academic Publishers, 1998.

[9] Jan Puzicha. *Multiscale Annealing for Grouping, Segmentation and Image Quantization*, volume 601 of *Fortschritt Berichte VDI Reihe 10*. VDI Verlag, 1999.

[10] Nicholas D. Socci, Daniel D. Lee, and H. Sebastian Seung. The rectified gaussian distribution. In Michael Jordan, Michael Kearns, and Sara Solla, editors, *Advances in Neural Information Processing Systems*, volume 10, pages 350–356. MIT Press, 1998.

[11] Naftaly Tishby, Fernando C. Pereira, and William Bialek. The information bottleneck method. In *Proc. of the 37th annual Allerton Conference on Communication, Control, and Computing*, 1999.   ,

Path Variation and Image Segmentation

Pablo Andrés Arbeláez and Laurent D. Cohen

CEREMADE, UMR CNRS 7534 Université Paris Dauphine
Place du maréchal de Lattre de Tassigny
75775 Paris cedex 16, France
arbelaez,cohen@ceremade.dauphine.fr

Abstract. We study a notion of variation for real valued two variable functions called the *path variation* and we discuss its application as a low-level image segmentation method. For this purpose, we characterize the path variation as an energy in the framework of minimal paths. In this context, the definition of an energy and the selection of a set of source points determine a partition of the image domain. The problem of choosing a relevant set of sources is addressed through a nonlinear diffusion filtering.

1 Introduction

The notion of *variation* or *total variation* for functions of one real variable was introduced by C. Jordan [ ] as early as in 1881. This functional has found application in various branches of mathematics [,], particularly, in the definition of the Stieltjes integral. In the regular framework, the variation of a function $f : [0, L] \rightarrow \mathbb{R}$ can be written as [ ]:

$$v(f) = \int_0^L |f'(s)|\, ds\ . \tag{1}$$

Several definitions of the variation have been proposed for functions of multiple variables; if $u : \Omega \subset \mathbb{R}^2 \rightarrow \mathbb{R}$ is a smooth function, a natural generalization of ( ) consists in replacing the derivative by the gradient:

$$V(u) = \int_\Omega \|\nabla u(x)\|\, dx\ . \tag{2}$$

In the context of image analysis, the general version of ( ), allowing discontinuities in the function, was first considered by Osher and Rudin [,]. In the last decade, the representation of an image as the sum of one term of bounded variation and one term due to noise has been widely adopted. Methods based on the minimization of the total variation have been successfully applied for image restoration and denoising purposes [, , ,].

In this paper, we study a notion of variation for real valued functions of two variables that, in contrast to the usual total variation, is defined pointwise. Precisely, we define the *path variation* between two points of the domain as

A. Rangarajan et al. (Eds.): EMMCVPR 2003, LNCS 2683, pp. 246–   , 2003.
© Springer-Verlag Berlin Heidelberg 2003

the minimal total variation of the function on all the paths that join them. Furthermore, we propose a discrete interpretation of the path variation and we discuss its application as a low-level segmentation tool.

Image segmentation is a fundamental issue in the field of computer vision. Its great complexity may be understood by the fact that partitioning an image domain into "meaningful" regions requires a level of interpretation of the image information. Therefore, the introduction of prior knowledge seems unavoidable in the segmentation process. However, a first pre-cognitive task is the extraction of the image structure provided by low-level cues.

In order to apply the path variation to the segmentation of monochrome images, we characterize this notion as an energy in the framework of minimal paths. In this context, an energy determines a partition of the image domain by considering the influence zones of a set of source points.

Then, we address the problem of selecting a set of sources that represent accurately the image structure. For this purpose, we consider the intensity extrema of a scale-space representation of the image.

This paper is organized as follows: the basic definitions of the minimal paths approach are given in Sect. 2. The path variation is presented in Sect. 3. In Sect. 4, we discuss the choice of a set of source points.

2   Definitions

This introductory section presents the general framework for the rest of the paper. Basic definitions are recalled and the notations settled.

2.1   Minimal Paths

Let $\Omega \subset \mathbb{R}^2$ be a compact connected domain in the plane and $x, y \in \Omega$ two points. A *path* from x to y designates an injective $\mathcal{C}^1$ function $\gamma : [0, L] \to \Omega$ such that $\gamma(0) = x$ and $\gamma(L) = y$. The image of γ is then a rectifiable simple curve in the domain. The path is parameterized by the arclength parameter s, i.e: $\|\dot{\gamma}(s)\| = 1, \forall s \in [0, L]$ and L represents the Euclidean length of the path. The set of paths from x to y is noted by Γ_{xy}.

Definition 1. *The **surface of minimal action**, or **energy**, of a potential function $P : \Omega \times \mathcal{S}^1 \to \mathbb{R}^+$, with respect to a source point $x_0 \in \Omega$, evaluated at x, is defined as*

$$E_0(x) = \inf_{\gamma \in \Gamma_{x_0 x}} \int_0^L P(\gamma(s), \dot{\gamma}(s)) \, ds \ .$$

When P depends only on the position $\gamma(\cdot)$ and is strictly positive, the field of geometrical optics provides the following physical interpretation of the energy: the potential $P : \Omega \to \mathbb{R}^+$ represents a refractive field of indices of an optical medium and E_0, called the *eikonal* in this context, supplies the optical length of the light rays. Then, the relation between the energy and the potential can be expressed by the *Eikonal Equation*:

$$\|\nabla E_0(x)\| = P(x) \ , \tag{3}$$

with boundary condition $E_0(x_0) = 0$.

In this particular case, the computation of the energy can be performed using Sethian's *Fast Marching* method [,]. Noticing that the information is propagating outwards from the sources, the Fast Marching uses an up-wind scheme to construct a correct approximation of the viscosity solution of ( ).

Energy minimizing paths have been used to address several problems in the field of computer vision, where the potential is generally defined as a function of the image. Examples include the global minimum for active contour models [ ], shape from shading [ ], continuous scale morphology [ ], virtual endoscopy [ ] and perceptual grouping [ ].

2.2   Energy Partitions

The energy with respect to a set of sources $S = \{x_i\}_{i \in J}$ is defined as the minimal individual energy:

$$E_S(x) = \inf_{i \in J} E_i(x) \ .$$

In the presence of multiple sources, a valuable information is provided by the interaction in the domain of a source x_i with the other elements of S, which is expressed through its *influence zone*:

$$Z_i = \{x \in \Omega \,|\, E_i(x) < E_j(x), \forall j \in J, \, j \neq i\} \ .$$

Thus, the influence zone, or briefly the *zone*, is a connected subset of the domain, completely determined by the energy and the rest of the sources. Their union is noted by:

$$Z(E, S) = \bigcup_{i \in J} Z_i \ .$$

The *medial set* is defined as the complementary set of $Z(E, S)$:

$$M(E, S) = \{x \in \Omega \,|\, \exists i, j \in J, \, i \neq j : E_S(x) = E_i(x) = E_j(x)\} \ .$$

Definition 2. *The **energy partition** of a domain Ω with respect to an energy E and a set of sources S, is defined as:*

$$\Pi(E, S) = Z(E, S) \bigcup M(E, S) \ .$$

As a first example, if the potential is constant, e.g. $P \equiv 1$, then the energy at x,

$$G_0(x) = \inf_{\gamma \in \Gamma_{x_0 x}} \int_0^L ds \ ,$$

becomes the geodesic distance to the source, or the Euclidean length of the shortest path between x_0 and x. Moreover, if the domain is convex, then G_0 coincides with the usual Euclidean distance to x_0. If a set of sources $S = \{x_i\}_{i \in J}$ is considered, then the medial set $M(G, S)$ corresponds to the Voronoi diagram and the zones $Z(G, S)$ to the Voronoi cells.

2.3   Mosaic Images

Therefore, in this context, the image segmentation problem is transferred to the definition of an energy from the image data and the selection of a set of sources. Nevertheless, in practice, digital images are subsampled on the discrete grid. Consequently, important parts of the medial set often fall in the intergrid space. For region based segmentation purposes, an alternative to surround this problem is to consider an energy partition composed only by zones. Thus, the elements of the medial set that would fall exactly in the grid are assigned to one of their neighboring influence zones.

   Then, an approximation of the image can be constructed by the assignation of a *model* to represent each influence zone. The model is determined by the distribution of the image values on the zone; simple models are the mean or median value on the influence zone and source's level. When the model is constant, the valuation of each zone by its model produces a piecewise constant approximation of the image, referred in the sequel as a *mosaic image*.

3   The Path Variation

In the usual approach for the application of minimal paths to image analysis, a large part of the problem consists in the design of a relevant potential for a specific situation and type of images. However, we adopt a different perspective and use the framework of the previous section for the study of a particular energy, whose definition depends only on geometric properties of the image.

3.1   Continuous Domain

Jordan introduced the notion of variation for functions of one real variable as follows [ ]:
Let $f : [0, L] \to \mathbb{R}$ be a function, $\sigma = \{s_0, ..., s_n\}$ a finite partition of $[0, L]$ such that $0 = s_0 < s_1 < ... < s_n = L$ and Φ the set of such partitions.
The *total variation* of f is defined as the (possible infinite) number given by the formula:

$$v(f) = \sup_{\sigma \in \Phi} \sum_{i=1}^{n} |f(s_i) - f(s_{i-1})| \ .$$

   Hence, for two variable functions, we consider the minimal total variation on all the paths that join two points of the domain [ ]:

Definition 3. *The **path variation** of a function $u : \Omega \subset \mathbb{R}^2 \to \mathbb{R}$ with respect to a source point $x_0 \in \Omega$, evaluated at x, is defined as*

$$V_0(u)(x) = \inf_{\gamma \in \Gamma_{x_0 x}} v(u \circ \gamma) \ .$$

Definition 4. *The space of functions of **bounded path variation** of Ω, noted by $BPV(\Omega)$ is defined by*

$$BPV(\Omega) = \{u : \Omega \to \mathbb{R} \mid \forall x_0, x \in \Omega, \ \exists \hat{\gamma} \in \Gamma_{x_0 x} : V_0(u)(x) = v(u \circ \hat{\gamma}) < \infty\} \ .$$

In the sequel, we suppose that u has bounded path variation. Note that, if $u \in BPV(\Omega)$, then the path variation of u between any couple of points is not only required to be finite but also to be realized by a path. Hence, Def. supposes the existence of geodesics for V. This assumption seems reasonable for digital images; however, it should be noted that the geodesics of the path variation are generally not unique:

A path $\gamma \in \Gamma_{xy}$ is said to be *monotone* for u if $u \circ \gamma$ is a monotone function. By definition, if a path is monotone for u, then it is a geodesic for $V(u)$. Conversely, every geodesic for $V(u)$ is a concatenation of monotone paths.

In the regular framework, the path variation can be characterized as an energy, in the sense of Def. :

Proposition 1. *If $u \in \mathcal{C}^1(\Omega) \bigcap BPV(\Omega)$, then the path variation $V_0(u)$ is the surface of minimal action of the potential $P = |D_{\dot{\gamma}} u|$, the absolute value of the directional derivative of u in the tangent direction of the path.*

Proof. If $f \in \mathcal{C}^1([0, L])$, then the total variation can be expressed in terms of its derivative [ ] by the formula:

$$v(f) = \int_0^L |f'(s)| \, ds \ .$$

Thus, if u is a continuously differentiable function, Def . can be reformulated as:

$$V_0(u)(x) = \inf_{\gamma \in \Gamma_{x_0 x}} \int_0^L |\frac{\partial(u \circ \gamma)}{\partial s}(s)| \, ds \ .$$

Hence, we obtain the following expression for the path variation:

$$V_0(u)(x) = \inf_{\gamma \in \Gamma_{x_0 x}} \int_0^L |D_{\dot{\gamma}} u(\gamma(s))| \, ds \ .$$

$\square$

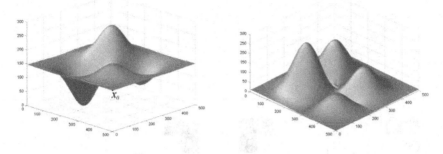

Fig. 1. Simple example: graphs of u and $V_0(u)$

The intuitive interpretation of the path variation is illustrated in Fig. :
consider a particle moving along the graph of the function depicted on the left
and starting at the source x_0. Then, as shown on the right, the value of $V_0(u)$,
evaluated at x, represents the minimal sum of ascents and descents to be travelled
to reach the point x.

The path variation expresses the same geometric notion as the *linear variation*, introduced in [ ], though in a different formulation, as a part of a geometric
theory for functions of two variables.

The *component* of u containing x, noted by K_x, designates the maximal connected subset of Ω such that $u(y) = u(x)$, $\forall y \in K_x$. The level of a component K
is noted by $u(K)$ and the set of components of u is noted by T_u. The components of a continuous function are closed and pairwise disjoint subsets of Ω. For
continuously differentiable functions, the components of the nonsingular levels
(i.e.: levels t such that $0 \notin \nabla u(u^{-1}(t))$) coincide with the level lines of u and can
be described as Jordan curves.

The importance of the components for the path variation is expressed by the
following proposition, whose proof is an immediate consequence of Def. .

Proposition 2. *The path variation acts on the component space T_u:*

$$\forall x, y \in \Omega, \ K_x = K_y \Rightarrow \forall x_0, \ V_0(u)(x) = V_0(u)(y) \ .$$

Therefore, each component of $V_0(u)$ is a union of components of u. Furthermore,
for a set of sources S, each element of $\Pi(V(u), S)$ is a union of components of
the function. Thus, since the energy partitions induced by the path variation
preserve this geometric structure of the function, $V(u)$ presents a particular
interest for image analysis. Additionally, the energy partitions induced by the
path variation are invariant under linear contrast changes.

Figure   illustrates the application of the path variation on two different
test functions. On the top row, a smooth function, given by the simple formula

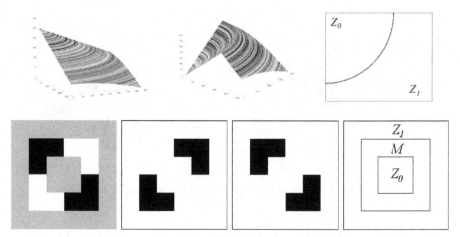

Fig. 2. Energy partitions of the path variation for two different test functions (see text)

$u(x) = c\|x - x_0\|$. The set of sources $S = \{x_0, x_1\}$, is composed by the upper left and the lower right corners of the domain. From left to right, we can observe the graph of u, the graph of $V_S(u)$ and the energy partition $\Pi(V(u), S)$. In this case, the components of the function are nested and the medial set $M(V(u), S)$, shown in black, corresponds to the component whose level is the average of the sources' levels.

In contrast, the function on the bottom-left of Fig. is piecewise constant; the corresponding gray levels were set to 0 for the black, 254 for the white and 127 for the gray. The two images on the middle show, in black, the level sets $[u \geq 200]$ and $[u \leq 100]$ respectively. Finally, bottom-right displays the energy partition obtained by taking the two gray components as sources. Notice that the component spaces of the two functions have different topologies. As a consequence, in the second example, even if the boundaries of the zones are composed by pieces of level lines, none of the squares determined by the energy partition is a level line of the function.

3.2 Discrete Domain

In this paragraph, we propose a discrete interpretation for the path variation. Thus, we consider that the image u has been sampled on a uniform grid. A first remark is that, since the potential of the path variation in Prop. depends not only on the position but also on the path direction, the Fast Marching method cannot be used for its implementation.

Nevertheless, in a discrete domain, the component structure of a function can be represented by an adjacency graph G, where the nodes correspond to discrete components and the links join neighboring components. Thus, G is the equivalent of T_u in the discrete space. Since V acts on the components of the function, we propose to construct the discrete path variation directly on G.

A path on G joining the components of two points p and q is a set $\gamma = \{K_0, ..., K_n\}$ such that $K_p = K_0$, $K_n = K_q$, K_i and K_{i-1} are neighbors, $\forall i = 1, ..., n$. The set of such paths is noted by Γ_{pq}^G. Each element of Γ_{pq}^G corresponds then to a class of discrete paths between p and q.

Thus, the expression of the discrete path variation of u at a point q with respect to the source p becomes

$$V_p(u)(q) = \min_{\gamma \in \Gamma_{pq}^G} \sum_{i=1}^{n} |u(K_i) - u(K_{i-1})| \ .$$

Hence, the calculation of $V_p(u)$ is reduced to finding the path of minimal cost on a graph. This classical problem can be solved using a greedy algorithm [,]. The complexity of this straightforward implementation for the path variation is then $O(Nlog(N))$, where N is the total number of discrete components of the image. Furthermore, if u takes integer values, the sorting step in the update of the narrow band can be suppressed and the complexity is reduced to $O(N)$.

4   Sources Selection

In order to use a surface of minimal action to address image segmentation problems, the choice of the sources is a critical issue. Indeed, since Def.   is based on an integration along the paths, the partitions determined by this type of energies are very sensitive to the location of the sources. Furthermore, replacing a source $x_i \in S$ by another point $x_i' \in Z_i$ usually modifies the corresponding energy partition.

Therefore, the set of sources must be physically representative of the image content. Ideally, for region based segmentation purposes, each zone should correspond to a meaningful feature in the image and their boundaries should coincide with the contours of the objects.

A first option is to address the problem interactively. In this case, a human operator decides which are the meaningful features in the image and the path variation is used to determine their contours. Thus, with this approach, the choice of the sources can be seen as the moment where semantic information is introduced in the segmentation process. This idea was also used in the well known *markers* method related to the watershed transform [ ].

Figure   displays, on the left, a set S, composed by 25 hand-placed sources for the *cameraman* test image. The source points, represented by white disks for better visualization, were chosen to provide a general description of the image, while including perceptually important details such as the face, the camera or the building on the background. On the right, we can observe the energy partition $\Pi(V(u), S)$. Note how the boundaries of the zones model accurately the contour information and, particularly, semantically important characteristics of edges such as corners and junctions.

Fig. 3. Example of hand-placed sources and corresponding energy partition

4.1   The Extrema Partition

A different problem is the choice of a set of sources without the intervention of a human operator. Figure   exemplifies this issue on the smooth image u on top-left. An acceptable segmentation of this "scene" should be composed by four approximately circular regions on a gray background. A solution is to consider the extrema of the four peaks as sources for the "features" and the border of the domain as the source representing the background. The image on top-right shows the set of sources, S, and the corresponding energy partition. On bottom-left, we can observe the graph of the energy $V_S(u)$. Finally, on bottom-right, we observe the corresponding mosaic image, when the zone model is intensity at the source.

Therefore, in the regular framework, the image extrema appear as natural candidates for the sources. The energy partition induced by the path variation and the set of extremal components, $\Pi(V(u), ext(u))$, will be called the *extrema partition* of the image u and the corresponding mosaic image, the *extrema mosaic*.

In real images, the choice of the path variation as the energy and the spatial distribution of the intensity extrema provide a compromise between content conservation and simplification in the extrema mosaic. This piecewise constant approximation of the image can be seen as a decomposition in elemental zones or as a first abstraction of the image information. The extrema mosaic may be used as a parameter-free presegmentation, where the contour information is preserved.

In certain cases, it may prove useful to repeat the process and construct the extrema mosaic of an extrema mosaic. However, an excessive iteration destroys the physical meaning of the intensity extrema and often results in an alteration of the original image structure.

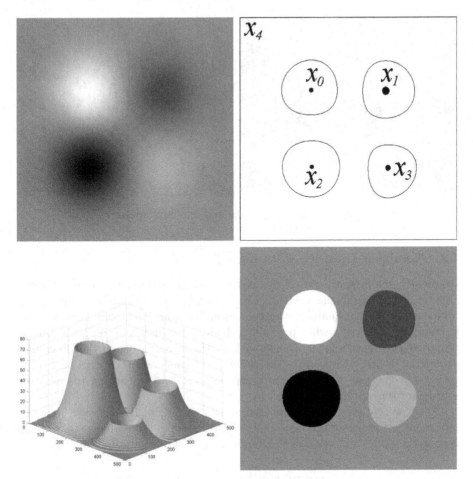

Fig. 4. Top: original image and energy partition. Bottom: graph of the energy and mosaic image

Figure   shows an example where the extrema mosaic was applied two times on a natural image. The ratio between the number of components in the original image and the final number of zones is in this case 42.35. On the left, we can observe the original image and, on the right, the second extrema mosaic. This image illustrates two properties of the extrema partition. First, an enhancement of the contrast information, as can be seen on the butterfly's wings. Second, a reduction of the blur in the background, caused by the absorption of blurred contours and transition components by neighboring zones.

Fig. 5. Original image and extrema mosaic

4.2 Nonlinear Diffusion Filtering

Frequently, the presence of textures and noise in natural images produces a large number of extrema in the intensity. Consequently, the extrema partition is often composed by a great quantity of small zones. The question is then how to reduce the number of extrema while preserving the image structure. In [ ], the authors proposed to preprocess the image with methods based on partial differential equations, in order to improve the watershed segmentation. In this paragraph, we discuss the use of a scale-space representation of the image to select the sources for our approach.

Thus, we consider the regularized version [,] of the classical approach proposed by Perona and Malik [ ]. In this method, a filtered image $u_t = u(x, t)$ is constructed as a solution of the nonlinear diffusion equation:

$$\frac{\partial u}{\partial t} = \operatorname{div}(g(|\nabla(G_\sigma * u)|^2)\nabla u) \ , \tag{4}$$

where G_σ denotes a Gaussian kernel of variance σ and $g(\cdot)$ is a positive *diffusivity function*. Reflecting boundary conditions are considered and the initial state $u_0 = u(x, 0)$ coincides with the original image.

For the examples presented, we used the diffusivity :

$$g(s) = \begin{cases} 1, \text{ if } s \leq 0 \\ 1 - exp\left(\frac{-3.315}{(s/\kappa)^4}\right), \text{ if } s > 0 \end{cases}$$

where κ is the contrast parameter that regulates the selective smoothing process. This diffusivity was reported in [ ] to lead to better results than the original functions in [ ].

The main properties of nonlinear diffusion filtering are illustrated in Fig. . The initial image u_0 was the extrema mosaic of the *cameraman*, shown on the left. The parameters of the diffusion were $\sigma = 1$ and $\kappa = 30$. The filtered image u_t, shown on the right, corresponds to the scale $t = 180$. In this method,

Fig. 6. Example of nonlinear diffusion filtering (see text)

intraregional smoothing is preferred to interregional smoothing. Thus, homogeneous regions are smoothed in the filtered image u_t, while the edge information is enhanced.

Therefore, the number of extrema in the filtered image, noted by $ext(u_t)$, decreases rapidly when the scale is augmented. These properties make of $ext(u_t)$ an interesting candidate for the set of sources of our energy partitions. Two choices are then possible, either consider the extrema partition of the filtered image, $\Pi(V(u_t), ext(u_t))$, or go back to the initial image u_0 and construct the partition $\Pi(V(u_0), ext(u_t))$.

Figure   illustrates this method for the choice of the sources, with the example of Fig. . The number of extremal components decreased from 8412 in the original image to 261 in the smoothed image. Top-left shows the extrema mosaic of u_t and top-right displays the mosaic image of $\Pi(V(u_0), ext(u_t))$. Notice how both energy partitions, shown on the bottom row, preserve the image structure, in spite of the reduction in the number of sources. The main difference lies in the regularization of the zones in the filtered image with respect to the zones obtained with the initial image.

In summary, the use of nonlinear diffusion produces in general a representative set the sources. However, an excessive filtering destroys the contour information. Thus, this method requires the tuning of the diffusion parameters. Finally, note that even homogeneous regions like the sky in Fig.   contain several extrema after the filtering.

The comparison between the results of Fig.   and the partition obtained with hand-placed sources in Fig.   suggests that other approaches for the choice of the sources may lead to better results.

Fig. 7. Sources selection by nonlinear diffusion (see text)

Alternatively, our approach can be seen as a parameter-free method to construct a partition with a small number of regions, starting from an image filtered by nonlinear diffusion.

5   Conclusion and Perspectives

In this paper, we discussed the application of the path variation to the segmentation of monochrome images. It should be noted that the use of the path variation for the construction of an energy partition assumes a certain homogeneity of the objects represented in the image. Therefore, in order to apply this approach to highly textured or noisy images, a pre-processing step should be considered.

Finally, present work includes the generalization of our approach to vector-valued images and the definition of alternative methods for the selection of the sources.

Acknowledgments

The first author wishes to thank P. Monasse and J.M. Morel for introducing him to the inspiring work of A.S. Kronrod.

References

[1] P. A. Arbeláez. The path variation. Technical report, CEREMADE, 2003.

[2] S. Beucher and F. Meyer. The morphological approach to segmentation: The watershed transformation. *Mathematical Morphology in Image Processing*, pages 433–481, 1992.

[3] P. Blomgren and T. F. Chan. Color tv: Total variation methods for restoration of vector-valued images. *IP*, 7(3):304–309, March 1998.

[4] F. Catté, P. L. Lions, J. M. Morel, and T. Coll. Image selective smoothing and edge detection by nonlinear diffusion. *SIAM J. Numer. Anal.*, 29(1):182–193, 1992.

[5] A. Chambolle and P. L. Lions. Image recovery via total variation minimization and related problems. *Numerische Mathematik*, 76:167–188, 1997.

[6] L. D. Cohen. Multiple contour finding and perceptual grouping using minimal paths. *Journal of Mathematical Imaging and Vision*, 14(3):225–236, 2001.

[7] L. D. Cohen and R. Kimmel. Global minimum for active contour models: A minimal path approach. *International Journal of Computer Vision*, 24(1):57–78, August 1997.

[8] T. Deschamps and L. D. Cohen. Fast extraction of minimal paths in 3d images and applications to virtual endoscopy. *Medical Image Analysis*, 5(4):281–299, 2001.

[9] F. Dibos and G. Koepfler. Global total variation minimization. *SIAM Journal of Numerical Analysis*, 37(2):646–664, 2000.

[10] E. W. Dijkstra. A note on two problems in connection with graphs. *Numerische Mathematic*, 1:269–271, 1959.

[11] E. Hewitt and K. Stromberg. *Real and Abstract Analysis*. Springer Verlag, 1969.

[12] C. Jordan. Sur la série de fourier. *C. R. Acad. Sci. Paris Sér. I Math.*, 92(5):228–230, 1881.

[13] R. Kimmel and A. M. Bruckstein. Global shape from shading. *CVIU*, 62(3):360–369, 1995.

[14] R. Kimmel, N. Kiryati, and A. M. Bruckstein. Distance maps and weighted distance transforms. *Journal of Mathematical Imaging and Vision*, 6:223–233, May 1996. Special Issue on Topology and Geometry in Computer Vision.

[15] A. S. Kronrod. On functions of two variables. *Uspehi Mathematical Sciences*, 5(35), 1950. In Russian.

[16] R. Kruse and A. Ryba. *Data structures and program design in C++*. Prentice Hall, New York, 1999.

[17] H. Lebesgue. *Leçons sur l'Intégration et la Recherche des Fonctions Primitives.* Gauthier Villars, 1928.

[18] I. P. Natansson. *Theory of Functions of a Real Variable.* Frederick Ungar Publishing, New York, 1964.

[19] S. Osher and L. I. Rudin. Feature-oriented image enhancement using shock filters. *NumAnal*, 27(4):919–940, 1990.

[20] P. Perona and J. Malik. Scale-space and edge detection using anisotrppic diffusion. *PAMI*, 12(7):629–639, 1990.

[21] L. I. Rudin and S. Osher. Total variation based image restoration with free local constraints. In *Proc. ICIP*, pages 31–35, 1994.

[22] L. I. Rudin, S. Osher, and E. Fatemi. Nonlinear total variation based noise removal algorithms. *Physica D*, 60:259–268, 1992.

[23] J. A. Sethian. *Level Set Methods and Fast Marching Methods.* Cambridge University Press, Cambridge, UK, 2 edition, 1999.

[24] J. Weickert. *Anisotropic Diffusion in Image Processing.* Teubner, 1998.

[25] J. Weickert. Efficient image segmentation using partial differential equations and morphology. *Pattern Recognition*, 34(9):1813–1824, 2001.

[26] J. Weickert, B. M. ter Haar Romeny, and M. A. Viergever. Efficient and reliable schemes for nonlinear diffusion filtering. *IP*, 7(3):398–410, March 1998.

A Fast Snake Segmentation Method
Applied to Histopathological Sections*

Adam Karlsson[1], Kent Stråhlén[2], and Anders Heyden[1]

[1] School of Technology and Society, Malmö University, Sweden,
Adam.Karlsson@ts.mah.se
[2] CellaVision AB, Ideon Research Park, Lund, Sweden,
Kent.Srahlen@cellavision.se

Abstract. Using snakes to segment images has proven to be a powerful tool in many different applications. The snake is usually propagated by minimizing an energy function. The standard way of updating the snake from the energy function is time consuming. This paper presents a fast snake evolution algorithm, based on a more efficient numeric scheme for updating the snake. Instead of inverting a matrix derived from approximating derivatives in a sampled snake, an analytical expression is obtained. The expression takes the form of a convolution with a filter given by an explicit formula. The filter function can then be sampled and used to propagate snakes in a fast and straightforward manner. The proposed method is generally applicable to snakes and is here used for propagating snakes in a gradient vector flow field. Experiments are carried out on images of histopathological tissue sections and the results are very promising.

1 Introduction

Segmentation is the process of dividing an image into different regions, e.g. separating the nucleus of a cell from the rest of the image and nuclei from each other in an image of a tissue section. Segmentation is perhaps the most crucial step in any image analysis system, since any automatic quantitative analysis of an image is difficult, without separating the relevant information from the irrelevant.

The main contribution of this paper is to further develop the algorithm used for propagating snakes in [ ]. The new and faster algorithms will be used as a semi-automatic, with implications for fully automatic, method for segmentation. Other approaches to fast snake algorithms use e.g. dynamic programming, cf. [ ].

The proposed method will be applied to histopathological sections. The tissue sections studied are Hematoxylin- and Eosin-stained sections of bladder tumors and normal urothelium. The type of snake investigated is the so-called GVF (Gradient Vector Flow) snake [ ], which is an important improvement over the traditional snakes in [ ].

* This work has been supported by the Swedish Research Council, project 621-2001-358.

A. Rangarajan et al. (Eds.): EMMCVPR 2003, LNCS 2683, pp. 261–   , 2003.
© Springer-Verlag Berlin Heidelberg 2003

1.1   Snakes

Active contour models are a group of methods used in image segmentation. The models all define some interface that moves according to internal forces, inherent to the interface itself and according to external forces derived from the image. The active contour models can be divided into two groups: parametric models and geometric models. The geometric models are e.g. the Level Set and the Fast Marching methods. Snakes is an example of a parametric model and this is the model we will deal with in this paper.

In the original paper [ ] on snakes a snake is defined as a curve $\mathbf{v}(s) = [x(s), y(s)]$, $s \in S = [0, 1]$, that moves through an image attempting to minimize the following energy functional

$$E[\mathbf{v}(s)] = \int_S \frac{1}{2} \left(\alpha |\mathbf{v}'(s)|^2 + \beta |\mathbf{v}''(s)|^2 \right) + E_{\text{ext}} \left(\mathbf{v}(s) \right) ds . \tag{1}$$

Here $\mathbf{v}'(s)$ and $\mathbf{v}''(s)$ denote the first and second order derivatives of $\mathbf{v}(s)$ with respect to s. The first order derivative can be considered as a measure of continuity and the second order derivative as a measure of the smoothness. Hence the weights α and β control the tension and rigidity of the snake. E_{ext} is a scalar field derived from an image with low values for the structures sought and can be regarded as the external energy. Likewise, the first term (i.e. the derivatives and the weights) of the integrand can be regarded as the internal energy of the snake. It is noted that α and β may be functions of s, although in this paper they will only be used as constants, and will therefore from here on be treated as such.

Compared to simpler segmentation techniques (e.g. thresholding, watershedding) active contour models have the important advantage of incorporating nonlocal information in the process of edge detection. Due to the formulation above in ( ), points in the image are considered in a spatially connected sense and a priori information about the contours is incorporated in a natural way. For example, if looking for objects that are nearly circular, high constraints on their continuity and smoothness should be applied.

1.2   The External Energy Function

As stated above an external energy field should have the property, that it assumes low values for features of interest. Since edges are the most commonly features sought typical examples of E_{ext} are

$$E_{\text{ext}} = -|\nabla I(x, y)|^2 \quad \text{and} \quad E_{\text{ext}} = -|\nabla G_\sigma(x, y) * I(x, y)|^2 , \tag{2}$$

where $I(x, y)$ denotes an intensity map derived from the image, ∇ denotes the gradient operator and G_σ denotes a Gaussian kernel with standard deviation σ.

1.3   Numerical Solution

Using the Euler equations it is found that a necessary condition for $\mathbf{v}$ to minimize the functional ( ) is

$$\alpha \mathbf{v}''(s) - \beta \mathbf{v}^{(4)}(s) - \nabla E_{\text{ext}}(\mathbf{v}(s)) = 0 . \tag{3}$$

Note that the equation also can be considered as a force balance equation

$$\mathbf{F}_{\text{int}} + \mathbf{F}_{\text{ext}} = 0 ,$$

where

$$\begin{cases} \mathbf{F}_{\text{int}} = \alpha \mathbf{v}''(s) - \beta \mathbf{v}^{(4)}(s) \\ \mathbf{F}_{\text{ext}} = -\nabla E_{\text{ext}}(\mathbf{v}(s)) \end{cases}$$

denote the internal force of the snake and the external force that draws the snake towards regions of interest respectively.

In order to find a solution to ( ) a new variable t is introduced, and $\mathbf{v}$ is considered as a function of t, interpreted as time, as well as of s. The partial derivative of $\mathbf{v}(s,t)$ with respect to t is then set equal to the left-hand side of ( ), giving the following two independent equations:

$$x_t(s,t) = \alpha x''(s,t) - \beta x^{(4)}(s,t) - \nabla E_{\text{ext}} \tag{4}$$

$$y_t(s,t) = \alpha y''(s,t) - \beta y^{(4)}(s,t) - \nabla E_{\text{ext}} \tag{5}$$

Discretizing these equations using $x_k = x(kh)$, with $x_0 = x_N$ for closed contours, and approximating the derivatives with finite differences, yields, where δ denotes the time-step:

$$\delta(x_k^n - x_k^{n-1}) = \frac{\alpha}{h^2}(x_{k+1}^n - 2x_k^n + x_{k-1}^n) -$$

$$\frac{\beta}{h^4}(x_{k+2}^n - 4x_{k+1}^n + 6x_k^n - 4x_{k-1}^n + x_{k-2}^n) - f_x(x_k^n, y_k^n) \tag{6}$$

and similarly $y_k = y(kh)$, with $y_0 = y_N$ for closed contours yields time-step:

$$\delta(y_k^n - y_k^{n-1}) = \frac{\alpha}{h^2}(y_{k+1}^n - 2y_k^n + y_{k-1}^n) -$$

$$\frac{\beta}{h^4}(y_{k+2}^n - 4y_{k+1}^n + 6y_k^n - 4y_{k-1}^n + y_{k-2}^n) - f_y(x_k^n, y_k^n) . \tag{7}$$

The equations in ( ) and ( ) can be rewritten in matrix form as

$$\begin{cases} (\mathbf{A} + \delta \mathbf{I})\mathbf{x}^n = \mathbf{x}^{n-1} - \mathbf{f_x}(\mathbf{x}^n, \mathbf{y}^n) \approx \mathbf{x}^{n-1} - \mathbf{f_x}(\mathbf{x}^{n-1}, \mathbf{y}^{n-1}) \\ (\mathbf{A} + \delta \mathbf{I})\mathbf{y}^n = \mathbf{y}^{n-1} - \mathbf{f_y}(\mathbf{x}^n, \mathbf{y}^n) \approx \mathbf{y}^{n-1} - \mathbf{f_y}(\mathbf{x}^{n-1}, \mathbf{y}^{n-1}) \end{cases} \tag{8}$$

where $\mathbf{x} = [x_0, \ldots, x_{N-1}]$, $\mathbf{y} = [y_0, \ldots, y_{N-1}]$ and $\mathbf{A}$ denotes a penta-diagonal banded matrix (since only x_i^n for $i = k - 2.k - 1, k - k + 1, k + 2$ appears in ( ) and similarly for). Assuming the image derived force field to be constant during a time step, evaluating it at time $n - 1$ rather than at time n gives the final approximation.

Comments on the Spatial Step: Note that by redefining α and β in ( ), h can be ignored. In fact, for all practical purposes we can set h to be equal to one in all computations below. In order for this to work, h must be kept constant. Since the points of the snake are dynamically updated, N must be adjusted after each step, to keep h approximately fixed. Thus the snake has to be resampled in each iteration.

Resampling the snake is also necessary in order to maintain a good representation of the continuous function that the discretization represents and to avoid variations in the resolution of the model, cf. [ ]. Furthermore resampling the snake solves another problem. By resampling the snake the possibility of snake points forming bundles, something that otherwise may have a negative impact on the final results, is avoided.

Comments on the Temporal Step: Note that if we use the point x_k^{n-1} instead of x_k^n, and similarly using y_k^{n-1} instead of y_k^n, on the right hand side of ( ), we get

$$\delta(x_k^n - x_k^{n-1}) = \frac{\alpha}{h^2}(x_{k+1}^{n-1} - 2x_k^{n-1} + x_{k-1}^{n-1}) -$$
$$\frac{\beta}{h^4}(x_{k+2}^{n-1} - 4x_{k+1}^{n-1} + 6x_k^{n-1} - 4x_{k-1}^{n-1} + x_{k-2}^{n-1}) - f_x(x_k^{n-1}, y_k^{n-1}) \ , \quad (9)$$

which can be solved directly. In fact it will reduce to a simple convolution, with a kernel of finite size, and an addition. This explicit method, however, is not as stable as the semi-implicit method introduced above for large time steps, cf. [ ] and also indicated in [ ]. One of the contributions of this paper is to show that also the semi-implicit method in ( ) can be expressed in terms of a convolution.

1.4 Gradient Vector Flow

One of the main draw-backs with using snakes is that the contour has to be initialized close to the final solution, in order to converge. One way to solve this problem is to introduce so called pressure forces, cf. [ ]. Other methods that has been proposed in the literature is dual-active contours, cf. [ ], and distance-potentials, cf. [ ]. However, the most promising extension to snakes seems to be the Gradient Vector Flow, cf. [ ].

The Gradient Vector Flow method introduces a new type of static external force field derived from an image. The external force is replaced by a vector valued function $\mathbf{g}(x, y) = [u(x, y), v(x, y)]$, where the force field $\mathbf{g}$ is called the Gradient Vector Flow (GVF) field. The corresponding dynamic snake equation is found by replacing the potential force $-\nabla E_{ext}$ in ( ) with $\mathbf{g}$, yielding

$$\mathbf{v}_t(s, t) = \alpha \mathbf{v}''(s) - \beta \mathbf{v}^{(4)}(s) + \mathbf{g} \ . \quad (10)$$

The parametric curve solving equation is consequently defined as a GVF snake, and the solution is found in exactly the same manner as for a traditional snake.

Since $\mathbf{g}(x, y)$ can not be expected to be a divergence free field in general, it can not be expressed as the gradient of a potential function. Therefore the GVF snake generally will not satisfy the Euler equation of the original snake energy minimization problem. However, the advantages due to this new formulation are so profound that they well make up for this loss of optimality.

The GVF field is defined as the vector field, $\mathbf{g}(x, y) = [u(x, y), v(x, y)]$, that minimizes the integral

$$\iint \mu(u_x^2 + u_y^2 + v_x^2 + v_y^2) + |\nabla f|^2 |\mathbf{g} - \nabla f|^2 dx dy \ , \tag{11}$$

where $f(x, y)$ denotes an edge map and μ denotes a scalar parameter determining the relative importance of the two terms of the integrand. The edge map $f(x, y)$ is a scalar field having the property that it is largest near the edges. Hence setting $f(x, y) = -E_{\text{ext}}$ gives a suitable edge map.

The Euler-equations for minimizing ( ) can be solved iteratively, cf. [ ]. Notably, the Euler-equations, in this case, give both necessary and sufficient conditions for the integral to be minimal, cf. [ ].

2   A Fast Iterative Scheme for Snake Evolution

Whether GVF-snakes or traditional snakes are used the iterative evolution of the snake involves solving two equations in each step, one for $\mathbf{x_t}$ and one for $\mathbf{y_t}$ of the type

$$(\mathbf{A} + \delta \mathbf{I})\, \mathbf{x_t} = \delta \mathbf{x_{t-1}} + \mathbf{G_x}\left(\mathbf{x_{t-1}}, \mathbf{y_{t-1}}\right) \ . \tag{12}$$

A straight-forward approach to solving this equation is to invert the matrix $(\mathbf{A} + \delta \mathbf{I})$, which would be acceptable provided that the calculation was just performed once. However, the snake is continuously resampled in order to maintain adequate resolution. This requires to update the size of the matrix each time the snake is resampled, which in turn makes it necessary to recalculate the inverse.

Since the matrix is quite large, calculating its inverse is a computationally costly operation. One solution is to use sparse methods for LU-decomposition, cf. [ ]. However, by examining the matrix it is possible to do better. The matrix $(\mathbf{A} + \delta \mathbf{I})$ is a square symmetric penta-diagonal banded matrix;

$$(\mathbf{A} + \delta \mathbf{I}) = \begin{bmatrix} h(0) & h(1) & h(2) & 0 & 0 & 0 & \cdots & 0 & h(2) & h(1) \\ h(1) & h(0) & h(1) & h(2) & 0 & 0 & \cdots & 0 & 0 & h(2) \\ h(2) & h(1) & h(0) & h(1) & h(2) & 0 & \cdots & 0 & 0 & 0 \\ 0 & h(2) & h(1) & h(0) & h(1) & h(2) & \cdots & 0 & 0 & 0 \\ \vdots & \vdots & \vdots & \vdots & \vdots & \vdots & \ddots & \vdots & \vdots & \vdots \\ h(1) & h(2) & 0 & 0 & 0 & 0 & \cdots & h(2) & h(1) & h(0) \end{bmatrix} , \tag{13}$$

where the entries $h(i)$ easily can be obtained from ( ). Consider $(\mathbf{A} + \delta \mathbf{I})$ operating on a vector $\mathbf{x}$. If $\mathbf{x}$ is expanded periodically to an N-periodic sequence we may express element number i of the result as

$$((\mathbf{A} + \delta\mathbf{I})\,\mathbf{x})_i = \sum_{k=-2}^{2} h\,(|k|)\,x\,(i+k) = \sum_{k=0}^{N-1} g\,(i-k)x\,(k)\ , \qquad (14)$$

where the last equality holds provided that the sequence g is the N-periodic equivalent of the first row in the matrix $(\mathbf{A} + \delta\mathbf{I})$. The right hand side of ( ) is the convolution of $\mathbf{x}$ with g. From the convolution theorem for periodic sequences we know that

$$\mathcal{F}_N\,(g * x) = \mathcal{F}_N\,(g)\,\mathcal{F}_N\,(x)\ , \qquad (15)$$

where $\mathcal{F}_N$ denotes the discrete Fourier transform. Thus $\mathbf{x}_t$ can be expressed as

$$\mathbf{x_t} = \mathcal{F}_N^{-1}\,(1./(\mathcal{F}_N g)\,\mathcal{F}_N \mathbf{R})\ , \qquad (16)$$

where $\mathbf{R}$ denote the right-hand side of ( ) and the operation $1./$ is defined as the element-wise division operation. This is in itself a fast method, but it is possible to improve it even further.

In ( ) it can be seen that $\mathbf{x}_t$ can be solved for by convolving $\mathbf{R}$ with a filter f according to

$$\mathbf{x_t} = \mathcal{F}_N^{-1}\,(1./\mathcal{F}_N g) * \mathbf{R} = f * \mathbf{R}\ , \qquad (17)$$

i.e. $f = \mathcal{F}_N^{-1}\,(1./\mathcal{F}_N g)$. Now, we can find an explicit expression for the filter. Observe that $(\mathbf{A} + \delta\mathbf{I})$ is the discrete approximation of the operator

$$\mathcal{A} = \delta - \alpha\frac{\partial^2}{\partial s^2} + \beta\frac{\partial^4}{\partial s^4}\ . \qquad (18)$$

Discretizing ( ) only in time and not in space we may write

$$\mathcal{A}x_t = \delta x_{t-1} + G_x\,(x_{t-1}, y_{t-1})\ , \qquad (19)$$

regarding x and y as continuous periodic functions. Taking the Fourier transform of ( ) gives

$$\mathcal{F}\,(\mathcal{A}x_t) = \mathcal{F}\,(\delta x_{t-1} + G_x\,(x_{t-1}, y_{t-1}))\ ,$$

and using ( ) we obtain

$$\left(\delta + \alpha\omega^2 + \beta\omega^4\right)\mathcal{F}x_t = \mathcal{F}\,(\delta x_{t-1} + G_x\,(x_{t-1}, y_{t-1}))\ . \qquad (20)$$

Since x_{t-1} and G_x are bounded, periodic functions, their Fourier transforms exist, at least in a distributional sense.

Solving for $\mathcal{F}x_t$ in ( ) and performing the inverse transformation results in

$$x_t = \mathcal{F}^{-1}\left(\frac{1}{\delta + \alpha\omega^2 + \beta\omega^4}\right) * (\delta x_{t-1} + G_x\,(x_{t-1}, y_{t-1}))\ . \qquad (21)$$

The inverse transform $f(t) = \mathcal{F}^{-1}\left(\frac{1}{\delta + \alpha\omega^2 + \beta\omega^4}\right)$ depends on the roots of the polynomial $\delta + \alpha\omega^2 + \beta\omega^4$. In the case of complex roots, denote these $\pm(u \pm iv)$

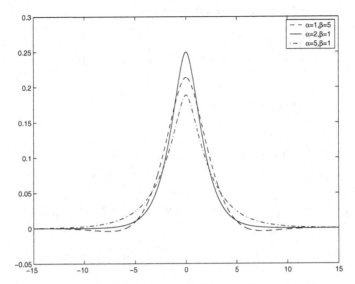

Fig. 1. The function $f(t)$ for three different values of the parameters

and let $\varphi = \arctan\left(u/v\right)$. In the case of real roots denote these $\pm\sqrt{m}, \pm\sqrt{n}$ and in the case of multiple roots denote them $\pm y$. The solution can be shown to be

$$
f\left(t\right) = \begin{cases}
\dfrac{e^{-v|t|}\,\sin(u|t|+\varphi)}{\sqrt{4\delta\beta-\alpha^{2}}\,\sqrt[4]{\frac{\delta}{\beta}}}, & \alpha^{2} < 4\beta\delta \\[2mm]
\dfrac{1}{4\beta y^{3}}\left(1+y\left|t\right|\right)e^{-y|t|}, & \alpha^{2} = 4\beta\delta \\[2mm]
\dfrac{1}{2\sqrt{\alpha^{2}-4\delta\beta}}\left(\dfrac{e^{-\sqrt{n}|t|}}{\sqrt{n}}-\dfrac{e^{-\sqrt{m}|t|}}{\sqrt{m}}\right), & \alpha^{2} > 4\beta\delta \\[2mm]
\dfrac{e^{-\sqrt{\frac{\delta}{\alpha}}|t|}}{2\sqrt{\alpha\delta}}, & \beta = 0
\end{cases}
\tag{22}
$$

The function $f(t)$ in ( ) for three different values of the parameters α and β are shown in Figure , with $\delta = 1$ in all cases. Note that the function $f(t)$ is rapidly decreasing. It is defined on $[-L/2, L/2]$, L being the period, corresponding to the arc length, with order of magnitude equal to hundred usually. Using this filter we have

$$
x_{t}\left(s\right) = f * R = R * f = \int_{-\infty}^{+\infty} R\left(s-\tau\right)f\left(s\right)d\tau \;,
\tag{23}
$$

with

$$
R\left(s\right) = \delta x_{t-1}\left(s\right) + G_{x}\left(x_{t-1}\left(s\right), y_{t-1}\left(s\right)\right) \;.
$$

Since $f(x) \geq 0$ is rapidly decreasing and symmetric (of the order $p(|x|) \cdot e^{-c|x|}$, for some first order polynomial p and constant $c > 0$, see ( )), and R is periodical, we can for each ϵ find a θ, such that

$$\left| \int_{|\tau| \geq \theta} R(s - \tau) f(\tau) \, d\tau \right| \leq \epsilon \left| \int_{|\tau| \leq \theta} R(s - \tau) f(\tau) \, d\tau \right| .$$

The proof is roughly as follows:

$$\left| \int_{|\tau| \geq \theta} R(s - \tau) f(\tau) \, d\tau \right| \leq \max_{|x| \leq L/2} |R(x)| \int_{|\tau| \geq \theta} f(x) dx \leq$$

$$\max_{|x| \leq L/2} |R(x)| \int_{|\tau| \geq \theta} p(|x|) e^{-c|x|} dx = 2 \cdot \max_{|x| \leq L/2} |R(x)| \int_{\tau \geq 0} p(x) e^{-cx} dx .$$

Partial integration, and noting that $p'(x)$ is a constant K, gives:

$$\left| \int_{|\tau| \geq \theta} R(s - \tau) f(\tau) \, d\tau \right| \leq$$

$$2 \cdot \max_{|x| \leq L/2} |R(x)| \left(\frac{1}{c} e^{-c\theta} p(\theta) + \frac{K}{c^2} e^{-c\theta} \right) . \tag{24}$$

It is now easy to see that a θ can be found, which satisfies the inequality. Say that

$$\left| \int R(s - \tau) f(\tau) d\tau \right| = A ,$$

then choose θ such that (   ) is smaller that $\frac{\epsilon}{1+\epsilon} A$ and the inequality holds.

Finally we obtain, using the above and approximating the integral (   ) with its Riemann sum,

$$\mathbf{x_t}(i) \approx \frac{1}{h} \sum_k R(i - k) f(kh) , \tag{25}$$

where the limit of k is such that $|kh| \leq \theta$ for a desired approximation ϵ. Observe that this is the first time that we make any approximations. Apart from the discretization in the time domain all calculations have been exact up to this step.

Empirical studies suggest that the results are satisfactory even when choosing a very small θ. Here we have chosen θ such that all values of $f(x)$ is less than 2% of the maximum of $f(x)$ for $|x| \geq \theta$. This somewhat crude method works well. This way of computing $\mathbf{x_t}$ allows for a fast algorithm, of the same order of complexity as the direct explicit method, see (   ). We have both got rid of the matrix inversion problem and obtained a filter which is symmetric and of very limited length, see Table .

Table 1. Table showing the number of non-zero elements in the convolution kernel using different α and β with $\delta = 1$. All elements with a magnitude smaller than 2 % of the largest value where set to zero

$\alpha\backslash\beta$	0	1	2	3	4
0	1	7	11	13	15
1	11	9	11	15	17
2	13	9	11	15	17
3	15	9	13	15	17
4	15	11	13	15	17

The approximation can be further refined by using a sliding mean of f instead of just sample at points:

$$\mathbf{x_t}(i) = \frac{1}{h}\sum_k R(i-k) \int_{k-h/2}^{k+h/2} f(x)\,dx \ . \tag{26}$$

A comparison between the filter, $f(t)$, in ( ) and a row of the inverted matrix (denoted Matrix), using $h = 1$, $\alpha = 2$, and $\beta = 3$ is shown in Figure . In the figure the somewhat more accurate approximation according to ( ), (denoted $\int f(t)dt$), is also shown. Note that the three functions are almost identical.

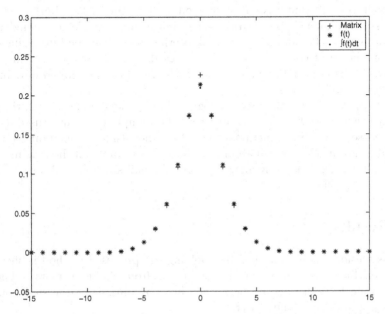

Fig. 2. Comparisons of three different ways of computing $f(t)$

3   Experiments

Images were acquired from Hematoxylin- and Eosin-stained tissue sections from bladder tumors and normal urothelium using a microscope. The purpose of the segmentation algorithm is to segment the nuclei in the images. The system used for the experiments was constructed as a semi-automatic tool, the user is required to specify a circle as a rough demarcation of the object of interest.

A small image of the region specified is cut out and this image undergoes an image processing chain which be summarized as: color reduction, edge map calculation, and calculation of the GVF-field. Finally, the snake is iterated starting from the specified circle.

The color reduction is performed by subtracting the red component from the blue component, which stands to reason since the acidophilic stain Hematoxylin is blue and has affinity for the nucleus, whilst Eosin is pink and basophilic, therefore staining the cytoplasm.

The edge map is computed from a gradient field, obtained by convolving the color reduced image with the gradient of a gaussian kernel with standard deviation σ. To take into account the directions of the gradient field the scalar product of the gradient field and a normalized circular field is used as edgemap. This results in a scalar field having high positive values for the edges whose normal direction is correct; i.e. a direction away from the chosen point, see Figure .

In order to suppress irrelevant information, the edge map is multiplied with a binary mask computed with Otsu's method [ ] and modified by a series of dilations. Due to high magnitude gradients in the nuclei, it is suitable to pre-process in two different ways depending on whether the snake is initialized inside or outside the nuclei's boundaries. When initializing outside the boundaries of the nucleus; $\sigma = 0.5$ and no additional filtering is used. When initializing inside the boundaries of the nucleus $\sigma = 1.5$ is used and a 3 by 3-pixel min-filter is applied to the edgemap, whereby solitary high values are filtered out. In both cases $\alpha = 2$ and $\beta = 3$ are used.

In accordance with the methodological developments in Section , the snake is convolved with a filter in each iteration. The simplest variant is used, i.e. just making use of the filter function as is (   ) and not using the integration in (   ). The filter is cut off for small absolute values (less than 2% of the maximal value of the filter). This yields symmetric filters of small sizes (e.g. 13 for $\alpha = 2$ and $\beta = 3$), see Table .

4   Results

In this section results obtained by applying the proposed method is shown for Hematoxylin- and Eosin-stained tissue sections from bladder tumors and normal urothelium. Experiments are performed both by initializing the snake outiside the object and inside the object.

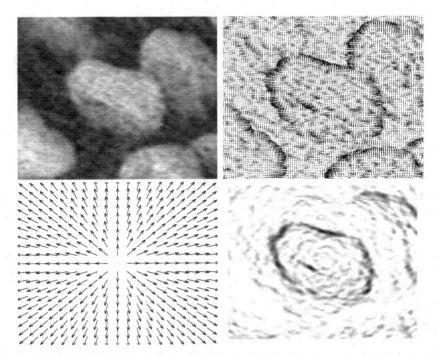

Fig. 3. Top row: The colorreduced image and its gradient field. Bottom row: A circular field and the edgemap obtained by scalar multiplication of the circular field with the gradient field

4.1   Initializing Outside the Boundaries of the Nucleus

Figure   is an example of two nuclei overlapping each other, and the snake being initialized outside the boundaries of the nucleus. The problem of separating these two nuclei cannot be solved using e.g. thresholding. The snake on the other hand solves it given a fair initialization.

What to be considered as "a fair initialization" requires some discussion. In simpler cases when a rough delimitation of the object may be found by means of e.g. thresholding, the snake will converge to a good result given any initialization outside the object. In tougher cases (e.g. Figure   ) the snake will of course not converge if for example initialized too close to the occluding nucleus' further edge or outside both nuclei. However, in almost all tried cases there is a wide range of initializations that produce the desired result, which gives at hand that the system works well as a semi-automatic tool.

4.2   Initializing within the Boundaries of the Nucleus

Figure   illustrates an important aspect about this segmentation technique. Two nuclei that overlap each other are shown. Most segmentation methods are based

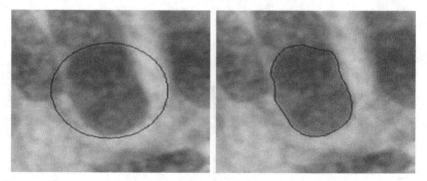

Fig. 4. Segmentation of one of two overlapping nuclei by intializing the snake outside of the actual nucleus

on the assumption that a pixel can belong to one and only one object. Using this technique no such limitations apply and two overlapping objects can both be perfectly segmented.

4.3   Aspects on Computational Time

The main improvement considering speed compared to standard methods, is the computations concerning the iterative evolution of the snake. Implemented in C and using an 800 MHz Pentium 3 processor the preprocessing performed on the cutout 111x111 pixel image is performed in less than 10 ms. To iterate the snake until convergence is done in about the same amount of the time for an average snake. This is very much thanks to the developments of Section , which keeps the number of calculations performed in each step at a minimum.

In every iteration we are convolving the the snake with a symmetric filter. Hence, the complexity of our algorithm depends on the number of iterations, I, the number of points of the snake, N, and the size of the filter, F, see Table . The complexity of the algorithm, counting the number of multiplications, is $IN(F+1)/2$. This is in same order of complexity as for the explicit method, which requires $IN \cdot 3$ multiplications, see Equation ( ).

It has been found that it takes less than 10^{-6}s per iteration and point to iterate the snake. Typically $50-100$ iterations are required, sometimes however as many as 400 are needed and a typical snake in this application consists of $100-150$ points; yielding execution times normally lower than 10 ms or in worst-case scenarios of about 60 ms.

The only slow part of the program is the calculation of the GVF-field that requires about 3 ms per iteration for the image size used, resulting in a total calculation time of 150 ms, when 50 iterations are used.

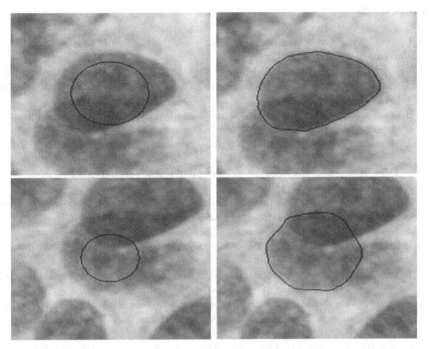

Fig. 5. Segmentation of two overlapping nuclei by initializing snakes inside the nuclei

5   Conclusions

The analysis that has been performed on the iterative evolution of snakes has made it possible to perform the calculations in a new way. Instead of inverting a rather big matrix, we have transformed the problem to a convolution with a filter. The filter is symmetric and of limited extension. This approach combines the simplicity and high speed of the explicit method with the stability and robustness of the implicit method.

The described method is not restricted to be used with the GVF-field but since the formulation of the GVF-field provides for very good convergence even with a rather poor initialization we obtain very good results. However, the calculation of the GVF-field is slow and therefore future work should address possibilities of speeding up the process of computing the GVF-field.

We have also presented a straightforward approach to segmenting overlapping objects. This approach brings a very important thing that few other segmentation methods handle. A subset of an image can be classified as belonging to two or more different objects.

We have presented experiments on the problem of segmenting nuclei in Hematoxylin- and Eosin-stained tissue sections from bladder tumors and normal urothelium, with very promising results.

References

[1] L. D. Cohen. On active contour models and balloons. *CVGIP: Image Understanding*, 53(2):211–218, 1991.

[2] L. D. Cohen and I. Cohen. Finite-element methods for active contour models and balloons for 2d and 3d images. *IEEE Trans. Pattern An. and Mach. Int.*, 15(11):1131–1147, 1993.

[3] S. T. Gunn and M. S. Nixon. A robust snake implementation; a dual active contour. *IEEE Trans. Pattern An. and Mach. Int.*, 19:63–88, 1997.

[4] M. Kass, A. Witkin, and D. Terzopoulos. Snakes: Active contour models. *Int. J. Computer Vision*, 1(4):321–331, 1987.   ,   ,

[5] S. Lobregt and M. A. Viergever. A discrete dynamic contour model. *IEEE Trans. on Medical Imaging*, 14(1):12–24, 1995.

[6] N. Otsu. A threshold selection method from gray-level histograms. *IEEE Trans. Systems, Man snd Cybernetics*, 9(1):62–66, 1979.

[7] J. L. Prince. personal communication, 2002.

[8] D. Terzopoulos. Regularization of inverse visual problems involving discontinuities. *IEEE Trans. Pattern An. and Mach. Int.*, 8(4):413–424, 1986.   ,

[9] D. J. Williams and M. Shah. A fast algorithm for active contours and curvature estimation. *CVGIP: Image Understanding*, 55(1):14–22, 1992.

[10] C. Xu. *Deformable models with applications to human cerebral cortex reconstruction from magnetic resonance images*. PhD thesis, Johns Hopkins University, April 2000.

[11] C. Xu and J. L. Prince. Gradient vector flow: A new external force for snakes. In *IEEE Proc. on Computer Vision and Pattern Recognition*, pages 66–71, 1997.

[12] C. Xu and J. L. Prince. Snakes, shapes and gradient vector flow. *IEEE Trans. on Image Processing*, 7(3):359–369, 1998.

[13] C. Xu and J. L. Prince. Global optimality of gradient vector flow. In *Proc. Conference on Information Sciences and Systems*, 2000.

A Compositionality Architecture
for Perceptual Feature Grouping

Björn Ommer and Joachim M. Buhmann

Rheinische Friedrich-Wilhelms-Universität
Institut für Informatik III, Römerstr. 164
D-53117 Bonn, Germany
{ommer,jb}@cs.uni-bonn.de
http://www-dbv.informatik.uni-bonn.de

Abstract. We propose a compositionality architecture for perceptual organization which establishes a novel, generic, algorithmic framework for feature binding and condensation of semanticemm information in images. The underlying algorithmic ideas require a hierarchical structure for various types of objects and their groupings, which are guided by gestalt laws from psychology. A rich set of predefined feature detectors with uncertainty that perform real-valued measurements of relationships between objects can be combined in this flexible Bayesian framework. Compositions are inferred by minimizing the negative posterior grouping probability. The model structure is founded on the fundamental perceptual law of *Prägnanz*. The grouping algorithm performs hierarchical agglomerative clustering and it is rendered computationally feasible by visual pop-out. Evaluation on the edgel grouping task confirms the robustness of the architecture and its applicability to grouping in various visual scenarios.

1 Introduction

Simple entities like points, isolated edgels or even small image patches provide only local, relatively unreliable information about objects in the image. This fact and the large number of such simple objects call for a processing step that concentrates information in few descriptive objects. The procedure focuses on the relevant entities in an image and increases the information content of single entities by forming complex *groupings* of simple ones. As a result, a hierarchy of compositions is created that contains objects of increasing robustness and growing relevance with respect to the whole image. This goal is exactly the primary objective of a composition system, as presented by Geman et al. [ ]. Although our system resembles in its structure more neural nets and graphical models than stochastic grammars as used in [,], the principle of compositionality constitutes a central part of our approach which follows from the philosophy of Geman. Psychological and neurophysiological concepts related to perceptual organization are ported and integrated into a uniform, algorithmic framework using methods common to computer science such as energy minimization and

A. Rangarajan et al. (Eds.): EMMCVPR 2003, LNCS 2683, pp. 275–   , 2003.
© Springer-Verlag Berlin Heidelberg 2003

compositionality. The goal is to obtain a universally applicable, robust grouping algorithm that can be used as a preprocessing step for subsequent applications such as search and retrieval of objects.

The above described processing has the underlying psychological motivation that a representation of the original image which is based on such groupings is *perceptually more salient* and *simpler* than unstructured sets of pixels or edgels. To create simple, stable, and perceptually salient groupings, Gestalt psychology proposes the fundamental principle of *Prägnanz* [,]. Moreover, numerous simple (compared to Prägnanz) *Gestalt laws* [,] exist that approximately entail Prägnanz. These laws (e.g. proximity of entities, their closure, or their similarity in orientation) form the basis for the implemented feature detectors, called *relations* in the following. These relations act as *sensors* that perceive a certain mutual relatedness of objects in a perceptually meaningful way.

In this paper we introduce a highly flexible algorithmic framework that provides a uniform embedding of arbitrary, uncertain feature detectors. Consequently we also have to control the interaction of a large number of these components. To unify and ease the design of different kinds of feature detectors, we define a uniform basic structure for these detectors which spans the probability space for feature groupings. The negative posterior grouping probability serves as a cost function which measures the quality of different perceptual organizations. The grouping algorithm performs hierarchical agglomerative clustering [ ] of these objects to minimize the grouping costs. To speed up the process, psychological concepts like visual pop-out efficiently prune the solution space.

As a result, our approach achieves the goal to reduce the dependence on single relations and, thereby, it is robustified against cues that are accidentally erroneous in certain situations. The analysis and processing of the numerous feature detectors produces a *sensor fusion* scheme that allows us to extract the various hints or cues for a grouping out of the scene.

The basic ideas on perceptual organization in computer vision relevant to the presented architecture are motivated by Lowe in [ ]. However, our approach differs from Lowe's and other related work [, ,] in the fundamental way the feature detectors are used: Our framework handles numerous features in a flexible way compared to the alternative approaches which base their grouping decisions on a very limited number of fixed cues. Williams and Thornber [ ] use a random walk process to formulate a new saliency measurement. By defining saliency measures for edgels, Shashua and Ullman [ ] separate edgels into highly salient figure elements and background elements of lower saliency. Jacobs [ ] computes the likelihood that a group of edgels is produced by a single object to direct a recognition system and improve its accuracy.

The strategy to implement a large number of uncertain feature detectors allows us to simplify the specification of concrete relations as far as possible. Related work by Amir and Lindenbaum [ ] on the integration of large numbers of sensors differs exactly in this system design step. While the relations in their approach are mainly treated as binary valued random variables (presence or absence of relationships between objects), that have to be specified by the user, we offer a Bayesian concept for real-valued, uncertain feature detectors. Thereby different features of wide ranging strength can be detected and compared.

The next section presents a discussion of Prägnanz to provide the foundation for the cost function. Thereafter our algorithmic framework for the integration of arbitrary relations into a common cost function will be described. Section   will present the perceptually optimized grouping algorithms. Finally the performance of the presented architecture will be evaluated in section   .

2 Prägnanz, Redundancy, and MDL

Fred Attneave [ ] has stated that the received visual input is highly redundant and that large parts of a scene are predictable, given only a small fraction of the overall stimulus. This is due to some restrictions in the visually perceivable world he attributes to *lawfulness* of nature.

Given (an estimate of) the complexity of the visually perceivable world (e.g. by measuring the relative frequency of certain involved phenomena), it is possible to acquire a set of rules that predict large parts of a scene on the basis of only a small number of detected features. These rules, which exploit redundancy, are just the Gestalt laws. Moreover, a grouping of maximal Prägnanz can be understood as an optimal exploitation of this redundancy [ ]. Consequently, this repetition of information within clusters can be avoided in the joint, probably even lossy encoding of the objects. The resulting strategy represents a realization of the minimum description length principle.

These ideas are illustrated by a brief example: Consider two straight edgels that are situated adjacent to each other, each represented by its respective end-points. A joint encoding of the grouping can be represented by three points, or in case of collinearity by only two points. More complex entities such as squares or templates for natural objects such as cars need even fewer parameters in proportion to the number of their elementary constituents. Generalizing this idea, Biederman [ ] proposed *geons*, a set of image primitives that can be used as components of complex visual scenarios. In conclusion, the goal of a grouping that obeys maximal Prägnanz can be reached by following the MDL principle and minimizing a corresponding cost function.

Splitting up Prägnanz: A direct specification of a cost function for Prägnanz is too complicated and we, therefore, replace the Prägnanz concept by directly measurable relations: Gestalt psychology proposes a number of Gestalt laws, which analyze similarity of objects in certain image features (e.g. color or orientation). Thereby, the relations detect the redundancies of the resulting grouping which favors the simplicity in image coding.

3 An Energy Function for Gestalt Principles

Outline of the Algorithm: The input to the grouping algorithm are *edgels*, short straight edge elements gained from a Canny edge detector. Furthermore color histograms in a small neighborhood on both sides of each edgel are computed. Thereafter the grouping algorithm uses various feature detectors to obtain information about the mutual relationship of objects in order to create a hierarchy of groupings. This procedure is mainly bottom-up, thereby not requiring additional knowledge about the scene.

3.1 Objects

To support the idea of minimizing the overall description length, this approach defines a hierarchy of objects of different complexity. Composite types of objects are defined via inclusion of simpler ones, e.g. curves are defined as compositions of edgels or other curves. The basic objects are *edgels* that result from a Canny edge detector. An edgel E is described by its two endpoints in Euclidian space, $\text{Ep}_i(E) \in \mathbb{R}^2, i \in \{-1, 1\}$. The goal is to group these objects to perceptually meaningful curves which are the second type of objects we use. These entities are applicable to widely differing scenarios and are therefore chosen to exemplify the general architecture subsequently. Other types of objects are grouped in a similar fashion using appropriate features. The endpoints of a curve C are recursively defined via its components, which are edgels or other curves. Assuming a grouping of two objects O_{-1}, O_1 that can be edgels or curves, the endpoint of entity O_α that is closest to the endpoints of the other object has the index

$$\text{cEp}(O_\alpha, O_{-\alpha}) := \operatorname*{argmin}_{i \in \{-1,1\}} \min_{j \in \{-1,1\}} \left\{ \left\| \text{Ep}_i(O_\alpha) - \text{Ep}_j(O_{-\alpha}) \right\|_2 \right\} . \tag{1}$$

The endpoints of C are then

$$\text{Ep}_i(C) := \text{Ep}_{-\text{cEp}(O_i, O_{-i})}(O_i), i \in \{-1, 1\} . \tag{2}$$

Moreover the additional feature of orientation is added to the endpoints of an edgel (the curves take over this parameter during the grouping):

$$\text{Ep}_i^{\text{orient}}(E) := \measuredangle \left\{ \text{Ep}_i(E) - \text{Ep}_{-i}(E); \ (1,0)^T \right\}, i \in \{-1, 1\} . \tag{3}$$

Each object, except for the singleton edgels, is a grouping of other objects. The goal is to group objects to perceptually meaningful compositions that constitute new objects. The hierarchy of the created compositions is logged in a rootless tree, the *dependency graph* of the participating objects. Each vertex corresponds to an object (the edgels form the leafs of this structure), while the arcs represent the grouping relationships between compositions and their subparts.

3.2 Relations

In the following, a generic and flexible framework for all different kinds of grouping cues will be presented. As a result a modular and adjustable cost function is obtained that measures the gain in Prägnanz given arbitrary features. Therefore each of the underlying relations corresponds to a technical *neuron* that perceives a specific mutual relatedness of objects from a previous level of the hierarchy mentioned above as its input. The outputs of sensors with the same entities as input are combined to obtain the overall grouping cost function. These measures are in turn used recursively for subsequent groupings via a feed-forward architecture of successively applied relations. Given this structure, perceptual organization can be understood literally as applying relations to their respective sensory input in order to *organize* these *percepts* in a dependency graph of objects.

The final output of each relation, the *vote*, corresponds to the probability that the considered objects belong to a joint object, given the information on their mutual relationship that is gathered by the relation. Letting r denote the output of the relation and using only two objects O_1 and O_2 for simplicity (each of these is a singleton or a grouping of objects), the probability of a perceptually favorable grouping is

$$P\left(O_1 \odot O_2 | r\left(O_1, O_2\right)\right) . \tag{4}$$

Here the symbol $\odot$ indicates that the objects join to form a new grouped object (e.g. a new composition $O := O_1 \odot O_2$).

In order to compute a relation it is splitted into two separate parts. At first a feature extration function is used to obtain information on the relationship between objects. This sensor data is then normalized and interpreted so that all different relations provide equation ( ) with an unified input. The output of the relation is the composition

$$r := \mathtt{sI} \circ \mathtt{sD} . \tag{5}$$

The first part computes the strength of a specified relationship of the objects (e.g. their relative orientation or similarity of color) given the data. This part corresponds to the input nodes of a perceptron and its output resembles the internal activity level, or the *action potential* of their neural counterparts. Letting $\mathfrak{O}$ denote the set of all objects and assuming for simplicity a compact codomain $[sd_{min}, sd_{max}]$, this feature extraction can be summarized as

$$\mathtt{sD} : \mathfrak{O} \times \mathfrak{O} \to [sd_{min}, sd_{max}] \subset \mathbb{R} . \tag{6}$$

This function comprises both the perception of relevant features of the objects and the computation of a relation specific distance measure. In order to combine different measures they have to be normalized, i.e., this normalization corresponds to the output function of a neuron,

$$\mathtt{sI} : [sd_{min}, sd_{max}] \to [0, 1] . \tag{7}$$

Subsequently, the grouping probability can be computed using the output of the relation and Bayesian decision theory [ ]

$$P(O_1 \odot O_2 | r) = \frac{p(r | O_1 \odot O_2) \cdot P(O_1 \odot O_2)}{p(r)} . \tag{8}$$

Using marginalization, the evidence can be written as

$$p(r) = \underbrace{p(r | O_1 \odot O_2)}_{\rightsquigarrow \text{ causal reason}} \cdot P(O_1 \odot O_2) + \underbrace{p(r | O_1 \emptyset O_2)}_{\rightsquigarrow \text{ accidentalness}} \cdot P(O_1 \emptyset O_2) . \tag{9}$$

In the following a Gaussian probability density function

$$\varphi(r) := \frac{1}{\sqrt{2\pi}\sigma}e^{-\frac{(r-\mu)^2}{2\sigma^2}}, \quad \mu \in [0,1], \quad \sigma \in \mathbb{R}_+ \tag{10}$$

is used as a parametric model of the likelihood of a relation, Φ being the cumulative distribution. The range of mean μ is restricted to the range of r. The likelihood is then a rectified Gaussian

$$p(r|O_1 \odot O_2) = \frac{\varphi(r)}{\Phi(1) - \Phi(0)} \ . \tag{11}$$

Furthermore, the mean μ is the expected value of the relation

$$\mu = E_{p(r|O_1 \odot O_2)}[r] \ , \tag{12}$$

given that the objects form a grouping. The variance σ^2 corresponds to the inverse significance of the relation and reflects its uncertainty. Having a distribution with a sharp peak, a response close to the optimum, $r(O_1, O_2) \approx \mu$, is a good indication for a reliable grouping.

In contrast to the likelihood, $p(r|O_1 \oslash O_2)$ indicates how likely it is that r takes on a certain value, given that the objects do not form a perceptually meaningful composition. In absence of further information, most relations permit the approximation of this *accidentalness* term by assuming that all outputs are equally likely in this case, c.f. [ ].

3.3   The Energy Function

The approach uses numerous relations that provide knowledge about different features in order to find out whether objects form a grouping. Therefore, sensors that are uncertain about a specific clustering of entities can be compensated by others. Given a *sensor fusion* of n different relations, a voting scheme (see figure) is proposed that pools them in the overall energy function

$$\mathcal{H}(O_1 \odot O_2|r_1, \ldots, r_n) = -\log\left[\prod_{i=1}^{n} P(O_1 \odot O_2|r_i)^{\frac{w_i}{\sum_{j=1}^{n} w_j}}\right] \ . \tag{13}$$

The weights w_i correct slight statistical dependencies between the features that are detected by different relations. If they are all independent, i.e., $p(r_i|r_{i+1}, \ldots, r_n, O_1 \odot O_2) = p(r_i|O_1 \odot O_2)$, all weights are equal and $\mathcal{H}$ leads to the same grouping decisions as $-\log P(O_1 \odot O_2|r_1, \ldots, r_n)$, c.f. [ ]. An example of such a correction is our model for the relation that detects the parallelism of the ends of two curves. Since it relies on similar features as the relation for collinearity, the weight is lower than the chosen standard value of 2. The management of the voting information is carried out in a knowledge base. With this framework each relation can be designed without much effort by specifying the two sensor functions and the parameters μ, σ, and the weight. Furthermore, these variables offer a uniform point of access to adjust the relations and their interaction.

The overall cost function for the current grouping of the complete image is formed by the set $\mathfrak{O}_l$ of all groupings in the latest level of the dependency graph,

$$\widehat{\mathcal{H}}(\mathfrak{O}_l | r_1, \ldots, r_n) = \sum_{O \in \mathfrak{O}_l} \mathcal{H}(O | r_1, \ldots, r_n) . \tag{14}$$

3.4   Implemented Relations

So far a number of relations have been specified to illustrate the potential of the presented architecture. In the following the design of some of these sensors will be described in detail. The implemented Gestalt laws are *proximity*, *similarity* of *orientation* and *color*, *good continuation*, and *closure* (see [,]).

Let $O_{-1}, O_1 \in \mathfrak{O}$ be two curves or edgels with endpoints $\mathrm{Ep}_i(O_j), i, j \in \{-1, 1\}$ and the corresponding grouping $O_{-1,1} := O_{-1} \odot O_2$. Furthermore, $\mathtt{maxDist} \in \mathbb{R}$ is set to the length of the image diagonal and the abbreviation

$$\widehat{\mathrm{cEp}}(O_i, O_{-i}) := \mathrm{Ep}_{\mathrm{cEp}(O_i, O_{-i})}(O_i), \quad i \in -1, 1 \tag{15}$$

is used. The relation for *proximity* of the endpoints of two curves or edgels is

$$\mathtt{sD}_{\mathrm{prox}}(O_{-1}, O_1) := \left\| \widehat{\mathrm{cEp}}(O_{-1}, O_1) - \widehat{\mathrm{cEp}}(O_1, O_{-1}) \right\|_2 \in [0, \mathtt{maxDist}] , \tag{16}$$

$$\mathtt{sI}_{\mathrm{prox}}(d) := d/\mathtt{maxDist} , \tag{17}$$

$$\mu_{\mathrm{prox}} := \mathtt{sI}(0), \ \sigma_{\mathrm{prox}} := \mathtt{sI}(\max\{t_l, \min\{t_h, \mathtt{avgDist}\}\}), \ \mathtt{w}_{\mathrm{prox}} := 2.3 . \tag{18}$$

To estimate $\mathtt{avgDist}$, the distances of a number of randomly located objects to their nearest neighbors (distance of endpoints) are averaged with threshold constants $t_l := 4, t_h := 40$.

Relative orientation (or parallelism) of the ends of two curves or edgels is modeled by

$$\mathtt{sD}_{\mathrm{orient}}(O_{-1}, O_1) := \left| \mathrm{Ep}_{\mathrm{cEp}(O_1, O_{-1})}^{\mathrm{orient}}(O_1) - \mathrm{Ep}_{\mathrm{cEp}(O_{-1}, O_1)}^{\mathrm{orient}}(O_{-1}) \right| \mod 2\pi , \tag{19}$$

$$\mathtt{sI}_{\mathrm{orient}}(\alpha) := 1 - \frac{|\pi - \alpha|}{\pi} , \tag{20}$$

$$\mu_{\mathrm{orient}} := 1, \ \sigma_{\mathrm{orient}} := \mathtt{sI}_{\mathrm{orient}}(10°/180° \cdot \pi), \ \mathtt{w}_{\mathrm{orient}} := 1.0 . \tag{21}$$

A simple, computationally feasible way to measure the gain in *closure* of object O_{-1} by grouping it with O_1 is modeled as follows:

$$\mathtt{gap}_s(O_{-1}, O_1) := \left\| \widehat{\mathrm{cEp}}(O_1, O_{-1}) - \widehat{\mathrm{cEp}}(O_{-1}, O_1) \right\|_2 , \tag{22}$$

$$\mathtt{gap}_o(O_{-1}, O_1) := \left\| \mathrm{Ep}_{-\mathrm{cEp}(O_1, O_{-1})}(O_1) - \mathrm{Ep}_{-\mathrm{cEp}(O_{-1}, O_1)}(O_{-1}) \right\|_2 , \tag{23}$$

$$\mathtt{sD}_{\mathrm{closure}}(O_{-1}, O_1) := \max \left\{ \frac{\mathtt{gap}_s(O_{-1}, O_1) + \mathtt{gap}_o(O_{-1}, O_1)}{\left\| \mathrm{Ep}_{-1}(O_{-1}) - \mathrm{Ep}_1(O_{-1}) \right\|_2}, l \right\} . \tag{24}$$

Of course equation (   ) is only applicable to objects that are not perfectly closed and a parameter $l := 2$ penalizes losses in closure above this bound equally. Therefore short curves, whose closure can fluctuate a lot when they are grouped, can still receive a fixed lower probability mass from the rectified gaussian introduced above. The remaining components of this relation are

$$sI_{closure}(g) := g/l \; , \tag{25}$$

$$\mu_{closure} := sI(0), \; \sigma_{closure} := sI(1/2), \; w_{closure} := 2.0 \; . \tag{26}$$

Furthermore, our system computes color histograms for small areas (depending on the length of an edgel) on both sides of an edgel E. The means $\bar{c}_{-1}^{E}, \bar{c}_{1}^{E} \in [0, 255]^3$ of these two histograms are added to the endpoint section of each edgel so that the curves inherit these features,

$$Ep_i^{color_j}(E) := \bar{c}_{i \cdot j}^{E}, i, j \in \{-1, 1\} \; . \tag{27}$$

Relying on the color information of the edgels, *similarity in color* of the local surroundings of two curves and *color contrast* of both sides of an edgel are used. Another implemented feature detector is the *collinearity* of the ends of two curves. In combination with relative orientation and proximity, an implementation of the Gestalt law of good continuation is formed by these three relations. Finally another relation performs the recursive *propagation* of grouping probabilities from the component objects in the dependency graph to their composition.

4   Grouping Algorithms

The grouping algorithm perceives a certain mutual relatedness of some objects by applying the relations. The resulting energy function provides the necessary information on which entities to combine.

The solution space in which the grouping algorithm searches, consists of groupings of the whole image. Each of these is represented by a level in the dependency graph and consists of all grouped objects that are necessary to describe the relevant aspects of the image. The grouping algorithm produces a new level in the graph by grouping entities from a previous level. The resulting hierarchical agglomerative clustering starts on the initial level that contains only edgels and returns the last level of the graph that represents the final grouping of the image. The algorithm performs a search for a perceptually favorable grouping by minimizing the energy function. Successive states of the clustering procedure in solution space correspond to successive levels in the dependency graph.

On the one hand a perceptually optimal grouping of the whole image is to be found eventually. On the other hand the search for such a solution has to be speeded up in order to obtain computationally feasible algorithms that find these groupings in the enormously large solution space in reasonable time. This poses a trade-off between optimality and feasibility. It is possible to come closer to both objectives simultaneously by placing perceptually motivated restrictions

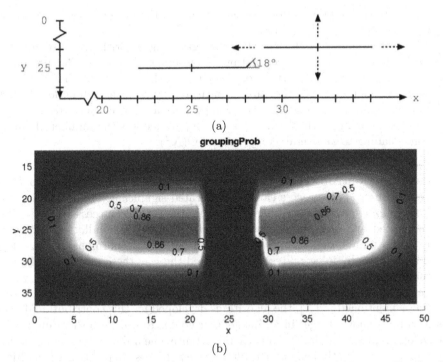

Fig. 1. (a) Two short curve segments, one moving about the other. The fixed one has a bend of 18° at one end. (b) Plot of the cost function $\exp -\mathcal{H}$ (labeled `groupingProb` in the figure) resulting from the application of the relations *proximity*, *relative orientation* and *collinearity* to these segments

(c.f. section) on the continuations of paths through solution space so that these lead to reasonably good solutions. In the following we will discuss the grouping of curves. The grouping of more complex objects proceeds in the same manner.

Greedy Approach: A significant decrease in complexity can be achieved by making grouping decisions in a *greedy* fashion. Provided the set of relations conveys enough information, groupings will persist once they are formed. In this case psychology indicates that the resulting speed up is *not* at the expense of optimality. The energy function $\mathcal{H}$ measures the gain in Prägnanz resulting from performing one additional grouping that is discriminating two successive states in solution space. In the above depicted case of persisting groupings this local optimization leads to a global optimum. Furthermore, the idea is to correct erroneous compositions in later stages by producing more complex objects than curves that are less prone to accidental influences. One cause for such a robustness is additional information about missing components that is available once a great fraction of a complex object has been detected. Therefore, complex compositions integrate information over large parts of the image. However, work on these concepts is still in progress.

To further improve the speed of the grouping algorithm, we reduce the branching factor by early commiting to grouping decisions: The procedure searches for a grouping partner of the curve with best $\mathcal{H}$, so that the composition yields improved Prägnanz, as measured by the energy function. If such a grouping has been found, the two components are not considered in further groupings. Starting with N curves each grouping reduces the number of curves by one, leading to an overall complexity of $\mathcal{O}(N^2)$.

Attention Control: The grouping algorithm applies the cost function $\mathcal{H}$ to pairs of curves. This process can be accelerated significantly by restricting the set of grouping partners and thereby limiting the possible successor states. This is motivated by observations on the way the (human) brain allots attention to the various inputs, thereby speeding up their perception enormously. Psychological and neurophysiological research analyzed the way these processes influence visual search [,]. One key point is that targets that have features which differ from the surrounding distractors can *pop-out* pre-attentively. In contrast to ideas mentioned in [ ], the algorithms developed for this contribution do not search for a known target in an image. Our goal is to speed up the grouping by developing processes similar to their pre-attentive neural counterparts that can group objects directly *without serially checking* all possible partners of an object as in regular pairwise grouping.

A uniform framework has been designed that uses some relations to compute a possibly multidimensional feature vector for each object. The features should constitute a relevant measure for both, *within-group attraction* and *between-group segregation*, so that groupable objects are similar in feature space. Therefore, the algorithm induces a partition of this space. The clusters are determined from an inverting of the relations so that groupable objects have at least one cell in common. The possible branchings of the decision tree of the previously presented grouping algorithm are significantly limited by performing this central clustering prematurely that assigns entities to the according cells. In contrast to the similarity measure used above, this preprocessing step computes the relevant features for each object on its own and not pairwise. Thereby only those groupings have to be reviewed by the pairwise procedure that have joint cells. Since only those groupings are neglected that would not have a chance to be grouped anyway, this acceleration still preserves the optimality and leaves the clustering resulting from the greedy approach unchanged.

The speed up is significantly higher than the acceleration that arises out of regular *shielding*. Shielding-effects occur when long range interactions are eclipsed by short, intermediate ones. The acceleration is due to the fact that a small set of grouping partners pops out immediately and no serial scanning is needed. Therefore the total complexity of the grouping algorithm reduces to $\mathcal{O}(N^{3/2})$. Images of size 400×400 pixels can thereby be processed in only a few seconds on a Pentium®II-400 with 128 Mb of RAM. Scenes of size 1000×1000

take only a few minutes to be grouped (depending on the choice of parameters and on the image this takes about one to three minutes).

5   Evaluation of the Framework

In the following, exactly the same grouping algorithm is applied to numerous different visual scenarios which emphasizes the flexibility of the architecture. Only the scale parameter and edgel density of the preprocessing edge detector are changed for the first image to illustrate the resulting phenomena. All other scenes are processed with a scale parameter $\sigma = 2$ of the edge detector. Distances are measured in pixel throughout this paper. To improve the legibility of the illustration we only visualize a certain fraction of the longest curves so that the output is not too densely filled with groupings. Again we are only using objects of type curve for these tests in order to present the architecture in its most general form.

Figures   a), c), and   a), c) show the original images, while figures   b), d), and   b), d) display the respective groupings. The first image illustrates the capabilities of the algorithm to group loosely coupled edgels coming from the edge detector. Moreover the scale parameter was set to 4 [pixel] for this image.

Figure   shows an image and the only minimally differing groupings of this original and of a version with added white noise. The signal to noise ratio is approximately 17 dB. Furthermore two images of similar cars viewed under different environmental conditions and perspectives were grouped (see figure   ) to illustrate the degree of invariance of certain curves against these effects.

Finally the grouping algorithm is tested using the human segmented images presented in [   ]. Fifteen original images with about seven hand segmentations available for each image are used to select only those edgels coming from the Canny detector that lie on the respective human produced grouping. These remaining edgels are grouped using our system. The number of resulting curves and their length are then compared with those that are generated by using an edge point linking strategy as is common in implementations of the Canny detector.

On average, our algorithm generates only a fourth ($28\% \pm 3\%$) of the number of curves which are produced by the linking method while both methods explain the same number of edgels in the hand segmentations. Similarly, our curves are 4.2 ± 0.17 times longer. It remains to mention that these results probably would further improve, if the used images would have been less textured, since the currently implemented relations do not exploit region information.

6   Conclusion and Further Work

In this contribution a novel, flexible algorithmic framework for perceptual feature grouping has been presented based on fundamental principles of perceptual organization. The groupings are integrated into a hierarchical architecture that has been designed on the philosophy of compositionality. Moreover, a sensor fusion scheme has been presented that is flexible, problem independent, and easily

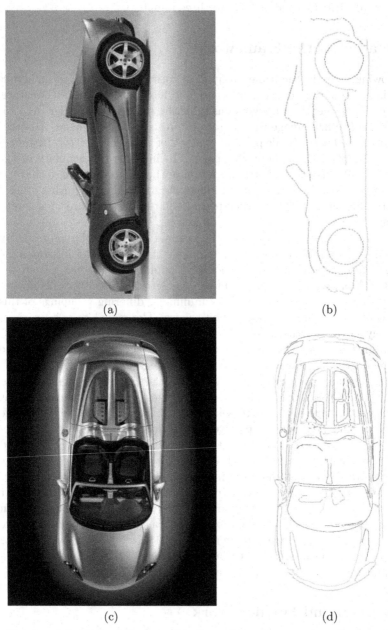

(a)   (b)

(c)   (d)

Fig. 2. (a) Original image. (b) Grouping after running Canny with $\sigma = 4$. Processing time is about 2 seconds on a PII-400 with 128Mb of RAM. (c) Original image. (d) Grouping after running Canny with $\sigma = 2$. Processing time is about 95 seconds

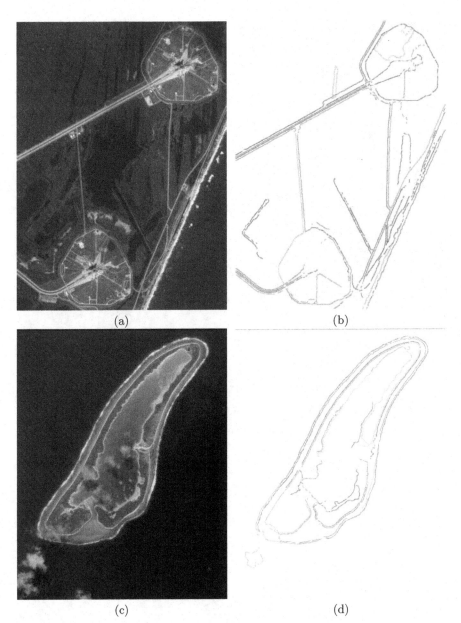

(a)   (b)

(c)   (d)

Fig. 3. (a) Original image from *www.spaceimaging.com* (b) Grouping after running Canny with $\sigma = 2$. Processing time is about 2.5 minutes. (c) Original image from *www.spaceimaging.com* (d) Grouping after running Canny with $\sigma = 2$. Processing time is about 3.5 minutes

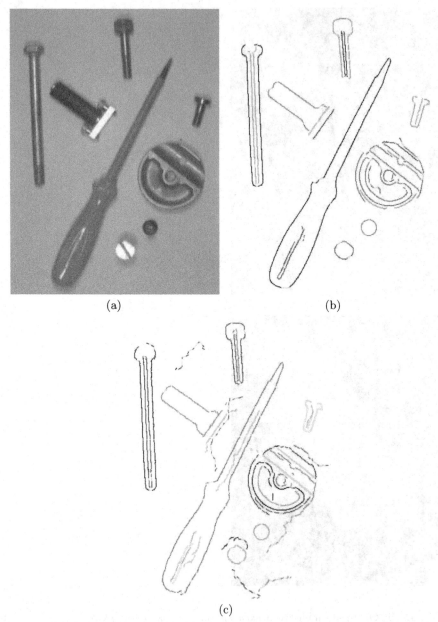

(a)

(b)

(c)

Fig. 4. (a) Original image. (b) Grouping after running Canny with $\sigma = 2$. Processing time is about 15 seconds. (c) Grouping of the noisy image after running Canny with $\sigma = 2$. Processing time is about 35 seconds

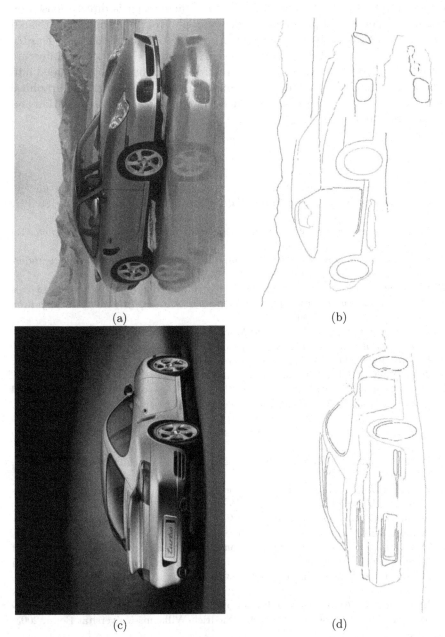

Fig. 5. (a) Original image. (b) Grouping after running Canny with $\sigma = 2$. Processing time is about 2 minutes. (c) Original image. (d) Grouping after running Canny with $\sigma = 2$. Processing time is about 70 seconds

extendable with respect to the feature detectors that are used. As a result an open design of an energy function has been obtained that is directly based on fundamental perceptual principles. Using concepts from psychology the related grouping algorithm has been designed and brought to a computationally feasible form. Finally real world experiments have demonstrated that the architecture meets the aspired properties. Moreover, the framework has been embedded into a number of commonly used techniques including neural networks and graphical models (c.f. [ ]) in order to gain new insights into perceptual organization and into the presented architecture.

References

[1] Arnon Amir and Michael Lindenbaum. A generic grouping algorithm and its quantitative analysis. *IEEE Trans. Pattern Anal. Machine Intell.*, 20(2):186–192, 1998.

[2] Fred Attneave. Some informational aspects of visual perception. *Psychological Review*, 61(3):183–193, 1954.

[3] Irving Biederman. Recognition-by-components: A theory of human image understanding. *Psychological Review*, 94(2):115–147, 1987.

[4] Elie Bienenstock. Notes on the growth of a composition machine. In *Proceedings of the Royaumont Interdisciplinary Workshop on Compositionality in Cognition and Neural Networks*, 1991.

[5] Vicki Bruce, Patrick R. Green, and Mark A. Georgeson. *Visual Perception: Physiology, Psychology, and Ecology*. Psychology Press, 3rd edition, 1996.

[6] Richard O. Duda, Peter E. Hart, and David G. Stork. *Pattern Classification*. John Wiley & Sons, New York, NY, 2nd edition, 2001.

[7] Stuart Geman, Daniel F. Potter, and Zhiyi Chi. *Composition Systems*. Technical report, Division of Applied Mathematics, Brown University, Providence, RI, 1998.

[8] E. Bruce Goldstein. *Sensation and Perception*. Wadsworth, 3rd edition, 1989.

[9] David W. Jacobs. Grouping for recognition. MIT AI Lab Memo 1177, MIT, Cambridge, MA, 1989.

[10] Zhaoping Li. A V1 model of pop out and asymmetry in visual search. In *Advances in Neural Information Processing Systems*, volume 11, 1999.

[11] David G. Lowe. *Perceptual Organization and Visual Recognition*. Kluwer Academic Publishers, Norwell, MA, 1985.

[12] David Martin, Charless Fowlkes, Doron Tal, and Jitendra Malik. A database of human segmented natural images and its application to evaluating segmentation algorithms and measuring ecological statistics. In *ICCV*, volume 8, July 2001.

[13] Björn Ommer. An algorithmic framework for visual grouping by perceptual organization. Diploma thesis, Rheinische Friedrich-Wilhelms-Universität Bonn, 2003.

[14] Amnon Shashua and Shimon Ullman. Structural saliency: The detection of globally salient structures using a locally connected network. In *ICCV*, 1988.

[15] Hemant D. Tagare, Kentaro Toyama, and Jonathan G. Wang. A maximum-likelihood strategy for directing attention during visual search. *IEEE Trans. Pattern Anal. Machine Intell.*, 23(5):490–500, 2001.

[16] Anne Treisman. Features and objects in visual processing. *Scientific American*, 254(11):114–125, 1986.

[17] Lance R. Williams and Karvel K. Thornber. A comparison of measures for detecting natural shapes in cluttered backgrounds. *Int. J. Computer Vision*, 34:81–96, 1999.

Using Prior Shape and Points
in Medical Image Segmentation

Yunmei Chen[1], Weihong Guo[1], Feng Huang[1],
David Wilson[1], and Edward A. Geiser[2]

[1] Department of Mathematics, University of Florida
Gainesville, FL. 32611
Phone: 352-392-0281-x.268
yun@math.ufl.edu
[2] Division of Cardiology, Department of Medicine, University of Florida
Gainesville, FL. 32611

Abstract. In this paper we present a new variational framework in level
set form for image segmentation, which incorporates both a prior shape
and prior fixed locations of a small number of points. The idea underlying the model is the creation of two energy terms in the energy function
for the geodesic active contours. The first energy term is for the shape,
the second for the locations of the points In this model, segmentation is
achieved through a registration technique, which combines a rigid transformation and a local deformation. The rigid transformation is determined explicitly by using shape information, while the local deformation
is determined implicitly by using image gradients and prior locations.
We report experimental results on both synthetic and ultrasound images.
These results compared with the results obtained by using a previously
reported model, which only incorporates a shape prior into the active
contours.

Keywords Prior shape and points, active contours, energy minimization, level set methods

1 Introduction

Segmentation of anatomical structures from medical images has very important
applications in diagnosis, surgical planning, navigation, and various medical eval-
uations. A multitude of segmentation algorithms have been proposed to tackle
these types of problems. They might be classified as edge-based, region-based,
or a combination of these two. The edge based methods (e.g. [KWT, CCCD,
MSV, CKS, KKOTY, YKKOT]) rely on the information of the edges, such as
high magnitude of image gradient. The region-based methods (e.g. [ZY, MS,
CV1, CV2, CSW, TYW]) make use of homogeneity on the statistics of the regions being segmented. The algorithm developed in [CSD] integrates gradient
and region information within a deformable boundary finding framework. The
Geodesic Active Region models proposed in [PD, P1, P2] integrates the edge
and region based segmentation methods in a variational approach.

A. Rangarajan et al. (Eds.): EMMCVPR 2003, LNCS 2683, pp. 291–   , 2003.

However, the analysis of medical images is frequently complicated by noise, dropout, confusing anatomical structures, motion, poor contrast along boundaries, and non-uniformity of regional intensities. For these kinds of images the segmentation algorithms using image information alone may not give a desired result. Thus, the model developed in this paper provides the opportunity for an expert to input a small number of points to initiate the method. Since the locations of these points would be be incorporated into the method, the methods described here would most likely be used as a semi-automated rather than fully automated method.

Recently, various approaches including deterministic setting and probabilistic context have been developed to use prior shape information in image segmentation (see [CBET, WS, CTCG, SD, T, YHC, CHTH, SKBG, MT93, VR], and references there). A survey of methods, which incorporate prior knowledge into deformable models in medical image analysis is provided in [MT96]. The approaches presented in the papers [LGF, C, CSW, MS, PR] are closely related to our current work. In these work the statistical shape knowledge were incorporated into either edge based or region based active contours. Leventon, Grimson and Faugeras [LGF] extended the technique of geometric active contours by incorporating shape information into the evolution process. A segmentation result was obtained first by the curve evolution driven by a force depending on image gradient and curvature, and then the shape prior was used to make a correction by maximizing a posterior estimate of shape and pose. Chen, et al. [C] modified the techniques discussed by [LGF] so that their variational method incorporates both high image gradients and shape information into the energy term of a geodesic active contour model. The shape term can also be used to recover a similarity transformation that maps the evolving interface to the prior shape. Cremers, Schnörr and Weickert [CSW] incorporated statistical shape knowledge into the Mumford-Shah segmentation scheme [MS] by minimizing a functional that includes the Mumford-Shah energy and the shape energy corresponding to the Gaussian probability. Recently, In [PR] Rousson and Paragios introduced a energy functional, that constrains the level set representations to follow a shape global consistency while preserving the ability to capture local deformation.

The experimental results have shown that all these models have their own strengths, and provide promising results for particular applications. However, due to the accuracy and efficiency requirement for medical image analysis, and the complexity of medical images, as well as the variability of the shapes of anatomic structures, how to use shape prior to get a better segmentation is still a challenging question. One of the most difficult problem is to determine local shape variations from the prior shape. One solution may be the use of nonrigid registration to assist segmentation (e.g. [VCW, RC]), but this approach requires reliable region or edge information in the image to find the velocity field. This technique is also computationally expensive.

The goal of the method presented in this report is to find an improved way to locate boundaries when they may vary widely from a prior shape and when they are to be detected in an image which may have significant signal loss. In particular, we are motivated by the problem of detecting the boundary of the left ventricle of the heart in echocardiographic image sequences. Cardiac ultrasound images are plagued with noise, signal dropout, and confusing intracavitary structures. Moreover, the shape of the boundary of the myocardium varies extensively from one patient image to another, and is not equivalent to the "average" of a set of training shapes. More importantly, for patients with cardiac disease the shape distortion of the myocardium from the "normal shape" cannot be ignored.

To get a desirable segmentation in some cardiac ultrasound images more prior knowledge than the expected shape is needed. For instance, in [DL] Dias and Leitao used temporal information from time sequence of images to assist the determination of the inner and outer contours in the areas of low contrast in echocardiographic images. In this note we consider the cases in which users have the knowledge about the locations of a few points on the boundary of the object of interest. We will use this information as a constrain in addition to shape constrain to control the evolution of active contours. Our basic idea is to extend the segmentation algorithm developed in [C] by incorporating the information on the location of a few "key" points in addition to shape prior into geometric active contours.

The idea of matching nonequivalent shapes by the combination of a rigid transformation and a point-wise local deformation developed in the papers [PRR, PR SY] will be applied to our formulation. In [SY] Soatto and Yezzi view a general deformation as the composition of a finite dimensional group action (e.g. rigid or affine transformation) and a local deformation, and introduced a notion of "shape average" as the entity that separates a group action from a deformation. In [PRR] Paragios, Rousson and Ramesh proposed a variational framework for global as well as local shape registration. Their optimization criterion accounts for global (rigid, affine) transformation and local pixel-wise deformation. A similar idea was also used by [PR] to define shape prior models in terms of level set representations. These ideas can be used to simultaneously approximate, register, and track nonequivalent shapes as they move and deform through time. However, the question of how to determine the local deformation has not been considered in these previous works.

We will employ these ideas into our algorithm by viewing the evolution of an active contour as a deformation of the interface, This deformation consists of a rigid transformation and a local deformation. We will use the "average shape" to determine the rigid transformation that better maps the interface to the prior shape, and use the image gradient and a few "key" points to determining the local deformation that provides more accurate segmentation. Based on these thoughts we propose a variational framework that is able to incorporate prior knowledge of the expected shape and a few points that boundary should pass through into active contours. We modify the energy function of geodesic active contour so that it depends on the image gradient and prior shape, as well as a few prior points. We only need a few points since we have information on expected shape. The modified energy function provides a satisfactory segmentation despite the presence of both large shape distortions and image dropout. To combine both prior shape (a global constraint) and prior points (a local constraint) into a single variational framework, we use a level set formulation. Further, we report experimental results on synthetic and ultrasound images.

Very recently we learned from the author about his work on user interactive level set method for image segmentation. In this work Paragios [P] introduced a framework for user-interaction within the propagation of curves using level set representations. The user-interaction term is introduced in the form of an evolving shape prior that transforms the user-edits to level set based propagation constraints. The work in [P] and in this notes both are based on the idea that the user interactive edits can be used as a constraint to correct local discrepancies. However, the formulations of the constraint in these two papers are different.

The reminder of this paper is organized as follows. In section 2 we briefly review geometric active contours and the model developed in [C]. We then propose the new model for incorporating both prior shape and points in active contours. Section 3 contains the numerical method, while section 4 provides experiment results. Section 5 concludes the paper.

2 Description of the Proposed Model

In this section we present our variational approach for joint segmentation and registration using a prior shape and the locations of a few points. The main idea of our model is to propagate a curve/surface by a velocity that depends on the image gradients, prior shape and locations, so that the propagation stops when the active contour/surface forms a shape similar to the shape prior, arrives at high gradients, and passes through the prior points. The notion of shape is independent of translation, rotation, and scaling. In particular, two contours C_1 and C_2 have the same shape, if there exists a scale μ, a rotation matrix R (with respect to an angle θ), and a translation T, such that C_1 coincides with $\mu R C_2 + T$.

To begin the description of the proposed model, we first briefly review the geodesic active contour model in [CKS, KKOTY], and the active contour with a shape prior in [C].

Let $C(p) = (x(p), y(p))$ ($p \in [0, 1]$) be a differentiable parameterized curve in an image I. The geometric active contour model minimizes the energy function:

$$E(C) = \int_0^1 g(|\nabla I|)(C(p))|C'(p)|dp, \qquad (2.1)$$

where

$$g(|\nabla I|) = \frac{1}{1 + \beta|\nabla G_\sigma * I|^2}, \qquad (2.2)$$

with a parameter $\beta > 0$, and $G_\sigma(x) = \frac{1}{\sigma}e^{-\frac{|x|^2}{4\sigma^2}}$. The minimum of this energy functional occurs when the trace of the curve is over points of high gradient in the image. Because object boundaries are often defined by such points, the active contour becomes stationary at the boundary. In its level set formulation this model can handle topological change. However, since this algorithm requires a high image gradient to be present along the boundary of the object to stop the curve evolution, it may "leak" through the "gaps" in the boundary, where it is not salient.

To overcome this problem a variational model was proposed in [C] that incorporates prior shape information in geodesic active contours. The feature of this model is the creation of a shape term in the energy functional (2.1). If $C^*(p)$ ($p \in [0,1]$) is a curve representing the expected shape of the boundary of interest, then the energy functional to be minimized in [C] is

$$E(C, \mu, R, T) = \int_0^1 \{g(|\nabla I|)(C(p)) + \frac{\lambda}{2}d_{C^*}^2(\mu RC(p) + T)\}|C'(p)|dp, \quad (2.3)$$

where (μ, R, T) are similarity transformation parameters, and $d_{C^*}(x, y)$ is the distance of the point (x, y) to C^*. The first term in the energy functional (2.3) is the same as the energy functional for geodesic active contours, which measures the amount of high gradient under the trace of the curve. The second term is the shape related energy, that measures the disparity in shape between the interface and the prior. The constant $\lambda > 0$ is a parameter, which balances the influence from the image gradient and shape. The curve C and the transformation parameters μ, R and T evolve to minimize $E(C, \mu, R, T)$. At the stationary point, the contour C lies over points of high gradient in the image and forms a shape close to C^*, and μ, R and T determine the "best" alignment of C to $\mu RC(p) + T$. The experimental results in [C] showed their model is able to get a satisfactory segmentation in the presence of gaps, even when the gaps are a substantial fraction of the overall boundary, if the shape of interest is similar to the shape of interest. However, if some parts of the boundary are not visible, and the shape of boundary has relatively larger geometric distortion from the prior, as shown in section 4, model (2.3) can not provide a desired segmentation, since the knowledge on expected shape does not provide correct information about how the gaps should be bridged.

In this note we intend to incorporate extra prior knowledge of the location of a few points on the boundary into segmentation process. These points are given at the location where the edge information is not salient and the local shape has relatively large variation from the prior one. Our idea is the creation of a new energy term, that measures the distances of the prior points from the interface, into the energy functional of the active contours in [C]. Similar to the approach developed in [C], to get a smooth curve C that captures higher gradients we minimize the arc-length of C in the conformal metric $ds = g(|\nabla I|)(C(p))|C'(p)|dp$, where $g(|\nabla I|)$ is defined in (2.2). To capture the shape prior C^*, we find a curve C and the transformation (μ, R, T), such that the curve $\mu RC + T$ and C^* are "best" aligned. To capture the prior points we minimize the distances of each prior point x_i ($i = 1, \ldots, m$) from the curve C.

We present our model in a variational level set formulation. First, as well known, the level set method initiated in [OS] allows for cusps, corners, and automatic topological changes, Secondly, it is more convenient to computer the distances of the prior points to the interface by using the level set form of the interface.

Let the contour C be the zero level set of a Lipschitz function u such that $C = \{x \in R^N : u(x) = 0\}$, with (inside of C) $= \{x \in R^N : u(x) > 0\}$, and (outside C) $= \{x \in R^N : u(x) < 0\}$. Let H be the Heaviside function $H(z) = 1$, if $z \geq 0$, otherwise $H(z) = 0$, and δ be the Dirac measure concentrated at 0, i.e. $\delta(z) = H'(z)$ in the sense of distribution. Then, the length of the zero level set of u in the conformal metric $ds = g(|\nabla I|)|C'(p)|dp$ can be computed by $\int_\Omega g(|\nabla I|)|\nabla H(u)| = \int_\Omega \delta(u)g(|\nabla I|)|Du|$. The disparity in shape between the zero level set of u and C^* can be evaluated by $\int_\Omega \delta(u)d^2_{C^*}(\mu Rx+T)dx$, where the distance function d_{C^*} is the same as that in (2.3). Moreover, the constrain for contour C passing through the prior points $x_1, \ldots, x_m$ can be simply represented by $u(x_i) = 0$, $(i = 1, \ldots, m)$. Now let $f_\gamma(x)$ be a smooth function defined on the image domain Ω, such that $0 \leq f_\gamma(x) \leq 1$, $f_\gamma(x) = 1$ for $x = x_i$ $(i = 1, \ldots, m)$. The function $f_\gamma(x)$ can be obtained by the convolution of f and η_γ, where f is a function taking value one on the points $x_1, \ldots, x_m$ and zero elsewhere, and η_γ is the standard mollifier. Now we can formulate our new variational approach as

$$\min_{u,\mu,R,T} E(u, \mu, R, T) = \min_{u,\mu,R,T} \{\alpha \int_\Omega \delta(u)g(|\nabla I|)|\nabla u|$$

$$+ \frac{\beta}{2} \int_\Omega \delta(u)d^2_{C^*}(\mu Rx + T)|\nabla u| + \frac{1}{2} \int_\Omega f_\gamma(x)u^2(x)\}dx, \tag{3.1}$$

where $\alpha > 0$ and $\beta > 0$ are parameters. The first two terms in this energy functional are the same as those in (2.3), which force the interface arriving at the location where the magnetite of image gradient is high, and forming a shape similar to the prior. The last term forces the interface passing through the given points, since minimizing the third term in (3.1) with sufficiently small γ results that u must be close to zero at the given points. Note that $f_\gamma(x)$ is non-zero only on the γ neighborhood of the given points, so the third term doesn't affect much the shape of the contour outside the γ neighborhood of the given points.

This model performs a joint segmentation and registration. The segmentation is assisted by the registration between the interface and shape prior. This registration is non-rigid that consists of a global transformation (rigid) and a local deformation. The global transformation is determined by minimizing the second term in (3.1), while the local deformation, is controlled by minimizing the first and last terms in (3.1).

The evolution equations associated with the Euler-Lagrange equations for (3.1) are

$$\frac{\partial u}{\partial t} = \delta(u)div((\alpha g + \frac{\beta}{2}d^2)\frac{\nabla u}{|\nabla u|}) - f_\gamma u, \tag{3.2}$$

$$\frac{\partial u}{\partial n} = 0, \quad x \in \partial\Omega, \ t > 0; \quad u(x,0) = u_0(x), \ x \in \Omega, \tag{3.3}$$

$$\frac{\partial \mu}{\partial t} = -\beta \int_\Omega \delta(u)d\nabla d \cdot (Rx)|\nabla u|dx, \ t > 0, \quad \mu(0) = \mu_0, \tag{3.4}$$

$$\frac{\partial \theta}{\partial t} = -\alpha \int_\Omega \delta(u)\mu d\nabla d \cdot (\frac{dR}{d\theta}x)|\nabla u|, \ t > 0, \quad \theta(0) = \theta_0, \tag{3.5}$$

$$\frac{\partial T}{\partial t} = -\beta \int_{\Omega} \delta(u) d\nabla d |\nabla u| dx, \quad t > 0, \quad T(0) = T_0, \tag{3.6}$$

where $d = d_{C^*}$, R is the rotation matrix in terms of the angle θ, and the function d is evaluated at $\mu Rx + T$.

3   Numerical Scheme

The solution of the proposed model (3.1) for fi is obtained by finding the steady state solution to the evolution problem (3.2)-(3.6). To solve the equations (3.2)-(3.6) numerically, as in [CV], we replace δ in (3.1)-(3.6) by the slightly regularized versions of them, denoted by:

$$H_\varepsilon(z) = \begin{cases} 1 & if z > \epsilon \\ 0 & if z < -\epsilon \\ \frac{1}{2}[1 + \frac{z}{\epsilon} + \frac{1}{\pi}sin(\frac{\pi z}{\epsilon})] & if |z| \le \epsilon \end{cases}$$

$$\delta_\epsilon(z) = H'_\epsilon(z) = \begin{cases} 0 & if |z| > \epsilon \\ \frac{1}{2\epsilon}[1 + cos(\frac{\pi z}{\epsilon})] & if |z| \le \epsilon \end{cases}$$

To discrete the equation of u, different from the scheme used in [C], here we use a implicit finite difference scheme. Let h be the step space, and $(x_i, y_i) = (ih, jh)$ be the grid points, for $1 \le i, j \le M$. Let $u_{i,j}^n = u(t_n, x_i, y_j)$ be an approximation of $u(t, x, y)$. The time derivative u_t at (i, j, t_n) is approximated by the forward difference scheme: $u_t(i, j, t_n) = \frac{u_{i,j}^{n+1} - u_{i,j}^n}{\Delta t}$, where Δt is the time step.

We adopt the algorithm for the discretization of the divergence operator from [ROF], and the implicit iteration from [AV]. Knowing u^n, we compute u^{n+1} by using the following discretization and linearization scheme of (3.2):

$$\frac{u_{i,j}^{n+1} - u_{i,j}^n}{\Delta t} = \delta_\epsilon(u_{i,j}^n)\{(\alpha g_{i,j}^n + \frac{\beta}{2}d_{i,j}^{n\,2})div(\frac{\nabla u_{i,j}^{n+1}}{|\nabla u|_{i,j}^{n+1}})$$

$$+\alpha\frac{(\nabla g \cdot \nabla u)_{i,j}^{n+1}}{|\nabla u|_{i,j}^{n+1}} + \beta d_{i,j}^n \frac{(\nabla d \cdot \nabla u)_{i,j}^{n+1}}{|\nabla u|_{i,j}^{n+1}}] - f_\gamma(u_{i,j}^n)u_{i,j}^{n+1},$$

where

$$div(\frac{\nabla u_{i,j}^{n+1}}{|\nabla u|_{i,j}^{n+1}}) = \Delta_-^x \left(\frac{\Delta_+^x u_{i,j}^{n+1}}{\sqrt{(\Delta_+^x u_{i,j}^{n+1})^2 + (\Delta^y u_{i,j}^{n+1})^2}} \right)$$

$$+ \left(\frac{\Delta_+^y u_{i,j}^{n+1}}{\sqrt{(\Delta^x u_{i,j}^{n+1})^2 + (\Delta_+^y u_{i,j}^{n+1})^2}} \right).$$

When we compute $u_{i,j}^{n+1}$, $u_{i+1,j}^{n+1}$ and $u_{i,j+1}^{n+1}$ were replaced by $u_{i+1,j}^n$ and $u_{i,j+1}^n$, respectively, since they are unknown. We use the forward or backward finite difference schemes adaptively to approximate $\nabla d \cdot \nabla u$ and $\nabla g \cdot \nabla u$. That is

$$(\nabla d \cdot \nabla u)_{i,j}^n = (max(\Delta^x d_{i,j}^n, 0)\Delta_+^x u_{i,j}^n + min(\Delta^x d_{i,j}^n, 0)\Delta_-^x u_{i,j}^n$$

$$+ max(\Delta^y d_{i,j}^n, 0)\Delta_+^y u_{i,j}^n + min(\Delta^y d_{i,j}^n, 0)\Delta_-^y u_{i,j}^n).$$

The term $\nabla g \cdot \nabla u$ is approximated in the same way.

To have the signed distance function near the front the technique of reinitialization developed and applied in [e.g. SSS, ZCMO, AV] is also used in our computation. This procedure is made by using a new function $v(x)$, which is the steady state solution to the equation

$$\frac{\partial v}{\partial s} = sign(u(\cdot, t))(1 - |\nabla v|), v(\cdot, 0) = u(\cdot, t),$$

as $u(\cdot, t)$ for the next iteration $t + \Delta t$.

The equation (3.4)-(3.6) are discretized as in [C] by using finite difference.

4   Experimental Results and Applications

In this section we report our experimental results on both synthetic and ultrasound images.

The aim of our first experiment is to verify that the active contour with the prior shape and points can fill in the "gaps" in a boundary in a meaningful way.

Figure 1a shows a typical binary image I with three points and an ellipse superimposed. The ellipse and points are used as the prior shape and points in this experiment, respectively. The object to be segmented is partially occluded, and the shape of its boundary is not equivalent to the prior shape. We want to determine whether or not the active contour with the prior shape and points can use the partial boundary to aid the process of filling in the rest.

The active contour was initialized by the solid curve displayed in figure 1c. Evolving the active contour according to (3.2)-(3.6) with the parameters $\alpha = 250$, $\beta = 15$, $\sigma = 0.5$ (in $g(x)$), $\mu_0 = 1$, $\theta_0 = 0$, $T_0 = (0,0)$, we get the stationary contour C (the dotted one) in figure 1c, and the transformation parameters $\mu = 0.91$, $\theta = -0.14$, and $T = (-0.5, 0.3)(pixels)$. We can see that even though complete gradient information is not available the contour C captures the high gradient in the image I, passes through three prior points, and forms a shape similar but not the same as the prior shape. To show the advantage of using prior points we compared the segmentation results obtained by using model (3.1) and (2.3). Figure 1b shows the segmentation result by using model (2.3). In figure 1b the solid contour is the initial contour, and the dotted one is the segmentation result. Since the prior points are not incorporated in the model (2.3), the segmented contour only captures the prior shape and high gradients. It can't accurately capture local shape variations.

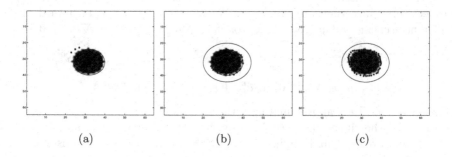

(a)   (b)   (c)

Fig. 1. (a) An image with the prior shape and three points superimposed;(b) The segmentation result using model (2.3) (dotted) and the initial contour (solid); (c) The segmentation result using model (3.1) (dotted) and the initial contour (solid)

The aim of the second experiment is to segment the endocardium (the inner boundary of the myocardium surrounding the left ventricle) in an apical two-chamber image of the heart (see figure figure 2a for a typical image). The endocardium is not completely visible in the image, and its shape is not the same as the "average shape" (the shape prior). Our task is to determine the endocardium using "average shape" and five points given by an expert.

The prior shape is created by the same way as that in [C]. It is obtained by averaging the aligned contours in a training set. The alignment of two contours C_1 and C_2 is made by finding the "best" scaling constant μ, rotation matrix R and translation vector T such that the overlapping area of the interiors of C_1 and $\mu R C_2 + T$ is maximized. If the shapes of the curves in the training set have a large variation, a clustering technique is required to group these curves into several groups. The shape priors for each group are obtained using this technique.

For this particular problem to create the prior shape, an expert echocardiographer traced endocardial boundaries on 112 image sequences for 66 patients. Aftere the boundaries were clustered, the average was computed. Figure 2b shows the "average contour" for one of the clusters (the dotted contour), the endocardium outlined by an expert (the solid contour), and five points on the expert's contour, The prior points are usually given at the location where the image gradients are low, and the local shape distortions are larger. Figure 2c presents the image $|\nabla G_\sigma * I|$. From this image we can see the dropout of image information at several parts of the endocardium.

To segment the endocardium in the image shown in figure 2d (it is the same as in figure 2a), the the active contour was initialized as the contour shown in figure 2a. This contour was evolved according to the equations (3.2)-(3.6) and it finally stopped at the location of the dotted contour in figure 2d. We also obtained the transformation parameters $\mu = 1.0024$, $\theta = -0.1710$, and $T = (-24.6163, 32.3165)$ (pixels). The solid contour in figure 2d is the expert's endocardium. Observe that the segmentation is close to the expert's contour. To see the shape variation between the solution of (3.1) and "average shape" we aligned the solution of (3.1) to the "average shape" using the solutions (μ, R, T) of (3.1). Figure 2e shows the disparity in shape between these two contours. The dotted contour is the transformed solution of (3.1), and the solid one is the "average shape". From figures 2d and 2e we can see that our active contour formed a shape different from the prior one in order to capture the high gradients and given points. Figure 2f provides the segmentation result obtained by using model (2.3). In this figure the dotted contour is the solution of (2.3), and the solid contour is the expert's endocardium. Comparing figure 2d with figure 2f, note that the solution of (3.1) is closer to the expert's contour than the solution of (2.3). Figure 2g presents the shape comparison between the solution of (2.3) and prior shape. In figure 2g the solid contour is the "average shape", and the dotted one is the transformed solution of (2.3), (the transformation parameters are the solution of (2.3)). From figures 2f and 2g we see that the solution of (2.3) can only capture the high image gradients and the "average shape", but it can't provide a desirable segmentation as the expert's endocardium.

The last experiment is a repetition of the second experiment on a second apical 2-chamber cardiac ultrasound image. We list the figures below for the results of this experiment in the same order as above. The segmentation C is given in figure 3d represented by the dotted contour, the transformation parameters are $\mu = 0.9883$, $\theta = -0.1981$, and $T = (-28.7246, 49.1484)$.

5   Conclusion

In this paper we proposed the addition of prior points to an active contour with shape in a variational framework and in level set formulation. The key idea was to introduce an energy term which measured the image gradients, the closeness of the shape between the active contour and a prior shape, as well as the distance of the prior point from the active contour. We used an implicit numerical scheme to solve the minimization problem. In the experiments with application to cardiac ultrasound images, the active contour could segment images in which the complete boundary was missing and the shape of tthe boundary has relatively large distortion from the prior. Besides the segmentation, the algorithm also provides estimates of translation, rotation, scale that map the active contour to the prior shape. These estimates are useful in aligning images.

The future work include the extension of model (3.1) to 3-d images, and more tests on normal and abnormal ultrasound images to improve the efficiency, accuracy, and stability of the proposed algorithm.

Moreover, several important theoretical questions remains open, and we are working on these questions. One of them is the existence and uniqueness for the model (3.1). Another question is whether the zero level set of the solution u of (3.2) is independent of the choice of the embedding of the initial contour. If this failed, the reinitialization will affect the zero level set of the solution of (3.1), so that the reinitialization can't be applied. We are working on these problems.

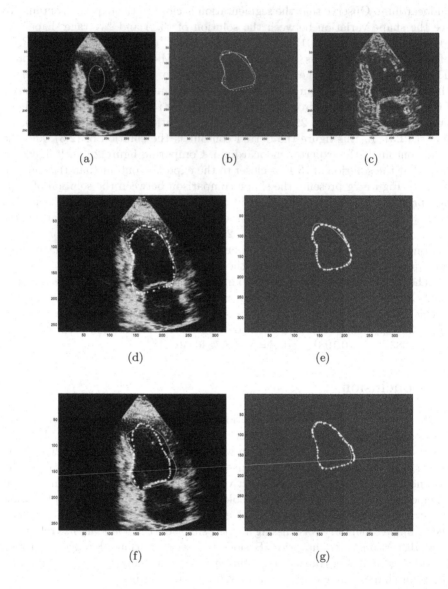

Fig. 2. (a). a typical 2-chamber ultrasound image with an initial contour; (b). Expert's endocardium (solid contour), "average shape" (dotted contour), and five points on the expert's contour; (c). The image $|\nabla G_\sigma * I|$; (d). The endocardium segmented by using model (3.1) (dotted) and the expert's contour (solid); (e) The transformed solution of (3.1) (dotted), and the "average shape"; (f). The endocardium segmented by using model (2.3) (dotted) and the expert's contour (solid); (g) The transformed solution of (2.3) (dotted), and the "average shape"

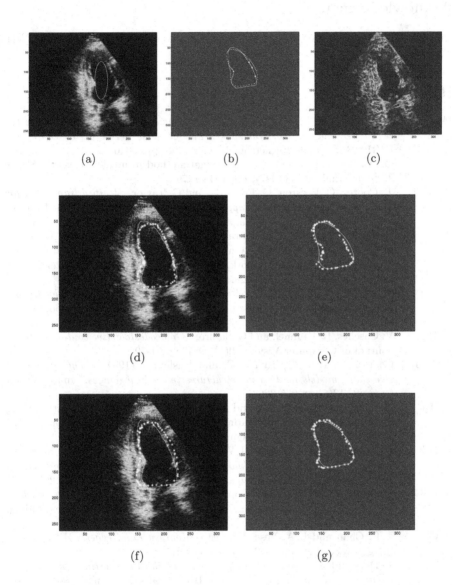

Fig. 3. (a). a typical 2-chamber ultrasound image with an initial contour; (b). Expert's endocardium (solid contour), "average shape" (dotted contour), and five points on the expert's contour; (c). The image $|\nabla G_\sigma * I|$; (d). The endocardium segmented by using model (3.1) (dotted) and the expert's contour (solid); (e) The transformed solution of (3.1) (dotted), and the "average shape"; (f). The endocardium segmented by using model (2.3) (dotted) and the expert's contour (solid); (g) The transformed solution of (2.3) (dotted), and the "average shape"

Acknowledgements

Yunmei Chen is partially supported by NIH grants P50-DC03888, and NIH NS42075.

References

[AF]   G. Aubert and L. Blanc-Feraud, *"An element proof of the equivalence between 2D and 3D classical snakes and geodesic active active contours"*, INRIA Rapport de Recherche, Janvier 1998, pp. 3340

[AV]   G. Aubert and L. Vese, "A variational method in image recovery", SIAM J. Num. Anal., 34/5(1997), pp. 1948-1979

[CBET]   T. Cootes, C. Beeston, G. Edwards, and C. Taylor, *"Unified framework for atlas matching using active appearance models "*, Int'l Conf. Inf. Proc. in Med. Imaging, Springer-Verlag, (1999), pp.322-333.

[C]   Y. Chen, H. Tagare, S. R. Thiruvenkadam, F. Huang, D.Wilson, A. Geiser, K.Gopinath and R.Briggs, Using prior shapes in geometric active contours in a variational framework, *International Journal of Computer Vision*, Vol.50 (3), (2002), pp. 315-328.

[CCCD]   V. Caselles, F. Catté, T. Coll and F. Dibos, *"A geometric model for active contours in image processing"*, Numerische Mathematik Vol.66, (1993), pp.1-31.

[CKS]   V. Caselles, R. Kimmel. and G. Sapiro, *"On geodesic active contours"*, Intel. Journal of Computer Vision, 22(1),1997, pp.61-79

[CHTH]   Cootes, T., Hill, A., Taylor, C. and Haslam, J.(1994). *"The use of active shape models for locating structures in medical images."* Image Vision Comput.,13(6),pp.255-366

[CSD]   A. Chakraborty, H. Staib, and J. Duncan, "Deformable boundary finding in medical images by integrating gradient and region information", IEEE Transactions on Medical Imaging, 15(6), (1996), pp. 859-870.

[CSW]   D. Cremers, F. Tischhauser, J. Weickert, and C. Schnorr, *"Diffusion-snakes: Introducing statistical shape knowledge into the Mumford-Shah functional "*, International Journal of Computer Vision, Vol.50 (3), (2002), pp. 295-315.

[CTCG]   T. Cootes, C. Taylor, D. Cooper and J. Graham, *"Active shape model - their training and application,* Computer Vision and Image Understanding, Vol. 61 (1995), pp. 38-59.

[CV]   T. F. Chan and L. A. Vese, *"Active contours without edges"*, IEEE Trans. Image Processing, 10(2) (2001), pp. 266-277.

[DL]   J. Dias and J. Leitao, *"Wall position and thickness estimation from sequences of echocardiograms images"*, IEEE Trans. Med. Imag., vol. 15, Feb. (1996), pp. 25-38.

[G]   E. Giusti, *Minimal Surfaces and Functions of Bounded Variation,* Birkhauser, 1985.

[HS]   Staib, L.H. and Duncan, J. S.(1992b), *"Deformable Fourier models for surface finding in 3D images."* In Robb, R.A(ed.), Proc, Second Conf. on Visualization in Biomedical Computing(VBC'92), Chapel Hill, NC, October, 1992, SPIE Proc., Vol 1808, pp.90-104. Bellingham, WA: SPIE

[LGF]   M. E. Leventon, W. E. L. Grimson, and O. Faugeras, *"Statistical Shape Influence in Geodesic Active Contours"*, Proc. IEEE Conf. Comp. Vision and Patt. Recog. (2000), pp.316-323.

[KWT]   M. Kass, A.Witkin, and D. Terzopoulos, *"Snakes: Active contour models, International Journal of Computer Vision"*, No. 1, 1988, pp 321-331.

[KKOTY] S. Kichenassamy, A. Kumar, P. Olver, A. Tannenbaum, and A. J. Yezzi, *"Gradient flows and geometric active contour models"*, Proc. ICCV'95, IEEE Computer Soc. Press, Cambridge, Mass., (1995), pp.810-815.

[McInerney] T. McInerney and D. Terzopoulos, *"Deformable models in medical image analysis: a survey"*, Medical Image Analysis, Vol.1(2),(1996), pp.91-108

[MS]   D. Mumford and J. Shah, *"Optimal approximation by piecewise smooth functions and associated variational problems"*, Comm. Pure Appl. Math., Vol. 42, (1989), pp.557-685.

[MSV]   R. Malladi, J. Sethian, and B. Vemuri, *"Shape modeling with front propagation: A level set approach"*, IEEE Trans. Pattern Anal. machine Intell. Vol. 17 (1995), pp.158-175.

[MT93] Metaxas, D. and Terzopoulos, D.(1993). *"Shape and nonrigid motion estimation through physics-based synthesis."* IEEE trans. Pattern Anal. Machine Intelligence, 15(6), pp.580-591

[MT96] Tim McInerney and Demetri Terzopoulos. *"Deformable models in medical image analysis: a survey."* Medical Image Analysis(1996) volume 1, number 2, pp.91-108

[OS]   S. Osher and J. A. Sethian, *"Fronts propagating with curvature-dependent speed: algorithm based on Hamilton-Jacobi formulation"*, Journal of Computational Physics, Vol. 70 (1988), pp.12-49.

[P]   N. Paragios, *"User-interactive level set method for image segmentation"*, submitted to ICCV2003.

[PD]   N. Paragios and R. Deriche, *"Geodesic active regions for supervised texture segmentation,* IEEE ICCV Cofu, Greece, (1999), pp.926-932.

[P1]   N. Paragios, *"Geodesic active regions and level set methods: contributions and applications in artificial vision"*, Ph.D. thesis, School of Computer Engineering, University of Nice/Sophia Antipolis, 2000.

[P2]   N. Paragios, *"A variational approach for the segmentation of the left ventricle in MR cardiac images,* Proceedings 1st IEEE Workshop on Variational and Level Set methods in Computer Vision, 13 July 2001, Vancouver, B. C., Canada, (2001), pp.153-160.

[PR]   N. Paragios and M.Rousson, *"Shape prior for level set representations"*, Proceeding of ECCV 2002.

[PRR]   N. Paragios, M. Rousson, and V. Ramesh, *"Marching distance functions: a shape-to-area variational approach for global-to-local registration"*, Computer Vision-ECCV2002, the 7th European Conference on Computer Vision, Copenhagen, Demark, May 2002 Proceeding pp. 775-789."

[RC]   F. Richard and L. Cohen, *"A New Image Registration Technique with Free Boundary Constraints: Application to Mammography"*, ECCV 2002, LNCS 2353, pp. 531-545.

[SD]   L. Staib and J. Duncan, *"Boundary finding with parametrically deformable contour methods"*, IEEE Trans. Patt. Analysis and Mach. Intell., Vol. 14(11), 1992. pp. 1061-1075

[SKBG] Szekel, G., Kelemen, A., Brechbuhler, Ch. and Gerig, G. (1996). *"Segmentation of 2-D and 3-D objects from MRI volume data using constrained elastic deformation of flexible Fourier surface models."* Medical Image Analysis, 1(1), pp.19-34.

[SSS]   M. Sussman, P. Smereka and S. Osher,"*A level set approach for comput-ing solutions to incompressible two phase flow*", J. Comput. Phys. Vol. 119(1994), pp. 146-159.

[SY]   S. Soatto and A. Yezzi, "*Deformation: deforming motion, shape average and joint registration and segmentation of images*, Proceeding of ECCV 2002.

[T]   H. D. Tagare, "*Deformable 2-D Template Matching Using implementation of the Mumford-Shah functional for image segmentation, denoising, in-terpolation, and magnification*", IEEE Transactions on Image Processing, 10(8),(2001),pp.1169-1186.

[TYW]   A. Tsai, A. Yezzi,Jr., and A. S. Willsky, "*Curve evolution implementation of the Mumford-Shah functional for image segmentation, denoising, interpo-lation, and magnification*", IEEE Transactions on Image Processing, 10(8), (2001), pp.1169 -1186.

[VCW]   B. C. Vemuri, Y. Chen, and Z. Wang, "*registration associated image smooth-ing and segmentation*", Proceeding of ECCV 2002.

[VR]   Vemuri, B. C. and Radisavljevie, A.(1994). "*Multiresolution stochastic hy-brid shape models with fractal priors.*" ACM Trans. on Graphics. 13(2), pp.177-207

[WS]   Y. Wang and L. Staih, "*Boundary funding with corresponding using sta-tistical shape models*", Proc. IEEE Conf. Comp. Vision and Patt. Recog. (1998), pp.338-345

[YHC]   A. Yuille, P. W. Hallinan, and D. S. Cohen,"*Feature extraction from faces using deformable templates*", Int. J. Computer Vision, Vol.8, (1992), pp.99-111

[YKKOT]   A. Yezzi, S. Kichenassamy, A. Kumar, P. J. Olver, and A. Tannenbaum, "A geometric snake model for segmentation of medical imagery", IEEE Trans. Medical Imaging 16 (1997). pp.199-209.

[ZCMO]   H. K. Zhao, T. Chan, B. Merriman and S. Osher,"*A variational level set approach to multiphase motion*", J. Comput. Phys. Vol.127, (1996), pp.179-195

[ZY]   S. C. Zhu and A. Yuille,"*Region Competition: unifying snakes, region grow-ing, and Bayes/MDL for multiband image segmentation*", IEEE PAMI, Vol.18, (1996), pp.884-900.

Separating a Texture from an Arbitrary Background Using Pairwise Grey Level Cooccurrences

Georgy Gimel'farb and Linjiang Yu

CITR, Dept. of Computer Science, University of Auckland
Auckland, New Zealand
g.gimelfarb@auckland.ac.nz
lyu011@ec.auckland.ac.nz

Abstract. The problem of finding a given texture in an arbitrary image is of a sound practical interest. We analyse possibilities of using characteristic pairwise pixel interactions in the texture to find similar regions in other images. The interactions have top-rank energies in a generic Gibbs random field model of the texture, each energy depending on relative frequency distribution of grey level cooccurrences. Experiments show that various stochastic and regular textures can be separated from a complex background using similarity between the characteristic frequency distributions.

1 Introduction

Decades of developing modern image analysis techniques yield a rich variety of different image models, features and similarity measures for supervised and unsupervised texture segmentation (e.g., [, ,] to mention just a few). Typical segmentation separates an image into regions containing each only a single homogeneous texture. The supervised segmentation assumes that training samples are available for learning characteristics of the textures and regions. The unsupervised segmentation considers the opposite case with no training data at all.

In many practical applications, such as computer analysis of remotely sensed images of the Earth's surface, the training information always exists but it is in principle incomplete. The task is to find only those regions that are similar to the available training samples [ ]. Such a "partially supervised" separation of only one or several desired textures from an arbitrary background differs from the traditional segmentation problems. Generally, the partially supervised segmentation has a direct relationship to the Bayesian statistical decision with an additional rejection class. The decision is based on pixelwise marginal posterior region probabilities, but in the case of separating a single texture, these latter cannot be derived in a traditional Bayesian way, from the prior probability models of textures and regions.

A. Rangarajan et al. (Eds.): EMMCVPR 2003, LNCS 2683, pp. 306– , 2003.

This paper proposes an alternative simple scheme of using the supervised learning with a non-parametric probabilistic texture model in order to separate an arbitrary image into the two regions, namely, the desired texture (represented by a given training sample) and its arbitrary background. Our approach is based on an energy-based measure of similarity between the textures.

2   Energy-Based Similarity of Textures

We restrict our consideration to only spatially homogeneous textures. Let such images be described as samples of a generic Gibbs random field (GGRF) with multiple pairwise pixel interactions [ ]. Under the GGRF model, relative frequency distributions of grey level cooccurrences for characteristic pixel pairs are sufficient statistics of each image, and similarity between the images relates directly to similarity between the distributions. Initially, the GGRF model involves the grey level cooccurrence distributions collected over the entire image, and pixel-wise interaction energies depend on the cooccurrences in a characteristic neighbourhood of each pixel.

2.1   Pixel-Wise Interaction Energies

Let $\mathbf{Q} = \{0, 1, \ldots, q_{\max}\}$ be a finite set of grey values. Let $\mathbf{R} = \{i = (x, y) : x = 1, \ldots, M; y = 1, \ldots, N\}$ be a finite arithmethic lattice supporting digital images $\mathbf{g} = [g_i : i \in \mathbf{R}; g_i \in \mathbf{Q}]$. The GGRF model relates the probability of each image $\mathbf{g}$ to a total energy $E(\mathbf{g})$ of translation invariant pairwise pixel interactions in the image. The energy is specified by a geometric structure and quantitative strengths of interactions in the pixel pairs.

Let $\mathbf{C}_a = \{(i, i + a) : i \in \mathbf{R}; +a \in \mathbf{R}$ be a family of all pixel pairs with the same inter-pixel displacement a in the lattice. These pairs are the simplest cliques of the neighbourhood graph linking the interacting pixels, and $\mathbf{C}_a$ is traditionally referred to as the clique family. Let $\mathbf{A}$ denote a set of the displacements a relating the interaction structure to the characteristic pixel neighbourhood $\mathbf{N_A} = \{i \pm a : a \in \mathbf{A}\}$. Let $V_a : \mathbf{Q}^2 \rightarrow (-\infty, \infty)$ be a potential function relating the strength of interactions in the clique $(i, i + a) \in \mathbf{C}_a$ to a grey level cooccurrence $(q = g_i, s = g_{i+a})$. Let $\mathbf{V} = \{\mathbf{V}_a : a \in \mathbf{A}\}$ denote the set of potentials $\mathbf{V}_a = [V_a(q, s) : (q, s) \in \mathbf{Q}^2]$ describing the interaction strengths.

Then the total interaction energy in the image $\mathbf{g}$ is

$$E(\mathbf{g}) = \sum_{a \in \mathbf{A}} E_a(\mathbf{g}) \quad \text{where} \quad E_a(\mathbf{g}) = \sum_{(i, i+a) \in \mathbf{C}_a} V_a(g_i, g_{i+a}) \propto \mathbf{V}_a \bullet \mathbf{F}_a(\mathbf{g})$$

is the partial interaction energy for the clique family $\mathbf{C}_a$. Here, $\mathbf{F}_a(\mathbf{g})$ is a relative frequency distribution of grey level cooccurrences for the clique family $\mathbf{C}_a$ over the image $\mathbf{g}$:

$$\mathbf{F}_a(\mathbf{g}) = \left[F_a(q, s) : (q, s) \in \mathbf{Q}^2; \sum_{(q,s) \in \mathbf{Q}^2} F_a(q, s) = 1 \right]$$

where

$$F_a(q, s|\mathbf{g}) = \frac{1}{|\mathbf{C}_a|} \sum_{(i,i+a)\in\mathbf{C}_a} \delta(g_i - q) \cdot \delta(g_{i+a} - s)$$

and $\delta(z) = 1$ for $z = 0$ and $\delta(z) = 0$ otherwise.

The characteristic subset $\mathbf{A}$ and the first approximation of the maximum likelihood estimates of the corresponding potentials $\mathbf{V}$ are analytically obtained for a given training sample $\mathbf{g}^\circ$ of the texture. The computations involve the top-rank interaction energies and corresponding relative frequency distributions of grey level cooccurrences [ ]. It is easily shown that the first approximation of the training partial energy $E_a(\mathbf{g}^\circ)$ is proportional to the variance of the relative sample frequency distribution:

$$E_a(\mathbf{g}^\circ) \propto \sum_{(q,s)\in\mathbf{Q}^2} \left(F_a(q, s|\mathbf{g}^\circ) - \frac{1}{256}\right)^2 \qquad (1)$$

In many cases, the textures are visually similar to the training image $\mathbf{g}^\circ$ if their characteristic cooccurrence distributions $\mathbf{F}(\mathbf{g}) = \{\mathbf{F}_a(\mathbf{g}) : a \in \mathbf{A}\}$ are closely similar to the training ones $\mathbf{F}(\mathbf{g}^\circ)$. This allows to use the GGRF model with the estimated characteristics $(\mathbf{A}, \mathbf{V})$ for generating realistic textures in such a way that frequency distributions $\mathbf{F}(\mathbf{g})$ for each generated sample closely approach the training ones $\mathbf{F}(\mathbf{g}^\circ)$ [ ].

The pixel-wise interaction energy in the GGRF model:

$$E_i(g_i|\mathbf{g}) = \sum_{a\in\mathbf{A}} (V_a(g_{i-a}, g_i) + V_a(g_i, g_{i+a})) \qquad (2)$$

relates directly to the conditional probability of the grey levels in every pixel:

$$\Pr(g_i = q|\mathbf{g}) = \frac{\exp(E_i(q|\mathbf{g}))}{\sum_{s\in\mathbf{Q}} \exp(E_i(s|\mathbf{g}))} \qquad (3)$$

Although the model itself describes the spatially homogeneous texture, the pixel-wise energies of Eq. ( ) and hence the pixel-wise signal probabilities of Eq. ( ) vary considerably over the training samples. It can be shown that such variations hold both with the analytic first approximation of the Gibbs potentials proportional to the centred training cooccurrence distributions $\mathbf{F}_a(\mathbf{g}^\circ)$ and with the actual maximum likelihood estimates of the potentials obtained by stochastic approximation.

Figure   shows 20 training samples of the size 100×100 for the natural stochastic and regular image textures from the well-known Brodatz's collection [ ] that are used below for experiments in the partially supervised texture segmentation: D004 Pressed cork, D005 Expanded mica, D006 Woven aluminium wire, D009 Grass lawn, D0012 Bark of tree, D020 French canvas, D029 Beach sand, D034 Netting, D036 Lizard skin, D053 Oriental straw cloth, D57 Hand-made paper, D066 Plastic pellets, D068 Wood grain, D080 Oriental straw cloth,

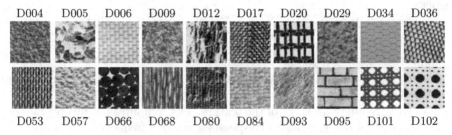

Fig. 1. Training textures 100×100

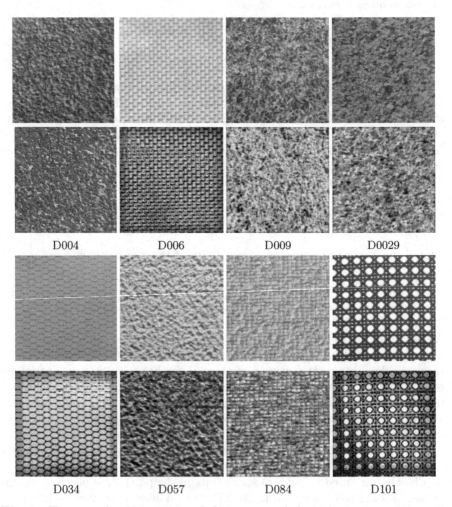

Fig. 2. Test samples 256×256 and their grey-coded pixel-wise interaction energies: the lower the energy, the darker the pixel

Table 1. Variations of the pixel-wise interaction energies per clique family over the test sample of the learned texture

Texture:	D004	D006	D009	D029	D034	D057	D084	D101
Number $|\mathbf{A}|$ of the clique families:	8	27	14	13	20	14	12	27
Minimum total energy:	-0.7	-1.9	-2.0	-1.9	-1.9	-1.9	-2.0	-1.9
Maximum total energy:	2.6	65.2	14.3	28.2	121.7	27.5	32.5	104.1

D84 Raffia, D093 Fur, D095 Brick wall, D101 Cane, and D102 Cane. Figure presents 8 test textures 256×256 and the maps of the pixel-wise energies of Eq. ( ) formed for these textures using the interaction structures and approximate potentials learned from the corresponding training samples. The energies vary in a very wide range (see Table), so that they cannot definitely act as the pixel-wise discriminative features of the texture.

2.2 Distance Distributions as Sufficient Statistics

In contrast to the pixel-wise energies, the distributions of grey level cooccurences collected in the moving window of a fixed size around each pixel of the training or test sample of the texture are similar to the like distributions collected over the entire training sample. For example, the average Euclidean distance per clique family between the distributions collected over the training sample and in the windows of the size 17×17 in the test sample of the same texture D004 in Figs. and varies in the range $[0.0001, 0.0082]$ whereas the possible maximum range of the distances is $[0.0, 2.0]$.

Because the model characteristics $(\mathbf{A}, \mathbf{V})$ depend on the relative training frequency distributions, the learned GGRF model is applicable for generating images of arbitrary size $|\mathbf{R}|$. In much the same way the distributions of characteristic grey level cooccurrences around each pixel can be considered as a pixel-wise non-parametric description of the texture. Therefore it is of an obvious interest to find out whether such a description can separate a single given texture from a complex arbitrary background.

Let $\mathbf{F}_{a,i}(\mathbf{g})$ denote the frequency distribution of the grey level cooccurrences for the clique family $\mathbf{C}_a$ in the square window of a fixed size around the pixel $i \in \mathbf{R}$. Let $D_{a,i}(\mathbf{F}_{a,i}(\mathbf{g}), \mathbf{F}_a(\mathbf{g}^\circ))$ be the Euclidean distance between the distributions $\mathbf{F}_{a,i}(\mathbf{g})$ and $\mathbf{F}_a(\mathbf{g}^\circ)$:

$$D_{a,i}(\mathbf{F}_{a,i}(\mathbf{g}), \mathbf{F}_a(\mathbf{g}^\circ)) = \sum_{(q,s)\in\mathbf{Q}^2} (F_{a,i}(q,s|\mathbf{g}) - F_a(q,s|\mathbf{g}^\circ))^2 \qquad (4)$$

This distance is changing over the image in accord with the changes in the local distributions $\mathbf{F}_{a,i}(\mathbf{g})$. But one may expect that for the training sample these changes will be scattered much less than the corresponding components of the local energy of pairwise pixel interactions in Eq. ( ). The adequate choice of

the window size ensuring relatively small variations of the distances of Eq. ( )
depends on the actual structure $\mathbf{A}$ of characteristic interactions.

The GGRF model belongs to the exponential family of distributions and, as
shown in [ ], it is the maximum entropy distribution provided that the maximum
likelihood estimates are used for the potentials. This allows to introduce a GGRF
model of textures having the relative frequency distributions of the distances as
sufficient statistics.

Let the Gibbs potential $V_a(D)$ depend on the quantised distance of Eq. ( ):
$D \in \{0, \Delta, 2\Delta, \ldots, U\Delta = 2\}$ where Δ is the quantising step. Then the corresponding GGRF model describing the texture in terms of the energy of the
spatially distributed pixel-wise distances has the interaction energy $E(\mathbf{g}) = \sum_{a \in \mathbf{A}} E_a(\mathbf{g})$ where $E_a(\mathbf{g})$ is the partial energy attributed to the partial distances
of Eq. ( ):

$$E_a(\mathbf{g}) = \sum_{i \in \mathbf{R}} V_a(D_{a,i}) \equiv \sum_{u=0}^{U} V_a(u\Delta)\Phi_a(u\Delta|\mathbf{g}) \qquad (5)$$

Here, $\Phi_a(u\Delta|\mathbf{g})$ is a component of the relative frequency distribution of the quan-
tised distances of Eq. ( ) between the local grey level cooccurrence distribution
in the moving window and the corresponding training distribution for the clique
family $\mathbf{C}_a$:

$$\mathbf{F}_{a,\text{dist}}(\mathbf{g}) = \left[\Phi_a(u\Delta|\mathbf{g}) : u = 0, 1, \ldots, U; \; \sum_{u=0}^{U} \Phi_a(u\Delta|\mathbf{g}) = 1 \right]$$

The relative frequency distribution $\mathbf{F}_{\text{dist}}(\mathbf{g}) = \{\mathbf{F}_{a,\text{dist}}(\mathbf{g}) : a \in \mathbf{A}\}$ of the
distances acts as the sufficient statistics in the latter GGRF model. The maxi-
mum entropy model of that type makes the training distribution $\mathbf{F}_{\text{dist}}(\mathbf{g}^\circ)$ the
mathematical expectation of the like distributions for all other images. The first
approximation of the maximum likelihood estimates of the potentials for the
latter model can be obtained in the same way as for the initial one in [ ]:

$$V_a(u\Delta) \propto \Phi_a(u\Delta|\mathbf{g}^\circ) - \Phi_{a,\text{irf}}(u\Delta)$$

where $\Phi_{a,\text{irf}}(u\Delta)$ is the component of the marginal probability of the quantised
distance $D = u\Delta$ for the samples of the independent random field.

In this case the pixel-wise similarity between the image window and the goal
texture is measured with the average distance between the distributions:

$$D\left(\mathbf{F}_i(\mathbf{g}), \mathbf{F}(\mathbf{g}^\circ)\right) = \frac{1}{|\mathbf{A}|} \sum_{a \in \mathbf{A}} D_{a,i}\left(\mathbf{F}_{a,i}(\mathbf{g}), \mathbf{F}_a(\mathbf{g}^\circ)\right) \qquad (6)$$

The distance in Eq. ( ) between the collected and training distributions can
be used to separate the desired texture from an arbitrary backbround, the window size having set limits on the minimal texture patches to separate from the
background.

In the simplest case, the window can be chosed as to obtain about $4-6$ measurements per individual degree of freedom. Because the distribution $\mathbf{F}_a(\ldots)$ contains $(q_{max}+1)^2$ individual frequencies of grey level cooccurrences, the window should have a linear size about $(2\ldots 2.4)\cdot(q_{max}+1)$. If comparable or smaller texture regions should be found, then less precise discrimination has to be used, e.g. by lowering the greyscale resolution. The experiments below use mostly eight levels ($q_{max}=8$) resulting in the window of the linear size $17\ldots 17$. Alternatively, the simpler initial GGRF model with distributions of signal differences in the cliques [ ] instead of cooccurrences can also help in reducing the window size.

From the computational viewpoint, a grey level cooccurrence distibution for a particular clique family takes $8\cdot(q_{max}+1)$ operations per window position, independently of the window size. Therefore the segmentation based on such "non-parametric" description is of moderate computational complexity. Also, the frequency distribution of the distances in Eq. ( ) for the training sample can specify a proper distance threshold for separating that texture from an arbitrary background.

3   Experimental Results

Our experiments use the training cooccurrence distributions for the characteristic interaction structures learned from the training samples 100×100 in Fig. . The training set of distributions is compared to the corresponding set of the "pixel-wise" distributions collected in the moving window 17×17 centred around each pixel in the test images.

Table 2. Relative number ε_{tx} of the missed texture pixels w.r.t. the texture area and relative number ε_{bg} of the falsely separated background pixels w.r.t. the background area

Search for	$\|\mathbf{A}\|$	ε_{tx},%	ε_{bg},%	Threshold
	Collage A in Figs. and			
D004	2	27.0	29.6	EM-based: 3 clusters
	8	1.3	58.5	EM-based: 3 clusters
	8	17.8	36.1	95% of the training distances
D009	2	99.9	2.6	EM-based: 3 clusters
	29	51.3	4.0	EM-based: 3 clusters
	29	26.3	29.6	95% of the training distances
D029	2	35.8	14.8	EM-based: 3 clusters
	13	34.9	16.4	EM-based: 3 clusters
	13	7.4	54.7	95% of the training distances
D057	2	0.0	6.1	EM-based: 3 clusters
	14	2.5	1.1	EM-based: 3 clusters
	14	9.3	0.2	95% of the training distances

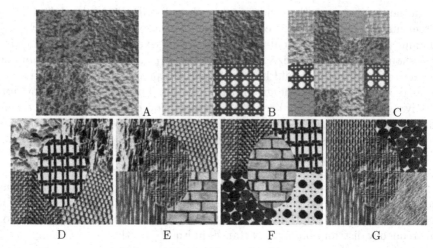

Fig. 3. Test collages 256 × 256: A - 4 textures: D004, D009, D029, and D057; B - 4 textures: D004, D006, D034, and D101; C - 8 textures: D004, D006, D009, D029, D034, D057, D084, and D101; D - 5 textures: D005, D012, D017, D020, and D036; E - 5 textures: D012, D036, D068, D080, and D095; F - 5 textures: D017, D020, D066, D095, and D102; G - 5 textures: D053, D066, D068, D080, and D093

Table 3. Relative number ε_{tx} of the missed texture pixels w.r.t. the texture area and relative number ε_{bg} of the falsely separated background pixels w.r.t. the background area

Search for	|**A**|	ε_{tx},%	ε_{bg},%	Threshold
Collage B in Figs. and				
D004	8	3.3	0.4	EM-based: 3 clusters
D006	27	26.9	0.0	EM-based: 3 clusters
D034	20	5.9	1.1	EM-based: 3 clusters
D101	27	17.3	0.5	EM-based: 3 clusters
Collage C in Figs. and				
D004	8	4.0	27.0	EM-based: 3 clusters
D057	14	34.3	3.9	EM-based: 3 clusters
D084	12	9.3	7.9	EM-based: 3 clusters
D101	27	23.7	0.4	EM-based: 3 clusters

Seven synthetic collages A – F of the size 256 × 256 formed from the selected textures are presented in Fig. , and Figs.   –   show the grey-coded maps of the pixel-wise distances of Eq. ( ) and the regions found by thresholding the distance maps (the smaller the distance, the darker the pixel).

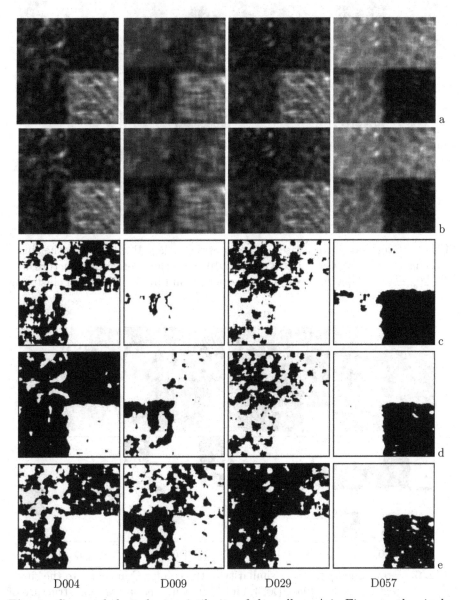

D004   D009   D029   D057

Fig. 4. Grey-coded pixel-wise similarity of the collage A in Fig.   to the single
training texture D004, D009, D029, and D057 with the interaction structure of 2
clique families (a) and of 8, 14, 13, and 14 (b), regions (c) found by thresholding
the distances in (a) by the EM-based clustering, and regions found by thresholding the distances in (c) by the EM-based clustering (d) and by selecting 95%
of the training distances (e)

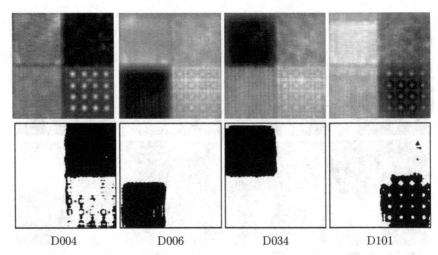

Fig. 5. Grey-coded pixel-wise similarity of the collage B in Fig.   to the single training texture D004, D006, D034, and D101 with the interaction structure of 8, 27, 20, and 27 clique families (a) and regions found by the EM-based clustering

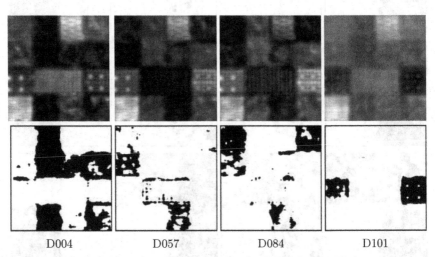

Fig. 6. Grey-coded pixel-wise similarity of the collage C in Fig.   to the single training texture D004, D057, D084, and D101 with the interaction structure of 8, 14, 12, and 27 clique families, and regions found by the EM-based clustering

We compared three variants of choosing the distance threshold: the Otsu algorithm [ ] approximating the distance distribution with two Gaussian clusters, the EM algorithm [ ] with two, three, or four Gaussian clusters, and the threshold selecting 95% or 99% of the training sample.

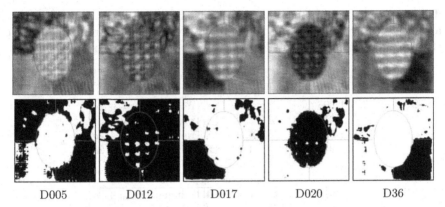

Fig. 7. Pixel-wise similarity of the collage D in Fig. and segmented regions for the training texture D005, D012, D017, D020, and D036 (the interaction structure of 5 clique families)

The best results were mostly obtained with the three-cluster EM approach. But the thresholds for 95%–99% of the training pixels or the threshold $D_{\mathrm{mean}}+2\sigma$ where D_{mean} is the mean training distance and σ is the standard deviation of these distances yield similar results. Tables – give the relative values of the missed area of the desired texture (that is, the texture area assigned to the background) and the relative background area falsely selected as the texture for the collages A – G in Fig. .

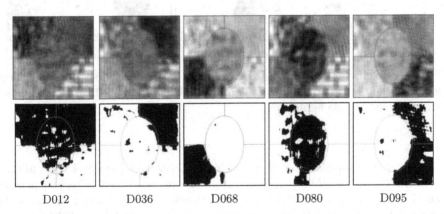

Fig. 8. Pixel-wise similarity of the collage E in Fig. and segmented regions for the training texture D012, D036, D068, D080, and D095 (the interaction structure of 5 clique families)

Table 4. Relative number ε_{tx} of the missed texture pixels w.r.t. the texture area and relative number ε_{bg} of the falsely separated background pixels w.r.t. the background area

Search for	$\|\mathbf{A}\|$	$\varepsilon_{tx},\%$	$\varepsilon_{bg},\%$	Threshold
Collage D in Figs. and				
D005	5	3.1	41.8	Training: $D_{mean}+2\sigma$
D012	5	2.5	79.6	Training: $D_{mean}+2\sigma$
D017	5	6.9	10.8	Training: $D_{mean}+2\sigma$
D020	5	4.0	8.5	Training: $D_{mean}+2\sigma$
D036	5	9.6	5.3	Training: $D_{mean}+2\sigma$
Collage E in Figs. and				
D012	5	7.0	49.4	Training: $D_{mean}+2\sigma$
D036	5	7.4	5.9	Training: $D_{mean}+2\sigma$
D068	5	14.6	0.1	Training: $D_{mean}+2\sigma$
D080	5	12.4	11.8	Training: $D_{mean}+2\sigma$
D095	5	7.2	16.8	Training: $D_{mean}+2\sigma$

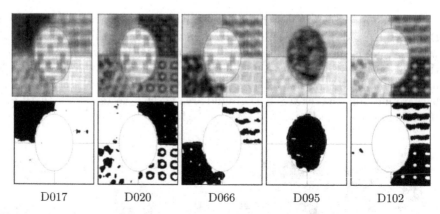

| D017 | D020 | D066 | D095 | D102 |

Fig. 9. Pixel-wise similarity of the collage F in Fig. and segmented regions for the training texture D017, D020, D066, D095, and D102 (the interaction structure of 5 clique families)

These experiments show that the locally collected grey level cooccurrence distributions can easily separate highly structured textures like regular mosaics D006, D034, D101, or D102. But if the textures have very similar characteristic distributions of grey level cooccurrences (e.g. D004, D009, and D029) or contain subregions similar to "dominating" grey level cooccurrences in the desired texture, then all such regions are separated brom the background and assigned to the desired texture. In particular, such regions are labelled as the desired texture in Figs. , , and . (e.g., the white uniform regions in Fig. or the grass-like textured ones in Fig.). For the latter two collages the relative errors

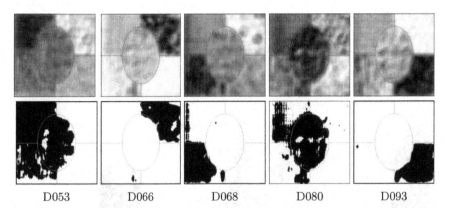

| D053 | D066 | D068 | D080 | D093 |

Fig. 10. Pixel-wise similarity of the collage G in Fig.   and segmented regions for the training texture D053, D066, D068, D080, and D93 (the interaction structure of 5 clique families)

Table 5. Relative number ε_{tx} of the missed texture pixels w.r.t. the texture area and relative number ε_{bg} of the falsely separated background pixels w.r.t. the background area

Search for	$\|\mathbf{A}\|$	$\varepsilon_{tx},\%$	$\varepsilon_{bg},\%$	Threshold
Collage F in Figs. and				
D017	5	7.2	0.5	Training: $D_{mean} + 2\sigma$
D020	5	6.3	13.2	Training: $D_{mean} + 2\sigma$
D066	5	6.0	8.1	Training: $D_{mean} + 2\sigma$
D095	5	5.5	2.0	Training: $D_{mean} + 2\sigma$
D102	5	8.3	11.6	Training: $D_{mean} + 2\sigma$
Collage G in Figs. and				
D053	5	0.8	41.9	Training: $D_{mean} + 2\sigma$
D066	5	12.0	0.8	Training: $D_{mean} + 2\sigma$
D068	5	13.2	2.6	Training: $D_{mean} + 2\sigma$
D080	5	11.5	18.2	Training: $D_{mean} + 2\sigma$
D093	5	11.7	0.1	Training: $D_{mean} + 2\sigma$

are as follows: $\varepsilon_{tx} = 7.3\%$, $\varepsilon_{bg} = 1.0\%$ for the collage in Fig.   and $\varepsilon_{tx} = 5.2\%$, $\varepsilon_{bg} = 3.2\%$ for the collage in Fig. , respectively.

It is worthy to note that the GGRF-based texture synthesis of the stochastic textures D004, D009, and D029 by approaching the training cooccurrence distributions results in quite realistic images although just the same distributions are not sufficient for separating these textures. Also, the desired texture cannot be effectively separated from other ones if the texture is not actually translation invariant (as, for instance, D005, D012, or D066) or the training sample is too small for recovering its characteristic interaction structure (say, in the case of

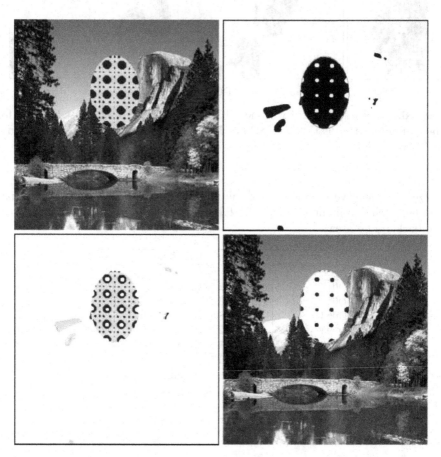

Fig. 11. Segmentation of the texture D102 using the threshold related to the distribution of distances for the training sample (top row: initial image and segmentation map; bottom row: the segmented texture and its background)

Fig. 12. Segmentation of the texture D102 using the threshold related to the distribution of distances for the training sample (top row: initial image and segmentation map; bottom row: the segmented texture and its background)

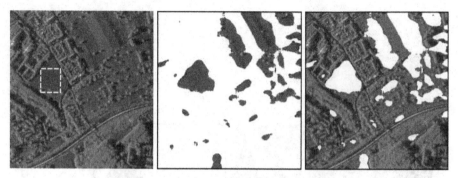

Fig. 13. SAR image of terrain with a shown training patch, the segmented regions similar to the patch (the EM-based thresholding of the distances), and the background region

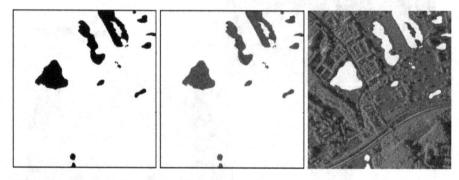

Fig. 14. Segmentation of the SAR image of terrain using the threshold related to the distance distribution for the training patch, the regions similar to the patch, and the background region

D020 or D095). Nonetheless, for many textures, especially for the "highly structured" ones, results of the proposed segmentation are quite satisfactory. The chosen textured regions are mostly similar to the desired texture, as it is evident from the "synthetic–natural" examples in Figs.   and Fig.   . The same similarity holds for the natural SAR image of the terrain in Figs.   and   .

4   Concluding Remarks

In total, in spite of its simplicity, the described approach yields in many cases a quite efficient separation of the single texture from an arbitrary background. Moreover, some segmentation errors can be easily fixed by taking account of the minimal expected size of the regions that could be selected.

This approach should be amplified in the following directions:

- more efficient estimation of the characteristic interaction structure because in the above experiments only the simplest choice of the top-energetic clique families was implemented
- choice of a better similarity measure to compare two sample frequency distributions collected over relatively small windows
- development of more efficient distance thresholding schemes

and so on. Because the approach is based on the easily collected training data, it is possible to relatively pre-order the textures of a particular practical interest with respect to their abilities of separating one from another on the basis of grey level cooccurrence distributions and then to search for only the groups of similar textures.

Acknowledgements

This work was supported by the Royal Society of New Zealand under Marsden Fund Grant UOA122 (9143/3600771) and by the University of Auckland Research Committee under Grant 9393/3600529. The authors are grateful to Prof. C.-E. Liedtke for the SAR image of the terrain.

References

[1] Barndorff-Nielsen, O.: Information and Exponential Families in Statistical Theory. John Wiley and Sons, New York, 1978.
[2] Brodatz, P.: *Textures: A Photographic Album for Artists an Designers.* Dover Publications, New Nork, 1966.
[3] Carson, C., Belongie, S., Greenspan, H., Malik, J.: Blobworld: image segmentation using expectation-maximization and its application to image querying. IEEE Trans. Pattern Analysis and Machine Intelligence 24 (2002) 1026–1038.
[4] Dempster, A., Lairld, N., Rubin, D.: Maximum likelihood from incomplete data via the EM algorithm. J. Royal Stat. Soc. 39B (1977) 1–38.
[5] Gimel'farb, G. L.: *Image Textures and Gibbs Random Fields.* Kluwer Academic Publishers, Dordrecht (1999).   ,   ,   ,
[6] Liedtke, C.-E.: Personal communication (2001).
[7] Otsu, N.: A threshold selection method from gray-level histograms. IEEE Trans. Systems, Man, Cybern. SMC-9 (1979) 62–66.
[8] Panjwani, D., Healey, G.: Markov random field models for unsupervised segmentation of textured color images. IEEE Trans. Pattern Analysis and Machine Intelligence 17 (1995) 939–954.
[9] Reed, T. R., du Buf, J. M. H.: A review on recent texture segmentation and feature extraction techniques. Computer Vision, Graphics, and Image Processing 57 (1993) 359–372.

Surface Recovery from 3D Point Data Using a Combined Parametric and Geometric Flow Approach

Peter Savadjiev, Frank P. Ferrie, and Kaleem Siddiqi

Centre for Intelligent Machines, McGill University
3480 University Street, Montréal, Québec H3A 2A7, Canada
{petersv,ferrie,siddiqi}@cim.mcgill.ca

Abstract. This paper presents a novel method for surface recovery from discrete 3D point data sets. In order to produce improved reconstruction results, the algorithm presented in this paper combines the advantages of a parametric approach to model local surface structure, with the generality and the topological adaptability of a geometric flow approach. This hybrid method is specifically designed to preserve discontinuities in 3D, to be robust to noise, and to reconstruct objects with arbitrary topologies. The key ideas are to tailor a curvature consistency algorithm to the case of a set of points in 3D and to then incorporate a flux maximizing geometric flow for surface reconstruction. The approach is illustrated with experimental results on a variety of data sets.

1   Introduction

Surface reconstruction from incomplete data sets is a classical problem in computer vision. The problem consists of finding a surface S that approximates a physical surface P by using a set of point coordinates sampled from the surface P. These point coordinates may be corrupted with noise, due to imperfections in the acquisition of the data. Like many other problems in computer vision, the problem of surface reconstruction is ill-posed. Prior knowledge about the world and the data acquisition process must therefore be used in order to make it solvable. A good algorithm for surface reconstruction should be robust to noise and result in smooth surfaces, while recovering important structural information from the data, such as edges, ridges and holes. The presence of such structural information in the reconstructed 3D model is very important for further, higher-level processing tasks, such as shape segmentation into parts, object recognition, etc. It should impose as little restrictions on the topology of the reconstructed object as possible. These issues are taken into consideration in the research presented in this paper.

The approach to surface reconstruction presented in this article combines two different philosophies, namely that of a parametric reconstruction approach, and that of a geometric flow reconstruction approach. Many algorithms for surface recovery are based on either one of the two types of approaches, but few have attempted to

A. Rangarajan et al. (Eds.): EMMCVPR 2003, LNCS 2683, pp. 325–340, 2003.

bring the two together in order to combine their advantages. Recently, Vemuri *et al.* [29, 30] have developed an interesting hybrid model which has been applied to the problem of surface recovery. However, it is not clear how their method can be tailored to preserve and model structural features such as discontinuities.

In this paper, we introduce a novel algorithm for surface reconstruction. This method is a combination between a curvature consistency algorithm, which is a parametric surface modeling approach [9, 17, 21], and a variation of the flux maximizing flow algorithm [28], which is a geometric flow algorithm implemented through the level-set method [22]. Our approach is novel for several reasons. It uses the degrees of freedom and the ease of manipulation of parameter-free geometric flow approaches, while incorporating knowledge from the local structure of the data obtained by fitting and refining local parametric patches [22]. Contrary to other flow based algorithms for surface recovery, our method is specifically designed to preserve discontinuities in 3D data, which are a very important source of information for higher-level vision processes such as shape segmentation and object recognition. We show that the inclusion of local structural information can improve the behavior of flow based algorithms for surface reconstruction. Furthermore, our approach is an improvement over the curvature consistency algorithm in that it results in a continuous surface rather than in a patchwork of overlapping surfaces. We extend the edge preserving formulation of curvature consistency [17] to 3D, which makes our technique robust to noise, while preserving discontinuities in 3D. Finally, our approach presents a novel application of the flux maximizing geometric flow.

1.1   Previous Work

Over the years, various approaches have been put forward in order to deal with surface recovery. Traditionally, parametric surface reconstruction approaches restrict the class of possible solutions to surfaces of a certain topology by fitting a model with a known (fixed) topology to the data so that it minimizes a particular error metric. This is usually done using energy-minimizing methods. Algorithms in this category can be classified by the type of model that is fit to the data. Popular choices include global models such as generalized splines [3, 25], volumetric primitives such as generalized cylinders or superquadrics, e.g. [24]. Alternatively, [9, 10, 17, 21] make use of local parameterizations by fitting a set of local parametric patches to the data. Several parametric surface recovery algorithms were developed from the concept of active deformable models (also known as active contours), introduced in [14], e.g. [18, 26].

An important inconvenience of parametric approaches is that they impose severe topological restrictions on the reconstructed surface, e.g. they require it to be homomorphic to a sphere. In this framework, it is very hard to model surfaces with a complicated topology.

Approaches in the computational geometry domain have been proposed, e.g. [1, 8], however they are very sensitive to noise in the data, regions of high curvature and outliers. Such methods reconstruct polygonal meshes. More recently, a different class of approaches that use implicit surfaces has received much interest, e.g. [2, 6, 13]. Working within the framework of variational implicit surfaces [27], Dinh *et al.* [7] use anisotropy in order to model sharp features in reconstructions. The process for locating edges and for classifying surface points as belonging to edges, corners, or flat regions is very sensitive to noise and outliers, hence tensor filtering is required in order to smooth the reconstruction. Medioni *et al.* [12, 19] have developed a separate methodology to infer structure from sparse data, known as tensor voting. It is a non-iterative process based on tensor calculus and non-linear voting. Gomes and Mojsilovic [11] propose a related variational solution to the problem implemented through an iterative algorithm.

The concept of active contours has been extended to the implicit surface representation independently by [4] and [16]. In the context of shape segmentation, they introduce geometric active contours, which are active contours represented implicitly as a level set of a higher-dimensional scalar function. An initial contour is made to evolve under forces depending on the contour's own geometric characteristics and on image-based external forces. More recently, Vemuri *et al.* [29, 30] have developed a hybrid shape modeling scheme which is based on the notion of a pedal curve. In their work, a global prior is introduced using a parameterized model, and local properties are fine-tuned using a geometric flow.

Geometric active contours have been applied to the problem of surface reconstruction from point data in [31, 33]. Zhao *et al.* [33] propose a variational method for implicit surface reconstruction that is based on a weighted minimal surface model that behaves like an elastic membrane wrapped over the data. Their flow formulation is actually a specific instance of the conformal flow originally introduced independently in [15] and [5] (see also [23] for more recent variants). Zhao *et al.* [33] use distance to the data as the weight in the conformal flow formulation of [15] and [5]. A drawback of the method in [33] is that it cannot model accurately pronounced concavities and convexities in the data, which results in the over-smoothing of corner discontinuities and in the loss of thin structures or surface borders. This is due to the use of a curvature-based regularization term which pushes the evolving curve away from high-curvature regions in the data. The algorithm in [33] is highly dependent on a good initial approximation to the real surface.

Implicit surface representations are independent of the underlying surface parameterization. This fact allows for topological flexibility in surface reconstruction algorithms, unfortunately it also makes it very difficult to exploit structural information in the data. It is not possible to model spring forces for example, or physical objects whose rigidity and tension vary along the surface, without additional surface point tracking. Structural information is lost, to the benefit of ease of manipulation. A comparison between geometric and parametric active contour models appears in [32].

2   Method Overview

The fundamental idea behind our algorithm is to reconstruct a surface by using a field of vectors normal to the surface. We assume that the input to our algorithm consists of a set of points in 3D (with x,y,z coordinates) located in a regularly spaced 3D voxel grid, in which voxels that correspond to point locations have been labeled accordingly. We assume that within a small neighbourhood, there is a local coordinate frame such that the data points in that neighbourhood have been sampled from a surface that can be described in the form $w = f(u,v)$, where (u,v,w) are the axes of the local coordinate frame. At each data point, we compute an initial estimate of the surface normal. We regularize this initial set of normal vectors by using a new extension of the curvature consistency algorithm which preserves discontinuities in 3D. Once we have obtained a smooth field of normal vectors, we use it to reconstruct the underlying surface by applying a variant of the flux maximizing flow algorithm of [28]. The flux maximizing flow is used to align an evolving surface in 3D to be normal to a given vector field.

3   Curvature Consistency with Edge Preservation

The curvature consistency algorithm achieves a stable surface representation by iteratively minimizing a functional related to the satisfaction of local constraints on the curvature of the surface. It was introduced in [21] for reconstruction in 3D voxel-based medical images. It was reformulated in [9, 17] in the context of surface reconstruction from 2½D range images, and in [10] for surface reconstruction from stereo depth data. It provides a patchwork of overlapping, interpolating functions each of which describes the surface locally.

The method makes use of a local surface model, which describes the local neighbourhood around point P on the surface with a quadric patch of the form

$$w = au^2 + buv + cv^2 , \qquad (1)$$

with origin at P and the w axis aligned with the surface normal at P, $\mathbf{N_p}$, as shown in Fig. 1. The information (parameters) associated with each patch are the location of the given point, the two principal directions of the paraboloid, the minimum and maximum curvatures (along the principal directions), and a coordinate frame (u,v,w) with the w axis aligned with the normal of the patch at point P, the u and v axis being aligned with the two principal directions. The u and v axis span the tangent plane at point P, T_p. All this information is stored in an "augmented Darboux frame" $D(P)$.

An initial set of such Darboux frames is computed at every data point from local estimates of surface normals, which can be obtained through various standard methods. We use least-squares fitting of local planes. Once the initial estimates are obtained from noisy data, the patchwork of surface descriptors are refined through iterative minimization of an energy functional that limits the variation of curvature with respect to the model of the surface. At convergence, each provides a consistent representation of its local surface region with respect to its neighbours.

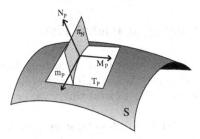

Fig. 1. Local surface representation – the augmented Darboux frame

The energy minimization is performed using variational relaxation. It is an iterative process which, at each iteration, operates by minimizing the difference between the description of the surface centered at point P given by $D(P)$, and that predicted by its neighbours Q_i $(i=1...n)$ believed to lie on the same continuous surface as P and which are within a threshold distance from P. This set of neighbours is known as the "contextual neighborhood" [21] and is discussed further below.

Thus, at each iteration, a neighbour Q_i provides a prediction $D_i(P)$ of the augmented Darboux frame at P. The traditional energy-minimization approach presented in [9, 21] gives update equations of the form

$$\hat{D}(P) = \frac{1}{n} \sum_{i=1}^{n} D_i(P).$$

(2)

In this update mechanism, each neighbour's prediction is given an equal weight in the update of the local surface descriptor. In this form of the equation, an implicit assumption of a continuous underlying surface is being made. While the effect of noise is minimized, discontinuities are smoothed over with each progressive iteration.

The authors in [17] derive a new form of Eq. (2) by casting the neighbourhood prediction update problem in estimation theoretic terms. Eq. (2) is modified such that each neighbour's contribution is weighted according to the prediction error variance, as determined by using a Kalman filter. The net effect is an anisotropic smoothing which preserves surface discontinuities. Thus, discontinuities are "learned" as the iterations proceed and do not need to be known in advance, as in [25], for example.

The edge preservation formulation of curvature consistency in [17] was designed specifically for 2½D range images. The extension to 3D of the edge-preserving formulation is straightforward, provided some technical adjustments are made to the concept of a "contextual neighborhood". In [17], the contextual neighborhood is determined simply by choosing the n closest neighbours of P in the embedding 2D grid. In 3D data, it is possible to have two or more surfaces that lie in close proximity to one another, without intersecting each other (e.g. the two sides of a thin object). Since refinement cannot proceed across surfaces, we cannot simply take the n closest 3D neighbors. Instead, we take those neighbors that are "sufficiently" close to the parabolic surface patch at P. In other words, the contextual neighborhood of P, consists of those neighboring points Q_i that are within radius r of P and whose local surface parameterization contains P, i.e. P is within an arbitrarily small distance from the local quadric surface patch $\Gamma = (u, v, \frac{1}{2}(\kappa_{Mi}u^2 + \kappa_{mi}v^2))$ fit at Q_i. This is the same definition of contextual neighborhood as in [21].

4   The Flux Maximizing Geometric Flow

With the motivation to address the problem of segmenting thin elongated structures in intensity images, Vasilevskiy and Siddiqi [28] derive the geometric flow which maximizes the rate of increase of flux of an auxiliary vector field through a curve or a surface.

Let $\mathbf{C}(p,t)$ be a smooth family of closed curves evolving in the plane. Here t parameterizes the family and p parameterizes the given curve. Without loss of generality, assume that $0 \leq p \leq 1$, i.e. that $C(0,t) = C(1,t)$. Consider also a vector field $V = (V_1(x,y), V_2(x,y))$ defined for each point (x,y) in R^2. The total inward flux of the vector field through the curve is given by the contour integral

$$Flux(t) = \int_0^1 \langle V, N \rangle \| C_p \| dp = \int_0^{L(t)} \langle V, N \rangle ds \tag{3}$$

where $L(t)$ is the Euclidean length of the curve.

Intuitively, the inward flux through a planar closed curve provides a measure of how well the curve is aligned with the direction perpendicular to the vector field. The main theoretical result of [28] is that the direction in which the inward flux of the vector field V through the curve C is increasing most rapidly is given by

$$\frac{\partial C}{\partial t} = div(V)N \tag{4}$$

where N is the normal vector field of C. In other words, the flow which maximizes the rate of increase of the total inward flux is obtained by moving each point of the curve in the direction of the inward normal by an amount proportional to the divergence of the vector field. In the resting flux maximizing configuration, the inward normals to the curve are everywhere aligned with the direction of the vector field.

It turns out that the volumetric extension of Eq. (4) has the same form as Eq. (4). Let $S : [0,1] \times [0,1] \to R^3$ denote a compact embedded surface with (local) coordinates (u,v). The authors of [28] show that the direction in which the inward flux of the vector field V through the surface S is increasing most rapidly is given by

$$\frac{\partial S}{\partial t} = div(V)N \tag{5}$$

where N is the normal vector field of S.

The authors of [28] apply the flux maximizing flow to blood vessel segmentation. We tailor the flux maximizing flow to our problem by considering the field of normal vectors defined on the data points to be the vector field V whose inward flux through the evolving surface is maximized. Once the normals information has been extracted from the Darboux frame at every point, we compute an approximation to the divergence of this vector field by using a consequence of the divergence theorem, which states that the divergence at a point is defined as the net outward flux per unit area, as the area about the point shrinks to zero. Via the divergence theorem,

$$\int_{\Delta a} div(V)da \equiv \int_R \langle V, N \rangle dr \tag{6}$$

where Δa is the area, R is the bounding surface and N is the *outward* normal at each point on the contour surface.

For our numerical implementation we use this flux formulation along the boundaries of small spheres of varying radii. The chosen flux value at a particular location is the maximum (magnitude) flux over the range of radii. Normalization across scales is trivial, one simply has to divide by the number of entries in the discrete sum that approximates Eq. (6). We thus obtain a scalar field defined over our 3D grid.

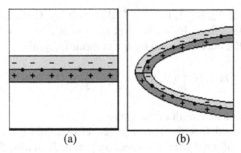

Fig. 2. Data points and their associated normal vectors, together with the flux sign distribution around them. (a) Positive and negative values form thin sheets on either side of the data points, the flux values are zero elsewhere. (b) The lack of a global notion of inside vs. outside may cause an interleaving of positive and negative sheets

Fig. 2 shows a schematic representation of a 2D planar cross-section through our 3D computational grid, for different data point configurations. As illustrated in Fig. 2(a), locations where the total outward flux (which is proportional to divergence) is positive form a thin sheet "under" the data points, and those where the total outward flux is negative form a thin sheet "above" the data points, assuming that "above" denotes the direction of the normal vectors and "under" denotes the direction opposite to it. Except for these two sheets "wrapping" the data points, the flux value is zero elsewhere. Because only local information is available, there is no reasonable notion of up vs. down on a surface, or exterior vs. interior on an object. Thus, there is always a 180° ambiguity of direction, and it is possible that the directions of the normal vectors flip from pointing "outward" to pointing "inward" from one region to another, as illustrated in Fig. 2(b). Thus, the sheets of positive and negative flux values are not necessarily continuous and can be interleaved.

According to the formulation in Eq. (5), evolving seeds initialized within a region with flux of a given sign will not leak into regions of the opposite sign, or into regions with a zero flux value. To avoid discontinuities in the reconstructed surface due to the ambiguity in normal directions, we remove the dependency on the sign of the flux value by taking its *square*. Thus, we use a numerical approximation of the following flow equation:

$$\frac{\partial \mathbf{S}}{\partial t} = div^2(\mathbf{V})\mathbf{N} \tag{7}$$

The presence of the square term in Eq. (7) implies that the flow formulation used in the hybrid method is not exactly a flux maximizing flow anymore, but rather a variant which is better adapted to deal with abrupt changes in the flux sign distribution. With this new flow formulation, we initialize a set of small seed spheres at locations where the flux magnitude is higher than a threshold, and we let them evolve according to Eq. (7). Starting the evolution at locations of high magnitude flux provides additional robustness to outliers, as outliers would be represented as isolated low magnitude flux values surrounded by zero magnitude flux values. Thus, the evolution would not spread to include them in the final reconstruction.

The flow described by Eq. (7) is implemented through the level-set representation for surfaces flowing according to functions of curvature [20]. Level-set methods represent an *n*-dimensional moving curve **C** as a level set of an *(n+1)*-dimensional scalar function ψ. Let **C** be moving with a speed F in the direction of its normal vector **N**, i.e. $\mathbf{C}_t = F\mathbf{N}$. One can show that

$$\psi_t + \mathbf{C}_t \cdot \nabla \psi = 0 . \tag{8}$$

Since the normal vector **N** is given by $\mathbf{N} = \nabla \psi / |\nabla \psi|$, by substitution one obtains the partial differential equation,

$$\psi_t + F|\nabla \psi| = 0 . \tag{9}$$

Eq. (9) is solved using a combination of straightforward discretization and numerical techniques derived from hyperbolic conservation laws [20].

The use of Eq. (7) to direct the flow of the seeds allows one to overcome the artifact depicted in Fig. 2(b), however it results in a surface that may be "thicker" than necessary, as the surface includes regions on both sides of the data points, as shown in Fig. 2. If the algorithm makes use of a global notion of outside vs. inside, it would be possible to remove the ambiguity in normal orientations, caused by using strictly local information to form initial estimates of the normal vectors. Then one may revert to using Eq. (5), which would potentially yield a thinner surface. However, the use of such a global notion implies imposing a global parametric model on the data, which goes against the philosophy of this work, which is to use only local parameterizations in order to allow the reconstruction of objects of arbitrary topology. Furthermore, it is not obvious how such a notion can be reliably computed, especially if there is more than one object in the scene. Alternative methods for thinning the surface are subject to future research, e.g. the computation of a medial surface of the "thick" reconstruction.

In the implementation presented in this paper, flux values at a point are calculated over the surface of small spheres centered at the points of interest. Since the recovery of the surface is entirely dependent on the accurate computation of flux values, future research may investigate the effect of calculating the flux through other types of surfaces, e.g. small ellipsoids or hyperboloids having the same curvature characteristics as the local surface patch at the data point.

5   Experiments and Results

In this section we present the results of an experiment that uses synthetic data to test the robustness to noise of our algorithm. We show that the application of our algorithm results in smooth reconstructions, which are qualitatively better than those obtained with the algorithm in [33].

Fig. 3(a) shows points on the surface of a hemisphere whose coordinates have been corrupted with Gaussian noise of mean 0.0, standard deviation of 1.0. The data is embedded in a 70×70×70 grid. We attempt to reconstruct the hemispherical surface using this data. As the first stage of our hybrid algorithm, we ran 15 iterations of curvature consistency. As the second and final stage of our hybrid algorithm, we applied the flux maximizing flow algorithm, using the normal vectors returned by curvature consistency. One can see the resulting surface in Fig. 3(c). The result obtained through our method, using only the flux maximizing flow and no iterations of curvature consistency to smooth the initial field of normal vectors, is shown in Fig. 3(b). It is a lot less smooth. For comparison, Fig. 3(d) shows the reconstruction from the same data obtained by using the algorithm of Zhao *et al.* [33]. The algorithm in [33] is very sensitive to noise. It does not converge to a smooth hemisphere, at some locations the surface collapses through the data points and vanishes, while at others it models the outliers in the data. These results show that the use of the local parametric information provided by the curvature consistency algorithm yields better reconstructions than the ones given either by the flux maximizing flow algorithm alone, or by the method in [33].

Our next experiment aims at showing how our method fares at recovering structure in 3D data, and at comparing it with that of Zhao *et al.* [33]. We use the Stanford bunny 3D model, which was obtained from [34]. The model is a triangle mesh with 35947 vertices and 69451 triangles that represent the surface of a bunny. We extracted the coordinates of the vertices of that mesh and we used them as a cloud of 3D points to test our algorithm. We embedded the vertices in a 160×160×160 grid. At such a grid resolution, the 35947 mesh vertices map to 30838 distinct voxels in the grid. The size of the grid was chosen as a trade-off between good data resolution and low space requirements. Fig. 4(a) shows a rendering of the voxelized data acquired from the model. Because the data is essentially noise-free, we ran our algorithm without making use of curvature consistency, we simply used the initial normal vector estimates and we ran the flux maximizing flow on them. The result of our reconstruction is shown in Fig 4(b). Fig. 4(c) shows the reconstruction obtained through the method in [33]. Note how our method captures better the discontinuities, the concavities/convexities in the data, in particular at the locations denoted by the arrows.

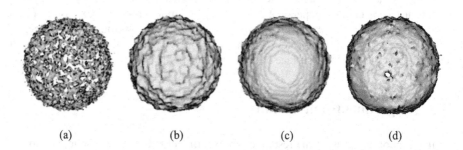

(a)   (b)   (c)   (d)

Fig. 3. (a) Data – the coordinates of the points on the hemisphere have been corrupted with zero mean Gaussian noise, standard deviation of 1.0. Reconstruction using (b) 0 iterations and (c) 15 iterations of curvature consistency in our method. (d) Reconstruction using the method of Zhao *et al.* [33]

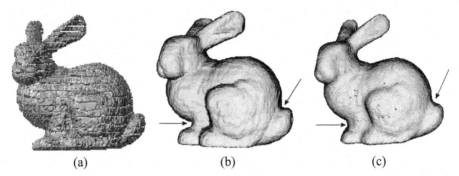

(a)   (b)   (c)

Fig. 4. The Stanford bunny. (a) Data extracted from the mesh model used in our experiments, embedded in a 160×160×160 grid. (b) Reconstruction of the Stanford bunny using our method (c) Reconstruction using the method of Zhao *et al.* [33]. Note how the structure in the data is better recovered through our method, in particular at the locations denoted by the arrows

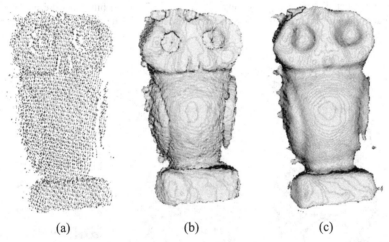

(a)   (b)   (c)

Fig. 5. (a) Owl dataset. (b) Reconstruction using our method. (c) Reconstruction using the method of Zhao *et al.* [33]. The reconstruction is smoother but does not recover discontinuities

We conducted another experiment using data acquired from a stone owl statuette through a laser range sensor. The data consists of 7648 data points distributed in a 250×162×83 voxel grid, and is shown in Fig. 5(a).

Fig. 5(b) shows the reconstruction from this data obtained with our method (using 100 iterations of curvature consistency). For comparison, we also include in Fig. 5(c) the results obtained by applying the method of Zhao *et al.* [33] on the same data. The result is smooth, but not satisfactory in terms of reconstructing the discontinuities in the data. Note how our algorithm recovers the pupil, the crease of the eye, the beak, the separation between head and body, as well as the wing, whereas the algorithm in [33] smooths them over.

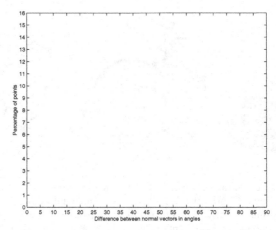

Fig. 6. Distribution of the difference in angles between the normal direction returned by curvature consistency at every data point and the normal direction on the corresponding point on the reconstructed surface of the bunny shown in Fig 7. Each bin gives the percentage of points that yield a difference falling within the bin. Median difference: 22.5°. Mean difference: 31.6°. Standard deviation: 24.2°

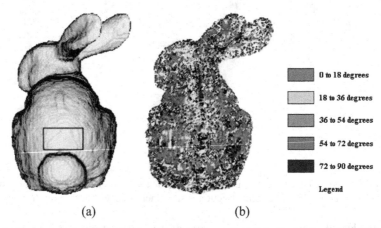

(a)   (b)

Fig. 7. (a) Reconstruction of the bunny. The box above the tail indicates the region from which the normal vectors returned by curvature consistency are shown in Fig. 8. (b) Spatial distribution of the normal vector differences in degrees. Note: figure should be viewed in color

We next present a quantitative comparison between the curvature consistency algorithm as such, and our hybrid algorithm. The purpose of this comparison is to show that our variant of the flux maximizing flow is able to overcome to some extent the drawbacks of the curvature consistency algorithm. For each data point, we compute the smallest angle formed between the normal vector returned by curvature consistency, and the corresponding normal computed on the reconstructed surface (obtained after running the flow given by Eq. (7)). Since the reconstructed surface does not necessarily pass through each data point, we compute the normal vector on the point on the reconstructed surface which is closest to the data point. Because we compute differences between orientations, not directions, the range of possible differences is constricted to $[0° - 90°]$.

A reconstruction of the Stanford bunny using our hybrid method (with one iteration of curvature consistency) is shown in Fig. 7(a). A histogram of the normal vector differences is shown in Fig. 6, and a spatial plot of the difference is shown in Fig. 7(b) (this figure should be viewed in color). It is possible to see that the agreement is good mostly everywhere except along the body midline. At these locations, one can observe the artifact described in Section 4 in Fig. 2(b), where the initial estimates of the normal vectors suddenly change their orientation from pointing outwards to pointing inwards. Due to the regularizing properties of the curvature consistency algorithm, a normal vector which is between two vectors that point in opposite directions (one inwards, the other outwards) will be set to point parallel to the surface. Hence, there is a difference of nearly 90° between the normal on the reconstructed surface, which is "correctly oriented", as seen in Fig. 7(a), and the normals returned by curvature consistency after one iteration, shown in Fig. 8. Fig. 8 shows a close-up on the normals of the bunny surface, from the region just above the tail indicated by the black box in Fig. 7(a). One can see that the normals change smoothly their orientation from pointing inwards to pointing outwards (going from left to right in the image). Due to the smooth transition in orientation, some normals are actually oriented parallel to the surface to be reconstructed. Our flux maximizing algorithm is able to overcome this drawback of the curvature consistency algorithm. Our algorithm can produce a surface that is oriented in the correct direction at locations where the normals returned by curvature consistency are not oriented correctly.

As discussed in Section 4, a drawback of our algorithm is that the resulting surface is "thick". By thinning the reconstructed surface and smoothing it further, one may obtain better structural properties on the surface. For example, one can expect an even better agreement between the orientation of the normals on the reconstructed surface and those returned by curvature consistency.

Our last experiment is designed to provide a quantitative measure of the localization of the reconstructed surface, by comparing it to a ground truth surface using a distance metric.

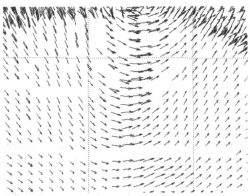

Fig. 8. A close-up on the normals on the surface of the bunny. The normals shown are taken from the back of the bunny, from the region indicated by the black box in Fig. 7(a)

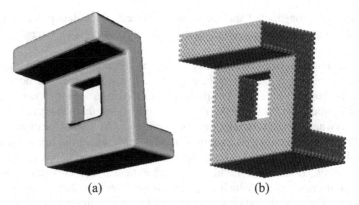

(a)   (b)

Fig. 9. (a) Ground truth surface. (b) Data sampled from the ground truth surface

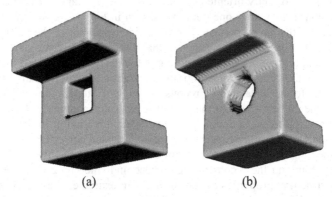

(a)   (b)

Fig. 10. (a) Reconstruction obtained through our hybrid method. $u_L = 0.9$, $Var_L = 0.13$, and $max_L = 1.4$. (b) Reconstruction achieved by the algorithm of Zhao *et al.*[33]. $u_L = 0.2$, $Var_L = 0.7$, and $max_L = 4.7$. See text for details

In the last experiment, synthetic data is used as ground truth in order to measure how well the reconstructed surface is localized with respect to the ground truth. The experiments make use of a simple distance metric L. Given a point on the ground truth surface, the metric L consists in measuring the Euclidean distance to the closest point on the reconstructed surface:

$$L = dist[G_i, R_i], \qquad (10)$$

where G_i [$i = 1 .. n$] are the points on the ground truth surface and n is the total number of points on the ground truth. For a given i, R_i is the point on the reconstructed surface closest to point G_i. Finally, *dist*[] is the Euclidean distance function. It is assumed that the ground truth surface is discretized and embedded in the same 3D grid as the reconstructed surface. It is thus possible to define a point on that surface as an individual voxel that belongs to it.

The distance metric L was applied to the reconstructions of the hemisphere shown in Fig. 3, using as ground truth the (noise free) hemispherical surface from which the data points shown in Fig. 3(a) were generated. The metric L was computed over the entire ground truth surface for the reconstructions shown in Figs. 3(c) and 3(d). For the reconstruction in Fig. 3(c), the mean of L, u_L, is 0.6, with a variance Var_L of 0.3, and a maximum value max_L of 3.7. All units are given in grid voxels, except for the units of variance. For the reconstruction in Fig. 3(d), $u_L = 1.5$, $Var_L = 0.7$, and $max_L = 4.7$. The difference between the values obtained for each reconstruction is due to the fact that, contrary to our algorithm, the algorithm in [33] is not designed to reconstruct surfaces from noisy data. Thus, our algorithm achieves a better reconstruction in the presence of noise.

The distance metric L was also applied in another experiment, presented next. The experiment makes use of the synthetic data shown in Fig. 9(b). The data consists of points sampled from the surface of a thick step with a rectangular hole in it (the original surface is shown in Fig. 9(a)), embedded in a 70×70×70 grid. Fig. 10(a) shows the reconstruction obtained from this dataset using our method, and Fig. 10(b) shows the reconstruction obtained with the algorithm of Zhao et al. [33]. One can see that our reconstruction models well the original ground truth (in particular the corners), except that it is thicker. The algorithm in [33], on the other hand, fails to recover some of the features of the surface. The evolving surface, "shrinking" over the data, wraps over the outward-oriented corners of the surface, but fails to enter the inward-oriented corners and smooths them over. If the surface is let to evolve further, it would collapse through the data points and create holes in the reconstruction, still without penetrating the inward-oriented corners. For the reconstruction shown in Fig. 10(a), $u_L = 0.9$, $Var_L = 0.13$, and $max_L = 1.4$. For the reconstruction shown in Fig. 10(b), $u_L = 0.2$, $Var_L = 0.7$, and $max_L = 4.7$. Thus, even though on average the method of Zhao et al. [33] provides a better surface localization around the (noise-free) data points, it nevertheless gives a worst-case performance which is a lot worse than the worst-case performance of our algorithm. This effect is apparent with a simple visual inspection of Figs. 9 and 10.

6   Summary and Conclusions

This paper was concerned with the problem of surface reconstruction from 3D sets of points. The paper showed that it is possible to combine the advantages of both parametric and geometric flow approaches into a single hybrid method. The hybrid method presented here is a combination of the curvature consistency algorithm and of the flux maximizing flow. It is designed to produce reconstructions of object surfaces of arbitrary topology. It is designed to preserve structure in the data (edges, ridges, and discontinuities in general), while being robust to noise. These properties are not found in standard geometric flow approaches, such as the method of Zhao et al. [33]. Our hybrid algorithm is able to overcome some of the drawbacks of curvature consistency. It also presents a new application of the flux maximizing flow.

Experimental results were presented to demonstrate these properties of the hybrid algorithm. Our algorithm has drawbacks and weaknesses that can be improved with future work. However, it does clearly demonstrate that the inclusion of local parametric information can improve the behavior of geometric flow algorithms, and that it is possible to use the topological modeling power of flow based algorithms together with the structural modeling power of parametric approaches to provide improved reconstruction results.

References

[1]   N. Amenta, M. Bern, and M. Kamvysselis. A new Voronoi-based surface reconstruction algorithm. In *Proc. SIGGRAPH'98*, pages 415-421, 1998.

[2]   C. Bajaj, F. Bernardini, and G. Xu. Automatic reconstruction of surfaces and scalar fields from 3d scans. In *Proc. SIGGRAPH'95*, pages 193-198, 1995.

[3]   A. Blake and A. Zisserman, *Visual Reconstruction*, MIT Press, Cambridge, Massachusetts, 1987.

[4]   V. Caselles, F. Catte, T. Coll, and F. Dibos. A geometric model for active contours in image processing. *Numerische Mathematik*, Vol. 66, pages 1-31, 1993.

[5]   V. Caselles, R. Kimmel, and G. Sapiro. Geodesic Active Contours. In *Proc. Int. Conf. on Computer Vision (ICCV)'95*, pages 694-699, 1995.

[6]   B. Curless and M. Levoy. A volumetric method for building complex models from range images. In *Proc. SIGGRAPH'96*, pages 303-312, 1996.

[7]   H. Q. Dinh, G. Turk, and G. Slabaugh. Reconstructing Surfaces Using Anisotropic Basis Functions. In *Proc. Int. Conf. on Computer Vision (ICCV) 2001*, pages 606-613, 2001.

[8]   H. Edelsbrunner and E. P. Mücke. Three dimensional α shapes. *ACM Trans. Graphics* 13, pages 43-72, 1994.

[9]   F. P. Ferrie, J. Lagarde, and P. Whaite. Darboux frames, snakes, and super-quadrics: Geometry from the bottom up. *IEEE Trans. on Pattern Analysis and Machine Intelligence*, Vol. 15, pages 771-784, 1993.

[10]   P. Fua and P. Sander. Reconstructing surfaces from unstructured 3d points. In *Proc. Image Understanding Workshop*, pages 615-625, 1992.

[11]   J. Gomes and A. Mojsilovic. A variational approach to recovering a manifold from sample points. In *Proc. European Conf. on Computer Vision (ECCV) 2002, LNCS 2351*, Vol 2, pages 3-17, 2002.

[12]   G. Guy and G. Medioni. Inference of Surfaces, 3D Curves, and Junctions from Sparse, Noisy, 3-D Data. *IEEE Trans. on Pattern Analysis and Machine Intelligence*, Vol. 19, pages 1265-1277, 1997.

[13]   H. Hoppe, T. DeRose, T. Duchamp, J. McDonald, and W. Stuetzle. Surface reconstruction from unorganized points. In *Proc. SIGGRAPH'92*, pages 71-78, 1992.

[14]   M. Kass, A. Witkin, and D. Terzopoulos. Snakes: active contour models. *International Journal of Computer Vision*, Vol. 1, pages 321-331, 1988.

[15]   S. Kichenassamy, A. Kumar, P. Olver, A. Tannenbaum, and A. Yezzi. Gradient flows and geometric active contour models. In *Proc. Int. Conf. on Computer Vision (ICCV)'95*, pages 810-815, 1995.

[16]   R. Malladi, J. A. Sethian, and B. C. Vemuri. Shape modeling with front propagation: A level set approach. *IEEE Trans. on Pattern Analysis and Machine Intelligence*, Vol. 17, pages 158-175, 1995.

[17]   S. Mathur and F. P. Ferrie. Edge Localisation in Surface Reconstruction Using Optimal Estimation Theory. In *Proc. Conf. on Computer Vision and Pattern Recognition (CVPR)'97*, pages 833-838, 1997.

[18] T. McInerney and D. Terzopoulos. A finite element model for 3D shape reconstruction and nonrigid motion tracking. In *Proc. Int. Conf. on Computer Vision (ICCV) '93*, pages 518-523, 1993.

[19] G. Medioni, M. S. Lee, and C. K. Tang. *A Computational Framework for Segmentation and Grouping*, Elsevier, 2000.

[20] S. J. Osher and J. A. Sethian. Fronts propagating with curvature dependent speed: Algorithms based on hamilton-jacobi formulations. *Journal of Computational Physics*, Vol. 79, pages 12-49, 1988.

[21] P. Sander and S. W. Zucker. "Inferring differential structure from 3-D images", *IEEE Trans. on Pattern Analysis and Machine Intelligence*, Vol. 12, pp. 833-854, 1990.

[22] P. Savadjiev. *Surface recovery from three-dimensional point data*. Master's thesis, Dept. of Electrical Engineering, McGill University, 2003.

[23] K. Siddiqi, Y. Bérubé-Lauzière, A. Tannenbaum, and S. W. Zucker. Area and length minimizing flows for shape segmentation. *IEEE Trans. on Image Processing*, Vol. 7, pages 433-443, 1998.

[24] F. Solina and R. Bajcsy. Recovery of Parametric Models from Range Images: The Case for Superquadrics with Global Deformations. *IEEE Trans. on Pattern Analysis and Machine Intelligence*, Vol. 12, pp. 131-147, 1990.

[25] D. Terzopoulos. Regularization of Inverse Visual Problems Involving Discontinuities. *IEEE Trans. on Pattern Analysis and Machine Intelligence*, Vol. 8, pp. 413-424, 1986.

[26] D. Terzopoulos and D. Metaxas. Dynamic 3D models with local and global deformations: deformable superquadrics. *IEEE Trans. on Pattern Analysis and Machine Intelligence*, Vol. 13, pages 703-714, 1991.

[27] G. Turk and J. F. O'Brien. Modeling with Implicit Surfaces that Interpolate. *ACM Trans. on Graphics*, Vol. 21, No. 4, pages 855-873, 2002.

[28] A. Vasilevskiy and K. Siddiqi. Flux maximizing geometric flows. *IEEE Trans. on Pattern Analysis and Machine Intelligence*, Vol. 24, pages 1565-1578, 2002.

[29] B.C. Vemuri and Y. Guo. Snake pedals: compact and versatile geometric models with physics-based control. *IEEE Trans. on Pattern Analysis and Machine Intelligence*, Vol. 22, pages 445-459, 2000.

[30] B.C. Vemuri, Y. Guo, and Z. Wang. Deformable pedal curves and surfaces: hybrid geometric active models for shape recovery. *International Journal of Computer Vision*, Vol. 44, pages 137-155, 2001.

[31] R. T. Whitaker. A level-set approach to 3D reconstruction from range data. *International Journal of Computer Vision*, Vol. 29, pages 203-231, 1998.

[32] C. Xu, A. Yezzi, and J. L. Prince. A summary of geometric level-set analogues for a general class of parametric active contour and surface models. In *Proc. IEEE Workshop on Variational and Level Set Methods*, pages 104-111, 2001.

[33] H. K. Zhao, S. Osher, and R. Fedkiw. Fast surface reconstruction using the level set method. In *Proc. IEEE Workshop on Variational and Level Set Methods*, pages 194-201, 2001.

[34] Stanford University 3D scanning repository: http://graphics.stanford.edu /data/3Dscanrep/

Geometric Analysis
of Continuous, Planar Shapes

Anuj Srivastava[1], Washington Mio[2], Eric Klassen[2], and Shantanu Joshi[3]

Department of Statistics, Florida State University, Tallahassee, FL
anuj@stat.fsu.edu
fax: 850-644-5271, phone: 850-644-8832
Department of Mathematics, Florida State University, Tallahassee, FL
Department of Electrical Engineering, Florida State University, Tallahassee, FL

Abstract. We propose two differential geometric representations of planar shapes using: (i) direction functions and (ii) curvature functions, of their boundaries. Under either representation, planar shapes are treated as elements of infinite-dimensional shape spaces. Pairwise differences between the shapes are quantified using the lengths of geodesics connecting them on the shape spaces. We specify the geometry of the two shape spaces and utilize numerical methods for finding geodesics on them. Some applications of this shape analysis are illustrated including: (i) interpolation between shapes, (ii) clustering of objects according to their shapes, and (iii) computation of intrinsic mean shapes.

1 Introduction

Shapes play a pivotal role in understanding objects in terms of their behavior and characteristics, such as their growth, health, identity, and functionality. Quantitative characterization of shapes is emerging as a major area of research, which will impact diverse applications. A major limitation in many current studies is the use of landmarks to define shapes. Shapes are encoded by a coarse, finite collection of points on the boundary of the objects, and the outcome and accuracy of the ensuing shape analysis is heavily dependent on the choices made. A more fundamental approach is to represent the continuous boundaries as curves, and then study their shape. However, this approach requires dealing with infinite-dimensional Riemannian manifolds, spaces for which the commonly used tools are not frequently available. Our goal is to develop mathematical formulations, optimization strategies, and statistical procedures to fundamentally address the outstanding issues in study of continuous, planar shapes.

The main idea presented in this paper is a computational analysis of differential geometric representations of **continuous** curves. Specifically, we: (i) derive two differential geometric representations of shapes represented by planar curves, (ii) develop algorithms for computing geodesic paths between arbitrary shapes on the resulting shape spaces, and (iii) apply this shape analysis to problems in object recognition and shape inferences. Shapes will be represented by real-valued functions that are elements of pre-defined Riemannian manifolds. In

A. Rangarajan et al. (Eds.): EMMCVPR 2003, LNCS 2683, pp. 341–   , 2003.

order to develop future statistical procedures for analyzing shapes, we will address the issues of defining and computing inferences (means, variances, etc.) on these shape spaces.

Tools for efficient shape analysis will impact many areas such as computer vision, structural genomics, medical imaging, and computational topology. The issue of representing, analyzing, learning, and interpolating amongst shapes is central to many problems in these applications. Recognition of objects using observed images is a well publicized problem in computer vision. Analyzing the shapes of contours can provide important clues about the identities of the objects in images. For instance, an algorithm in shape analysis can help in automated recognition of marine animals from their contours. This requires tools to represent and analyze shapes of planar curves. Additionally, if the shapes are inferred from noisy data, statistical formulations and inferences become important. For example, one may need to compute an average shape under a given probability model on shapes. Or, given two probability models on a shape manifold, we may need to test the hypothesis whether a given observation is from one model or the other. An example is to associate a butterfly with one of the known species using shapes of its wings.

1.1 Past Research in Shape Analysis

There have been many exemplary efforts in characterization and quantification of object shapes. D'Arcy Thompson [ ] studied shape variations in, among other things, florets, fishes, mountains, and heights of schoolboys. In recent years, the credit for initiating a mathematical theory of shapes goes to David Kendall and his colleagues [, , ,]. In addition, a rich analysis of shapes exists due to the independent works of Bookstein [ ], Mardia, Kent and colleagues [ ], and many others. They study shapes using finite landmarks (points in Euclidean space) and establish equivalences with respect to shape preserving transformations, i.e. rigid rotation and translation, and non-rigid uniform scaling. The resulting quotient space (a finite-dimensional Riemannian manifold) is called the *shape space*; different shapes correspond to different points in this space and a quantification of shapes differences is accomplished using metrics based on geodesic lengths.

Another fundamental approach is due to Grenander's characterization of shapes [,], that treats shapes as points on an infinite-dimensional, differentiable manifold, and the variation between the shapes are modeled by the action of Lie groups on this manifold. Low-dimensional groups, such as rotation, translation and scaling, change the object instances keeping the shape fixed (see for example [ ]), while the high dimensional groups, such as diffeomorphism groups, alter the shapes ([ ]. This representation forms a mathematical basis of *deformable templates* as treated in [,]. Use of diffeomorphisms in matching images (or shapes) has also been described in [, , ,]. Such tools have found remarkable success in analysis of anatomical shapes. However, one limitation is their need for embedding shapes in larger Euclidean spaces, e.g. curves in $\mathbb{R}^2$, surfaces in $\mathbb{R}^3$. After embedding, one derives diffeomorphic transformations between two Euclidean spaces such that the embedded shapes transform from one to another. Computational cost of diffeomorphic solutions is rather large, and this paper suggests more efficient algorithms based on intrinsic transformations amongst the shapes without requiring Euclidean embeddings.

In [,], Younes quantifies differences of planar (open and closed) shapes using metrics derived from the energy needed to deform a shape into another via elastic deformations that allow both stretching and bending. The consideration of both forms of elastic energy has the advantage of (infinitesimally) yielding more natural matchings between shapes, however, the shape deformations obtained in [,] applied to closed shapes may involve intermediate open shapes. The computational cost of finding the most efficient deformations through closed shapes appears to be very high. In contrast, we take only the bending energy into account, and the corresponding Riemannian metric is defined directly on a space of closed curves. This simplification allows us to analyze the geometry of the space of closed shapes and compute shortest paths (geodesics) between closed shapes in an efficient manner.

In this paper, we seek more general characterizations of shapes in the following two senses: (i) the curves under study will be viewed as a continuum, thus avoiding the difficult issue of automatically finding landmarks, and (ii) we will avoid the Euclidean embedding of shapes and will deal more intrinsically with the shape spaces. Although the curves in $\mathbb{R}^2$ can be conveniently parameterized by their arc lengths, there are still several ways of representing these parameterized curves. In this paper we study two such representations: one using the direction functions and another using the curvature functions, and analyze planar shapes on the two resulting shape spaces.

This paper is organized as follows: Section 2 describes two mathematical representations of closed, planar curves and Section 3 studies the differential geometry of the two resulting shape spaces. Section 4 presents techniques for constructing geodesics between arbitrary shapes on these manifolds while Section 5 demonstrates some applications of the resulting shape metrics.

2   Geometric Representations of Planar Shapes

We consider shapes whose contours are given by closed curves with a single component, which are viewed as closed immersed curves in the plane $\mathbb{R}^2$. Curves that differ by rigid motions (rigid rotation and translation in $\mathbb{R}^2$) and uniform scaling (of $\mathbb{R}^2$) are considered to represent the same shape, so we will need representations that are invariant to these transformations. Scaling can be quickly resolved by fixing the length of the curves to be, say 2π, but other invariances require some consideration.

There are several ways to represent planar curves. All curves $\alpha\colon [0, 2\pi] \to \mathbb{R}^2$ will be parameterized by the arc length, that is, $|\alpha'(s)| = 1$, for every s. The two coordinate functions of α are denoted as $(\alpha_1(s), \alpha_2(s))$. Associated with each α, there is a *tangent indicatrix* $v\colon [0, 2\pi] \to \mathbb{S}^1 \subset \mathbb{R}^2$ given by $v(s) = \alpha'(s)$, where $\mathbb{S}^1$ denotes the unit circle. We can write the tangent indicatrix in the form

$$v(s) = v_1(s) + iv_2(s) = e^{i\theta(s)}, \tag{1}$$

where $\theta\colon [0, 2\pi] \to \mathbb{R}$ and $i = \sqrt{-1}$. We are identifying $\mathbb{R}^2$ with the complex plane $\mathbb{C}$ in the usual way. We refer to θ as a *direction function* or *angle function* for the given curve. For each s, $\theta(s)$ gives the angle that the vector $\alpha'(s)$ makes with the positive x-axis. The *curvature* of α at $s \in [0, 2\pi]$ is defined by $\kappa(s) = \theta'(s)$. Eqn. ( ) only determines θ up to the addition of integer multiples of 2π although the function κ is clearly independent of the direction function used.

In this paper we use $\mathbb{L}^2$ to denote the space of all real-valued, square-integrable functions on $[0, 2\pi)$. Also, we will use the inner product $\langle f_1, f_2 \rangle = \int_0^{2\pi} f_1(s) f_2(s) ds$ on $\mathbb{L}^2$, and $\|f\|$ denotes the norm $\sqrt{\langle f, f \rangle}$ for an $f \in \mathbb{L}^2$.

There are at least two ways of representing planar curves: one using the direction function θ and another using the curvature function κ. We will analyze shapes under both representations.

1. **Case 1**: Shape Representation using Direction Functions

   To motivate the discussion, we first assume that all curves are smooth. Let $\theta\colon [0, 2\pi] \to \mathbb{R}$ be a (smooth) direction function of a curve α as defined in Eqn. 1. To isolate and focus on the curves of interest, we will impose the following restrictions.

   (a) Addition of a constant to the function θ results in a rotation of the corresponding curve in the plane. Since shapes are invariant to planar rotations, we restrict to those θ that have mean value of π, i.e.,

   $$\frac{1}{2\pi} \int_0^{2\pi} \theta(s)\, ds = \pi \ . \tag{2}$$

   Any constant can be used here, but we chose π to have the identity function $\theta_0(s) = s$ as the direction function associated with the unit circle.

   (b) To result in a closed curve, θ must satisfy the *closure condition*:

   $$\int_0^{2\pi} \exp(i\, \theta(s))\, ds = 0 \ . \tag{3}$$

   The regularity condition we impose on curves representing shapes is that they be absolutely continuous and admit square integrable direction functions defined almost everywhere. We define the *preshape space* $\mathcal{C}_1 \subset \mathbb{L}^2$ to be the set of all elements of $\mathbb{L}^2$ that satisfy the two conditions given above. More formally, define a map $\phi_1 = (\phi_1^1, \phi_1^2, \phi_1^3)\colon \mathbb{L}^2 \to \mathbb{R}^3$ by

   $$\phi_1^1(\theta){=}\frac{1}{2\pi} \int_0^{2\pi} \theta(s)\, ds, \quad \phi_1^2(\theta){=}\int_0^{2\pi} \cos(\theta(s))\, ds, \quad \phi_1^3(\theta){=}\int_0^{2\pi} \sin(\theta(s))\, ds. \tag{4}$$

   Then, $\mathcal{C}_1$ can be written as $\phi_1^{-1}(\pi, 0, 0)$. It can be shown that $d\phi_1$ is surjective and, by the implicit function theorem, $\mathcal{C}_1$ is a submanifold of $\mathbb{L}^2$ of codimension three.

   Remark 1. For absolutely continuous curves whose direction functions are defined almost everywhere and are square integrable, there is a well-defined assignment $[\alpha] \mapsto \theta$, where $[\ ]$ denotes pre-shape class, i.e., the class modulo scaling and rigid motions. For smooth curves, we choose smooth direction functions satisfying ( ). This is extended to more general curves using limiting techniques. In practice, we often use smooth approximations to planar shape contours.

$\mathcal{C}_1$ is termed as a pre-shape space since it is possible to have multiple elements of $\mathcal{C}_1$ representing the same shape. This variability is due to the choice of the reference point $(s = 0)$ along the curve. For $x \in \mathbb{S}^1 = [0, 2\pi]$, with 0 and 2π identified, and $\theta \in \mathcal{C}_1$, define $(x \cdot \theta)(s) = \theta(s - x \,(\mathrm{mod}\ 2\pi))$. This operation corresponds to moving the initial point $(s = 0)$ on the closed curve by a distance of x along the curve. Different placements of $s = 0$ on a curve result in different parametrizations of the curve, and hence, we call this group $(\mathbb{S}^1)$ the *re-parametrization group*. Re-parametrizations leave shapes unchanged, therefore, shapes will be represented by elements of the quotient space $\mathcal{S}_1 = \mathcal{C}_1/\mathbb{S}^1$. $\mathcal{S}_1$ is the space of planar shapes under direction-function representations. To analyze planar shapes, we will study its geometry and compute geodesics between its elements.

2. **Case 2**: Shape Representation using Curvature Functions
   Another attractive way to represent planar curves is through their curvature functions since two curves have the same curvature function if and only if they differ by a rigid motion of the plane. To isolate the curves of interest, we specify the shape space as follows.
   The *rotation index* of a curve α is the integer given by $\imath(\alpha) = \frac{\theta(2\pi) - \theta(0)}{2\pi}$, whose magnitude is independent of the direction function chosen. For simple closed curves to the first order, i.e., curves without self-intersections other than the endpoints such that $\alpha(0) = \alpha(2\pi)$ and $v(0) = v(2\pi)$, the rotation index is known to be ± 1 (see e.g. [ ], p. 396), with the sign depending on the direction of the parametrization. Therefore, we restrict our attention to the case $\imath(\alpha) = 1$. We are interested in curvature functions that represent planar closed curves of rotation index 1, i.e., curves with $\alpha(0) = \alpha(2\pi)$ and $\theta(2\pi) - \theta(0) = 2\pi$. We wish to express these two conditions in terms of the curvature of α.

   (a) Since $\theta(2\pi) - \theta(0) = \int_0^{2\pi} \kappa(s) \, ds = \langle \kappa, 1 \rangle$, the condition on κ can be written as

   $$\int_0^{2\pi} \kappa(s) \, ds = \langle \kappa, 1 \rangle = 2\pi. \tag{5}$$

   (b) If $\theta(s)$ is an angle function of a curve α with curvature κ, $\alpha(2\pi) - \alpha(0) = \int_0^{2\pi} e^{i\theta(s)} \, ds$, and using $\theta(s) = \int_0^s \kappa(x) \, dx$,

   $$\alpha(2\pi) - \alpha(0) = \int_0^{2\pi} \exp\left(i \int_0^s \kappa(x) \, dx \right) ds$$
   $$= \int_0^{2\pi} \cos\left(\int_0^s \kappa(x) \, dx \right) ds + i \int_0^{2\pi} \sin\left(\int_0^s \kappa(x) \, dx \right) ds.$$

Thus, the closure condition can be written in terms of κ as

$$\int_0^{2\pi} \cos \left(\int_0^s \kappa(x)\,dx \right) ds = 0 \text{ and } \int_0^{2\pi} \sin \left(\int_0^s \kappa(x)\,dx \right) ds = 0. \quad (6)$$

We define a pre-shape space $C_2 \subset \mathbb{L}^2$ as the collection of all curvature functions $\kappa \in \mathbb{L}^2$ satisfying conditions ( ) and ( ). Formally, define a map $\phi_2 = (\phi_2^1, \phi_2^2, \phi_2^3) : \mathbb{L}^2 \to \mathbb{R}^3$ by

$$\phi_2^1(\kappa) = \int_0^{2\pi} \kappa(s)\,ds, \quad \phi_2^2(\kappa) = \int_0^{2\pi} \cos \left(\int_0^s \kappa(x)\,dx \right) ds,$$

$$\phi_2^3(\kappa) = \int_0^{2\pi} \sin \left(\int_0^s \kappa(x)\,dx \right) ds \ . \quad (7)$$

Then, C_2 is a codimension three submanifold of $\mathbb{L}^2$ given by $\phi_2^{-1}(2\pi, 0, 0)$. The change of initial point can be viewed as an action of the unit circle $\mathbb{S}^1$ on C_2 and the shape space S_2 is the quotient space $C_2/\mathbb{S}^1$.

S_1 and S_2 are two shape spaces corresponding to two representations of planar shapes. They differ in their geometry and hence in the ensuing characterization of shapes. We will derive algorithms for analyzing shapes under both representations.

3   Geometries of Pre-shape Spaces

Our goal is to analyze shapes and perform statistical inferences on the shape spaces S_1 and S_2. An important tool in that process is a technique for computing geodesic paths between arbitrary points on the pre-shape spaces C_1 and C_2. Complicated geometries of C_1, C_2 disallow explicit expressions for geodesics. One can approximate the geodesics by drawing infinitesimal geodesic curves in the larger space, namely $\mathbb{L}^2$, and then projecting them onto C_1 and C_2, respectively. Therefore, we need a mechanism for projecting points from $\mathbb{L}^2$ to C_1 and C_2. In order to perform these projections, we will need to specify the tangent spaces, or equivalently the normal spaces, of these manifolds.

3.1   Tangent/Normals to Preshape Spaces

Rather than specifying the tangent spaces on these manifold, it is easier to describe the spaces of normals to C_1 and C_2, inside $\mathbb{L}^2$. The normal bundles in the two cases are specified using the ϕ maps as follows:

1. **Case 1:** For the map $\phi_1 : \mathbb{L}^2 \mapsto \mathbb{R}^3$ as specified in Eqn. , the directional derivative $d\phi_1$, at a point $\theta \in \mathbb{L}^2$ and in the direction of an $f \in \mathbb{L}^2$, is

$$d\phi_1^1(f) = \frac{1}{2\pi} \int_0^{2\pi} f(s)\,ds = \left\langle f, \frac{1}{2\pi} \right\rangle$$

$$d\phi_1^2(f) = -\int_0^{2\pi} \sin(\theta(s))f(s)ds = -\langle f, \sin(\theta) \rangle$$

$$d\phi_1^3(f) = \int_0^{2\pi} \cos(\theta(s))f(s)ds = \langle f, \cos(\theta) \rangle. \tag{8}$$

This calculation implies that $d\phi_1 : \mathrm{L}^2 \to \mathbb{R}^3$ is surjective, for any θ, as claimed earlier. By Eqn. , a vector $f \in \mathrm{L}^2$ is tangent to $\mathcal{C}_1$ at θ if and only if f is orthogonal to the subspace spanned by $\{1, \sin(\theta), \cos(\theta)\}$, and hence, these three functions span the normal space at $\theta \in \mathcal{C}_1$. Implicitly, the tangent space is given as: $T_\theta(\mathcal{C}_1) = \{f \in \mathrm{L}^2 | f \perp \mathrm{span}\{1, \cos(\theta), \sin(\theta)\}\}$.

2. **Case 2**: Similar to the previous case, the derivative of the map $\phi_2 : \mathrm{L}^2 \mapsto \mathbb{R}^3$ is found to be

$$d\phi_2^1(f) = \langle f, 1 \rangle, \quad d\phi_2^2(f) = \langle f, -d_2 + \alpha_2 \rangle, \quad d\phi_2^3(f) = \langle f, d_1 - \alpha_1 \rangle. \tag{9}$$

where $\alpha(s) = (\alpha_1(s), \alpha_2(s))$ is a curve with curvature function κ and $\alpha(2\pi) = (d_1, d_2)$ assuming $\alpha(0) = (0, 0)$. As earlier, $\phi_2 : \mathrm{L}^2 \to \mathbb{R}^3$ is surjective and by Eqn. , a vector $f \in \mathrm{L}^2$ is tangent to $\mathcal{C}_2$ at κ if and only if f is orthogonal to the subspace spanned by $\{1, -d_2 + \alpha_2, d_1 - \alpha_1\}$. Taking appropriate linear combinations, we conclude that $\{1, \alpha_1, \alpha_2\}$ form a basis of the normal space to $\mathcal{C}_2$ at κ. The tangent space is given by: $T_\kappa(\mathcal{C}_2) = \{f \in \mathrm{L}^2 | f \perp \mathrm{span}\{1, \alpha_1, \alpha_2\}\}$.

3.2 Projections on Preshape Spaces

Given arbitrary points in L^2, we need a mechanism for finding the nearest points on the manifolds $\mathcal{C}_1$ and $\mathcal{C}_2$. We will do so using the notion of level sets of the maps ϕ_i, for $i = 1, 2$.

1. **Case 1**: For each $b \in \mathbb{R}^3$, consider the set $\phi_1^{-1}(b) = \{\theta \in \mathrm{L}^2 | \phi_1(\theta) = b\}$. Of course, the level set for $b_1 = (\pi, 0, 0)$ is the preshape space $\mathcal{C}_1$. If we are at a point $\theta \in \mathrm{L}^2$, we define a displacement $d\theta$ that takes us closest to $\mathcal{C}_1$ moving in the direction orthogonal to the level set of θ. Since $d\phi_1 : \mathrm{L}^2 \to \mathbb{R}^3$ is surjective for any θ, it maps the normal space to the level set of θ isomorphically onto $\mathbb{R}^3$. Thus, if $d\theta$ is a normal vector at θ such that $\phi_1(\theta) + d\phi_1(d\theta)$ equals the desired point $b_1 \in \mathbb{R}^3$, $d\theta$ can be approximated to first order as follows. Let J_1 be the Jacobian matrix of ϕ_1 restricted to the 3-dimensional normal space to the level set of θ, which is given in the basis $\{1, \sin\theta, \cos\theta\}$ and the standard basis of $\mathbb{R}^3$ by the 3×3 matrix

$$J_1 = \begin{bmatrix} \langle \frac{1}{2\pi}, 1 \rangle & \langle \frac{1}{2\pi}, \sin(\theta) \rangle & \langle \frac{1}{2\pi}, \cos(\theta) \rangle \\ -\langle \sin(\theta), 1 \rangle & -\langle \sin(\theta), \sin(\theta) \rangle & -\langle \sin(\theta), \cos(\theta) \rangle \\ \langle \cos(\theta), 1 \rangle & \langle \cos(\theta), \sin(\theta) \rangle & \langle \cos(\theta), \cos(\theta) \rangle \end{bmatrix}. \tag{10}$$

If $r_1(\theta) = b_1 - \phi_1(\theta)$ is the residual vector, the desired vector $d\theta$ is given by $d\theta = \beta_1 + \beta_2 \sin(\theta) + \beta_3 \cos(\theta)$, where $\beta = J_1(\theta)^{-1} r_1(\theta)$. We implement this by updating the curve using $\theta = \theta + d\theta$, and iterating until the norm $|r_1(\theta)|$ converges to zero. This projection is denoted by $\mathbb{P}_1 : \mathrm{L}^2 \mapsto \mathcal{C}_1$.

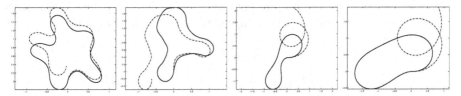

Fig. 1. Example of projecting curves onto preshape spaces. Firs two panels show the case of projections onto C_1 while the last two panels are for C_2. Broken lines denote the original curves and solid lines plot the projected curves

2. **Case 2**: The appropriate displacement $d\kappa$ is found using the 3×3 Jacobian matrix

$$J_2 = \begin{bmatrix} 2\pi & \langle 1, \alpha_1 \rangle & \langle 1, \alpha_2 \rangle \\ -2\pi d_2 + \langle 1, \alpha_2 \rangle - \langle d_2, \alpha_1 \rangle + \langle \alpha_2, \alpha_1 \rangle & -\langle d_2, \alpha_2 \rangle + \langle \alpha_2, \alpha_2 \rangle \\ 2\pi d_1 + \langle 1, \alpha_1 \rangle & \langle d_1, \alpha_1 \rangle - \langle \alpha_1, \alpha_1 \rangle & \langle d_1, \alpha_2 \rangle - \langle \alpha_1, \alpha_2 \rangle \end{bmatrix} \quad (11)$$

and the residual vector $r_2(\kappa) = b_2 - \phi_2(\kappa)$, where $b_2 = (2\pi, 0, 0)$. Set $d\kappa = \beta_1 + \beta_2\alpha_1 + \beta_3\alpha_2$, where $\beta = J_2(\kappa)^{-1}r_2(\kappa)$. Update using $\kappa = \kappa + d\kappa$ and iterate till $|r_2(\kappa)|$ becomes small enough. Denote this projection by $\mathbb{P}_2 : \mathbb{L}^2 \mapsto C_2$.

Shown in Figure   are some examples of projecting curves in the larger spaces to the preshape spaces. The two leftmost panels are examples of projections from $\mathbb{L}^2$ onto C_1 and the two rightmost panels are examples of projections from $\mathbb{L}^2$ onto C_2. Broken lines show the curves for the original points in $\mathbb{L}^2$ while the solid lines show the projected points.

3.3   Geodesics on Preshape Spaces

The next step is to construct shortest paths by numerically approximating geodesic flows on the preshape spaces. We will approximate geodesics on C_1 and C_2 by taking small increments in the larger space $\mathbb{L}^2$, and then projecting them using $\mathbb{P}_1$ and $\mathbb{P}_2$.

1. **Case 1**: For a point $\theta \in C_1$, let $f \in T_\theta(C_2)$ be a tangent direction. We want to generate a geodesic path (generated by a one-parameter flow) starting from θ and in the direction f; denote this flow by $\Psi(\theta, t, f)$ where t is the time parameter. We will compute this flow for discrete times $t = \delta, 2\delta, 3\delta, \ldots$, for a small $\delta > 0$. Setting $\Psi(\theta, 0, f) = \theta$, take the first increment to reach $\theta + \delta f$ in $\mathbb{L}^2$ and apply the projection $\mathbb{P}_1$ to this point. Set $\Psi(\theta, \delta, f) = \mathbb{P}_1(\theta + \delta f)$ to get the next point along the geodesic. Iterating this process provides successive points along the geodesic Ψ in C_1. One remaining issue is that we need to transport the tangent vector f to the new points along the geodesic to perform iterations. This can be achieved by projecting f to the tangent

spaces at these points. For example, let $\tilde{\theta}$ be a point along the geodesic path and we want to find $\tilde{f}$ that is tangent to $\mathcal{C}_1$ at $\tilde{\theta}$ and is a parallel transport of f. This can be accomplished using:

$$\tilde{f} = \|f\| \frac{g}{\|g\|}, \quad \text{where} \quad g = f - \sum_{k=1}^{3} \langle f, h_k \rangle \, h_k \tag{12}$$

and where h_ks form an orthonormal basis of the space $\text{span}\{1, \cos(\tilde{\theta}), \sin(\tilde{\theta})\}$. An algorithm summarizing the steps for constructing a geodesic path on $\mathcal{C}_1$ is as follows:

Algorithm 1 *Start with a point $\theta \in \mathcal{C}_1$ and a direction $f \in T_\theta(\mathcal{C}_1)$. Set $j = 0$ and $\Psi(\theta, j, f) = \theta$, and choose a small $\delta > 0$.*
(a) Set $j = j + 1$. Compute the increment $\Psi(\theta, (j - 1)\delta, f) + \delta f$ and set $\Psi(\theta, j\delta, f) = \mathbb{P}_1(\Psi(\theta, (j - 1)\delta, f) + \delta f)$.
(b) Transport f to the new point by using $\Psi(\theta, j\delta, f)$ for $\tilde{\theta}$ in Eqn. . Go to step (a) with $f = \tilde{f}$.

An inspection of the differential equation satisfied by geodesics shows that the proposed numerical scheme for constructing geodesics with prescribed initial conditions is just (a slight variant of) the classical Euler's method applied to the geodesic flow on pre-shape spaces. Alternately, one can use a higher order Runge-Kutta method with adaptive step-size control, for more robust and precise numerical solutions.

2. **Case 2**: The construction of geodesics on $\mathcal{C}_2$ is similar to the previous case with the direction functions replaced by the curvature functions. The only exception is that in Eqn.   the h_ks form an orthonormal basis of the space $\text{span}\{1, \alpha_1, \alpha_2\}$, where α is the curve generated by the curvature function $\tilde{\kappa}$ at which the tangent is being transported.

3.4   Geodesics on Shape Spaces

The shape spaces $\mathcal{S}_1$ and $\mathcal{S}_2$ are orbit spaces of the action of the re-parametrization group $\mathbb{S}^1$ on $\mathcal{C}_1$ and $\mathcal{C}_2$, respectively. We define a metric on $\mathcal{S}_i$ $(i = 1, 2)$ by declaring the distance between two points to be the minimum distance between points on the corresponding orbits in $\mathcal{C}_i$, with distances in $\mathcal{C}_i$ given by lengths of minimal paths. These length minimizing curves in $\mathcal{C}_i$ descend to "geodesics" in the shape space $\mathcal{S}_i$.

1. **Case 1**: If $\theta_a, \theta_b \in \mathcal{S}_1$, and $\tilde{\theta}_a, \tilde{\theta}_b \in \mathcal{C}_1$ are pre-shapes representing θ_a and θ_b,

$$d(\theta_a, \theta_b) = \min_{\alpha, \beta \in \mathbb{S}^1} \{ d(\alpha \cdot \tilde{\theta}_a, \beta \cdot \tilde{\theta}_b) \}.$$

Since the re-parametrization group acts on $\mathcal{C}_1$ by isometries, $d(\theta_a, \theta_b) = \min_{\beta \in \mathbb{S}^1} \{ d(\tilde{\theta}_a, \beta \cdot \tilde{\theta}_b) \}$. Thus, to find a geodesic realizing the distance between θ_a and θ_b, it suffices to consider geodesics in $\mathcal{C}_1$ starting at $\tilde{\theta}_a$ and ending at a preshape in the orbit of $\tilde{\theta}_b$. First observe that any such minimal length geodesic must be orthogonal to every $\mathbb{S}^1$-orbit it meets, for otherwise, we can deform it into curves of shorter length satisfying the required boundary conditions. Although we do not present full details, it is easy to describe such deformation. Let the geodesic be given by $\tilde{\theta}(s,t) = \tilde{\theta}^t(s)$, where s and t are the arc-length and "time" parameters, respectively. For each t, $\tilde{\theta}_t$ is the tangent vector to the given path in $\mathcal{C}_1$. If $\nu^t(s)$ is the orthogonal projection of $\tilde{\theta}_t$ onto the tangent direction to the $\mathbb{S}^1$-orbit of $\tilde{\theta}^t$, slightly deforming each $\tilde{\theta}^t$ along its $\mathbb{S}^1$-orbit proportionally to $-\nu^t(s)$, we shorten the length of the curve. Furthermore, one can show that if a geodesic is orthogonal to a single $\mathbb{S}^1$-orbit, it is actually orthogonal to every $\mathbb{S}^1$-orbit it meets. In practice, this orthogonality condition can be imposed by observing that the tangent space $T_{\tilde{\theta}}(\mathbb{S}^1 \cdot \tilde{\theta})$ to the $\mathbb{S}^1$-orbit at $\tilde{\theta}$ is the 1-dimensional subspace of $T_{\tilde{\theta}}(\mathcal{C}_1)$ spanned by $\{\tilde{\theta}'\}$ (this discussion only applies to preshapes that have square integrable first derivative). The algorithm for constructing geodesics in $\mathcal{S}_1$ – or more precisely, geodesics in $\mathcal{C}_1$ satisfying the orthogonality condition – is identical to Algorithm , except that in Eqn. the vector g is now given by $g = f - \sum_{k=1}^{4} \langle f, h_k \rangle h_k$, where $\{h_k\}$ is an orthonormal basis of the space span$\{1, \cos(\tilde{\theta}), \sin(\tilde{\theta}), \tilde{\theta}'\}$.

2. **Case 2**: The construction of geodesics on $\mathcal{S}_2$ is similar, except that the basis of $T_\kappa(\mathbb{S}^1 \cdot \kappa)$ is given by $\{\kappa'\}$.

4   Numerical Methods for Finding Geodesics

So far we have described a technique for approximating geodesic paths in the two shape spaces. However, the main task of finding a geodesic path between any two given shapes still remains. This problem can be stated as follows:

Problem Statement: Given two shapes $\theta_1, \theta_2 \in \mathcal{C}_1$, or $\kappa_1, \kappa_2 \in \mathcal{C}_2$, how does one construct a geodesic that is always orthogonal to $\mathbb{S}^1$-orbits and it starts from one shape and reaches the other, or a re-parametrization of the other, in unit time?

Consider the case of $\mathcal{S}_1$ first. Let Ψ be the desired one-parameter flow from θ_1 to θ_2. For any $f \in T_{\theta_1}(\mathcal{C}_1)$ such that $f \perp \theta_1'$, the algorithm described in Section 3.4 generates a discrete geodesic path in $\mathcal{S}_1$. Therefore, the real issue is to find that appropriate direction $f \in T_{\theta_1}(\mathcal{C}_1)$ such that $f \perp \theta_1'$ and a geodesic in that direction passes through the $\mathbb{S}^1$-orbit of θ_2. In other words, the problem is to solve for an $f \in T_{\theta_1}(\mathcal{C}_1)$ such that $f \perp \theta_1'$, $\Psi(\theta_1, 0, f) = \theta_1$ and $\Psi(\theta_1, 1, f) = s \cdot \theta_2$, for some $s \in \mathbb{S}^1$. One can treat the search for this appropriate direction as an optimization problem over the $T_{\theta_1}(\mathcal{C}_1)$. The cost function for minimizing is given by the functional $H[f] = \inf_{s \in \mathbb{S}^1} \|\Psi(\theta_1, 1, f) - (s \cdot \theta_2)\|^2$, and we are looking for that $f \in T_{\theta_1}(\mathcal{C}_1)$ for which: (i) $\langle f, \theta' \rangle$, $H[f]$ are zero and (ii) $\|f\|$ is minimum among all such tangents. Since the space $T_{\theta_1}(\mathcal{C}_1)$ is infinite dimensional, this optimization is not straightforward.

One idea is to use a finite-dimensional approximation of the elements of $T_{\theta_1}(\mathcal{C}_1)$ to find the optimal direction. Since $f \in \mathbb{L}^2$, it has a Fourier decomposition and we can solve the optimization problem over a finite number of Fourier coefficients. Approximate any $f \in T_{\theta_1}(\mathcal{C}_1)$ according to $f(s) \approx \sum_{n=0}^{m}(a_n \cos(ns) + b_n \sin(ns))$, for a large positive integer m. Under this approximation the cost function modifies to: $\tilde{H} : \mathbb{R}^{2m+1} \mapsto \mathbb{R}_+$,

$$\tilde{H}(a,b) = \inf_{\tau \in \mathbb{S}^1} \|\Psi(\theta_1, 1, f_1(s)) - (\tau \cdot \theta_2)\|^2 , \text{ where } f_1 = f - \langle f, \theta'_1 \rangle \theta'_1,$$

$$\text{and } f(s) = \sum_{n=0}^{m} a_n \cos(ns) + b_n \sin(ns) .$$

To minimize $\tilde{H}$ we use a gradient technique by approximating the gradients according to: for $\epsilon > 0$ small

$$\frac{\partial \tilde{H}}{\partial a_n} \approx \frac{\tilde{H}(a + \epsilon e_n, b) - \tilde{H}(a,b)}{\epsilon} \text{ and } \frac{\partial \tilde{H}}{\partial b_n} \approx \frac{\tilde{H}(a, b + \epsilon e_n) - \tilde{H}(a,b)}{\epsilon}, \quad (13)$$

where $e_n \in \mathbb{R}^{m+1}$ is a unit vector with one in n^{th} location and zeros everywhere else.

Algorithm 2 *For a given initial shape θ_1 and the target shape θ_2, let $a, b \in \mathbb{R}^{m+1}$ be arbitrary initial coefficients.*

1. *Set $f_1 = \langle f, \theta'_1 \rangle \theta'_1$ where $f(s) = \sum_{n=0}^{m} a_n \cos(ns) + b_n \sin(ns)$.*
2. *Find the re-parametrization element $\tau \in \mathbb{S}^1$ that minimizes the quantity $\|\Psi(\theta_1, 1, f_1) - (\tau \cdot \theta_2)\|^2$.*
3. *For $n = 0, 1, \ldots, m$ compute $\frac{\partial \tilde{H}}{\partial a_n}$ and $\frac{\partial \tilde{H}}{\partial b_n}$ according to Eqn.   .*
4. *Update vectors a and b using small $\Delta > 0$:*

$$a = a - \Delta(\nabla_a \tilde{H}), \quad b = b - \Delta(\nabla_b \tilde{H}) .$$

5. *If not converged, return to Step 1.*

Shown in Figure   are two examples of shape matching using this algorithm. The leftmost curve in each picture corresponds to θ_1 and the rightmost curve is generated by the direction function θ_2. Drawn in between are nine curves denoting nine equally spaced points along the geodesic path connecting θ_1 and θ_2 in $\mathcal{S}_1$. Using $m = 75$ coefficients, and 100 (equispaced) samples along the curves, it takes two to three seconds in matlab on a Pentium III to find a geodesic between two shapes. The approach for computing geodesics in $\mathcal{S}_2$ is similar after using a Fourier decomposition of $f \in T_{\kappa_1}(\mathcal{C}_2)$. Shown in Figure   are two examples of the geodesic paths in $\mathcal{S}_2$.

5   Applications of Shape Analysis

In this section, we demonstrate the strengths of this shape analysis in some practical situations. Before we describe these applications, we discuss some implementation issues:

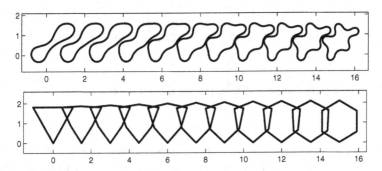

Fig. 2. Evolution of curves corresponding to a geodesic path in $\mathcal{S}_1$ connecting θ_1 (leftmost) to θ_2 (rightmost)

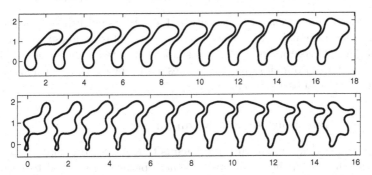

Fig. 3. Evolution of shapes along a geodesic path in $\mathcal{S}_2$

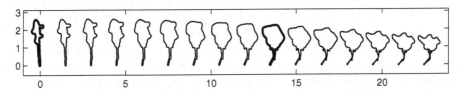

Fig. 4. Interpolation and extrapolation on the shape space given the two shapes drawn in bold lines

1. Shapes to be analyzed are most commonly available in the form of a set of coordinates in $\mathbb{R}^2$. Since the two representations utilized here require arclength parameterizations, we need to find a continuous function $\alpha(s)$ that matches the given coordinates. This can be achieved by first finding the direction function at the given points and then fitting a smooth function $\theta(s)$. The degree of smoothness has to be balanced with the computational cost of this fitting. Once we have the direction function $\theta(s)$, the curvature function $\kappa(s)$ can be computed using finite differences.

Fig. 5. Right panel displays the intrinsic mean shape of the other four shapes

2. In implementation, the inner product between functions is approximated as follows: $\langle f_1, f_2 \rangle = \int_0^{2\pi} f_1(s)f_2(s)ds \approx \sum_{i=1}^T f_1(i\delta)f_2(i\delta)\delta$, where $\delta = 2\pi/T$.
3. Even though the shapes are analyzed using the direction functions and the curvature functions, we need to compute the coordinate function for displaying them. One can use either $\alpha(0) = (0,0)$ or $\frac{1}{2\pi}\int_0^{2\pi} \alpha(s)ds = 0$.

To demonstrate our ideas, we have utilized a database of fish shapes generated by the researchers at Univ of Surrey, UK [,]. This database consists of the (coordinates of) contour points of fish shapes extracted from images. There are a total of 1100 contours for different species of marine creatures although we will use only a small subset of them here.

5.1 Shape Interpolation and Mean Shapes

An important advantage of this approach is that it provides shortest paths between the shapes on the shape spaces. These paths can be used to interpolate between shapes, extrapolate a shape change, and compute a mean shape under a probability distribution on shapes. Furthermore, it can lead to sophisticated statistical inferences such as confidence intervals, hypothesis testing, and Markov chain Monte Carlo type tools on such shape spaces. In this paper we demonstrate the use of geodesic flows in shape interpolation and mean evaluation. Shown in Figure is a geodesic path in $\mathcal{S}_1$ between the two shapes drawn in bold lines. Shapes in between the two can be used to interpolate between them, and the shapes on the right can be used to predict future shapes along that path.

Shown in Figure is an example of computing intrinsic means of the four shapes in $\mathcal{S}_1$ by adapting an algorithm described in [ ].

5.2 Clustering of Objects Using Shapes

In many applications, the goal is to classify and cluster objects according to their shapes. Examples include object classification, shape-based database search, and object detection in images. Using Algorithm , we first compute a geodesic path between any two shapes in $\mathcal{S}_1$ and then compute the norm of the tangent vector to denote the geodesic length. We have computed this geodesic length pairwise for a subset of the database containing 25 fishes shown in Figure . In this implementation, we have used 75 Fourier components to approximate the tangent vector f. To illustrate the task of clustering objects using this metric, we have

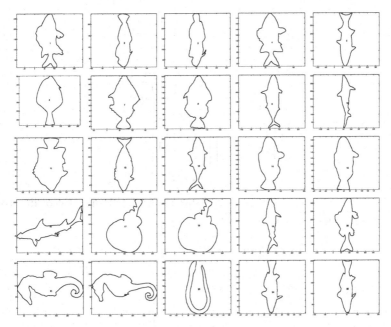

Fig. 6. 25 sample fish contours taken from the Fish Database used here for shape studies. The shapes are numbered from top left to bottom right with successive numbers along the rows

applied the dendrogram clustering algorithm supplied with Matlab. The result, shown in the Figure , seems to agree with the perceptual similarities between the fishes. For instance, Fishes 24 and 25 are paired together, and so are Fishes 10 and 19, Fishes 7 and 8, and Fishes 17 and 18, respectively. Also, Fish 23 is most different in shape from the others according to this metric. One anomaly in this clustering seems to be between Fishes 14 and 15, as they are not paired together despite the similarity in their shapes.

5.3 Shape Recognition

Geodesic lengths on shape spaces provide metrics for shape recognition. Consider a dataset, or a training set, of pre-categorized shapes and a set of new test shapes. Using the nearest neighbor criterion, and finding the nearest shapes in the training set, one can assign a shape category to a test shape. Shown in Fig are some examples of the nearest neighbors for five test shapes (top panels). The middle and the bottom panels display the corresponding nearest and the second nearest shapes in the training set, respectively. The training set consisted of 70 shapes from the fish database.

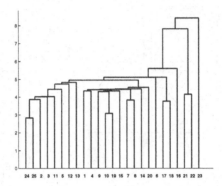

Fig. 7. Dendrogram clustering of 25 fishes shown in Figure   according to their shapes using geodesic lengths in $\mathcal{S}_1$

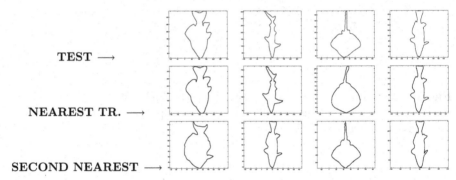

Fig. 8. Recognition of shapes using training data. Top panels are test shapes, middle panels are nearest training shapes, and the bottom panels are the second nearest

6 Conclusion

We have presented two geometric representations of the shapes of planar, closed curves. After forcing shape invariances, we obtain two shape spaces in which elements denote planar shapes. Difference between two shapes are computed using the geodesic paths on these shape spaces. In addition to generating shape metrics, these techniques are useful in computing intrinsic means of shapes, interpolating and extrapolating between shapes, and future statistical hypothesis testing for shape recognition.

References

[1] Y. Amit, U. Grenander, and M. Piccioni. Structural image restoration through deformable templates. *J. American Statistical Association*, 1991.

[2] F. L. Bookstein. Size and shape spaces for landmark data in two dimensions. *Statistical Science*, 1:181–242, 1986.

[3] M. P. Do Carmo. *Differential Geometry of Curves and Surfaces*. Prentice Hall, Inc., 1976.

[4] I. L. Dryden and K. V. Mardia. *Statistical Shape Analysis*. John Wiley & Son, 1998.

[5] C. R. Goodall. Procrustes methods in the statistical analysis of shapes. *Journal of Royal Statistical Society B*, 53:285–339, 1991.

[6] U. Grenander. *General Pattern Theory*. Oxford University Press, 1993.

[7] U. Grenander and M. I. Miller. Computational anatomy: An emerging discipline. *Quarterly of Applied Mathematics*, LVI(4):617–694, 1998.

[8] U. Grenander, M. I. Miller, and A. Srivastava. Hilbert-schmidt lower bounds for estimators on matrix lie groups for atr. *IEEE Transactions on PAMI*, 20(8):790–802, 1998.

[9] David G. Kendall. Shape manifolds, procrustean metrics and complex projective spaces. *Bulletin of London Mathematical Society*, 16:81–121, 1984.

[10] H. Le. Locating frechet means with application to shape spaces. *Advances in Applied Probability*, 33(2):324–338, 2001.

[11] H. L. Le and D. G. Kendall. The riemannian structure of euclidean shape spaces: a novel environment for statistics. *Annals of Statistics*, 21(3):1225–1271, 1993.

[12] M. I. Miller and L. Younes. Group actions, homeomorphisms, and matching: A general framework. *International Journal of Computer Vision*, 41(1/2):61–84, 2002.

[13] F. Mokhtarian, S. Abbasi, and J. Kittler. Efficient and robust shape retrieval by shape content through curvature scale space. In *Proceedings of First International Conference on Image Database and MultiSearch*, pages 35–42, 1996.

[14] F. Mokhtarian, S. Abbasi, and J. Kittler. Robust and efficient shape indexing through curvature scale space. In *Proceedings of Sixth British Machine Vision Conference*, pages 53–62, 1996.

[15] Christopher G. Small. *The Statistical Theory of Shape*. Springer, 1996.

[16] D. W. Thompson. *On Growth and Form: The Complete Revised Edition*. Dover, 1992.

[17] A. Trouve. Diffemorphisms groups and pattern matching in image analysis. *International Journal of Computer Vision*, 28(3):213–221, 1998.

[18] L. Younes. Computable elastic distance between shapes. *SIAM Journal of Applied Mathematics*, 58:565–586, 1998.

[19] L. Younes. Optimal matching between shapes via elastic deformations. *Journal of Image and Vision Computing*, 17(5/6):381–389, 1999.

Curvature Vector Flow to Assure Convergent Deformable Models for Shape Modelling*

Debora Gil and Petia Radeva

Computer Vision Center (CVC), Edifici O, Campus UAB
08193 Bellaterra, Barcelona, Spain
{debora,petia}@cvc.uab.es
fax/tel: 93 581 16 70 /93 581 30 36

Abstract. Poor convergence to concave shapes is a main limitation of snakes as a standard segmentation and shape modelling technique. The gradient of the external energy of the snake represents a force that pushes the snake into concave regions, as its internal energy increases when new inflexion points are created. In spite of the improvement of the external energy by the gradient vector flow technique, highly non convex shapes can not be obtained, yet. In the present paper, we develop a new external energy based on the geometry of the curve to be modelled. By tracking back the deformation of a curve that evolves by minimum curvature flow, we construct a distance map that encapsulates the natural way of adapting to non convex shapes. The gradient of this map, which we call curvature vector flow (CVF), is capable of attracting a snake towards any contour, whatever its geometry. Our experiments show that, any initial snake condition converges to the curve to be modelled in optimal time.

1   Introduction

Shape modelling arises in many fields of computer vision and graphics [, ,], to mention just a few. The most efficient way of producing smooth models of shapes is by means of a snake [, ,]. Snakes are curves that minimize an energy functional. In classic snakes [ ], this functional splits into an external energy, depending on the set of points to be approached, and an internal one that serves to smoothly interpolate the curve to be modelled when no information is available. Geodesic snakes [,] blend both the internal and external energies and seek for the curve of minimal length in a Riemannian manifold with the external energy as metric. In any case the minimum of the energy functional is obtained by gradient descent of an initial contour. Hence the definition of the external energy is crucial for a successful model of the shape.

Distance maps are one of the most used external energies, simple and quick to compute. Curves of level zero correspond to the contour of interest and the snake moves in the direction opposite to the gradient of the distance map. Unfortunately, the geometry of the curve of level zero may produce maps with null

---

* This work is partially supported by the "Ministerio de Ciencia y Tecnologia" grant
TIC2000-1635-C04-04.

A. Rangarajan et al. (Eds.): EMMCVPR 2003, LNCS 2683, pp. 357–   , 2003.

gradients along some curves. The snake gets caught in these local minima and produces a wrong model of the shape. There are several ways of addressing this problem. We can initialize the snake close to the final shape so that we make sure that it is far away from these local minima. This is certainly not a very elegant approach for automated procedures. Some authors [,] suggest searching for the global minimum of the energy, but global minimums of real images are hard to find in an efficient way without manual intervention. The most sensible solution up to now consists in using the Gradient Vector Flow (GVF) or the Generalized Gradient Vector Flow (GGVF) to obtain a regularized version of the gradient of the external energy [ ], [,] that only admits isolated zeros. The technique succeeds in producing smooth gradients in the whole image that guide the snake to the final contour for a large variety of geometries. However the vector field obtained with GVF may have saddle points which also trap the snake. No technique will remove saddle points because they are inherent to the distance map. We need a new definition of the distance map.

The novelty of this work is that we study distance maps from a geometric point of view, which clearly shows the limitations of the current external forces. By means of the formulas developed, we build a new distance map to closed contours.

An analysis of the Euclidean distance map points out that propagating a shape with constant speed produces shocks in the map that difficult using its gradient as external force in the snake equation. In this paper we propose a distance map that takes into account the local geometry of the closed contour we want to approach. A back-tracking of the evolution of the contour of level zero by minimum curvature flow [ ] is the natural geometric way of converging to non-convex regions. Since the PDE associated to this evolution is of elliptic type, we can assure that propagation of non convex regions will not develop shocks during the process. In this manner we build a distance map having the contour of level zero as unique local minimum. The gradient of the map, called Curvature Vector Flow, is capable of attracting any initial interior or exterior curve towards the contour of interest, independently of its geometric features.

Experiments done on synthetic shapes and contours extracted from real images, show that CVF adapts snakes to any geometry of the curve to be modelled, provided the initial snake lies completely either in the interior or exterior of the shape to model. Comparing to other external forces (GVF and Euclidean distance map), not only is CVF the most efficient and accurate but also the graphs of the snake total energy present a smoother asymptotic behavior. This minimizes the snake oscillation in a neighborhood of the equilibrium state and provides CVF with a stop criterion either in terms of the magnitude of the energy or in terms of stabilization of the iterative numerical scheme. Shapes that CVF yields represent accurate smooth models of the contours. Further, using B-spline parametric snakes a compact representation is obtained.

The paper is organized as follows: the theoretical analysis of shape propagation is given in Section ; advantages and drawbacks of the Euclidean distance map and GVF are described in Sections   and   , respectively; the formu-

lation of CVF in Section   . Applications to shape modelling are presented in
Section   and, finally, Section   is devoted to conclusions and further research.

2   Shape Propagation

Distance maps encode the evolution of the curve of level zero, γ_0, under a geometric flow defined, generically, by a parabolic PDE:

$$\gamma_t(u,t) = \beta(u,t)\overrightarrow{n} \ . \tag{1}$$

with initial condition $\gamma(u,0) = \gamma_0(u)$ a closed curve and $\overrightarrow{n}$ denoting the
unit inward normal. Each level curve of a given distance, d, corresponds to the
solution to ( ) at time $t = d$. This point of view, reduces the study of distance
maps to the analysis of the propagation of the zero level curve governed by means
of a geometric flow. We will use the machinery developed in [ ] in order to study
the drawbacks of the Euclidean distance map and define a more natural way of
propagating shapes that will produce distance maps capable of guiding a snake
to any closed curve. Since a plane curve is defined, up to rigid transformations,
by its unit tangent, a pleasant way of handling geometric flows is by means of the
equation of the angle of the unit tangent, θ, in the arc length, s, parameterization.
The advantage of this formulation is that we reduce the study of the properties
of ( ) to the analysis of a single equation, so that standard results on PDE's can
be applied. The parabolic PDE for θ when the curve solves ( ) is given by:

$$\theta_t(s,t) = \partial_s(\beta) + \left(\int_0^s \beta\theta_s ds \right) \theta_s \ . \tag{2}$$

with initial condition the angle of the unit tangent, θ_0, of the initial curve.
An important remark is that the first order term arises due to the change of
parameter, and, hence, it is present in any geometric flow.

2.1   Euclidean Distance Maps

In Euclidean distance maps, propagation of the initial curve, γ_0, is equivalent to
mathematical morphology with a circle of radius 1 as structural element. Erosion
corresponds to the inward propagation and dilation to the outward one. Hence
the geometric flow associated [ ] [ ] is given by:

$$\gamma_t = \pm\overrightarrow{n} \ .$$

The minus sign corresponds to the dilation and the plus to the erosion. Since,
in this case, $\beta = \pm 1$ is constant, the corresponding equation ( ) for θ is simply:

$$\theta_t(s,t) = \pm(\int_0^s \theta_s ds)\theta_s \ . \tag{3}$$

This equation is a first order non-linear PDE that is solved [ ] by means of the
computation of the characteristic curves, that is, those curves in the s-t plane,

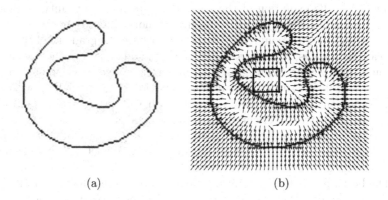

Fig. 1. Highly non-convex curve (a) and gradient of Euclidean distance map (b)

$\alpha(u)$, such that the function solving ( ) keeps constant, that is $\theta(\alpha(u)) \equiv const$. Assuming this last condition for $\alpha(u) = (s(u), t(u))$, we obtain that:

$$0 = \frac{d}{du}(\theta(s(u), t(u)) = t_u\theta_t + s_u\theta_s = t_u(\pm(\int_0^s \theta_s ds)\theta_s) + s_u\theta_s = (\pm t_u\theta + s_u)\theta_s .$$

Since the equality holds for all points in the characteristic, we have that α solves the first order PDE:

$$\pm t_u\theta + s_u = 0$$

And, consequently, its tangent vector fulfils the following system of ODE's:

$$\left.\begin{array}{rcl} t_u &=& 1 \\ s_u &=& \pm\theta \end{array}\right\}$$

Therefore, the characteristics through a point $(s_0, 0)$ are parameterized as:

$$\alpha(u) = (\pm\theta_0 u + s_0, u) .$$

where θ_0 equals $\theta_0(s_0, 0)$ and is constant along the characteristics.

This means that we have straight lines in a plane which slopes, $\theta_0(s_0)$, do not need to be a monotonous function of the curve parameter. Variation of the characteristics slope along the initial curve is given by the derivative of the angle θ_0'. Since the initial curve is parameterized by its arc length, we have that the sign of the curvature of the initial curve determines whether the slopes increase or decrease. For convex curves, characteristics slope are either increasing (inward propagation) or decreasing (outward propagation) along the curve. Hence, two different characteristics never cross during the curve propagation and the distance map is a smooth map. However, for non-convex shapes, changes in the monotonicity of the slopes induced by the curve inflexion points make characteristics meet each other in finite positive time (squared region of fig. (b)) .

At this time, the evolution of the angle develops a discontinuity or shock and the corresponding curve is not smooth any more. Indeed shocks in the angle domain translate into points or, even, curves where the gradient of the distance map cancels, that is, they correspond to crests and valleys of the distance map. Although this property is used in computer vision for extraction of shape skeletons [,], it constitutes a main hindrance for shape modelling with snakes. Highly non-convex shapes (see fig. (a)) with the angle turning around more than π between two consecutive inflexion points produce distance maps with crests of positive slope (fig. (a)). These crests and valleys induce local minima in the snake energy functional that our deformable model, which seeks for zeros of the energy gradient, will never cross.

The best approach up to our knowledge to overcome the null gradient problem along curves is by means of the use of a regularized gradient (that only cancels at isolated points) as external force. Such regularization is obtained by means of the GVF [ ] or its generalized faster version GGVF [ ].

2.2   Gradient Vector Flow and Saddle Points

The GVF/GGVF technique [,] consists in substituting the gradient of the external energy, ∇E_e, by the vector field $v(x)$ that is the steady-state of the reaction-diffusion vector equation:

$$u_t = g(|\nabla E_e|)\nabla u - h(|\nabla E_e|)(u - \nabla E_e) \text{ with } u(x,0) = \nabla E_e \qquad (4)$$

The weighting functions, $g(\cdot)$ and $h(\cdot)$ are monotonically non-increasing and non-decreasing functions of the norm $|\nabla E_e|$, respectively. An important remark is that $h(0) = 0$. In this manner, the equilibrium vector field smoothly extends ∇E_e, thanks to the Laplacian, keeping close to the original gradient when it is significant enough. It can be used either to extend the edge map to the whole image or to regularize a gradient of a distance map. The main difference between GVF and GGVF is that the latter field keeps enough force as to drive the snake until the edge.

Notice that, in any of the two cases (GVF or GGVF), at parts of null gradient the equilibrium point is an harmonic function. Harmonic functions [ ] do not admit accumulation of zeros and, thus, our vector field v will only have isolated points with $|v| = 0$. This important feature solves the problem of the distance map null gradient along curves (fig. (b)). However, in both cases the geometry of the contours introduces saddle points in the vector field v, as the close up in fig. (c) illustrates. These false minima of the snake energy trap, once again, the snake and prevent the deformable contour from entering into concave regions where the angle of the unit tangent, θ, turns around more than π.

For regularization of gradients of Euclidean distance maps, saddle points appear because of shock formation during the propagation of the curve of level zero. In the case of extension of image gradients we find a similar problem. The Laplacian is an isotropic linear constant way of extending information. Therefore in every image region such that the contour/edge of interest is concave and the

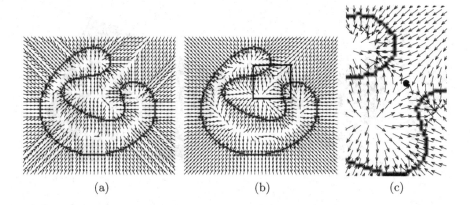

Fig. 2. Gradient of Euclidean distance map to non-convex curve (a), GGVF (b) and saddle point of GGVF (c)

angle of the image gradient (parallel to the unit normal of the curve) turns more than π, two opposite directions meet (fig. (c)) and we have a saddle point.

In order to eliminate saddle points we need changing the propagation of shapes, so that the geometry of the contour to be extended is taken into account.

2.3   Curvature Vector Flow

Let us analyze the problem of the Euclidean distance map. From an analytic point of view, we see that equation ( ) is a non-linear first order PDE, prone to develop shocks during the evolution. From a geometric one, it lies on the fact that we are propagating the curve at constant speed whatever its geometric features. In other words, the structural element used in the mathematical morphology is a circle of constant radius, which means that all points in the curve travel equal distance at the same time. We argue that the evolution should consider different metrics depending on the local geometry around each point so that structural circular elements of non constant radius are used. And what characterizes the local geometry of a curve better than curvature?. We propose [ ] a distance map based on the Mean Curvature Flow, that is, the evolution of the curve of level zero under the PDE given by:

$$\gamma_t = \kappa \overrightarrow{n} \ . \tag{5}$$

This equation makes points on the curve travel a distance that depends on the magnitude of the curvature, the higher its absolute value, the faster and further the point will move. From the mathematical morphology point of view we make the radius of the structural circle depend on the absolute value of the curvature. Now, can we assure, analytically speaking, that our evolution will stay

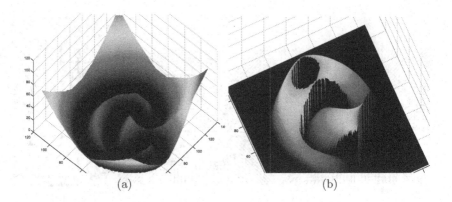

Fig. 3. Detail of Euclidean distance map, showing a crest of positive slope (a) and detail of Elliptic Distance Map (b)

smooth for all times?. On one hand we have that the equation ( ) associated to θ in arc length parameter has turned into a PDE of parabolic elliptic type:

$$\theta_t = \theta_{ss} + (\int_0^s \theta_s^2 ds)\theta_s \ . \tag{6}$$

Hence by general theory on PDE's [ ], we already know that our Curvature Distance Map (CDM) will be infinitely differentiable. Intuitively, the Laplacian that equation ( ) contains introduces curvature into the characteristic lines, so that two characteristics do not intersect any more. Besides, the large amount of literature [ ], [,] on MCF, states that any initial curve evolves smoothly towards a convex shape, circular in the limit, before collapsing to a point. This is the key point to the definition of CDM.

Evolution by negative curvature   **Evolution by positive curvature**
$$\gamma_t = \min((\kappa, 0))\overrightarrow{n} \qquad\qquad \gamma_t = \max((\kappa, 0))\overrightarrow{n}$$
$$\tag{7}$$

We will define separately the outward and inward propagation in order to ensure maximal accuracy in the position of the snake. The analysis of Section points out that convex shapes do not develop shocks during their propagation. An evolution of a non convex shape by negative curvature [ ] stops as soon as the curve becomes convex. Therefore, for the outward propagation, we will evolve the initial shape under the flow given by ( ) until it stabilizes. The tracking of the curve for each time produces the level sets of the outward CDM for the non convex regions. To complete the outward CDM, we use an outward Euclidean distance map to the stable state of the flow by negative curvature. For the inward propagation we use evolution under positive curvature ( ) until the curve becomes circular and then we use the Euclidean distance map to this circle to complete the inward propagation.

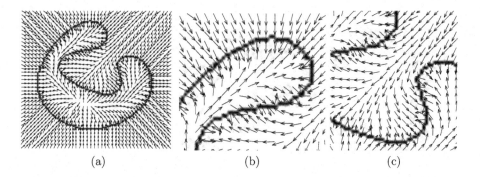

Fig. 4. Gradient of the Elliptic Distance Map (a) and close-ups from the interior (b) and exterior (c)

Since there are not any self intersections between the level curves of CDM, we obtain maps (fig.   (b)) without curves of null gradient or saddle points (fig.   (a)). The gradient of this map, CVF, drives the snake [ ] to the zero level curve of CDM whatever its geometry. Details of CVF shown in figure   illustrate the absence of either saddle points or null gradients in both, the interior (fig.   (b)) and exterior (fig.   (c)) regions of a highly non-convex curve.

3   Applications to Shape Modelling

In this section we apply CVF to smooth shape representation. Given a closed curve in the plane, we approach it by means of a parametric B-spline snake that uses CVF as external force. In the case of discontinuous curves, CVF is computed over their closing obtained by dilation. We recall the reader that a parametric snake [   ] is a curve $\gamma(u) = (x(u), y(u))$ that minimizes the energy functional:

$$E(\gamma) = \int_{\gamma} (E_{int} + E_{ext})du = \int_{\gamma} (\alpha ||\gamma'||^2 + \beta ||\gamma''||^2 + E_{ext})du \ ,$$

where the external energy depends on the image object to model and can be either a distance map or a function of the original image gradient. The parameters α and β determine the stiffness of the deformable model and are in the range $[0, 1]$. In any case the optimal curve is obtained by means of the Euler-Lagrange equations associated to E, which are equivalent to solving a linear system:

$$Ax = -\nabla E_{ext} \ .$$

The numeric iterative scheme is given by:

$$x_{t+1} = (A + \lambda I)^{-1} (\lambda x_t - \nabla E_{ext})$$

where I denotes the identity matrix, A the stiffness matrix [   ] and λ is a viscosity parameter. An important remark is that stability of the finite difference

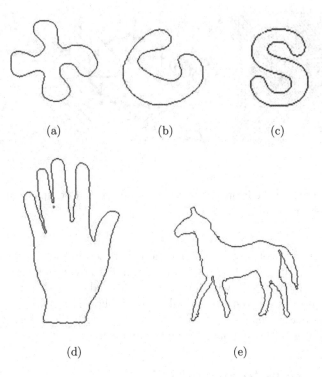

(a)   (b)   (c)

(d)   (e)

Fig. 5. Set of test shapes: clover (a), highly non-convex curve (b), character 'S' (c), hand (d) and horse (e)

scheme depends upon the viscosity parameter, which must be increased if α, β decrease. This viscosity parameter determines the speed of convergence, the higher it is, the slower the snake converges. We consider the snake has reached its final state when its total energy stabilizes.

3.1 Results

Experiments focus on the efficiency and accuracy of CVF when non-convex contours are modelled. Accuracy has been computed in terms of snake convergence, given by the snake maximum Euclidean distance to the original closed contours. Efficiency is given by the CPU-time the initial snake takes to reach its final state. Since the stop criterion is in terms of the stabilization of the external energy, the asymptotic behavior of the functional E is also a measure of the method efficiency. An oscillating graph for E hinders stopping the deformable model with the former stop criterion and the final snake must be obtained after a fixed number of iterations.

We have tested the external potentials for different values of the snake parameters, α and β, in order to check if the energies could support large values

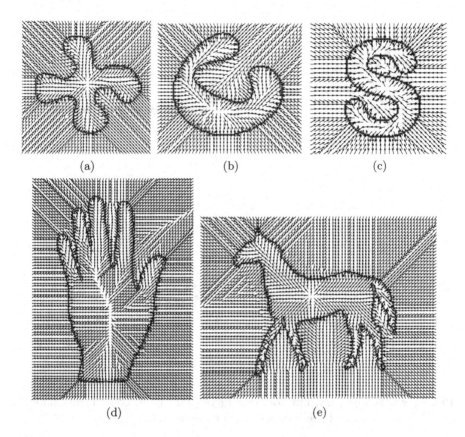

Fig. 6. CVF on clover (a), highly non-convex curve (b), character 'S' (c), hand (d) and horse (e)

and still guarantee convergence of the snake to the curve of interest. As noticed before, supporting large values for α, β is also a signal of efficiency, since the larger these parameters are, the faster the snake converges. The snake has been initialized inside and outside the object of interest. We have compared CVF to the results obtained using a GVF-regularized gradient of the Euclidean distance map (DM) and GVF applied to the edge map.

The shapes chosen are depicted in figure . The external force given by CVF is shown in figure . Convergence of snakes for the different external forces is shown in figure   and the final model obtained is depicted in figure   .

In terms of an accurate model of the shape, CVF is the only external energy that adapts the deformable model to all curves, whatever position (inside or outside the object of interest) of the initial snake. The other two external energies fail to obtain an accurate model when the initial snake lies inside the object of interest. Convergence to the character 'S' and horse in fig.   and the final shapes of fig.   illustrate this bad-pose of the snake inner convergence with

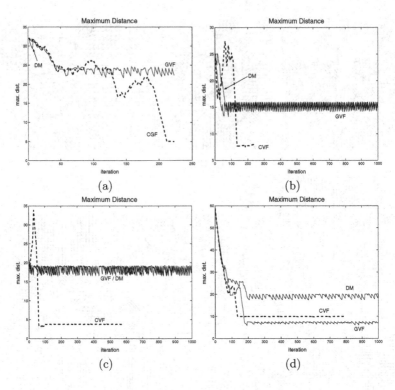

Fig. 7. Snake accuracy, interior convergence for highly non convex shape (a) and the clover (b) and the corresponding exterior convergence (c) and (d)

GVF and DM. In the case of the character 'S', saddle points of both GVF and DM, make the snake oscillate at closed shapes which fail to reach the extremal boundary of the 'S'. Irregularities in the gradient of the horse external energy, produces open final snakes (fig. (b),(c)) approaching only a part of the animal's contour. Notice the accuracy and smoothness of the final model of the horse achieved with CVF (last row of fig. (a)). In the case of an outer initial snake, GVF succeeds in adapting to non convex shapes such that the angle θ does not turn more that π between two consecutive inflexion points (like the clover of fig. (b)). However the snake gets trapped at the saddle points that highly non convex shapes (second row of fig. (b)) produce in the vector field. The external force field obtained by a regularization of the gradient of DM using GVF is the worst performer. Even for small values of α and β, the external force is not strong enough to attract the snake to non-convex shapes, even in the case of shapes (like the clover of fig. (c)) with the angle θ turning less than π between two consecutive inflexion points. Figure   summarizes these results in the form of maximum Euclidean distance to the contour of interest versus number of iterations. Notice significant differences of the maximum distance between CVF

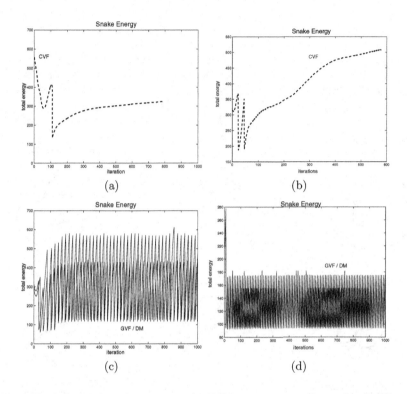

Fig. 8. Evolution of snake energy, CVF exterior convergence for highly non-convex shape (a), the clover (b) and the corresponding GVF/DM convergence (c) and (d)

and DM/GVF in the case of convergence to highly non-convex shapes (fig. (a),(c)).

Concerning efficiency, CVF is, again the best performer, since attains accurate models in optimal time, meanwhile GVF is the worst of the methods. Times for DM have not been taken into account since the method does not produce good enough segmentations as to be taken into account. The main reason for this difference in times lies on the fact that, due to the smoothness of the map, deformable models guided by CVF do not need, in general to be re sampled during evolution. On the other side, since GVF does not take into account the geometry of shapes, the snake sampling must be refined at points where two opposite directions compete (that is when entering into concave regions) in order to guarantee convergence to a closed contour. This increases the computational time of GVF up to four times CVF time in the case of the hand or the horse. Also in terms of the stiffness parameters, α and β, CVF is the most efficient. Our tests done for different values of the stiffness parameters show that CVF supports, in general, values in the whole range of $[0, 1]$. Only in extreme cases

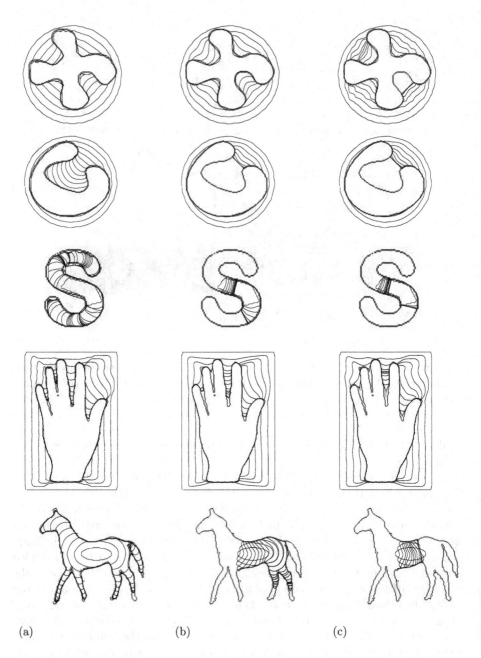

(a)   (b)   (c)

Fig. 9. Snake convergence, CVF (a), GVF (b) and regularized DM (c)

(a)   (b)   (c)

Fig. 10. Models of shapes obtained with CVF (a), GVF (b) and regularized DM (c)

like inner convergence to the horse and outer convergence to the hand, α and β must be smaller than 0.3 if we want a reliable final model.

Another issue worth to be considered is the asymptotic behavior of the snake convergence. Figure   shows the evolution of the snake energy in time for convergence to the clover and the highly non-convex shape of fig. , in the case of a CVF guided snake (fig. (a),(b)) and a DM/GVF one (fig. (c),(d)). Notice that deformations under CVF present a smoother asymptotic behavior, compared to the highly oscillating graphics of DM and GVF. This oscillating behavior strengths when the snake gets trapped at saddle points. A smooth energy implies a strong advantage since a stop criterion in terms of the snake total energy is a robust way of determining the final state for CVF guided snakes.

4   Conclusions and Future Work

Shape modelling and reconstruction is an issue frequently addressed in different fields of computer vision and graphics. Snakes or deformable models are a common way of obtaining smooth shape models. The external force is crucial in order to ensure the snake convergence. In the present paper we have introduced a new distance map to closed contours. Based on the grounds that a distance map represents the evolution of an initial curve in time under a geometric PDE, we propose using the mean curvature flow to avoid shock formation. The gradient of this map is a smooth external force that guides in a natural manner the snake to the shape of interest. The fact that the force field takes into account the geometry of the final curve, makes convergence robust whatever the concavity of this curve is. The only requirement is that the initial snake must be either inside or outside the shape of interest. Experiments show the higher accuracy and efficiency of our model of shapes compared to the most commonly used external force fields in the framework of parametric snakes. Comparing to geodesic active contours, our CVF converges faster to a comparable segmenting snake.

We are aware that requiring closed contours is a main limitation of CVF. However we argue that ensuring convergence and a smooth potential should be essential requirements for any external energy. In order to apply CVC to object segmentation, special treatment must be made to noisy images well as to uncompleted contours. In [ ] we present a more general framework for segmentation purposes where we embed CVF to segment real images with concave objects.

References

[1] V. Caselles, F. Catte, T. Coll, F. Dibos, *A geometric model for active contours.* Numerische Mathematik, 66, pg.1-31, 1993.
[2] V. Caselles, R.Kimmel, G. Sapiro *Geodesic Active Contours.* Int. J. Comp. Vision.
[3] L. D. Cohen, R. Kimmel, *Global minimum for active contour models: A minimal path approach.* Int. Journal Comp. Vision, 24 (1), pp. 57-78, Aug. 1997.

[4] D. Gil, P. Radeva. *Regularized curvature flow*. CVC Tech. Report n° 63, 2002.

[5] D. Gil, P. Radeva. *Curvature based Distance Maps*. CVC Tech. Report n° 70, 2003.   ,

[6] D. Gil, P. Radeva. *Anisotropic Contour Completion*, ICIP'03 (submmited).

[7] L. C. Evans. *Partial Differential equations*. Berkeley Math. Lect. Notes, vol. 3B.
      ,

[8] D. R. Forsey, R. H. Bartels. *Surface Fitting with Hierarchical Splines*, Computer Graphics, April 1995.

[9] M. A. Grayson. *The heat equation shrinks embedded plane curves to round points*. J. Differential Geometry, Vol. 26, pp. 285-314, 1986.

[10] M. Gage, R. S. Hamilton. *The heat equation shrinking convex plane curves*. J. Differential Geometry, Vol. 23, pp. 69-96, 1986.

[11] M. Gage. *Curve shortening makes convex curves circular*. Invent. Math, vol 76, pp. 357-364, 1984.

[12] F.Guichard, J. M.Morel *Mathematical Models in Image Processing*. Advanced Courses on Mathematical Aspects on Image Processing.

[13] H. Hoppe, T. DeRose, T. Duchamp, M. Halstead, H. Jin, J. McDonald, J. Scheweitzer, and W. Stuetzle, *Piecewise smooth surface reconstruction*, Proc. ACM SIGGRAPH, pp. 295-302, July 1994.

[14] M.Kass, A.Witkin and D.Terzopoulos, "Snakes: Active Contour Models", *Int. Journal of Computer Vision*, vol. 1, pp. 321-331, 1987.   ,

[15] Ch. Knoll, M. Alcañiz, V. Grau, C. Montserrat, M. C. Juan, *Outlining of the prostate using snakes with shapes restrictions based on the wavelet transform*. Pattern Recognition, 32, pp. 1767-1781, 1999.

[16] W. Rudin. *Complex and Real Analysis*. McGraw-Hill, Inc.

[17] R.Malladi, J. A. Sethian. *Image Processing: Flows under min-max curvature and mean curvature*. Graph. Models and Image Process., vol. 58 (2), Mar. 1996.   ,

[18] G. Sapiro, B. B. Kimia, R. Kimmel, D. Shaked, A. Bruckstein. *Implementing continuous-scale morphology*. Pattern Recognition, vol. 26(9), 1992.

[19] K. Siddiqi, A. Tannenbaum, S. W. Zucker. *A Hanmiltonian Aaproach to the Eikonal Equation*, EMMCVPR'99, Lecture Notes in comp. Science, 1654.

[20] Ch.Sun, S. Pallotino, *Circular shortest path on regular grids*, Asian Conference on Computer Vision, pp. 852-857, Melbourne, Australia, Jan. 2002.

[21] Z. S. G. Tari, J. Shah, H. Pien. *Extraction of shape skeletons from grayscale images*. Comp. Vision and Image Understanding, vol. 66, pp. 133-146, May 1997.

[22] C.Xu and J. L. Prince *Snakes, shapes and gradient vector flow*. IEEE Trans. on Image Proc., vol. 7(3), pp. 359-369, March 1998.   ,

[23] N.Paragios, O.Mellina-Gottardo, V.Ramesh, *Gradient Vector Flow Fast Geodesic Active Contours*. Comp. Vision, ICCV 2001.

[24] C.Xu and J. L. Prince *Generalized gradient vector flow external forces for active contours*. Signal Processing, An International Journal, vol. 71(2), pp. 132-139, 1998.   ,

[25] D. Zhang, M. Herbert, *Harmonic shape images: a representation for 3-d free-form surfaces based on energy minimization*, EMMCVPR'99, Lect. Notes in Comp. Science, 1654.

Definition of a Signal-to-Noise Ratio
for Object Segmentation
Using Polygonal MDL-Based Statistical Snakes

François Goudail[1], Philippe Réfrégier[1], and Olivier Ruch[2]

[1] Fresnel Institute, Physics and Image Processing group
Dom. Univ. St Jérôme, 13397 MARSEILLE Cedex 20
francois.goudail@fresnel.fr
http://www.fresnel.fr/PHYTI/
[2] Thales Optronique S.A., Rue Guynemer - BP 55 - 78283 Guyancourt Cedex

Abstract. We address the problem of the characterization of segmentation performance of Minimum Description Length snake techniques in function of the noise which affects the image. It is shown that a parameter quantifying the contrast between the object of interest and the background can be defined from the Bhattacharyya distance. This contrast parameter is very general since it applies to several different noise statistics which belong to the exponential family. We illustrate its relevancy with a segmentation application using a polygonal snake descriptor.

Nowadays, more and more new sensors and imaging systems are appearing. These systems provide images perturbed with noises having different statistical characteristics. For example, the noise perturbing Synthetic Aperture Radar (SAR) images can be modelled with Gamma statistics, whereas low-photon flux systems are affected by Poisson distributed perturbations. When processing such images, it is useful to define a contrast parameter between an object of interest and the background. This permits to characterize the difficulty of the processing tasks, and thus the performance to be expected from processing algorithms. We propose in this paper to define such a contrast parameter by using information-theoretic distances between the probability density functions (pdf) of the graylevels of the object and of the background for segmentation with Minimum Description Length snake techniques. This parameter will be valid for a number of different noise statistics belonging to the exponential family. For example, it will permit to compare the difficulty of processing tasks in the presence of Gamma and Gaussian-distributed noises.

In order to evaluate the candidates contrast measures, we will consider a segmentation application using active contours. An active contour, or "snake", is a continuous curve which has the ability to evolve in order to match an object in the image [ ]. We will focus here on the polygonal statistical snake [, ,] which is designed to segment a single object in very noisy images. Since it is based on a statistical description of the data, it can be adapted to the statistics of the noise present in the image. Moreover, if the noise statistics belongs to

A. Rangarajan et al. (Eds.): EMMCVPR 2003, LNCS 2683, pp. 373–   , 2003.
© Springer-Verlag Berlin Heidelberg 2003

the exponential family [ ], the computational load can be minimized to yield a fast segmentation method [ ]. Recently, a method has been proposed to determine the sufficient number of polygon nodes required to correctly segment the object. Initially introduced by Figueiredo et al. in [ ] for B-spline contour description, this method is based on the Minimum Description Length (MDL) principle and an original optimization procedure. It has been adapted in [ ] to polygonal contour descriptors.

After briefly reviewing this MDL-based snake, we will address the problem of defining a contrast parameter for characterizing its performance in the presence of different noise statistics.

1   MDL-Based Polygonal Statistical Snake

In this section, we briefly review the MDL-based statistical snake [,] and illustrate its performance on real-world images. We show in particular that this method improves the segmentation performance compared to approaches where the number of nodes is not estimated.

1.1   MDL-Based Segmentation Criterion

In the following mathematical developments, for the sake of simplicity, one-dimensional notation will be used for image coordinates and bold font symbols will denote N-component vectors. Let us consider a scene $\mathbf{s} = \{s_i | i \in [1, N]\}$ composed of two regions: an object and a background. Let $\mathbf{w} = \{w_i | i \in [1, N]\}$ denote a binary window function that defines a certain shape for the object, so that $w_i = 1$ within this shape and $w_i = 0$ elsewhere. The image is thus divided into two regions: $\Omega_a = \{i \in [1, N] | w_i = 1\}$ and $\Omega_b = \{i \in [1, N] | w_i = 0\}$. The gray levels of the object and of the background are considered as independent random variables respectively distributed with probability density functions (pdf) $P_{\mu_a}(x)$ (for the object region) and $P_{\mu_b}(x)$ (for the background region). μ_a and μ_b are the statistical parameters which describe the graylevel fluctuations in the two regions.

The purpose of segmentation is therefore to determine the shape $\mathbf{w}$ which best matches the real shape of the object in the scene. This shape will be modelled with a k-node polygon and $\mathbf{w}$ is then a polygon-bounded support function, one-valued on and within the snake and zero-valued elsewhere. In the previous approaches reported in [, ,] the number k of nodes was arbitrarily chosen and the estimation of the target shape $\mathbf{w}$ was performed by maximizing the likelihood function determined from the image $\mathbf{s}$ and an hypothesis for the shape $\mathbf{w}$. In order to estimate the number of nodes k of the object, we propose to use an approach analogous to the one developed in Figueiredo et al. [ ], which consists in minimizing the length Δ of the description of the image (this approach is well known as the Minimum Description Length (MDL) principle introduced by Rissanen, see [ ] for example). Since the image is divided in three parts (the target, the background and the contour), Δ is the sum of three terms: the length Δ_a of the description of the target gray levels, the length Δ_b of the description of the background gray levels and the length Δ_w of the description of the polygon $\mathbf{w}$.

Let us first provide an approximation of Δ_w. The number of possible locations for one node is N. Thus, for k nodes, the number of different sets of locations is N^k and we will consider that it is an approximation of the number of different polygons. The number of bits necessary to describe the polygon (if all polygons are assumed to be equally likely) is thus approximately $\log_2(N^k)$ (where $\log_2$ is the base 2 logarithm), which can be considered as the complexity of the polygon.

Let us now determine the expression of Δ_a and Δ_b. According to Shannon theory [ ], the average number of bits needed to describe N_l random variables distributed with pdf $P_{\boldsymbol{\mu}_l}(x)$ is $\Delta_l \simeq N_l S_l$, where S_l is the entropy of the pdf and is given by $S_l = -\int P_{\boldsymbol{\mu}_l}(x) \log_2 \left[P_{\boldsymbol{\mu}_l}(x) \right] dx - \log_2(q)$, where q is the quantization precision. Since the contribution of $\log_2(q)$ only consists in adding a constant term in the description length, it will not be taken into account in the following. The average number of bits needed to describe the object region (resp. the background region) is thus $\Delta_a \simeq N_a S_a$ (resp. $\Delta_b \simeq N_b S_b$). The total description length is then:

$$\Delta \simeq N_a S_a + N_b S_b + k \log_2(N). \tag{1}$$

Practically speaking, the data entropy is estimated from the data by using the empirical mean instead of the statistical average: $N_l S_l \simeq - \sum_{i \in \Omega_l} \log_2 \left[P_{\boldsymbol{\mu}_l}(i) \right]$ where $l = a$ or b. Consequently, the term $-N_a S_a - N_b S_b$ is nothing but the base 2 log-likelihood $\ell_2[\mathbf{s}|\mathbf{w}, \boldsymbol{\mu}_a, \boldsymbol{\mu}_b]$ of the hypothesis that the shape of the target in the image $\mathbf{s}$ is $\mathbf{w}$. In the following, we will rather make use of the natural logarithm likelihood $\ell_e[.]$.

In practice, $\ell_e[\mathbf{s}|\mathbf{w}, \boldsymbol{\mu}_a, \boldsymbol{\mu}_b]$ cannot be directly computed since the statistical parameters $\boldsymbol{\mu}_a, \boldsymbol{\mu}_b$ of the graylevel pdf in the two regions are unknown. We will adopt the same approach as in [ ], which consists in considering their maximum likelihood estimates $\hat{\boldsymbol{\mu}}_a(\mathbf{s}, \mathbf{w})$ and $\hat{\boldsymbol{\mu}}_b(\mathbf{s}, \mathbf{w})$. The pseudo-loglikelihood obtained by injecting these estimates into the expression of the loglikelihood is thus $\ell(\mathbf{s}, \mathbf{w}) = \ell_e[\mathbf{s}|\mathbf{w}, \hat{\boldsymbol{\mu}}_a(\mathbf{s}, \mathbf{w}), \hat{\boldsymbol{\mu}}_b(\mathbf{s}, \mathbf{w})]$. This pseudo-loglikelihood can be written as: $\ell(\mathbf{s}, \mathbf{w}) = -J(\mathbf{s}, \mathbf{w}) + A$ where A accounts for the constant terms which do not depend on $\mathbf{s}$ nor $\mathbf{w}$. Finally, the MDL principle leads to the minimization of:

$$\Delta' = J(\mathbf{s}, \mathbf{w}) + k \ln(N). \tag{2}$$

We have reported in Table   the definitions of the different graylevel statistics that we will consider in this paper and in Table   the expression of $J(\mathbf{s}, \mathbf{w})$ for each of them.

1.2   Optimization Procedure

Δ' in Eq.   represents the criterion to minimize in order to estimate the shape of the object. It is a function of both k and $\mathbf{w}$. This double optimization problem is not trivial and the adopted strategy may have strong influence on the quality

Table 1. Pdf of the graylevel statistics used in this paper and their corresponding parameters. $\delta(x)$ is the Dirac distribution, $\mathbf{N}$ is the set of integers and $n! = n(n-1)..2.1$

Law	Pdf	Parameters: μ_u
Bernoulli	$p\delta(x) + (1-p)\delta(1-x)$	p
Poisson	$\sum_{n \in \mathbf{N}} \delta(x-n)e^{-\lambda}\frac{\lambda^n}{n!}$	λ
Gamma	$\left(\frac{L}{\mu}\right)^L \frac{x^{L-1}}{\Gamma(L)}exp[-\frac{L}{\mu}x]$	μ, L
Gaussian	$\frac{1}{\sqrt{2\pi}\sigma}exp[-\frac{(x-m)^2}{2\sigma^2}]$	m, σ

and on the relevance of the application of the MDL principle. The simplest strategy consists in determining the shapes $\hat{\mathbf{w}}^{(k)}$ which optimize the criterion Δ' for different fixed values of k and selecting the value of k which leads to the minimal value of Δ' [ ].

However, this method appears to be inefficient in our case. Let us illustrate this point with a synthetic image of a boat (whose shape is polygonal with 10 nodes) corrupted with speckle noise of order 1 (that is, Gamma pdf with $L = 1$, see Figure 1.a and 1.b). Figure 1.c presents the shape obtained after the convergence of the snake with the true number of nodes ($k = 10$), when the multiresolution strategy described in [ ] is used. We can see that the obtained contour is a poor approximation of the true shape. In fact, in order to obtain a correct estimation of the shape, one has to use a larger number of nodes. For example, Figure 1.d represents the contour estimate obtained with $k = 192$ nodes. All the details of the shape have been correctly segmented, but it is clear that the number of nodes is excessive. These results show that the simple strategy which consists in increasing progressively the resolution of the snake does not make it possible to estimate the exact number of nodes of a polygonal shape.

To overcome this problem, a new approach has been proposed in [ ]: An *up and down multiresolution* strategy which consists of two basic steps. Since efficient convergence is obtained when the number of nodes is large, we first perform a segmentation with a multiresolution strategy, by increasing the number of nodes up to a point where the distance between two consecutive nodes does not exceed a small value d_f (typically a few pixels) [ ]. The continuous curve reported in Figure 2 shows the evolution of the value of Δ' as k increases. At

Table 2. Expression the criterion $J(\mathbf{s}, \mathbf{w})$ involved in the MDL snake criterion for the pdf listed in Table . One has $\widehat{p_u} = \widehat{\lambda_u} = \widehat{\mu_u} = \widehat{m_u} = \frac{1}{N} \sum_{i \in \Omega_u} s_i$ for $u = a$ or b, $\widehat{\sigma_u^2} = \frac{1}{N} \sum_{i \in \Omega_u} (s_i - \widehat{m_u})^2$ and $\widehat{\sigma^2} = \frac{1}{N} (N_a \widehat{\sigma_a^2} + N_b \widehat{\sigma_b^2})$. The two last rows correspond to Gaussian noise, when the variances in the two regions are supposed different on the regions Ω_a and Ω_b (fourth row) and when they are supposed equal, which corresponds to the case of additive Gaussian noise (fifth row), since these two cases lead to different expressions of the pseudo-likelihoods

Pdf	$J(\mathbf{s}, \mathbf{w})$	$f(x)$
Bernoulli	$N_a f(\widehat{p_a}) + N_b f(\widehat{p_b})$	$-x \ln(x) - (1 - x) \ln(1 - x)$
Poisson	$N_a f(\widehat{\lambda_a}) + N_b f(\widehat{\lambda_b})$	$-x \ln x$
Gamma	$N_a f(\widehat{\mu_a}) + N_b f(\widehat{\mu_b})$	$L \ln(x)$
Gaussian	$N_a f(\widehat{\sigma_a^2}) + N_b f(\widehat{\sigma_b^2})$	$\frac{1}{2} \ln(x)$
Gaussian with identical variances	$N f(\widehat{\sigma^2})$	$\frac{1}{2} \ln(x)$

the end of this process, we typically end up with an over-estimated number of nodes k_0 and a segmentation result such as that in Figure 2.d for example.

The second step is a complexity reduction technique and consists in pruning the contour. For this purpose, we sequentially consider each node of the contour and determine the value of the criterion Δ' obtained if this node is removed. Then, the pruned contour is defined by suppressing the node which leads to the minimal value of Δ' and a new convergence of the snake is performed on this contour. The process is continued until the number of nodes is smaller than a limit value (typically 4 or 5). We have reported in Figure 2, with dashed line, the value of Δ' obtained using this procedure. One can observe that it is very efficient for the considered image since one obtains the true number of nodes ($k = 10$), although k was varying in a large domain (between more than 200 and 5). We show in Figure 1.e the final result of the MDL segmentation of the boat.

This method is also efficient to segment objects which are not polygonal, as for example the three shapes on a textured background appearing in Figure .a. Figure .b represents the result of the first step of the optimization process and .c the final result obtained after having pruned the nodes in excess. We can

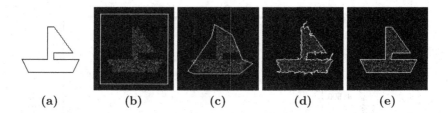

Fig. 1. (**a**) Boat whose shape is a polygon with 10 nodes in a 128 × 128 pixel image. (**b**) Speckled image of the boat of (**a**) with a contrast equal to 4 (*in white*: initialization of the contour). (**c**) Final state of the snake after optimization of the log-likelihood with the multiresolution strategy when the number of nodes on the contour is equal to the true one: $k = 10$. (**d**) Final state of the snake when the number of nodes on the contour is equal to $k = 192$. (**e**) Final state of the snake after optimization of the MDL criterion with the *up and down multiresolution* strategy

see that although the two shape in the lower part of the image is not polygonal, they have been correctly segmented with a little number of nodes. On the star-shaped object, the nodes concentrate in the cusps, where more nodes are required to correctly define the local curvature. Moreover, one can remark that the MDL snake is "soft" enough to segment the three separated object. However, since it is by construction intended to describe a single object, the three segmented shapes are linked by thin contour elements, so that they form a single object. A generalization of the MDL active contour to the automatic partition of an image into several regions with an "active grid" has been proposed in [ ].

Besides providing a parsimonious description of the object shape, the proposed MDL-based segmentation scheme also yields better quantitative segmentation performance. This performance can be evaluated by computing a distance between the contour estimate and the real shape of the object. There are many ways of defining this distance, such as for example Hausdorff distances [ ], each of which having specific properties [ ]. For the sake of simplicity, we will use throughout this article a simpler distance, the number of misclassified pixels (NMP). The NMP is the number of pixels which belong to the object region but are outside the estimated contour, plus the number of pixels which belong to the background but which lie inside the estimated contour. We can see on Figure that the NMP obtained after the *up and down multiresolution* process (on the boat image in Figure 1.b) is lower than that obtained with the increasing resolution optimization process.

2 Determining a Contrast Parameter for Segmentation

In practical applications of image segmentation, it is important to be able to characterize the performance that can be expected when processing a given image. This is usually done by specifying a contrast parameter, which is a function

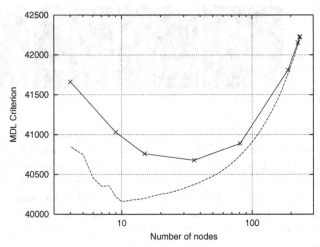

Fig. 2. Continuous line: values of the MDL criterion Δ' obtained with a direct approach. Dashed line: values of the MDL criterion Δ' obtained with the proposed *up and down multiresolution* strategy

of the image parameters that synthesizes their influence on segmentation performance. There are several ways to define such parameter, that we briefly recall in the following.

2.1 Defining a Contrast Parameter

When an image processing problem is formulated in a Bayesian framework, the sources of randomness are well defined, which makes it possible to rigorously determine some "reduced parameters" on which the processing performance uniquely depends [,   ,   ]. Indeed, let us assume that the scene is composed of two regions a and b, whose graylevels are random variables distributed with pdf $P_{\boldsymbol{\mu}_a}(x)$ and $P_{\boldsymbol{\mu}_b}(x)$. The pdf parameter vectors $\boldsymbol{\mu}_a$ and $\boldsymbol{\mu}_b$ will be called the *image parameters*. Let us consider an algorithm which performs a given processing task on this image (detection, segmentation, etc.), and whose performance is quantified by a measure $\mathcal{M}(\boldsymbol{\mu}_a, \boldsymbol{\mu}_b)$. For example, this performance measure can be the probability of detection in detection applications or the NMP in segmentation applications. The ideal would be to determine the expression of $\mathcal{M}(\boldsymbol{\mu}_a, \boldsymbol{\mu}_b)$, but this problem is intractable in the general case. One can then determine a function $\mathbf{CP}(\boldsymbol{\mu}_a, \boldsymbol{\mu}_b)$ so that $\mathcal{M}(\boldsymbol{\mu}_a, \boldsymbol{\mu}_b) = f(\mathbf{CP}(\boldsymbol{\mu}_a, \boldsymbol{\mu}_b))$. If $\mathbf{CP}(\boldsymbol{\mu}_a, \boldsymbol{\mu}_b)$ is a scalar function and $f(x)$ is bijective, knowing $\mathbf{CP}(\boldsymbol{\mu}_a, \boldsymbol{\mu}_b)$ is a measure of the difficulty of the considered task. A very classical example of this situation is the detection of a constant signal of mean m_a over a background of mean m_b embedded in zero-mean Gaussian noise of variance σ^2. If the considered performance measure $\mathcal{M}(\boldsymbol{\mu}_a, \boldsymbol{\mu}_b)$ is the probability of detection, it is well know that it only depends on the following function: $CP(m_a, m_b, \sigma^2) = \frac{|m_a - m_b|^2}{\sigma^2}$.

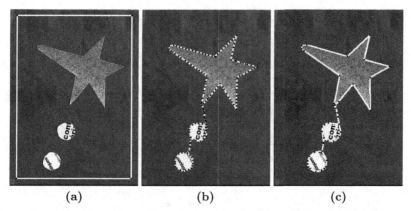

(a)   (b)   (c)

Fig. 3. Segmentation of a real image acquired with a CCD camera. The nodes of the polygon are represented in black. **(a)** : Image and initial contour. **(b)** : Contour obtained after the first step of the *up and down* optimization process (with $d_f = 2\ pixels$). **(c)** : MDL contour estimate obtained after the second step

In many cases, it can be difficult to exhibit such a function. However, it is still often possible to determine a vectorial function $\mathbf{CP}(\boldsymbol{\mu}_a, \boldsymbol{\mu}_b)$ whose dimensionality is lower than that of the parameter vector $(\boldsymbol{\mu}_a, \boldsymbol{\mu}_b)$. This can be done by using the group-invariance properties of the pdf which describe the graylevels of the image [ ]. For example, it has been shown that in polarimetric images formed in coherent light, the graylevels can be described by 2-D circular complex Gaussian random vectors defined by their 2×2 hermitic covariance matrices. The dimension of the parameter space $(\boldsymbol{\mu}_a, \boldsymbol{\mu}_b)$ is thus 8, but it is possible exhibit a contrast parameter $\mathbf{CP}(\boldsymbol{\mu}_a, \boldsymbol{\mu}_b)$ of dimension 2 by using group-invariance concepts [ ], thus achieving considerable dimensionality reduction of the problem.

As further examples, let us consider the pdf belonging to the exponential family that are listed in Table . The parameters $(\boldsymbol{\mu}_a, \boldsymbol{\mu}_b)$ for each of these pdf and the reduced parameters (in other words, $\mathbf{CP}(\boldsymbol{\mu}_a, \boldsymbol{\mu}_b)$) that can be arrived at by using the group-invariance approach described in [ ] are shown in Table . It can be noticed that for Bernoulli and Poisson noise, no reduced parameter can be determined ; for Gamma noise, the number of parameters is reduced from 3 to 2 and in the Gaussian case, it is reduced from 4 to 2. In all cases, $\mathbf{CP}(\boldsymbol{\mu}_a, \boldsymbol{\mu}_b)$ cannot be reduced to a single value. The group-invariance method for determining the contrast parameter is rigorous, in the sense that the relation between $\mathbf{CP}(\boldsymbol{\mu}_a, \boldsymbol{\mu}_b)$ and the performance measure is exact, but it does not lead to a scalar contrast parameter. Moreover, with this approach, the expression of the contrast parameter is only valid for a given type of pdf. It does not allow for comparing the segmentation performance in the presence of two different types of noise, say, Gaussian and Poisson for example.

It is thus useful to consider methods that yield a contrast parameter which is scalar and general to any pdf. Such a contrast parameter will of course

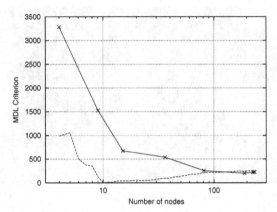

Fig. 4. Evaluation of segmentation quality (NMP) obtained with the two-step optimization process on the synthetic image represented in Figure 1.b. The values of the NMP are plotted as a function of k, in continuous lines for the first step of the process and in dotted lines for the second step

be approximate in general. A classical way of doing so is to use information-theoretic distances between the pdf's describing the object and the background graylevels [, , ,]. Some of these distances provide bounds on classical performance measures. For example, the Kullback-Leibler distance can be used to define a bound on the probability of detection through the Stein's lemma [ ], and the Chernoff distance leads to bounds on the probability of error [,]. Here, we are interested by characterizing the segmentation quality with the number of misclassified pixels (NMP) defined in Section . Since bounds on this performance measure are difficult to exhibit, we will compare the performance of three different information-theoretic measures as expressions of the contrast parameter: The Fisher ratio, the Kullback divergence and the Bhattacharyya

Table 3. Expression the reduced parameters for different types of graylevel statistics. Please note that in the case of Bernoulli noise and of Poisson noise, one cannot define any rigorous reduced parameter

Pdf	Parameters	Reduced parameter(s)
Bernoulli	p_a, p_b	p_a, p_b
Poisson	λ_a, λ_b	λ_a, λ_b
Gamma	μ_a, μ_b, L	$r = \frac{\mu_a}{\mu_b}$, L
Gaussian	$m_a, m_b, \sigma_a, \sigma_b$	$\alpha = \frac{\sigma_a^2}{\sigma_b^2}$, $\beta = \frac{(m_a - m_b)^2}{\sigma_b^2}$

distance. Let us first recall the definition of these three measures and some of their properties.

Fisher Ratio: The Fisher ratio is simply the ratio of the squared difference of the means m_a and m_b of the two pdf over the sum of their variances σ_a^2 and σ_b^2, so that

$$\mathcal{F} = \frac{(m_a - m_b)^2}{\sigma_a^2 + \sigma_b^2} \tag{3}$$

The Fisher ratio represents the rigorous signal to noise ratio when the pdf of the two regions are Gaussian with identical variances. If it is not the case, it still represents an empirical evaluation of the "separability" between the two distributions and is often used as an empirical estimate of the signal-to-noise ratio. Other expressions of the divergence between pdf which have more interesting and general properties are used in the domain of information theory. We will consider two of them in the following.

Kullback Divergence: The Kullback-Leibler measure between continuous-valued statistical distributions is defined as:

$$\mathcal{D}[P_{\boldsymbol{\mu}_a} \| P_{\boldsymbol{\mu}_b}] = \int P_{\boldsymbol{\mu}_a}(x) \ln \left[\frac{P_{\boldsymbol{\mu}_a}(x)}{P_{\boldsymbol{\mu}_b}(x)} \right] dx \tag{4}$$

The Kulback-Leibler measure has an interpretation in terms of detection performance through the Stein's Lemma [ ]. However, it is a directed distance, in the sense that the distributions $P_{\boldsymbol{\mu}_a}(x)$ and $P_{\boldsymbol{\mu}_a}(x)$ do not play symmetric roles, which may be an undesirable property for a contrast parameter. We will thus consider the Kullback divergence (also called divergence, or J-divergence), which is a symmetrized version of the Kullback-Leibler measure and is defined as :

$$\mathcal{K} = \mathcal{D}[P_{\boldsymbol{\mu}_a} \| P_{\boldsymbol{\mu}_b}] + \mathcal{D}[P_{\boldsymbol{\mu}_b} \| P_{\boldsymbol{\mu}_a}] \tag{5}$$

Bhattacharyya Distance: The Bhattacharyya distance is defined as follows :

$$\mathcal{B} = -\ln \left[\int \sqrt{P_{\boldsymbol{\mu}_a}(x) P_{\boldsymbol{\mu}_b}(x)} \, dx \right] \tag{6}$$

This distance is symmetric, but it must be noted that it is not a distance in the topological sense, since it does not respect the triangle inequality. However, following the usage, we will still denote it "Bhattacharyya distance". This distance provides lower and higher bounds on the probability of error in detection, and more generally in two-hypothesis Bayesian decision problems. The Bhattacharyya distance is a special case of the more general Chernoff distance defined as :

$$\mathcal{C}(s) = -\ln \left[\int P_{\boldsymbol{\mu}_a}^s(x) P_{\boldsymbol{\mu}_b}^{1-s}(x) \, dx \right] \tag{7}$$

Table 4. Expression of the Fisher ratio $\mathcal{F}$, the Kullback divergence $\mathcal{K}$ and the Bhattacharyya distance $\mathcal{B}$ for different graylevel statistics. The signification of the pdf parameters is defined in Table , that of the reduced parameters r, α and β in Table , and $q = 1 - p$

Law	$\mathcal{F}$	$\mathcal{K}$	$\mathcal{B}$
Bernoulli	$\dfrac{(p_a - p_b)^2}{p_a q_a + p_b q_b}$	$(p_a - p_b) \ln \left[\dfrac{p_a q_b}{p_b q_a} \right]$	$- \ln \left[\sqrt{p_a p_b} + \sqrt{q_a q_b} \right]$
Poisson	$\dfrac{(\lambda_a - \lambda_b)^2}{\lambda_a + \lambda_b}$	$(\lambda_a - \lambda_b) \ln \left[\dfrac{\lambda_a}{\lambda_b} \right]$	$\dfrac{1}{2} \left(\sqrt{\lambda_a} - \sqrt{\lambda_b} \right)^2$
Gamma	$L \dfrac{(r-1)^2}{r^2 + 1}$	$L \left(\sqrt{r} - \dfrac{1}{\sqrt{r}} \right)^2$	$L \ln \left[\dfrac{1}{2} \left(\sqrt{r} + \dfrac{1}{\sqrt{r}} \right) \right]$
Gaussian	$\dfrac{\beta}{1 + \alpha}$	$\dfrac{1}{2} \dfrac{\beta(1+\alpha)}{\alpha}$ $+ \dfrac{1}{2} \left(\sqrt{\alpha} - \dfrac{1}{\sqrt{\alpha}} \right)^2$	$\dfrac{1}{4} \dfrac{\beta}{1+\alpha}$ $+ \dfrac{1}{2} \ln \left[\dfrac{1}{2} \left(\sqrt{\alpha} + \dfrac{1}{\sqrt{\alpha}} \right) \right]$

with s varying between 0 and 1. The Bhattacharyya distance is the Chernoff distance for $s = 0.5$. The main drawback of the Chernoff distance is that it depends on the parameter s. However, it can be shown that in many cases, the Chernoff distance varies very smoothly around $s = 0.5$, so that the Bhattacharyya distance is usually a good approximation of the Chernoff distance over a wide range of values of s [ ].

We have listed in Table   the expressions of the three considered measures for the graylevel statistics of interest in this paper.

2.2   Contrast Parameter for Segmentation

In order to determine which of the three candidate measures is the most appropriate to define a contrast parameter, we have performed the following simulations. We have considered two polygonal objects: a square (4 nodes) and a boat with the same shape as in Figure 1 (10 nodes). The two objects are embedded in 64×64 images. We will consider the noise statistics defined in Table . For the Gaussian noise, we consider the cases where the variances in the target and in the background regions are identical and where they are different, which leads to two different expressions of the MDL criterion (see Table).

We perform the simulation as follows. For each type of noise, we select different combinations of parameters μ_a and μ_b. For each of these configurations, we generate 500 noisy images as in Figure 1.b and segment them with the MDL-based snake adapted to the noise statistics using the proposed *up and down*

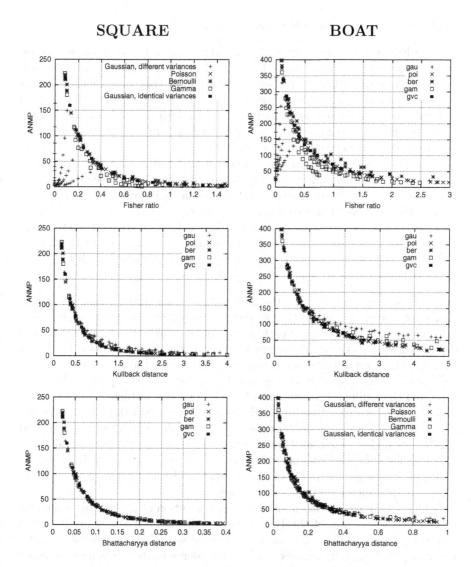

Fig. 5. Average number of misclassified pixels (ANMP) as a function of three measures: the Fisher ratio, the Kullback divergence and the Bhattacharyya distance. Two different objects are considered

multiresolution optimization procedure with a final inter-node interval $d_f = 3$. We compute the number of misclassified pixels (NMP) on each of these segmentation results and average the values obtained over the 500 realizations to obtain the averaged NMP (ANMP). Finally, we plot the ANMP as a function of the measure $\mathcal{D}(\boldsymbol{\mu}_a, \boldsymbol{\mu}_b)$, where $\mathcal{D}$ is one of the three candidate measures. The resulting curves are shown in Figure .

Some remarks can be done about these graphs:

- The Fisher ratio constitutes a good expression of the contrast parameter for some types of noise statistics. It is in particular the case for Gaussian with identical variances on the object and on the background, since in this case it is the rigorous signal-to-noise ratio. However, it completely fails for other types of noises, in particular Gamma with low order and Gaussian with different variances, when averages are equal. In fact, the Fisher ratio is not adapted to multiplicative noise.
- The Kullback distance performs much better and can handle the case of multiplicative noise. However, for the complex shape of the boat, there are some deviations in the case of highly multiplicative noise, that is, low-order speckle and Gaussian with different variances.
- The Bhattacharyya distance seems to be the best choice for a contrast parameter. This means that whatever the noise statistics and the parameter values, two configurations leading to the same Bhattacharyya distance correspond to the same segmentation performance.

In conclusion, we can see that the Bhattacharyya distance constitutes a good choice for a contrast parameter in the considered segmentation applications. We have also noticed that the performance of the different contrast parameters depend on noise statistics. For example, in the case of Bernoulli noise, the Fisher ratio and the Kullback divergence perform correctly. On the other hand, they fail for Gaussian noise. In order to interpret these results, we have plotted the Fisher ratio and the Kullback measure as a function of the Bhattacharyya distance in Figure . It can be seen that for the Bernoulli noise, the relations between $\mathcal{F}$ and $\mathcal{B}$ and $\mathcal{K}$ and $\mathcal{B}$ are close to bijection, which explains that the three measures constitute good expressions of the contrast parameter for this type of noise. On the other hand, in the Gaussian case, these relations are far from being bijective: this explains the poorer ability of Fisher ratio and Kullback divergence to define a contrast parameter for this type of noise.

Finally, we have plotted on Figure the evolution of the estimated number of nodes as a function of the Bhattacharyya distance for the segmentation of the boat, which consists of 10 nodes. It can be seen that for low values of the contrast parameter, the number of nodes is underestimated. It is a phenomenon classically encountered in model order estimation problems: when the signal gets noisier, the selected order tends to decrease, since less confidence is put on the data. It can also be noted that when the constrast is high, the estimated number of nodes tends to be higher than the true one. We conjecture that this is due to the fact that on the point of view of discrete geometry, the considered object is not a "true" polygon. In this range of contrast values, it can be also noted that the estimated number of nodes in the presence of Gaussian noise is significantly higher than for the other types of noises for a given value of the contrast.

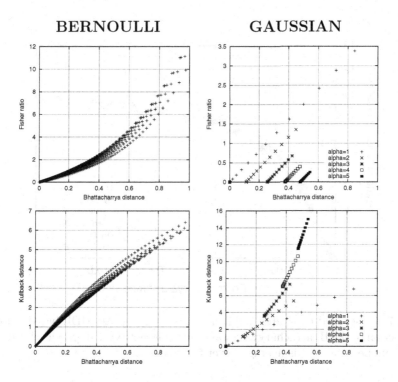

Fig. 6. Plot of the Fisher ratio and of the Kullback divergence as a function of the Bhattacharyya distance for Bernoulli and Gaussian noises. For Bernoulli noise, one has considered all the combinations of p_a and p_b in $[0.01, 0.99]$ with 0.01 step. For Gaussian noise, we have considered five different values of the reduced parameter α (see Table): $1, 2, 3, 4, 5$ and for each of them several values of $(m_a - m_b)$ in the interval $[0, 2.7]$

3   Conclusion

We have proposed a contrast parameter to characterize the segmentation performance obtained with MDL-based snake. This contrast parameter is based on the Bhattacharyya distance between the pdf of the graylevel fluctuations in the object and in the background regions. Its main advantage is to be valid for a wide family of different noise statistics. It can thus be used for characterizing a given imaging systems but also for choosing between different imaging configurations. Indeed, if the imaging system, and thus the type of noise, is fixed, this contrast parameter makes it possible to characterize the segmentation performance obtained for different noise parameters. On the other hand, if one has to choose between different possible imaging systems (coherent/incoherent imaging for example) which are perturbed by different noise statistics, this contrast parameter allows for comparing the performance obtained with the different types of noise.

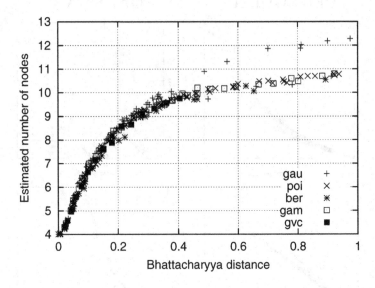

Fig. 7. Averaged estimated number of nodes using the MDL-based snake as a function of the Bhattacharyya distance for different types of graylevel statistics. The number of nodes is averaged over 500 realizations

There is a wide area for development of this subject. Firstly, the proposed contrast parameter could be generalized to characterize segmentation performance in the presence of other types of perturbations, such as noise induced by image compression or deleted pixels [ ], and to other types of image processing tasks. It has been shown elsewhere [,] that this expression of the contrast is also useful to characterize small target detection performance. In the context of segmentation, it would also be interesting to consider a more general expression of the contrast which takes into account the object size and the complexity of its shape.

References

[1] M. Kass, A. Witkin, and D. Terzopoulos, "Snakes: Active contour models," International Journal of Computer Vision **1**, 321–331 (1988).
[2] O. Germain and Ph. Réfrégier, "Optimal snake-based segmentation of a random luminance target on a spatially disjoint background," Opt. Lett. **21**, 1845–1847 (1996).   ,
[3] C. Chesnaud, V. Pagé, and Ph. Réfrégier, "Robustness improvement of the statistically independent region snake-based segmentation method," Opt. Lett. **23**, 488–490 (1998).   ,   ,
[4] C. Chesnaud, Ph. Réfrégier, and V. Boulet, "Statistical region snake-based segmentation adapted to different physical noise models," IEEE Trans. Pattern Analysis and Machine Intelligence **21**, 1145–1157 (1999).   ,   ,   ,

[5] T. S. Ferguson, "Exponential families of distributions," in *Mathematical Statistics, a decision theoretic approach*, pages 125–132 (Academic Press, New York and London, 1967).

[6] M. Figueiredo, J. Leitão, and A. K. Jain, "Unsupervised contour representation and estimation using B-splines and a minimum description length criterion," IEEE Trans. Image Processing **9**, 1075–1087 (2000).   ,

[7] O. Ruch and Ph. Réfrégier, "Minimal-complexity segmentation with a polygonal snake adapted to different optical noise models," Opt. Lett. **41**, 977–979 (2001).

,

[8] O. Ruch and Ph. Réfrégier, "Comparison of Hausdorff distances performances in dissimilarity measurements for silhouette discrimination," in *Automatic Target Recognition, XI*, F. A. Sadjadi, ed., SPIE **4379**, 454–465 (2001).   ,

[9] J. Rissanen, *Stochastic Complexity in Statistical Inquiry* (World Scientific, Singapore, 1989).

[10] C. E. Shannon, "A mathematical theory of communication," Bell Syst. Tech. J. **27**, 379– 423 ; 623 – 656 (1948).

[11] F. Galland, N. Bertaux, and Ph. Réfrégier, "Merge, Move and Remove MDL based segmentation for synthetic aperture radar images," in *Proceedings of ACIVS*, IEEE, 307–314 (September 2002).

[12] D. P. Huttenlocher, G. A. Klanderman, and W. J. Rucklidge, "Comparing images using the Hausdorff distance," IEEE Trans. on Pattern Analysis and Machine Intelligence **15**, 850–863 (1993).

[13] A. O. Hero and C. Guillouet, "Robust detection of SAR/IR targets via invariance," in *Proceedings of the IEEE International Conference on Image Processing*, IEEE, New York **3**, 472–475 (1997).

[14] H. S. Kim and A. O. Hero, "Comparison of GLR and invariant detectors under structured clutter covariance," IEEE Trans. Image Processing **10**, 1509–1520 (2001).

[15] Ph. Réfrégier and F. Goudail, "Invariant polarimetric contrast parameters for coherent light," J. Opt. Soc. Am. A **19**, 1223–1233 (2002).   ,

[16] S. A. Kassam, "Optimal quantization for signal detection," IEEE Trans. Comm. **25**, 479–484 (1977).

[17] H. V. Poor and J. B. Thomas, "Application of Ali-Silvey distance measures in the design of general quantizers for binary decision systems," IEEE Trans. Comm. **25**, 893–900 (1977).

[18] A. D. Lanterman, A. J. O'Sullivan, and M. I. Miller, "Kullback-Leibler distances for quantifying clutter and models," Optical Eng. **38**, 2143–2146 (1996).

[19] A. Jain, P. Moulin, M. I. Miller, and K. Ramchandran, "Information-theoretic bounds on target recognition performance based on degraded image data," IEEE Trans. Pattern Analysis and Machine Intelligence **24**, 1153–1166 (2002).   ,

,

[20] T. M. Cover and J. A. Thomas, *Elements of Information Theory* (Wiley-interscience, New York, 1991).   ,

[21] H. V. Poor, *An introduction to signal detection and estimation* (Springer Verlag, New York, 1994).

[22] H. H. Barrett, C. K. Abbey, and E. Clarkson, "Objective assessment of image quality. III. ROC metrics, ideal observers and likelihood generating functions," J. Opt. Soc. Am. A **15**, 1520–1535 (1998).

[23] F. Goudail, N. Roux, and Ph. Réfrégier, "Performance parameters for detection in low-flux coherent images," Optics Letters **28**, 81–83 (2003).

Minimization of Cost-Functions
with Non-smooth Data-Fidelity Terms
to Clean Impulsive Noise

Mila Nikolova

[1] CNRS URA820–ENST Dpt. TSI, ENST, 46 rue Barrault, 75013 Paris, France
[2] CMLA UMR 8536–ENS de Cachan, 61 av. President Wilson, 94235 Cachan Cedex
nikolova@tsi.enst.fr
http://tsi.enst.fr/~nikolova/

Abstract. We consider signal and image restoration using convex cost-functions composed of a non-smooth data-fidelity term and a smooth regularization term. First, we provide a convergent method to minimize such cost-functions. Then we propose an efficient method to remove impulsive noise by minimizing cost-functions composed of an ℓ_1 data-fidelity term and an edge-preserving regularization term. Their minimizers have the property to fit exactly uncorrupted (regular) data samples and to smooth aberrant data entries (outliers). This method furnishes a new approach to the processing of data corrupted with impulsive noise. A crucial advantage over alternative filtering methods is that such cost-functions can convey adequate priors about the sought signals and images—such as the presence of edges. The numerical experiments show that images and signals are efficiently restored from highly corrupted data.

1 Introduction

We consider the problem where, given data $y \in \mathbb{R}^q$, the estimate $\hat{x} \in \mathbb{R}^p$ of an unknown image or signal is defined as the minimizer of a regularized convex cost-function $\mathcal{F}_y : \mathbb{R}^p \to \mathbb{R}$ which combines a data-fidelity term $\Psi_y : \mathbb{R}^p \to \mathbb{R}$ and a regularization term $\mathcal{Q} : \mathbb{R}^p \to \mathbb{R}$, weighted by a parameter $\beta > 0$:

$$\mathcal{F}_y(x) = \Psi_y(x) + \beta \mathcal{Q}(x), \quad \text{where} \quad \Psi_y(x) = \sum_{i=1}^{q} \psi_i(a_i^T x - y_i). \tag{1}$$

Here, $a_i^T : \mathbb{R}^p \to \mathbb{R}$ is a linear operator, for every $i = 1, \ldots, q$. The cost-function $\mathcal{F}_y$ is systematically assumed to satisfy the hypotheses given next.

H1 *For every $i = 1, \ldots, q$, the function $\psi_i : \mathbb{R} \to \mathbb{R}$ is convex, $\mathcal{C}^1$ on $\mathbb{R} \setminus \{0\}$ and its left-side and right-side derivatives at zero, denoted $\psi_i'(0^-)$ and $\psi_i'(0^+)$, respectively, satisfy* $\quad \psi_i'(0^-) < 0 < \psi_i'(0^+)$.

---

[1] Since ψ_i is convex, $\psi_i(0^+) = \lim_{\varepsilon \searrow 0} (\psi_i(\varepsilon) - \psi_i(0)) / \varepsilon$ and $\psi_i(0^-) = \lim_{\varepsilon \searrow 0} (\psi_i(-\varepsilon) - \psi_i(0)) / (-\varepsilon)$ are well defined and finite [ ]. We write $\varepsilon \searrow 0$ to specify that ε goes to zero by positive values.

A. Rangarajan et al. (Eds.): EMMCVPR 2003, LNCS 2683, pp. 391–   , 2003.
© Springer-Verlag Berlin Heidelberg 2003

H2 *The family $\{a_i : i = 1, \ldots, q\}$ is linearly independent.*

If $q < p$, let $a_i^T : \mathbb{R}^p \to \mathbb{R}$, for $i = q+1, \ldots, p$, be such that $\{a_i : i = 1, \ldots, p\}$ spans $\mathbb{R}^p$. Let A be the $p \times p$ matrix such that for every $i = 1, \ldots, p$ its ith row is a_i^T. For every $i = 1, \ldots, p$, let $e_i \in \mathbb{R}^p$ denote the ith vector of the standard basis of $\mathbb{R}^p$. Using the change of variables $z = Ax - \tilde{y}$, where $\tilde{y} = \sum_{i=1}^{q} y_i e_i + \sum_{i=q+1}^{p} 0 \, e_i$, we will consider $F_y(z) = \mathcal{F}_y\left(A^{-1}(z + \tilde{y})\right)$,

$$F_y(z) = \sum_{i=1}^{q} \psi_i(z_i) + \beta Q_y(z), \quad \text{where } Q_y(z) = \mathcal{Q}(A^{-1}(z + \tilde{y})). \tag{2}$$

$\mathcal{F}_y$ and F_y are equivalent since $\mathcal{F}_y$ reaches its minimum at $\hat{x} \in \mathbb{R}^p$ if, and only if, F_y reaches its minimum at $\hat{z} = A\hat{x} - \tilde{y}$.

H3 *The function $\mathcal{Q}$ in ( ), or equivalently Q_y in ( ), is convex and $\mathcal{C}^1$-continuous.*

H4 *For every $y \in \mathbb{R}^q$, the function F_y in ( ) is 0-coercive,* $\lim\limits_{\|z\| \to +\infty} F_y(z) = \infty$.

In the following, $\|.\|$ denotes the ℓ_2-norm and $\|.\|_1$ the ℓ_1-norm. Notice that Q_y (and also $\mathcal{Q}$) is required to be neither coercive, nor positive.

H5 *For all $y \in \mathbb{R}^q$ and $\rho > 0$, there is $\eta > 0$ such that for every $i = 1, \ldots, p$,*

$$Q_y(z + t e_i) - Q_y(z) \geq t D_i Q_y(z) + \eta t^2, \quad \forall z \text{ such that } \|z\| \leq \rho, \ \forall t \in [-\rho, \rho],$$

where $D_i Q_y$ denotes the ith partial derivative of Q_y.

So, Q_y is strongly convex [ ] only along the directions $\mathrm{span}\{e_i\}$, for $i = 1, \ldots, p$, whereas globally Q_y can be non-strictly convex. In signal and image restoration $\mathcal{Q}$ is usually of the form [ ]

$$\mathcal{Q}(x) = \sum_{i=1}^{r} \varphi(g_i^T x), \tag{3}$$

where $g_i^T : \mathbb{R}^p \to \mathbb{R}$, for $i = 1, \ldots, r$, yield the differences between neighboring samples of x and $\varphi : \mathbb{R} \to \mathbb{R}$ is a potential function. We will denote by G the $r \times p$ matrix such that for every $i = 1, \ldots, r$, its ith row is g_i^T. Several frequently used $\mathcal{C}^1$, convex potential functions φ are [, , , , ,]

$$\varphi(t) = |t|^\alpha, \ 1 \leq \alpha \leq 2, \tag{4}$$
$$\varphi(t) = \sqrt{\alpha + t^2}, \tag{5}$$
$$\varphi(t) = 1 + |t|/\alpha - \log\left(1 + |t|/\alpha\right), \tag{6}$$
$$\varphi(t) = \log(\cosh(t/\alpha)), \tag{7}$$

where $\alpha > 0$ is a parameter. These functions are known to be *edge-preserving* since the minimizer $\hat{x}$ can involve large differences $|g_i^T \hat{x}|$ at the locations of edges [, , , ,]. The equivalent form ( ) now corresponds to

$$Q_y(z) = \sum_{i=1}^{r} \varphi\left(b_i^T(z + y)\right), \tag{8}$$

where b_i^T is the ith row of the matrix $B = GA^{-1}$, for every $i = 1, \ldots, r$. Since φ is $\mathcal{C}^1$ and convex, H clearly holds. If moreover $p = q$, H holds as well. Notice that the functions φ in ( )-( ) are strongly convex on any bounded interval—for any $\delta > 0$, there is a constant $\eta_\delta > 0$, such that $\varphi(t) - \varphi(\tau) \geq \varphi'(\tau)\,(t - \tau) + \eta_\delta (t - \tau)^2$, for all $t \in [-\delta, \delta]$ and $\tau \in [-\delta, \delta]$. It is easy to see that if φ is $\mathcal{C}^1$ and satisfies the latter inequality, Q_y in ( ) satisfies H .

The introduction of nonsmooth data-fidelity terms in regularized cost-functions of the form ( ) is unusual, since only a few papers make an exception to this, e.g. [,]. Our interest in such cost-functions is due to the property that typically, their minimizers $\hat{x}$ fit *exactly* a certain number of the data entries, i.e. $\hat{h} = \{i : a_i^T \hat{x} = y_i\}$ is nonempty [ ]. Based on it, we propose in § an efficient method to selectively smooth outliers by minimizing cost-functions of the form ( ), where $\Psi_y(x) = \|x - y\|_1$ and $\mathcal{Q}$ is as in ( ). We analyze the minimizers of these cost-functions in order to explain the method. We show that they keep unchanged all regular data samples ($\hat{x}_i = y_i$) whereas the outliers incur edge-preserving smoothing based exclusively on the neighboring *regular* data samples. This method is very robust and accurate. The experiments in § show that it gives rise to significant improvement in signal and image restoration over usual order-statistic filtering methods. Some more details on the method, as well as the proofs of all statements given in this paper, can be found in [ ].

2   Minimization Method

Being convex by H and H , and 0-coercive by H , the function F_y (and also $\mathcal{F}_y$), has a minimum for every $y \in \mathbb{R}^q$. This minimum is both local and global [ ].

Theorem 1. *Let H , H and H hold. The function F_y in ( ) reaches its minimum at $\hat{z} \in \mathbb{R}^p$ if, and only if,*

$$-\psi_i'(0^+) \leq \beta D_i Q_y(\hat{z}) \leq -\psi_i'(0^-) \quad \text{if } i \in \hat{h}, \tag{9}$$

$$\psi_i'(\hat{z}_i) + \beta D_i Q_y(\hat{z}) = 0 \qquad \text{if } i \in \hat{h}^c, \tag{10}$$

$$D_i Q_y(\hat{z}) = 0 \qquad \text{if } i \in \{1, \ldots, p\} \setminus (\hat{h}^c \cup \hat{h}), \tag{11}$$

where $\hat{h}$ is defined by

$$\hat{h} = \{i \in \{1, \ldots, q\} : \hat{z}_i = 0\}, \tag{12}$$

and $\hat{h}^c$ is its complement in $\{1, \ldots, q\}$. Moreover, for any $i \in \hat{h}^c$, we have

$$\beta D_i Q_y(\hat{z} - \hat{z}_i e_i) < -\psi_i'(0^+) \Rightarrow \hat{z}_i > 0,$$

$$\beta D_i Q_y(\hat{z} - \hat{z}_i e_i) > -\psi_i'(0^-) \Rightarrow \hat{z}_i < 0.$$

In § we see that $\hat{h}$ is usually non-empty. Notice that under our assumptions, the minimum of F_y may be non-strict. E.g., this can occur when B is singular and $\{\psi_i\}_{i=1}^q$ are not strictly convex.

Proposition 1. *Let F_y be of the form ( ) where Q_y is as given in ( ). Let H , H and H be satisfied. Let $\hat{z} \in \mathbb{R}^p$ satisfy ( ), ( ) and ( ). Suppose also that*

(i) φ is strictly convex on $\mathbb{R}$;

(ii) the set $\hat{h}^0 = \{i \in \hat{h}$ such that ( ) is strict$\}$ is nonempty;

(iii) for every $u \in \ker B$, there is $i \in \hat{h}^0$, such that $u_i \neq 0$.

Then the minimum reached by F_y at $\hat{z}$ is strict.

All functions φ given in ( )-( ) satisfy (i). We see in §　that (ii) is usually satisfied. When A is the identity and $\{g_i^T\}_{i=1}^r$ yield the first-order differences between neighboring samples, $\ker B = \ker G = \mathrm{span}\{\mathbb{1}\}$ where $\mathbb{1}_i = 1$ for all $i = 1, \ldots, r$, hence (iii) holds. So, the minimum of F_y is usually strict.

Since F_y is non-smooth, the calculation of $\hat{z}$ needs a special care. To this end, we consider a relaxation-based minimization which extends a method proposed in [ ] (p. 73). In [ ], $\psi_i(t) = \alpha_i|t|$, with $\alpha_i \geq 0$, for all $i = 1, \ldots, p$, and Q_y is strictly convex and 0-coercive. In our context, $\{\psi_i\}_{i=1}^q$ are more general, and Q_y may be non-strictly convex and non-coercive; so the arguments of [ ] for the convergence of the minimization scheme are not applicable any longer.

Let $z^{(0)} \in \mathbb{R}^p$ be a starting point. At every iteration $k = 1, 2, \ldots$, the new iterate $z^{(k)}$ is obtained from $z^{(k-1)}$ by calculating successively all its entries $z_i^{(k)}$, for $i = 1, \ldots, p$, according to the scheme:

$$\text{for any } i = 1, \ldots, p, \quad F_y(z_1^{(k)}, z_2^{(k)}, \ldots, z_{i-1}^{(k)}, z_i^{(k)}, z_{i+1}^{(k-1)}, \ldots, z_p^{(k-1)})$$
$$= \min_{t \in \mathbb{R}} F_y(z_1^{(k)}, z_2^{(k)}, \ldots, z_{i-1}^{(k)}, t, z_{i+1}^{(k-1)}, \ldots, z_p^{(k-1)}). \quad (13)$$

Let $z_{[i]}^{(k)} \in \mathbb{R}^p$ denote the intermediate solution at step i of iteration k,

$$z_{[i]}^{(k)} = \left(z_1^{(k)}, z_2^{(k)}, \ldots, z_{i-1}^{(k)}, z_i^{(k)}, z_{i+1}^{(k-1)}, \ldots, z_p^{(k-1)} \right).$$

The calculation of $z_{[i]}^{(k)}$ amounts to finding $z_i^{(k)} \in \mathbb{R}$ such that

$$f_i(z_i^{(k)}, z_{[i-1]}^{(k)}) \leq f_i(t, z_{[i-1]}^{(k)}), \quad \forall t \in \mathbb{R}, \quad (14)$$

where $f_i(.; z) : \mathbb{R} \to \mathbb{R}$ reads

$$f_i(t; z) = \psi_i(t) + \beta Q_y(z + (t - z_i)e_i), \quad \forall i = 1, \ldots, q,$$
$$\text{if } q < p, \quad f_i(t; z) = \beta Q_y(z + (t - z_i)e_i), \quad \forall i = q+1, \ldots, p.$$

Under H , H , H and H , for every $z \in \mathbb{R}^p$ and $i = 1, \ldots, p$, the function $t \to f_i(t; z)$ is strictly convex and 0-coercive. Hence, $z_i^{(k)}$ in ( ) is well defined and unique [ ]. It is determined using Theorem :

– if $i \in \{1, \ldots, q\}$, calculate $\quad \xi_i^{(k)} = \beta D_i Q_y(z_{[i-1]}^{(k)} - z_i^{(k-1)}e_i);$

if $-\psi_i'(0^+) \leq \xi_i^{(k)} \leq -\psi_i'(0^-)$ then $z_i^{(k)} = 0$,

otherwise $z_i^{(k)}$ satisfies $\psi_i'(z_i^{(k)}) + \beta D_i Q_y(z_{[i-1]}^{(k)} + (z_i^{(k)} - z_i^{(k-1)})e_i) = 0$,

where $\begin{cases} z_i^{(k)} > 0 \text{ if } \xi_i^{(k)} < -\psi_i'(0^+), \\ z_i^{(k)} < 0 \text{ if } \xi_i^{(k)} > -\psi_i'(0^-); \end{cases}$

– if $q < p$ and $i \in \{q+1, \ldots, p\}$, then $z_i^{(k)}$ is the solution of
$$\mathrm{D}_i Q_y(z_{[i-1]}^{(k)} + (z_i^{(k)} - z_i^{(k-1)})e_i) = 0.$$

Knowing the sign of $z_i^{(k)}$, when $z_i^{(k)} \neq 0$, is essential, since $t \to \psi'(t)$ is discontinuous at zero. The convergence of ( ) is considered next.

Theorem 2. *Let $F_y : \mathrm{I\!R}^p \to \mathrm{I\!R}$ be of the form ( ) and suppose that* H , H , H , H *and* H *are satisfied. For $k \to \infty$, the sequence $z^{(k)}$ defined by ( ) converges to a $\hat{z}$ such that $F_y(\hat{z}) \leq F_y(z)$, for all $z \in \mathrm{I\!R}^p$.*

3   Processing of Impulsive Noise and Outliers

We focus on cost-functions $\mathcal{F}_y : \mathrm{I\!R}^p \to \mathrm{I\!R}$ of the form ( ) where $p = q$, $\psi_i(t) = |t|$ and $a_i = e_i$, for all $i = 1, \ldots, p$, and $\mathcal{Q}$ is of the form ( ). Specifically, we consider

$$\mathcal{F}_y(x) = \sum_{i=1}^{p} |x_i - y_i| + \beta \mathcal{Q}(x), \quad \text{where} \quad \mathcal{Q}(x) = \frac{1}{2} \sum_{i=1}^{p} \sum_{j \in \mathcal{N}_i} \varphi(x_i - x_j). \quad (15)$$

Here $\mathcal{N}_i$ denotes the set of the neighbors of i, for every $i = 1, \ldots, p$. As usually, we have $i \notin \mathcal{N}_i$ and $j \in \mathcal{N}_i \Leftrightarrow i \in \mathcal{N}_j$, for all i and j in $\{1, \ldots, p\}$ [,]. If x is an 1D signal, $\mathcal{N}_i = \{i, i+1\}$, if $i = 2, \ldots, p-1$; for a 2D image, $\mathcal{N}_i$ is the set of the 4, or the 8 pixels adjacent to i. If $\#$ denotes cardinality, put

$$N = \overset{p}{\underset{i=1}{\max}} \, \#\mathcal{N}_i. \quad (16)$$

We assume that $\#\mathcal{N}_i = N$ for every i which is not on the boundaries of x. The function φ in ( ) is $\mathcal{C}^1$, convex and symmetric, as those in ( )-( ).

We will use ( ) to process data $y \in \mathrm{I\!R}^p$ corrupted with impulsive noise. Outliers are characterized by their dissimilarity with respect to neighboring samples. Typically, we have *salt-and-pepper noise*—the corrupted samples take either the maximal, or the minimal value of the allowable dynamic range of the original signal or image [,]. Impulsive noise cleaning involves two sub-problems which are to reliably detect the outliers and to smooth them while preserving the important features of the original signal or image, such as edges and texture.

Let $y \in \mathrm{I\!R}^p$ contain outliers. Suppose that $\mathcal{F}_y$ reaches its minimum at $\hat{x}$ and put $\hat{h} = \{i : \hat{x}_i = y_i\}$. The idea of our method is that *every y_i, for $i \in \hat{h}$, is uncorrupted (i.e. regular)*, since $\hat{x}_i = y_i$; in contrast, *every y_i, for $i \in \hat{h}^c$, can be an outlier* since $\hat{x}_i \neq y_i$, in which case $\hat{x}_i$ is an estimate of the original (uncorrupted) sample. Thus, we introduce the *outlier detector* function

$$y \to \hat{h}^c = \{i \in \{1, \ldots, p\} : \hat{x}_i \neq y_i\}, \quad (17)$$

where $\hat{x}$ is such that $\mathcal{F}_y(\hat{x}) \leq \mathcal{F}_y(x)$, $\forall x \in \mathrm{I\!R}^p$.

The rationale of our method relies on the properties of the minimizers $\hat{x}$ of $\mathcal{F}_y$.

Corollary 1. *For $y \in \mathbb{R}^p$ given, consider $\mathcal{F}_y$ of the form ( ), where φ is C^1 and convex. The function $\mathcal{F}_y$ reaches its minimum at $\hat{x} \in \mathbb{R}^p$ if, and only if,*

$$i \in \hat{h} \Rightarrow \left| \sum_{j \in \mathcal{N}_i} \varphi'(y_i - \hat{x}_j) \right| \leq \frac{1}{\beta}, \tag{18}$$

$$i \in \hat{h}^c \Rightarrow \sum_{j \in \mathcal{N}_i} \varphi'(\hat{x}_i - \hat{x}_j) = \frac{\sigma_i}{\beta}, \quad for \ \sigma_i = \text{sign} \left(\sum_{j \in \mathcal{N}_i} \varphi'(y_i - \hat{x}_j) \right) \tag{19}$$

and $\hat{h} = \{i \in \{1, \ldots, p\} : \hat{x}_i = y_i\}$.

Since ( ) is false for every $i \in \hat{h}^c$, we see that $\sigma_i \in \{-1, 1\}$ in ( ).

Lemma 1. *Let $\mathcal{F}_y$, $\hat{h}$ and σ_i, for all $i \in \hat{h}^c$, be as in Corollary . Define $Y_{\hat{x}}$ by*

$$Y_{\hat{x}} = \left\{ \gamma \in \mathbb{R}^p : \begin{array}{ll} \gamma_i = y_i & if \ i \in \hat{h}, \\ \sigma_i \gamma_i \geq \sigma_i y_i & if \ i \in \hat{h}^c. \end{array} \right\} \tag{20}$$

Then for every $\gamma \in Y_{\hat{x}}$, the function $\mathcal{F}_\gamma$ reaches its minimum at $\hat{x}$.

All functions $\mathcal{F}_\gamma$, corresponding to $\gamma \in Y_{\hat{x}}$, reach their minimum at the same $\hat{x}$, even if $\gamma_i \to \sigma_i \infty$, for any $i \in \hat{h}^c$. Thus, any $\hat{x}_i$ for $i \in \hat{h}^c$ (the estimate of an outlier) is *independent* of the exact value of γ_i (the outlier).

Given a vector $v \in \mathbb{R}^p$ and a subset $h = \{h_1, \ldots, h_{\#h}\} \subset \{1, \ldots, p\}$, we will write $v_h \in \mathbb{R}^{\#h}$ for the restriction of v to those of its entries whose indexes are in h, i.e. $v_h(i) = v(h_i)$ for $i = 1, \ldots, \#h$.

If data are slightly corrupted, many outliers are isolated (i.e., if y_i is an outlier, there is no outlier on $\mathcal{N}_i$). When data are highly corrupted, many outliers are neighbors and we expect that $\hat{h}^c$ involves many neighboring indexes. Let us represent $\hat{h}^c$ as a union of connected components with respect to $\{\mathcal{N}_i : i \in \{1, \ldots, p\}\}$, say ω_k for $k = 1, \ldots, m$. Given ω—a connected component of $\hat{h}^c$—let f_y be the function which for every $x_\omega \in \mathbb{R}^{\#\omega}$ yields

$$f_y(x_\omega) = \sum_{i \in \omega} \sum_{j \in \mathcal{N}_i \cap \hat{h}} \varphi(x_i - y_j) + \frac{1}{2} \sum_{i \in \omega} \sum_{j \in \mathcal{N}_i \cap \omega} \varphi(x_i - x_j) - \frac{\sigma_i x_i}{\beta}. \tag{21}$$

By ( ) and ( ), all $\hat{x}_i$, for $i \in \omega$, satisfy the following system of $\#\omega$ equations :

$$D_i f_y(\hat{x}_\omega) = 0, \quad \text{where } \sigma_i = \text{sign} \left(\sum_{j \in \mathcal{N}_i \cap \hat{h}} \varphi'(y_i - y_j) + \sum_{j \in \mathcal{N}_i \cap \omega} \varphi'(y_i - \hat{x}_j) \right), \quad \forall i \in \omega. \tag{22}$$

---

[2] $\omega = \{i\}$ is a singleton if $\mathcal{N}_i \subset \hat{h}$. Otherwise, for every $i, j \in \omega$ there are $i_j \in \omega$, for $j = 1, \ldots, n$, such that $i_1 \in \mathcal{N}_i, i_2 \in \mathcal{N}_{i_1}, \ldots, j \in \mathcal{N}_{i_n}$; moreover, for every $i \in \omega$, if $\mathcal{N}_i \cap \hat{h}^c$ is nonempty, then $\mathcal{N}_i \cap \hat{h}^c \subset \omega$.

[3] Let $\omega = \{i_1, \ldots, i_n\}$, then $x_\omega = \{x_{i_1}, \ldots, x_{i_n}\}$. To avoid ambiguity, let us precise that $D_i f_y(x_\omega) = \frac{\partial f_y}{\partial x_{i_j}}(\hat{x}_\omega)$ if $i = i_j$.

The influence of an y_i for $i \in \omega$ (an outlier) on the minimizer $\hat{x}_\omega$ of f_y (and thus on $\hat{x}$) is reduced to the binary value σ_i. Notice that $\hat{x}_\omega$ is a function of the data samples y_j for $j \in N_\omega$, where N_ω is the adjacent neighborhood of ω, namely $N_\omega = \left(\bigcup_{i \in \omega} \mathcal{N}_i \right) \setminus \omega \subset \hat{h}$. Thus, any $\hat{x}_{\omega_k}$ is independent of all y_j for $j \notin \mathcal{N}_{\omega_k} \cup \omega_k$ and of any $\hat{x}_{\omega_j}$ for $j \neq k$.

Lemma 2. *Let φ be C^1 and strictly convex. Let $\hat{h} \subset \{1, \ldots, p\}$ and $\hat{h}^c \neq \emptyset$. For ω a connected component of $\hat{h}^c$, let $\hat{x}_\omega$ be such that ( ) is satisfied. Then*

(a) f_γ is strictly convex, for every $\gamma \in \mathbb{R}^p$;
(b) there is $\xi > 0$ and a C^0-function $\mathcal{X}_\omega$ such that if $\|\gamma - y\| < \xi$, then $D_i f_\gamma(\mathcal{X}_\omega(\gamma)) = 0$, for all $i \in \omega$.

Thus, $\hat{x}_\omega$ is the unique minimizer of the strictly convex function f_y.

Remark 1. The function f_y in ( ) is an almost classical regularized cost-function: its first term favors the closeness of $\hat{x}_\omega$ to the regular data samples y_{N_ω} and its second term is a smoothness constraint on $\hat{x}_\omega$; the last term introduces a small bias in the direction of σ_i. If $\#\omega = 1$, say $\omega = \{i\}$, the second term is absent and $\hat{x}_i$ is a compromise between all y_j for $j \in \mathcal{N}_i$ (controlled by the last term). If $\#\omega > 1$, $\hat{x}_\omega$ is a compromise between y_{N_ω} and the smoothness constraint. Based on the results on edge-preserving regularization [, , ,], we can foresee that *edges in $\hat{x}_\omega$ (and thus in $\hat{x}$) are better restored if φ is a good edge-preserving function.* E.g., for φ in ( )-( ), noticing that $\varphi(t) \to |t|$ as $\alpha \searrow 0$, we see that for α small enough, every $\hat{x}_i$, for $i \in \omega$, tends to be close either an y_j, or to an $\hat{x}_j$, for $j \in \mathcal{N}_i$.

Theorem 3. *For $y \in \mathbb{R}^p$ given, let $\mathcal{F}_y$ be of the form ( ), where φ is C^1 and strictly convex. Let $\mathcal{F}_y$ reach its minimum at $\hat{x}$. Define $\hat{h}$ and σ_i, for every $i \in \hat{h}^c$, as in Corollary . Suppose that $\hat{h}$ is nonempty and that for every $i \in \hat{h}$, the inequality in ( ) is strict. Then there is $\rho > 0$ such that if $Y_{\hat{h}}$ reads*

$$Y_{\hat{h}} = \left\{ \gamma \in \mathbb{R}^p : \begin{array}{ll} |\gamma_i - y_i| \leq \rho & \forall i \in \hat{h} \\ \sigma_i \gamma_i \geq \sigma_i y_i - \rho & \forall i \in \hat{h}^c \end{array} \right\},$$

then for every $\gamma \in Y_{\hat{h}}$, the relevant $\mathcal{F}_\gamma$ reaches its minimum at an $\hat{\chi} \in \mathbb{R}^p$ such that

$$\{i \in \{1, \ldots, p\} : \hat{\chi}_i = \gamma_i\} = \hat{h}. \tag{23}$$

Moreover, $\operatorname{sign}\left(\sum_{j \in \mathcal{N}_i} \varphi'(\gamma_i - \hat{\chi}) \right) = \sigma_i$, *for every $i \in \hat{h}^c$, if $\gamma \in Y_{\hat{h}}$.*

Several consequences of the statements given above are worth to emphasize.

(a) By ( ), the subset $Y_\infty \subset \mathbb{R}^p$ given below is *the set of all outlier-free data,*

$$Y_\infty = \left\{ y \in \mathbb{R}^p : \left| \sum_{j \in \mathcal{N}_i} \varphi'(y_i - y_j) \right| \leq \frac{1}{\beta}, \quad \forall i = 1, \ldots, p \right\}, \tag{24}$$

since for every $y \in Y_\infty$, the function $\mathcal{F}_y$ reaches its minimum at $\hat{x} = y$ and $\hat{h}^c$ is empty. Observe that Y_∞ is of dimension p and contains all constant data, as well as *signals and images with smoothly varying and textured areas, edges (of size limited by $1/\beta$) and non-impulsive noise.*

(b) By Theorem , $\mathbb{R}^p$ contains *open domains* $Y_{\hat{h}}$ corresponding to different sets $\hat{h}$. Real data do belong to such domains and give rise to minimizers which fit exactly a certain number of the data entries, i.e. for which $\hat{h}$ is nonempty.

(c) Regular data samples (y_i for $i \in \hat{h}$) are fitted exactly, according to ( ).

(d) Since φ' is increasing on $\mathbb{R}$ and $\varphi'(0) = 0$, ( ) provides the threshold to decide whether a sample y_i is an outlier or not: if y_i is too dissimilar with respect to its neighbors—$y_j \in \mathcal{N}_i \cap \hat{h}$ (regular data) and $\hat{x}_j \in \mathcal{N}_i \cap \hat{h}^c$ (estimates of outliers)—( ) fails. Since this comparison is conducted only with respect to *faithful* neighbors, *the detection of outliers is reliable, even if $\mathcal{N}_i$ is restricted.*

(e) The outliers are smoothed by minimizing implicit functions f_y of the form ( ). The estimate $\hat{x}_\omega$ for a connected component $\omega \subset \hat{h}^c$ of outliers is given on $Y_{\hat{h}}$ by an implicit, continuous function $\mathcal{X}_\omega$ which depends only on the neighboring regular data samples $y_{\mathcal{N}_\omega}$ and is independent of y_i for all $i \in \omega$ (outliers), even if $y_i \to \sigma_i \infty$. Thus, *the minimizers $\hat{x}$ of $\mathcal{F}_y$ are highly resistant to aberrant data.*

(f) The shape of the connected components ω_k of $\hat{h}^c$ depends on the particular realization of the impulsive noise. The possibility of estimating patches of outliers of any size and shape is an essential advantage over filtering methods where the size of the window is fixed. Its importance is crucial for highly corrupted data.

(g) Theorem   shows that *the outlier detector in ( ) is stable under small perturbations of the regular data samples (y_i for $i \in \hat{h}$) and is insensitive to the magnitude of the outliers (y_i for $i \in \hat{h}^c$).*

Remark 2. Edge-preserving functions φ are almost affine when $|t|$ is large [,]. Then $t \to \varphi'(t)$ has a slow increase for $|t|$ large and in many cases—e.g. in ( )-( )—φ' is bounded. In the latter case we must have

$$\beta > \left(N \sup_{t \in \mathbb{R}} |\varphi'(t)| \right)^{-1}, \tag{25}$$

where N is given in ( ). Otherwise, Corollary   shows that for every $y \in \mathbb{R}^p$, the function $\mathcal{F}_y$ reaches its minimum at $\hat{x} = y$.

How Outliers Are Processed. Assume that φ is $\mathcal{C}^2$, symmetric and $\varphi''(t) > 0$, for all $t \in \mathbb{R}$, and that ( ) is satisfied. Let $i \in \{1, \dots, p\}$ be such that no $j \in \mathcal{N}_i$ is on the boundaries of x. For $\sigma_i = 1$, define the function $\mathcal{X}_i : \mathbb{R}^p \to \mathbb{R}$ by

$$\sum_{j \in \mathcal{N}_i} \varphi'(\mathcal{X}_i(y) - y_j) = \frac{\sigma_i}{\beta}, \quad \forall y \in \mathbb{R}^p. \tag{26}$$

Notice that $\mathcal{X}_i$ is well defined and continuous. Let us now define the subset

$$Y_i = \left\{ y \in \mathbb{R}^p : \left| \begin{array}{l} |\sum_{k \in \mathcal{N}_j} \varphi'(y_j - y_k)| < 1/\beta, \ \forall j \in \mathcal{N}_i \cup \{i\}, \\[2mm] |\sum_{k \in \mathcal{N}_j \setminus \{i\}} \varphi'(y_j - y_k) + \varphi'(y_j - \mathcal{X}_i(y))| < 1/\beta, \ \forall j \in \mathcal{N}_i. \end{array} \right. \right\} \tag{27}$$

It is easy to see that Y_i contains an open subset of $\mathbb{R}^p$. Let $y \in Y_i$ and $\mathcal{F}_y$ reach its minimum at $\hat{x}$. Put $\hat{h} = \{i : \hat{x}_i = y_i\}$. Consider now that $\gamma \in \mathbb{R}^p$ reads

$$\gamma = y + t e_i, \quad \text{for} \ \ t \in [0, +\infty).$$

We will analyze how $\hat{\chi}$, the minimizer of the corresponding $\mathcal{F}_\gamma$, varies as a function of γ.

$0 \le t \le \mathcal{X}_i(y) - y_i$. The minimizer $\hat{\chi}$ of $\mathcal{F}_\gamma$ reads

$$\begin{aligned} \hat{\chi}_i &= \gamma_i = y_i + t, \\ \hat{\chi}_j &= \gamma_j = y_j, \quad &\forall j \in \mathcal{N}_i, \\ \hat{\chi}_k &= \hat{x}_k, \quad &\forall k \in \{1, \ldots, p\} \setminus (i \cup \mathcal{N}_i). \end{aligned} \tag{28}$$

$t > \mathcal{X}_i(y) - y_i$. Now $\hat{\chi}$ is given by

$$\begin{aligned} \hat{\chi}_i &= \mathcal{X}_i(\gamma) < \gamma_i, \\ \hat{\chi}_j &= \gamma_j = y_j, \quad &\forall j \in \mathcal{N}_i, \\ \hat{\chi}_k &= \hat{x}_k, \quad &\forall k \in \{1, \ldots, p\} \setminus (i \cup \mathcal{N}_i). \end{aligned} \tag{29}$$

In this case, $\{i : \hat{\chi}_i \neq \gamma_i\} = \hat{h}^c \cup \{i\}$: an isolated outlier is detected at i. Moreover, $\hat{\chi}_i$ incurs smoothing since $0 < \hat{\chi}_i < \gamma_i$.

Hence, $\theta = \mathcal{X}(y) - y_i$ is the threshold for the detection of an isolated outlier at i. From ( )-( ) it is seen that θ is a function of all y_j for $j \in \mathcal{N}_i$. Next we consider some typical configurations.

Constant area. Let $i \in \{1, \ldots, p\}$ be such that no $j \in \mathcal{N}_i$ belongs to the boundaries of x. Without loss of generality, consider that $y_k = 0$ for all $k \in \left(\bigcup_{j \in \mathcal{N}_i} \mathcal{N}_j \right) \cup \mathcal{N}_i$. Let $\theta > 0$ be such that

$$\varphi'(\theta) = \frac{1}{\beta N}. \tag{30}$$

Based on the analysis presented above,

$$\begin{aligned} |y_i| \le \theta &\ \Rightarrow\ \hat{x}_j = y_j, \quad &\forall j \in \mathcal{N}_i \cup \{i\}, \\ |y_i| > \theta &\ \Rightarrow\ \begin{cases} \hat{x}_i = \theta \operatorname{sign}(y_i), \\ \hat{x}_j = y_j, \end{cases} \quad &\forall j \in \mathcal{N}_i. \end{aligned}$$

Supposing that φ is C^2 and admits 3 derivatives, we have $\varphi'(\hat{x}_i) = \varphi''(0)\,\hat{x}_i + \hat{x}_i^2 \varepsilon(\hat{x}_i)$, where $\varepsilon(\hat{x}_i)$ goes to zero as $\hat{x}_i \to 0$. Then $\hat{x}_i = \left(\varphi'(\hat{x}_i) - \hat{x}_i^2 \varepsilon(\hat{x}_i) \right) / \varphi''(0)$. Grossly speaking, the more $\varphi''(0)$ is large, the more smoothing is improved, i.e. $\hat{x}_i$ is closer to zero. For the functions φ in ( )-( ), we notice that $\varphi''(0)$ increases when α goes to zero. This confirms the conclusion of Remark .

Breakpoint in an 1D signal. Let $y \in \mathbb{R}^p$ and let for some $i \in \{3, \ldots, p-2\}$,

$$y_{i-2} = y_{i-1} = 0 \quad \text{and} \quad y_{i+1} = y_{i+2} = \delta > 0.$$

We consider that $\beta < 1/\varphi'(\delta)$. Let θ be the constant such that

$$\varphi'(\theta) + \varphi'(\theta - \delta) = \frac{1}{\beta}. \tag{31}$$

Then $\theta > \delta$ (otherwise, $\varphi'(\theta) + \varphi'(\theta - \delta) < 1/\beta$). It is not difficult to check that

$$y_i \in [0, \theta] \Rightarrow \begin{cases} \hat{x}_{i-1} = y_{i-1} = 0, \\ \hat{x}_i = y_i, \\ \hat{x}_{i+1} = y_{i+1} = \delta, \end{cases} \quad \text{whereas} \quad y_i > \theta \Rightarrow \begin{cases} \hat{x}_{i-1} = y_{i-1} = 0, \\ \hat{x}_i = \theta \in (\delta, y_i), \\ \hat{x}_{i+1} = y_{i+1} = \delta. \end{cases}$$

The conditions for an edge between two constant areas in a 2D image are basically the same.

Minimization Algorithm. We calculate $\hat{x}$ as $\hat{x} = \hat{z} + y$ where $\hat{z}$ minimizes F_y, the equivalent form for $\mathcal{F}_y$ introduced in ( ), namely

$$F_y(z) = \sum_{i=1}^{p} |z_i| + \beta Q_y(z), \quad \text{where} \quad Q_y(z) = \frac{1}{2} \sum_{i=1}^{p} \sum_{j \in \mathcal{N}_i} \varphi(z_i + y_i - z_j - y_j).$$

Based on Theorem , we expect that $\hat{z}_i = 0$ for a certain number of indexes. This suggests we initialize with $z^{(0)} = 0$. At each iteration k, for every $i = 1, \ldots, p$, we calculate

$$\xi_i^{(k)} = \beta \sum_{j \in \mathcal{N}_i} \varphi'(y_i - z_j - y_j), \quad \text{where} \quad z = z_{[i]}^{(k)}; \tag{32}$$

$$\begin{cases} \left| \xi_i^{(k)} \right| \leq 1 \Rightarrow z_i^{(k)} = 0, \\ \left| \xi_i^{(k)} \right| > 1 \Rightarrow \text{find } z_i^{(k)}, \text{ such that } \operatorname{sign}(z_i^{(k)}) = -\operatorname{sign}(\xi_i^{(k)}), \\ \qquad \text{by solving} \quad \beta \sum_{j \in \mathcal{N}_i} \varphi'(z_i^{(k)} + y_i - z_j - y_j) = \operatorname{sign}(\xi_i^{(k)}). \end{cases}$$

All conditions of Theorem   being satisfied, the sequence $z^{(k)}$ converges to the sought $\hat{z}$ as $k \to \infty$.

Remark 3. The calculation of any $z_i^{(k)}$ involves only the samples belonging to $\mathcal{N}_i$. So, at each step we can update simultaneously any subset of entries $\{i_1, \ldots, i_K\}$ $\subset \{1, \ldots, p\}$ such that $i_j \cap N_{i_k} = \emptyset$ for all $j, k \in \{1, \ldots, K\}$ with $j \neq k$.

4   Experiments

Processing of a Signal with Impulsive Noise. The original signal x^* in Fig. (a) is composed of polynomial pieces separated by sharp edges. The data y in Fig. (b) are corrupted with 45% uniformly distributed salt-and-pepper noise.

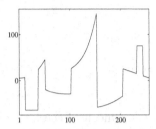 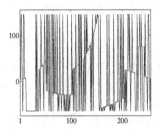

(a) Original signal x^*.   (b) Data y with 45%salt-and-pepper noise.

Fig. 1. Piece-wise polynomial signal in 45% salt-and-pepper noise

The results in Fig.   (a)-(b) are obtained by minimizing classical cost-functions of the form $\mathcal{F}_y(x) = \|x - y\|^2 + \beta \sum_{i=1}^{p-1} |x_i - x_{i+1}|^\alpha$. The signal in (a) corresponds to $\alpha = 1.3$ and $\beta = 150$, the one in (b) corresponds to $\alpha = 1$ (total-variation regularization [ ]) and $\beta = 180$. Cost-functions of this kind are not adapted to impulsive noise and the results are unsatisfactory. Order-statistic (OS) filters are particularly effective at removing outliers [,   ,   ,   ,   ]. We present experiments with median filter, center-weighted median (CWM) filter   and permutation-weighted (PWM) filter . For each method, the restorations which are displayed correspond to the set of parameters (window size, number of iterations, recursivity, other parameters) leading to the best result. The signal in (c) is calculated with a 7 window recursive median filter. It exhibits a stair-case effect and some of the edges are misplaced. The result in Fig.   (d) is obtained with a 9-window recursive CWM for $\alpha = 2$. The restoration in (e) correspond to a PWM filter with the same window and $\alpha = 4$. All restorations obtained using OS filters—(c), (d) and (e)—exhibit important defects. This can be explained by the fact that filtering cannot efficiently take into account prior for signals containing both edges and homogeneous zones. The signal displayed in (f) is calculated by minimizing $\mathcal{F}_y(x) = \sum_{i=1}^p |x_i - y_i| + \frac{\beta}{2} \sum_i \left(\sum_{j \in N_i} \varphi(x_i - x_j) + \gamma \sum_{j \in N_i'} \varphi(x_i - x_j) \right)$, where $\mathcal{N}_i = \{i - 1, i + 1\}$ and $\mathcal{N}_i' = \{i - 2, i + 2\}$, and $\varphi(t) = \sqrt{\alpha + t^2}$. The parameters are $\gamma = 0.6$, $\alpha = 0.2$ and $\beta = 1.2$. Notice that very similar restorations are obtained for different sets of parameters.

Cleaning of a Picture with Impulsive Noise. The original image x^* is shown in Fig.   (a). We consider its restoration from data corrupted with uniformly distributed salt-and-pepper noise. In Fig.   (b), only 10% of the pixels are corrupted. Then we consider data with as much as 45% noise corruption,

---

4 CWM filter is defined using a window $\mathcal{N}_i \cup \{i\}$ and a replication parameter $\alpha \in \mathbb{N}$. The output at i is the median of the set of all y_j, for $j \in \mathcal{N}_i$, and the current sample y_i replicated α times. Thus, α is the weight of the central sample.

5 PWM filter is defined using a window $\mathcal{N}_i \cup \{i\}$ and a rank threshold α. The output at i is y_i if the rank of y_i among all samples in the window is rated between α and $\#\mathcal{N}_i - \alpha$; otherwise, it is the median of all y_j for $j \in \mathcal{N}_i \cup \{i\}$.

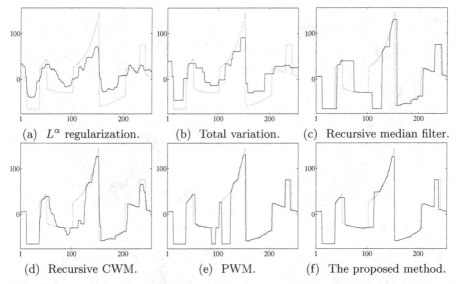

(a) L^α regularization.   (b) Total variation.   (c) Recursive median filter.

(d) Recursive CWM.   (e) PWM.   (f) The proposed method.

Fig. 2. Restoration using different methods: restored signal (—), original signal (- -)

(a) Original image x^* (size 300×300).   (b) Data y (10% salt-and-pepper noise).

Fig. 3. Original picture and data with 10% salt-and-pepper noise

shown in Fig.   (a). For all methods, the parameters are tuned to yield the best result.

Data with 10% salt-and-pepper noise. The denoising results are displayed in Fig.   . All OS methods—(a), (b) and (c)—are obtained with a 3×3 window. The image in (a) corresponds to one iteration of median filter. Its resolution is

(a) Median filtering ($\|\hat{x}-x^*\|_2 = 4147$).   (b) Recursive CWM ($\|\hat{x}-x^*\|_2 = 3613$).

(c) PWM ($\|\hat{x}-x^*\|_2 = 3891$).   (d) The proposed method ($\|\hat{x}-x^*\|_2 = 2904$).

Fig. 4. Denoising of the picture with 10% salt-and-pepper noise

poor. The image in (b) is calculated using a recursive CWM for $\alpha = 3$. The one in (c) corresponds to a PWM filter for $\alpha = 4$. These images are slightly blurred, the texture of the sea is deformed, and several outliers still remain (their removal would increase the distortion considerably). The image $\hat{x}$ in (d) is obtained by minimizing $\mathcal{F}_y$ as given in ( ), with $\varphi(t) = |t|^\alpha$, $\mathcal{N}_i$ the set of the 4 adjacent neighbors, and $\alpha = 1.1$ and $\beta = 0.3$. All details are well preserved and the image is difficult to distinguish from the original x^*. Indeed, for 56% of the pixels, $\hat{x}_i = y_i = x_i^*$ exactly, and for 86% of the pixels, $|\hat{x}_i - x_i^*| < 0.02 \, (\max_i x^* - \min_i x^*)$.

Data with 45% salt-and-pepper noise. The image in Fig.   (b) is obtained after 2 iterations of a 3×3 window recursive median filter. This image has a poor resolution and exhibits a stair-case effect. The result in (c) is calculated using a 5×5 window recursive CWM filter for $\alpha = 7$. The image in (d) results from

(a) Data y (45% salt-and-pepper noise).   (b) Recursive median ($\|\hat{x}-x^*\|_2 = 7825$).

(c) Recursive CWM ($\|\hat{x}-x^*\|_2 = 7497$).   (d) PWM ($\|\hat{x}-x^*\|_2 = 6265$).

Fig. 5. Picture with 45% salt-and-pepper noise

a 7×7 window PWM filter for $\alpha = 14$. Although the images in (c) and (d) are better restored, the resolution is poor, there are artifacts along the edges and the texture of the sea is destroyed.

The images in Fig.   are the minimizers of the same cost-function $\mathcal{F}_y$, see ( ), with $\mathcal{N}_i$ the set of the 4 nearest neighbors, $\varphi(t) = |t|^\alpha$ and $\alpha = 1.3$. The image in (a) corresponds to $\beta = 0.18$ and the one in (b) to $\beta = 0.2$. The quality of these restorations is clearly improved: the contours are neater, the texture of the sea in better preserved and some details on the boat can be distinguished.

(a) $\alpha = 1.3$, $\beta = 0.18$ ($\|\hat{x} - x^*\|_2 = 6064$).   (b) $\alpha = 1.3$, $\beta = 0.2$ ($\|\hat{x} - x^*\|_2 = 6126$).

Fig. 6. The proposed method (the minimizer $\hat{x}$ of $\mathcal{F}_y$)

5   Conclusion

We present a convergent method to minimize convex cost-functions composed of a non-smooth data-fidelity term and a smooth regularization term. Then we propose a method to remove impulsive noise from signals and images by minimizing a cost-function composed of an ℓ_1 data-fidelity and a smooth, edge-preserving regularization term. This provides a new framework in the field of the processing of data corrupted with impulsive noise. Our method is justified by the specific properties of the minimizers of the cost-functions we consider. An important advantage over filtering methods is that the detection of outliers is based on a global cost-function, accounting for the priors on the underlying signal or image—such as the presence of edges and homogeneous zones. The minimizer is independent of the exact values of the outliers and stable with respect to variations of the regular data samples. The experiments show that the outliers are efficiently recovered and smoothed while the regular data samples are well preserved, even if the data are highly corrupted.

References

[1] Hiriart-Urruty, J. B., Lemaréchal, C.: Convex analysis and Minimization Algorithms, vol. I and II. Springer-Verlag, Berlin (1996)   ,   ,   ,
[2] Besag, J. E.: Digital image processing : Towards Bayesian image analysis. Journal of Applied Statistics**16** (1989) 395–407   ,
[3] Bouman, C., Sauer, K.: A generalized Gaussian image model for edge-preserving MAP estimation. IEEE Transactions on Image Processing**2** (1993) 296–310
[4] Li, S.: Markov Random Field Modeling in Computer Vision. 1 edn. Springer-Verlag, New York (1995)   ,

[5] Black, M., Rangarajan, A.: On the unification of line processes, outlier rejection, and robust statistics with applications to early vision. International Journal of Computer Vision**19** (1996) 57–91   ,

[6] Vogel, C. R., Oman, M. E.: Iterative method for total variation denoising. SIAM Journal of Scientific Computing**17** (1996) 227–238

[7] Teboul, S., Blanc-Féraud, L., Aubert, G., Barlaud, M.: Variational approach for edge-preserving regularization using coupled pde's. IEEE Transactions on Image Processing**7** (1998) 387–397   ,   ,

[8] Charbonnier, P., Blanc-Féraud, L., Aubert, G., Barlaud, M.: Deterministic edge-preserving regularization in computed imaging. IEEE Transactions on Image Processing**6** (1997) 298–311   ,   ,

[9] Alliney, S., Matej, S., Bajla, I.: On the possibility of direct Fourier reconstruction from divergent-beam projections. IEEE Transactions on Medical Imaging**MI-12** (1993) 173–181

[10] Alliney, S.: A property of the minimum vectors of a regularizing functional defined by means of absolute norm. IEEE Transactions on Signal Processing**45** (1997) 913–917

[11] Nikolova, M.:   Minimizers of cost-functions involving nonsmooth data-fidelity terms. Application to the processing of outliers. SIAM Journal of Numerical Analysis**40** (2001) 965–994

[12] Nikolova, M.: Minimization of cost-functions with non-smooth data-fidelity terms. application to the processing of impulsive noise. Technical report, (CMLA—ENS de Cachan, Report N°. 2003-01)

[13] Glowinski, R., Lions, J., Trémolières, R.:   Analyse numérique des inéquations variationnelles. 1 edn. Volume 1. Dunod, Paris (1976)

[14] Geman, D. In: Random fields and inverse problems in imaging. Lecture notes in mathematics edn. Volume 1427. École d'Été de Probabilités de Saint-Flour XVIII - 1988, Springer-Verlag (1990) 117–193

[15] Abreu, E., Lightstone, M., Mitra, S. K., Arakawa, K.: A new efficient approach for the removal of impulse noise from highly corrupted images. IEEE Transactions on Image Processing**5** (1996) 1012–1025

[16] Bovik, A. C.: Handbook of image and video processing. Academic Press, New York (2000)   ,

[17] Rudin, L., Osher, S., Fatemi, C.: Nonlinear total variation based noise removal algorithm. Physica **60 D** (1992) 259–268

[18] Ko, S. J., Lee, Y. H.: Adaptive center weighted median filter. IEEE Transactions on Circuits and Systems **38** (1998) 984–993

[19] Sun, T., Neuvo, Y.: Detail-preserving based filters in image processing. Pattern-Recognition Letters **15** (1994) 341–347

[20] Arce, G. R., Hall, T. A., Barner, K. E.: Permutation weighted order statistic filters. IEEE Transactions on Image Processing**4** (1995) 1070–1083

[21] Yin, L., Yang, R., Gabbouj, M., Neuvo, Y.: Weighted median filters: a tutorial. IEEE Transactions on Circuit Theory**41** (1996) 157–192

A Fast GEM Algorithm for Bayesian Wavelet-Based Image Restoration Using a Class of Heavy-Tailed Priors[⋆]

José M. Bioucas-Dias

Instituto de Telecomunicações
Instituto Superior Técnico, Torre Norte, Piso 10
Av. Rovisco Pais, 1049-001 Lisboa, PORTUGAL
ioucas@lx.it.pt
Phone: 351 21 8418466

Abstract. The paper introduces modelling and optimization contributions on a class of Bayesian wavelet-based image deconvolution problems. Main assumptions of this class are: 1) space-invariant blur and additive white Gaussian noise; 2) prior given by a linear (finite of infinite) decomposition of Gaussian densities. Many heavy-tailed priors on wavelet coefficients of natural images admit this decomposition. To compute the *maximum a posteriori* (MAP) estimate, we propose a *generalized expectation maximization* (GEM) algorithm where the missing variables are the Gaussian modes. The maximization step of the EM algorithm is approximated by a *stationary second order iterative method*. The result is a GEM algorithm of $O(N \log N)$ computational complexity. In comparison with state-of-the-art methods, the proposed algorithm either outperforms or equals them, with low computational complexity.

1 Introduction

Image deconvolution is a longstanding linear inverse problem with applications in remote sensing, medical imaging, astronomy, seismology, and, more generally, in image restoration [ ].

The challenge in many linear inverse problems is that they are ill-posed, i.e., either the linear operator does not admit inverse or it is near singular yielding highly noise sensitive solutions. To cope with the ill-posed nature of these problems, a large number of traditional techniques has been developed, most of them under the regularization or the Bayesian frameworks [, , , ,].

The heart of the regularization and Bayesian approaches is the *a priori* knowledge expressed by the prior/regularization term. A "good" prior should express knowledge about images being described. For example, the *weak membrane* [ ], in the regularization setup, and the *compound Gauss Markov random field* [ ],

---

[⋆] This work was supported by the Fundação para a Ciência e Tecnologia, under the project POSI/34071/CPS/2000.

in the Bayesian setup were conceived to model piecewise-smooth images. This was an improvement over the classical quadratic priors.

Wavelet-based approaches have recently been adopted to solve linear inverse problems [, , , , , , ,]. Underlying this direction is the parsimonious representation provided by the wavelet transform of a large class of natural images [ ]: images are essentially described by a few large wavelet coefficients. This fact has fostered Bayesian and regularization approaches where the prior favors a few large wavelet coefficients and many nearly zero ones (the so-called heavy-tailed priors).

In formulating linear space-invariant inverse problems in the wavelet domain, one is frequently faced with linear operations resulting from the composition of Toeplitz operators with the wavelet transforms. This composed operator is not diagonal and introduces unbearable computational complexity in the wavelet-based deconvolution schemes. Recent works [ ] and [ ] have circumventing this difficulty by recognizing that each of these operations *per se* can be computed efficiently with fast algorithms.

1.1 Proposed Approach

We introduce a wavelet-based Bayesian solution to image deconvolution. The observation mechanism comprehends space-invariant blur and additive Gaussian noise. The wavelet coefficients are assumed to be independent with density given by a linear (finite of infinite) combination of Gaussian densities. This class of densities models many heavy-tailed priors, namely, the *Gaussian mixture models* (GMM), the Jeffreys' non-informative prior [ ], the Laplacian prior, the equivalent *garrote* prior (see [ ] and papers therein).

To compute the MAP estimate, we propose an EM algorithm where the missing variables are the Gaussian modes. The maximization step of the EM algorithm includes a huge non-diagonal linear system with unbearable computational complexity. To avoid this difficulty we approximate the linear system solution by a few iterations of a *stationary second order iterative method*. The resulting scheme is a *generalized expectation maximization* (GEM) algorithm, achieving convergence in a few tens of iterations. The fast Fourier transform (FFT) and the discrete wavelet transform (DWT) are the heaviest computations on each GEM step. Thus the overall algorithm complexity is $O(N \log N)$.

In a set of experiments, the proposed algorithm either equals or outperforms state-of-the-art methods [, , , ,].

The paper is organized as follows. Section formulates the restoration problem in the wavelet domain under the Bayesian framework. Section 3 introduces a class of heavy-tailed priors that can be expressed as linear combination of Gaussian terms. It is shown that this class contains many of the heavy-tailed priors used in wavelet-based image denoising and restoration. Still in Section 3, it is introduced a *generalized expectation maximization* algorithm aimed at the fast computation of the *maximum a posteriori* image estimate. Finally, Section 4 presents experimental results illustrating the effectiveness of the proposed methodology.

2   Problem Formulation

Let us denote $\mathbf{x}$ and $\mathbf{y}$ as vectors containing the true and the observed image gray levels, respectively, arranged in column lexicographic ordering. We assume, without loss of generality, that images are square of size N (number of pixels).

The observation model herein considered is

$$\mathbf{y} = \mathbf{Hx} + \mathbf{n}, \tag{1}$$

where $\mathbf{H}$ is a square block-Toeplitz matrix accounting for space-invariant blur and $\mathbf{n}$ is a sample of zero-mean white Gaussian noise vector with density $p(\mathbf{n}) = \mathcal{N}(\mathbf{n}|\mathbf{0}, \sigma^2\mathbf{I})$ [$\mathcal{N}(\mathbf{z}|\mathbf{m}, \mathbf{C})$ denotes the Gaussian multivariate density of mean $\mathbf{m}$ and covariance $\mathbf{C}$ evaluated at $\mathbf{z}$, and $\mathbf{I}$ is the identity matrix].

Let $\mathbf{W}$ denote the orthogonal discrete wavelet transform (DWT) and $\boldsymbol{\theta} = \mathbf{Wx}$ the wavelet coefficients of $\mathbf{x}$. Since $\mathbf{W}$ is orthogonal, expression ( ) can be written as

$$\mathbf{y} = \mathbf{HW}^T\boldsymbol{\theta} + \mathbf{n}. \tag{2}$$

The density of the observed vector $\mathbf{y}$ given $\boldsymbol{\theta}$ is then $p(\mathbf{y}|\boldsymbol{\theta}) = \mathcal{N}(\mathbf{y}|\mathbf{HW}^T\boldsymbol{\theta}, \sigma^2\mathbf{I})$. Given a prior $p(\boldsymbol{\theta})$, the maximum a posteriori (MAP) estimate of $\boldsymbol{\theta}$ is given by

$$\widehat{\boldsymbol{\theta}} = \arg\max_{\boldsymbol{\theta}} \left\{ \log p(\mathbf{y}|\boldsymbol{\theta}) + \log p(\boldsymbol{\theta}) \right\} \tag{3}$$

$$= \arg\max_{\boldsymbol{\theta}} \left\{ \frac{-\|\mathbf{y} - \mathbf{HW}^T\boldsymbol{\theta}\|^2}{2\sigma^2} + \log p(\boldsymbol{\theta}) \right\}. \tag{4}$$

As in many recent works, we assume that the wavelet coefficients are mutually independent and identically distributed, i.e.,

$$p(\boldsymbol{\theta}) = \prod_{i=1}^{N} p(\theta_i).$$

The independence assumption is motivated by the high degree of decorrelation exhibited by wavelet coefficients of natural images. Although decorrelation does not imply independence, the former has led to very good results.

If $\mathbf{H} = \mathbf{I}$, i.e., there is no blur, the image restoration at hand fall into a denoising problem. In this case the maximization ( ) reduces to N decoupled coefficient-wise maximizations, what can be efficiently solved exploiting the orthogonality of $\mathbf{W}$ and using fast implementations of the DWT (see, e.g. [,]).

If $\mathbf{H} \neq \mathbf{I}$, i.e., there exists blur, the maximization ( ) cannot be decoupled. Furthermore, matrix $\mathbf{HW}^T$ of size $N \times N$ introduces complexity beyond reasonable. In the next section we develop a GEM algorithm that avoids direct manipulation of matrix $\mathbf{HW}^T$.

3   A GEM Algorithm
that Avoids Direct Manipulation of $\mathbf{HW}^T$

Let us assume that the prior on each wavelet coefficient is given by

$$p(\theta) = E_z[p(\theta|z)], \tag{5}$$

where z is a continuous or discrete random variable, and

$$p(\theta|z) = \mathcal{N}[\theta|0, \sigma^2(z)]. \tag{6}$$

Many of the heavy-tailed priors used in wavelet-based image denosing/restoration admit the decomposition implicit in the right-hand side of ( ). Some examples are listed below (see [ ])

- Gaussian mixture models (GMM): $z \in \{1, \ldots n\}$ and $P(z = i)$ is the probability of $\theta \sim \mathcal{N}[\theta|0, \sigma^2(i)]$
- Laplacian prior: $p(z) = \gamma \exp(-\gamma z)$, with $z > 0$, and $\sigma^2(z) = z$
- Jeffreys prior: $p(z) \propto 1/z$, with $z > 0$, and $\sigma^2(z) = z$.
- Any even prior such that $p(\sqrt{\theta})$ is *completely monotone* (see [ ]).

Random vectors $\mathbf{z} \equiv (z_1, \ldots, z_N)$ and $(\mathbf{y}, \mathbf{z})$ play the role of *missing data* and *complete data*, respectively, in our GEM formulation. The EM algorithm generates a nondecreasing sequence [ ] $\{p(\mathbf{y}, \widehat{\boldsymbol{\theta}}_t), |t = 0, 1, \ldots\}$, where $\{\widehat{\boldsymbol{\theta}}_t, |t = 0, 1, \ldots\}$ is generated by the two-step iteration

E-step:

$$Q(\boldsymbol{\theta}, \widehat{\boldsymbol{\theta}}_t) = E\left[\log[p(\mathbf{y}, \mathbf{z}, \boldsymbol{\theta})|\mathbf{y}, \widehat{\boldsymbol{\theta}}_t\right] \tag{7}$$

$$= \frac{-\|\mathbf{y} - \mathbf{H}\mathbf{W}^T\boldsymbol{\theta}\|^2}{2\sigma^2} - \frac{1}{2}\boldsymbol{\theta}^T\mathbf{D}_t\boldsymbol{\theta} + c^{te},$$

where $\mathbf{D}_t \equiv \text{diag}\{E[(\sigma^{-2}(z_1), \ldots, \sigma^{-2}(z_N))|\widehat{\boldsymbol{\theta}}_t]\}$ and c^{te} stands for constant.

M-step:

$$\widehat{\boldsymbol{\theta}}_{t+1} = \arg\max_{\boldsymbol{\theta}} Q(\boldsymbol{\theta}, \widehat{\boldsymbol{\theta}}_t) \tag{8}$$

$$= \left(\sigma^2\mathbf{D}_t + \mathbf{W}\mathbf{H}^T\mathbf{H}\mathbf{W}^T\right)^{-1}\mathbf{W}\mathbf{H}^T\mathbf{y}. \tag{9}$$

M-step ( ) is impracticable from the computational point of view, as it amounts to solving the linear system $\mathbf{A}_t\boldsymbol{\theta} = \mathbf{y}'$, where $\mathbf{A}_t \equiv \sigma^2\mathbf{D}_t + \mathbf{W}\mathbf{H}^T\mathbf{H}\mathbf{W}^T$ and $\mathbf{y}' = \mathbf{W}\mathbf{H}^T\mathbf{y}$, of size N^2 and involving the matrix $\mathbf{H}\mathbf{W}^T$. We tackle this difficulty by replacing the maximization ( ) with a few steps of an iterative procedure that increments $Q(\boldsymbol{\theta}, \widehat{\boldsymbol{\theta}}_t)$, with respect to $\boldsymbol{\theta}$. The resulting scheme is thus a GEM algorithm.

Let $\mathbf{A}_t = \mathbf{C}_t - \mathbf{R}$ be a *splitting* [ ] of $\mathbf{A}_t$, where $\mathbf{C}_t \equiv (\sigma^2\mathbf{D}_t + \mathbf{I})$ and $\mathbf{R} \equiv (\mathbf{I} - \mathbf{W}\mathbf{H}^T\mathbf{H}\mathbf{W}^T)$. Assuming that $\mathbf{A}_t$ is positive definite, then the *second-order iterative method* defined by

$$\begin{aligned}
\mathbf{r}_i &= \mathbf{A}_t\boldsymbol{\xi}_i - \mathbf{y}' & i = 0, 1, \ldots \\
\boldsymbol{\xi}_1 &= \boldsymbol{\xi}_0 - \beta_0\mathbf{C}_t^{-1}\mathbf{r}_0 & \\
\boldsymbol{\xi}_{i+1} &= \alpha\boldsymbol{\xi}_i + (1-\alpha)\boldsymbol{\xi}_{i-1} - \beta\mathbf{C}_t^{-1}\mathbf{r}_i & i = 1, 2, \ldots,
\end{aligned} \tag{10}$$

converges to the solution of $\mathbf{A}\boldsymbol{\theta} = \mathbf{y}'$, if and only if

$$\begin{cases} 0 < \alpha < 2 \\ 0 < \beta < 2\alpha/\lambda_N, \end{cases} \tag{11}$$

where $0 < \lambda_1 \le \lambda_2 \le \cdots \le \lambda_N$ are the eigenvalues of $\mathbf{C}_t^{-1}\mathbf{A}_t$ (see Theorem 5.9 of [, ch. 5]). The optimal convergence factor is

$$\rho_{opt} \equiv [1 - \sqrt{\lambda_1/\lambda_N}][1 + \sqrt{\lambda_1/\lambda_N}]$$

and is achieved for

$$\begin{cases} \alpha = \rho_{opt}^2 + 1 \\ \beta = 2\alpha/(\lambda_1 + \lambda_N) \\ \beta_0 = \beta/\alpha. \end{cases}$$

Some algebra applied to the third line of ( ) leads to

$$\boldsymbol{\xi}_{i+1} = (\alpha - \beta)\boldsymbol{\xi}_i + (1 - \alpha)\boldsymbol{\xi}_{i-1}$$
$$+ \beta\mathbf{C}_t^{-1}\left\{\boldsymbol{\xi}_i + \mathbf{W}\mathbf{H}^T\left(\mathbf{y} - \mathbf{H}\mathbf{W}^T\boldsymbol{\xi}_i\right)\right\} \qquad i = 1, 2, \ldots \tag{12}$$

Expression shown in the second line of ( ) is also given by ( ) with $\alpha = 1$ and $\beta = \beta_0$. Given that $\mathbf{C}_t = (\sigma^2\mathbf{D}_t + \mathbf{I})$ is diagonal, the product $\mathbf{W}\mathbf{H}^T\mathbf{H}\mathbf{W}^T\boldsymbol{\xi}_i$, necessary to determine the residual $\mathbf{r}_i$, is the heaviest computation in each iteration ( ). We note however that $\mathbf{W}\mathbf{H}^T\mathbf{H}\mathbf{W}^T\boldsymbol{\xi}_i$ can be computed efficiently, since there exists fast implementations $[O(N)]$ of the DWT and of the inverse DWT [ ], and the product of a Toeplitz matrix by a vector can also be computed efficiently, by embedding $\mathbf{H}$ in a larger block-circulant matrix. Block-circulant matrices are diagonalized by the 2D discrete Fourier transform. Therefore, by using the 2D fast Fourier transform, the complexity of the product of a Toeplitz matrix by a vector is $[O(N \log N)]$ [ ].

A pertinent question is the choice of the number of iterations, say p, of the optimization step (O-step) assuring that Q increases, i.e., $Q(\boldsymbol{\xi}_p, \widehat{\boldsymbol{\theta}}_t) > Q(\widehat{\boldsymbol{\theta}}_t, \widehat{\boldsymbol{\theta}}_t)$. A very simple solution to this problem consists in computing $Q(\boldsymbol{\xi}_i, \widehat{\boldsymbol{\theta}}_t)$ after each iteration ( ) and check if $Q(\boldsymbol{\xi}_i, \widehat{\boldsymbol{\theta}}_t) > Q(\widehat{\boldsymbol{\theta}}_t, \widehat{\boldsymbol{\theta}}_t)$. Note that this procedure adds only a small computational complexity to the GEM algorithm, since the heaviest step in determining the quadratic function $Q(\xi_i, \widehat{\boldsymbol{\theta}}_t)$ given by ( ) is the computation of $\mathbf{H}\mathbf{W}^T\boldsymbol{\theta}$, also needed to compute ξ_i in ( ).

Figure , part a), illustrates the behavior of $Q(\boldsymbol{\xi}_i, \widehat{\boldsymbol{\theta}}_t)$ and $\log p(\widehat{\boldsymbol{\theta}}_t|\mathbf{y})$ for an image of size 256×256, blur uniform of size 9×9, and blurred signal-to-noise ratio of $40\,dB$. Notice that, for a given $\widehat{\boldsymbol{\theta}}_t$, the plotted values of $Q(\boldsymbol{\xi}_i, \widehat{\boldsymbol{\theta}}_t)$ are strictly increasing. Part b) plots $\log p(\widehat{\boldsymbol{\theta}}_t|\mathbf{y})$ as function of the total number of iterations ( ), parameterized by p (number of iterations ( ) per O-step). Curves for $p = 5$

---

[1] From now on we refer to O-step instead of M-step, because $Q(\boldsymbol{\theta}, \widehat{\boldsymbol{\theta}}_t)$ is not maximized with respect to $\boldsymbol{\theta}$, but only increased.

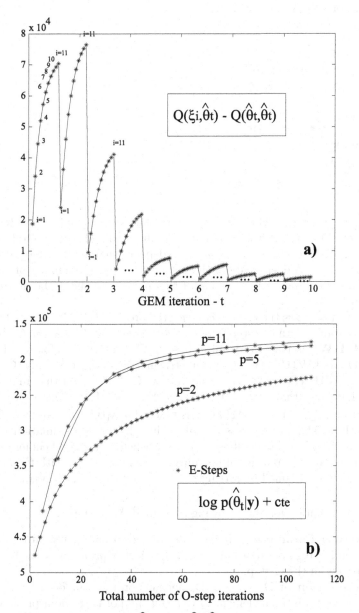

Fig. 1. a) Evolution of $Q(\boldsymbol{\xi}_i, \widehat{\boldsymbol{\theta}}_t) - Q(\widehat{\boldsymbol{\theta}}_t, \widehat{\boldsymbol{\theta}}_t)$, for $i = 1, 2, \ldots, 11$ and $t = 0, 1, \ldots, 10$; b) Evolution of $\log p(\widehat{\boldsymbol{\theta}}_t | \mathbf{y})$ (up to a constant c^{te}) parameterized with p (O-step iterations)

Algorithm 1 Generalized Expectation Maximization Algorithm

Initialization: $\widehat{\boldsymbol{\theta}}_0$ {Wiener filter},
1: **for** $t := 0$ to *StopRule* **do**
2:     {E-Step}
3:     $\mathbf{D}_t := \text{diag}\{E[(\sigma^{-2}(z_1), \ldots, \sigma^{-2}(z_N))|\widehat{\boldsymbol{\theta}}_t]\}$
4:     {O-step (Increases $Q(\boldsymbol{\theta}, \widehat{\boldsymbol{\theta}}_t)$)}
5:     $\boldsymbol{\xi}_0 := \widehat{\boldsymbol{\theta}}_t$, *Compute* $\mathbf{r}_0$, $\boldsymbol{\xi}_1$ { see ( ) }
6:     **for** $i := 1$ to 4 **do**
7:         $\mathbf{r}_i = \mathbf{A}_t \boldsymbol{\xi}_i - \mathbf{y}'$
8:         $\boldsymbol{\xi}_{i+1} = \alpha \boldsymbol{\xi}_i + (1 - \alpha) \boldsymbol{\xi}_{i-1} - \beta \mathbf{C}_t^{-1} \mathbf{r}_i$
9:     **end for**
10:     $\widehat{\boldsymbol{\theta}}_{t+1} = \boldsymbol{\xi}_5$
11: **end for**

---

and for $p = 11$ are very close, whereas curve for $p = 2$ is well below the others. This pattern of behavior was systematically observed and seems to indicate that for $p \geq p_{min}$, the evolution of $\log p(\widehat{\boldsymbol{\theta}}_t|\mathbf{y})$ depends mainly on the total number of iterations ( ). A deep study of the balance between the number of inner and outer iterations is beyond the scope of this paper and should be addressed in future work.

Algorithm 1 shows the pseudo-code for the proposed GEM scheme. The number of iterations of the O-step is set to 4. Given that $\mathbf{C}_t^{-1}\mathbf{A}_t = \mathbf{C}_t^{-1}\sigma^2\mathbf{D}_t + \mathbf{C}_t^{-1}\mathbf{W}\mathbf{H}^T\mathbf{H}\mathbf{W}^T$ is positive definite, $0 \leq \lambda_i(\mathbf{C}_t^{-1}\sigma^2\mathbf{D}_t) \leq 1$, for $i = 1, \ldots, N$, and $\mathbf{C}_t$, $\mathbf{D}_t$, and $\mathbf{W}\mathbf{H}^T\mathbf{H}\mathbf{W}^T$ are symmetric matrices, we have $0 < \lambda_i(\mathbf{C}_t^{-1}\mathbf{A}_t) \leq 1 + \lambda_i(\mathbf{C}_t^{-1}\mathbf{W}\mathbf{H}^T\mathbf{H}\mathbf{W}^T)$. Noting that $0 < \lambda_i(\mathbf{C}_t^{-1}) \leq 1$ and that matrix $\mathbf{W}$ is unitary, it follows that $0 < \lambda_i(\mathbf{C}_t^{-1}\mathbf{A}_t) \leq 1 + \lambda_N(\mathbf{H}\mathbf{H}^T)$. The approximation $\widetilde{\lambda}_1 = 0.01$ and $\widetilde{\lambda}_N = 1 + \lambda_N(\mathbf{H}^T\mathbf{H})$ was taken, for $\lambda_1(\mathbf{C}_t^{-1}A_t)$ and $\lambda_N(\mathbf{C}_t^{-1}A_t)$, respectively. It should be stressed that, although this approximation might be rough, it assures that inequalities ( ) are satisfied and is good enough to boost the converge rate by an order of magnitude when comparing with *the first order iterative method* obtained by setting $\alpha = 1$ in ( ) (see [, ch. 5])).

We call attention for the following aspects of Algorithm 1:

- **Unknown Parameters:** If there are unknown parameters in the observation model (e.g., observation noise σ^2) or in the prior, they can be inferred iteratively in the O-step.
- **Computation of $\mathbf{D}_t$:** Matrix $\mathbf{D}_t$ depends on the type of prior. Below, we list a generic diagonal element $d_t = E[\sigma^2(z)|\theta_t]$ of $\mathbf{D}_t$ for four priors (see [, ,]):

$$\text{Gaussian mixture } d_t = \frac{\sum_{i=1}^{n} \frac{P(z=i)}{\sigma_i^2} p(\theta_t | z = i)}{p(\theta_t)}$$

$$\text{Laplacian prior } d_t = 2\gamma |\theta_t|^{-1}$$

$$\text{Jeffreys prior } d_t = |\theta_t|^{-2}$$

$$\text{Garrote prior } d_t = \frac{-|\theta_t| + \sqrt{\theta_t^2 + 4a\sigma^2}}{2|\theta_t|\sigma^2}$$

The denoising algorithm introduced in [ ] is equivalent to the Garrote prior with $a = 3$. The present formulation opens the door to adapting parameter a to data.

- **Translation-Invariant Restoration:** Translation-invariant (TI) wavelet-based methods outperform the orthogonal DWT based ones, as the former significantly reduce the *blocky* artifacts associated to the dyadic shifts inherent to the orthogonal DWT basis functions [ ]. In the present setup, replacing the orthogonal DWT with the TI-DWT does not alter the GEM nature of the developed algorithm, as the optimization step still increment the objective function $Q(\boldsymbol{\theta}, \widehat{\boldsymbol{\theta}}_t)$.

4   Experimental Results

We now present a set of four experiments illustrating the performance of Algorithm 1. Original images are cameraman (experiments 1, 2, and 3,) and lena (experiment 4) both of size 256×256. Estimation results are compared with state-of-the-art methods [,   ,   ,   ,   ]. In all experiments, we employ TI-DWT, with Haar wavelets (Daubechies-2), and the equivalent Garrote prior with $a = 3$ as it yields the best results among priors compared in paper [ ]. Noise is assumed unknown and the stopping rule is

$$\frac{\|\widehat{\mathbf{x}}_{t+1} - \widehat{\mathbf{x}}_t\|_2}{\|\widehat{\mathbf{x}}_t\|_2} < 2 \times 10^{-3}\sigma^2.$$

In the first experiment we take the setup of [ ]: blur uniform of size 9×9 and signal-to-noise-ratio of the blurred image (BSNR) set to BSNR=40 dB. In the second and third experiments we consider the setup of [,   ]: point spread function of blur $h_{ij} = (1 + i^2 + j^2)$, for $i, j = -7, \ldots, 7$, and noise variances set to $\sigma^2 = 2$ for experiment 2 and $\sigma^2 = 8$ for experiment 3. Finally, in experiment 4, we use the setup of [ ]: 5×5 separarable blur filter with weights $[1, 4, 6, 4, 1]/16$ and noise of standard variance $\sigma = 7$.

Table   shows the signal-to-noise improvements (ISNR) of the proposed approach and methods [,   ,   ,   ,   ], for the four experiments. Algorithm 1 outperforms the others in all experiments. The number of GEM iterations to satisfy the stop criterion was 55, 10, 8, and 3, for the experiments 1, 2, 3, and 4, respectively.

Fig. 2. Camera-man: a) Original image; b) Blurred noisy image (blur (9×9) uniform, BSNR=40 dB); c) Restored image with Algorithm 1 (ISNR = 8.1dB)

Fig. 3. a) Original image; b) Blurred noisy image (blur $h_{ij} = (1 + i^2 + j^2)$, for $i, j = -7, \ldots, 7$, and noise variance set to $\sigma^2 = 8$); c) Restored image with Algorithm 1 (ISNR = 5.17dB)

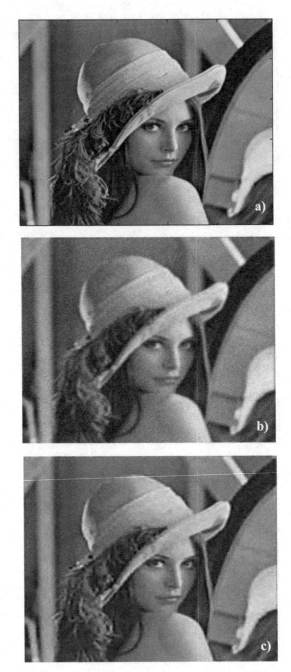

Fig. 4.   a) Original image; b) Blurred noisy image (separable blur filter (blur with with weights $[1, 4, 6, 4, 1]/16$ and noise of standard variance $\sigma = 7$); b) Restored imaged Algorithm 1 (ISNR = 2.73dB)

Table 1. SNR improvements (ISNR) of the proposed algorithm (Algoritm 1) and methods [, , , ,]

Method	ISNR (dB)			
	Exp1	Exp2	Exp3	Exp4
Algoritm 1	8.10	7.47	5.17	2.73
Figueiredo & Nowak [ ]	7.02	7.22	5.06	2.42
Neelamani et al. [ ]	7.30	–	–	–
Banham & Katsaggelos [ ]	6.70	–	–	–
Jalobeanu et al. [ ]	–	6.75	4.85	–
Liu & Moulin [ ]	–	–	–	1.08

Figure a) shows the cameraman image, part b) is a degraded version (blur (9×9) uniform, BSNR=40 dB), and part c) is the restored image with Algorithm 1, corresponding to a ISNR of 8.1dB.

Figure a) shows the cameraman image, part b) is a degraded version ($h_{ij} = (1 + i^2 + j^2)$, for $i, j = -7, \ldots, 7$, and noise variance set to $\sigma^2 = 8$), and part c) is the restored image with Algorithm 1, corresponding to a ISNR of 5.17dB.

Figure a) shows the lena image, part b) is a degraded version (blur with weights $[1, 4, 6, 4, 1]/16$ and noise of standard variance $\sigma = 7$), and part c) is the restored image with Algorithm 1, corresponding to a ISNR of 2.73dB.

5   Concluding Remarks

We developed a new fast Bayesian wavelet-based algorithm to image deconvolution. To compute the MAP estimate, we adopted a GEM optimization algorithm that employs a *second order stationary iterative* procedure to approximate the M-step of the EM algorithm. The total complexity is $O(N \log N)$ (N is the number of image pixels). In a set of experiments the proposed methodology competes with state-of-the-art methods.

References

[1] A. Jain. *Fundamentals of Digital Image Processing*. Prentice Hall, Englewood Cliffs, 1989.   ,

[2] S. Geman and D. Geman. Stochastic relaxation, Gibbs distribution and the Bayesian restoration of images. *IEEE Transactions on Pattern Analysis and Machine Intelligence*, PAMI-6(6):721–741, November 1984.

[3] T. Poggio, V. Torre, and C. Koch. Computational vision and regularization theory. *Nature*, vol. 317:314–319, 1985.

[4] D. Terzopoulos. Regularization of inverse visual problems involving discontinuities. *IEEE Transactions on Pattern Analysis and Machine Intelligence*, PAMI-8(4):413–424, July 1986.

[5] A. Katsaggelos, editor. *Digital Image Restoration*. Spriger-Verlag, New York, 1991.

[6] A. Katsaggelos, J. Biemond, R. Schafer, and R. Mersereau. A regularized iterative image restoration algorithm. *IEEE Transactions on Signal Processing*, 39(4):914–929, April 1991.

[7] A. Blake and A. Zisserman. *Visual Reconstruction.* MIT Press, Cambridge, M. A., 1987.

[8] F. Jeng and J. Woods. Compound Gauss-Markov random fields for image processing. In A.Katsaggelos, editor, *Digital Image Restoration*, pages 89–108. Springer Verlag, 1991.

[9] D. Donoho. Nonlinear solution of linear inverse problems by wavelet-vaguelette decompositions. *Journal of Applied and Computational Harmonic Analysis*, 1:100–115, 1995.

[10] M. Banham and A. Katsaggelos. Spatially adaptive wavelet-based multiscale image restoration. *IEEE Transactions on Image Processing*, 5:619–634, 1996.

[11] F. Abramovich, T. Sapatinas, and B. Silverman. Wavelet thresholding via a Bayesian approach. *Journal of the Royal Statistical Society (B)*, 60, 1998.

[12] J. Liu and P. Moulin. Complexity-regularized image restoration. *Proc. IEEE Int. Conf. on Image Proc*, pages 555–559, 1998.

[13] Y. Wan and R. Nowak. A wavelet-based approach to joint image restoration and edge detection. In *SPIE Conference on Wavelet Applications in Signal and Image Processing VII*, Denver, CO, 1999. SPIE Vol. 3813.

[14] J. Kalifa and S. Mallat. Minimax restoration and deconvolution. In P. Muller and B. Vidakovic, editors, *Bayesian Inference in Wavelet Based Models.* Springer-Verlag, New York, 1999.

[15] A. Jalobeanu, N. Kingsbury, and J. Zerubia. Image deconvolution using hidden Markov tree modeling of complex wavelet packets. In *Proceedings of the IEEE International Conference on Image Processing – ICIP'2001*, Thessaloniki, Greece, 2001.

[16] M. Figueiredo and R. Nowak. An em algorithm for wavelet-based image restoration. *IEEE Transactions on Image Processing*, 2003. Accepted for publication (available in htt://www.lx.it.pt/~mtf/).

[17] S. Mallat. *A Wavelet Tour of Signal Processing.* Academic Press, San Diego, 1998.

[18] R. Neelamani, H. Choi, and R. Baraniuk. Wavelet-based deconvolution using optimally inversion for ill-conditioned systems. In *Wavelet Applications in Signal and Image Processing*, volume 3169, pages 389–399, Oct. 2001.

[19] C. Robert. *The Bayesian Choice. A Decision-Theoritic Motivation.* Springer-Verlag, 1994.

[20] M. Figueiredo and R. Nowak. Wavelet-based image estimation: an empirical Bayes approach using Jeffreys' noninformative prior. *IEEE Transactions on Image Processing*, 10(9):1322–1331, 2001.

[21] R. Neelamani, H. Choi, and R. Baraniuk. Wavelet-based deconvolution for ill-conditioned systems. *IEEE Transactions on Image Processing*, 2001 (submitted).

[22] P. Moulin and J. Liu. Analysis of multiresolution image denoising schemes using generalized - Gaussian and complexity priors. *IEEE Transactions on Information Theory,*, 45:909–919, 1999.

[23] F. Girosi. Models of noise and robust estimates. Massachusetts Institute of Technology. Artificial Intelligence Laboratory (Memo 1287) and Center for Biological and Computational Learning (Paper 66), 1991.

[24] A. Dempster, N. Laird, and D. Rubin. Maximum likelihood estimation from incomplete data via the EM algorithm. *Journal of the Royal Statistical Society B*, 39:1–38, 1977.

[25] O. Axelsson. *Iterative Solution Methods*. Cambridge University Press, New York, 1996.   ,   ,

[26] R. Coifman and D. Donoho. Translation invariant de-noising. In *Wavelets and Statistics*, Lecture Notes in Statistics, pages 125–150, New York, 1995. Springer-Verlag.

Diffusion Tensor MR Image Restoration*

Z. Wang[1], B.C. Vemuri[1], and Y. Chen[2]

[1] Dept. of CISE, University of Florida, Gainesville, Fl. 32611
[2] Dept. of Mathematics, University of Florida, Gainesville, Fl. 32611

Abstract. Diffusion tensor magnetic resonance imaging (DT-MRI) can provide the fundamental information required to visualize structural connectivity. However, this high-dimensional data can be rather noisy and requires restoration. In this paper, we present a novel unified formulation involving a variational principle for simultaneous smoothing and estimation of the diffusion tensor field from DT-MRI. This tensor field is estimated directly from the measurements using a combination of L^p smoothness and positive definiteness constraints respectively. The data term we employ is the Stejskal-Tanner equation instead of its linearized version as usually employed in the published literature. In addition, we impose the positive definite constraint via the Cholesky decomposition of the tensors in the field. Our unified variational principle is discretized and solved numerically using the limited memory quasi-Newton method. Algorithm performance is depicted via both synthetic and real data experiments.

1 Introduction

Diffusion is a process of molecular motion caused by random thermal agitation and in the context of the work presented in this paper, refers to the random translatory motion of water molecules in the anatomy being imaged with the MR. In 3D, water diffusivity can be approximated by a matrix $\mathbf{D}(3 \times 3)$ called the diffusion tensor which is correlated to the local geometry and organization of the microscopic environment. General principle is that water diffuses preferably along ordered tissues like the white matter in the brain.

Diffusion tensor MRI is a relatively new MR imaging modality from which anisotropy of water diffusion can be inferred quantitatively [ ], thus providing a method to study the tissue microstructure e.g., white matter connectivity in the brain in vivo. Diffusion weighted echo intensity image S_l and the diffusion tensor $\mathbf{D}$ are related through the Stejskal-Tanner equation [ ] as given by:

$$S_l = S_0 e^{-\mathbf{b_l}:\mathbf{D}} = S_0 e^{-\sum_{i=1}^{3}\sum_{j=1}^{3} b_{ij} D_{ij}} \tag{1}$$

where $\mathbf{b_l}$ is the diffusion weighting of the $l-th$ magnetic gradient, ":" denotes the generalized dot product for matrices. Equation ( ) can be rewritten as

$$log(S_l) = log(S_0) - \mathbf{b_l} : \mathbf{D} \tag{2}$$

---

* This research was in part funded by the NIH grant RO1-NS42075.

A. Rangarajan et al. (Eds.): EMMCVPR 2003, LNCS 2683, pp. 421–   , 2003.
© Springer-Verlag Berlin Heidelberg 2003

which is now in a log-linearized form. Given several (at least seven) non-collinear diffusion weighted intensity measurements, $\mathbf{D}$ can be estimated via multivariate regression models from either equations. Diffusion anisotropy can then be computed to show microstructural and physiological features of tissues [ ]. Especially in highly organized nerve tissue, like white matter, diffusion tensor provides a complete characterization of the restricted motion of water through the tissue that can be used to infer fiber tracts. The development of diffusion tensor acquisition, processing, and analysis techniques provides the framework for creating fiber tract maps based on this complete diffusion tensor analysis [,].

For automatic fiber tract mapping, the diffusion tensor field must be smoothed without losing relevant features. Currently there are two popular techniques for achieving this goal, one is to smooth the raw data S_l while preserving relevant detail and then estimate diffusion tensor D from the smoothed raw data (Parker et.al., [,]). The raw data in this case consists of several diffusion weighted images acquired for varying magnetic field strengths and directions. It should be noted that at least seven values at each 3D grid point in the data domain are required to estimate the six unknowns in the symmetric 2-tensor and one scale parameter S_0. The raw data smoothing or de-noising can be formulated using variational principles which in turn requires solution to PDEs or some times using PDEs which are not necessarily arrived at from variational principles (see [, , ,] and others in [ ]).

Another approach to restore the diffusion tensor field is to smooth the principal diffusion direction after the diffusion tensor has been estimated from the raw noisy measurements S_l. In Poupon et al. [ ], an energy function based on a Markovian model was used to regularize the noisy dominant eigenvector field computed directly from the noisy estimates of D from the measurements S_l. Coulon et.al., [ ] proposed an iterative restoration scheme for principle diffusion direction based on direction map restoration. Other sophisticated vector field restoration methods [, , ,] can potentially be applied to the problem of restoring the dominant eigen-vector fields computed from the noisy estimates of D. Recently, Chefd'Hotel et.al., [ ] presented an interesting geometric solution to the problem of smoothing a noisy D that was computed from S_l using the log-linearized model described above. They assume that the given (computed) tensor field D from S_l is positive definite and develop a clever approach based on manifold theory to achieve smoothing where the smoothed tensor field is constrained to be positive semi-definite.

We propose a novel unified variational principle to simultaneously estimate and smooth the diffusion tensor D with positiveness constraints. The novelty lies in being able to directly (single step) estimate a smooth D from the noisy measurements S_l with the preservation of the positiveness constraint on D. In contrast, earlier approaches used a two step method involing, (i) computation of a D from S_l using a linear least-squares approach and then (ii) computing a smoothed D via either smoothing of the eigen-values and eigen-vectors of D or using the matrix flows approach in [ ]. The problem with the two step approach to computing D is that the estimated D in the first step using the log-linearized model need not be positive definite or even semi-definite. Also, the noise model in this case is incorrect as the noise in the measurements is on S_l and not on $\log S_l$. Moreover, it is hard to trust the fidelity of the eigen values and vectors computed from such matrices even if they are to be smoothed subsequently prior to mapping out the nerve fiber tracts. Briefly, our model involves a nonlinear data term based on the original (not linearized) Stejskal-Tanner equation ( ), an L^p norm based matrix-valued image smoothing scheme with the positiveness of the diffusion tensor being ensured via a Cholesky factorization of D in the minimizer.

2   Simultaneous Estimation and Smoothing of the Diffusion Tensor

Our solution to the recovery of a smooth diffusion tensor field from the measurements S_l is posed as a variational principle involving a nonlinear data fidelity term with a Cholesky factorization of the diffusion tensor and an L^p norm smoothness constraint on the diffusion tensor to be estimated. The novelty of our formulation lies in the use of a unified framework for recovering and smoothing of the tensor field from the data S_l. The nonlinear data term is obtained directly from the Stejskal-Tanner equation describing the physics of the tensor field model for the diffusion weighted imaging and the positiveness constraint on the diffusion tensor to be estimated is enforced via the use of the Cholesky factorization.

Let $S_0(\mathbf{X})$ be the response intensity when no diffusion-encoding gradient is present, $\mathbf{D}(\mathbf{X})$ the unknown symmetric positive definite tensor, $\mathbf{LL^T}(\mathbf{X})$ be the Cholesky factorization of the diffusion tensor with L being a lower triangular matrix, $S_l, l = 1, .., N$ is the response intensity image measured after application of a magnetic gradient of known strength and direction and N is the total number of intensity images each corresponding to a direction of the applied magnetic gradient. The variational principle for estimating and smoothing $\mathbf{D}(\mathbf{X})$ is given by

$$\min \mathcal{E}(S_0, \mathbf{L}) = \int_\Omega \sum_{l=1}^N (S_l - S_0 e^{-\mathbf{b_l}:\mathbf{LL^T}})^2 d\mathbf{X}$$
$$+ \int_\Omega (\alpha |\nabla S_0(\mathbf{X})|^p + \beta |\nabla \mathbf{L}(\mathbf{X})|^p) d\mathbf{X} \tag{3}$$

where Ω is the image domain, α, β are regularization parameters, $\mathbf{b_l}$ is the diffusion weighting of the lth magnetic gradient and ":" is the generalized inner product of matrices. The first term is the data fidelity term which is obtained directly from Stejskal-Tanner equation, the second and the third term are L^p smoothness constraint on S_0 and $\mathbf{L}$ respectively, where $p > 6/5$ for S_0 and $p \geq 1$ for $\mathbf{L}$. These values are chosen to facilitate the mathematical proof of existence of a solution. $|\nabla \mathbf{L}|^p = \sum_d |\nabla L_d|^p$, where $d = xx, yy, zz, xy, yz, xz$ are indices to the six nonzero components of $\mathbf{L}$.

2.1 The Nonlinear Data Model

The equation ( ) depicts the relation between diffusion weighted echo intensity image S_l and the diffusion tensor $\mathbf{D}$. However, all of the current methods in published literature use a multivariate linear regression technique based on equation ( ) to estimate the diffusion tensor $\mathbf{D}$ [ ]. It was pointed out in [ ] that these results agree with nonlinear regression based on the original Stejskal-Tanner equation ( ). However, if the signal to noise ratio (SNR) is low and the number of intensity images S_l is not very large (unlike in [ ] where $N = 315$ or $N = 294$), the result from multivariate linear regression will differ from the nonlinear regression significantly. A robust estimator belonging to the M-estimator family was used by Poupon et.al., [ ], however, its performance is not discussed in detail. In [ ]), Westin et. al., present an analytical solution obtained from equation ( ) by using a dual tensor basis, however, it should be noted that this can only be used for computing the tensor D when there is no noise in the measurements S_l or the SNR is extremely high.

Our aim is to provide an accurate estimation of diffusion tensor D for practical clinical use, where the SNR may not be high and the total number of intensity images N is restricted to a moderate number. The nonlinear data fidelity term based on original Stejskal-Tanner equation ( ) is fully justified for use in these situations.

2.2 The L^p Smoothness Constraint

In [ ], Blomgren et.al., show that L^p smoothness constraint does not admit discontinuous solutions as the TV-norm when $p > 1$. However, when p is chosen close to 1, its behavior is close to the TV-norm when restoring edges. In our unified model, we require $p > 6/5$ for regularizing S_0 and $p \geq 1$ for $\mathbf{L}$ to ensure existence of the solution. We can still choose a proper p which is as close to 1 as possible to have a good edge preserving smoothing scheme. We choose $p = 1.205$ for S_0 and $p = 1.00$ for $\mathbf{L}$ in our experiments.

2.3 Comments on Existence of the Solution

Consider the problem:

$$\min_{(S_0,\mathbf{L})\in\mathcal{A}} \mathcal{E}(S_0,\mathbf{L}) = \int_\Omega \sum_{l=1}^{N}(S_l - S_0 e^{-\mathbf{b}_l:\mathbf{LL}^\mathbf{T}})^2 d\mathbf{X}$$

$$+\int_\Omega (\alpha|\nabla S_0(\mathbf{X})|^p + \beta|\nabla\mathbf{L}(\mathbf{X})|^p)d\mathbf{X} \tag{4}$$

Where $\mathcal{A} = \{(S_0,\mathbf{L}) \mid \mathbf{L} \in BV(\Omega),\ L_d \in L^2(\Omega), d = xx,yy,zz,xy,yz,xz$ and $S_0 \in W^{1,p}(\Omega), p > 6/5\}$. $BV(\Omega)$ denotes the space of bounded variation functions on the domain Ω, $L^2(\Omega)$ is the space of square integrable functions on Ω and $W^{1,p}(\Omega)$ denotes the Sobolev space of order p [ ].

Theorem 1 *Suppose $S_l \in L^2(\Omega)$, then the minimization problem ( ) has a solution $(S_0, \mathbf{L}) \in \mathcal{A}$.*

Proof Outline Let $(S_0^{(n)}, \mathbf{L}^{(n)})$ be a minimizing sequence. We can have a convergent subsequence from the compact embedding theorem [ ]. We also can prove the following:

– Lower semi-continuity of the L^p smoothness constraint terms.
– Continuity of the data fidelity term for $S_0 \in W^{1,p}(\Omega)$ when $p > 6/5$ and $\Omega \subset \Re^3$.

Thus, we have the convergence of the minimizing subsequence which is the solution of the minimization problem ( )([ ]).

Finding a solution using the unified model is much more difficult than when dealing with the problems of recovering and smoothing separately). However, there are benefits of posing the problem in a unified framework, namely, one does not accumulate the errors from a two stage process. Moreover, the unified framework incorporates the nonlinear data term which is more appropriate for low SNR values prevalent when b is high. Also, the noise model is correct for the nonlinear data model unlike the log-linearized case. Lastly, in the unified formulation, it is possible to pose mathematical questions of existence and uniqueness of the solution – which was not addressable previously.

2.4   The Positive Definite Constraint

The diffusion tensor D is supposed to be a positive definite matrix however, due to the noise in the measurements, S_l, it is hard to recover a D that retains this property unless explicitly included as a constraint. In general, a matrix $\mathbf{A} \in \Re^{n \times n}$ is said to be positive definite if $\mathbf{x}^T \mathbf{A} \mathbf{x} > 0$, for all $\mathbf{x} \neq \mathbf{0}$ *and* $\in \Re^n$. By applying the Cholesky factorization theorem, which states that: *If $\mathbf{A}$ is a symmetric positive definite matrix then, there exists a unique factorization $\mathbf{A} = \mathbf{L}\mathbf{L}^T$ where, $\mathbf{L}$ is a lower triangular matrix with positive diagonal elements.* After doing the Cholesky factorization, we have transfered the inequality constraint on the matrix $\mathbf{D}$ to an inequality constraint on the diagonal elements of L. This is still hard to satisfy theoretically because, the set on which the minimization takes place is an open set. However, in practise, with finite precision arithmetic, testing for a positive definiteness constraint is equivalent to testing for positive semi-definiteness. To answer the question of positive semi-definiteness, a stable method would yield a positive response even for nearby symmetric matrices. This is because, $\tilde{\mathbf{D}} = \mathbf{D} + \mathbf{E}$ with $\| \mathbf{E} \| \leq \epsilon \| \mathbf{D} \|$, where ϵ is a small multiple of the machine precision. Because, with an arbitrarily small perturbation, a semi-definite matrix can become definite, it follows that in finite precision arithmetic, testing for definiteness is equivalent to testing for semi-definiteness. Thus, we repose the positive definiteness constraint on the diffusion tensor matrix as, $\mathbf{x}^T \mathbf{D} \mathbf{x} \geq 0$ which is satisfied when $\mathbf{D} = \mathbf{L}\mathbf{L}^T$.

3   Numerical Methods

We discretized the variation principle ( ) directly and applied the limited memory Quasi-Newton method to find a numerical solution. The discretized variational principle is given by,

$$R_{l,ijk} = S_{l,ijk} - S_{0,ijk}e^{-\mathbf{b_1}\cdot\mathbf{L_{ijk}}\mathbf{L_{ijk}^T}}$$

$$|\nabla S_0|_{ijk} = \left[\sqrt{(\Delta_x^+ S_0)^2 + (\Delta_y^+ S_0)^2 + (\Delta_z^+ S_0)^2 + \epsilon}\right]_{ijk}$$

$$|\nabla L_d|_{ijk} = \left[\sqrt{(\Delta_x^+ L_d)^2 + (\Delta_y^+ L_d)^2 + (\Delta_z^+ L_d)^2 + \epsilon}\right]_{ijk}$$

$$d = xx, yy, zz, xy, yz, xz$$

$$|\nabla \mathbf{L}|_{ijk}^p = |\nabla L_{xx}|_{ijk}^p + |\nabla L_{yy}|_{ijk}^p + |\nabla L_{zz}|_{ijk}^p$$
$$+ |\nabla L_{xy}|_{ijk}^p + |\nabla L_{yz}|_{ijk}^p + |\nabla L_{xz}|_{ijk}^p. \tag{5}$$

Where Δ_x^+, Δ_y^+ and Δ_z^+ are forward difference operators, ϵ is a small number to avoid singularities of L^p norm when $p < 2$. We then have

$$\min_{S_0,\mathbf{L}} \mathcal{E}(S_0,\mathbf{L}) = \sum_{i,j,k} \sum_{l=1}^{N} R_{l,ijk}^2$$
$$+ \sum_{i,j,k} (\alpha|\nabla S_0|_{ijk}^p + \beta|\nabla\mathbf{L}|_{ijk}^p) \tag{6}$$

Numerical optimization techniques can be applied to solve the above discrete minimization problem. Due to the large number of unknown variables in the minimization, we apply the limited memory Quasi-Newton technique [ ]. Quasi-Newton like methods compute the approximate Hessian matrix at each iteration of the optimization by using only the first derivative information. In Limited-Memory Broyden-Fletcher-Goldfarb-Shano (BFGS), search direction is computed without storing the approximated Hessian matrix.

Let $x = (S_0,\mathbf{L})$ be the vector of variables, $f(x) = E(S_0,\mathbf{L})$ the energy function to be minimized. At kth iteration, let $s_k = x_{k+1} - x_k$ be the update of the variable vector x, $y_k = \nabla f_{k+1} - \nabla f_k$ the update of the gradient and H_k^{-1} the approximation of inverse of the Hessian. Using the Sherman-Morrison-Woodbury formula [ ], we have the following expression for the inverse of the approximate Hessian H_k^{-1}

$$H_{k+1}^{-1} = H_k^{-1} - \frac{H_k^{-1}y_k y_k^T H_k^{-1}}{y_k^T H_k^{-1} y_k} + \frac{s_k s_k^T}{y_k^T s_k} \tag{7}$$

We now have the following L-BFGS two-loop recursion iterative procedure which computes the search direction $H_k^{-1}\nabla f_k$ efficiently by using last m pair of (s_k, y_k) (see [ ])

$q \leftarrow \nabla f_k;$
for $i = k-1, k-2, ..., k-m$

$$\alpha_i \leftarrow \rho_i s_i^T q;$$
$$q \leftarrow q - \alpha_i y_i;$$
end(for)
$$r \leftarrow (H_k^0)^{-1} q;$$
for $i = k - m, k - m - 1, ..., k - 1$
$$\beta \leftarrow \rho_i y_i^T r;$$
$$r \leftarrow r + s_i(\alpha_i - \beta)$$
end(for)
stop with result $H_k^{-1} \nabla f_k = r$.

Where $\rho_k = \frac{1}{y_k^T s_k}$ and $(H_k^0)^{-1}$ is the initial approximation of the inverse of the Hessian, we set $(H_k^0)^{-1} = \gamma_k I$ where $\gamma_k = \frac{s_{k-1}^T y_{k-1}}{y_{k-1}^T y_{k-1}}$.

The gradient of our energy function can be computed analytically as,

$$\nabla f(x) = \left(\frac{\partial \mathcal{E}(S_0, \mathbf{L})}{\partial S_0}, \frac{\partial \mathcal{E}(S_0, \mathbf{L})}{\partial L_{xx}}, \frac{\partial \mathcal{E}(S_0, \mathbf{L})}{\partial L_{yy}}, \frac{\partial \mathcal{E}(S_0, \mathbf{L})}{\partial L_{zz}}, \right.$$
$$\left. \frac{\partial \mathcal{E}(S_0, \mathbf{L})}{\partial L_{xy}}, \frac{\partial \mathcal{E}(S_0, \mathbf{L})}{\partial L_{yz}}, \frac{\partial \mathcal{E}(S_0, \mathbf{L})}{\partial L_{xz}} \right) \qquad (8)$$

Where

$$\frac{\partial \mathcal{E}(S_0, \mathbf{L})}{\partial S_{0,ijk}} = 2 \sum_{l=1}^{N} R_{l,ijk} \frac{\partial R_{l,ijk}}{\partial S_{0,ijk}} + \sum_{i',j',k'} \frac{\partial |\nabla S_0|_{i'j'k'}^p}{\partial S_{0,ijk}}$$

$$\frac{\partial \mathcal{E}(S_0, \mathbf{L})}{\partial L_{d,ijk}} = 2 \sum_{l=1}^{N} R_{l,ijk} \frac{\partial R_{l,ijk}}{\partial L_{d,ijk}} + \sum_{i',j',k'} \frac{\partial |\nabla L_d|_{i'j'k'}^p}{\partial L_{d,ijk}}$$

$$d = xx, yy, zz, xy, yz, xz \qquad (9)$$

Here $\sum_{i',j',k'}$ is over a neighborhood of the voxel (i, j, k) where the forward differences involves the variables $S_{0,ijk}$ or $L_{d,ijk}$. Each term in equation ( ) can be computed analytically, for example

$$\frac{\partial R_{l,ijk}}{\partial L_{xx,ijk}} = S_{0,ijk} e^{-\mathbf{b_l} : \mathbf{L_{ijk}} \mathbf{L_{ijk}^T}} *$$
$$(2b_{l,xx} L_{xx,ijk} + 2b_{l,xy} L_{xy,ijk} + 2b_{l,xz} L_{xz,ijk})$$

4   Experimental Results

In this section, we present two sets of experiments on the application of the proposed unified model. One is on synthetic DT-MRI data and the other is on a normal rat brain DT-MRI data.

4.1   Synthetic DT-MRI Data

We designed the synthetic experiments to show how the choice of parameters will affect the results of the proposed method, and compare the accuracy of the proposed methods with other methods.

The synthetic anisotropic tensor field is on a 3D lattice of size 32x32x8, each slice is the same as shown in figure (a). S_0 is fixed to a value of 10.0 in the whole volume. The l-th diffusion weighted image S_l corresponding to the diffusion weighting b_l are then generated by adding a Gaussian noise based on equation ( ) at each voxel $\mathbf{x}$ by:

$$S_l(\mathbf{x}) = S_0(\mathbf{x})e^{-b_l:\mathbf{D}(\mathbf{x})} + n(\mathbf{x}), \quad n(\mathbf{x}) \sim N(0,\sigma) \tag{10}$$

where $N(0,\sigma)$ is a zero mean Gaussian noise with standard deviation σ. We choose the 7 commonly used gradient direction configurations (see [ ]) and 3 different field strengths in each direction for b_l values. The noise we added has a $\sigma = S_0 * 0.1$.

To quantitatively assess the proposed unified model, we compute certain scalar measures such as fractional anisotropy (FA) [ ], which is defined as $FA = \frac{\sqrt{(\lambda_1 - \overline{\lambda})^2 + (\lambda_2 - \overline{\lambda})^2 + (\lambda_3 - \overline{\lambda})^2}}{\sqrt{\lambda_1^2 + \lambda_2^2 + \lambda_3^2}}$, where, λ_1, λ_3 and $\overline{\lambda}$ are the largest, smallest and average eigen values of the diffusion tensor $\mathbf{D}$ respectively. FA values range from 0 to 1, where, larger values indicate more anisotropy. Let Δ_{FA} be the difference of FA values between the estimated diffusion tensor field and the original known tensor field, and θ_{DEV} be the angle(in degrees) between the dominant eigen vector of the estimated diffusion tensor field and the original tensor field.

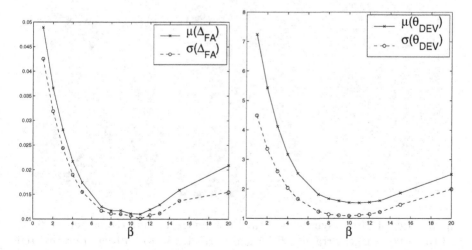

Fig. 1. Results when $\alpha = 1.0$ and β changes. Left: Mean and variance of Δ_{FA}. Right: Mean and variance of θ_{DEV}

In figure , we fix $\alpha = 1.0$ and show the effect of varying β which controls the degree of smoothing in **L**. It is evident that initially, the smoothing results improve as β increases, then they reach an optimum when β is around 11.0, after that the smoothing results deteriorate with further increases in β. This agrees with the intuition that neither under smoothing nor over smoothing will give a satisfying result. We found empirically that the choice of α does not significantly affect the result of the restored **D** and thus we simply set $\alpha = 1.0$.

Next, we compare the results of the proposed method with other methods. In figure , we use the ellipsoid visualization technique to show the original diffusion tensor field and restored diffusion tensor field using the following methods: linear regression from equation ( ), nonlinear regression from equation ( ), weighted TV-norm (WTV-norm) method [ ], modified WTV-Norm method and our current proposed method respectively. The modified WTV-Norm (MWTV-Norm) method is used to smooth the raw data first and then **D** is estimated using a nonlinear regression method. The parameters of each method are chosen to yield the best results in each case. It is evident from this figure that the MWTV-Norm method and the new unified model both yield very good estimates of the original tensor field. *However, further experimentation using the previously mentioned quantitative measures reveals the superiority of the proposed unified model.*

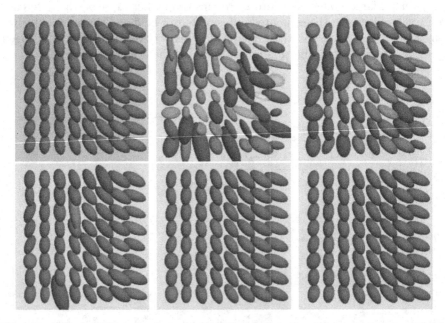

Fig. 2. Results from synthetic data: First image is the original tensor field, and the other images arranged from left to right, top to bottom are estimated tensor field using the following methods: linear regression, nonlinear regression, WTV-Norm, MWTV-Norm and the proposed model

Table 1. Comparison of different methods

Method	$\mu(\Delta_{FA})$	$\sigma(\Delta_{FA})$	$\mu(\theta_{DEV})$	$\sigma(\theta_{DEV})$
Linear	0.0870	0.0725	17.730	12.755
Nonlinear	0.0654	0.0570	9.908	6.467
WTV-Norm	0.0274	0.0367	3.270	4.758
MWTV-Norm	0.0114	0.0166	1.853	1.805
Unified Model	0.0111	0.0107	1.533	1.084

Table   shows the mean and standard deviation for these two measures when computed using various methods discussed thus far. A better estimator is one that yields values of these scalar measures closer to zero. From table , we can see the unified model yields lower values than all the methods including the the modified WTV-Norm method, although the difference between them in figure ( ) is not apparent.

4.2   DT-MRI from a Normal Rat Brain

The normal rat brain data we used here has 21 diffusion weighted images measured using the same configuration of b_i as in the previous example, each image is a 128x128x78 volume data. We extract 20 slices in the region of interest, namely the corpus callosum, for our experiment. Figure   depicts images of the six independent components of the estimated diffusion tensor, the computed FA, the trace($\mathbf{D}$) and S_0 (echo intensity without applied gradients) obtained using our proposed unified model with $p = 1.0$ for the smoothing of $\mathbf{L}$ and $p = 1.205$ for the smoothing of S_0. As a comparison, figure   shows the same images computed using linear least squares fitting based on the linearized Stejskal-Tanner equation from the raw data. In addition, we present results of comparison of our proposed model with $p = 2.0$ for the smoothing of both $\mathbf{L}$ and S_0 figure . For display purposes, we use the same brightness and contrast enhancement for displaying the corresponding images in all the figures. The effectiveness of edge preserving smoothing in our method with the proper choices of p values is clearly evident in the off-diagonal components of $\mathbf{D}$. The quality of results obtained is reasonably satisfactory for visual inspection purposes, however intensive quantitative validation of the mapped fibers needs to be performed and will be the focus of our future efforts.

5   Conclusions

In this paper, we presented a new and unified approach for simultaneous smoothing and estimation of the diffusion tensor field with positive definiteness constraint from DT-MRI. The Cholesky decomposition was used to incorporate the positive definiteness constraint on the diffusion tensors being estimated. Existence of a solution for the unified model was sketched and a numerical solution

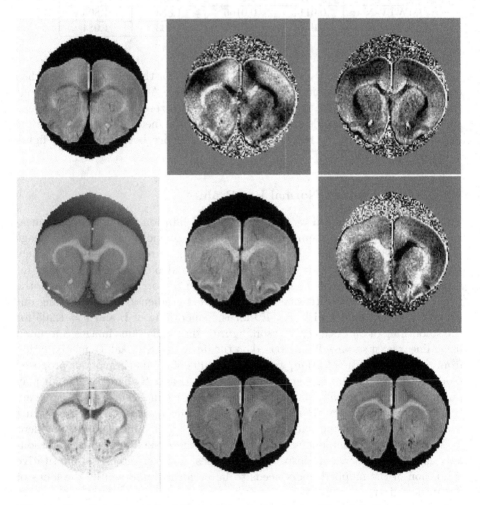

Fig. 3. Results of normal rat brain estimated using multivariate linear regression without smoothing. First row, left to right: D_{xx}, D_{xy} and D_{xz}. Second row, left to right: S_0, D_{yy} and D_{yz}. Third row, left to right: FA, $<\mathbf{D}>$ and D_{zz}

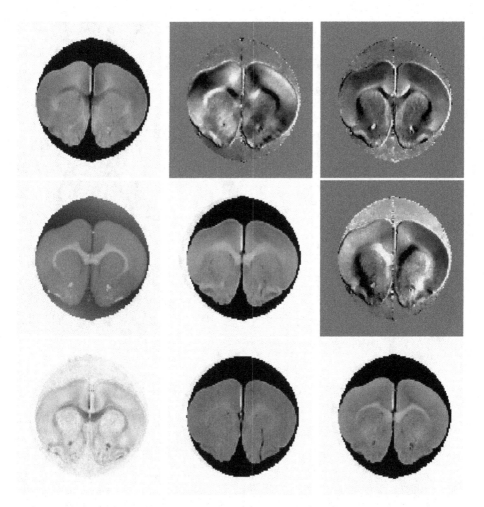

Fig. 4. Results for a normal rat brain, estimated using the new proposed unified model with L^p norm. First row, left to right: D_{xx}, D_{xy} and D_{xz}. Second row, left to right: S_0, D_{yy} and D_{yz}. Third row, left to right: FA, $<\mathbf{D}>$ and D_{zz}

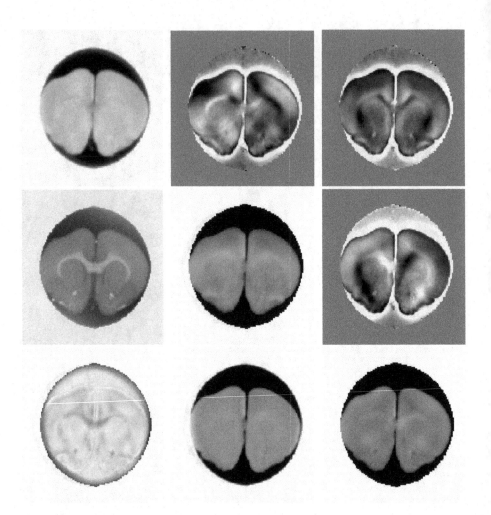

Fig. 5. Results for a normal rat brain, estimated using the new proposed unified model with L^2 norm. First row, left to right: D_{xx}, D_{xy} and D_{xz}. Second row, left to right: S_0, D_{yy} and D_{yz}. Third row, left to right: FA, $< \mathbf{D} >$ and D_{zz}

involving the limited memory Quasi-Newton for the discretized variation principle was presented. Finally, results of a synthetic experiment and results of estimating the diffusion tensor and computed fractional anisotropy from a normal a rat brain data were depicted. The estimated diffusion tensors are quite smooth without the loss of essential features when inspected visually. Quantitative comparison of the restored diffusion tensor in the synthetic data case clearly indicates the benefits of our model over existing models of smoothing and estimation. Our future work will focus on performing validation for real data sets.

Acknowledgments

Authors would like to thank Timothy McGraw in providing assistance on the WTV experiments and Evren Ozarslan and Dr. Mareci for discussions on the physics of imaging as well as the data.

References

[1] L. Alvarez, P. L. Lions, and J. M. Morel, "Image selective smoothing and edge detection by nonlinear diffusion. ii," *SIAM J. Numer. Anal.*, vol. 29, no. 3, pp. 845-866, June 1992.

[2] P. J. Basser, J. Mattiello and D. Lebihan, "Estimation of the Effective Self-Diffusion Tensor from the NMR Spin Echo," *J. Magn. Reson.*, series B 103, pp. 247-254, 1994.   ,

[3] P. J. Basser and C. Pierpaoli, "Microstructural and Physiological Features of Tissue Elucidated by Quantitative-Diffusion-Tensor MRI," *J. Magn. Reson.*, series B 111, pp. 209-219, 1996.   ,

[4] P. Blomgren, T. F. Chan and P. Mulet, "Extensions to Total Variation Denoising,", Tech. Rep.97-42, UCLA, September 1997.

[5] C. Chefd'hotel, D. Tschumperle', Rachid Deriche, Olivier D. Faugeras, "Constrained Flows of Matrix-Valued Functions: Application to Diffusion Tensor Regularization," *ECCV*, Vol. 1, pp. 251-265, 2002.

[6] V. Caselles, J. M. Morel, G. Sapiro, and A. Tannenbaum, *IEEE TIP*, special issue on PDEs and geometry-driven diffusion in image processing and analysis, Vol 7, No. 3, 1998.

[7] T. F. Chan, G. Golub, and P. Mulet, "A nonlinear primal-dual method for TV-based image restoration," in *Proc. 12th Int. Conf. Analysis and Optimization of Systems: Images, Wavelets, and PDE's*, Paris, France, June 26-28, 1996, M. Berger et.al., Eds., no. 219, pp. 241-252.

[8] T. E. Conturo, N. F. Lori, T. S. Cull, E. Akbudak, A. Z. Snyder, J. S. Shimony, R. C. McKinstry, H. Burton, and M. E. Raichle, "Tracking neuronal fiber pathways in the living human brain," in *Proc. Natl. Acad. Sci. USA 96*, 10422-10427 (1999)

[9] O. Coulon, D. C. Alexander and S. R. Arridge, "A Regularization Scheme for Diffusion Tensor Magnetic Resonance Images," *IPMI*, 2001, pp. 92-105, Springer-Verlag .

[10] L. C. Evans, "Partial Differential Equations," *Graduate Studies in Mathematics*, American Mathematical Society, 1997.   ,

[11] G.H. Golub and CF van Loan, *Matrix Computations*, The Johns Hopkins University Press, 2nd ed. 1989.

[12] D. K. Jones, A. Simmons, S. C. R. Williams, and M. A. Horsfield, "Non-invasive assessment of axonal fiber connectivity in the human brain via diffusion tensor MRI," *Magn. Reson. Med.*, 42, 37-41 (1999).

[13] R. Kimmel, R. Malladi and N. A. Sochen, "Images as Embedded Maps and Minimal Surfaces: Movies, Color, Texture, and Volumetric Medical Images," *IJCV*, 39(2), pp. 111-129, 2000.

[14] T. E. McGraw, B. C. Vemuri, Y. Chen, M. Rao and T. Mareci, "LIC for visualization of fiber tract maps," *Vth International Conference on Medical Image Computing and Computer-Assisted Intervention (MICCAI)*, Tokyo, Japan, Sept. 2002.

[15] J. Nocedal and S. J. Wright, *Num. Optimization*, Springer, 2000.

[16] A. Pang and K. Smith, "Spray Rendering: Visualization Using Smart Particles," *IEEE Visualization 1993 Conference Proceedings*, 1993, pp. 283-290.

[17] G. J. M. Parker, J. A. Schnabel, M. R. Symms, D. J. Werring, and G. J. Baker, "Nonlinear smoothing for reduction of systematic and random errors in diffusion tensor imaging," *Magn. Reson. Imag.* 11, 702-710, 2000.

[18] P. Perona and J. Malik, "Scale-space and edge detection using anisotropic diffusion," *IEEE TPAMI*, vol. 12, no. 7, pp. 629–639, 1990.

[19] Perona, P., "Orientation diffusions," *IEEE TIP*, vol.7, no.3, pp. 457-467, 1998.

[20] C. Poupon, J. F. Mangin, C. A. Clark, V. Frouin, J. Regis, D. Le Bihan and I. Block, "Towards inference of human brain connectivity from MR diffusion tensor data,", *Med. Image Anal.*, vol. 5, pp. 1-15, 2001.   ,

[21] L. I. Rudin, S. Osher, and E. Fatemi, "Nonlinear variation based noise removal algorithms," *Physica D*, vol. 60, pp. 259-268, 1992.

[22] B. Tang, G. Sapiro and V. Caselles, "Diffusion of General Data on Non-Flat Manifolds via Harmonic Maps Theory: The Direction Diffusion Case," *IJCV*, 36(2), pp. 149-161, 2000.

[23] D. Tschumperle and R. Deriche. "Regularization of orthonormal vector sets using coupled PDE's," *Proceedings of IEEE Workshop on Variational and Level Set Methods in Computer Vision*, pp. 3-10, July 2001

[24] B. C. Vemuri, Y. Chen, M. Rao, T. McGraw, Z. Wang and T. Mareci, "Fiber Tract Mapping from Diffusion Tensor MRI," *Proceedings of IEEE Workshop on Variational and Level Set Methods in Computer Vision*, pp. 81-88, July 2001   ,

[25] J. Weickert, "A review of nonlinear diffusion filtering," *Scale-space theory in computer vision*, 1997, vol. 1252, of *Lecture Notes in Computer Science*, pp. 3–28, Springer-Verlag.

[26] C. F. Westin, S. E. Maier, H. Mamata A. Nabavi, F. A. Jolesz and R. Kikinis, "Processing and visualization for diffusion tensor MRI," *Med. Image Anal.*, vol. 6, pp. 93-108, 2002.   ,

[27] S. Zhang, C. Demiralp and D. Laidlaw, " Visualizing diffusion tensor MRI using stream tubes and stream surfaces," in IEEE Trans. on Visualization and Computer Graphics, 2003, in press.

A MAP Estimation Algorithm
Using IIR Recursive Filters*

João M. Sanches** and Jorge S. Marques

IST/ISR, Torre Norte, Av. Rovisco Pais, 1049-001, Lisbon, Portugal

Abstract. The MAP method is a wide spread estimation technique used in many signal processing problems, e.g., image restoration, denoising and 3D reconstruction. When there is a large number of variables to estimate, the MAP method often leads to a huge set of linear or non-linear equations which must be numerically solved using time consuming algorithms.

This paper proposes a fast method to compute the MAP estimates in large scale problems, based on the solution of a linear set of equations by low pass filtering the ML solution. A family of space varying IIR filters with data dependent coefficients is derived from the MAP criterion. This approach can be extended to other types of filters derived under different assumptions about the prior or using other design strategies. The filter approach proposed in this paper is much faster than the classic solution and provides additional insights about the structure of the problem.

Experimental results are provided to assess the performance of the proposed methods with Gaussian and non Gaussian noise models.

1 Introduction

The maximum likelihood (ML) method is widely used to estimate signals from noisy data. For instance, in image processing, the ML method is often used to solve problems of image restoration [ ], denoising [ ], deblurring [ ], 2D and 3D reconstruction [ ]. In medical imaging, statistical methods [ ], e.g., the ML method, became popular techniques especially after the work of Shepp and Vardi on emission tomography [ ].

However, the ML estimates tend to be noisy and the convergence of the algorithm is slow due to the ill-conditioned nature of the estimation problem [ ]. In the case of 2D or 3D reconstruction, the lack of data is the main difficulty, since we do not have enough information to obtain an accurate estimate for each unknown variable [ ]. To overcome these difficulties the ML criterion is often replaced by Bayesian methods (e.g., the MAP method) using prior knowledge about the unknown variables. This leads to an improvement of the numerical

---

* This work was partially supported by FCT in the scope of project POSI-33726-CPS-2000.

** Corresponding author: João Sanches, IST/ISR, Torre Notre, Av. Rovisco Pais, 1049-001 Lisboa, Portugal, Email:jmrs@alfa.ist.utl.pt, Phone:+351 21 8418195.

A. Rangarajan et al. (Eds.): EMMCVPR 2003, LNCS 2683, pp. 436–   , 2003.
© Springer-Verlag Berlin Heidelberg 2003

stability of the optimization algorithms as to better estimates of the unknown variables if the prior distribution is correctly chosen [,].

Gibbs distributions are one of the most popular choices to represent the prior information. This class of priors leads to simple formulations of the estimation problem. The equivalence with Markov random fields allows to easily obtain the joint probability distribution from a set of local distributions [ ].

This paper shows that the MAP estimation of signals can be obtained by filtering the ML estimate with space varying IIR filters. This result is derived assuming a Gibbs prior with quadratic potential functions. The proposed solution is based on two recursive filters with space varying coefficients: a causal IIR filter and an anti-causal IIR filter. It is shown, that the cutoff frequencies of the proposed filters are adaptively adjusted according to the number of observations and to sufficient statistics of the signal.

The MAP filters proposed in this paper are applied to reconstruction problems from noisy observations corruped by Gaussian and non Gaussian (Rayleigh) noise. Experimental results are provided to compare the proposed solution to the classic algorithms.

2   Problem Formulation

Let $X = \{x_i\}$ be a sequence of N unknown variable to be estimated and $Y = \{y_i\}$ a sequence of observations. Each element of Y, y_n is, itself, a set of n_i observations of x_i. In typical problems of image restoration $n_i = 1$, which means that there is one observation per pixel. On the contrary, in 3D reconstruction, the number of observations per voxel varies from voxel to voxel. For instance, in free-hand 3D ultrasound the number of observations associated to non inspected voxels is zero ($n_i = 0$). On the contrary if given voxel is intersected by several cross sections $n_i > 1$.

In this paper the MAP method is used to estimate X from the observations Y. This method estimates X by minimizing an energy function,

$$\hat{X} = arg \min_U E(Y, X) \tag{1}$$

where

$$E(X, Y) = -l(X, Y) - \log p(X) \tag{2}$$

$l(X, Y) = \log(p(Y|X)$ is the likelihood function, and $p(X)$ is the a prior distribution associated to the unknown variables.

For sake of simplicity let us assume that y_i is normal distributed (later we will consider other distributions), with $p(y_i) = N(x_i, \sigma^2)$ corresponding to the following observation model

$$y_i = x_i + w_i \tag{3}$$

with $p(w_i) = N(0, \sigma^2)$. If the observations are independent, the log-likelihood function is given by

$$l = C - \frac{\beta}{2} \sum_{i,k} (y_{ik} - x_i)^2 \qquad (4)$$

where $\beta = 1/\sigma^2$ and y_{ik} is the kth observation of the unknown x_i.

The prior $p(X)$ used in ( ) plays an important role in the estimation process when there is lack of information about the variables X (n_i small), since the ML estimates are very poor in this case [ ].

In this paper we will consider that $p(x)$ is a Gibbs distribution with quadratic potential functions [,]. This is equivalent to assuming that the vector X is a Markov random field [,]. Therefore

$$p(X) = \frac{1}{Z} e^{\sum_i V_i(X)} \qquad (5)$$

where Z is the partition function and $V_i(X)$ is the potential function associated to the i-th unknown. Assuming that X is a 1D signal and assuming that each variable x_i has two neighbors, x_{i-1}, x_{i+1},

$$p(X) = \frac{1}{Z} e^{-\frac{\alpha}{2} \sum_i (x_i - x_{i-1})^2} \qquad (6)$$

The parameter α defines the strength of the links among neighbors and it is pre-defined. Therefore, the energy function to be minimized is

$$E(Y, X) = \frac{\beta}{2} \sum_{i,k} (y_{i_k} - x_i)^2 + \frac{\alpha}{2} \sum_i (x_i - x_{i-1})^2 \qquad (7)$$

The constants C and Z were discarded because they do not contribute to the solution.

3   Optimization

To minimize ( ) the following stationary conditions must be met

$$\frac{\partial E(Y, X)}{\partial x_i} = 0 \qquad (8)$$

which lead to the following set of linear equations

$$x_i = (1 - k_i) x_i^{ML} + k_i \bar{x}_i \qquad i = 1, ..., N \qquad (9)$$

where x_i^{ML} is the maximum likelihood estimation of x_i, k_i is a parameter that depends on the data and $\bar{x}_i$ is the average value of the neighbors of x_i

$$x_i^{ML} = \frac{1}{n_i} \sum_{k=1}^{n_i} y_{i_k}^2 \tag{10}$$

$$k_i = \frac{1}{1 + \frac{\beta n_i}{2\alpha}} \tag{11}$$

$$\bar{x}_i = \frac{x_{i-1} + x_{i+1}}{2} \tag{12}$$

To minimize the border effects it is assumed that $x_0 = x_2$ and $x_{N+1} = x_{N-1}$. Taking this into account, ( ) can be written as follows

$$Ax = b \tag{13}$$

where

$$A = \begin{bmatrix} 1 & -k_1 & 0 & 0 & 0 \dots & 0 & 0 & 0 & 0 \\ -k_2/2 & 1 & -k_2/2 & 0 & 0 \dots & 0 & 0 & 0 & 0 \\ 0 & -k_3/2 & 1 & -k_3/2 & 0 \dots & 0 & 0 & 0 & 0 \\ \dots & \dots & \dots & \dots & \dots \dots & \dots & & \dots & \dots \\ 0 & 0 & 0 & 0 & 0 \dots & -k_{N-2}/2 & 1 & -k_{N-2}/2 & 0 \\ 0 & 0 & 0 & 0 & 0 \dots & 0 & -k_{N-1}/2 & 1 & -k_{N-1}/2 \\ 0 & 0 & 0 & 0 & 0 \dots & 0 & 0 & -k_N & 1 \end{bmatrix}$$

and

$$b = [(1 - k_1)x_1^{ML}, (1 - k_2)x_2^{ML}, ..., (1 - k_N)x_N^{ML}]^T \tag{14}$$

The estimation of ( ) amounts to the solution of a linear system of equations which can be performed by using either iterative (e.g. Gauss elimination method) or non iterative methods (e.g. Gauss-Seidel method). Since the number of unknowns is often very large (e.g. on the order of a million) iterative methods are preferred since they provide an approximate solution with acceptable computational effort. In order to obtain an efficient solution the structure of A can be considered.

In the next section we will show that the system ( ) can be solved using two space varying IIR filters, obtained from ( ).

4   IIR Filter

Equation ( )

$$x_i = (1 - k_i)x_i^{ML} + \frac{k_i}{2}(x_{n-1} + x_{n+1}) \tag{15}$$

defines a non causal recursive filter [ ] with x_i^{ML} as input. Assuming that k_i is constant the filter impulsive response, g_i, can be computed. The general form is

$$g_i = Ca^{|i|} \tag{16}$$

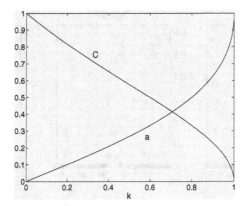

Fig. 1. Impulse response parameters

where C and a are computed replacing ( ) in ( ) and making $x_i^{ML} = \delta(i)$

$$\begin{cases} Ca^0 = (1-k) + \frac{k}{2}(Ca^{|-1|} + Ca^{|1|}) & i = 0 \\ Ca^i = \frac{k}{2}(Ca^{i-1} + Ca^{i+1}) & i \neq 0 \end{cases}$$

$$\begin{cases} C = \frac{1-k}{1-ak} \\ a^2 - \frac{2}{k}a + 1 = 0 \end{cases}$$

leading to

$$\begin{cases} a = \frac{1 \pm \sqrt{1-k^2}}{k} \\ C = \frac{1-k}{-(\pm)\sqrt{1-k^2}} \end{cases}$$

Since $0 \leq k \leq 1$ and $C > 0$, only one solution is feasible, i.e.,

$$\begin{cases} a = \frac{1 - \sqrt{1-k^2}}{k} \\ C = \frac{1-k}{\sqrt{1-k^2}} \end{cases}$$

Fig. shows the dependence of a and C on $k \in [0, 1]$. As it can be observed, a is monotonic increasing with k and limited to the interval $[0, 1]$.

Fig. shows the impulsive response ( ) and the solution of ( ) for several values of k. As it can be seen, both solutions are identical, except for k close to 1 ($k > 0.99$). These differences are due to border effects. In fact, equation ( ) is not valid at $n = 1$ and $n = N$.

The impulsive response defined by ( ) can not be used in a recursive way because it is not wedge supported [ ]. Therefore, we will decompose it as a sum of two wedge supported impulsive responses, one causal and other anti-causal, i.e., one depending only on past inputs and outputs and other depending only on future inputs and outputs [ ]. Therefore,

$$g_n = g_n^+ + g_n^- \tag{17}$$

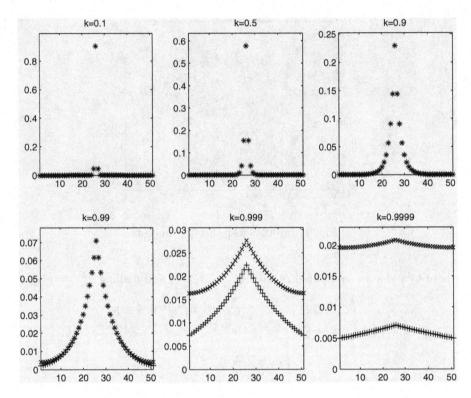

Fig. 2. Impulsive response computed from (   ) (x) and from (   ) (+)

where

$$g_n^+ = \begin{cases} Ca^n & n > 0 \\ \frac{C}{2} & n = 0 \\ 0 & n < 0 \end{cases}$$

$$g_n^- = \begin{cases} 0 & n > 0 \\ \frac{C}{2} & n = 0 \\ Ca^{-n} & n < 0 \end{cases}$$

where it was assumed $g_0^+ = g_0^-$ to impose symmetry. Applying the Z transform to the previous equation we obtain

$$G(Z) = G(Z)^+ + G(Z)^- \tag{18}$$

$$G(Z)^+ = \frac{C}{2} \frac{1 + aZ^{-1}}{1 - aZ^{-1}} \tag{19}$$

$$G(Z)^- = \frac{C}{2} \frac{1 + aZ}{1 - aZ} \tag{20}$$

The solution of ( ) is the sum of two terms

$$x_i = x_i^+ + x_i^- \tag{21}$$

where

$$x_i^+ = g_i^+ * x_i^{ML} = \frac{C_i}{2}(x_i^{ML} + a_i x_{i-1}^{ML}) + a_i x_{i-1} \tag{22}$$

is a causal space varying recursive filter and

$$x_i^- = g_i^- * x_i^{ML} = \frac{C_i}{2}(x_i^{ML} + a_i x_{i+1}^{ML}) + a_i x_{i+1} \tag{23}$$

is an anti-causal space varying recursive filter where

$$\begin{cases} a_i = \frac{1-\sqrt{1-k_i^2}}{k_i} \\ C = \frac{1-k_i}{\sqrt{1-k_i^2}} \end{cases}$$

The MAP estimates defined in ( ) can be obtained as follows. First the maximum likelihood estimates X^{ML} is computed. Then the ML estimate are filtered with a causal filter $G(Z)^+$ and with an anti-causal filter $G(Z)^-$. The solution is obtain by adding both results.

5   Frequency Analysis

It is now clear that the regularization imposed by the prior is equivalent to filtering the ML estimates with a first order low-pass filter that smoothes the transitions, reducing the noise present in the maximum likelihood estimation.

The low-pass filters ( ) and ( ) present a 0.5 gain at d.c., a pole located at a and a zero at $-a$ (see Fig.). The cutoff frequency, depending on the pole

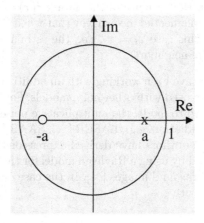

Fig. 3. Pole and zero position of $G(z)$

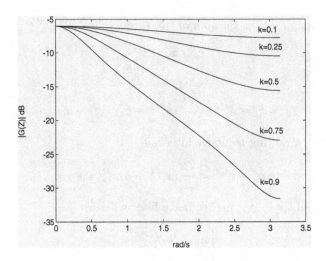

Fig. 4. Bode diagrams of $G(Z)$ for several different values of k

position, depends on the data and on the parameter α of the prior as it can be observed on ( ) and ( ) (see Figs. ,). Therefore, the following conclusions can be stated:

1) Since $0 \le a \le 1$, the pole of the first order filter is always inside the unit circle and the filter is always stable.
2) The parameter k (parameter a) (see eq.( )) decreases with the number of data points n_i, i.e., the bandwidth of the filter increases with the amount of available data and decreases as the number of data points goes to zero. The algorithm compensates the lack of confidence in the data by decreasing the filter bandwidth (see Fig.).
3) The bandwidth of the filter decreases when the regulatization parameter α increases and when the variance of the data, $\sigma^2(x) = 1/\beta$, increases.
4) The algorithm is implemented in such way that when there is no data, $n_i = 0$, $k = 1$ ($a = 1$). In this case $x_i = \bar{x}_i$, i.e., the estimate depends only on the average value of the neighbors.

Until this point we have been working with an additive Gaussian noise. However, the method can be used with other noise models. For instance, the Rayleigh distribution is often used to model the multiplicative noise present in signals obtained using coherent radiation, e.g., LASER [ ], SAAR [ ] or ultrasound [ ]. In a previous work, the authors have derived expressions similar to ( ) in the context of 3D ultrasound by using a Rayleigh model for the multiplicative speckle noise present in the ultrasound images [ ]. In the case of the Rayleigh observations ( ) is still valid with

---

[1] Note that a(k) is monotonic with k.

$$\begin{cases} x_i^{ML} = \frac{1}{2n_i} \sum_k (y_i^k)^2 \\ k_i = \frac{1}{1+\frac{n_i}{2\alpha(x_i^{ML})^2}} \end{cases}$$

In this case k_i depends on the number of observations, n_i, as before, but it also depends on the ML estimate. Therefore an additional property is valid.

5) the bandwidth decreases with the increase of x_i^{ML}, i.e., as stronger regularization is applied for large values of x_i^{ML} than for smaller values (the noise amplitude is larger in high intensity regions). This behaviour is a consequence of the multiplicative type of noise associated to the Rayleigh distribution.

As shown, the MAP estimation problem can be interpreted as a space varying filtering process. Adopting a Gibbs prior with a quadratic potential the MAP estimation process can be implemented by using two first order IIR filters. This approach can also be used to derive other type of filters associated, for instance, to higher order Gibbs priors, which allow the improvement of the estimation performance at transitions (see [ ]).

In the next section two examples of application are presented using synthetic and real data.

6   Experimental Results

Experimental tests were performed to evaluate the algorithm in 1D and 2D signal restoration, with synthetic and real data.

Each problem is solved using the standard MAP method and the fast algorithm based on space-varying IIR filters proposed in this paper. Examples with Gaussian and non-Gaussian (Rayleigh) noise are considered.

6.1   Synthetic Data

Let us consider a synthetic signal defined as follows,

$$x_i = \begin{cases} 150 & 50 \le i \le 100 \\ 50 & otherwise \end{cases}$$

The observation vector Y is obtained by adding Gaussian white noise $\eta_i = N(0, 20^2)$ to each sample (see Fig.).

The MAP solution was computed by both methods, i.e, by solving ( ) and by low pass filtering using ( ).

Both solutions are displayed in Fig. . Since both curves coincide they can not be distinguish. To minimize the border effects, the unknowns x_0 and x_{N+1},

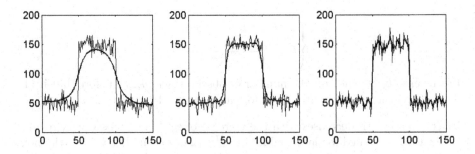

Fig. 5. Synthetic data: Noisy and filtered data for $\alpha = 1, 0.1, 0.001$

used in equations ( ) and ( ) respectively were defined as follows

$$x_0 = \frac{1}{2w} \sum_{i=1}^{w} x_i^{ML} \tag{24}$$

$$x_{N+1} = \frac{1}{2w} \sum_{i=N-w}^{N} x_i^{ML} \tag{25}$$

i.e., x_0 and x_{N+1} are initialized with half of the average value of the ML estimates inside window with length $w = 5$.

The two solutions are not identical. However, their difference is so small that can not be observed in Fig. . The two solutions are almost identical within the interval $[0, 150]$, except in the vicinity of the boundaries.

6.2 Ultrasound Image

This example considers the problem of noise reduction in ultrasound images, using a multiplicative model for the noise (Rayleigh model). The MAP estimates of the original image was computed by both methods, i.e., by solving the linear set of equations ( ), obtained by linearization of the non linear cost function ( ), and by using the IIR filters defined in ( ). X^{ML} and k are computed using ( ).

We have used the following separable filter to process the ultrasound image

$$G(Z_1, Z_2)_{2D} = G(Z_1)G(Z_2) \tag{26}$$

where $G(Z)$ is given by ( ). Separable filters allow fast filtering procedures based on two steps: in the first step the filter $G(Z)$ is applied to each column of the ultrasound image and, in a second step $G(Z)$ is applied to each row of the image obtained in the previous step. Fig. shows an ultrasound image (left), and the MAP estimates obtained by the IIR filter (right). The results achieved by solving ( ) are nor shown since they are similar.

Fig. shows the matrix of coefficients k_i. As noted before, the Rayleigh distribution, corresponding to a multiplicative type of noise, make the coefficients

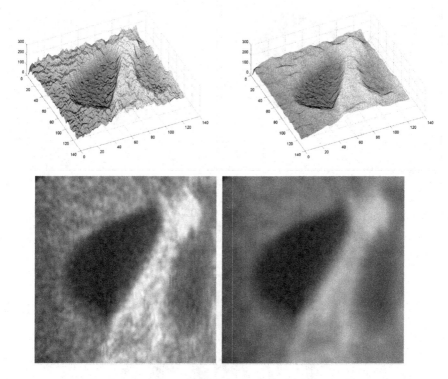

Fig. 6. First column: ultrasound image, Second column: MAP estimates

depend not only on the amount of data, but also on the data itself (see ( )). Therefore, the lighter zones of Fig. correspond to regions where the cutoff frequency of the IIR filter is smaller and consequently the regularization effect imposed by the prior is higher. On the contrary, in the darker regions, corresponding to the darker regions on the original ultrasound image, the regularization effect imposed by the prior is smaller.

Fig. shows the image obtained by computing the absolute difference of the images computed by the matrix inversion method and by the filtering method. The difference is small, except at the transitions and at the borders. The signal do noise ratio is $SNR = S_A - S_\Delta = 43.64dB$. S_A is the energy of the image X_A estimated using equation ( ) and computed as $S_A = 10 \log_{10}(X_A.X_A')$. $S_\Delta = 10 \log_{10}[(X_A - X_F)(X_A - X_F)']$ is the energy of the error image displayed in Fig. . X_F is the image estimated using equation ( ). The largest difference between X_A and X_F is observed at the origin due borders effect (as expected).

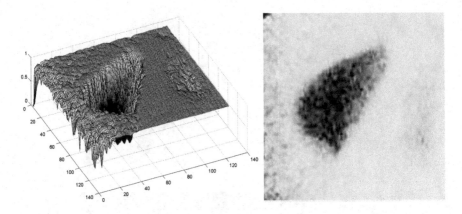

Fig. 7. Matrix of coefficients k_i

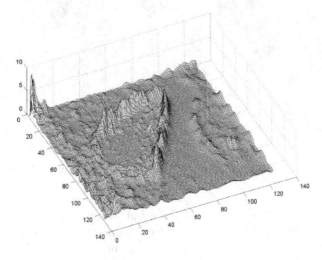

Fig. 8. Error image($SNR = 43.64dB$)

7   Conclusions

This paper formulates the MAP estimation of signals as a filtering problem and shows that the MAP estimates can be obtained by a two step approach. The first step computes the ML estimates of the signal using standard estimation methods. In the second step the ML estimates are low pass filtered by an IIR filter. This can be performed by using two recursive filters: a forward causal filter and a backward anti-causal filter.

The filter coefficients depend on the number of observations available for each unknown variable. In the case of non Gaussian noise (Rayleigh distributed), the coefficients also depend on the sufficient statistics of the signal.

The numerical methods presented in the paper showed that the proposed algorithm based on recursive filtering is faster and produces results identical to the ones obtained by solving the MAP equations using stand numerical methods. Furthermore, this approach can be extended to higher order filters corresponding to other Gibbs priors with better performances at transitions [20]. This can also be seen as a useful tool for the design of prior distributions based on filtering theory.

References

[1] V. E.Johnson, W. H. Wong, X. Hu and C. Chen, Image Restoration Using Gibbs Priors: Bondary Modeling, Treatment of Blurring, and selection of Hyperparameters, IEEE PAMI, vol.13, no.5, May 1991. 436

[2] D. L. Snyder, M.I Miller, L. J. Thomas and D. G. Politte, Noise and Edge Artifacts in Maiximum-Likelihood Reconstructions for Emission Tomography, IEEE Trans. on Medical Imaging, vol. MI-6, no.3, September 1987. 436

[3] A. K. Jain, Fundamentals of Digital Image Processing, Prentice-Hall, Inc., Englewood Cliffs, NJ, 1989. 436

[4] E. S. Chornoboy, C. J. Chen, M. I. Miller, T. R. Miller and D. L. Snyder, An Evaluation of Maxim Likelihood Reconstruction for SPECT, IEEE Trans. on Medical Imaging, vol.9, no.1, March 1990. 436

[5] T. A. Gooley and H. H. Barret, Evaluation of Statistical Methods of Image Reconstruction Through ROC Analysis, IEEE Trans. on Medical Imaging, vol.11, no.2, June 1992. 436

[6] L. A.Shepp and Y.Vardi, Maximum Likelihood Reconstruction for Emission Tomography, IEEE Trans. on Medical Imaging, vol.MI-1, no.2, October 1982. 436

[7] T.Herbert and R. Leahy, A Generalized EM Algorithm for 3-D Bayesian Reconstruction from Poisson Data Using Gibbs Priors, IEEE Trans. on Medical Imaging, vol.8, no.2, June 1989. 436

[8] A. K. Katsaggelos, Digital Image Restoration, Springer Series in Information Sciences, Springer-Verlag, 1991. 436, 438

[9] D. S. Lalush and B. M. W. Tsui, Simulation Evaluation of Gibbs Prior Distributions for Use in Maximum A Posteriori SPECT Reconstructions, IEEE Trans. on Medical Imaging, vol.11, no.2, June 1992. 437

[10] P. J. Green, Bayesian Reconstructions From Emission Tomography Data Using a Modified EM Algorithm, IEEE Trans. on Medical Imaging, vol.9, no.1, March 1990. 437

[11] S. Geman and D. Geman, Stochastic Relaxation, Gibbs Distributions, and the Bayesian Restoration of Images, IEEE Trans on Pattern Analysis and Machine Intelligence, vol.PAMI-6, no.6, pp. 721-741, November 1984. 437, 438

[12] S. Z.Li, Close-Form Solution and Parameter Selection for Convex Minimization-Based Edge-Preserving Smoothing, IEEE Trans. on PAMI, vol. PAMI-20, no.9, pp.916-932, September 1998. 438

[13] Jorge S. Marques, Pattern Recognition. Statistical and Neuronal Approches, IST Press, 1999. 438

[14] Jae. S. Lim, Two-Dimensional Signal and Image Processing, PTR Prentice Hall, Englewood Cliffs, New Jersey. 439, 440

[15] R. Deriche. Using Canny's criteria to derive a recursively implemented optimal edge detector. The International Journal of Computer Vision, 1(2):167-187, May 1987.

[16] J. Abbot and F. Thurstone, Acoustic Speckle: Theory and Experimental Analysis, Ultrasound Imaging vol.1, pp.303-324, 1979.

[17] J. Dias, T. Silva, J. Leitão,Adaptive Restoration of Speckled SAR Images Using a Compound Random Markov Field, Procedings ICIP98 Chicago,vol.II,pp.79-83,October 1998.

[18] C. Burckhardt, Speckle in Ultrasound B-Mode Scans, IEEE Trans. on Sonics and Ultrsonics, vol. SU-25, no.1, pp.1-6, January 1978.

[19] J. Sanches and J. S. Marques, A Fast MAP Algorithm for 3D Ultrasound, Proceedings Third International Workshop on Energy Minimization Methods in Computer Vision and Pattern Recognition, EMMCVPR2001, pp.63-74, Sophia Antipolis, France, September 2001.

[20] J. Sanches and J. S. Marques, A MAP IIR Filter for 3D Ultrasound, ICIP2002, Rochester, New York, pp.II-957-960,September 2002.   ,

Estimation of Rank Deficient Matrices
from Partial Observations:
Two-Step Iterative Algorithms*

Rui F. C. Guerreiro and Pedro M. Q. Aguiar

Institute for Systems and Robotics / IST, Lisboa, Portugal
{rfcg,aguiar}@isr.ist.utl.pt
http://www.isr.ist.utl.pt/~{rfcg,aguiar}

Abstract. Several computer vision applications require estimating a
rank deficient matrix from noisy observations of its entries. When the
observation matrix has no missing data, the LS solution of such problem
is known to be given by the SVD. However, in practice, when several
entries of the matrix are not observed, the problem has no closed form
solution. In this paper, we study two iterative algorithms for minimizing
the non-linear LS cost function obtained when estimating rank deficient
matrices from partial observations. In the first algorithm, the iterations
are the well known *Expectation* and *Maximization* (EM) steps that have
succeeded in several estimation problems with missing data. The second algorithm, which we call *Row-Column* (RC), estimates, in alternate
steps, the row and column spaces of the solution matrix. Our conclusions
are that RC performs better than EM in what respects to the robustness
to the initialization and to the convergence speed. We also demonstrate
the algorithms when inferring 3D structure from video sequences.

1 Introduction

Recent approaches to several computer vision problems require determining linear or affine low dimensional subspaces from noisy observations. These problems include object recognition [,], applications in photometry [, ,],
image alignment [,], and the recovery of 3D rigid structure from video sequences [, , , , , , , , ,].
   In general, such low dimensional subspaces are found by estimating rank
deficient matrices from noisy observations of their entries. When the observation matrix is completely known, the solution to this problem is easily obtained
from its *Singular Value Decomposition* (SVD) [ ]. However, in practice, the
observation matrix may be incomplete, *i.e.*, some of its entries may be unknown (unobserved). Take as an example the recovery of 3D structure from
video. The observation matrix collects 2D trajectories of projections of feature
points [, , , , ,] or other primitives [, , ,]. In real life video

---

* This work was partially supported by FCT project POSI/SRI/41561/2001,
FCT POSI – QCA III.

A. Rangarajan et al. (Eds.): EMMCVPR 2003, LNCS 2683, pp. 450–   , 2003.

clips, these projections are not visible along the entire image sequence due to the occlusion and the limited field of view. Thus, the observation matrix is in general incomplete.

In this paper, we address the problem of estimating a rank deficient matrix from noisy observations of a subset of its entries. This problem hasn't been much addressed in the computer vision literature. References [ ] and [ ] propose sub-optimal solutions. In [ ], the missing values of the observation matrix are "filled in", in a sequential way, by using SVDs of observed submatrices. In [ ], the author proposes a method to combine the constrains that arise from the observed submatrices of the original matrix. A bidirectional optimization scheme was proposed in [ ]. In this paper, we study two distinct two-step iterative algorithms, developed for this problem. The first algorithm is based in a well known method to deal with missing data – the *Expectation-Maximization* (EM) [ ]. Although the authors don't refer it, the bidirectional scheme in [ ] is also an EM-based algorithm. However, as detailed below, the EM algorithm we propose is more general and computationally simpler than the one in [ ]. Our second two-step iterative scheme is similar to Wiberg's algorithm [ ] and related to the one used in [ ] to model polyhedral objects. It computes, alternately, in closed form, the row space matrix and the column space matrix whose product is the solution matrix. We call this the *Row-Column* (RC) iterative algorithm.

In the paper, we illustrate the behavior of both algorithms with simple cases and evaluate their performance with more extensive experiments. In particular, we study the impact of the initialization on the algorithm's behavior. From these experiments, we conclude that the RC algorithm is more robust than EM in what respects to the sensibility to the initialization. Furthermore, the number of iterations needed for good convergence and the computational cost of each iteration are both smaller for RC than for EM. Obviously, the performances of both EM and RC improve when the initial estimate provided to the algorithms is more accurate. Any sub-optimal method, e.g. the ones in [,], can be used to compute such an initialization. Our experience shows that, with a simple initialization procedure, even for high levels of noise and large amount of missing data, both iterative algorithms converge: **i)** to the global optimum; and **ii)** in a very small number of iterations.

We apply the EM and RC estimation algorithms to the problem of recovering 3D rigid structure from video sequences, when the observation matrix misses entries due to occlusion. Our experiments show that fitting the rank deficient matrix to the entire observation matrix (which misses several entries) leads to better 3D reconstructions than those obtained by combining partial 3D models estimated by fitting submatrices to smaller subsets of data (each corresponding to a subset of features that were visible in a subset of frames). A preliminary version of parts of this work was presented in [ ]. MatLab© implementations of the algorithms we describe in this paper are available at [ ].

Paper Organization In Section , we introduce the *Least Squares* (LS) cost function associated with the problem of estimating a rank deficient matrix from noisy observations of a subset of its entries. Sections and describe the EM and

RC iterative algorithms that minimize the non-linear LS cost function. In Section   , we illustrate the behavior of the EM and RC algorithms with simple cases that enable graphical representations and demonstrate their good performance when dealing with arbitrary matrices. In Section   we apply our algorithms to the problem of recovering 3D rigid structure from video sequences. Section concludes the paper.

2   Problem Formulation

Given an observation $\boldsymbol{W}$ of a $M \times N$ rank deficient matrix $\widetilde{\boldsymbol{W}}$, say rank $R <$ $\min(M, N)$, corrupted by white Gaussian noise, the ML estimate $\widehat{\boldsymbol{W}}$ of $\widetilde{\boldsymbol{W}}$ is

$$\widehat{\boldsymbol{W}} = \arg \min_{\widetilde{\boldsymbol{W}} \in \mathcal{S}_R} \left\| \boldsymbol{W} - \widetilde{\boldsymbol{W}} \right\|_F, \tag{1}$$

where $\|.\|_F$ represents the Frobenius norm and $\mathcal{S}_R$ denotes the space of the $M \times N$ rank R matrices. The solution $\widehat{\boldsymbol{W}}$ of ( ) is known – it is obtained from the SVD of $\boldsymbol{W} = \boldsymbol{U} \boldsymbol{\Sigma} \boldsymbol{V}$, after selecting the R largest singular values [ ]. We denote this optimal rank reduction operation, $i.e.$, the projection onto $\mathcal{S}_R$, by $\boldsymbol{W} \downarrow \mathcal{S}_R$:

$$\widehat{\boldsymbol{W}} = \boldsymbol{W} \downarrow \mathcal{S}_R = \boldsymbol{U}_{M \times R} \, \boldsymbol{\Sigma}_{R \times R} \, \boldsymbol{V}_{R \times N}. \tag{2}$$

When the observation matrix $\boldsymbol{W}$ misses a subset of its entries, the ML estimation of $\widetilde{\boldsymbol{W}}$ leads to the minimization of a generalized version of ( ),

$$\widehat{\boldsymbol{W}} = \arg \min_{\widetilde{\boldsymbol{W}} \in \mathcal{S}_R} \left\| \left(\boldsymbol{W} - \widetilde{\boldsymbol{W}} \right) \odot \boldsymbol{M} \right\|_F, \tag{3}$$

where $\odot$ represents the elementwise product, also known as the Hadamard product, and the $M \times N$ matrix $\boldsymbol{M}$ is a binary mask that accounts for the known entries of the observation matrix $\boldsymbol{W}$, $i.e.$, $m_{ij} = 1$ if w_{ij} is known and $m_{ij} = 0$ otherwise. The existence of unknown entries in $\boldsymbol{W}$ prevents us to use the SVD of $\boldsymbol{W}$ as in ( ) to minimize ( ). In Sections   and   we introduce two iterative algorithms that minimize the nonlinear cost function ( ).

3   Expectation-Maximization Algorithm

The *Expectation-Maximization* (EM) approach to estimation problems with missing data works by enlarging the set of parameters to estimate – the data that is missing is jointly estimated with the other parameters. The joint estimation is performed, iteratively, in two alternate steps: **i)** the *E-step* estimates the missing data given the previous estimate of the other parameters; **ii)** the *M-step* estimates the other parameters given the previous estimate of the missing data, see [ ] for a review on the EM algorithm.

In our case, given an initial estimate $\widehat{\boldsymbol{W}}_0$, the EM algorithm estimates in alternate steps: **i)** the missing entries of the observation matrix $\boldsymbol{W}$; **ii)** the rank R

matrix $\widehat{\boldsymbol{W}}$ that best matches the "complete" data. The algorithm performs these two steps until convergence, $i.e.$, until the error measured by the Frobenius norm in ( ) stabilizes.

E-Step – Estimation of the Missing Data Given $\widehat{\boldsymbol{W}}_{k-1}$, the ML estimates of the missing entries $\{w_{ij} : m_{ij} = 0\}$ of $\boldsymbol{W}$ are simply the corresponding entries $\widehat{w}_{ij}$ of $\widehat{\boldsymbol{W}}_{k-1}$. We then build a complete observation matrix $\overline{\boldsymbol{W}}_k$, whose entry $\overline{w}_{ij}$ equals the corresponding entry w_{ij} of the observation matrix $\boldsymbol{W}$ if w_{ij} was observed or its estimate $\widehat{w}_{ij}$ if w_{ij} is unknown,

$$\overline{w}_{ij} = \begin{cases} w_{ij} \text{ if } m_{ij} = 1 \\ \widehat{w}_{ij} \text{ if } m_{ij} = 0, \end{cases} \tag{4}$$

or, in matrix notation,

$$\overline{\boldsymbol{W}}_k = \boldsymbol{W} \odot \boldsymbol{M} + \widehat{\boldsymbol{W}}_{k-1} \odot [\mathbf{1} - \boldsymbol{M}]. \tag{5}$$

M-Step – Estimation of the Rank Deficient Matrix We are now given the complete data matrix $\overline{\boldsymbol{W}}_k$ with the estimates of the missing data from the E-step. The ML estimate of the rank R matrix $\widetilde{\boldsymbol{W}}$, $i.e.$, the rank R matrix $\widehat{\boldsymbol{W}}_k$ that best matches $\overline{\boldsymbol{W}}_k$ in the Frobenius norm sense, is then obtained from the SVD of $\overline{\boldsymbol{W}}_k$, as in ( ),

$$\widehat{\boldsymbol{W}}_k = \overline{\boldsymbol{W}}_k \downarrow \mathcal{S}_R. \tag{6}$$

In [ ], the authors develop a bidirectional algorithm to factor out an observation matrix with missing data, in the context of recovering rigid SFM. Their bidirectional algorithm is in fact an EM algorithm developed to the specific strategy of treating the 3D translation separately. In opposition, the EM algorithm just described is general, i.e, it solves any rank deficient matrix approximation problem with missing data. Furthermore, our E-step in ( ) is simpler than the corresponding step of [ ] that requires inverting matrices.

4 Row-Column Algorithm

We now describe the $Row\text{-}Column$ (RC) algorithm – another iterative approach, similar to Wiberg's algorithm [ ], to the estimation of a rank deficient matrix that best matches an incomplete observation. From our experience, summarized in Section   , the RC algorithm is not only computationally cheaper than EM, avoiding SVD computations and exhibiting faster convergence, but also more robust than EM to initializations far from the solution.

For the RC algorithm, we parameterize the rank R matrix $\widetilde{\boldsymbol{W}}$ as the product

$$\widetilde{\boldsymbol{W}} = \widetilde{\boldsymbol{A}}_{M \times R} \, \widetilde{\boldsymbol{B}}_{R \times N} \in \mathcal{S}_R, \tag{7}$$

where $\widetilde{A}$ determines the column space of $\widetilde{W}$ and $\widetilde{B}$ its row space. The estimate $\widehat{W}$ of $\widetilde{W}$ is obtained by minimizing the cost function in ( ) with respect to (wrt) the column space and row space matrices, $i.e.$, $\widehat{W} = AB$, where

$$\{A, B\} = \arg \min_{\widetilde{A}, \widetilde{B}} \left\| \left(W - \widetilde{A}\widetilde{B} \right) \odot M \right\|_F. \tag{8}$$

By using this parameterization, we have mapped the constrained minimization ( ) wrt $\widetilde{W} \in \mathcal{S}_R$ into the unconstrained minimization ( ) wrt $\widetilde{A}$ and $\widetilde{B}$.

We minimize ( ) in two alternate steps: **i)** the R-*step* assumes the column space matrix A is known and estimates the row space matrix B; **ii)** the C-*step* estimates B for known A. The algorithm is initialized by computing A from an initial estimate $\widehat{W}_0$ and it runs until the value of the norm in ( ) stabilizes.

When there is no missing data, $i.e.$, when $M = \mathbf{1}_{M \times N}$, the solutions for the RC steps above are simply obtained by using the *pseudoinverse* [ ],

$$B_k = \left(A_{k-1}^T A_{k-1} \right)^{-1} A_{k-1}^T W, \qquad A_k = W B_k^T \left(B_k B_k^T \right)^{-1}. \tag{9}$$

If we write steps R and C together as a recursion on one of the matrices A or B, say, on the column space in A, we get

$$A_k = W W^T A_{k-1} \left(A_{k-1}^T W W^T A_{k-1} \right)^{-1} A_{k-1}^T A_{k-1}, \tag{10}$$

which shows that, in this simpler case, our RC algorithm is in fact implementing the application of the *power method* [ ] to the matrix $W W^T$ (the factor $(A_{k-1}^T W W^T A_{k-1})^{-1} A_{k-1}^T A_{k-1}$ is the normalization). The power method has been widely used to avoid the computation of the entire SVD when fitting rank deficient matrices to complete observations. We will see that, even when there is missing data, steps R and C admit closed-form solution and the overall algorithm generalizes the power method in a very simple way.

R-Step – Estimation of the Row Space For known A, the minimization of ( ) wrt B can be rewritten in terms of each of the N columns $\{b_n, n = 1 \ldots N\}$ of B,

$$b_n = \arg \min_{\widetilde{b}_n} \left\| \left(w_n - A\widetilde{b}_n \right) \odot m_n \right\|_F, \tag{11}$$

where the lowercase boldface letters denote columns of the matrices with the same uppercase letters. Exploiting the structure of the vector m_n, we now rearrange the minimization in ( ) in such a way that its solution becomes obvious. First, we note that the binary vector m_n in ( ) is just selecting the entries of the error vector $(w_n - A\widetilde{b}_n)$ that affect the error norm. Then, by making explicit that selection in terms of the entries of w_n that contain known data and the corresponding relevant entries of A, we rewrite ( ) as

$$b_n = \arg \min_{\widetilde{b}_n} \left\| w_n \odot m_n - (A \odot M_n) \widetilde{b}_n \right\|_F, \tag{12}$$

where M_n is a $M \times R$ matrix with all R columns equal to m_n, i.e., it is a short notation for $M_n = m_n 1_{1 \times R}$.

The minimization in (   ) is now a linear LS problem. Its solution b_n is then obtained by using the pseudoinverse of matrix $A \odot M_n$,

$$b_n = \left[(A \odot M_n)^T (A \odot M_n) \right]^{-1} (A \odot M_n)^T (w_n \odot m_n), \qquad (13)$$

which is simplified by omitting repeated binary maskings,

$$b_n = \left[A^T (A \odot M_n) \right]^{-1} A^T (w_n \odot m_n). \qquad (14)$$

The set of N estimates $\{b_n, n = 1 \ldots N\}$ as in (   ) generalizes the well known pseudoinverse LS solution in (   ) to problems with missing data.

C-Step – Estimation of the Column Space Given B, the estimate of each row a_m of the column space matrix A is obtained by proceeding in a similar way as in the R-step. We get, for each $m = 1 \ldots M$,

$$a_m = (w_m \odot m_m) B^T \left[(B \odot M_m) B^T \right]^{-1}, \qquad (15)$$

where in this case, for commodity, lowercase boldface letters denote rows rather than columns, and $M_m = 1_{R \times 1} m_m$.

5   Experimental Analysis

In this Section, we describe experiments that illustrate the behavior of the EM and CR algorithms and demonstrate their good performance.

2×2 Matrices We start by a simple case that allows an illustrative graphical representation – estimating the 2×2 rank 1 matrix $\widetilde{W}$ that best matches an observation W that misses one of its entries. In this case, the estimation error measured by the Frobenius norm in (   ) and (   ) can be expressed in terms of a single parameter θ. In fact, let the 2×2 rank 1 matrix $\widetilde{W}$ be written in terms of its column and row spaces as in (   ),

$$\widetilde{W} = a_{2 \times 1} b_{1 \times 2} \in \mathcal{S}_1. \qquad (16)$$

Without loss of generality, impose that the row vector b has unit norm and write it in terms of a row angle θ, $b = [\cos \theta, \sin \theta]$. Now denote the minimum of (   ) wrt the column space a for fixed row space b, i.e., for fixed θ, by $a(W, \theta)$, given by (   ). The estimation error in (   ) and (   ) is then rewritten as a function of θ,

$$\text{error}(\theta) = \left\| (W - a(W, \theta) \left[\cos \theta \ \sin \theta \right]) \odot M \right\|_F. \qquad (17)$$

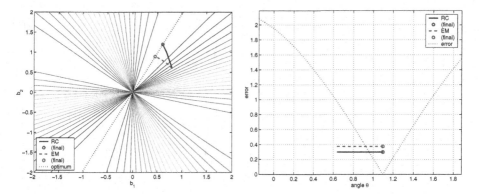

Fig. 1. Typical good behavior. Left: EM and RC trajectories. Right: error function

Note that for any set of three entries of a 2×2 matrix, there is always a value for the forth entry that makes the rank of the matrix equal to one, *i.e.*, there is always a 2×2 rank 1 matrix $\widetilde{W}$ that fits exactly the observed entries of W. Thus, we have $\min \text{error}(\theta) = 0$.

The following examples illustrate the impact of the initialization on the behavior of the algorithms with experiments that use the same observations,

$$\widetilde{W} = \begin{bmatrix} -1 & -1.95 \\ 2 & 3.9 \end{bmatrix} \in \mathcal{S}_1, \qquad M = \begin{bmatrix} 1 & 1 \\ 1 & 0 \end{bmatrix}, \qquad W = \begin{bmatrix} -1 & -1.95 \\ 2 & ? \end{bmatrix}, \qquad (18)$$

where "?" represents the unobserved entry w_{22} of the observation matrix W.

Typical Good Behavior of EM and RC Using the initial estimate

$$\widehat{W}_0 = \begin{bmatrix} -1 & -1.95 \\ 2 & 0 \end{bmatrix}, \qquad (19)$$

we describe the evolution of the estimates $\widehat{W}_k$ of the rank 1 matrix $\widetilde{W}$ by plotting two equivalent representations of $\widehat{W}_k$: **i)** its row space $b = [b_1, b_2]$; and **ii)** the corresponding angle θ as defined above. The left plot of Fig.   shows the level curves of the error function as function of the row vector $b = [b_1, b_2]$, superimposed with the evolution of the estimates of b for EM (dashed line) and RC (solid line). In this plot, the dotted line (optimum) are the row vectors that lead to zero estimation error. The right plot of Fig.   represents the same error function, now as a function of θ, as defined in ( ), (dotted line) superimposed with the locations of the θ estimates for EM (dashed line) and RC (solid line).

From the left plot of Fig.   , we see that both EM and RC trajectories start at the same point (due to the equal initialization) and converge to points in the optimal line. As expected, the EM estimates of the row space vector have constant unit norm (due to the normalization in the SVD) while the RC estimates don't.

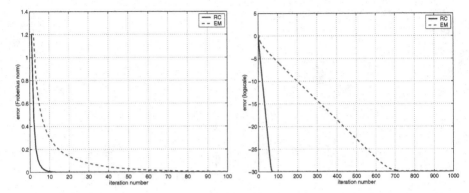

Fig. 2. Typical good behavior. Left: estimation error. Right: the same in logscale

The good behavior of the algorithms is confirmed by the right plot of Fig.   that shows that both algorithms converge to a value of θ that makes error$(\theta) = 0$, *i.e.*, that minimizes error(θ).

To evaluate the convergence speed, we plot in Fig.   the evolution of the estimation error along the iterative process for both algorithms (in the left, in linear scale, in the right, in logarithmic scale). From Fig. , we see that RC converges in a smaller number of iterations than EM. Our experience with larger matrices in practical applications have confirmed the faster convergence of RC.

Large Entries in Rows or Columns that Miss Data We now illustrate a drawback of the EM algorithm. Using the same data and the initial estimate

$$\widehat{\boldsymbol{W}}_0 = \begin{bmatrix} -1 & -1.95 \\ 2 & 22 \end{bmatrix}, \tag{20}$$

we get the first 1000 iterations of Fig. , which is as described above for Fig. .

From the left plot of Fig. , we see that, while RC converges to the optimal line, the estimates given by the EM almost doesn't change along the iterative process. This can also be seen in the right plot of Fig. , which shows that RC converges to the θ such that error$(\theta) = 0$, while EM, after 1000 iterations is still far from $\arg\min$ error(θ). The left plot of Fig.   shows the evolution of the estimation errors. See that while the error of RC converges to zero in a few iterations, the error of EM almost doesn't decrease during the first 100 iterations.

The bad behavior of EM is due to the large initial guess for w_{22} (note that $\widehat{w}_{0_{22}}$ is large when compared with the known entries of $\boldsymbol{W}$). Remember that EM starts by estimating the rank 1 matrix that best matches the initial guess $\widehat{\boldsymbol{W}}_0$. This rank 1 matrix is the matrix associated with the largest singular value of $\widehat{\boldsymbol{W}}_0$, which is highly constrained by the large spurious entry $\widehat{w}_{0_{22}} = 22$ (note that while the singular values of the solution matrix $\widetilde{\boldsymbol{W}}$ are $\sigma_1(\widetilde{\boldsymbol{W}}) \simeq 4.9$ and $\sigma_2(\widetilde{\boldsymbol{W}}) = 0$,

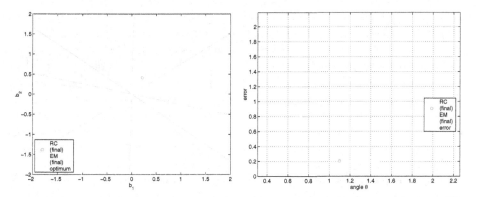

Fig. 3. Large initialization. Left: EM and RC trajectories. Right:error function

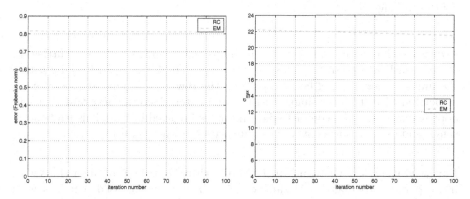

Fig. 4. Large initialization. Left: estimation error. Right: largest singular value of $\widehat{W}_k$

the singular values of the initial guess $\widehat{W}_0$ are $\sigma_1(\widehat{W}_0) \simeq 22.2$ and $\sigma_2(\widehat{W}_0) \simeq 0.8$ due to the large entry $\widehat{w}_{0_{22}} = 22$). Then, EM replaces the known entries of W in the new estimate (obtaining thus an estimate that is very close to the initial guess) and repeats the process. To better illustrate this very slow convergence of EM, we represent, in the right plot of Fig. , the evolution of the largest singular value of the estimate $\widehat{W}_k$ for both algorithms. We see that while, as expected, the largest singular value of the RC estimates converges to the largest singular value of the solution $\widetilde{W}$, $\sigma_1(\widetilde{W}) \simeq 4.9$, the largest singular value of the first 100 iterations of the EM estimates changes very slowly from its initial value $\sigma_1(\widehat{W}_0) \simeq 22.2$.

The behavior just described also happens in situations other than the initial guesses of the unknown entries being too large when compared to the other entries. In fact, we observed the same behavior in situations where the observation

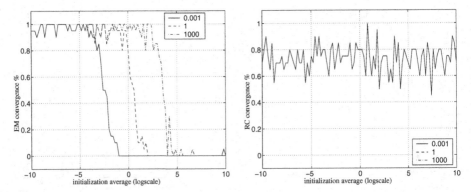

Fig. 5. Percentage of convergent experiments as a function of the mean value of the initial random guesses for the unknown entries. Left: results for the EM algorithm with matrices whose entries have mean 10^{-3}, 1, and 10^3. Right: results for the RC algorithm

matrix had large entries in rows or columns that contained missing entries. In these situations, due to those large entries, even small values for initial guess of the unknown entries had large impact on the row and column singular vectors associated with the large singular values that determined the best rank deficient approximations to the complete data matrices involved in EM. This lead to the same kind of very slow convergence illustrated in Fig.   and Fig. .

Large Matrices with Random Initialization We tested the algorithms with noisy partial observations of rank deficient matrices. We used matrices with dimensions ranging from 2×2 to 200×200 and rank from 1 to 6. The percentage of missing entries ranged from 10% to 80%. We initialized both EM and RC with random values for the unknown entries.

To illustrate the influence of the initialization on the convergence of the algorithms, Fig.   shows the percentage of experiments that converged (to an estimate close enough to the ground truth) in less than 100 iterations, as a function of the mean value of the random guesses for the unknown entries. Although representative for the entire range of experiments done, the results in the plots of Fig.   were obtained with noisy observations of 24×24 rank 4 matrices that missed 70% of their entries. The left plot of Fig.   shows three lines, each obtained by using EM with data generated with a ground truth matrix whose elements had mean 0.001, 1, and 1000. The percentages of convergence for the RC algorithm are in the right plot.

The left plot of Fig.   shows that the EM algorithm converges almost always if the mean value of the initial guesses for the missing entries is smaller than the mean value of the observed entries. When we increase the values of the initial estimates of the missing entries, the percentage of convergence decreases abruptly, becoming close to zero when those values become much larger than the ones of the observed entries. This is in agreement with the behavior illustrated in the example of Fig. . In opposition, the right plot of Fig. shows that the behavior of the RC algorithm is somewhat independent of the order of magnitude of the initialization. The experiments that lead to a non-convergent behavior of RC were such that the matrices whose inverse is computed in ( ) and ( ) were close to singular. We thus conclude that it is very important in practical applications to provide good initial estimates for both EM and RC algorithms.

Finally, we note that the relevance of a good initialization goes behind avoiding non-convergent behavior. In fact, we observed that both the amount of missing data and the noise level have strong impact on the algorithm's convergence speed. Thus, when dealing with large percentages of missing entries and high levels of noise, as it may arise in practice, a better initialization not only improves the chance of a convergent behavior but also leads to a faster convergence.

Heuristic Initialization We now use an initial guess $\widehat{W}_0$ obtained by combining the column and row spaces given by the SVDs of the known submatrices of W [ ]. In our tests, with this simple initialization procedure, 100% of the runs of EM and RC converged to the ground truth matrix in a very small number of iterations, typically less than 10, even for high levels of noise.

The plot of Fig. represents the average entry estimation error, defined as $\overline{error}(\widehat{W}) = \|(\widehat{W} - \widetilde{W}) \odot M\|_F / \sqrt{\sum_{i,j} m_{ij}}$, where $\sum_{i,j} m_{ij}$ accounts for the number of observed entries, after 20 iterations of EM and RC algorithms, for noisy observations of a 24×24 rank 4 matrix $\widetilde{W}$, with 70% missing data, as a function of noise standard deviation. We see that the average entry estimation errors after 20 iterations are below 10^{-8} for noise standard deviation ranging from $10^{-2.5}$ to $10^{2.5}$ (the mean value of the entries of the ground truth matrix $\widetilde{W}$ is 1). This shows that, with a simple initialization procedure, both EM and RC algorithms converge to the optimal solution, even for very noisy observations. Furthermore, we conclude that the main impact of the observation noise is on the EM and RC convergence speeds – the slightly higher average error values on the right region of the plot of Fig. indicates that the estimates were still converging to the optimal solution after 20 iterations.

Computational Cost As referred above, the EM and RC algorithms converge in a very small number of iterations when initialized by the heuristic procedure in [ ]. We now report an experimental evaluation of the computational costs of each iteration of EM and RC as functions of the observation matrix dimension.

We used $N \times 24$ observation matrices with missing data corresponding to a $(N-4) \times 20$ submatrix. The plots in Fig. represent the number of MatLab© floating point operations (FLOPS) and the computation time per iteration, as functions of N. From the left plot, we see that the number of FLOPS per iteration of the EM algorithm is larger than one of the RC algorithm. Furthermore, the FLOPS count for EM increases exponentially with N (due to the SVD computation) while for RC it increases linearly with N. Thus, although the computation

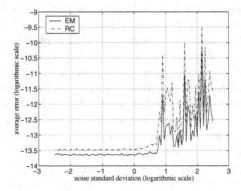

Fig. 6. Estimation errors for EM and RC as functions of the noise standard deviation

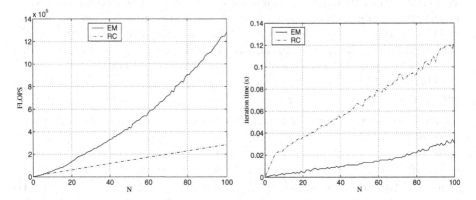

Fig. 7. Computational cost of each iteration of EM and RC. Left: number of MatLab© floating point operations (FLOPS). Right: computation time

times in the right plot of Fig.   are smaller for EM than for RC (the reason being the very efficient MatLab© implementation of the SVD), we conclude that RC is computationally simpler than EM. RC is even as simple as the methods to deal with complete matrices, since the most efficient way to compute the SVD is to use the power method [ ] of which RC is a simple generalization.

6   Application: 3D Structure from Video Sequences

We illustrate the application of the matrix estimation algorithms to the problem of recovering 3D rigid shape and 3D motion from video. As with the majority of current approaches, we infer the 3D positions of a set of features points and the 3D motion of the camera by first determining the 2D trajectories of the feature points on the image plane. Among the approaches to compute the 3D rigid

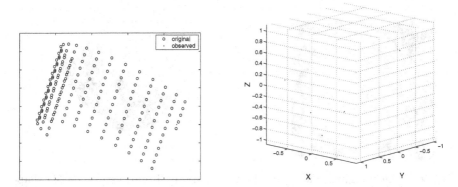

Fig. 8. Cylinder sequence. Left: one synthetic frame. Right: estimates of the 3D positions of the features points

structure parameters from the 2D projections, we use the *factorization method* of Tomasi and Kanade [ ], now popular due to its robustness and simplicity. In this method, the observed trajectories are collected in an observation matrix W that is rank deficient in a noiseless situation. The parameters describing the 3D shape and 3D motion are estimated from the factors of the rank deficient matrix $\widetilde{W}$ that best matches W. In [ ], the authors use the SVD to compute $\widetilde{W}$ when W is completely observed. In practice, however, due to the limited field of view and the occlusion, the observation matrix W may miss several of its entries. We use our algorithms to compute $\widetilde{W}$ when W has missing data. This way, we take into account the rigidity of the scene along the entire video sequence, leading to a more constrained problem (and a more accurate solution) than the one obtained by processing independently several small subsets of frames. We describe below experiments with synthesized and real video sequences.

Synthetic Data – Cylinder We synthesized noisy versions of the 2D trajectories of 372 feature points located on the 3D surface of a rotating cylinder. Then, we simulated occlusion and inclusion by removing significant segments of those trajectories. The left plot of Fig.   shows one of the 50 synthesized frames. The small circles denote the noiseless projections and the points denote their noisy version, *i.e.*, the data that is observed. Note that only an incomplete view portion of the cylinder is observed in each frame.

The data from the cylinder sequence was then collected on a 100×372 observation matrix W with 9537 unknown entries ($\simeq 26\%$ of the total number). We used the RC algorithm to estimate the rank deficient matrix $\widetilde{W}$ that best matched W and computed the 3D structure by using the factorization method [ ]. The right plot of Fig.   plots the final estimate of the 3D shape. We see that the complete cylinder is recovered. Due to the incorporation of the rigidity constraint, the 3D positions of the features points are accurately estimate even in the presence of very noisy observations (compare the plots in Fig.   ).

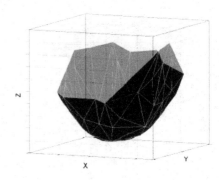

Fig. 9. Ping-pong ball video clip. Left: first frame. Right: estimated 3D shape

Real Video – Ping-Pong Ball We used a real-life video clip available at [   ]. This clip shows a rotating ping-pong ball with painted dots. The left image of Fig.   shows the first of the 52 video frames of the ball sequence. We used simple correlation techniques to track a set of 64 feature points. Due to the camera-ball 3D rotation, the region of the ball that is visible changes along time, leading to an observation matrix with $\simeq 41\%$ missing entries. By proceeding as described for the previous experiment, we estimated the 3D shape shown on the right image of Fig.   , which shows that our method succeeded in recovering the spherical surface of the ball.

Real Video – Rubik's Cube This video clip – see two representative frames on the left and middle images of Fig.   – shows a Rubik's cube rotating around a vertical axis. In the leftmost image of Fig.   , we superimposed with the video frame the visible features and the initial parts of their trajectories. Due to the occlusion, feature points enter and leave the scene. To emphasize the advantages of using the algorithms described in this paper, we first applied to a segment of the Rubik's cube video clip the factorization method of Tomasi and Kanade [ ] for complete data, obtaining the 3D shape represented on the left side of Fig.   . This model was obtained with 28 features and 18 frames.

We then collected the entire set of the visible parts of the trajectories of 64 features across 85 frames in a 170×64 incomplete observation matrix W. The structure of the missing part of W is coded by the 170×64 binary mask M represented on the right side of Figure   . The number of missing entries in W was about 62%. Since the 3D motion in this video clip is a 3D rotation, the observation matrix would be rank 3 in a noiseless situation [ ]. We used the RC algorithm to estimate the rank 3 matrix that best matches the incomplete data in W and then the factorization method to compute the 3D shape shown on the right image of Fig.   . This simple example illustrates how RC algorithm trivializes the usually hard task of merging partial estimates of a 3D model. In the right image of Fig.   , the top face is missing because the position the cube model is shown in that image was not seen in the original video clip.

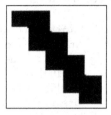

Fig. 10. Rubik's cube video clip. Left: frame with visible features and corresponding partial trajectories. Middle: another frame. Right: binary mask matrix M representing the incomplete data – black regions correspond to entries $m_{ij} = 1$ meaning that w_{ij} is observed, *i.e.*, feature j is visible in frame i; white regions represent the opposite

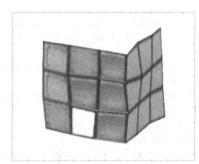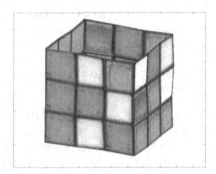

Fig. 11. Texture mapped 3D shape recovered from the Rubik's cube video clip. Left: incomplete model obtained by using the factorization method of Tomasi and Kanade [1]. Right: complete shape recovered by our method – factorization with missing data

The advantage of using RC or EM to recover 3D rigid structure is two-fold. First, while recovering a complete 3D model by fusing partial models as the one on the left side of Fig.   is a complex task, our method recovers directly the complete model shown on the right side of Fig.   . Second, rather than processing subsets of the set of features and frames at disjoint steps, our method uses all the information available in a global way, leading to more accurate 3D shapes as illustrated by the 3D models in Fig.   .

7   Conclusion

We developed two iterative algorithms, *Expectation-Maximization* (EM) and *Row-Column* (RC), that estimate rank deficient matrices from partial observations. Our experiments showed that both algorithms converged to the correct estimate whenever initialized by a simple procedure and that RC algorithm is computationally cheaper and more robust than EM. We used RC to recover 3D structure from video sequences with self-occluding objects.

References

[1] Basri, R., Ullman, S.: The alignment of objects with smooth surfaces. Computer Graphics, Vision, and Image Processing: Image Understanding **57** (1988)

[2] Ullman, S., Basri, R.: Recognition by linear combinations of models. IEEE TPAMI **13** (1991)

[3] Shashua, A.: Geometry and photometry in 3D visual recognition. MIT TR 1401, Massachussets Institute of Technology, MA, USA (1992)

[4] Moses, Y.: Face recognition: generalization to novel images. PhD thesis, Weizmann Institute of Science (1993)

[5] Belhumeur, P., Kriegman, D.: What is the set of images of an object under all possible lighting conditions ? In: IEEE CVPR. (1996)

[6] Zelnik-Manor, L., Irani, M.: Multi-frame alignement of planes. In: IEEE CVPR, Fort Collins CO, USA (1999)

[7] Zelnik-Manor, L., Irani, M.: Multi-view subspace constraints on homographies. In: IEEE ICCV, Kerkyra, Greece (1999)

[8] Tomasi, C., Kanade, T.: Shape and motion from image streams under orthography: a factorization method. International Journal of Computer Vision **9** (1992)

[9] Sturm, P., Triggs, B.: A factorization based algorithm for multi-image projective structure and motion. In: Proc. of ECCV, Cambridge, UK (1996)

[10] Poelman, C. J., Kanade, T.: A paraperspective factorization method for shape and motion recovery. IEEE TPAMI **19** (1997)

[11] Morita, T., Kanade, T.: A sequential factorization method for recovering shape and motion from image streams. IEEE TPAMI **19** (1997)

[12] Aguiar, P. M. Q., Moura, J. M. F.: Factorization as a rank 1 problem. In: IEEE CVPR, Fort Collins CO, USA (1999)

[13] Irani, M., Anandan, P.: Factorization with uncertainty. In: Proc. of ECCV, Dublin, Ireland (2000)

[14] Shapiro, L.: Affine Analysis of Image Sequences. Cambridge University Press, Cambridge, UK (1995)

[15] Quan, L., Kanade, T.: A factorization method for affine structure from line correspondences. In: IEEE CVPR, San Francisco CA, USA (1996)

[16] Morris, D., Kanade, T.: A unified factorization algorithm for points, line segments and planes with uncertainty models. In: IEEE ICCV. (1998)

[17] Aguiar, P. M. Q., Moura, J. M. F.: Three-dimensional modeling from two-dimensional video. IEEE Transactions on Image Processing **10** (2001)

[18] Golub, G. H., Van-Loan, C. F.: Matrix Computations. The Johns Hopkins University Press (1996)

[19] Jacobs, D.: Linear fitting with missing data: Applications to structure-from-motion and to characterizing intensity images. In: IEEE CVPR, St Barbara, USA (1997)

[20] Maruyama, M., Kurumi, S.: Bidirectional optimization for reconstructing 3D shape from an image sequence with missing data. In: IEEE ICIP, Kobe, Japan (1999)

[21] McLachlan, G., Krishnan, T.: The EM Algorithm and Extensions. John Wiley & Sons, New York (1997)

[22] Wiberg, T.: Computation of principal components when data are missing. In: Proc. of the Second Symposium Computational Statistics, Berlin, Germany (1976)

[23] Shum, H., Ikeuchi, K., Reddy, R.: Principal component analysis with missing data
      and its applications to polyhedral object modeling. IEEE TPAMI **17** (1995)
[24] Guerreiro, R. F. C., Aguiar, P. M. Q.: 3D structure from video streams with par-
      tially overlapping images. In: IEEE ICIP, New York, USA (2002)   ,
[25] http: //www.isr.ist.utl.pt/~aguiar/code.html (2002)
[26] http: //www-2.cs.cmu.edu/~cil/vision.html (2002)

Contextual and Non-combinatorial Approach to Feature Extraction

Toshiro Kubota

Computer Science and Engineering, University of South Carolina
Columbia, SC 29208, USA
kubota@cse.sc.edu

Abstract. Extracting features from an image is the first step in many computer vision applications. Traditionally, features represent physical or visual primitives such as edges and corners. In this paper, we augment the definition to include any attributes that conveniently describe the correlation and contextual relation between the primitive and its neighbors. The augmentation allows us to design a more detailed probability distribution model. If the distribution model is differentiable with respect to each attribute of a feature, a simple local search will find a feature set that is a local maximum in the joint probability distribution. Therefore, the final representation is free from noise and aliasing that perturbs the representation away from the local maximum. We can apply the approach to many low level vision tasks. In this paper, we demonstrate our approach with sub-pixel contour representation and surface reconstruction problems.

1 Introduction

Feature extraction in computer vision and image analysis is to extract important geometrical primitives from an image or images. In subsequent stages, the extracted features are grouped and each set of grouped features is further analyzed and interpreted. Thus, errors in the feature extraction stage will degrade the performance of the whole vision system.

It is a well accepted assumption that nearby features are well correlated. Theoretically, this is a good thing, as we can confine features to those that satisfy the correlation condition. We can concisely write the feature extraction problem as the following.

$$\hat{F} = \arg\max_{F} \Pr(F|O) \tag{1}$$

where Pr denotes the probability, O denotes observation or an image, F is a set of features, and $\hat{F}$ is an estimate of F.

The main difficulty of solving ( ) is that the dimension of the joint PDF, $\Pr(F|O)$, is extremely high for non-trivial cases. Thus, any common statistical techniques are not applicable without some approximation. A common approach

A. Rangarajan et al. (Eds.): EMMCVPR 2003, LNCS 2683, pp. 467–   , 2003.

is to introduce the following approximation to the problem; each feature in a feature set is extracted individually from the observation within some neighborhood around the feature. Then the feature extraction problem becomes

$$\hat{f}_i = \arg\max_{f_i} \Pr(f_i|O_i) \quad \forall i \tag{2}$$

where f_i is a feature indexed by i and O_i is the observation within the neighborhood of f_i. The approximated approach can be viewed as maximizing the product of marginal PDFs:

$$\hat{F} = \arg\max_{F} \prod_i^N \Pr(f_i|O_i) \tag{3}$$

The approximation reduces the dimension of each PDF significantly, as $|O_i| \ll O$ and $|f_i| \ll |F|$. A penalty of the above approximation is that a feature extraction system no longer considers the joint correlation among features, and the $\prod_i \Pr(f_i|O_i)$ contains many spurious peaks that do not exist in the original joint PDF. Denote a set of peaks in the marginal distribution, $\Pr(f_i|O_i)$, as $\left\{\tilde{f}_i\right\}$. Then every cartesian product of $\left\{\tilde{f}_1\right\} \times \dots \times \left\{\tilde{f}_N\right\}$ forms a peak in ( ). The correlation is often explored at the next feature grouping stage where spurious feature configurations are pruned and corrected as much as possible. However, the problem is combinatorial and very difficult to solve.

An alternative approach is to introduce a Markovian assumption, which states that f_i is dependent only on other features and the observation within some local neighborhood. With the Markovian assumption, the joint PDF can be written as a product of smaller PDFs known as Gibbs distribution due to the Hammersley-Clifford theorem. With this representation, we can explore an approach where each feature in turn increases the joint PDF, while other features are fixed. As each feature only influences a small number of components in the Gibbs distribution, the problem becomes more tractable.

A major issue of the above approach is the design of the Gibbs distribution, which is often decomposed into two terms: data dependent conditional term and data independent prior term. The latter term imposes some smoothness to the result. The formulation is motivated by a common assumption that underlying signal varies smoothly while noise gives non-smooth components to the observed data. However, for image analysis tasks, the signal does contain abrupt changes at object boundaries, and the above formulation tends to lose this important structural information. Therefore, a primary challenge is to formulate the potential in such a way that the solution removes noise while preserving structural information.

In this paper, we *augment* the feature representation by incorporating many relevant information that aids an accurate description of the prior term. The augmentation allows more sophisticated prior to be defined. We demonstrate that, with a proper design, the system can preserve important structural information while removing noise without relying on the conditional term.

Contributions of the paper can be summarized in three-fold. First, it presents a new way of representing a feature and dealing with the feature extraction problem in general. Second, it offers an efficient algorithm to extract a feature set that corresponds to a local maximum in the joint PDF. Third, it presents applications of the framework to contour representation and surface reconstruction problems. With the particular implementations described in this paper for these problems, the observation only affects the initial condition of the search. As the algorithm is guaranteed to find a local maximum in the joint PDF, the final representation is free from noise and aliasing in the observation that perturbs the feature set away from the local maximum. Another benefit of the proposed framework applied to these specific problems is that the representations are continuous and no longer tied to the original discrete lattices where the observation is obtained. Thus, the representations provide an estimates of the true data set in the continuous domain.

The rest of the paper is organized as following. Section 2 provides some relevant works, which help us to illustrate our technique. Section 3 discusses our feature extraction approach. We prove that our approach finds a local maximum of the joint PDF. Section 4 applies the approach to sub-pixel curve representation and surface representation problems. Finally, Section 5 summarizes the paper and provides conclusive remarks.

2   Related Works

2.1   General Feature Extarction

A large number of feature extraction techniques have been proposed in literature in the past 4 decades. Most of earlier approaches are simple local spatial operators. Thus, they explicitly or implicitly introduce the approximation of ( ). Examples are edge detectors[,   ], edge fitting[,   ], and edge grouping[,   ]. Global operators such as Hough transform and data clustering techniques pose difficulties in adapting to fine local variations.[,   ]. Later approaches, notably the probabilistic relaxation (PR)[,   ,   ], Markov random fields (MRF) [,   ,], and variational methods [,   ,   ], incorporate joint correlation via iterative local interactions, and are closely related to our approach.

The probabilistic relaxation treats feature extraction problems as selecting the most plausible set of labels where each label represents a particular state of a feature. For each pair of labels of two nearby features, a compatibility measure is provided, which measures how the label of one feature is compatible to the label of the other feature. The objective is to find an optimal set of labels that maximizes the sum of compatibility measures for the feature set, and the PR effectively finds a near optimal solution by maximizing an expected sum of the compatibility measure. The technique has been applied to many vision tasks including edge extraction[ ], pattern matching[ ], and segmentation[ ].

In our opinion, the main shortcoming associated with the PR is that it is difficult to assign a compatibility measure to each pair of labels for each pair of

features. The total of $l \times l \times n$ such measures is needed where l is the number
of labels and n is the number of nearby features. We also argue that insufficient
performance of the PR arises due to a discrete nature of its feature space. In the
next section, we show that solutions can be found more easily when the feature
space is differentiable.

The MRF based approaches assume a Markovian property in its joint PDF.
In accordance with the Hammersley-Clifford theorem, such PDF is represented
as a Gibbs distribution[ ],

$$\Pr(f) = Z_f^{-1} \exp(-\sum_{c \in C} V_c(f)) \tag{4}$$

where Z_f is a partition function, C is a set of cliques of the pixel lattice, and $V_c(f)$
is a clique potential of f associated with clique c. A major problem of the above
model is that it is difficult to compute the partition function. Various Monte-
Carlo based techniques have been proposed and successfully applied to derive
a steady state distribution without explicitly computing the partition function.
With the MRF approaches, the feature space is discrete and the state transition
is also discrete.

Variational approaches refer to those that express the problem in terms of
an energy or cost function and find a solution by minimizing the function using Euler-Lagrange derivatives. The techniques have been applied to boundary extraction[ ], image restoration[,], shape from shading[ ], and stereo
correspondence[ ], to name a few. They are similar to our approach as features
are defined in continuous domains and a solution is sought using gradient de-
scent/ascent. However, typical variational techniques only consider feature vectors of one or two dimensions. Our approach supports feature vectors of higher
dimensions and allows to treat parameters in the energy function as a part of
the features. Thus, it can eliminates a tedious process of finding a good set of
parameters for a particular task.

2.2   Shape Representation

In Section 4, we apply our feature extraction framework to a shape representation
problem. The shape is first represented by a set of spline curves interpolating
edge points extracted by an edge detector, and second as a set of surface patches
interpolating gray-scale pixel values. The objective of both cases is to remove
noise and refine the representation while preserving underlying structures in the
observation.

It has been an active area of research to accurately represent shape contours from noisy observation. The field has been especially active in recent years
in conjunction with medical imaging and biological structure modeling. Popular methods include active contour[ ], level-set[ ], scale-space[ ], and active
shape[ ] models. Our technique resembles the active contour model as a set
of feature points refine their spatial locations iteratively. However, the feature
points converge to a non-trivial configuration without any bias toward observation when our technique is applied, while they collapse to a single point when

the active contour model is applied. The bias is a convenient and effective way of adjusting the model to dynamic environment, however it also complicates the behavior of the model and adds extra parameters that need to be adjusted. The bias can be easily incorporated to our framework so that the model can track moving objects, for example. However, it is not an absolute requirement as other methods such as the active contour.

Estimating a continuous surface from discrete samples is also an important research area in computer vision and image processing. The problem is closely related to data interpolation and super-resolution image expansion. Popular 2D interpolation methods include biliner interpolation, bicubic interpolation, and non-uniform rational B-spline (NURBS). They are often employed in computer graphics to model smooth surfaces, but are not suited for computer vision applications as they remove important high-frequency information.

Various high-frequency preserving interpolation techniques have been proposed in literature. Aramini developed a computationally efficient bicubic splines that preserved high-frequency contents better than the conventional cubic splines [ ]. Nguyen et al. treated the problem in a regularization framework, and derived a suitable regularization parameter using generalized cross validation[ ]. Schultz and Stevenson employed a Bayesian based robust estimator for the super-resolution problem.[ ]. More recently, super-resolution techniques using multiple image frames and/or learning from a set of training data have been proposed to improve single image based techniques [, , ,].

The surface representation technique described in this paper preserves sharp edges while reduces the amount of random noise. It is a single image based approach and there is no learning phase involved. The technique uses quadratic polynomial patches for interpolation, and adaptively adjusts the shapes of the patches as well as the 3D positions of the patches.

3 Approach

3.1 Fundamentals

We call F a feature set where each element of the feature set is a feature vector, f_i, $1 \le i \le N$. Each feature vector is a vector of random numbers called attributes where each attribute is in a compact subset of a real line. Assume that every feature vector is L dimensional. Then, $f_i \in R^L$, $\forall i$, and $F \in R^{NL}$. A feature set corresponds to a point in a space called *feature space*. We then define mappings, $\phi_i : R^{NL} \to R^L$ as

$$\phi_i(F) = \arg \max_{f_i} \Pr(f_i | \{f_j\}_{j \neq i}, O), \quad 1 \le i \le N \tag{5}$$

and $\Phi : R^{NL} \to R^{NL}$ as

$$\Phi(F) = (\phi_1(F), ..., \phi_N(F)) \tag{6}$$

In short, Φ maps a feature set to another set where each feature vector maximizes the conditional probability given other features. With the definition, we can make the following observations on Φ.

Theorem 1. *When $\Pr(F|O)$ is differentiable with respect to each feature attribute, then the followings are true.*

1. *A fixed point of Φ maximizes the conditional probability, $\Pr(f_i|\{f_j\}_{j\neq i}, O)$, $\forall i$.*
2. *A fixed point of Φ is a local maximum of the joint probability, $\Pr(F|O)$, in the feature space.*

Proof. The first statement is obvious from the definition of ϕ_i and Φ, as a fixed point of Φ implies a fixed point of every ϕ_i and a fixed point of ϕ_i maximizes the conditional probability by definition. The second one is true because if a point in the feature space is not a local maximum of $\Pr(F|O)$, then there exists an attribute, say a_{ik} that is the kth attribute of f_i, with $\partial \Pr(F|O)/\partial a_{ik} \neq 0$. But

$$\frac{\partial \Pr(F|O)}{\partial a_{ik}} = \Pr(\{f_j\}_{j\neq i}|O)\frac{\partial \Pr(f_i|\{f_j\}, O)}{\partial a_{ik}} \neq 0, \tag{7}$$

thus $\partial \Pr(f_i|\{f_j\}, O)/\partial a_{ik} \neq 0$. The point is not a fixed point of ϕ_i, and therefore not a fixed point of Φ.

In general, an analytical solution to each ϕ_i may not be available. Then ϕ_i can be replaced with

$$\phi_i(F) = \Pr(f_i|\{f_j\}_{j\neq i}, O) + r\frac{\partial \Pr(f_i|\{f_j\}_{j\neq i}, O)}{\partial f_i} \tag{8}$$

where r is an ascent rate. The theorem still holds.

An accurate conditional PDF for natural environment is difficult to obtain. As the goal of our feature extraction system is to find a reasonable feature configuration represented as a local maximum of the joint PDF, we can replace the PDF with another differentiable function that shares the same extremum points with the PDF. Such a function is less constrained than the joint PDF, as it does not have to be non-negative and its integration does not have to amount to 1. For example, $\log \Pr(F|O)$ is a common transformation that preserves the extrema.

We also conjecture that feature sets at the local maxima of the joint PDF satisfy physical constraints and smoothness assumptions often introduced in many other feature extraction algorithms. Some popular constraints and assumptions include camera's projective geometry, rigid body assumption, geometric invariants, smooth surface assumption, and smooth motion assumption. By accepting the conjecture, we can bypass PDFs, which are often hard to derive, and work directly with common constraints and assumptions. Currently, we work directly on problem dependent constraints, and employ a quantity, $H(f_i|\{f_j\}, O)$, that measures how well f_i satisfy the constraints given the observation and the configuration of other features. We call the quantity *constraint measure*, which is analogous to the support measure of the PR. It is our future work to incorporate a learning process to the framework so that the system can learn the joint PDF of the environment in a self-organizing manner.

We are interested in decomposing H into a sum of weaker constraints comprised of smaller number of neighbor features. The decomposition not only simplifies the design of the constraint but also lessens the sensitivity of the constraint measure to partial occlusion of nearby features; the constraint measure degrades only linearly with the number of missing weaker constraints. An extreme case is when the constraint is decomposed into a set of pair-wise constraints. In the case, the constraint measure degrades linearly with the number of missing features. Such formulation resembles compatibility measures of the PR, and allows a neural network like efficient implementation. However, we remark that some tasks may require two or more nearby features to specify a weaker constraint properly.

3.2   Design Procedure

There are two design issues for applying the above general framework to a specific feature extraction task. First, feature attributes and constraints appropriate for the task need to be identified, and a constraint measure that is differentiable with respect to each feature attribute needs to be formulated. Second, the observation, which is often a set of images, needs to be mapped to the feature space. The mapping is required so that the observation can specify an initial point of search in the feature space or bias the constraints toward the mapped point.

In the examples shown in Section 5, we impose an assumption that contours and surfaces can be modeled with a set of quadratic curves and patches, respectively. We then form a pair-wise constraint measure of two features based on the assumption. The quadratic assumption may seem rather artificial and we provides no justification of its correctness. However, our intension is to show an effectiveness of our approach to general feature extraction problems and other kinds of constraints can easily be incorporated into the framework.

Once the two issues are resolved for a particular task, a generic procedure shown below (Algorithm) can be applied to derive a good set of features. Note that the do-until loop within the for loop derives an appropriate ascent rate. When the rate is too large, the process will pass a local maximum. In the case, it will bring the point half-way back and reevaluate how well a new point satisfy the constraint. The convergence can be measured by the amount of change in $\sum_i H(f_i)$.

4   Examples

This section presents some examples of applying the above approach to feature extraction tasks. We have selected contour representation and surface reconstruction problems, which are important for many subsequent tasks including registration, shape learning and object recognition.

We emphasize that the objective of two examples described below is not to reconstruct original structures with numerical accuracy, but to refine the representation of a feature set to a more probable one in terms of constraints imposed in the examples. Numerically faithful reproduction of surfaces is an important engineering problem and has a large number of applications in reverse engineering, damage assessment and cartography. However, for general vision problems such as recognition, navigation, and scene interpretation, high numerical accuracy is not essential. We demonstrate that with proper selection of constraints, the procedure given in Section 3 can remove noise and aliasing significantly while preserve the underlying structures of the observed data. Thus, it can facilitate subsequent vision tasks such as registration, grouping, correspondence and recognition.

```
program FeatureExtract(O,r) //observation (O) and ascent rate (r)
    F={fi}=initial feature set from observation
    do
        for each feature vector, fi
            real H1=H(fi,F) //evaluate the constraint measure
            vector d=grad(H(fi,F)) // find the gradient direction
            vector fnew=fi+r*d
            do  //find an appropriate ascent rate
                real H2=H(fnew,F)
                if(H2<H1)  //descent rate too high
                    fnew=(fnew+fi)/2  //go half way back
            until H2>=H1
            fi=fnew
        endfor
    until convergence
```

Algorithm 1 *Procedure for Feature Extraction*

4.1   Contour Representation

Contours are often used to define the shape of objects in many computer vision applications. Typically they are represented by a set of landmark points and parametric curves interpolating them. The landmark points are often extracted by some low level operator that extracts points along the boundary of an object. We employ quadratic polynomials to interpolate two adjacent landmark points. With the formulation, a contour segment around a feature point $p_i = (x_i, y_i)$ is represented parametrically as

$$x(t) = x_i(t) + a_i t^2 + b_i t, \ y(t) = y_i(t) + c_i t^2 + d_i t \tag{9}$$

where t is a parameter, and a_i, b_i, c_i, and d_i are coefficients. Note that the curve passes p_i at $t = 0$. We select the coefficients so that the curve penetrates two adjacent feature points at $t = -1$ and $t = 1$. Then

$$a_i = \frac{1}{2}(x_{i+1} + x_{i-1}) - x_i, \ b_i = \frac{1}{2}(x_{i+1} - x_{i-1}),$$

$$c_i = \frac{1}{2}(y_{i+1} + y_{i-1}) - y_i, \ d_i = \frac{1}{2}(y_{i+1} - y_{i-1}).$$

Each landmark point is represented with two attributes, x and y coordinates of the point. The system adjusts the attributes so that the set of landmark is more probable in terms of the joint PDF or more consistent with the imposed constraint. We suggest a constraint that two interpolating polynomials adjacent to each other have the same first order derivative at the landmark points. In another word, $p_i'(t = -1) = p_{i-1}'(t = 0)$ and $p_i'(t = 1) = p_{i+1}'(t = 0)$. The constraint is met when the following conditions are satisfied for every p_i:

$$3y_i = -y_{i-2} + y_{i-1} + 3y_{i+1}, \ 3y_i = -y_{i+2} + 3y_{i-1} + y_{i+1},$$

$$3x_i = -x_{i-2} + x_{i-1} + 3x_{i+1}, \ 3x_i = -x_{i+2} + 3x_{i-1} + x_{i+1}.$$

We formulate a constraint measure for p_i as (note a negative sign at each item)

$$\phi_i(p_i|\{p_j\}_{j \neq i}) = -(3y_i + y_{i-2} - y_{i-1} - 3y_{i+1})^2 - (3y_i + y_{i+2} - 3y_{i-1} - y_{i+1})^2$$

$$-(3x_i + x_{i-2} - x_{i-1} - 3x_{i+1})^2 - (3x_i + x_{i+2} - 3x_{i-1} - x_{i+1})^2.$$

The measure is non-positive and is zero when p_i satisfies the constraint. We can derive an updated rule for p_i by differentiating the constraint by each attribute. Thus,

$$\dot{y}_i \propto \frac{\partial \phi_i}{\partial y_i} \propto -y_{i+2} - y_{i-1} + 4y_{i+1} + 4y_{i-1} - 6y_i \tag{10}$$

and

$$\dot{x}_i \propto \frac{\partial \phi_i}{\partial x_i} \propto -x_{i+2} - x_{i-1} + 4x_{i+1} + 4x_{i-1} - 6x_i. \tag{11}$$

Now the feature extraction procedure described in Section 3 can be applied, and the performance of the algorithm can be tested. We test it with both synthetic and natural data. First, feature points are generated around some parametric curves and observe how the points converge to a more plausible form. Three sets of feature points are generated around a straight line, a circle, and a sine curve, respectively. They are shown in the top row of Figure . Results of our feature extraction process are shown in the bottom row of Figure . The amount of noise is reduced significantly in the converged form, and each result represents a form that satisfies the imposed constraint. For comparison, a cubic spline interpolator is used to interpolate two adjacent feature points. The results are shown in the middle row of Figure . The cubic interpolator cannot remove noise as effectively as our technique.

We have applied the technique to natural images. The top-left image in Figure is an input to the procedure. We employ Canny's edge detector to delineate an initial feature points. The bottom left image in Figure shows the initial set of feature points at a 4x4 expansion rate. The bottom right image in the figure is the result of our feature extraction process. Note that the purpose of the process is not numerically faithful reproduction of the contours, but refinement of their representations so that they are more plausible with respect to the contextual constraints imposed on them. We believe that contours on the right image are easier to be handled in subsequent vision processes than the left counterparts.

Fig. 1. The figure shows results of curve fitting using both cubic spline and the proposed technique. The top row shows three noisy patterns: line, circle and sine curve. The second row shows interpolation results using cubic splines. The third row shows results of our technique

4.2   Surface Reconstruction

We can extend the above contour representation technique to a higher dimension, particularly to 2D geometric surfaces in 3D. We are interested in reconstructing surfaces from a two dimensional image. Thus, the underlying problem is to estimate the height or pixel intensity field Z addressed by 2D coordinate (X, Y). It is easy, however, to extend the algorithm to a more general parametric form of $(x(s,t), y(s,t), z(s,t))$. Here we employ a quadratic polynomial patch to represent each small area of a 2D surface. We can express a patch around a feature point at (X_i, Y_i, Z_i) as

$$z_i(x,y) = Z_i + A_i(x-X_i)^2 + B_i(x-X_i) + C_i(y-Y_i)^2 + D_i(y-Y_i) + E_i(x-X_i)(y-Y_i) \tag{12}$$

where A_i, B_i, C_i, D_i, and E_i are coefficients and x and y are 2D coordinates.

We assume that the following constraints are most likely satisfied in natural environments.

- C^0 continuation at mid-point of two adjacent feature points, and
- C^1 continuation at mid-point of two adjacent feature points

This assumption may not be strictly a valid one, however, other constraints can be easily incorporated into the framework. Each feature is defined by the

Fig. 2. The figure shows a result of the proposed technique to a natural image. A small gray scale image at the top is an input. Initial contours are extracted with Canny operator and displayed at a 4x4 expansion shown in the left. Final contours are shown in the right

following set of attributes: $f_i = (X_i, Y_i, Z_i, A_i, B_i, C_i, D_i, E_i)$. According to the constraints, a pair-wise constraint measure is given by (note a negative sign at each term):

$$h_{ij} = -(z_i - z_j)^2 - \left(\frac{\partial z_i}{\partial x_i} - \frac{\partial z_j}{\partial x_j}\right)^2 - \left(\frac{\partial z_i}{\partial y_i} - \frac{\partial z_j}{\partial y_j}\right)^2, \tag{13}$$

which is evaluated at the mid-point between f_i and f_j. The constraint measure of f_i is $H_i = \sum_{j \in N_i} h_{ij}$ where N_i denotes the neighborhood of f_i. Since the equations of z_i and z_j are simply quadratic forms as given in ( ), the constraint measure can be differentiated with respect to every attribute. For example,

$$\frac{\partial H_i}{\partial X_i} = 2 \sum_j (z_i - z_j) \left(-A_i(X_j - X_i) - \frac{B_i}{2} - E_i\left(\frac{Y_j - Y_i)}{2}\right)\right) +$$

$$(z_i - z_j) \left(A_j(X_i - X_j) + \frac{B_j}{2} + E_j\left(\frac{Y_i - Y_j)}{2}\right)\right) +$$

$$\left(\frac{\partial z_i}{\partial x_i} - \frac{\partial z_j}{\partial x_j}\right)(A_i + A_j) - \left(\frac{\partial z_i}{\partial y_i} - \frac{\partial z_j}{\partial y_j}\right)(E_i + E_j).$$

First, the surface fitting procedure is applied to a small test data set, which has 8x8 data points and has a constant 4x4 square region at the center. A significant amount of noise is added to the test image. First, quadratic polynomial surfaces of ( ) are fitted at each feature point without any refinement in feature representation and the result is shown in the left of Figure . The figure visualizes

Fig. 3. The figure shows surface plots of interpolated surfaces comprised of 32x32 sample points. The left plot is prior to the surface fitting procedure, and the right one is after the fitting procedure

the structure of the initial data set. The feature extraction procedure is applied for 10 iterations and interpolated with derived quadratic patches. The result is shown in the right of Figure .

Second, the procedure is applied to another noisy square pattern but with a larger number of data points. The top left image in Figure   shows a 64x64 test image. The remaining three images in the figure are results of bi-linear interpolation (top-left) , Aramini's high-resolution bicubic spline interpolation (bottom-right), and our surface fitting procedure (bottom-left), respectively, resampled at a 4x4 expansion rate. The test demonstrates that the proposed technique preserves corners and boundaries while removing noise more effectively than other two methods.

The proposed technique, however, is more computationally expensive, as it runs in a iterative fashion while other two methods are non-iterative. The proposed technique took about 3 seconds to process the test image on a Pentium 4 1.69GHz PC, while both bi-linear and bicubic methods took less than 1 sec.

Finally, the technique is applied to a natural image shown in Figure . The region enclosed by a box is expanded at a 4x4 rate in the figure using the three methods as in Figure . The results are arranged in the same order as Figure .

The results with both bi-linear and bicubic methods still contain a large amount of aliasing (jagged edges) around strong edges such as the wrist-hand of the statue. We have extracted 8x8 region from the region and visualized in 3D mesh plots shown in Figure . The top left is a plot of the original 8x8 sample points. The remaining figures are plots of the bilinear interpolation result (top-right), bicubic interpolation result, and our surface fitting result, respectively. As the interpolation was done at a 4x4 expansion rate, the plots have 32x32 data points. Our surface fitting technique produced most smooth surface while preserving the discontinuity.

Fig. 4. The figure shows results of surface interpolation techniques to a noisy synthetic pattern. The top left image is a noisy input pattern expanded by 4x4 with pixel duplication. The top right image is the result of bilinear interpolation. The bottom left is the result of Aramini's high-resolution bicubic spline interpolation[ ]. The bottom right shows the result of the proposed quadratic surface fitting

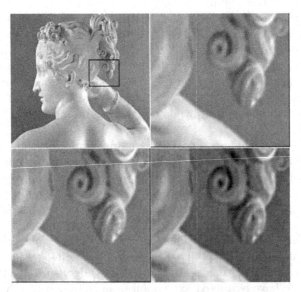

Fig. 5. The figure shows results of surface interpolation techniques to a natural image. The top left image is an image where a portion within a square is taken for interpolation. The top right image is the result of bilinear interpolation. The bottom left is the result of Aramini's high-resolution bicubic spline interpolation. The bottom right shows the result of the proposed quadratic surface fitting

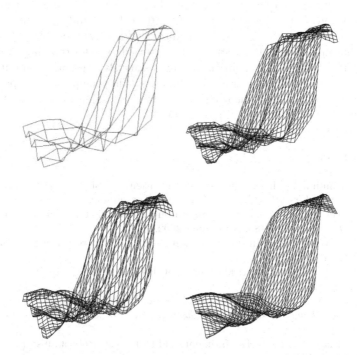

Fig. 6. The figure shows blown-up views of the interpolation results shown in Figure . An 8x8 region around the wrist-hand of the image is plotted for scrutiny. The top left is a plot of the original data. The top-right is a plot of the bilinear interpolation result. The bottom-left is a plot of the bicubic interpolation result. The bottom-right is a plot of our surface fitting result

5   Conclusion

The paper describes a new feature extraction framework that takes contextual correlation into account and runs in an efficient non-combinatorial manner. The framework reduces the amount of parameter 'tweaking', as most parameters can be considered as a feature attributes.

The technique is similar to probabilistic relaxation, as each feature iteratively update its state so that a constraint is better satisfied given the configuration of neighbor features. The state space of a feature set in our framework is continuous, while that of the PR is intrinsically discrete. It is also related to variational methods, as both employ local gradient based search. They are different, as our technique incorporates a multi-dimensional feature vector representation, while typical variational techniques only consider at most two dimensional feature vectors.

The framework is applied to sub-pixel contour representation and surface fitting problems, which are important for many computer vision applications.

Both contour representation and surface fitting algorithms find a near optimal representation that is locally quadratic and both C^0 and C^1 continuous. The algorithms converge to a non-trivial solution without any bias from given data, while it has an option of incorporating an external force for tracking applications. See [ ] for details. The algorithms run iteratively, thus are computationally more expensive than non-iterative techniques. This computational penalty can be remedied by carefully incorporating new observation into the system while the feature set is being refined iteratively.

References

[1] M. Aramini.   Efficient image magnification by bicubic spline interpolation. *http://members.bellatlantic.net/ vze2vrva/design.html.*   ,

[2] S. Baker and T. Kanade. Limits on super-resolution and how to break them. *PAMI*, 24(9):1167–1183, September 2002.

[3] D. H. Ballard. Generalizing the hough transform to detect arbitrary shapes. *PR*, 13(2):111–122, 1981.

[4] J. Besag. On the statistical analysis of dirty pictures. *J. Royal Statistical Soc., Ser. B*, 48:259–302, 1986.

[5] C. Bishop, A. Blake, and B. Marthi. Super-resolution enhancement of video. In *Proc. Artificial Intelligence and Statistics*, to appear, Key West, Florida, 2003.

[6] M. J. Black, G. Sapiro, D. Marimont, and D. Heeger. Robust anisotropic diffusion. *IP*, 7(3):421–432, 1998.   ,

[7] A. Blake and A. Zisserman. *Visual Reconstruction*. MIT Press, Cambridge, MA, 1987.   ,

[8] J. F. Canny.   A computational approach to edge-detection. *PAMI*, 8:679–700, 1986.

[9] R. H. Davies, C. J. Twining, T. F. Cootes, J. C. Waterton, and C. J. Taylor. A minimum description length approach to statistical shape modeling. *MedImg*, 21(5):525–537, May 2002.

[10] M. Elad and A. Feuer. Super-resolution reconstruction of image sequences. *PAMI*, 21(9):817, September 1999.

[11] O. D. Faugeras and R. Keriven. Variational-principles, surface evolution, pdes, level set methods, and the stereo problem. *IP*, 7(3):336–344, March 1998.

[12] D. Geiger and F. Girosi. Parallel and deterministic algorithms from MRF's: Surface reconstruction. *PAMI*, 13(5):401–412, 1991.

[13] S. Geman and D. Geman.   Stochastic relaxation, Gibbs distribution, and the Bayesian restoration of images. *PAMI*, 6(6):721–741, 1984.   ,

[14] M. W. Hansen and W. E. Higgins. Relaxation methods for supervised image segmentation. *PAMI*, 19(9):949–962, September 1997.

[15] M. Hueckel. A local visual operator which recognizes edges and lines. *JACM*, 20(4):634–647, October 1973.

[16] R. A. Hummel and S. W. Zucker. On the foundations of relaxation labeling processes. *PAMI*, 5(3):267–287, May 1983.

[17] A. K. Jain and F. Farrokhnia. Unsupervised texture segmentation using Gabor filters. *PR*, 24(12):1167–1186, 1991.

[18] M. Kass, A. P. Witkin, and D. Terzopoulos. Snakes: Active contour models. *IJCV*, 1(4):321–331, January 1988.

[19] B. B. Kimia, A. R. Tannenbaum, and S. W. Zucker. Shapes, shocks, and deformations i: The components of 2-dimensional shape and the reaction-diffusion space. *IJCV*, 15(3):189–224, July 1995.

[20] J. V. Kittler and J. Illingworth. Relaxation labelling algorithms – a review. *IVC*, 3:206–216, 1985.

[21] T Kubota. Robust feature extraction: A new framework for visual information processing. Technical Report CSCE TR-2002-015, Department of Computer Science and Engineering, University of South Carolina, 2002.

[22] D. G. Lowe. *Perceptual organization and visual recognition*. Kluwer Academic Publisher, Hingham MA 02043, USA, 1985.

[23] D. Mumford and J. Shah. Boundary detection by minimizing functionals. In *CVPR'85*, pages 22–26, San Francisco, CA, 1985.   ,

[24] N. Nguyen, P. Milanfar, and G. Golub. A computationally efficient superresolution image reconstruction algorithm. *IP*, 10(4):573–583, April 2001.

[25] P. Papachristou, M. Petrou, and J. V. Kittler. Edge postprocessing using probabilistic relaxation. *SMC-B*, 30(3):383–402, June 2000.

[26] W. T. Freeman; J. A. Haddon; E. C. Pasztor. Example-based super-resolution. *IEEE Computer Graphics and Applications*, 22(2):56–65, 2002.

[27] A. Rosenfeld, R. A. Hummel, and S. W. Zucker. Scene labeling by relaxation operations. *SMC*, 6(6):420–433, June 1976.

[28] S. Sarkar and K. L. Boyer. Perceptual organization in computer vision: A review and a proposal for a classificatory structure. *SMC*, 23(2):382–399, March 1993.

[29] R. R. Schultz and R. L. Stevenson. A bayesian approach to image expansion for improved definition. *IP*, 3(3):233–242, March 1994.

[30] J. A. Sethian. *Level Set Methods: evolving interfaces in geometry, fluid dynamics, computer vision, and material science*. Cambridge University Press, New York, NY, 1996.

[31] Y. Shan and G. W. Boon. Sub-pixel location of edges with non-uniform blurring: a finite closed-form approach. *IVC*, 18(13):1015–1023, October 2000.

[32] S. M. Smith and J. M. Brady. Susan: A new approach to low-level image-processing. *IJCV*, 23(1):45–78, May 1997.

[33] R. C. Wilson and E. R. Hancock. Structural matching by discrete relaxation. *PAMI*, 19(6):634–648, June 1997.

[34] P. L. Worthington and E. R. Hancock. Needle map recovery using robust regularizers. *IVC*, 17(8):545–557, June 1999.

Generalizing the Motzkin-Straus Theorem to Edge-Weighted Graphs, with Applications to Image Segmentation

Massimiliano Pavan and Marcello Pelillo

Dipartimento di Informatica, Università Ca' Foscari di Venezia
Via Torino 155, 30172 Venezia Mestre, Italy
{mapavan,pelillo}@dsi.unive.it

Abstract. The Motzkin-Straus theorem is a remarkable result from graph theory that has recently found various applications in computer vision and pattern recognition. Given an unweighted undirected graph G with adjacency matrix A, it establishes a connection between the local/global solutions of the following quadratic program:

$$\begin{aligned} \text{maximize} \quad & \boldsymbol{x}^{\mathrm{T}} A \, \boldsymbol{x}/2 \\ \text{subject to} \quad & \boldsymbol{e}^{\mathrm{T}} \boldsymbol{x} = 1, \ \boldsymbol{x} \in \mathbb{R}_+^n \end{aligned}$$

where $\boldsymbol{e} = (1, ..., 1)^{\mathrm{T}}$, and the maximal/maximum cliques of G. Given an edge-weighted undirected graph G and the corresponding weight matrix A, in this paper we address the following question: What kind of (combinatorial) structures of G are associated to the (continuous) local solutions of our quadratic program? We show that these structures correspond to a "weighted" generalization of maximal cliques, thereby providing a first step towards an edge-weighted generalization of the Motzkin-Straus theorem. Moreover, we show how these structures can be relevant in clustering as well as image segmentation problems. We present experimental results on real-world images which show the effectiveness of the proposed approach.

1 Introduction

Let $G = (V, E)$ be a simple undirected (and unweighted) graph, where $V = \{1, \ldots, n\}$ is the vertex set and $E \subseteq \binom{V}{2}$ is the edge set, $\binom{V}{2}$ denoting the set of all two-element subsets of V. A *clique* of G is a subset of V in which all vertices are pairwise adjacent. A clique C is called *maximal* if no strict superset of C is a clique, i.e., no vertex external to C is adjacent to more than $|C| - 1$ vertices of C (here, and in the sequel, $|C|$ denotes the cardinality of a set C). If, in addition, no external vertex of C is adjacent to exactly $|C| - 1$ vertices of C, then a maximal clique C will be called *strictly maximal*. Finally, a maximum cardinality clique (or, simply, a *maximum clique*) is a clique whose cardinality is the largest possible. Clearly, a maximum clique is also maximal but the converse need not be true. The maximum size of a clique in G is called the *clique number* (of G) and

A. Rangarajan et al. (Eds.): EMMCVPR 2003, LNCS 2683, pp. 485–   , 2003.
© Springer-Verlag Berlin Heidelberg 2003

is denoted by $\omega(G)$. The problem of determining a maximum clique of a graph (or finding its clique number) is a classical combinatorial optimization problem with a variety of practical applications. It is known to be NP-hard for arbitrary graphs and, according to recent theoretical results, so is the problem of approximating it within a constant factor. We refer to [ ] for a recent review concerning algorithms, applications and complexity issues of this important problem.

Let

$$\Delta = \{\boldsymbol{x} \in \mathbb{R}^n : \boldsymbol{x} \geq \boldsymbol{0} \text{ and } \boldsymbol{e}^{\mathsf{T}}\boldsymbol{x} = 1\}$$

be the standard simplex of $\mathbb{R}^n$, where $\boldsymbol{e}$ is a vector of appropriate length consisting of unit entries (hence $\boldsymbol{e}^{\mathsf{T}}\boldsymbol{x} = \sum_i x_i$), and consider the following quadratic function which is sometimes called the *Lagrangian* of graph G:

$$f_G(\boldsymbol{x}) = \sum_{\{i,j\}\in E} x_i x_j \ . \tag{1}$$

In 1965, Motzkin and Straus [ ] established a remarkable connection between the maxima of the Lagrangian of a graph over Δ and its clique number. Specifically, if $\boldsymbol{x}^*$ is a maximizer of f_G in Δ, they showed that the clique number $\omega(G)$ of G is related to $f_G(\boldsymbol{x}^*)$ according to the following formula:

$$\omega(G) = \frac{1}{1 - 2f_G(\boldsymbol{x}^*)} \ . \tag{2}$$

Additionally, they proved that a subset of vertices S is a maximum clique of G if and only if its (unweighted) *characteristic vector* $\boldsymbol{x}^{S,\mathrm{u}}$, which is the vector in Δ defined as:

$$x_i^{S,\mathrm{u}} = \begin{cases} 1/|S|, & \text{if } i \in S \\ 0, & \text{otherwise} \end{cases}$$

is a global maximizer of f in Δ. Recently, a similar connection has been established between *maximal* cliques of G and *local* maximizers of f_G [,].

The connection established by the Motzkin-Straus theorem between a purely combinatorial problem and a continuous one, although probably motivated by genuine mathematical curiosity, is indeed a fruitful one both from a theoretical and a practical standpoint. For example, in their original paper Motzkin and Straus used their result to provide an alternative proof of Turán's classical theorem, and Wilf [ ] derived from it new bounds on the clique size. Computationally, the result has also proven to be extremely useful since it motivated several clique-finding heuristics (see, e.g., [ ] and references therein). Moreover, the Motzkin-Straus theorem has recently found various applications in computer vision and pattern recognition, especially in graph matching and related problems [, ,].

---

[1] Actually, in their original paper, Motzkin and Straus proved just the "only-if" part of this theorem. The converse direction is however a straightforward consequence of their result [ ].

During the last few years, several generalizations of the Motzkin-Straus theorem have been proposed including, for example, Bomze's spurious-free regularized version [ ], Gibbons et al.'s extension to vertex-weighted graphs [ ], based on a suggestion by Lovász, and Sós and Straus' generalization to hypergraphs [ ].

The objective of this paper is twofold. First, we provide a further extension of the Motzkin-Straus theorem. Specifically, given an edge-weighted simple undirected graph $G = (V, E)$ with (positive) weight function $w : E \to \mathbb{R}_+^*$, we consider the *weighted Lagrangian* of G defined as:

$$f(\boldsymbol{x}) \equiv f_{G,w}(\boldsymbol{x}) = \sum_{\{i,j\} \in E} w(i,j) x_i x_j \qquad (3)$$

and we address the following question: What kind of combinatorial structures of G, if any, are associated to the maximizers of its weighted Lagrangian $f_{G,w}$ on the simplex Δ? We show that such structures do exist and correspond to a "weighted" generalization of maximal (and maximum) cliques, thereby providing a first step towards an edge-weighted generalization of the Motzkin-Straus theorem.

Moreover, we present an application of our result to image segmentation, a classic problem in computer vision and pattern recognition [ ]. An image can be represented as a *similarity* (edge-weighted) graph, where the vertices represent individual pixels, the edges neighborhood relations, and the weights on the edges reflect the similarity between pixel appearances. Recently there has been an increasing interest in graph-theoretic segmentation algorithms based on clustering (see, e.g., [, , , , ,]), which basically consist of searching for certain combinatorial structures in the similarity graph. Here, we propose a new clustering framework based on our "weighted" generalization of maximal (and maximum) cliques and show how this approach leads to competitive results in segmenting intensity as well as color real-world images.

2   Preliminaries

Let $G = (V, E)$ be an edge-weighted simple undirected graph of order n and let $A = (a_{ij})$ be the corresponding *weighted adjacency matrix*, which is the $n \times n$ symmetric matrix defined as:

$$a_{ij} = \begin{cases} w(i,j), & \text{if } \{i,j\} \in E \\ 0, & \text{otherwise.} \end{cases}$$

We shall consider the following standard quadratic program:

$$\begin{array}{ll} \text{maximize} & f(\boldsymbol{x}) = \frac{1}{2}\boldsymbol{x}^\mathsf{T} A\, \boldsymbol{x} \\ \text{subject to} & \boldsymbol{x} \in \Delta \end{array} \qquad (4)$$

whose objective function is nothing but the weighted Lagrangian of G, as defined in ( ).

---

[2] By convention, we write $w(i,j)$ instead of $w(\{i,j\})$.

A point $x^* \in \Delta$ is said to be a *global* solution of program ( ) if $f(x^*) \geq f(x)$, for all $x \in \Delta$. It is said to be a *local* solution if there exists an $\varepsilon > 0$ such that $f(x^*) \geq f(x)$ for all $x \in \Delta$ whose distance from x^* is less than ε, and if $f(x^*) = f(x)$ implies $x^* = x$, then x^* is said to be a *strict* local solution.

Given a vector $x \in \mathbb{R}^n$, the *support* of x is defined as the set of indices corresponding to its non-zero components, that is:

$$\sigma(x) = \{i \in V : x_i \neq 0\} \tag{5}$$

A point $x \in \Delta$ satisfies the Karush-Kuhn-Tucker (KKT) conditions for problem ( ), i.e. the first-order necessary conditions for local optimality [ ], if there exist $n + 1$ real constants (Lagrange multipliers) $\mu_1, \ldots, \mu_n$ and λ, with $\mu_i \geq 0$ for all $i = 1 \ldots n$, such that:

$$(Ax)_i - \lambda + \mu_i = 0 \tag{6}$$

for all $i = 1 \ldots n$, and

$$\sum_{i=1}^{n} x_i \mu_i = 0 . \tag{7}$$

Note that, since both x_i and μ_i are nonnegative for all $i = 1 \ldots n$, the latter condition is equivalent to saying that $i \in \sigma(x)$ implies $\mu_i = 0$. Hence, the KKT conditions can be rewritten as:

$$(Ax)_i \begin{cases} = \lambda, & \text{if } i \in \sigma(x) \\ \leq \lambda, & \text{otherwise} \end{cases} \tag{8}$$

for some real constant λ (indeed, it is immediate to see that $\lambda = x^T A\, x$). A point $x \in \Delta$ satisfying ( ) will be called a *KKT point* throughout.

We shall find it useful to introduce some new notations. If $S \subseteq V$, we denote by A_S the submatrix of A formed by the rows and the columns indexed by the elements of S. Additionally, we define the matrix B_S as:

$$B_S = \begin{pmatrix} 0 & e^T \\ e & A_S \end{pmatrix}$$

and, assuming $S = \{i_1, \ldots, i_m\}$ with $i_1 < \cdots < i_m$, the matrix $^j B_S$ is defined to be:

$$^j B_S = \begin{pmatrix} 0 & e^T \\ e & A_S^1\ A_S^2\ \cdots\ A_S^{j-1}\ \mathbf{0}\ A_S^{j+1}\ A_S^{j+2}\ \cdots\ A_S^n \end{pmatrix}$$

where A_S^i denotes the i-th column of A_S. With these notations, note that the KKT equality conditions in ( ) amount to saying that there exists a real number λ such that:

$$B_\sigma (\lambda, x_{i_1}, \ldots, x_{i_m})^T = (1, 0, \ldots, 0)^T \tag{9}$$

where $\sigma = \sigma(x) = \{i_1, \ldots, i_m\}$ with $i_1 < \cdots < i_m$.

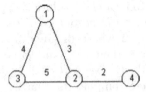

Fig. 1. An example edge-weighted graph

3   The Combinatorics of Standard Quadratic Programs

Our goal in this paper is to provide a combinatorial interpretation of the solutions of program ( ). Basically, our main result is centered around the intuitive idea that the assignment of edge-weights induces, in some way to be described, an assignment of weights on the vertices.

To grasp the intuition behind this idea, consider the graph in Figure 1 and the subgraph induced by the set $S = \{1, 2, 3\}$. Observe that the edges incident to vertex 1 are the lightest ones (within the subgraph), the heaviest ones are incident to vertex 3 and those incident to 2 are the lightest as well as the heaviest ones. This induces a sort of natural ranking among the vertices of S, which is captured by the notions introduced below. In order to formalize how such induction of node-weights takes place, we need some preliminary definitions. Let $S \subseteq V$ be a non-empty subset of vertices and $i \in V$. The *(average) weighted degree* of i w.r.t. S is defined as:

$$\text{awdeg}_S(i) = \frac{1}{|S|} \sum_{j \in S} a_{ij} . \tag{10}$$

Observe that $\text{awdeg}_{\{i\}}(i) = 0$ for any $i \in V$. Moreover, if $j \notin S$ we define:

$$\phi_S(i, j) = a_{ij} - \text{awdeg}_S(i) . \tag{11}$$

Note that $\phi_{\{i\}}(i, j) = a_{ij}$, for all $i, j \in V$ with $i \neq j$. Referring to the graph in Figure 1 we have:

$$\phi_{\{1,2\}}(1, 3) = a_{13} - \text{awdeg}_{\{1,2\}}(1) = 4 - \frac{0+3}{2} = \frac{5}{2} .$$

We are now in a position to formalize the notion of induction of node-weights.

---

[3] Note that, although we consider graphs with no self-loops, in computing the average weighted degree of $i \in S$ we divide by $|S|$ instead of $|S| - 1$, and this can lead to somehow counterintuitive results. For example, referring to the graph in Figure 1, $\text{awdeg}_{\{1,2\}}(1) = \frac{0+3}{2} < 3$.

Definition 1. *Let $S \subseteq V$ be a non-empty subset of vertices and $i \in S$. The weight of i w.r.t. S is*

$$\mathrm{w}_S(i) = \begin{cases} 1, & \text{if } |S| = 1 \\ \displaystyle\sum_{j \in S \setminus \{i\}} \phi_{S \setminus \{i\}}(j, i)\, \mathrm{w}_{S \setminus \{i\}}(j), & \text{otherwise.} \end{cases} \tag{12}$$

Moreover, the total weight *of S is defined to be:*

$$W(S) = \sum_{i \in S} \mathrm{w}_S(i). \tag{13}$$

Note that $\mathrm{w}_{\{i,j\}}(i) = \mathrm{w}_{\{i,j\}}(j) = a_{ij}$, for all $i, j \in V$ $(i \neq j)$. For example, in Figure 1 we have:

$$\begin{aligned} \mathrm{w}_{\{1,2,3\}}(3) &= \phi_{\{1,2\}}(1,3)\,\mathrm{w}_{\{1,2\}}(1) + \phi_{\{1,2\}}(2,3)\,\mathrm{w}_{\{1,2\}}(2) \\ &= [4 - (0+3)/2]3 + [5 - (0+3)/2]3 = 18. \end{aligned}$$

The following useful lemma characterizes the notions introduced above in terms of determinants. The proof proceeds by induction and exploits elementary properties of the determinant (see [ ] for details).

Lemma 1. *Let $S = \{i_1, \ldots, i_m\} \subseteq V$ be a non-empty subset of vertices and, w.l.o.g., assume $i_1 < \cdots < i_m$. Then, we have:*

$$\mathrm{w}_S(i_h) = (-1)^m \det\left({}^h B_S\right), \tag{14}$$

for any $i_h \in S$. Moreover:

$$W(S) = (-1)^m \det(B_S). \tag{15}$$

The next lemma, which follows easily from the previous one, provides an alternative way of computing the $\mathrm{w}_S(i)$'s.

Lemma 2. *For any non-empty subset of vertices $S \subseteq V$ and $i \in S$ we have:*

$$\mathrm{w}_S(i) = \sum_{j \in S \setminus \{i\}} (a_{ij} - a_{hj})\, \mathrm{w}_{S \setminus \{i\}}(j) \tag{16}$$

for all $h \in S \setminus \{i\}$.

The next definition is instrumental to characterize the solutions of our standard quadratic program ( ) in terms of combinatorial structures of G.

Definition 2. *We say that a non-empty subset of vertices S admits a* weighted characteristic vector *$\boldsymbol{x}^S$ if it has non-null total weight $W(S)$, in which case we set:*

$$x_i^S = \begin{cases} \dfrac{\mathrm{w}_S(i)}{W(S)}, & \text{if } i \in S \\ 0, & \text{otherwise.} \end{cases} \tag{17}$$

For example, consider the graph in Figure 1 and the set $S = \{1, 2, 3\}$. Since $w_S(1) = 10$ and $w_S(2) = 16$, we have:

$$x^S = (10/44, 16/44, 18/44, 0)^T \approx (0.23, 0.36, 0.41, 0)^T$$

and this confirms our intuitive ranking of the vertices in S based on the weights of the incident edges. The total weight of a subset of vertices $W(S)$ depends clearly on the topology of the graph and on the weights assigned to the edges, and can well be zero. Hence, a subset of vertices need not always admit a characteristic vector. For example, it is simple to see that any subset of at least two mutually non-adjacent vertices does not admit a characteristic vector.

The next two results establish useful connections between KKT points of program ( ) and weighted characteristic vectors.

Lemma 3. *Let $\sigma = \sigma(x)$ be the support of a vector $x \in \Delta$ which admits weighted characteristic vector x^σ. Then x satisfies the KKT equality conditions in ( ) if and only if $x = x^\sigma$. Moreover, in this case, we have:*

$$\frac{w_{\sigma \cup \{j\}}(j)}{W(\sigma)} = (Ax)_j - (Ax)_i = -\mu_j \tag{18}$$

for all $i \in \sigma$ and $j \notin \sigma$, where the μ_j's are the (nonnegative) Lagrange multipliers of program ( ) as defined in Section .

Proof. Note that conditions ( ), which are equivalent to the KKT equality conditions in ( ), can be regarded as a system of linear equations in the unknowns λ and x_i's ($i \in \sigma$). For Lemma , the system has a unique solution since $\det(B_\sigma) \neq 0$. Hence, supposing $\sigma = \{i_1, \ldots, i_m\}$ and, w.l.o.g., $i_1 < \cdots < i_m$, from Cramer's rule and Lemma we have:

$$x_{i_h} = \frac{\det\left({}^h B_\sigma\right)}{\det(B_\sigma)} = \frac{(-1)^m w_\sigma(i_h)}{(-1)^m W(\sigma)} = \frac{w_\sigma(i_h)}{W(\sigma)}$$

for any $1 \leq h \leq m$. Therefore $x = x^\sigma$.

The fact that $(Ax)_j - (Ax)_i = -\mu_j$, for $i \in \sigma$ and $j \notin \sigma$, follows immediately from equation ( ). Finally, applying Lemma we obtain:

$$\begin{aligned}
\frac{w_{\sigma \cup \{j\}}(j)}{W(\sigma)} &= \frac{\sum_{h \in \sigma}(a_{jh} - a_{ih})w_\sigma(h)}{W(\sigma)} \\
&= \sum_{h \in \sigma} a_{jh} x_h^\sigma - \sum_{h \in \sigma} a_{ih} x_h^\sigma \\
&= (Ax^\sigma)_j - (Ax^\sigma)_i
\end{aligned}$$

which concludes the proof, since $x = x^\sigma$. $\qquad\square$

Proposition 1. *Let $x \in \Delta$ be a vector whose support has positive total weight $W(\sigma)$, and hence admitting weighted characteristic vector x^σ. Then, x is a KKT point for ( ) if and only if the following conditions hold:*

1. $x = x^\sigma$
2. $\mathrm{w}_{\sigma \cup \{j\}}(j) \leq 0$, for all $j \notin \sigma$.

Proof. Vector x satisfies the KKT conditions ( ) if and only if $x = x^\sigma$ (cfr. Lemma) and $(Ax)_j \leq (Ax)_i$ for any $j \notin \sigma$ and $i \in \sigma$, but from ( ) the latter condition amounts to saying that $\mathrm{w}_{\sigma \cup \{j\}}(j) \leq 0$, since $\mathrm{W}(\sigma) > 0$. □

The notion of a weighted characteristic vector is too weak to characterize (strict) local solutions of program ( ). A strengthened, but still insufficient, notion is given by the following:

Definition 3. *A non-empty subset of vertices S is said to be* good *if:*

1. $\mathrm{w}_S(i) > 0$, *for all* $i \in S$
2. $\mathrm{W}(T) > 0$, *for any non-empty* $T \subseteq S$

A good subset of vertices S is said to be maximally good, *if no strict superset of S is good.*

It is evident that any good subset of vertices admits weighted characteristic vector, and it always belongs to the simplex Δ. Note that the subset of vertices $S = \{1, 2\}$ in Figure 1 is good for $\mathrm{w}_S(1) = \mathrm{w}_S(2) = 3 > 0$.

By using the bordered Hessian test [ ] from nonlinear programming, it is possible to prove the following instrumental result (cfr. [ ]).

Lemma 4. *Let* $S \subseteq V$ *be a subset of m vertices. Then,* $\mathrm{W}(T) > 0$ *for any non-empty subset* $T \subseteq S$ *if and only if* A_S *is negative definite in the subspace* $\{y \in \mathbb{R}^m : \sum_{i=1}^m y_i = 0\}$.

The following is our first connection between solutions of the continuous problem ( ) and combinatorial structures of G.

Lemma 5. *If a vector* $x^* \in \Delta$ *is a strict local solution for program ( ), then its support* $\sigma = \sigma(x^*)$ *is good.*

Proof. From the strict local maximality of x^* it follows, after some algebra, that the submatrix A_σ is negative definite in the subspace $\{y \in \mathbb{R}^m : \sum_{i=1}^m y_i = 0\}$, where $m = |\sigma|$, and from Lemma   this happens if and only if the second condition for a set to be good is satisfied. It remains to show that $\mathrm{w}_S(i) > 0$ for all $i \in S$, but this follows directly from Lemma   (in fact, x^* is a KKT point) and the definition of weighted characteristic vector. □

It is simple to show that the converse of the previous result does not necessarily hold, that is a good set need not correspond to a strict local solution of ( ). In order to provide such a reverse connection we need to refine the goodness notion.

Definition 4. *A good subset of vertices S is said to be* dominant *if, for any node* $i \notin S$, *we have* $\mathrm{w}_{S \cup \{i\}}(i) < 0$.

For example, in the graph of Figure 1 the subset of vertices $S = \{1, 2, 3\}$ is dominant since it is good and $\mathrm{w}_{S \cup \{4\}}(4) = -88 < 0$.

The next theorem, which is the main result of this paper, establishes a correspondence between dominant sets and (strict) local solutions of program ( ). It is a generalization of a result proved independently by Pelillo and Jagota [ ] and Gibbons et al. [ ] which represent the "local" counterpart of the original Motzkin-Straus theorem [ ], which is "global" in nature.

Theorem 1. *If S is a dominant subset of vertices, then its weighted characteristics vector x^S is a strict local solution of program ( ).*

Conversely, if x^* is a strict local solution of program ( ) then its support $\sigma = \sigma(x^*)$ is dominant, provided that $\mathrm{w}_{\sigma \cup \{i\}}(i) \neq 0$ for all $i \notin \sigma$.

Proof. If S is dominant, then from Proposition it follows that x^S is a KKT point for ( ). Moreover, by Lemma , we have that the j-th nonnegative Lagrange multiplier μ_j $(j \notin S)$ is positive if and only if $\mathrm{w}_{S \cup \{j\}}(j) < 0$. Therefore, the second-order sufficient conditions for local optimality [ ] together with Lemma imply that x^S is a strict local solution for program ( ).

On the other hand, if x^* is a strict local solution of ( ) then $\sigma = \sigma(x^*)$ is good, from Lemma . Moreover, Proposition states that $x^* = x^\sigma$ and $\mathrm{w}_{\sigma \cup \{j\}}(j) \leq 0$, for all $j \notin \sigma$. Therefore, the fact that σ is dominant follows trivially from the hypotheses.   □

Unfortunately, the previous result does not say anything concerning the combinatorial interpretation of x^* when $\mathrm{w}_{\sigma \cup \{i\}}(i) = 0$ for some $i \notin \sigma$. As in the unweighted case [ ], this has to do with the presence of "spurious" solutions in ( ), namely maximizers of the weighted Lagrangian whose support does not admit a weighted characteristic vector.

4   Back to the Unweighted Case

In this section, we return to the original setting of Motzkin and Straus, namely to unweighted graphs where $w(i, j) = 1$ for all $\{i, j\} \in E$, and we show that all the concepts introduced previously do correspond to standard graph-theoretic notions related to that of a clique (due to lack of space we omit proofs, which can be found in [ ]).

To this end, note that if $C \subseteq V$ is a clique of an unweighted graph $G = (V, E)$, then for any $j \notin C$ we have:

$$\mathrm{w}_{C \cup \{j\}}(j) = \deg_C(j) - |C| + 1$$

where, if S is a subset of vertices and $j \in V$, $\deg_S(j) = |\{i \in S : \{i, j\} \in E\}|$ denotes the degree of j w.r.t. S. This follows easily by induction on the cardinality of C and by the observation that for a clique C, and for any $i \in C$ and $j \notin C$, we have

$$\phi_C(i, j) = \begin{cases} \frac{1}{m} & \text{if } \{i, j\} \in E \\ \frac{1}{m} - 1 & \text{otherwise.} \end{cases}$$

Using these properties, it is simple to prove that, for any clique C of G, the following facts hold:

1. $w_C(i) = 1$, for any $i \in C$, and hence $W(C) = |C|$.
2. C is a maximal clique if and only if $w_{C \cup \{j\}}(j) \leq 0$ for any $j \notin C$.
3. C is a strictly maximal clique if and only if $w_{C \cup \{j\}}(j) < 0$ for any $j \notin C$.

From the above properties the next proposition follows.

Proposition 2. *Let $S \subseteq V$ be a subset of vertices of an unweighted graph. Then, the following properties hold:*

1. *S is a clique if and only if it is good;*
2. *S is a maximal clique if and only if it is maximally good;*
3. *S is a strictly maximal clique if and only if it is dominant.*

Hence, S is a maximum clique if and only if it is a good set having largest cardinality.

Finally, note that if C is a clique then it admits a weighted characteristic vector and this coincides with its unweighted counterpart, i.e., $x^C = x^{C,u}$.

5   Dominant Sets as Clusters

In this section, we show how dominant sets can be interpreted as "clusters" of homogeneous elements. We represent the data to be clustered as an undirected edge-weighted graph with no self-loops $G = (V, E)$, where $V = \{1, \ldots, n\}$ is the vertex set, $E \subseteq V \times V$ is the edge set, and let $w : E \to \mathbb{R}_+^*$ be the (positive) weight function. Vertices in G correspond to data points, edges represent neighborhood relationships, and edge-weights reflect similarity between pairs of vertices.

A common informal definition states that "a cluster is a set of entities which are *alike*, and entities from different clusters are not alike" [, p. 1]. Hence, a cluster should satisfy two fundamental conditions: (a) it should have high internal homogeneity; (b) there should be high inhomogeneity between the entities in the cluster and those outside. When the entities are represented as an edge-weighted graph, these two conditions amount to saying that the weights on the edges within a cluster should be large, and those on the edges connecting the cluster nodes to the external ones should be small.

Now, all the concepts defined in Section   can be easily interpreted in terms of cluster-related notions. To begin, $\text{awdeg}_S(i)$, where S is a subset of vertices containing i, can be thought as a measure of the average similarity between node i and its neighbors in S. Similarly, if $j \notin S$, the value of $\phi_S(i, j)$ can be seen as a measure of the similarity between nodes j and i, with respect to the average similarity between node i and its neighbors in S. Note that $\phi_S(i, j)$ can be either positive or negative. Similarly, referring to Definition , we can think of $w_S(i)$ as a measure of the overall similarity between vertex i and the vertices

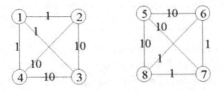

Fig. 2. An example edge-weighted graph

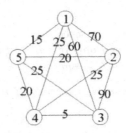

Fig. 3. The subset of vertices $\{1, 2, 3\}$ is dominant

of $S \setminus \{i\}$, with respect to the overall similarity among the vertices in $S \setminus \{i\}$. For example, in the graph of Figure 2 it turns out that $w_{\{1,2,3,4\}}(1) < 0$ and $w_{\{5,6,7,8\}}(5) > 0$ and this can be intuitively grasped by looking at the amount of edge-weight associated to vertices 1 and 5: that associated to vertex 1 is significantly smaller than that of subset $\{2, 3, 4\}$; conversely, that associated to vertex 5 is significantly greater than that of subset $\{6, 7, 8\}$.

The preceding qualitative observations suggest that any good subset of vertices satisfies the first main property of a cluster, namely high internal homogeneity (see conditions 1 and 2 in Definition , which concern the similarities between internal nodes). Moreover, recall that for any dominant subset of vertices S we have by definition $w_{S \cup \{i\}}(i) < 0$ for every node $i \notin S$ (see Definition). This condition, which regards similarities between internal and external nodes, formalizes the second main property of a cluster, i.e., high external inhomogeneity. Therefore, qualitatively speaking, a dominant set (which is also good by definition) does satisfy the two main conditions for a set of elements to be a cluster.

To illustrate, in the graph of Figure 3 the subset of vertices $\{1, 2, 3\}$ is dominant, and this may be intuitively explained by observing that the edge weights "internal" to that set (60, 70 and 90) are larger than those between internal and external vertices (which are between 5 and 25). As the example suggests, the main property of a dominant set is that the overall similarity among internal nodes is higher than that between external and internal nodes, and this fact is the main motivation of considering a dominant set as a cluster of nodes.

By virtue of Theorem dominant sets are in correspondence with (strict) solutions of quadratic program ( ). This is interesting because recently other

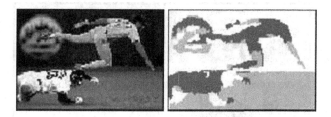

Fig. 4. An 83×125 intensity image (left) and its segmentation (right). Parameter setting: $\sigma = 0.14$. Minimal region size of interest is 11

quadratic programming formulations have been proposed for clustering and segmentation, though motivated by the different idea of finding cuts in a similarity graph [ ] or computing eigenvalues and eigenvectors of the weighted adjacency matrix [ ]. In particular, note that we use the same objective function as Sarkar and Boyer [ ] but differ from them in the feasible region (namely, we look for solutions in the standard simplex whereas they consider the sphere). Note also that there is no combinatorial interpretation of Sarkar and Boyer's clusters.

Finally, recall from Proposition   that our definition of a dominant set is indeed equivalent to that of a (strictly) maximal clique when applied to unweighted graphs; this is a further motivation to consider dominant sets as clusters, since maximal cliques are a classic formalization of the notion of a cluster [, , ,   ].

6   Application to Image Segmentation

We apply our clustering methodology to the segmentation of intensity and color images. The image to be segmented is represented as a *similarity* edge-weighted undirected graph $G = (V, E)$, where the vertices $V = \{1, \dots, n\}$ correspond to individual pixels and the edge-weights reflect the "similarity" between pairs of vertices. As customary, we define a similarity measure between pixels (i.e., the weight function w of G) based on brightness/color proximity. Specifically, in our experiments the similarity between pixels i and j was measured by:

$$w(i,j) = \exp\left(\frac{-\|\mathbf{F}(i) - \mathbf{F}(j)\|_2^2}{\sigma^2}\right)$$

where σ is a positive real number which affects the decreasing rate of w, and $\mathbf{F}(i)$ is defined as the intensity value at node i, normalized to a real number in the interval $[0, 1]$, for segmenting brightness images, and as $\mathbf{F}(i) = [v, vs\sin(h), vs\cos(h)](i)$, where h, s, v are the HSV values of pixel i, for color segmentation.

In principle, our clustering algorithm consists of iteratively finding a dominant set in the graph (i.e., a solution to program ( )) and then removing it from the graph, until all vertices have been clustered. Indeed, in the experiments reported here, to avoid the formation of small meaningless clusters, we repeated

Fig. 5. A 94 × 115 intensity image (left) and its segmentation (right). Parameter setting: $\sigma = 0.15$. Minimal region size of interest is 11

the process until 90% of the pixels were clustered, the remaining ones being assigned to the closest clusters, in terms of brightness/color proximity.

The continuous optimization method we use to solve problem ( ) is called *replicator equations*, a class of dynamical systems arising in evolutionary game theory [ ]. Such systems are attractive as can be coded in a few lines of any high-level programming language, can easily be implemented in a parallel network of locally interacting units, and offer the advantage of biological plausibility. In our simulations, we used the following discrete-time model (here $A = (a_{ij})$ is the weighted adjacency matrix of the similarity graph):

$$x_i(t+1) = \frac{x_i(t)\pi_i(t)}{\sum_{j=1}^{n} x_j(t)\pi_j(t)} \tag{19}$$

for $i = 1 \ldots n$, where

$$\pi_i(t) = \sum_{j=1}^{n} a_{ij}x_j(t) \ .$$

which corresponds to a well-known discretization of *first-order* replicator equations (see, e.g., [ ]). It is readily seen that the simplex Δ is invariant under these dynamics, which means that every trajectory starting in Δ will remain in Δ for all future times. Moreover, it can be proved that, since A is symmetric, the objective function $f(x) = \frac{1}{2}x^{\mathrm{T}}Ax$ of program ( ) is strictly increasing along any nonconstant trajectory of replicator equations ( ) [ ].

These properties naturally suggest using replicator equations as a useful heuristic for finding a dominant set. In all our examples, the process was started from the simplex barycenter and stopped after a few iterations (typically, no more than three). To improve the segmentation results, after convergence small isolated regions were incorporated into larger ones (see figure's captions for details).

Figures 4 to 7 show the results obtained with our segmentation algorithm on various natural brightness and color images. The left side of each figure shows the original image and the right one shows the corresponding segmentation, where connected pixels having the same gray level are intended to belong to

Fig. 6. An 125 × 83 color image (left) and its segmentation (right). Parameter setting: $\sigma = 0.11$. Minimal region size of interest is 16

the same region. On average, the algorithm took only a few seconds to return a segmentation, on a machine equipped with a 750 MHz Intel Pentium III.

Figure 4 shows an intensity image taken during a baseball game that has been used originally by Shi and Malik [ ] and other authors [,]. As can be seen, unlike other algorithms [, ,], ours was able to separate the grassy region from the back wall in a nice way. The uniforms of the two players (which have significant variation due to folds in the cloth) are also segmented in a satisfactory way, and smaller but important components such as the arms and gloves are also correctly segmented. Like other algorithms [,], however, ours did not succeed in distinguishing between the Mets emblem and the left leg of the top player. Also, note that the helmet of the bottom player is incorrectly merged with the back wall. Overall, these results compare well with those presented in [,], and are substantially better than those obtained with an optimally-tuned standard split-and-merge algorithm [ ].

Figure 5 shows the facade of a building. Again, the segmentation produced by our algorithm is of good quality. Specifically, the sky, the windows, the banners, and the wall (except from some noisy components around the central and right window on the first level) are all correctly segmented. Note also that the shadow of the balcony, the central door, and the window on the left-hand side are erroneously put in a unique component.

Figures 6 and 7 show results on color images taken from the COREL database. Figure 6 shows the image of a spaceman. Note how the segmentation is very clean despite substantial color variation. Essentially, the algorithm found three large regions: a large component for the black sky, another one for the earth, and a third one for the astronaut. Note also that some spurious regions were also found in the earth and in the man areas.

Finally, Figure 7 (used also in [ ]) shows an image of the Eiffel tower at night. Here, the algorithm was able to partition the image into meaningful components. It found a large component for the sky and, within the tower, it distinguished

Fig. 7. A 121 × 82 color image (left) and its segmentation (right). Parameter setting: $\sigma = 0.325$. Minimal region size of interest is 10

between the bright and the dark areas. However, note that the dark area in the bottom part of the image was incorrectly merged with the lower dark part of the tower. The quality of our segmentation looks comparable to the one reported by Felzenszwalb and Huttenlocher in [ ]: they were able to separate the lower dark area from the tower, but failed in clearly distinguishing the dark from the bright tower regions.

7   Conclusions

We have investigated the combinatorial properties of the solutions of a wide subclass of quadratic programming problems, thereby providing a first step towards a generalization of the Motzkin-Straus theorem to edge-weighted graphs. Essentially, we have shown that (strict) maximizers of the weighted Lagrangian on the standard simplex are in correspondence with certain combinatorial structures that we called dominant sets. These are the edge-weighted counterpart of strictly maximal cliques in unweighted graphs.

We have also shown how the concept of a dominant set can be relevant in clustering as well as image segmentation problems. Experimentally, we have demonstrated the potential of our approach for intensity and color image segmentation. The framework, however, is general and can be applied in a variety of computer vision and pattern recognition domains such as, for example, texture segmentation and perceptual grouping.

References

[1] J. G. Auguston and J. Minker. An analysis of some graph theoretical clustering techniques. *J. ACM*, 17(4):571–588, 1970.
[2] I. M. Bomze. Evolution towards the maximum clique. *J. Global Optim.*, 10:143–164, 1997.

[3] I. M. Bomze, M. Budinich, P. M. Pardalos, and M. Pelillo. The maximum clique problem. In D.-Z. Du and P. M. Pardalos, editors, *Handbook of Combinatorial Optimization (Suppl. Vol. A)*, pages 1–74. Kluwer, Boston, MA, 1999.

[4] P. F. Felzenszwalb and D. P. Huttenlocher. Efficient graph-based image segmentation. Preprint available at http://www.cs.cornell.edu/~dph/papers/seg-revised.pdf.

[5] D. Forsyth and J. Ponce. *Computer Vision: A Modern Approach*. Prentice-Hall, Englewood Cliffs, NJ, 2002.

[6] Y. Gdalyahu, D. Weinshall, and M. Werman. Sef-organization in vision: Stochastic clustering for image segmentation, perceptual grouping, and image database organization. *IEEE Trans. Pattern Anal. Machine Intell.*, 23(10):1053–1074, 2001.

[7] L. E. Gibbons, D. W. Hearn, P. M. Pardalos, and M. V. Ramana. Continuous characterizations of the maximum clique problem. *Math. Oper. Res.*, 22:754–768, 1997.

[8] C. C. Gotlieb and S. Kumar. Semantic clustering of index terms. *J. ACM*, 15(4):493–513, 1968.

[9] A. K. Jain and R. C. Dubes. *Algorithms for Clustering Data*. Prentice Hall, Englewood Cliffs, NJ, 1988.

[10] D. G. Luenberger. *Linear and Nonlinear Programming*. Addison-Wesley, Reading, MA, 1984.

[11] T. S. Motzkin and E. G. Straus. Maxima for graphs and a new proof of a theorem of Turán. *Canad. J. Math.*, 17:533–540, 1965.

[12] M. Pavan, M. Pelillo, and E. Jabara. On the combinatorics of standard quadratic optimization. Forthcoming, 2003.

[13] M. Pelillo. Replicator equations, maximal cliques, and graph isomorphism. *Neural Computation*, 11(8):2023–2045, 1999.

[14] M. Pelillo. Matching free trees, maximal cliques, and monotone game dynamics. *IEEE Trans. Pattern Anal. Machine Intell.*, 24(11):1535–1541, 2002.

[15] M. Pelillo and A. Jagota. Feasible and infeasible maxima in a quadratic program for maximum clique. *J. Artif. Neural Networks*, 2:411–420, 1995.

[16] M. Pelillo, K. Siddiqi, and S. W. Zucker. Matching hierarchical structures using association graphs. *IEEE Trans. Pattern Anal. Machince Intell.*, 21(11):1105–1120, 1999.

[17] V. V. Raghavan and C. T. Yu. A comparison of the stability characteristics of some graph theoretic clustering methods. *IEEE Trans. Pattern Anal. Machine Intell.*, 3:393–402, 1981.

[18] S. Sarkar and K. L. Boyer. Quantitative measures of change based on feature organization: Eigenvalues and eigenvectors. *Computer Vision and Image Understanding*, 71(1):110–136, 1998.

[19] J. Shi and J. Malik. Normalized cuts and image segmentation. *IEEE Trans. Pattern Anal. Machine Intell.*, 22(8):888–905, 2000.

[20] V. T. Sós and E. G. Straus. Extremal of functions on graphs with applications to graphs and hypergraphs. *J. Combin. Theory B*, 32:246–257, 1982.

[21] J. W. Weibull. *Evolutionary Game Theory*. MIT Press, Cambridge, MA, 1995.

[22] H. S. Wilf. Spectral bounds for the clique and independence numbers of graphs. *J. Combin. Theory B*, 40:113–117, 1986.

[23] Z. Wu and R. Leahy. An optimal graph theoretic approach to data clustering: Theory and its application to image segmentation. *IEEE Trans. Pattern Anal. Machine Intell.*, 15(11):1101–1113, 1993.

Generalized Multi-camera Scene Reconstruction Using Graph Cuts

Vladimir Kolmogorov[1], Ramin Zabih[1], and Steven Gortler[2]

[1] Computer Science Department, Cornell University, Ithaca, NY 14853
[2] Computer Science Department, Harvard University, Cambridge, MA 02138

Abstract. Reconstructing a 3-D scene from more than one camera is a classical problem in computer vision. One of the major sources of difficulty is the fact that not all scene elements are visible from all cameras. In the last few years, two promising approaches have been developed [,] that formulate the scene reconstruction problem in terms of energy minimization, and minimize the energy using graph cuts. These energy minimization approaches treat the input images symmetrically, handle visibility constraints correctly, and allow spatial smoothness to be enforced. However, these algorithm propose different problem formulations, and handle a limited class of smoothness terms. One algorithm [ ] uses a problem formulation that is restricted to two-camera stereo, and imposes smoothness between a pair of cameras. The other algorithm [ ] can handle an arbitrary number of cameras, but imposes smoothness only with respect to a single camera. In this paper we give a more general energy minimization formulation for the problem, which allows a larger class of spatial smoothness constraints. We show that our formulation includes both of the previous approaches as special cases, as well as permitting new energy functions. Experimental results on real data with ground truth are also included.

1 Introduction

Reconstructing an object's 3-dimensional shape from a set of cameras is a classic vision problem. In the last few years, it has attracted a great deal of interest, partly due to a number of new applications both in vision and in graphics that require good reconstructions. The problem is quite difficult, in large part because not all scene elements are visible from all cameras.

In this paper, we approach the scene reconstruction problem from the point of view of energy minimization. We build upon two recent algorithms [,] that give an energy minimization formulation of the scene reconstruction problem, and then minimize the energy using graph cuts. Both of these algorithms treat the input images symmetrically, handle visibility constraints correctly, and allow spatial smoothness to be enforced. Moreover, due to the use of graph cuts to perform the energy minimization, they are fast enough to be practical. However, the algorithms [,] use different problem formulations, and handle limited classes of smoothness terms. We propose a new problem energy minimization

A. Rangarajan et al. (Eds.): EMMCVPR 2003, LNCS 2683, pp. 501–   , 2003.

approach that includes both these methods as special cases, as well as permitting a larger class of energy functions.

We begin with a review of related work, including a discussion of the algorithms of [,]. In section   we give a precise definition of the problem that we wish to solve, and define the energy that we will minimize. Section   shows that our problem formulation contains the two previous methods [,] as special cases. In section   we describe how to use graph cuts to compute a strong local minimum of our energy. Experimental data is presented in section .

2   Related Work

The problem of reconstructing a scene from multiple cameras has received a great deal of attention in the last few years. One extensively-explored approach to this problem is voxel occupancy. In voxel occupancy [,] the scene is represented as a set of 3-dimensional voxels, and the task is to label the individual voxels as filled or empty. Voxel occupancy is typically solved using silhouette intersection, usually from multiple cameras but sometimes from a single camera with the object placed on a turntable [ ]. It is known that the output of silhouette intersection even without noise is not the actual 3-dimensional shape, but rather an approximation called the visual hull [ ].

2.1   Voxel Coloring and Space Carving

Voxel occupancy, however, fails to exploit the consistent appearance of a scene element between different cameras. This constraint, called *photo-consistency*, is obviously quite powerful. Two well-known recent algorithms that have used photo-consistency are voxel coloring [ ] and space carving [ ].

Voxel coloring makes a single pass through voxel space, first computing the visibility of each voxel and then its color. There is a constraint on the camera geometry, namely that no scene point is allowed to be within the convex hull of the camera centers. As we will see in section , our approach handles all the camera configurations where voxel coloring can be used. Space carving is another voxel-oriented approach that uses the photo-consistency constraint to prune away empty voxels from the volume. Space carving has the advantage of allowing arbitrary camera geometry.

One major limitation of voxel coloring and space carving is that they lack a way of imposing spatial coherence. This is particularly problematic because the image data is almost always ambiguous. Another (related) limitation comes from the fact that these methods traverse the volume making "hard" decisions concerning the occupancy of each voxel they analyze. Because the data is ambiguous, such a decision can easily be incorrect, and there is no easy way to undo such a decision later on.

2.2   Energy Minimization Approaches

It is well known that stereo, like many problems in early vision, can be elegantly stated in terms of energy minimization. The energy minimization problem has traditionally been solved via simulated annealing [,], which is extremely slow in practice.

While energy minimization has been widely used for stereo, only a few papers [, ,] have used it for scene reconstruction. The energy minimization formalism has several advantages. It allows a clean specification of the problem to be solved, as opposed to the algorithm used to solve it. In addition, energy minimization naturally allows the use of soft constraints, such as spatial coherence. In an energy minimization framework, it is possible to cause ambiguities to be resolved in a manner that leads to a spatially smooth answer. Finally, energy minimization avoids being trapped by early hard decisions.

In the last few years powerful energy minimization algorithms have been developed based on graph cuts [, , , ,]. These methods are fast enough to be practical, and yield quite promising experimental results for stereo [,]. Unlike simulated annealing, graph cut methods cannot be applied to an arbitrary energy function; instead, for each energy function to be minimized, a careful graph construction must be developed. In this paper, instead of building a special purpose graph we will use some recent results [ ] that give graph constructions for a quite general class of energy functions.

Although [ ] and [ ] use energy minimization via graph cuts, their focus is quite different from ours. [ ] uses an energy function whose global minimum can be computed efficiently via graph cuts; however, the spatial smoothness term is not discontinuity preserving, and so the results tend to be oversmoothed. Visibility constraints are not used. [ ] computes the global minimum of a different energy function as an alternative to silhouette intersection (i.e., to determine voxel occupancy). Their approach does not deal with photoconsistency at all, nor do they reason about visibility.

Our method is also related to the work of [ ], which also relies on graph cuts. They extend the work of [ ], which focused on traditional stereo matching, to allow an explicit label for occluded pixels. While the energy function that they use is of a similar general form to ours, they do not treat the input images symmetrically. While we effectively compute a disparity map with respect to each camera, they compute a disparity map only with respect to a single camera.

3   Graph Cut Algorithms for Scene Reconstruction

The results we will present generalize two recent papers: an algorithm for two-camera stereo with occlusions [ ], and an algorithm for multi-camera scene reconstruction [ ]. Both of these algorithms treat the input images symmetrically, handle visibility constraints correctly, and allow spatial smoothness to be enforced. The major difference between them lies in their problem formulations, and in the class of smoothness terms they permit.

The stereo with occlusions algorithm of [   ] uses a problem formulation that is restricted to two cameras. In their representation, a pair of pixels from the two images that may potentially correspond is called an *assignment*. An assignment is *active* when the corresponding scene element is visible in both images. The goal of the algorithm is to find the set of active assignments. There is a hard constraint that a given pixel is involved in at most one active assignment. A pixel that is involved in no active assignments is occluded, and there is a term in the energy function that introduces a penalty for each occluded pixel. Spatial smoothness is imposed with a term that involves assignments; hence, smoothness involves a pair of cameras at a time.

The multi-camera scene reconstruction algorithm given in [   ] can handle an arbitrary number of cameras. The problem is represented with a set of depth labels (typically planes). Each pixel in each camera must be assigned a depth label, such that the energy is minimized. Spatial smoothness is imposed with a term that involves a single camera at once.

3.1   Graph Cuts

Let $\mathcal{G} = \langle \mathcal{V}, \mathcal{E} \rangle$ be a weighted graph with two distinguished terminal vertices $\{s, t\}$ called the source and sink. A *cut* $\mathcal{C} = \mathcal{V}^s, \mathcal{V}^t$ is a partition of the vertices into two sets such that $s \in \mathcal{V}^s$ and $t \in \mathcal{V}^t$. (Note that a cut can also be equivalently defined as the set of edges between the two sets.) The cost of the cut, denoted $|\mathcal{C}|$, equals the sum of the weights of the edges between a vertex in $\mathcal{V}^s$ and a vertex in $\mathcal{V}^t$.

The minimum cut problem is to find the cut with the smallest cost. This problem can be solved very efficiently by computing the maximum flow between the terminals, according to a theorem due to Ford and Fulkerson [ ]. There are a large number of fast algorithms for this problem (see [ ], for example). The worst case complexity is low-order polynomial; however, in practice the running time is nearly linear for graphs with many short paths between the source and the sink, such as the one we will construct.

3.2   The Expansion Move Algorithm

Energy minimization algorithms that rely on graph cuts essentially perform a problem reduction. The algorithms with the best performance [,   ,   ] rely on the expansion move algorithm introduced by [ ]. For a given disparity α, an expansion move increases the set of pixels that are assigned the disparity α. The algorithm selects (in a fixed order or at random) a disparity α, and then finds the configuration within a single α-expansion move. If this decreases the energy, then we go there; if there is no α that decreases the energy, we are done. The expansion move algorithm is thus a simple local improvement algorithm, that computes a local minimum in a strong sense: the output is a configuration such that no expansion move can decrease the energy.

The only difficult part of the expansion move algorithm is to find the configuration within a single expansion move that most decreases the energy. This is done by computing the minimum cut on an appropriately defined graph. The precise details vary depending upon the technical definition of a configuration and the exact form of the energy function.

4   Problem Formulation

Now we will formalize the problem we are trying to solve. We will introduce two mappings describing the geometry of the scene, and enforce hard constraints between them. These mappings will be similar to the ones used in [ ] and [ ], respectively.

Suppose we are given n calibrated images of the same scene taken from different viewpoints (or at different moments of time). Let $\mathcal{P}_i$ be the set of pixels in the camera i, and let $\mathcal{P} = \mathcal{P}_1 \cup \ldots \cup \mathcal{P}_n$ be the set of all pixels. A pixel $p \in \mathcal{P}$ corresponds to a ray in 3D-space. Our first mapping f will describe depths for all pixels. More formally, the labeling f is a mapping from $\mathcal{P}$ to $\mathcal{L}$ where $\mathcal{L}$ is a discrete set of labels corresponding to different depths. In the current implementation of our method, labels correspond to increasing depth from a fixed camera.

A pair $\langle p, l \rangle$ where $p \in \mathcal{P}$, $l \in \mathcal{L}$ corresponds to some point in 3D-space. We will refer to such pairs as *3D-points*.

Our method has the same limitation as the earlier graph cut multi-camera algorithm [ ] and voxel coloring [ ]. Namely, there must exist a function $\mathcal{D}$: $R^3 \mapsto R$ such that for all scene points P and Q, P occludes Q in a camera i only if $\mathcal{D}(P) < \mathcal{D}(Q)$. If such a function exists then labels correspond to level sets of this function. In our current implementation, we make a slightly more specific assumption, which is that the cameras must lie in one semiplane looking at the other semiplane. The interpretation of labels will be as follows: each label corresponds to a plane in 3D-space, and a 3D-point $\langle p, l \rangle$ is the intersection of the ray corresponding to the pixel p and the plane l.

Let us introduce the set of interactions I consisting of (unordered) pairs of 3D-points $\langle p_1, l_1 \rangle$, $\langle p_2, l_2 \rangle$ "close" to each other in 3D-space. Several possible criteria for "closeness" are discussed in [ ]. In general, I can be an arbitrary set of pairs of 3D-points satisfying the following constraint:

– Only 3D-points at the same depth can interact, i.e.if $\{\langle p_1, l_1 \rangle, \langle p_2, l_2 \rangle\} \in I$ then $l_1 = l_2$.

To simplify the notation, we will denote interactions in I as $\langle p, q, l \rangle$ where p, q are pixels and l is a depth label.

Since 3D-points $\langle p, l \rangle$ and $\langle q, l \rangle$ are close to each other, the interaction $\langle p, q, l \rangle$ approximately corresponds to a single point in 3D-space (it can be, for example, the middle point between $\langle p, l \rangle$ and $\langle q, l \rangle$). We can describe the geometry of the scene by specifying which interactions are visible. Let us introduce another mapping $g : I \to \{0, 1\}$. $g(\langle p, q, l \rangle)$ will be 1 if this interaction is visible in both pixels p and q, and 0 otherwise. This mapping allows us to introduce the data term (i.e. the photoconsistency constraint) very naturally: we will enforce photoconsistency between p and q only if the interaction $\langle p, q, l \rangle$ is *active*, i.e. $g(\langle p, q, l \rangle) = 1$.

The mapping g is very similar to the mapping used in the stereo with occlusions method [ ]. Note that in their work each assignment is characterized by a disparity $q_x - p_x$, which generalizes to a depth label in our framework.

4.1   Our Energy Function

Now we will define the energy function that we minimize. It will consist of five terms:

$$E(f, g) = E_{data}(g) + E_{smooth}^{(1)}(f) + E_{smooth}^{(2)}(g) + E_{vis}(f) + E_{consistency}(f, g)$$

The terms $E_{smooth}^{(1)}$ and E_{vis} were used in [ ]. The terms $E_{smooth}^{(2)}$ and E_{data} are similar to the ones used in [ ]. The new term $E_{consistency}$ will enforce consistency between the mappings f and g.

Data Term The data term will be

$$E_{data}(g) = \sum_{i \in I} D_i(g(i))$$

where $D_i(0) = K$ for some constant K and $D_i(1)$ depends on intensities of pixels p and q involved in the interaction i. We can have, for example, $D_{\langle p,q,l \rangle}(1) = (Intensity(p) - Intensity(q))^2$.

Smoothness Terms Two smoothness terms enforce smoothness on two fields f and g, respectively. They involve a notion of neighborhood; we assume that there are two neighborhood systems: one on pixels

$$\mathcal{N}_1 \subset \{\{p, p'\} \mid p, p' \in \mathcal{P}\}$$

and one on interactions

$$\mathcal{N}_2 \subset \{\{i, i'\} \mid i, i' \in I\}.$$

$\mathcal{N}_1$ can be the usual 4-neighborhood system: pixels p and p' are neighbors if they are in the same image and $|p'_x - p_x| + |p'_y - p_y| = 1$. $\mathcal{N}_2$ can be defined similarly; interactions $\langle p, q, l \rangle$ and $\langle p', q', l \rangle$ are neighbors if p and p' are neighbors (or they are the same pixel): $|p'_x - p_x| + |p'_y - p_y| \leq 1$. The only requirement on $\mathcal{N}_2$ is that neighboring interactions must have the same depth label.

We will write the first smoothness term as

$$E_{smooth}^{(1)}(f) = \sum_{\{p,p'\} \in \mathcal{N}_1} V_{\{p,p'\}}(f(p), f(p'))$$

We will require the term $V_{\{p,q\}}$ to be a metric. This imposes smoothness while preserving discontinuities, as long as we pick an appropriate robust metric. For example, we can use the robustified L_1 distance $V(l_1, l_2) = \min(|l_1 - l_2|, R)$ for constant R. Note that this smoothness term involves only a single camera, as does [ ].

The second smoothness term can be written as

$$E_{smooth}^{(2)}(g) = \sum_{\{i,i'\}\in\mathcal{N}_2} V_{\{i,i'\}} \cdot T(g(i) \neq g(i'))$$

where $T(\cdot)$ is 1 if its argument is true and 0 otherwise. Note that this smoothness term involves pairs of cameras, as does [ ].

Visibility Term This term will encode the visibility constraint: it will be zero if this constraint is satisfied, and infinity otherwise. We can write this using another set of interactions I_{vis} which contains pairs of 3D-points violating the visibility constraint:

$$E_{visibility}(f) = \sum_{\langle p,f(p)\rangle, \langle q,f(q)\rangle \in I_{vis}} \infty$$

We require the set I_{vis} to meet following condition:

- Only 3D-points at different depths can interact, i.e. if $\{\langle p_1, l_1\rangle, \langle p_2, l_2\rangle\} \in I_{vis}$ then $l_1 \neq l_2$.

The visibility constraint says that if a 3D-point $\langle p, l\rangle$ is present in a configuration f (i.e. $l = f(p)$) then it "blocks" views from other cameras: if a ray corresponding to a pixel q goes through (or close to) $\langle p, l\rangle$ then its depth is at most l. Again, we need a definition of "closeness". We will use the set I for this purpose. Thus, the set I_{vis} can be defined as follows: it will contain all pairs of 3D-points $\langle p, l\rangle$, $\langle q, l'\rangle$ such that $\langle p, l\rangle$ and $\langle q, l\rangle$ interact (i.e. they are in I) and $l' > l$.

Consistency Term The last term will enforce consistency between two mappings f and g. It can be formulated as follows: if an interaction $\langle p, q, l\rangle$ is active, then the label for pixels p and q must be l. We can write this as

$$E_{consistency}(f, g) = \sum_{\langle p,q,l\rangle \in I} \infty \cdot T(g(\langle p, q, l\rangle) = 1 \;\wedge\; (f(p) \neq l \;\vee\; f(q) \neq l))$$

5   Relation to Previous Methods

In this section we show that multi-camera reconstruction algorithm of [ ] and the stereo with occlusions algorithm of [ ] are special cases of our general framework.

5.1   Multi-camera Reconstruction Algorithm

Let us consider our energy function with the second smoothness term $E^{(2)}_{smooth}$ omitted. We now show that this is equivalent to the energy used in the multi-camera reconstruction algorithm [ ].

We can view our energy as function of only one mapping f if we assume that g is determined from the minimality condition:

$$\tilde{E}(f) = E(f, g(f)) \quad \text{with} \quad g(f) = \arg\min_g E(f, g)$$

Let us consider an interaction $i = \langle p, q, l \rangle \in I$. Since g is not involved in the smoothness constraint, the value $g(i)$ will depend only on $f(p)$ and $f(q)$. Namely, if $f(p) \neq l$ or $f(q) \neq l$ then $g(i)$ must be 0 because of the consistency constraint between f and g. Now suppose that $f(p) = f(q) = l$. In this case the value $g(i)$ will be determined from the minimality condition: it will be 0 if $D_i(0) < D_i(1)$, and it will be 1 if $D_i(0) > D_i(1)$. Thus, the data term for interaction i becomes

$$\tilde{E}_{data(i)}(f) = D_i(0) + D(p, q) \cdot T(f(p) = f(q) = l)$$

where $D(p, q) = min(D_i(1) - D_i(0), 0)$. This is exactly the expression for data term used in [ ] except for the constant $D_i(0)$.

5.2   Stereo with Occlusions Algorithm

Now let us consider our energy with the first smoothness term $E^{(1)}_{smooth}$ omitted. We will show that in the case of stereo our formulation is equivalent to the stereo with occlusions algorithm [ ].

As before, we will view our energy as a function of only one mapping g (with f determined from the minimality condition). It is easy to see that the smoothness term $E^{(2)}_{smooth}$ is equivalent to the smoothness term used in [ ], and the sum of two terms $E_{vis}(f(g)) + E_{consistency}(f(g), g)$ is equivalent to the hard uniqueness constraint in [ ]. (The uniqueness constraint says that each pixel can be involved in at most one active assignment).

[ ] has an additional term which basically counts the number of occlusions. However, it is easy to see that having a penalty C for an occlusion is equivalent to having a penalty $C/2$ for an interaction (or assignment) being inactive. Thus, our data term term is equivalent to the sum of data and occlusion terms in [ ], which concludes the argument.

6   Graph Construction

We now show how to efficiently minimize E among all configurations using graph cuts. The output of our method will be a local minimum in a strong sense. In particular, consider an input configuration (f, g) and a disparity α. Another configuration (f', g') is defined to be within a single α-*expansion* of (f, g) if two conditions are satisfied:

- All pixels must either keep their depth labels, or change it to α. In other words, for any pixel $p \in \mathcal{P}$ either $f'(p) = f(p)$ or $f'(p) = \alpha$.
- All inactive interactions whose depth is different from α must remain inactive. In other words, for any interaction $\langle p, q, l \rangle \in I$ conditions $g(\langle p, q, l \rangle) = 0$ and $l \neq \alpha$ imply $g'(\langle p, q, l \rangle) = 0$.

This notion of an expansion move was proposed by [ ], and forms the basis for several very effective stereo algorithms [, ,].

Our algorithm is very straightforward; we simply select (in a fixed order or at random) a disparity α, and we find the unique configuration within a single α-expansion move (our local improvement step) that gives the largest decrease in the energy $E(f, g)$. If this decreases the energy, then we go there; if there is no α that decreases the energy, we are done. Except for the problem formulation and the choice of energy function, this algorithm is identical to the methods of [,].

One restriction on the algorithm is that the initial configuration must satisfy the visibility and consistency constraints (i.e. the initial energy must be finite). This will guarantee that all subsequent configurations will have finite energies, i.e. they will satisfy these constraints as well.

The critical step in our method is to efficiently compute the α-expansion with the smallest energy. In this section, we show how to use graph cuts to solve this problem.

6.1   Energy Minimization Using Graph Cuts

Instead of doing an explicit problem reduction, we will use a result from [ ] which says that for energy functions of binary variables of the form

$$E(x_1, \ldots, x_n) = \sum_i E^i(x_i) + \sum_{i<j} E^{i,j}(x_i, x_j) \tag{1}$$

it is possible to construct a graph for minimizing it if and only if each term $E^{i,j}$ satisfies the condition

$$E^{i,j}(0,0) + E^{i,j}(1,1) \leq E^{i,j}(0,1) + E^{i,j}(1,0). \tag{2}$$

If these conditions are satisfied then the graph $\mathcal{G}$ is constructed as follows. We add a node v_i for each variable x_i. For each term $E^i(x_i)$ and $E^{i,j}(x_i, x_j)$ we add edges as described in [ ].

Every cut on such a graph corresponds to some configuration $x = (x_1, \ldots, x_n)$, and vice versa: if $v_i \in \mathcal{V}^s$ then $x_i = 0$, otherwise $x_i = 1$. Edges on a graph were added in such a way that the cost of any cut is equal to the energy of the corresponding configuration plus a constant. Thus, the minimum cut on $\mathcal{G}$ yields the configuration that minimizes the energy.

6.2 α-Expansion

In this section we will show how to convert our energy function into the form of equation . Note that it is not necessary to use only terms $E^{i,j}$ for which $i < j$ since we can swap the variables if necessary without affecting condition .

In an α-expansion, active interactions may become inactive, and inactive interactions whose depth is α may become active. Suppose that we start off with an initial configuration (f^0, g^0) satisfying the visibility and consistency constraints. The active interactions for a new configuration within one α-expansion will be a subset of $I^0 \cup I^\alpha$, where $I^0 = \{\langle p, q, l \rangle \in I \mid g^0(\langle p, q, l \rangle) = 1 \text{ and } l \neq \alpha\}$ and $I^\alpha = \{\langle p, q, \alpha \rangle \in I\}$.

It is easy to see that any configuration (f, g) within a single α-expansion of the initial configuration (f^0, g^0) can be encoded by two binary vectors $x = \{x_p \mid p \in \mathcal{P}\}$ and $y = \{y_i \mid i \in I^\alpha \cup I^0\}$. We will use the following formula for correspondence between binary vectors and configurations:

$$\forall p \in \mathcal{P} \quad f(p) = \begin{cases} f^0(p) & \text{if } x_p = 0 \\ \alpha & \text{if } x_p = 1 \end{cases}$$

$$\forall i \in I^0 \quad g(i) = 1 - y_i$$
$$\forall i \in I^\alpha \quad g(i) = y_i$$
$$\forall i \notin I^0 \cup I^\alpha \quad g(i) = 0$$

Let us denote a configuration defined by vectors (x, y) as (f^x, g^y). We now have the energy of binary variables:

$$\tilde{E}(x, y) = \tilde{E}_{data}(y) + \tilde{E}^{(1)}_{smooth}(x) + \tilde{E}^{(2)}_{smooth}(y) + \tilde{E}_{vis}(x) + \tilde{E}_{consistency}(x, y)$$

where

$$\tilde{E}_{data}(y) = E_{data}(g^y),$$
$$\tilde{E}^{(1)}_{smooth}(x) = E^{(1)}_{smooth}(f^x),$$
$$\tilde{E}^{(2)}_{smooth}(y) = E^{(2)}_{smooth}(g^y),$$
$$\tilde{E}_{vis}(x) = E_{vis}(f^x),$$
$$\tilde{E}_{consistency}(x, y) = E_{consistency}(f^x, g^y).$$

We can now consider each term separately, and show that each satisfies condition ( ).

1. Data term.

$$\tilde{E}_{data}(y) = \sum_{i \in I^0} D_i(1 - y_i) + \sum_{i \in I^\alpha} D_i(y_i)$$

Condition ( ) is satisfied since each term in this sum depends only on one variable.

2. First smoothness term.

$$\tilde{E}^{(1)}_{smooth}(x) = \sum_{\{p,p'\}\in\mathcal{N}_1} V_{\{p,p'\}}(f^x(p), f^x(p')).$$

Let's consider a single term $E^{p,p'}(x_p, x_{p'}) = V_{\{p,p'\}}(f^x(p), f^x(p'))$. We assumed that $V_{\{p,p'\}}$ is a metric; thus, $V_{\{p,p'\}}(\alpha, \alpha) = 0$ and $V_{\{p,p'\}}(f(p), f(p')) \leq V_{\{p,p'\}}$ $(f(p), \alpha) + V_{\{p,p'\}}(\alpha, f(p'))$, or $E^{p,p'}(1,1) = 0$ and $E^{p,p'}(0,0) \leq E^{p,p'}(0,1) +$ $E^{p,p'}(1,0)$. Therefore, condition ( ) holds.

3. Second smoothness term.

$$\tilde{E}^{(2)}_{smooth}(y) = \sum_{\{i,i'\}\in\mathcal{N}_2} V_{\{i,i'\}} \cdot T(g^y(i) \neq g^y(i'))$$

Let's consider a single term $E^{i,i'}(y_i, y_{i'}) = V_{\{i,i'\}} \cdot T(g^y(i) \neq g^y(i'))$. Since the depths of i and i' are the same, they either both belong to I^0 or both belong to I^α. In both cases condition $g^y(i) \neq g^y(i')$ is equivalent to condition $y_i \neq y_{i'}$. Thus, $E^{i,i'}(0,0) = E^{i,i'}(1,1) = 0$ and $E^{i,i'}(0,1) = E^{i,i'}(1,0) = V_{\{i,i'\}} \geq 0$, so condition ( ) holds.

4. Visibility term.

$$\tilde{E}_{vis}(x) = \sum_{\langle p, f^x(p)\rangle, \langle q, f^x(q)\rangle \in I_{vis}} \infty$$

$$= \sum_{\langle p,l_p\rangle, \langle q,l_q\rangle \in I_{vis}} T(f^x(p) = l_p \wedge f^x(q) = l_q) \cdot \infty.$$

Let's consider a single term $E^{p,q}(x_p, x_q) = T(f^x(p) = l_p \wedge f^x(q) = l_q) \cdot \infty$. $E^{p,q}(0,0)$ must be zero since it corresponds to the visibility cost of the initial configuration and we assumed that the initial configuration satisfies the visibility constraint. Also $E^{p,q}(1,1)$ is zero (if $x_p = x_q = 1$, then $f^x(p) = f^x(q) = \alpha$ and, thus, the conditions $f^x(p) = l_p$ and $f^x(q) = l_q$ cannot both be true since I_{vis} includes only pairs of 3D-points at different depths). Therefore, condition ( ) holds since $E^{p,q}(0,1)$ and $E^{p,q}(1,0)$ are non-negative.

5. Consistency term.

$$\tilde{E}_{consistency}(x, y) = \sum_{\langle p,q,l\rangle \in I} \infty \cdot T(g^y(\langle p,q,l\rangle) = 1 \wedge (f^x(p) \neq l \vee f^x(q) \neq l))$$

The term involving interaction $i = \langle p,q,l\rangle$ can be rewritten as the sum $E^{p,i}(x_p, y_i) + E^{q,i}(x_q, y_i)$ where $E^{p,i}(x_p, y_i) = \infty \cdot T(g^y(i) = 1 \wedge f^x(p) \neq l)$ and $E^{q,i}(x_q, y_i) = \infty \cdot T(g^y(i) = 1 \wedge f^x(q) \neq l)$. Let's consider one of the terms, for example $E^{p,i}$. Two cases are possible:

5A. $l \neq \alpha$. If $f^0(p) \neq l$ then $E^{p,i} \equiv 0$, otherwise $E^{p,i}(x_p, y_i) = \infty \cdot T(y_i = 0 \wedge x_p = 1)$, so $E^{p,i}(1,0) = \infty$ and $E^{p,i}(0,0) = E^{p,i}(1,1) = E^{p,i}(0,1) = 0$.

5B. $l = \alpha$. In this case $E^{p,i}(x_p, y_i) = \infty \cdot T(y_i = 1 \wedge x_p = 0)$, so $E^{p,i}(0,1) = \infty$ and $E^{p,i}(0,0) = E^{p,i}(1,1) = E^{p,i}(1,0) = 0$.

7   Experimental Results

We performed experiments for the two special cases discussed in section . We will refer to the case in section   as "algorithm I" and the case in section as "algorithm II".

We used the same datasets used in [   ]: the "head and lamp" image from Tsukuba University, the flower garden sequence and the Dayton sequence. We also used the same geometry, i.e. depth labels, interaction sets I and I_{vis} and the neigborhood system $\mathcal{N}_1$ for algorithm I. Our choice of the neighborhood system $\mathcal{N}_2$ for algorithm II is a slight variation of that of [   ]: interactions $\langle p_1, q_1, l\rangle$ and $\langle p_2, q_2, l\rangle$ are neighbors if pixels p_1 and p_2 in a specified camera are neighbors according to $\mathcal{N}_1$.

Our choice of parameters for algorithms I and II is the same as in [   ] and [   ], respectively. In both cases the energy depends only on one parameter λ, which we picked empirically for different datasets. As in [   ], we stop after three iterations.

The results for algorithm II on the flower garden and Dayton datasets contain scattered pixels with no depth labels (or, more precisely, assigning any depth label to such pixels results in the same value of the energy function). Such pixels are probably due to the high noise in these datasets (or their miscalibration). We performed some postprocessing of the results: we assign to such pixels the label of the closest labeled pixel.

The table below show dataset sizes, number of interacting pairs of cameras that we used, and running times obtained on 450MHz UltraSPARC II processor. For all datasets we used 16 depth labels. The max flow implementation we used is one specifically designed for the kinds of graphs that arise in vision [ ].

dataset	number of images	number of interactions	image size	running time (I)	running time (II)
Tsukuba	5	4	384 x 288	369 secs	532 secs
Tsukuba	5	10	384 x 288	837 secs	1584 secs
Flower garden	8	7	352 x 240	693 secs	680 secs
Dayton	5	4	384 x 256	702 secs	481 secs

We have computed the error statistics for the Tsukuba dataset, which are shown in the table below.

	Errors	Gross errors
4 interactions (I)	6.13%	2.75%
4 interactions (II)	5.02%	1.40%
10 interactions (I)	4.53%	2.30%
10 interactions (II)	5.30%	2.36%
Boykov-Veksler-Zabih [ ]	9.76%	3.99%

We determined the percentage of the pixels where the algorithm did not compute the correct disparity (the "Errors" column), or a disparity within ±1 of the correct disparity ("Gross errors"). For comparison, we have included the results from the best known algorithm for stereo reported in [   ], which is the method of [ ].

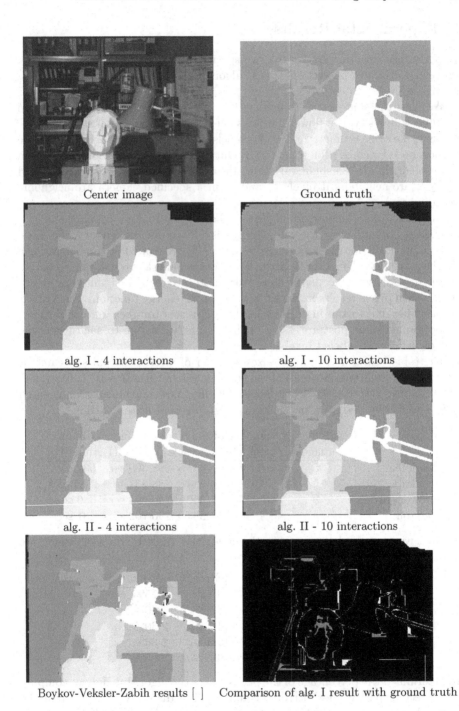

Center image

Ground truth

alg. I - 4 interactions

alg. I - 10 interactions

alg. II - 4 interactions

alg. II - 10 interactions

Boykov-Veksler-Zabih results [ ]   Comparison of alg. I result with ground truth

Fig. 1. Results on Tsukuba dataset

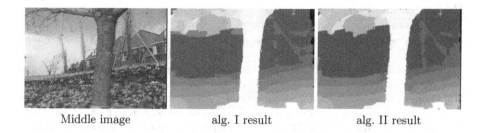

Middle image   alg. I result   alg. II result

Fig. 2. Results on the flower garden sequence

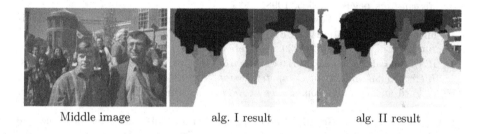

Middle image   alg. I result   alg. II result

Fig. 3. Results on the Dayton sequence

The images are shown in figure . The image at bottom right shows the areas where algorithm I differs from ground truth (black is no difference, gray is a difference of ± 1, and white is a larger difference). Inspecting the image shows that we in general achieve greater accuracy at discontinuities; for example, the camera in the background and the lamp are more accurate. The major weakness of our output is in the top right corner, which is an area of low texture. The behavior of our method in the presence of low texture needs further investigation.

8   Conclusions and Future Work

We have described a new energy minimization framework for multi-camera scene reconstruction. The energy can be efficiently minimized using graph cuts, and gives good experimental results. Furthermore, the new framework generalizes two previous algorithms, as well as permitting new energy functions that combine two distinct kinds of spatial smoothness constraints. More work is needed to determine if these new energy functions have experimental advantages over the previous methods that we have generalized.

Acknowledgements

This research was supported by the National Science Foundation under grant IIS-9900115.

References

[1] Ravindra K. Ahuja, Thomas L. Magnanti, and James B. Orlin. *Network Flows: Theory, Algorithms, and Applications.* Prentice Hall, 1993.

[2] Stephen Barnard. Stochastic stereo matching over scale. *International Journal of Computer Vision,* 3(1):17–32, 1989.

[3] Yuri Boykov and Vladimir Kolmogorov. An experimental comparison of min-cut/max-flow algorithms for energy minimization in computer vision. In *Workshop on Energy Minimization Methods in Computer Vision and Pattern Recognition,* volume 2134 of *LNCS,* pages 359–374, September 2001.

[4] Yuri Boykov, Olga Veksler, and Ramin Zabih. Markov Random Fields with efficient approximations. In *IEEE Conference on Computer Vision and Pattern Recognition,* pages 648–655, 1998.

[5] Yuri Boykov, Olga Veksler, and Ramin Zabih. Fast approximate energy minimization via graph cuts. *IEEE Transactions on Pattern Analysis and Machine Intelligence,* 23(11):1222–1239, November 2001.   ,   ,   ,   ,

[6] R. Cipolla and A. Blake. Surface shape from the deformation of apparent contours. *International Journal of Computer Vision,* 9(2):83–112, November 1992.

[7] L. Ford and D. Fulkerson. *Flows in Networks.* Princeton University Press, 1962.

[8] S. Geman and D. Geman. Stochastic relaxation, Gibbs distributions, and the Bayesian restoration of images. *IEEE Transactions on Pattern Analysis and Machine Intelligence,* 6:721–741, 1984.

[9] H. Ishikawa and D. Geiger. Occlusions, discontinuities, and epipolar lines in stereo. In *European Conference on Computer Vision,* pages 232–248, 1998.

[10] S. B. Kang, R. Szeliski, and J. Chai. Handling occlusions in dense multi-view stereo. In *IEEE Conference on Computer Vision and Pattern Recognition,* 2001.
,
[11] Vladimir Kolmogorov and Ramin Zabih. Visual correspondence with occlusions using graph cuts. In *International Conference on Computer Vision,* pages 508–515, 2001.   ,   ,   ,   ,   ,   ,   ,   ,

[12] Vladimir Kolmogorov and Ramin Zabih. Multi-camera scene reconstruction via graph cuts. In *European Conference on Computer Vision,* volume 3, pages 82–96, 2002.   ,   ,   ,   ,   ,   ,   ,

[13] Vladimir Kolmogorov and Ramin Zabih. What energy functions can be minimized via graph cuts? In *European Conference on Computer Vision,* volume 3, pages 65–81, 2002. Revised version to appear in *IEEE Transactions on Pattern Analysis and Machine Intelligence.*   ,

[14] K. N. Kutulakos and S. M. Seitz. A theory of shape by space carving. *International Journal of Computer Vision,* 38(3):197–216, July 2000.

[15] A. Laurentini. The visual hull concept for silhouette-based image understanding. *IEEE Transactions on Pattern Analysis and Machine Intelligence,* 16(2):150–162, February 1994.

[16] W. N. Martin and J. K. Aggarwal. Volumetric descriptions of objects from multiple views. *IEEE Transactions on Pattern Analysis and Machine Intelligence,* 5(2):150–158, March 1983.

[17] S. Roy and I. Cox. A maximum-flow formulation of the n-camera stereo correspondence problem. In *International Conference on Computer Vision,* 1998.

[18] Daniel Scharstein and Richard Szeliski. A taxonomy and evaluation of dense two-frame stereo correspondence algorithms. *International Journal of Computer Vision*, 47:7–42, April 2002.

[19] S. M. Seitz and C. R. Dyer. Photorealistic scene reconstruction by voxel coloring. *International Journal of Computer Vision*, 35(2):1–23, November 1999.   ,

[20] Dan Snow, Paul Viola, and Ramin Zabih. Exact voxel occupancy with graph cuts. In *IEEE Conference on Computer Vision and Pattern Recognition*, pages 345–352, 2000.

[21] R. Szeliski. Rapid octree construction from image sequences. *Computer Vision, Graphics and Image Processing*, 58(1):23–32, July 1993.

[22] Richard Szeliski and Ramin Zabih. An experimental comparison of stereo algorithms. In B. Triggs, A. Zisserman, and R. Szeliski, editors, *Vision Algorithms: Theory and Practice*, number 1883 in LNCS, pages 1–19, Corfu, Greece, September 1999. Springer-Verlag.   ,

Graph Matching Using Spectral Seriation

Antonio Robles-Kelly* and Edwin R. Hancock

Department of Computer Science, University of York
York, Y01 5DD, UK
{arobkell,erh}@cs.york.ac.uk

Abstract. This paper is concerned with computing graph edit distance. One of the criticisms that can be leveled at existing methods for computing graph edit distance is that it lacks the formality and rigour of string edit distance computation. Hence, our aim is to convert graphs to string sequences so that standard string edit distance techniques can be used. To do this, we use a graph spectral seriation method to convert the adjacency matrix into a string or sequence order. We pose the problem of graph-matching as maximum *a posteriori* probability alignment of the seriation sequences for pairs of graphs. This treatment leads to an expression for the edit costs. We compute the edit distance by finding the sequence of string edit operations which minimise the cost of the path traversing the edit lattice. The edit costs are defined in terms of the *a posteriori* probability of visiting a site on the lattice. We demonstrate the method with results on a data-set of Delaunay graphs.

1   Introduction

Graph-matching is a task of pivotal importance in high-level vision since it provides a means by which abstract pictorial descriptions can be matched to one-another. Unfortunately, since the process of eliciting graph structures from raw image data is a task of some fragility due to noise and the limited effectiveness of the available segmentation algorithms, graph-matching is invariably approached by inexact means [,]. The search for a robust means of inexact graph-matching has been the focus of sustained activity over the last two decades. Early work drew heavily on ideas from structural pattern recognition and re-volved around extending the concept of string edit distance to graphs [,]. One of the criticisms that can be aimed at this early work is that it lacks the formal rigour of the corresponding work on string edit distance. However, recently, Bunke and his co-workers have returned to the problem and have shown the relationship between graph edit distance and the size of the maximum common subgraph [ ].

An alternative approach to the problem is to convert graphs to string sequences and to use the existing theory of string edit distance. The problem of converting a graph to a sequence is known as seriation. Stated succinctly, it is the task of ordering the set of nodes in a graph in a sequence such that strongly

* Supported by CONACYT, under grant No. 146475/151752.

correlated nodes are placed next to one another. The problem is important in a number of areas including data visualisation and bioinformatics, where it is used for DNA sequencing. The seriation problem can be approached in a number of ways. Clearly the problem of searching for a serial ordering of the nodes, which maximally preserves the edge ordering is one of exponential complexity. As a result approximate solution methods have been employed. These involve casting the problem in an optimisation setting. Hence techniques such as simulated annealing and mean field annealing have been applied to the problem. It may also be formulated using semidefinite programming, which is a technique closely akin to spectral-graph theory since it relies on eigenvector methods. However, recently Atkins, Boman and Hendrikson [ ] have shown how to use an eigenvector of the Laplacian matrix to sequence relational data. There is an obvious parallel between this method and the use of eigenvector methods to locate steady state random walks on graphs.

The aim in this paper is to exploit this seriation method to develop a spectral method for computing graph edit distance. The task of posing the inexact graph matching problem in a matrix setting has proved to be an elusive one. This is disappointing since a rich set of potential tools are available from the field of mathematics referred to as spectral-graph theory. This is the term given to a family of techniques that aim to characterise the global structural properties of graphs using the eigenvalues and eigenvectors of the adjacency matrix [ ]. In the computer vision literature there have been a number of attempts to use spectral properties for graph-matching, object recognition and image segmentation. Umeyama has an eigendecomposition method that matches graphs of the same size [ ]. Borrowing ideas from structural chemistry, Scott and Longuet-Higgins were among the first to use spectral methods for correspondence analysis [ ]. They showed how to recover correspondences via singular value decomposition on the point association matrix between different images. In keeping more closely with the spirit of spectral graph theory, Shapiro and Brady [ ] developed an extension of the Scott and Longuet-Higgins method, in which point sets are matched by comparing the eigenvectors of the point proximity matrix. Horaud and Sossa[ ] have adopted a purely structural approach to the recognition of line-drawings. Their representation is based on the immanental polynomials for the Laplacian matrix of the line-connectivity graph. Shokoufandeh, Dickinson and Siddiqi [ ] have shown how graphs can be encoded using local topological spectra for shape recognition from large data-bases. In a recent paper, Luo and Hancock [ ] have returned to the method of Umeyama and have shown how it can be rendered robust to differences in graph-size and structural errors. Commencing from a Bernoulli distribution for the correspondence errors, they develop an expectation-maximisation algorithm for graph-matching. Correspondences are recovered in the M or maximisation step of the algorithm by performing singular value decomposition on the weighted product of the adjacency matrices for the graphs being matched. The correspondence weight matrix is updated in the E or expectation step. However, due to its iterative nature, the method is relatively slow and is sensitive to initialisation.

By using the spectral seriation method, we are able to convert the graph into a string. This opens up the possibility of performing graph matching by performing string alignment by minimising the Levenshtein or edit distance [,   ]. We can follow Wagner [ ] and use dynamic programming to evaluate the edit distance between strings and hence recover correspondences. It is worth stressing that although there been attempts to extend the string edit idea to trees and graphs [,   ,   ,   ], there is considerable current effort aimed at putting the underlying methodology on a rigourous footing.

2   Graph Seriation

Consider the graph $G = (V, E)$ with node index-set V and edge-set $E = \{(i,k)|(i,k) \in V \times V, i \neq k\}$. Associated with the graph is an adjacency matrix A whose elements are defined as follows

$$A(j_i, j_k) = \begin{cases} 1 & \text{if } (i,k) \in E \\ 0 & \text{otherwise} \end{cases} \tag{1}$$

Our aim is to assign the nodes of the graph to a sequence order which preserves the edge ordering of the nodes. This sequence can be viewed as an edge connected path on the graph. Let the path commence at the node j_1 and proceed via the sequence of edge-connected nodes $X = \{j_1, j_2, j_3, ...\}$ where $(j_i, j_{i-1}) \in E$. With these ingredients, the problem of finding the path can be viewed as one of seriation, subject to edge connectivity constraints.

As noted by Atkins, Boman and Hendrikson [ ], many applied computational problems, such as sparse matrix envelope reduction, graph partitioning and genomic sequencing, involve ordering a set according to a permutation $\varrho = \{\varrho(j_1), \varrho(j_2), \ldots, \varrho(j_{|V|})\}$ so that strongly related tokens are placed next to one another. The seriation problem is that of finding the permutation ϱ that satisfies the condition

$$\varrho(j_i) < \varrho(j_k) < \varrho(j_l) \Rightarrow \{A(j_i, j_k) \geq A(j_i, j_l) \wedge A(j_k, j_l) \geq A(j_i, j_l)\}$$

This task has been posed as a combinatorial optimisation problem which involves minimising the penalty function

$$g(\varrho) = \sum_{i=1}^{|V|} \sum_{k=1}^{|V|} A(j_i, j_k)\big(\varrho(j_i) - \varrho(j_k)\big)^2$$

for a real symmetric adjacency matrix A.

Unfortunately, the penalty function $g(\varrho)$, as given above, does not impose edge connectivity constraints on the ordering computed during the minimisation process. Furthermore, it implies no directionality in the transition from the node indexed j_i to the one indexed j_{i+1}. To overcome these shortcomings, we turn our attention instead to the penalty function

$$g(\varrho) = \sum_{i=1}^{|V|-1} A(j_i, j_{i+1})\big(\varrho(j_i) - \varrho(j_{i+1})\big)^2 \tag{2}$$

where the nodes indexed j_i and j_{i+1} are edge connected. After some algebra, it is straightforward to show that

$$g(\varrho) = \sum_{i=1}^{|V|-1} A(j_i, j_{i+1})(\varrho(j_i)^2 + \varrho(j_{i+1})^2) - 2\sum_{i=1}^{|V|-1} A(j_i, j_{i+1})\varrho(j_i)\varrho(j_{i+1}) \quad (3)$$

It is important to note that $g(\varrho)$ does not have a unique minimiser. The reason for this is that its value remains unchanged if we add a constant amount to each of the co-efficients of ϱ. We also note that it is desirable that the minimiser of $g(\varrho)$ is defined up to a constant λ whose solutions are polynomials in the elements of A. Therefore, we subject the minimisation problem to the constraints

$$\lambda\varrho(j_i)^2 = \sum_{k=1}^{|V|} A(j_k, j_i)\varrho(j_k)^2 \text{ and } \sum_{k=1}^{|V|} \varrho(j_k)^2 \neq 0 \quad (4)$$

Combining the conditions given in Equation   with the definition of the penalty function given in Equation , it is straightforward to show that the permutation ϱ satisfies the condition

$$\sum_{k=1}^{|V|}\sum_{i=1}^{|V|-1} \left(A(j_k, j_i) + A(j_k, j_{i+1})\right)\varrho(j_k)^2 = \lambda\sum_{i=1}^{|V|-1} (\varrho(j_i)^2 + \varrho(j_{i+1})^2) \quad (5)$$

Using matrix notation, we can write the above equation in the more compact form

$$\Omega A\phi = \lambda\Omega\phi \quad (6)$$

where $\phi = \{\varrho(j_1)^2, \varrho(j_2)^2, \ldots, \varrho(j_{|V|})^2\}^T$ and Ω is the $(N-1) \times N$ matrix

$$\Omega = \begin{bmatrix} 1 & 1 & 0 & \ldots & 0 \\ 0 & 1 & 1 & \ddots & \vdots \\ \vdots & \ddots & \ddots & \ddots & 0 \\ 0 & \ldots & 0 & 1 & 1 \end{bmatrix} \quad (7)$$

Hence it is clear that locating the permutation ϱ that minimises $g(\varrho)$ can be posed as an eigenvalue problem, and that ϕ is an eigenvector of A. This follows from the fact that Equation   can be obtained by multiplying both sides of the eigenvector equation $A\phi = \lambda\phi$ by Ω. Furthermore, due to the norm condition of the eigenvector, the constraint $\sum_{k=1}^{|V|} \varrho(j_k)^2 \neq 0$ is always satisfied. Taking this analysis one step further, we can pre-multiply both sides of Equation   by ϕ^T to obtain the matrix equation $\phi^T\Omega A\phi = \lambda\phi^T\Omega\phi$. As a result, it follows that

$$\lambda = \frac{\phi^T\Omega A\phi}{\phi^T\Omega\phi} \quad (8)$$

We note that the elements of the permutation ϱ are required to be real. Consequently, the co-efficients of the eigenvector ϕ are always non-negative. Since the elements of the matrices Ω and A are positive, it follows that the quantities $\phi^T \Omega A \phi$ and $\phi^T \Omega \phi$ are positive. Hence, the set of solutions reduces itself to those that are determined up to a constant $\lambda > 0$. As a result, the co-efficients of the eigenvector ϕ are linearly independent of the all-ones vector $\mathbf{e} = (1, 1..., 1)^T$.

With these observations in mind, we focus on proving the existence of a permutation that minimises $g(\varrho)$ subject to the constraints in Equation , and demonstrating that this permutation is unique. To this end we use the Perron-Frobenius theorem [ ]. This concerns the proof of existence regarding the eigenvalue $\lambda^* = \max_{i=1,2,...,|V|}\{\lambda_i\}$ of a primitive, real, non-negative, symmetric matrix A, and the uniqueness of the corresponding eigenvector ϕ^*. The Perron-Frobenius theorem states that the eigenvalue $\lambda^* > 0$ has multiplicity one. Moreover, the co-efficients of the corresponding eigenvector ϕ^* are all positive and the eigenvector is unique. As a result the remaining eigenvectors of A have at least one negative co-efficient and one positive co-efficient. Since, ϕ^* is also known to be linearly independent of the all-ones vector $\mathbf{e}$, the leading eigenvector of A is the minimiser of $g(\varrho)$.

The elements of the leading eigenvector ϕ^* can be used to construct a serial ordering of the nodes in the graph. We commence from the node associated with the largest component of ϕ^*. We then sort the elements of the leading eigenvector such that they are both in the decreasing magnitude order of the co-efficients of the eigenvector, and satisfy edge connectivity constraints on the graph. The procedure is a recursive one that proceeds as follows. At each iteration, we maintain a list of nodes visited. At iteration k let the list of nodes be denoted by $\mathcal{L}_k$. Initially, $\mathcal{L}_0 = j_o$ where $j_0 = \arg\max_j \phi^*(j)$, i.e. j_0 is the component of ϕ^* with the largest magnitude. Next, we search through the set of first neighbours $\mathcal{N}_{j_o} = \{k|(j_0, k) \in E\}$ of j_o to find the node associated with the largest remaining component of ϕ^*. The second element in the list is $j_1 = \arg\max_{l \in \mathcal{N}_{j_o}} \phi^*(l)$. The node index j_1 is appended to the list of nodes visited and the result is $\mathcal{L}_1$. In the kth (general) step of the algorithm we are at the node indexed j_k and the list of nodes visited by the path so far is $\mathcal{L}_k$. We search through those first-neighbours of j_k that have not already been traversed by the path. The set of nodes is $C_k = \{l|l \in \mathcal{N}_{j_k} \wedge l \notin \mathcal{L}_k\}$. The next site to be appended to the path list is therefore $j_{k+1} = \arg\max_{l \in C_k} \phi^*(l)$. This process is repeated until no further moves can be made. This occurs when $C_k = \emptyset$ and we denote the index of the termination of the path by T. The serial ordering of the nodes of the graph X is given by the ordered list or string of nodes indices $\mathcal{L}_T$.

In practice we will be interested in finding the edit distance for a pair of graphs $G_M = (V_M, E_M)$ and $G_D = (V_D, E_D)$. The leading eigenvectors of the corresponding adjacency matrices A_M and A_D are respectively ϕ_M^* and ϕ_D^*. The string representation of the graph G_M is denoted by X and that for the graph G_D by Y.

There are similarities between the use of the leading eigenvector for seriation and the use of spectral methods to find the steady state random walk on a graph. There are more detailed discussions of the problem of locating the steady state random walk on a graph in the reviews by Lovasz [ ] and Mohar [ ]. An important advantage of the seriation approach adopted in this paper is that it does impose edge connectivity constraints and can hence be used to convert graphs to strings in a manner which is suitable for computing edit distance.

3 Probabilistic Framework

We are interested in computing the edit distance between the graphs $G_M = (V_M, E_M)$ referred to as the model graph and the graph $G_D = (V_D, E_D)$ referred to as the data-graph. The seriations of the two graphs are denoted by $X = \{x_1, x_2, ..., x_{|V_M|}\}$ for the model graph and $Y = \{y_1, y_2, ..., y_{|V_D|}\}$ for the data graph. These two strings are used to index the rows and column of an edit lattice. The rows of the lattice are indexed using the data-graph string, while the columns are indexed using the model-graph string. To allow for differences in the sizes of the graphs we introduce a null symbol ϵ which can be used to pad the strings. We pose the problem of computing the edit distance as that of finding a path $\Gamma = < \gamma_1, \gamma_2, ... \gamma_k, ..., \gamma_L >$ through the lattice. Each element $\gamma_k \in (V_D \cup \epsilon) \times (V_M \cup \epsilon)$ of the edit path is a Cartesian pair. We constrain the path to be connected on the edit lattice. In particular, the transition on the edit lattice from the state γ_k to the state γ_{k+1} is constrained to move in a direction that is increasing and connected in the horizontal, vertical or diagonal direction on the lattice. The diagonal transition corresponds to the match of an edge of the data graph to an edge of the model graph. A horizontal transition means that the data-graph index is not incremented, and this corresponds to the case where the traversed nodes of the model graph are null-matched. Similarly when a vertical transition is made, then the traversed nodes of the data-graph are null-matched.

Suppose that $\gamma_k = (a, b)$ and $\gamma_{k+1} = (c, d)$ represent adjacent states in the edit path between the seriations X and Y. According to the classical approach, the cost of the edit path is given by

$$d(X, Y) = C(\Gamma) = \sum_{\gamma_k \in \Gamma} \eta(\gamma_k \to \gamma_{k+1}) \qquad (9)$$

where $\eta(\gamma_k \to \gamma_{k+1})$ is the cost of the transition between the states $\gamma_k = (a, b)$ and $\gamma_{k+1} = (c, d)$. The optimal edit path is the one that minimises the edit distance between string, and satisfies the condition $\Gamma^* = \arg\min_\Gamma C(\Gamma)$ and hence the edit distance is $d(X, Y) = C(\Gamma^*)$. Classically, the optimal edit sequence may be found using Dijkstra's algorithm or by using the quadratic programming method of Wagner and Fisher [ ].

However, in this paper we adopt a different approach. We aim to find the edit path that has maximum probability given the available leading eigenvectors of the data-graph and model-graph adjacency matrices. Hence, the optimal path is the one that satisfies the condition

$$\Gamma^* = \arg\max_\Gamma P(\Gamma | \phi_X^*, \phi_Y^*) \qquad (10)$$

To develop this decision criterion into a practical edit distance computation scheme, we need to develop the *a posteriori* probability appearing above. We commence by using the definition of conditional probability to re-write the *a posteriori* path probability in terms of the joint probability density $P(\phi_X^*, \phi_Y^*)$ for the leading eigenvectors and the joint density function $P(\phi_X^*, \phi_Y^*, \Gamma)$ for the leading eigenvectors and the edit path. The result is

$$P(\Gamma|\phi_X^*, \phi_Y^*) = \frac{P(\phi_X^*, \phi_Y^*, \Gamma)}{P(\phi_X^*, \phi_Y^*)} \tag{11}$$

We can rewrite the joint density appearing in the numerator to emphasise the role of the components of the adjacency matrix leading eigenvectors and the component edit transitions explicit

$$P(\Gamma|\phi_M^*, \phi_D^*) = \frac{P(\phi_X^*(1), \phi_X^*(2), ..., \phi_Y^*(1), \phi_Y^*(2)..., \gamma_1, \gamma_2, ...)}{P(\phi_M^*, \phi_D^*)} \tag{12}$$

To simplify the numerator, we make a conditional independence assumption. Specifically, we assume that the components of the leading eigenvector of the adjacency matrices, depend only on the edit transition γ_k associated with their node-indices. Hence, we can perform the factorisation

$$P(\Gamma|\phi_M^*, \phi_D^*) = \frac{\left\{\prod_{k=1}^{L} P(\phi_X^*(a), \phi_Y^*(b)|\gamma_k)\right\} P(\gamma_1, \gamma_2, \ldots, \gamma_L)}{P(\phi_X^*, \phi_Y^*)} \tag{13}$$

where $P(\gamma_1, \gamma_2, ..., \gamma_L)$ is the joint prior for the sequence of edit transitions and (a, b) is the coordinate pair on the edit lattice associated with the state γ_k. To simplify the joint prior, we assume that transitions between sites that are not adjacent on the edit lattice are conditionally independent. As a result

$$P(\gamma_1, \gamma_2, \ldots, \gamma_L) = P(\gamma_L) \prod_{k=1}^{L-1} P(\gamma_k|\gamma_{k+1}) \tag{14}$$

This takes the form of a factorisation of conditional probabilities for transitions between sites on the edit lattice $P(\gamma_k|\gamma_{k+1})$, except for the term $P(\gamma_L)$ which results from the final site visited on the lattice. To arrive at a more homogeneous expression, we use the definition of conditional probability to re-express the joint conditional measurement density for the adjacency matrix leading eigenvectors in the following form

$$P(\phi_X^*(a), \phi_Y^*(b)|\gamma_k) = \frac{P(\gamma_k|\phi_X^*(a), \phi_Y^*(b)) P(\phi_X^*(a), \phi_Y^*(b))}{P(\gamma_k)} \tag{15}$$

Substituting Equations ( ) and ( ) into Equation ( ) we find

$$P(\Gamma|\phi_X^*, \phi_Y^*) = \left\{\prod_{k=1}^{L} P(\gamma_k|\phi_X^*(a), \phi_Y^*(b)) \frac{P(\gamma_k, \gamma_{k+1})}{P(\gamma_k) P(\gamma_{k+1})}\right\}$$

$$\times \frac{\prod_{k=1}^{L} P(\phi_X^*(a), \phi_Y^*(b))}{P(\phi_X^*, \phi_Y^*)} \tag{16}$$

Since, the joint measurement density $P(\phi_X^*, \phi_Y^*)$ does not depend on the edit path, it does not influence the decision process and we remove it from further consideration. Hence, the optimal path across the edit lattice is

$$\Gamma^* = \arg\max_{\gamma_1,\gamma_2\ldots,\gamma_L}\left\{\prod_{k=1}^{L}P(\gamma_k|\phi_X^*(a),\phi_Y^*(b))\frac{P(\gamma_k,\gamma_{k+1})}{P(\gamma_k)P(\gamma_{k+1})}\right\} \tag{17}$$

The information concerning the structure of the edit path on the lattice is captured by the quantity

$$R_{k,k+1} = \frac{P(\gamma_k,\gamma_{k+1})}{P(\gamma_k)P(\gamma_{k+1})} \tag{18}$$

To establish a link with the classical edit distance picture presented in Section , we can re-write the optimal edit path as a minimisation problem involving the negative logarithm of the *a posteriori* path probability. The optimal path is the one that satisfies the condition

$$\Gamma^* = \arg\min_{\gamma_1,\gamma_2\ldots,\gamma_L}\left\{\sum_{k=1}^{L}\left[-P(\gamma_k|\phi_X^*(a),\phi_Y^*(b))-\ln R_{k,k+1}\right]\right\} \tag{19}$$

As a result the elementary edit cost $\eta(\gamma_k \to \gamma_{k+1}) = \eta((a,b) \to (c,d))$ from the site (a,b) and the edit lattice to the site (c,d) is

$$\eta(\gamma_k \to \gamma_{k+1}) = -\big(\ln P(\gamma_k|\phi_X^*(a),\phi_Y^*(b))+\ln P(\gamma_{k+1}|\phi_*^X(c),\phi_*^Y(d))+\ln R_{k,k+1}\big) \tag{20}$$

4   Lattice Transition Probabilities

We have recently reported a methodology which lends itself to the modelling of the edge compatibility quantity $R_{k,k+1}$ [ ]. It is based on the idea of constraint corruption through the action of a label-error process.

The model leads to an expression for the compatibility that is devoid of free parameters and which depends on the edge-set in the graphs being matched. Details of the derivation of the model are omitted from this paper for reasons of brevity. The compatibility contingency table is

$$R_{k,k+1} = \begin{cases} \rho_M\rho_D & \text{if } \gamma_k \to \gamma_{k+1} \text{ if } (a,c) \in E_D \text{ and } (b,d) \in E_M \\ \rho_M & \text{if } \gamma_k \to \gamma_{k+1} \text{ if } (a,c) \in E_D \text{ and } (b = \epsilon \vee d = \epsilon) \\ \rho_D & \text{if } \gamma_k \to \gamma_{k+1} \text{ if } (a = \epsilon \vee c = \epsilon) \text{ and } (b,d) \in E_M \\ 0 & \text{if } (a = \epsilon \vee c = \epsilon) \text{ and } (b = \epsilon \vee d = \epsilon) \end{cases} \tag{21}$$

4.1   A Posteriori Correspondence Probabilities

The second model ingredient is the *a posteriori* probability of visiting a site on the lattice. Here we assume that the differences in the components of the adjacency matrix leading eigenvectors are drawn from a Guassian distribution. Hence,

$$P(\gamma_k | \phi_X^*(a), \phi_Y^*(b)) = \begin{cases} \frac{1}{\sqrt{2\pi}\sigma} \exp\left\{ -\frac{1}{2\sigma^2}(\phi_X^*(a) - \phi_Y^*(b))^2 \right\} & \text{if } a \neq \epsilon \text{ and } b \neq \epsilon \\ \alpha & \text{if } a = \epsilon \text{ or } b = \epsilon \end{cases} \quad (22)$$

4.2   Minimum Cost Path

Once the edit costs are computed, we proceed to find the path that yields the minimum edit distance. Our adopted algorithm makes use of the fact that the minimum cost path along the edit lattice is composed of sub-paths that are also always of minimum cost. Hence, following Levenshtein [ ] we compute a $|V_D| \times |V_M|$ transition-cost matrix Ψ. The elements of the matrix are computed recursively using the formula

$$\psi_{i,j} = \begin{cases} \eta(\gamma_i \rightarrow \gamma_j) & \text{if } j = 1 \text{ and } i = 1 \\ \eta(\gamma_i \rightarrow \gamma_j) + \psi_{i,j-1} & \text{if } i = 1 \text{ and } j \geq 2 \\ \eta(\gamma_i \rightarrow \gamma_j) + \psi_{i-1,j} & \text{if } j = 1 \text{ and } i \geq 2 \\ \eta(\gamma_i \rightarrow \gamma_j) + \min(\psi_{i-1,j}, \psi_{i,j-1}, \psi_{i-1,j-1}) & \text{if } i \geq 2 \text{ and } j \geq 2 \end{cases} \quad (23)$$

The matrix Ψ is a representation of the accumulated minimal costs of the path along the edit lattice constrained to horizontal, vertical and diagonal transitions between adjacent coordinates. The minimum cost path can be proven to be that of the path closest to the diagonal of the matrix [ ]. As a result, the edit distance is given by the bottom rightmost element of the transition-cost matrix. Hence, $d(X,Y) = \Psi(|V_D|, |V_M|)$.

5   Experiments

We have experimented with our new matching method on an application involving clustering a database containing different perspective views of a number of 3D objects. In doing this, we aim to determine which distance measure results in a cluster assignment which best corresponds to the three image sequences. The objects used in our study are model houses. The different views are obtained as the camera circumscribes the object. The three object sequences used in our experiments are the CMU-VASC sequence, the INRIA MOVI sequence and a sequence of views of a model Swiss chalet, that we collected in-house. In our experiments we use ten images from each of the sequences. To construct graphs for the purposes of matching, we have first extracted corners from the images using the corner detector of Luo, Cross and Hancock [ ]. The graphs

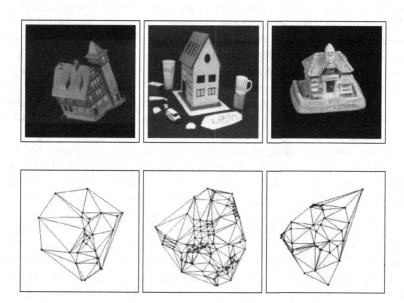

Fig. 1. Example frames and graphs of the sequences used for the experiments

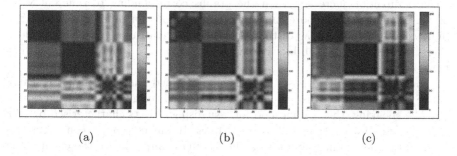

(a)   (b)   (c)

Fig. 2. Edit distance matrices

used in our experiments are the Delaunay triangulations of these corner points. In the top row of Figure , we show the first frame of the sequences used in our experiments. The corresponding graphs are displayed in the bottom row. For the 30 graphs contained in the database, we have computed the complete set of 30 × 29 =870 distances between each of the distinct pairs of graphs.

Next, we compare our results with those obtained when using the distances computed using two alternative methods. The first of these, is the negative log-likelihood function computed using the EM algorithm reported by Luo and

Hancock [ ]. This similarity measure uses purely structural information. The method shares with our edit distance framework the use of a statistical method to compare modal structure of two adjacency matrics. However, unlike our method which uses only the leading eigenvector of the adjacency matrix, this method uses the full pattern of singular vectors of a weighted correlation of the two adjacency matrices. In addition, the method is an iterative one which alternates between computing singular vectors in the M or maximisation step and re-computing the correspondence weight matrix in the E or expectation step. The second of the distance measures is computed using a spectral embedding of the graphs [ ]. The method involves embedding the graphs in an pattern space spanned by the leading eigenvalues of the adjacency matrix. According to this method, the distance between graphs is simply the L2 norm between points in this pattern space [ ]. This pairwise graph similarity measure again shares with our new method the feature of using spectral properties of the adjacency matrix.

In Figure a we show the distance matrix computed using our algorithm. The distance matrix obtained using the negative log-likelihood measure of Luo and Hancock [ ] is shown in Figure b, while the distance matrix computed from the spectral embedding is shown in Figure c. In each distance-matrix the element with row column indices i, j corresponds to the pairwise similarity between the graph indexed i and the graph indexed j in the data-base. In each matrix the graphs are arranged so that the row and column index increase monotonically with viewing angle. The blocks of views for the different objects follow one another. From the matrices in Figure , it is clear that as the difference in viewing direction increases, then the graphs corresponding to different views of the same object are more similar than the graphs for different objects. The different objects appear as distinct blocks in the matrices. Within each block, there is substructure (sub-blocks) which correspond to different characteristic views of the object.

For visualisation purposes, we have performed multidimensional scaling (MDS) on the pairwise distance matrices to embed the graphs in an eigenspace. Broadly speaking, this is a method for visualising objects characterised by pairwise distance rather than by ordinal values. It hinges around computing the eigenvectors of a similarity matrix, The leading components of the eigenvectors are the co-ordinates associated with the graphs. The method can be viewed as embedding the graphs in a pattern space using a measure of their pairwise similarity to one another. We plot the positions of the graphs on the plane corresponding to the two leading dimensions of the resulting eigenspace. We display two different sets of embeddings. The first consists of the embedding constructed using the entire similarity matrix for the three different objects. We do this in order to determine whether the eigenspace captures the structural differences between the sets of graphs for the distinct objects in our experimental dataset. In Figure , from left to right, we show the embeddings corresponding to the distance matrices computed using our algorithm, the negative log-likelihood computed using the algorithm of Luo and Hancock [ ] and the spectral featurevectors extracted from the adjacency matrix [ ].

The second set of embeddings are for the different views of the same object only. Our aim here is to determine whether the eigenspace captures in a systematic way the structural differences encountered as the object undergoes changes of viewpoiint. In the top row of Figure   we show the embeddings of the three objects that are obtained when we use the edit distance reported in this paper. The embeddings corresponding to the eigenspaces computed using the negative log-likelihood [ ] and the spectral feature vectors [ ] are shown in the middle and bottom rows.

We have also applied the pairwise clustering clustering algorithm of Robles-Kelly and Hancock [   ] to the similarity data for the complete data-base of graphs. Our aim is to investigate which distance measure results in the best set of graph-clusters. The pairwise clustering algorithm requires distances to be represented by a matrix of pairwise affinity weights. Ideally, the smaller the distance, the stronger the weight, and hence the mutual affinity to a cluster. The affinity weights are required to be in the interval $[0, 1]$. Hence, for the pair of graphs indexed $i1$ and $i2$ the affinity weight is taken to be

$$W_{i1,i2} = \exp\left(-k\frac{d_{i1,i2}}{\max(D)}\right) \qquad (24)$$

where k is a constant and $d_{i1,i2}$ is the element indexed $i1, i2$ of the matrix D of distances between distinct pairs of graphs (i.e the edit distance between the graph indexed $i1$ and the graph indexed $i2$). The clustering process is an iterative one that maintains two sets of variables. The first of these is a set of cluster membership indicators $s_{i\omega}^{(n)}$ which measures the affinity of the graph indexed i to the cluster indexed ω at iteration n of the algorithm. The second, is an estimate of the affinity matrix based on the current cluster-membership indicators $W^{(n)}$. These two sets of variables are estimated using interleaved updates steps, which are formulated to maximise a likelihood function for the pairwise cluster configuration.

The initial and final similarity matrices generated by the clustering process for each of the distance measures studied are shown in Figure   . In the top panel we show the initial and final similarity matrices obtained using our edit distance

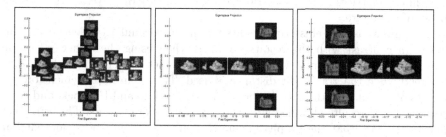

Fig. 3. Eigenspace projections for each of the distance matrices used

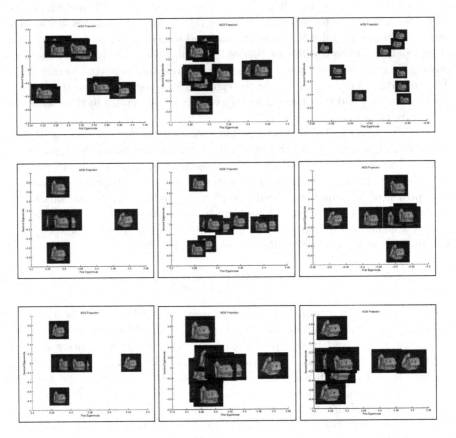

Fig. 4. Eigenspace projections for each of the three different clusters

to compute the affinity matrix elements $W_{i,j}$. Similarly, the middle panel shows the affinity matrices obtained using the distances yielded by the negative log-likelihood function for the structural graph matching algorithm (SGM). Finally, the affinity matrices for the spectral feature vectors are displayed in the bottom panel of the figure.

We summarise the clustering results for the three similarity measures in Table . In contrast with the results obtained when using the structural graph matching algorithm, Only two images of the Chalet sequence have been mis-assigned when the graph edit distance is used. This is an improvement on the results obtained with the log-likelihood function of Luo and Hancock, and comparable to the results obtained with the spectral feature vectors. The errors are due to the fact that the graphs in question are morphologically more similar to the graphs in the CMU and MOVI sequence than to those in the Chalet sequence. Nevertheless a success rate of 93.3% is obtained when edit distance

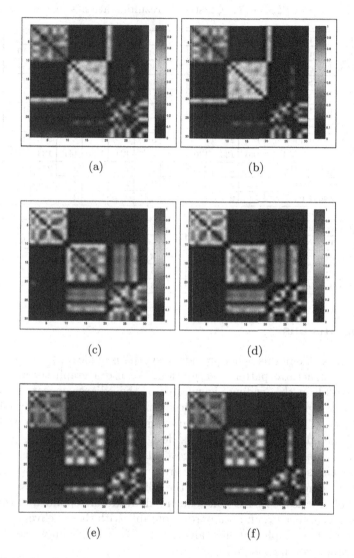

(a)   (b)

Fig. 5. Initial and final similarity matrices associated to the clustering process

is used for the affinity matrix computation. Our method compares favourably when computational cost is taken into account. This is because our method only requires the computation of the leading eigenvector while the spectral feature vectors require the complete eigenstructure to be computed. In consequence, the edit distance takes in average 2.6 times less time to compute than the spectral feature vectors.

Table 1. Clustering results statistics

CMU Sequence										
Image Number	1	2	3	4	5	6	7	8	9	10
Number of Nodes	30	32	32	30	30	32	30	30	30	31
Cluster (SGM)	1	1	1	1	1	1	1	1	1	1
Cluster (MDS)	1	1	1	1	1	1	1	1	1	1
Cluster (ED)	1	1	1	1	1	1	1	1	1	1
MOVI Sequence										
Image Number	1	2	3	4	5	6	7	8	9	10
Number of Nodes	140	134	130	136	137	131	139	141	133	136
Cluster (SGM)	2	2	2	2	2	2	2	2	2	2
Cluster (MDS)	2	2	2	2	2	2	2	2	2	2
Cluster (ED)	2	2	2	2	2	2	2	2	2	2
Chalet Sequence										
Image Number	1	2	3	4	5	6	7	8	9	10
Number of Nodes	40	57	92	78	90	64	113	100	67	59
Cluster (SGM)	3	3	2	2	2	3	2	2	3	3
Cluster (MDS)	4	3	3	3	3	3	2	3	3	3
Cluster (ED)	1	3	3	3	3	3	2	3	3	3

6 Conclusions

The work reported in this paper provides a synthesis of ideas from spectral graph-theory and structural pattern recognition. We use a graph spectral seriation method based on the leading eigenvector of the adjacency matrix to convert graphs to strings. We match the resulting string representations by minimising edit distance. The edit costs needed are computed using a simple probabilistic model of the edit transitions which is designed to preserve the edge order on the correspondences. The minimum cost edit sequence may be used to locate correspondences between nodes in the graphs under study.

We have demonstrated that both the edit sequence and the associated distance are of practical use. The edit sequence delivers correspondences that are robust to structural error, and compare favourably with those delivered by a number of alternative graph-matching algorithms. The edit distances can be used to cluster graphs into meaningful classes.

References

[1] K. Siddiqi A. Shokoufandeh, S. J. Dickinson and S. W. Zucker. Indexing using a spectral encoding of topological structure. In *Proceedings of the Computer Vision and Pattern Recognition*, 1998.
[2] Luo Bin and E. R. Hancock. Procrustes alignment with the em algorithm. In *8th International Conference on Computer Analysis of Images and Image Patterns*, pages 623–631, 1999.
[3] R. C. Wilson Bin Luo and E. R. Hancock. Spectral feature vectors for graph clustering. In *S+SSPR 2002*, 2002.   ,

[4] R. Wilson Bin Luo and E. Hancock. Eigenspaces for graphs. *International Journal of Image and Graphics*, 2(2):247–268, 2002.   ,

[5] H. Bunke. On a relation between graph edit distance and maximum common subgraph. *Pattern Recognition Letters*, 18(8):689–694, 1997.

[6] Fan R. K. Chung. *Spectral Graph Theory*. American Mathematical Society, 1997.

[7] M. A. Eshera and K. S. Fu. A graph distance measure for image analysis. *IEEE Transactions on Systems, Man and Cybernetics*, 14:398–407, 1984.

[8] R. Horaud and H. Sossa. Polyhedral object recognition by indexing. *Pattern Recognition*, 28(12):1855–1870, 1995.

[9] E. G. Roman J. E. Atkins and B. Hendrickson. A spectral algorithm for seriation and the consecutive ones problem. *SIAM Journal on Computing*, 28(1):297–310, 1998.   ,

[10] L. Lovász. Random walks on graphs: a survey. *Bolyai Society Mathematical Studies*, 2(2):1–46, 1993.

[11] V. I. Levenshtein. Binary codes capable of correcting deletions, insertions and reversals. *Sov. Phys. Dokl.*, 6:707–710, 1966.   ,

[12] Bin Luo and E. R. Hancock. Structural graph matching using the EM algorithm and singular value decomposition. *To appear in IEEE Trans. on Pattern Analysis and Machine Intelligence*, 2001.   ,

[13] B. Mohar. Some applications of laplace eigenvalues of graphs. In G. Hahn and G. Sabidussi, editors, *Graph Symmetry: Algebraic Methods and Applications*, NATO ASI Series C, pages 227–275, 1997.

[14] R. Myers, R. C. Wilson, and E. R. Hancock. Bayesian graph edit distance. *PAMI*, 22(6):628–635, June 2000.

[15] B. J. Oommen and K. Zhang. The normalized string editing problem revisited. *PAMI*, 18(6):669–672, June 1996.

[16] A. Robles-Kelly and E. R. Hancock. A maximum likelihood framework for iterative eigendecomposition. In *Proc. of the IEEE International Conference on Conputer Vision*, pages 654–661, 2001.

[17] A. Sanfeliu and K. S. Fu. A distance measure between attributed relational graphs for pattern recognition. *IEEE Transactions on Systems, Man and Cybernetics*, 13:353–362, 1983.   ,

[18] G. Scott and H. Longuet-Higgins. An algorithm for associating the features of two images. In *Proceedings of the Royal Society of London*, number 244 in B, 1991.

[19] L. G. Shapiro and R. M. Haralick. Relational models for scene analysis. *IEEE Transactions on Pattern Analysis and Machine Intelligence*, 4:595–602, 82.   ,

[20] L. S. Shapiro and J. M. Brady. A modal approach to feature-based correspondence. In *British Machine Vision Conference*, 1991.

[21] S. Umeyama. An eigen decomposition approach to weighted graph matching problems. *PAMI*, 10(5):695–703, September 1988.

[22] R. S. Varga. *Matrix Iterative Analysis*. Springer, second edition, 2000.

[23] R. A. Wagner and M. J. Fisher. The string-to-string correction problem. *Journal of the ACM*, 21(1), 1974.   ,

[24] J. T. L. Wang, B. A. Shapiro, D. Shasha, K. Zhang, and K. M. Currey. An algorithm for finding the largest approximately common substructures of two trees. *PAMI*, 20(8):889–895, August 1998.

Author Index